PROFESSIONAL
PARALLEL PROGRAMMING WITH C#

PROFESSIONAL

Parallel Programming with C#

MASTER PARALLEL EXTENSIONS WITH .NET 4

Gastón C. Hillar

WILEY

Wiley Publishing, Inc.

Professional Parallel Programming with C#

Published by
Wiley Publishing, Inc.
10475 Crosspoint Boulevard
Indianapolis, IN 46256
www.wiley.com

Published by Wiley Publishing, Inc., Indianapolis, Indiana

Published simultaneously in Canada

ISBN: 978-0-470-49599-5

ISBN: 978-1-118-02812-4 (ebk)

ISBN: 978-1-118-02977-0 (ebk)

ISBN: 978-1-118-02978-7 (ebk)

Manufactured in the United States of America

10 9 8 7 6 5 4 3 2 1

For general information on our other products and services, please contact our Customer Care Department within the United States at (877) 762-2974, outside the United States at (317) 572-3993 or fax (317) 572-4002.

Wiley also publishes its books in a variety of electronic formats. Some content that appears in print may not be available in electronic books.

Library of Congress Control Number: 2010930961

To my wonderful wife, Vanesa, who has somehow learned to put up with marathon writing sessions. And to my loving son, Kevin, who always managed to put a smile on my face after a long day.

CREDITS

ACQUISITIONS EDITOR
Paul Reese

PROJECT EDITORS
Ed Connor
Ginny Munroe

TECHNICAL EDITOR
Doug Parsons

PRODUCTION EDITOR
Kathleen Wisor

COPY EDITOR
Kathryn Duggan

EDITORIAL DIRECTOR
Robyn B. Siesky

EDITORIAL MANAGER
Mary Beth Wakefield

FREELANCER EDITORIAL MANAGER
Rosemarie Graham

ASSOCIATE DIRECTOR OF MARKETING
David Mayhew

PRODUCTION MANAGER
Tim Tate

VICE PRESIDENT AND EXECUTIVE GROUP PUBLISHER
Richard Swadley

VICE PRESIDENT AND EXECUTIVE PUBLISHER
Barry Pruett

ASSOCIATE PUBLISHER
Jim Minatel

PROJECT COORDINATOR, COVER
Katie Crocker

PROOFREADER
Paul Sagan, Word One New York

INDEXER
Robert Swanson

COVER IMAGE
© David Marchal/istockphoto.com

COVER DESIGNER
Michael Trent

ABOUT THE AUTHOR

 **GASTÓN C. HILLAR** has been working with computers since he was eight. He began programming with the legendary Texas TI-99/4A and Commodore 64 home computers in the early '80s. He received a bachelor's degree from UADE University, where he graduated with honors, and a Master of Business Administration from UCEMA University, where he graduated with an outstanding thesis.

Gastón has been researching parallel programming, multiprocessor, and multicore since 1997. He has 14 years of experience designing and developing diverse types of complex parallelized solutions that take advantage of multicore with C# and .NET Framework. He has been working with Parallel Extensions since the first Community Technology Preview (CTP). He is heavily involved with consulting, training, and development on the .NET platform, focusing on creating efficient software for modern hardware. He regularly speaks on software development at conferences all over the world. In 2009, he was awarded an Intel® Black Belt Software Developer award.

Gastón has written four books in English, contributed chapters to two other books, and has written more than 40 books in Spanish. He contributes to Dr Dobb's at www.drdobbs.com and Dr. Dobb's Go Parallel programming portal at www.ddj.com/go-parallel/, and is a guest blogger at Intel Software Network (http://software.intel.com).

He has worked as a developer, architect, and project manager for many companies in Buenos Aires, Argentina. Now, he is an independent IT consultant working for several American, German, Spanish, and Latin American companies, and a freelance author. He is always looking for new adventures around the world.

He lives with his wife, Vanesa, and his son, Kevin. When not tinkering with computers, he enjoys developing and playing with wireless virtual reality devices and electronics toys with his father, his son, and his nephew, Nico.

You can reach him at: gastonhillar@hotmail.com and follow him on Twitter at: http://twitter.com/gastonhillar. Gastón's blog is at http://csharpmulticore.blogspot.com.

ABOUT THE TECHNICAL EDITOR

DOUG PARSONS is a software architect and the director of Ohio Operations for NJI New Media. His expertise is in web development with a specialization in political websites. Most notably, he has worked on the 2008 John McCain presidential campaign website, and more recently, he has worked on Mitt Romney's official book tour website. In his down time, he enjoys spending time with his lovely fiancée, Marisa, and their puppies.

ACKNOWLEDGMENTS

PARALLEL PROGRAMMING IS ONE of the most difficult topics to write about. It is usually difficult to isolate subjects without having to reference many closely related topics. However, I had a lot of help during all the necessary stages to produce a high-quality book on a very challenging topic.

Special thanks go to Paul Reese, Edward Connor, Ginny Munroe, and Rosemarie Graham — they had a lot of patience, and they allowed me to make the necessary changes to the chapters in order to include the most accurate and appropriate information. The book required a lot of work, and they understood that writing an advanced book about parallel programming is a bit different from writing books about other programming topics. They worked very hard to make this book possible. In addition, I must thank Doug Parsons and Kathryn Duggan. You will notice their improvements when you read each sentence. They allowed me to convert a draft into a proof with their valuable feedback.

I wish to acknowledge Stephen Toub, Principal Program Manager of the Parallel Computing Platform team at Microsoft, who provided me with invaluable feedback for all the chapters. I was able to improve the examples and the contents by incorporating Stephen's insightful comments. This book would have been very difficult to finish without Stephen's help. His team's blog is at `http://blogs.msdn.com/b/pfxteam/`. The blog is an essential resource for keeping up-to-date with Parallel Extensions improvements and usage.

I must also thank Daniel Moth, member of the Microsoft Technical Computing group. Daniel helped me to improve the chapter that covers the new and exciting debugging features included in Visual Studio 2010. His feedback allowed me to incorporate a fascinating chapter into this book.

Special thanks go to Aaron Tersteeg and Kathy Farrel, managers of the excellent Parallel Programming community at Intel Software Network. I had the opportunity to enrich my knowledge in parallel computing topics through this great community. I wouldn't have been able to write this book without listening to and watching the Parallel Programming Talk shows (`www.intel.com/software/parallelprogrammingtalk`) that kept me up-to-date with the parallel computing trends.

Some of the information in this book is the result of intensive discussions I had at the Intel Black Belt Annual Meetups — I would like to acknowledge James Reinders, Dr. Clay Breshears, Jim Dempsey, and Doug Holland for sharing their wisdom. Doug also shares with me a passion for .NET, and I learned a great deal about his first experiences with Parallel Extensions via his blog: An Architect's Perspective (`http://blogs.msdn.com/b/dohollan/`).

I must also thank Jon Erickson, editor of the Dr. Dobb's website (`www.drdobbs.com`). Jon gave me the opportunity to contribute to both Dr. Dobb's and Dr. Dobb's Go Parallel (`www.ddj.com/go-parallel/`) in order to share my experience with other developers and architects. This book incorporates the great feedback received from my contributions.

I wish to acknowledge Hector A. Algarra, who always helped me to improve my writing skills.

Special thanks go to my wife, Vanesa S. Olsen, my son, Kevin, my nephew, Nicolas, my father, Jose Carlos, my sister, Silvina, and my mother, Susana. They were my greatest supporters during the production of this book.

And finally, thanks to all of you for selecting this book. I hope the parallel programming knowledge that you gain from it will help you develop powerful, high-performance applications, and responsive user interfaces.

CONTENTS

FOREWORD

aParllel prgoamrmnig s i ahdr. Hmm, let me try that again. Parallel programming is hard.

While truly a silly example, my first sentence exemplifies some of the difficulties we, as developers, face while writing multithreaded code. As I write this foreword, my hands typing on my laptop are effectively two distinct, physical processes, and if you further consider each of my fingers as an individual entity, the count would instead be 10. I'm generally acknowledged to be a fast typist, and in order to type at over 100 words per minute, my brain manages to coordinate all of my fingers, flowing them concurrently toward their next targets, yet still (most of the time) ensuring that their output is correctly serialized according to the spelling of the words my mind is willing my hands to render. I deliberately suspended that coordination to deliver that first sentence, such that my hands were no longer synchronizing correctly. The result is a barely readable representation of my thoughts. Luckily, it was easily debugged.

Parallel programming is indeed hard, or at least it has been historically. With the tools that have been available, only a small percentage of software developers have been proficient enough in the art to successfully develop and debug multithreaded applications. And yet, since the advent of modern computers, developers who need to write responsive user interfaces, build scalable services, or take advantage of multiple processing cores for performance have been forced to deal with concurrency, forced to develop software at the level of threads, mutexes, and semaphores. The difficulties here abound: oversubscription, race conditions, deadlocks, live locks, two-step dances, priority inversions, lock convoys, contention, and false sharing, just to name a few.

With all of these complications and with the recent industry shift toward multicore and manycore, parallel programming has received a lot of attention from companies that build development platforms, with Microsoft chief among them. Several years ago, the Parallel Computing Platform team at Microsoft emerged with a clear vision and purpose: to make building parallelized software easier. Developers should be able to easily express the parallelism that exists in their applications and allow the underlying framework, run-time, and operating system to implement that parallelism for them, mapping the expressed parallelism down to the hardware for correct and efficient execution. The first wave of supported components from the Parallel Computing Platform team was released in April 2010 as part of Visual Studio 2010; whether you're using native or managed code, this release provides foundational work to simplify the development of parallel applications. For developers using managed code, this includes the Task Parallel Library, Parallel LINQ, the new Parallel Stacks and Parallel Tasks debugging windows, a Concurrency Visualizer that yields deep insights into the execution of your multithreaded applications, and more.

Even with all of this new support, parallel programming still requires in-depth knowledge. In an age in which communication abounds in the form of 140-character quips, I personally find there's no better medium for conveying that in-depth knowledge than in a quality book. Luckily, you're reading one right now. Here, Gastón Hillar delivers a comprehensive book that covers all aspects of developing parallel applications with Visual Studio 2010 and the .NET Framework 4. From task-based programming to data parallelism to managing shared state to debugging parallel programs, and from the Task Parallel Library to Parallel LINQ to the ThreadPool to new coordination and synchronization primitives, Gastón provides a welcome and in-depth tour through the vast support for parallel programming that now exists in .NET Framework 4 and Visual Studio 2010.

This book contains information that can provide you with solid foundational knowledge you'll want when developing parallel applications. Congratulations on taking your first steps into this brave new manycore world.

—STEPHEN TOUB
Principal Program Manager
Parallel Computing Platform
Microsoft Corporation

Redmond, WA
September 2010

INTRODUCTION

In 2007, Microsoft released the first Community Technology Preview (CTP) of Parallel Extensions for the .NET Framework. The old .NET Framework multithreading programming model was too complex and heavyweight for the forthcoming multicore and manycore CPUs. I had been researching parallel programming, multiprocessor, and multicore since 1997, so I couldn't help installing the first CTP and trying it. It was obvious that it was going to be an exciting new way of expressing parallelism in future C# versions.

Visual Studio 2010 ships with version 4 of the .NET Framework, the first release to include Parallel Extensions. C# 4 and .NET Framework 4 allow you to shift to a modern task-based programming model to express parallelism. It is easier to write code that takes advantage of multicore microprocessors. Now, you can write code that scales as the number of available cores increases, without having to work with complex managed threads. You are able to write code that runs tasks, and the Common Language Runtime (CLR) will inject the necessary threads for you. It is easy to run data parallelism algorithms taking advantage of multicore.

At the time of this writing, multicore microprocessors are everywhere. Servers, desktop computers, laptops and notebooks, netbooks, mobile Internet devices (MIDs), tablets, and even smartphones use multicore microprocessors. The average number of cores in each microprocessor is going to increase in the forthcoming years. Are you going to lose the opportunity to transform this multicore power into application performance?

Parallel programming must become part of your skill set to effectively develop applications for modern hardware in C#. I spent more than three years working with the diverse versions of Parallel Extensions until Visual Studio 2010 was officially released. I enjoyed developing parallelized applications with C#, and I did my best to include explanations for the most common scenarios in this book.

Visual Studio 2010 provides an IDE prepared for a parallel developer, and C# is an excellent fit for the new task-based programming model.

WHO THIS BOOK IS FOR

This book was written to help experienced C# developers transform the multicore power found in modern microprocessors into application performance by using the Parallel Extensions introduced in .NET Framework 4. For those who are just starting the transition from the previous multithreading model to those who have worked with concurrent and parallel code for a while and need to gain a deeper understanding, this book provides information on the most common parallel programming skills and concepts you need.

This book offers a wide-ranging presentation of parallel programming concepts, but parallel programming possibilities with C# and .NET Framework 4 are so large and comprehensive that no single book can cover them all. The goal of this book is to provide a working knowledge of key technologies that are important to C# developers who want to take advantage of multicore and manycore architectures. It provides adequate knowledge for an experienced C# developer to work in many high-level parallelism areas. The book covers the new task-based programming model. Some developers who are interested in distributed parallelism and low-level concurrent programming topics may choose to add to their knowledge by supplementing this book with other books dedicated entirely to these technology areas.

This book provides background information that is very important to avoid common parallel programming pitfalls; therefore, it is best to read it without skipping chapters. Moreover, you should finish reading a chapter before considering the code shown in the middle of that chapter as a best practice. As each chapter introduces new features for Parallel Extensions, the examples are enhanced with simpler and more efficient coding techniques.

This book assumes that you are an experienced C# and .NET Framework 4 developer and focuses on parallel programming topics. If you don't have experience with advanced object-oriented programming, lists, arrays, closures, delegates, lambda expressions, LINQ, typecasting, and basic debugging techniques, you may need additional training to fully understand the examples shown.

WHAT THIS BOOK COVERS

This book covers the following key technologies and concepts:

➤ Modern multicore and manycore shared-memory architectures

➤ High-level, task-based programming with Task Parallel Library (TPL), C#, and .NET Framework 4

➤ Parallel Language Integrated Query (PLINQ)

➤ Most common coordination data structures and synchronization primitives for task-based programming

➤ Visual Studio 2010 debugging and profiling capabilities related to parallel programming

➤ Additional libraries, tools, and extras that help you master multicore programming in real-life applications

This book does not cover the old multithreaded programming model or distributed parallelism.

HOW THIS BOOK IS STRUCTURED

It is critical to master certain topics first. Unless you have previous experience with the new task-based programming model introduced in .NET Framework 4, you should read the book chapter by chapter. Each chapter was written with the assumption that you have read the previous chapter. However, if you have previously worked with TPL and PLINQ, you will be able to read and understand the content included in the chapters related to parallel debugging and tuning.

The book is divided into the following 11 chapters and three appendixes:

Chapter 1, "Task-Based Programming" — Explore the new task-based programming model that allows you to introduce parallelism in .NET Framework 4 applications. Parallelism is essential to exploit modern multicore and manycore architectures. This chapter describes the new lightweight concurrency models and important concepts related to concurrency and parallelism. It is important to read this chapter, because it includes the necessary background information in order to prepare your mind for the next 10 chapters and three appendixes.

Chapter 2, "Imperative Data Parallelism" — Start learning the new programming models introduced in C# 4 and .NET Framework 4 and apply them with pure data parallel problems. This chapter is about some of the new classes, structures, and enumerations that allow you to deal with data parallelism scenarios. Run the examples to understand the performance improvements.

Chapter 3, "Imperative Task Parallelism" — Start working with the new `Task` instances to solve imperative task parallelism problems and complex algorithms with simple code. This chapter is about the new classes, structures, and enumerations that allow you to deal with imperative task parallelism scenarios. Implement existing algorithms in parallel using basic and complex features offered by the new task-based programming model. Create parallel code using tasks instead of threads.

Chapter 4, "Concurrent Collections" — Task-based programming, imperative data, and task parallelism require arrays, lists, and collections capable of supporting updates concurrently. Work with the new concurrent collections to simplify the code and to achieve the best performance. This chapter is about the new classes and the new interface that allows you to work with shared concurrent collections from multiple tasks. It explains how to create parallel code that adds, removes, and updates values of different types in lists with diverse ordering schemes and structures.

Chapter 5, "Coordination Data Structures" — Synchronize the work performed by diverse concurrent tasks. This chapter covers some classic synchronization primitives and the new lightweight coordination data structures introduced in .NET Framework 4. It is important to learn the different alternatives, so that you can choose the most appropriate one for each concurrency scenario that requires communication and/or synchronization between multiple tasks. This is the most complex chapter in the book and one of the most important ones. Be sure to read it before writing complex parallelized algorithms.

Chapter 6, "PLINQ: Declarative Data Parallelism" — Work with declarative data parallelism using Parallel Language Integrated Query (PLINQ) and its aggregate functions. You can use PLINQ to simplify the code that runs a mix of task and data decomposition. You can also execute the classic parallel Map Reduce algorithm. This chapter combines many of the topics introduced in previous chapters and explains how to transform a LINQ query into a PLINQ query. In addition, the chapter teaches different techniques to tune PLINQ's parallel execution according to diverse scenarios.

Chapter 7, "Visual Studio 2010 Task Debugging Capabilities" — Take full advantage of the new task debugging features introduced in Visual Studio 2010. This chapter describes how the new windows display important information about the tasks and their relationships with the source code and the threads assigned to support their execution. Use these new windows to detect and solve potential bugs when working with parallelized code in .NET Framework 4.

Chapter 8, "Thread Pools" — Understand the differences between using tasks and directly requesting work items to run in threads in the thread pool. If you work with a thread pool, you can take advantage of the new improvements and move your code to a task-based programming model. This chapter is about the changes in the CLR thread pool engine introduced in .NET Framework 4 and provides an example of a customized task scheduler.

Chapter 9, "Asynchronous Programming Model" — Leverage the advantages of mixing the existing asynchronous programming models with tasks. This chapter provides real-life examples that take advantage of the simplicity of tasks and continuations to perform concurrent asynchronous jobs related to the existing asynchronous programming models. In addition, the chapter teaches one of the most complex topics related to concurrent programming: the process of updating the User Interface (UI) from diverse tasks and threads. The chapter explains patterns to update the UI in both Windows Forms and Windows Presentation Foundation (WPF) applications.

Chapter 10, "Parallel Testing and Tuning" — Leverage the new concurrency profiling features introduced in Visual Studio 2010 Premium and Ultimate editions. It is very important to learn the common, easy-to-detect problems related to parallelized code with .NET Framework 4. This chapter explains the different techniques used to create and run parallel tests and benchmarks. It also teaches you to refactor an existing application according to the results of each profiling session.

Chapter 11, "Vectorization, SIMD Instructions, and Additional Parallel Libraries" — Take advantage of other possibilities offered by modern hardware related to parallelism. .NET Framework 4 does not offer direct support to SIMD or vectorization. However, most modern microprocessors provide these powerful additional instructions. Thus, you can use libraries optimized to take advantage of the performance improvements provided by these instructions. This chapter explains how to integrate Intel Math Kernel Library into task-based programming code using C#. In addition, it explains how to optimize critical sections using Intel Integrated Performance Primitives.

Appendix A, ".NET 4 Parallelism Class Diagrams" — This appendix includes diagrams for the classes, interfaces, structures, delegates, enumerations, and exceptions that support parallelism with the new lightweight concurrency model and the underlying threading model. There are also references to the chapters that explain the contents of these diagrams in more detail.

Appendix B, "Concurrent UML Models" — This appendix gives you some examples of how you can use UML models to represent designs and code prepared for concurrency. You can extend the classic models by adding a few simple and standardized visual elements.

Appendix C, "Parallel Extensions Extras" — Parallel Extensions Extras is a complementary project that isn't part of the .NET Framework 4 classes, but was developed by Microsoft as part of the parallel programming samples for .NET Framework 4. This appendix includes diagrams and brief descriptions for the classes and structures that constitute the Parallel Extensions Extras.

WHAT YOU NEED TO USE THIS BOOK

To get the most out of this book, you'll need Visual Studio 2010 Premium or Ultimate Edition, which includes .NET Framework 4 and the concurrency profiling features. You may use Visual Studio 2010 Standard Edition instead, but the concurrency profiling features aren't available in this edition. Nor should you use Visual C# 2010 Express Edition, because it doesn't provide the necessary debugging windows to work with task-based programming.

In addition, you'll need at least two physical cores in your developer computer to understand the examples shown in the book. However, if you want to test scalability, at least three physical cores is a better option.

Windows 7 and Windows 2008 R2 introduced significant enhancements in their schedulers to improve scalability in multicore and manycore systems. The book is based on applications running on these Windows versions. If you work with previous Windows versions, the results might differ.

CONVENTIONS

To help you get the most from the text and keep track of what's happening, we've used a number of conventions throughout the book.

 Notes, tips, hints, tricks, and asides to the current discussion are offset and placed in italics like this.

As for styles in the text:

➤ We *highlight* new terms and important words when we introduce them.

➤ We show keyboard strokes like this: Ctrl+A.

➤ We show file names, URLs, and code within the text like so: `persistence.properties`.

➤ We present code in two different ways:

```
We use a monofont type with no highlighting for most code examples.
We use bold to emphasize code that's particularly important in the present context.
```

SOURCE CODE

As you work through the examples in this book, you may choose either to type in all the code manually or to use the source code files that accompany the book. All of the source code used in this book is available for download at `www.wrox.com`. Once at the site, simply locate the book's title (either by using the Search box or by using one of the title lists) and click the Download Code link on the book's detail page to obtain all the source code for the book.

 Because many books have similar titles, you may find it easiest to search by ISBN. This book's ISBN is 978-0-470-49599-5.

Once you download the code, just decompress it with your favorite compression tool. Alternately, you can go to the main Wrox code download page at www.wrox.com/dynamic/books/download. aspx to see the code available for this book and all other Wrox books.

ERRATA

We make every effort to ensure that there are no errors in the text or in the code. However, no one is perfect, and mistakes do occur. If you find an error in one of our books, like a spelling mistake or faulty piece of code, we would be very grateful for your feedback. By sending in errata, you may save another reader hours of frustration, and at the same time, you will be helping us provide even higher-quality information.

To find the errata page for this book, go to www.wrox.com and locate the title using the Search box or one of the title lists. Then, on the book details page, click the Book Errata link. On this page, you can view all errata that have been submitted for this book and posted by Wrox editors. A complete book list, including links to each book's errata, is also available at www.wrox.com/misc-pages/book-list.shtml.

If you don't spot "your" error on the Book Errata page, go to www.wrox.com/contact/techsupport .shtml and complete the form there to send us the error you have found. We'll check the information and, if appropriate, post a message to the book's errata page and fix the problem in subsequent editions of the book.

P2P.WROX.COM

For author and peer discussion, join the P2P forums at p2p.wrox.com. The forums are a web-based system for you to post messages relating to Wrox books and technologies and interact with other readers and technology users. The forums offer a subscription feature to email you topics of interest of your choosing when new posts are made to the forums. Wrox authors, editors, other industry experts, and your fellow readers are present on these forums.

At http://p2p.wrox.com, you will find a number of different forums that will help you not only as you read this book, but also as you develop your own applications. To join the forums, just follow these steps:

1. Go to p2p.wrox.com and click the Register link.

2. Read the terms of use and click Agree.

3. Complete the required information to join as well as any optional information you wish to provide and click Submit.

4. You will receive an email with information describing how to verify your account and complete the joining process.

 You can read messages in the forums without joining P2P, but in order to post your own messages, you must join.

Once you join, you can post new messages and respond to messages other users post. You can read messages at any time on the web. If you would like to have new messages from a particular forum emailed to you, click the Subscribe To This Forum icon by the forum name in the forum listing.

For more information about how to use the Wrox P2P, be sure to read the P2P FAQs for answers to questions about how the forum software works as well as many common questions specific to P2P and Wrox books. To read the FAQs, click the FAQ link on any P2P page.

1

Task-Based Programming

WHAT'S IN THIS CHAPTER?

➤ Working with shared-memory multicore

➤ Understanding the differences between shared-memory multicore and distributed-memory systems

➤ Working with parallel programming and multicore programming in shared-memory architectures

➤ Understanding hardware threads and software threads

➤ Understanding Amdahl's Law

➤ Considering Gustafson's Law

➤ Working with lightweight concurrency models

➤ Creating successful task-based designs

➤ Understanding the differences between interleaved concurrency, concurrency, and parallelism

➤ Parallelizing tasks and minimizing critical sections

➤ Understanding rules for parallel programming for multicore architectures

➤ Preparing for NUMA architectures

This chapter introduces the new task-based programming that allows you to introduce parallelism in applications. Parallelism is essential to exploit modern shared-memory multicore architectures. The chapter describes the new lightweight concurrency models and important concepts related to concurrency and parallelisms. It includes the necessary background information in order to prepare your mind for the next 10 chapters.

WORKING WITH SHARED-MEMORY MULTICORE

In 2005, Herb Sutter published an article in *Dr. Dobb's Journal* titled *"The Free Lunch Is Over: A Fundamental Turn Toward Concurrency in Software"* (www.gotw.ca/publications/concurrency-ddj.htm). He talked about the need to start developing software considering concurrency to fully exploit continuing exponential microprocessors throughput gains. Microprocessor manufacturers are adding *processing cores* instead of increasing their clock frequency. Software developers can no longer rely on the free-lunch performance gains these increases in clock frequency provided.

Most machines today have at least a dual-core microprocessor. However, *quad-core* and *octal-core* microprocessors, with four and eight cores, respectively, are quite popular on servers, advanced workstations, and even on high-end mobile computers. More cores in a single microprocessor are right around the corner. Modern microprocessors offer new multicore architectures. Thus, it is very important to prepare the software designs and the code to exploit these architectures. The different kinds of applications generated with Visual C# 2010 and .NET Framework 4 run on one or many *central processing units* (CPUs), the main microprocessors. Each of these microprocessors can have a different number of cores, capable of executing instructions.

You can think of a multicore microprocessor as many interconnected microprocessors in a single package. All the cores have access to the main memory, as illustrated in Figure 1-1. Thus, this architecture is known as *shared-memory* multicore. Sharing memory in this way can easily lead to a performance bottleneck.

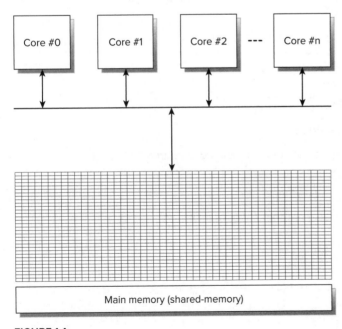

FIGURE 1-1

Multicore microprocessors have many different complex micro-architectures, designed to offer more parallel-execution capabilities, improve overall throughput, and reduce potential bottlenecks. At the same time, multicore microprocessors try to shrink power consumption and generate less heat. Therefore, many modern microprocessors can increase or reduce the frequency for each core according to their workload, and they can even sleep cores when they are not in use. Windows 7 and Windows Server 2008 R2 support a new feature called *Core Parking*. When many cores aren't in use and this feature is active, these operating systems put the remaining cores to sleep. When these cores are necessary, the operating systems wake the sleeping cores.

Modern microprocessors work with dynamic frequencies for each of their cores. Because the cores don't work with a fixed frequency, it is difficult to predict the performance for a sequence of instructions. For example, Intel Turbo Boost Technology increases the frequency of the active cores. The process of increasing the frequency for a core is also known as *overclocking*.

If a single core is under a heavy workload, this technology will allow it to run at higher frequencies when the other cores are idle. If many cores are under heavy workloads, they will run at higher frequencies but not as high as the one achieved by the single core. The microprocessor cannot keep all the cores overclocked a lot of time, because it consumes more power and its temperature increases faster. The average clock frequency for all the cores under heavy workloads is going to be lower than the one achieved for the single core. Therefore, under certain situations, some code can run at higher frequencies than other code, which can make measuring real performance gains a challenge.

Differences Between Shared-Memory Multicore and Distributed-Memory Systems

Distributed-memory computer systems are composed of many microprocessors with their own private memory, as illustrated in Figure 1-2. Each microprocessor can be in a different computer, with different types of communication channels between them. Examples of communication channels are wired and wireless networks. If a job running in one of the microprocessors requires remote data, it has to communicate with the corresponding remote microprocessor through the communication channel. One of the most popular communications protocols used to program parallel applications to run on distributed-memory computer systems is *Message Passing Interface* (MPI). It is possible to use MPI to take advantage of shared-memory multicore with C# and .NET Framework. However, MPI's main focus is to help developing applications run on clusters. Thus, it adds a big overhead that isn't necessary in shared-memory multicore, where all the cores can access the memory without the need to send messages.

Figure 1-3 shows a distributed-memory computer system with three machines. Each machine has a quad-core microprocessor, and a shared-memory architecture for these cores. This way, the private memory for each microprocessor acts as a shared memory for its four cores.

A distributed-memory system forces you to think about the distribution of the data, because each message to retrieve remote data can introduce an important latency. Because you can add new machines (nodes) to increase the number of microprocessors for the system, distributed-memory systems can offer great scalability.

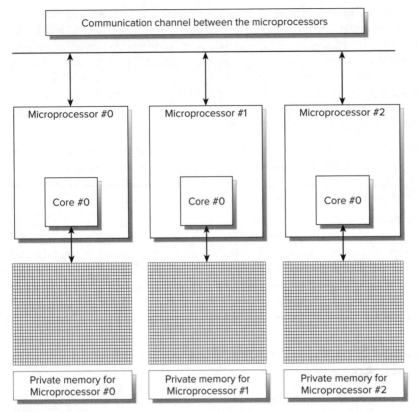

FIGURE 1-2

Parallel Programming and Multicore Programming

Traditional *sequential code*, where instructions run one after the other, doesn't take advantage of multiple cores because the serial instructions run on only one of the available cores. Sequential code written with Visual C# 2010 won't take advantage of multiple cores if it doesn't use the new features offered by .NET Framework 4 to split the work into many cores. There isn't an automatic parallelization of existing sequential code.

Parallel programming is a form of programming in which the code takes advantage of the parallel execution possibilities offered by the underlying hardware. Parallel programming runs many instructions at the same time. As previously explained, there are many different kinds of parallel architectures, and their detailed analysis would require a complete book dedicated to the topic.

Multicore programming is a form of programming in which the code takes advantage of the multiple execution cores to run many instructions in parallel. Multicore and multiprocessor computers offer more than one processing core in a single machine. Hence, the goal is to do more in less time by distributing the work to be done in the available cores.

Modern microprocessors can execute the same instruction on multiple data, something classified by Michael J. Flynn in his proposed *Flynn's taxonomy* in 1966 as *Single Instruction, Multiple Data* (SIMD). This way, you can take advantage of these *vector processors* to reduce the time needed to execute certain algorithms.

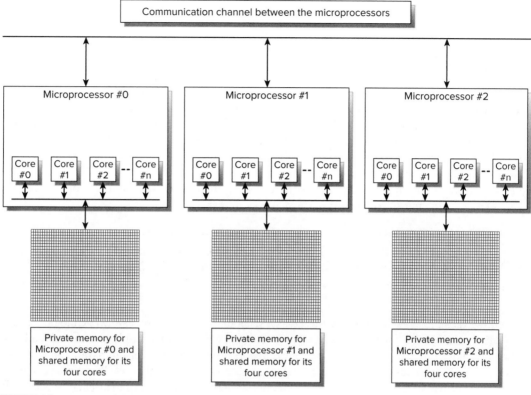

FIGURE 1-3

This book covers two areas of parallel programming in great detail: shared-memory multicore programming and the usage of vector-processing capabilities. The overall goal is to reduce the execution time of the algorithms. The additional processing power enables you to add new features to existing software, as well.

UNDERSTANDING HARDWARE THREADS AND SOFTWARE THREADS

A multicore microprocessor has more than one *physical core* — real independent processing units that make it possible to run instructions at the same time, in parallel. In order to take advantage of multiple physical cores, it is necessary to run many processes or to run more than one thread in a single process, creating multithreaded code.

However, each physical core can offer more than one *hardware thread*, also known as a *logical core* or *logical processor*. Microprocessors with Intel Hyper-Threading Technology (HT or HTT) offer many architectural states per physical core. For example, many microprocessors with four physical cores with HT duplicate the architectural states per physical core and offer eight hardware threads. This technique is known as *simultaneous multithreading* (SMT) and it uses the additional architectural states to optimize and increase the parallel execution at the microprocessor's instruction level. SMT isn't restricted to just two hardware threads per physical core; for example, you could have four hardware threads per core. This doesn't mean that each hardware thread represents a physical core. SMT can offer performance improvements for multithreaded code under certain scenarios. Subsequent chapters provide several examples of these performance improvements.

Each running program in Windows is a *process*. Each process creates and runs one or more *threads*, known as *software threads* to differentiate them from the previously explained hardware threads. A process has at least one thread, the *main thread*. An operating system scheduler shares out the available processing resources fairly between all the processes and threads it has to run. Windows scheduler assigns processing time to each software thread. When Windows scheduler runs on a multicore microprocessor, it has to assign time from a hardware thread, supported by a physical core, to each software thread that needs to run instructions. As an analogy, you can think of each hardware thread as a swim lane and a software thread as a swimmer.

> *Each software thread shares the private unique memory space with its parent process. However it has its own stack, registers, and a private local storage.*

Windows recognizes each hardware thread as a schedulable logical processor. Each logical processor can run code for a software thread. A process that runs code in multiple software threads can take advantage of hardware threads and physical cores to run instructions in parallel. Figure 1-4 shows software threads running on hardware threads and on physical cores. Windows scheduler can decide to reassign one software thread to another hardware thread to load-balance the work done by each hardware thread. Because there are usually many other software threads waiting for processing time, load balancing will make it possible for these other threads to run their instructions by organizing the available resources. Figure 1-5 shows Windows Task Manager displaying eight hardware threads (logical cores and their workloads).

> *Load balancing refers to the practice of distributing work from software threads among hardware threads so that the workload is fairly shared across all the hardware threads. However, achieving perfect load balance depends on the parallelism within the application, the workload, the number of software threads, the available hardware threads, and the load-balancing policy.*

> *Windows Task Manager and Windows Resource Monitor show the CPU usage history graphics for hardware threads. For example, if you have a microprocessor with four physical cores and eight hardware threads, these tools will display eight independent graphics.*

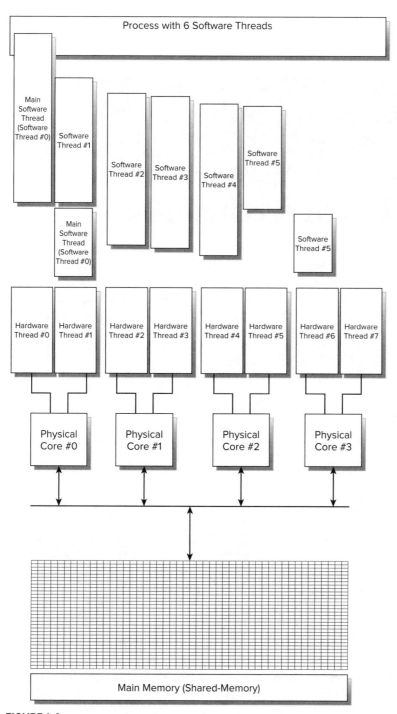

FIGURE 1-4

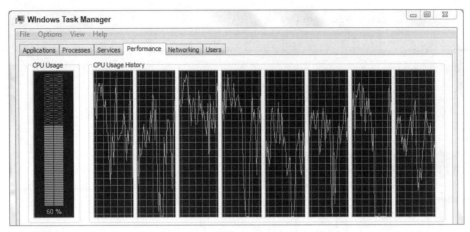

FIGURE 1-5

Windows runs hundreds of software threads by assigning chunks of processing time to each available hardware thread. You can use Windows Resource Monitor to view the number of software threads for a specific process in the Overview tab. The CPU panel displays the image name for each process and the number of associated software threads in the Threads column, as shown in Figure 1-6 where the `vlc.exe` process has 32 software threads.

Image	PID	Description	Status	Threads	CPU	Average CPU
perfmon.exe	5576	Resource and Per...	Running	19	0	0.72
vlc.exe	1456	VLC media player	Running	32	1	0.50
System Interrupts	-	Deferred Procedur...	Running	-	1	0.48
WINWORD.EXE	7660	Microsoft Office W...	Running	9	0	0.25
SynTPEnh.exe	4512	Synaptics TouchP...	Running	6	0	0.12
dwm.exe	4236	Desktop Window ...	Running	6	0	0.12
csrss.exe	568	Client Server Runti...	Running	11	0	0.10
audiodg.exe	4860		Running	5	0	0.10
explorer.exe	4284	Windows Explorer	Running	36	0	0.08
SnippingTool.exe	8164	Snipping Tool	Running	15	0	0.06

FIGURE 1-6

Core Parking is a Windows kernel power manager and kernel scheduler technology designed to improve the energy efficiency of multicore systems. It constantly tracks the relative workloads of every hardware thread relative to all the others and can decide to put some of them into sleep mode.

Core Parking dynamically scales the number of hardware threads that are in use based on workload. When the workload for one of the hardware threads is lower than a certain threshold value, the Core Parking algorithm will try to reduce the number of hardware threads that are in use by parking some of the hardware threads in the system. In order to make this algorithm efficient, the kernel scheduler gives preference to unparked hardware threads when it schedules software threads. The kernel scheduler will try to let the parked hardware threads become idle, and this will allow them to transition into a lower-power idle state.

Core Parking tries to intelligently schedule work between threads that are running on multiple hardware threads in the same physical core on systems with microprocessors that include HT. This scheduling decision decreases power consumption.

Windows Server 2008 R2 supports the complete Core Parking technology. However, Windows 7 also uses the Core Parking algorithm and infrastructure to balance processor performance between hardware threads with microprocessors that include HT. Figure 1-7 shows Windows Resource Monitor displaying the activity of eight hardware threads, with four of them parked.

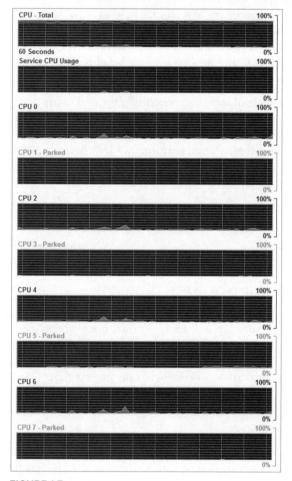

FIGURE 1-7

Regardless of the number of parked hardware threads, the number of hardware threads returned by .NET Framework 4 functions will be the total number, not just the unparked ones. Core Parking technology doesn't limit the number of hardware threads available to run software threads in a process.

Under certain workloads, a system with eight hardware threads can turn itself into a system with two hardware threads when it is under a light workload, and then increase and spin up reserve hardware threads as needed. In some cases, Core Parking can introduce an additional latency to schedule many software threads that try to run code in parallel. Therefore, it is very important to consider the resultant latency when measuring the parallel performance.

UNDERSTANDING AMDAHL'S LAW

If you want to take advantage of multiple cores to run more instructions in less time, it is necessary to split the code in parallel sequences. However, most algorithms need to run some sequential code to coordinate the parallel execution. For example, it is necessary to start many pieces in parallel and then collect their results. The code that splits the work in parallel and collects the results could be sequential code that doesn't take advantage of parallelism. If you concatenate many algorithms like this, the overall percentage of sequential code could increase and the performance benefits achieved may decrease.

Gene Amdahl, a renowned computer architect, made observations regarding the maximum performance improvement that can be expected from a computer system when only a fraction of the system is improved. He used these observations to define *Amdahl's Law*, which consists of the following formula that tries to predict the theoretical maximum performance improvement (known as *speedup*) using multiple processors. It can also be applied with parallelized algorithms that are going to run with multicore microprocessors.

```
Maximum speedup (in times) = 1 / ((1 - P) + (P/N))
```

where:

➤ P is the portion of the code that runs completely in parallel.

➤ N is the number of available execution units (processors or physical cores).

According to this formula, if you have an algorithm in which only 50 percent (P = 0.50) of its total work is executed in parallel, the maximum speedup will be 1.33x on a microprocessor with two physical cores. Figure 1-8 illustrates an algorithm with 1,000 units of work split into 500 units of sequential work and 500 units of parallelized work. If the sequential version takes 1,000 seconds to complete, the new version with some parallelized code will take no less than 750 seconds.

```
Maximum speedup (in times) = 1 / ((1 - 0.50) + (0.50 / 2)) = 1.33x
```

The maximum speedup for the same algorithm on a microprocessor with eight physical cores will be a really modest 1.77x. Therefore, the additional physical cores will make the code take no less than 562.5 seconds.

```
Maximum speedup (in times) = 1 / ((1 - 0.50) + (0.50 / 8)) = 1.77x
```

Figure 1-9 shows the maximum speedup for the algorithm according to the number of physical cores, from 1 to 16. As you can see, the speedup isn't linear, and it wastes processing power as the number of cores increases. Figure 1-10 shows the same information using a new version of the algorithm in which 90 percent (P = 0.90) of its total work is executed in parallel. In fact, 90 percent of parallelism is a great achievement, but it results in a 6.40x speedup on a microprocessor with 16 physical cores.

```
Maximum speedup (in times) = 1 / ((1 - 0.90) + (0.90 / 16)) = 6.40x
```

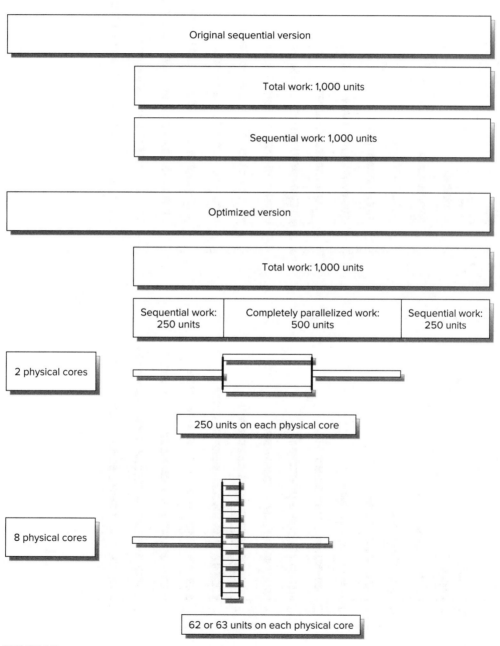

Original sequential version

Total work: 1,000 units

Sequential work: 1,000 units

Optimized version

Total work: 1,000 units

Sequential work: 250 units | Completely parallelized work: 500 units | Sequential work: 250 units

2 physical cores

250 units on each physical core

8 physical cores

62 or 63 units on each physical core

FIGURE 1-8

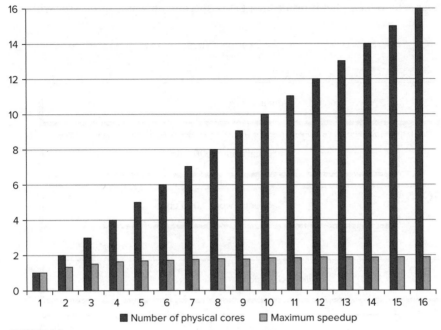

FIGURE 1-9

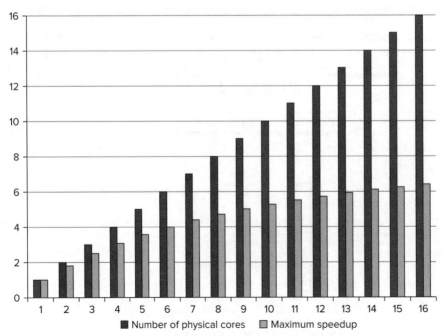

FIGURE 1-10

Amdahl's Law takes into account changes in the number of physical cores, but it doesn't consider potential new features that you could add to existing applications to take advantage of the additional parallel processing power. For example, you can create new algorithms that take advantage of the additional cores while you run other algorithms in parallel that don't achieve great performance improvements when they run with more than three cores. You can create designs that consider different parallelism scenarios to reduce the impact of Amdahl's Law. The applications have to evolve as the hardware offers new capabilities.

CONSIDERING GUSTAFSON'S LAW

John Gustafson noticed that Amdahl's Law viewed the algorithms as fixed, while considering the changes in the hardware that runs them. Thus, he suggested a reevaluation of this law in 1988. He considers that speedup should be measured by scaling the problem to the number of processors and not by fixing the problem size. When the parallel-processing possibilities offered by the hardware increase, the problem workload scales.

Gustafson's Law provides the following formula with the focus on the problem size to measure the amount of work that can be performed in a fixed time:

```
Total work (in units) = S + (N × P)
```

where:

> ➤ S represents the units of work that run with a sequential execution.

> ➤ P is the size of each unit of work that runs completely in parallel.

> ➤ N is the number of available execution units (processors or physical cores).

You can consider a problem composed of 50 units of work with a sequential execution. The problem can also schedule parallel work in 50 units of work for each available core. If you have a microprocessor with two physical cores, the maximum amount of work is going to be 150 units.

```
Total work (in units) = 50 + (2 × 50) = 150 units of work
```

Figure 1-11 illustrates an algorithm with 50 units of work with a sequential execution and a parallelized section. The latter scales according to the number of physical cores. This way, the parallelized section can process scalable, parallelizable 50 units of work. The workload in the parallelized section increases when more cores are available. The algorithm can process more data in less time if there are enough additional units of work to process in the parallelized section. The same algorithm can run on a microprocessor with eight physical cores. In this case, it will be capable of processing 450 units of work in the same amount of time required for the previous case:

```
Total work (in units) = 50 + (8 × 50) = 450 units of work
```

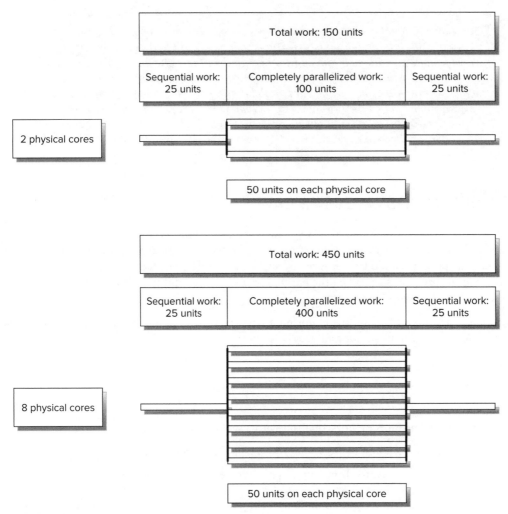

FIGURE 1-11

Figure 1-12 shows the speedup for the algorithm according to the number of physical cores, from 1 to 16. This speedup is possible provided there are enough units of work to process in parallel when the number of cores increases. As you can see, the speedup is better than the results offered by applying Amdahl's Law. Figure 1-13 shows the total amount of work according to the number of available physical cores, from 1 to 32.

> *Sometimes, the amount of time spent in sequential sections of the program depends on the problem size. In these cases, you can scale the problem size in order to improve the chances of achieving better speedups than the ones calculated by Amdahl's Law. However, some problems have limits in the volume of data to be processed in parallel that can scale. When this happens, you can add new features to take advantage of the parallel processing power available in modern hardware, or you can work with different designs. Subsequent chapters teach many techniques to prepare algorithms to improve the total work calculated by Gustafson's Law.*

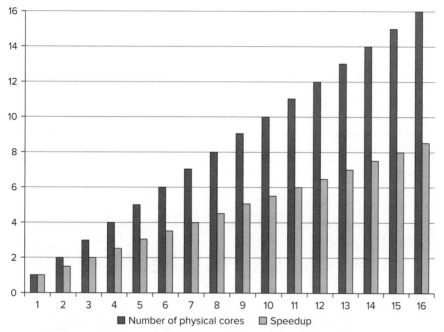

FIGURE 1-12

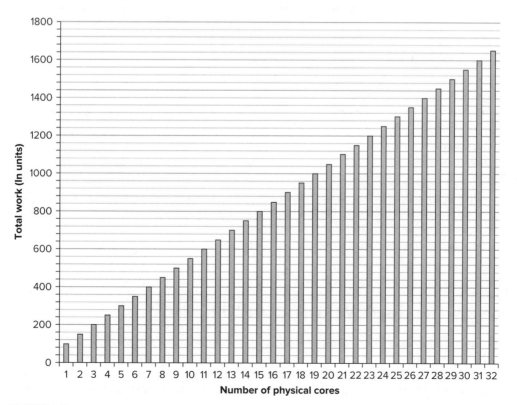

FIGURE 1-13

Figure 1-14 illustrates many algorithms composed of several units of work with a sequential execution and parallelized sections. The parallelized sections scale as the number of available cores increases. The impact of the sequential sections decreases as more scalable parallelized sections run units of work. In this case, it is necessary to calculate the total units of work for both the sequential and parallelized sections and then apply them to the formula to find out the total work with eight physical cores:

```
Total sequential work (in units) = 25 + 150 + 100 + 150 = 425 units of work
Total parallel unit of work (in units) = 50 + 200 + 300 = 550 units of work
Total work (in units) = 425 + (8 × 550) = 4,825 units of work
```

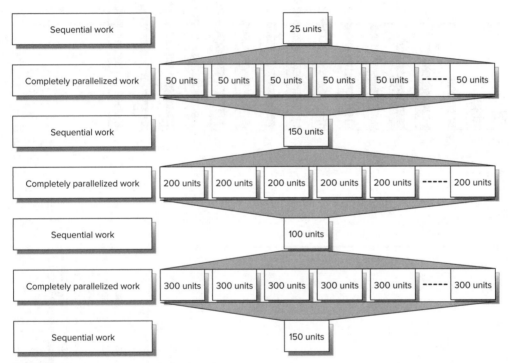

FIGURE 1-14

A sequential execution would be capable of executing only 975 units of work in the same amount of time:

```
Total work with a sequential execution (in units) =
25 + 50 + 150 + 200 + 100 + 300 + 150 = 975 units of work
```

WORKING WITH LIGHTWEIGHT CONCURRENCY

Neither Amdahl's Law nor Gustafson's Law takes into account the overhead introduced by parallelism. Nor do they consider the existence of patterns that allow the transformation of sequential parts into new algorithms that can take advantage of parallelism. It is very important to reduce the sequential code that has to run in applications to improve the usage of the parallel execution units.

In previous .NET Framework versions, if you wanted to run code in parallel in a C# application (a process) you had to create and manage multiple threads (software threads). Therefore, you had to write complex *multithreaded* code. Splitting algorithms into multiple threads, coordinating the different units of code, sharing information between them, and collecting the results are indeed complex programming jobs. As the number of logical cores increases, it becomes even more complex, because you need more threads to achieve better scalability.

The multithreading model wasn't designed to help developers tackle the multicore revolution. In fact, creating a new thread requires a lot of processor instructions and can introduce a lot of overhead for each algorithm that has to be split into parallelized threads. Many of the most useful structures and classes were not designed to be accessed by different threads, and, therefore, a lot of code had to be added to make this possible. This additional code distracts the developer from the main goal: achieving a performance improvement through parallel execution.

Because this multithreading model is too complex to handle the multicore revolution, it is known as *heavyweight concurrency*. It adds an important overhead. It requires adding too many lines of code to handle potential problems because of its lack of support of multithreaded access at the framework level, and it makes the code complex to understand.

The aforementioned problems associated with the multithreading model offered by previous .NET Framework versions and the increasing number of logical cores offered in modern microprocessors motivated the creation of new models to allow creating parallelized sections of code. The new model is known as *lightweight concurrency*, because it reduces the overall overhead needed to create and execute code in different logical cores. It doesn't mean that it eliminates the overhead introduced by parallelism, but the model is prepared to work with modern multicore microprocessors. The heavyweight concurrency model was born in the multiprocessor era, when a computer could have many physical microprocessors with one physical core in each. The lightweight concurrency model takes into account the new microarchitectures in which many logical cores are supported by some physical cores.

The lightweight concurrency model is not just about scheduling work in different logical cores. It also adds support of multithreaded access at the framework level, and it makes the code much simpler to understand.

Most modern programming languages are moving to the lightweight concurrency model. Luckily, .NET Framework 4 is part of this transition. Thus, all the managed languages that can generate .NET applications can take advantage of the new model.

CREATING SUCCESSFUL TASK-BASED DESIGNS

Sometimes, you have to optimize an existing solution to take advantage of parallelism. In these cases, you have to understand an existing sequential design or a parallelized algorithm that offers a reduced scalability, and then you have to refactor it to achieve a performance improvement without introducing problems or generating different results. You can take a small part or the whole problem and create a *task-based design*, and then you can introduce parallelism. The same technique can be applied when you have to design a new solution.

You can create successful task-based designs by following these steps:

1. Split each problem into many subproblems and forget about sequential execution.

2. Think about each subproblem as any of the following:

> **Data that can be processed in parallel** — Decompose data to achieve parallelism.
>
> **Data flows that require many tasks and that could be processed with some kind of complex parallelism** — Decompose data and tasks to achieve parallelism.
>
> **Tasks that can run in parallel** — Decompose tasks to achieve parallelism.

3. Organize your design to express parallelism.

4. Determine the need for tasks to chain the different subproblems. Try to avoid dependencies as much as possible.

5. Design with concurrency and potential parallelism in mind.

6. Analyze the execution plan for the parallelized problem considering current multicore microprocessors and future architectures. Prepare your design for higher scalability.

7. Minimize critical sections as much as possible.

8. Implement parallelism using task-based programming whenever possible.

9. Tune and iterate.

The aforementioned steps don't mean that all the subproblems are going to be parallelized tasks running in different threads. The design has to consider the possibility of parallelism and then, when it is time to code, you can decide the best option according to the performance and scalability goals. It is very important to think in parallel and split the work to be done into tasks. This way, you will be able to parallelize your code as needed. If you have a design prepared for a classic sequential execution, it is going to take a great effort to parallelize it by using task-based programming techniques.

> *You can combine task-based designs with object-oriented designs. In fact, you can use object-oriented code to encapsulate parallelism and create parallelized objects and components.*

Designing With Concurrency in Mind

When you design code to take advantage of multiple cores, it is very important to stop thinking that the code inside a C# application is running alone. C# is prepared for concurrent code, meaning that many pieces of code can run inside the same process simultaneously or with an interleaved execution. The same class method can be executed in concurrent code. If this method saves a state in a static variable and then uses this saved state later, many concurrent executions could yield unexpected and unpredictable results.

As previously explained, parallel programming for multicore microprocessors works with the shared-memory model. The data resides in the same shared memory, which could lead to unexpected results if the design doesn't consider concurrency.

It is a good practice to prepare each class and method to be able to run concurrently, without *side effects*. If you have classes, methods, or components that weren't designed with concurrency in mind, you would have to test their designs before using them in parallelized code.

Each subproblem detected in the design process should be capable of running while the other subproblems are being executed concurrently. If you think that it is necessary to restrict concurrent code when a certain subproblem runs because it uses legacy classes, methods, or components, it should be made clear in the design documents. Once you begin working with parallelized code, it is very easy to incorporate other existing classes, methods, and components that create undesired side effects because they weren't designed for concurrent execution.

Understanding the Differences between Interleaved Concurrency, Concurrency, and Parallelism

Figure 1-15 illustrates the differences between interleaved *concurrency* and *concurrency* when there are two software threads and each one executes four instructions. The interleaved concurrency scenario executes one instruction for each thread, interleaving them, but the concurrency scenario runs two instructions in parallel, at the same time. The design has to be prepared for both scenarios. Concurrency requires physically simultaneous processing to happen.

> *Parallelism entails partitioning work to be done, running processing on those pieces concurrently, and joining the results. Parallelizing a problem generates concurrency.*

Parallelized code can run in many different concurrency and interleaved concurrency scenarios, even when it is executed in the same hardware configuration. Thus, one of the great challenges of a parallel design is to make sure that its execution with different possible valid orders and interleaves will lead to the correct result, otherwise known as *correctness*. If you need a specific order or certain parts of the code don't have to run together, it is necessary to make sure that these parts don't run concurrently. You cannot assume that they don't run concurrently because you run it many times and it produces the expected results. When you design for concurrency and parallelism, you have to make sure that you consider correctness.

In the next chapter, you will learn more about the differences between concurrency and parallelism by looking at various code samples.

Parallelizing Tasks

Visual C# 2010 and .NET Framework 4 make it easy to transform task-based designs into parallelized code. However, it is very important to understand that the parallelized code requires specific testing and tuning procedures in order to achieve the expected goals. You will learn about them through the rest of the book.

When you parallelize the tasks, the overhead introduced by parallelism can have an important impact and may require testing different alternatives. As previously explained, modern multicore microprocessors are extremely complex, and it is necessary to test the results offered by different parallelizing techniques until you can make your choice. In fact, the same happens with sequential code, but the difference is that you already know that a `foreach` loop is slower than a `for` loop. While parallelizing tasks, a parallelized version of a `for` loop can offer many different performance results according to certain parameters that determine the way the parallelized tasks are executed. Once you experience these scenarios, you will be able to consider them when you have to write the code for similar problems and analogous task-based designs.

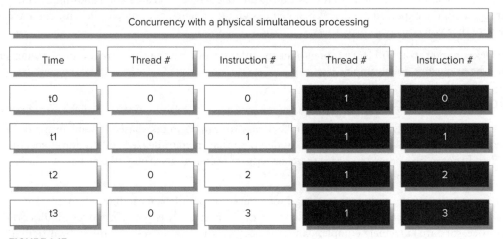

Interleaved concurrency		
Time	Thread #	Instruction #
t0	0	0
t1	1	0
t2	0	1
t3	1	1
t4	0	2
t5	1	2
t6	0	3
t7	1	3

Concurrency with a physical simultaneous processing				
Time	Thread #	Instruction #	Thread #	Instruction #
t0	0	0	1	0
t1	0	1	1	1
t2	0	2	1	2
t3	0	3	1	3

FIGURE 1-15

It is usually necessary to chain multiple tasks where the code can split the work to be done into tasks, execute actions in parallel, collect results, and then repeat many cycles like this one. Before deciding that parallelism isn't a good alternative for a specific problem, try to create a diagram with its potentially concurrent execution as if you may run it with 1,000 cores. If some completely parallelized parts of an algorithm don't offer the expected scalability, you have the chance to run them in parallel with other tasks.

Minimizing Critical Sections

Both Amdahl's Law and Gustafson's Law recognized sequential work as an enemy of the overall performance in parallelized algorithms. The serial time between two parallelized sections that needs a sequential execution is known as a *critical section*. Figure 1-16 identifies four critical sections in one of the diagrams used to analyze Gustafson's Law.

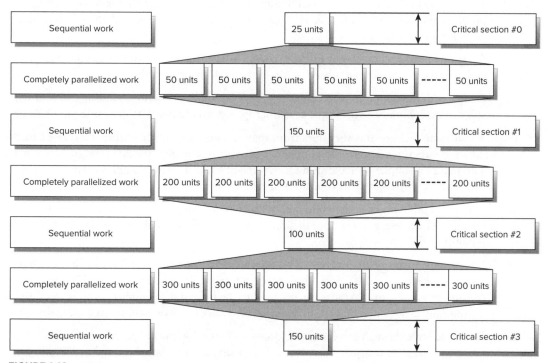

FIGURE 1-16

When you parallelize tasks, one of the most important goals in order to achieve the best performance is to minimize these critical sections. Most of the time, it is impossible to avoid some code that has to run with a sequential execution between two parallelized sections, because it is necessary to launch the parallel jobs and to collect results. However, optimizing the code in the critical sections and removing the unnecessary ones is even more important than the proper tuning of parallelized code.

When you face an execution plan with too many critical sections, remember Amdahl's Law. If you cannot reduce them, try to find tasks that could run in parallel with the critical sections. For example, you can pre-fetch data that is going to be consumed by the next parallelized algorithm in parallel with a critical section to improve the overall performance offered by the solution. It is very important that you consider the capabilities offered by modern multicore hardware to avoid thinking you have just one single execution unit.

Understanding Rules for Parallel Programming for Multicore

James Reinders published an article in *Dr. Dobb's Journal* entitled *"Rules for Parallel Programming for Multicore"* (www.drdobbs.com/hpc-high-performance-computing/201804248). He enumerated eight rules to help developers with multicore programming. His rules are also useful to create parallel applications with C# and .NET Framework 4, as described here:

1. **Think parallel** — This rule is about designing with parallelism in mind, as explained in previous sections.

2. **Program using abstraction** — You can take advantage of the new features offered by the Task Parallel Library (TPL) in .NET Framework 4 to make your high-level code reflect a problem and not complex low-level thread management techniques. *Chapter 2: Imperative Data Parallelism* introduces TPL.

3. **Program in tasks (chores), not threads (cores)** — TPL allows you to write code to implement task-based designs without worrying about the underlying threads.

4. **Design with the option to turn concurrency off** — When you write code using TPL, it will still run on computers with single-core microprocessors (those with only one physical core).

5. **Avoid using locks** — It is very important that you take advantage of the new classes, methods, and structures designed to eliminate the need for complex synchronization mechanisms. TPL makes it simpler to avoid using heavyweight locks in many complex scenarios, and it offers new lightweight synchronization mechanisms.

6. **Use tools and libraries designed to help with concurrency** — Visual Studio 2010 offers new tools to debug, test, and tune parallelized code. You will learn about various tools and libraries in this book.

7. **Use scalable memory allocators** — TPL provides scalable memory allocators in the *Common Language Runtime* (CLR), and it uses them automatically when working with tasks and threads. However, to maximize the usage of cache memories, you must analyze the different partitioning possibilities and try to avoid consuming excessive memory in each task.

8. **Design to scale through increased workloads** — Once you master parallel extensions, it is going to be easy to consider Gustafson's Law with the new classes offered by TPL. If you prepare your design for future scalability, you will be able to write the code to scale as the number of cores increases. Windows 7 and Windows Server 2008 R2 support up to 256 hardware threads or logical processors; therefore, there is room for scalability.

PREPARING FOR NUMA AND HIGHER SCALABILITY

In recent years, the most widespread model for multiprocessor support, *symmetric multiprocessor* (SMP), left the pole position to *non-uniform memory access* (NUMA) architectures. One of the great problems with SMP was that the processor bus became a limitation to future scalability, because each processor has equal access to memory and *input/output* (I/O).

With NUMA, each processor gains access to the memory it is close to faster than to the memory that is farther away. NUMA offers better scalability when the number of processors is more than four. In Windows scale-up-technology terms, NUMA is organized as follows (see Figure 1-17 for a diagram of this organization):

➤ A single computer or machine can have one or more groups.

➤ Each group has one or more NUMA nodes.

➤ Each NUMA node has one or more physical processors or sockets (a real microprocessor). The different microprocessors that compose a NUMA node have access to a local memory and I/O.

➤ Each processor or socket has one or more physical cores, because it's usually a multicore microprocessor.

➤ Each physical core can offer one or more logical processor or hardware threads.

Figure 1-18 shows a computer with one group composed of two NUMA nodes. Each NUMA node has two microprocessors that have access to their local memory and I/O. If a thread running on physical core #0 for processor #0 in NUMA node #0 needs to access data located in the local memory for NUMA node #1, it will have to use the shared bus between the two NUMA nodes, which will be slower than accessing its local memory.

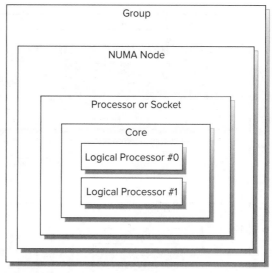

FIGURE 1-17

With NUMA, computers have more than one system bus. A certain set of processors uses each available system bus. Hence, each set of processors can access its own memory and its own I/O channels. As previously explained, they are still capable of accessing the memory owned by the other sets of processors, with appropriate coordination schemes. However, it is obviously more expensive to access the memory owned by the foreign NUMA nodes than to work with the memory accessed by the local system bus (the NUMA node's own memory).

NUMA hardware requires specific optimizations. The applications have to be aware of NUMA hardware and its configurations. Hence, they can run concurrent tasks and threads that have to access similar memory positions in the same NUMA node. The applications must avoid expensive memory accesses, and they have to favor concurrency, taking into account the memory needs.

Windows 7 and Windows Server 2008 R2 introduced the aforementioned concept of a processor group. A thread, process, or interrupt can indicate a preference for an operation on a particular core, processor, node, or group. However, there is no support for this kind of low-level definition in either TPL or C#. TPL is optimized to work with NUMA, and it tries to run the threads that support parallelism in the most convenient core and to use the local memory as much as possible. Therefore, your parallelized code is going to be NUMA-ready, though you can still face some unexpected performance problems when the threads that support the parallelized code have to access memory in foreign NUMA nodes.

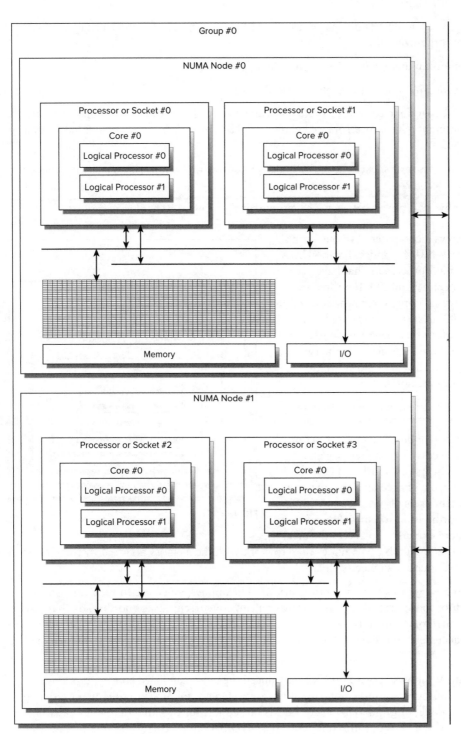

FIGURE 1-18

Windows API offers many functions to work with NUMA architectures, but they aren't compatible with managed threads. Therefore, you don't have to use them when working with C# and TPL.

Coreinfo is a simple yet powerful command-line utility that shows you very useful information about the processors, their organization, and the cache topology. It displays information about the mapping between logical processors or hardware threads and the physical cores. In addition, it shows information about the NUMA nodes, groups, sockets, and all the cache levels. You can easily save the information about the underlying hardware before running your performance tests, and you can determine whether a NUMA architecture is causing performance problems. You can download Coreinfo v2.0 at http://technet.microsoft.com/en-us/sysinternals/cc835722 .aspx. Then, you can unzip the executable file and run it from the command line (Start ⇨ All Programs ⇨ Accessories ⇨ Command Prompt).

The utility uses the GetLogicalProcessorInformation Windows API function to obtain all the information and display it on the screen. Listing 1-1 shows the results of running CoreInfo v2.0 on a computer with a single Intel Core i7 microprocessor. There is a single socket with four physical cores, detailed in the Logical to Physical Processor Map. However, because this CPU offers Intel Hyper-Threading Technology, Coreinfo tells you it is Hyperthreaded. Coreinfo uses an asterisk (*) to represent a mapping. In this case, there are four physical cores with two hardware threads each; therefore, they appear with two asterisks each (**). In addition, there is a unified 8MB Level 3 cache memory. The eight hardware threads share this cache; therefore, Coreinfo shows eight asterisks (********) on the left side of the last line under Logical Processor to Cache Map. This means that the cache is mapped to all these hardware threads and their physical cores.

LISTING 1-1: Information displayed by CoreInfo v2.0 for a single Intel Core i7

```
Logical to Physical Processor Map:
**------  Physical Processor 0 (Hyperthreaded)
--**----  Physical Processor 1 (Hyperthreaded)
----**--  Physical Processor 2 (Hyperthreaded)
------**  Physical Processor 3 (Hyperthreaded)

Logical Processor to Socket Map:
********  Socket 0

Logical Processor to NUMA Node Map:
********  NUMA Node 0

Logical Processor to Cache Map:
**------  Data Cache         0, Level 1,   32 KB, Assoc   8, LineSize  64
**------  Instruction Cache  0, Level 1,   32 KB, Assoc   4, LineSize  64
**------  Unified Cache      0, Level 2,  256 KB, Assoc   8, LineSize  64
--**----  Data Cache         1, Level 1,   32 KB, Assoc   8, LineSize  64
--**----  Instruction Cache  1, Level 1,   32 KB, Assoc   4, LineSize  64
--**----  Unified Cache      1, Level 2,  256 KB, Assoc   8, LineSize  64
```

```
----**--   Data Cache          2, Level 1,    32 KB, Assoc    8, LineSize  64
----**--   Instruction Cache   2, Level 1,    32 KB, Assoc    4, LineSize  64
----**--   Unified Cache       2, Level 2,   256 KB, Assoc    8, LineSize  64
------**   Data Cache          3, Level 1,    32 KB, Assoc    8, LineSize  64
------**   Instruction Cache   3, Level 1,    32 KB, Assoc    4, LineSize  64
------**   Unified Cache       3, Level 2,   256 KB, Assoc    8, LineSize  64
********   Unified Cache       4, Level 3,     8 MB, Assoc   16, LineSize  64

Logical Processor to Group Map:
********   Group 0
```

Listing 1-2 shows the results of running CoreInfo v2.0 on a computer with two Intel Core i7 microprocessors in two NUMA nodes. Each NUMA node has one socket with eight hardware threads.

LISTING 1-2: Information displayed by CoreInfo v2.0 for two NUMA nodes with a single Intel Core i7 inside each one

```
Logical to Physical Processor Map:
**--------------   Physical Processor 0 (Hyperthreaded)
--**------------   Physical Processor 1 (Hyperthreaded)
----**----------   Physical Processor 2 (Hyperthreaded)
------**--------   Physical Processor 3 (Hyperthreaded)
--------**------   Physical Processor 4 (Hyperthreaded)
----------**----   Physical Processor 5 (Hyperthreaded)
------------**--   Physical Processor 6 (Hyperthreaded)
--------------**   Physical Processor 7 (Hyperthreaded)


Logical Processor to Socket Map:
********--------   Socket 0
--------********   Socket 1

Logical Processor to NUMA Node Map:
********--------   NUMA Node 0
--------********   NUMA Node 1

Logical Processor to Cache Map:
**--------------   Data Cache          0, Level 1,    32 KB, Assoc    8, LineSize  64
**--------------   Instruction Cache   0, Level 1,    32 KB, Assoc    4, LineSize  64
**--------------   Unified Cache       0, Level 2,   256 KB, Assoc    8, LineSize  64
--**------------   Data Cache          1, Level 1,    32 KB, Assoc    8, LineSize  64
--**------------   Instruction Cache   1, Level 1,    32 KB, Assoc    4, LineSize  64
--**------------   Unified Cache       1, Level 2,   256 KB, Assoc    8, LineSize  64
----**----------   Data Cache          2, Level 1,    32 KB, Assoc    8, LineSize  64
----**----------   Instruction Cache   2, Level 1,    32 KB, Assoc    4, LineSize  64
----**----------   Unified Cache       2, Level 2,   256 KB, Assoc    8, LineSize  64
------**--------   Data Cache          3, Level 1,    32 KB, Assoc    8, LineSize  64
------**--------   Instruction Cache   3, Level 1,    32 KB, Assoc    4, LineSize  64
------**--------   Unified Cache       3, Level 2,   256 KB, Assoc    8, LineSize  64
```

```
********--------   Unified Cache       4, Level 3,    8 MB, Assoc 16, LineSize 64
--------**------   Data Cache          5, Level 1,   32 KB, Assoc  8, LineSize 64
--------**------   Instruction Cache   5, Level 1,   32 KB, Assoc  4, LineSize 64
--------**------   Unified Cache       5, Level 2,  256 KB, Assoc  8, LineSize 64
----------**----   Data Cache          6, Level 1,   32 KB, Assoc  8, LineSize 64
----------**----   Instruction Cache   6, Level 1,   32 KB, Assoc  4, LineSize 64
----------**----   Unified Cache       6, Level 2,  256 KB, Assoc  8, LineSize 64
------------**--   Data Cache          7, Level 1,   32 KB, Assoc  8, LineSize 64
------------**--   Instruction Cache   7, Level 1,   32 KB, Assoc  4, LineSize 64
------------**--   Unified Cache       7, Level 2,  256 KB, Assoc  8, LineSize 64
--------------**   Data Cache          8, Level 1,   32 KB, Assoc  8, LineSize 64
--------------**   Instruction Cache   8, Level 1,   32 KB, Assoc  4, LineSize 64
--------------**   Unified Cache       8, Level 2,  256 KB, Assoc  8, LineSize 64
--------********   Unified Cache       9, Level 3,    8 MB, Assoc 16, LineSize 64


Logical Processor to Group Map:
****************   Group 0
```

It is very important to test different partition techniques when working with NUMA architectures, in order to avoid the frequent need to access memory in foreign NUMA nodes. It is all about latency.

DECIDING THE CONVENIENCE OF GOING PARALLEL

Sometimes, parallelism isn't the best choice to optimize an algorithm. Parallelism makes sense when you can achieve a significant performance improvement compared with a sequential execution. There is no silver bullet to determine whether parallelism is convenient or not — it depends on the features and the performance requirements for a specific solution. For example, if a parallelized algorithm reduces the time needed to complete a job by 30 percent, it could be insignificant when its sequential version needs fractions of seconds. However, if you achieve the same performance improvement for a batch process that needs 18 hours to complete, you could run it less than 13 hours, and it would make a lot of sense to go parallel.

You can consider the parallel execution of additional features to improve existing applications. You can design solutions to be more responsive to the user via asynchronous tasks and threads that can also take advantage of parallelism.

Parallel programming is more complex than classic sequential programming. However, once you begin creating task-based designs and writing parallel code, it is difficult to avoid thinking parallel again.

The rest of this book dives deep into the different possibilities offered by Visual C# 2010 and .NET Framework 4 to translate a task-based design into parallelized code and to solve all the problems that could appear in this process.

SUMMARY

This chapter introduced the shared-memory multicore and NUMA architectures. It explained the details about the new lightweight concurrency and parallelism models and the need to think parallel while designing a solution and before writing the code. This chapter also discussed some classic laws related to parallel optimizations and scalability limits. To summarize this chapter:

➤ You can split algorithms into parallel tasks to take advantage of multiple hardware threads.

➤ You can work with simpler and more efficient lightweight concurrency models.

➤ You can improve your designs to avoid the scalability limitations explained by Amdahl's Law.

➤ You may consider Gustafson's Law.

➤ You have to minimize critical sections that reduce scalability.

➤ You have to design with concurrency, interleaved concurrency, and parallelism in mind.

➤ You must consider the overhead required to parallelize code.

➤ You can face unexpected performance problems with NUMA architectures.

➤ You have to consider everything learned so far about modern hardware architectures when writing parallelized code.

Imperative Data Parallelism

Visual C# 2010 (C# 4.0) and .NET Framework 4 offer exciting features designed to tackle the multicore and manycore complexity. However, because they include completely new features, programmers and architects must learn a new programming model.

This chapter is about some of the new classes, structures, and enumerations that allow you to deal with data parallelism scenarios. Instead of focusing on the most complex problems related to parallel programming, this chapter shows you how to create parallel code and describes the new concepts related to each scenario. This way, you will more fully understand the performance improvements.

LAUNCHING PARALLEL TASKS

With previous .NET Framework versions, it was difficult to develop applications capable of taking full advantage of multicore microprocessors. It was necessary to launch, control, manage, and synchronize multiple threads using complex structures that were capable of handling some concurrency but not the modern multicore systems.

.NET Framework 4 introduces the new *Task Parallel Library* (TPL), born in the multicore age and prepared to work with the new lightweight concurrency model explained in Chapter 1, "Task-Based Programming."

Supporting Data Parallelism, Task Parallelism, and Pipelining the TPL provides a lightweight framework to enable developers to work with different parallelism scenarios, implementing task-based designs instead of working with heavyweight and complex threads. These scenarios include the following:

➤ **Data parallelism** — There is a lot of data, and the same operations must be performed on each piece, as illustrated in Figure 2-1. For example, encrypting 100 Unicode strings using the Advanced Encryption Standard (AES) algorithm with a 256-bits key.

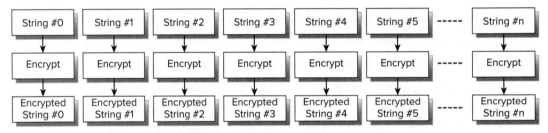

FIGURE 2-1

➤ **Task parallelism** — There are many different operations that can run concurrently, taking advantage of parallelism, as illustrated in Figure 2-2. For example, generating hash codes for files, encrypting Unicode strings, and creating thumbnail representations of images.

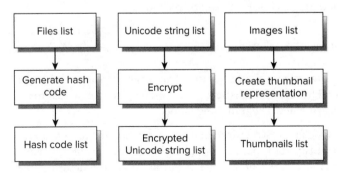

FIGURE 2-2

➤ **Pipelining** — This is a mix of task and data parallelism, as illustrated in Figure 2-3. It is the most complex scenario, because it always requires the coordination between multiple concurrent specialized tasks. For example, encrypting 100 Unicode strings using the AES algorithm with a 256-bits key and then generating a hash code for each encrypted string. This pipeline could be implemented running two concurrent tasks: the encryption and the hash code generation. Each encrypted Unicode string would enter into a queue in order to be processed by the hash-code-generation algorithm.

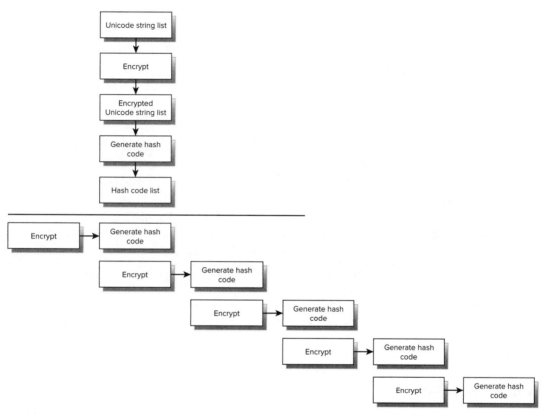

FIGURE 2-3

There are also mixed scenarios that combine the aforementioned ones. The easiest way to understand how to work with parallel tasks is by using them. Subsequent chapters will cover the most common scenarios with detailed examples.

System.Threading.Tasks.Parallel Class

TPL introduced a new namespace, `System.Threading.Tasks`. It offers access to classes, structures, and enumerations introduced in .NET Framework 4. Therefore, it is a good idea to use this namespace whenever you want to work with TPL:

```
using System.Threading.Tasks;
```

Available for download on Wrox.com

code snippet is Snippet2_1

This way, you can avoid large references. For example, instead of writing `System.Threading` `.Tasks.Parallel.Invoke`, you can write `Parallel.Invoke`. In order to simplify things, the code snippets in this chapter assume that the `Parallel.Invoke` directive is being used.

The main class is `Task`, which represents an asynchronous and concurrent operation. However, it is not necessary to work directly with instances of `Task` in order to create parallel code. Sometimes, the best option is to create parallel loops or regions. In these cases, instead of working with the lower-level `Task` instances, you can work with the following methods offered by the `Parallel` static class (`System.Threading.Tasks.Parallel`):

➤ `Parallel.For` — Offers a *load-balanced*, potentially parallel execution of a fixed number of independent `For` loop iterations.

> *A load-balanced execution will try to distribute work among tasks so that all tasks are kept busy most of the time. It tries to minimize the task idle time.*

➤ `Parallel.ForEach` — Offers a load-balanced, potentially parallel execution of a fixed number of independent `For Each` loop iterations. This method supports custom partitioners that enable you to have total control over the data distribution.

➤ `Parallel.Invoke` — Offers the potentially parallel execution of the provided independent actions.

These methods are very useful when refactoring existing code to take advantage of potential parallelism. However, it is very important to understand that it is not as simple as replacing a `for` statement with `Parallel.For`.

Parallel.Invoke

The easiest way to try to run many methods in parallel is by using the new `Invoke` method provided by the `Parallel` class. For example, supposing that you have the following four independent methods that perform a format conversion, and you are sure it is safe to run them concurrently:

➤ `ConvertEllipses`

➤ `ConvertRectangles`

➤ `ConvertLines`

➤ `ConvertText`

You can use the following line in order to launch these parameterless methods that return void and take advantage of potential parallelism:

```
Parallel.Invoke(ConvertEllipses,
    ConvertRectangles,
    ConvertLines,
    ConvertText);
```

code snippet is Snippet2_1

In this case, the code will create a delegate that points to each method. The definition of the `Invoke` method receives a params array of `Action` (`System.Action[]`) to execute in parallel.

The following code produces the same results using lambda expressions to run the methods:

```
Parallel.Invoke(() => ConvertEllipses(),
    () => ConvertRectangles(),
    () => ConvertLines(),
    () => ConvertText());
```

code snippet is Snippet2_2

You can also use lambda expressions and anonymous delegates to run the methods, as shown in the following code example:

```
Parallel.Invoke(
    () =>
    {
        ConvertEllipses();
        // Do something else adding more lines
    },
    () =>
    {
        ConvertRectangles();
        // Do something else adding more lines
    },
    delegate()
    {
        ConvertLines();
        // Do something else adding more lines
    },
    delegate()
    {
        ConvertText();
    });
```

code snippet is Snippet2_3

> *One of the great advantages of using lambda expressions or anonymous delegates is that they allow you to define complex multiline methods to run in parallel without needing to create additional methods. If you are going to be working with parallel programming using TPL, it is very important that you master delegates and lambda expressions.*

No Specific Execution Order

The following explanations apply to any of the previously shown code listings. The `Parallel`
`.Invoke` method will not return until each of the four methods has completed in any of the previously shown code listings. However, completion could occur even with exceptions.

The method will try to start the four methods concurrently, taking advantage of the multiple *logical cores* offered by one or more physical microprocessors. However, their real concurrent execution will depend on many factors. In this case, there are four methods. This means that `Parallel.Invoke` needs at least four logical cores available to be able to run the four methods concurrently. Logical cores, also known as *hardware threads*, are explained in Chapter 1. Remember that it is very important to understand the new multicore hardware that runs your parallelized code.

Having four logical cores doesn't guarantee that the four methods are going to start at the same time. The underlying scheduling logic could delay the initial execution of some provided methods if one or more cores are too busy. It is indeed very difficult to make accurate predictions about the execution order, because the underlying logic will try to create the most appropriate execution plan according to the available resources at run-time.

Figure 2-4 shows just three of the possible concurrent execution scenarios that could take place according to different hardware configurations or diverse workloads. Note that the same code doesn't require a fixed time to run; therefore, the `ConvertText` method could take more time than the `ConvertLines` method, even using the same hardware configuration and input data stream.

The first diagram represents an almost ideal situation: the four methods running in parallel. It is very important to consider the necessary time to schedule the concurrent tasks, which adds an initial overhead to the overall time.

The second diagram shows a different scenario. There are just two concurrent lanes, and there are four methods to run. On one lane, when `ConvertEllipses` finishes, `ConvertRectangles` starts. On the other lane, when `ConvertLines` finishes, `ConvertText` starts. `Parallel.Invoke` takes more time than the previous scenario to run all the methods.

The third diagram shows another scenario with three concurrent lanes. However, it takes almost the same time as in the second diagram because, in this case, the `ConvertLines` method takes more time to run. Thus, `Parallel.Invoke` takes almost the same time to run all the methods as in the previous scenario, even using one additional parallel lane.

> *The code written to run concurrently using* `Parallel.Invoke` *must not rely on a specific execution order. If you have concurrent code that needs a specific execution order, you can work with other mechanisms provided by the TPL. I'll cover them in detail later in this chapter and with many advanced topics in the following chapters.*

It is very easy to understand the execution order problem if you run the console application shown in Listing 2-1 many times on a computer with at least two physical cores.

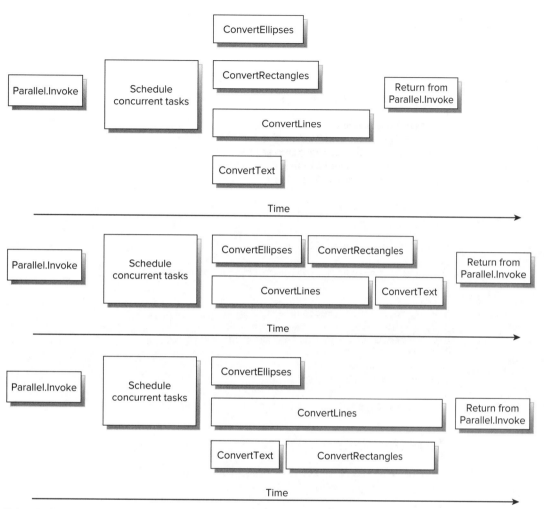

FIGURE 2-4

LISTING 2-1: Simple console application showing the execution order problems of concurrent code with Parallel.Invoke

```
using System;
using System.Collections.Generic;
using System.Linq;
using System.Text;
using System.Threading.Tasks;

namespace Listing2-1
```

continues

LISTING 2-1 *(continued)*

```
{
    class Program
    {
        static void Main(string[] args)
        {
            Parallel.Invoke(
                () => ConvertEllipses(),
                () => ConvertRectangles(),
                () => ConvertLines(),
                () => ConvertText());

            System.Console.ReadLine();
        }

        static void ConvertEllipses()
        {
            System.Console.WriteLine("Ellipses converted.");
        }

        static void ConvertRectangles()
        {
            System.Console.WriteLine("Rectangles converted.");
        }

        static void ConvertLines()
        {
            System.Console.WriteLine("Lines converted.");
        }

        static void ConvertText()
        {
            System.Console.WriteLine("Text converted.");
        }
    }
}
```

For example, consider the following sequential code version of the `Parallel.Invoke` line:

```
ConvertEllipses();
ConvertRectangles();
ConvertLines();
ConvertText();
```

code snippet is Snippet2_4

The results written on the output console would be the same on different multicore computers, as shown here, because the execution order is exactly the same:

```
Ellipses converted.
Rectangles converted.
Lines converted.
Text converted.
```

However, if you run the `Parallel.Invoke` version, the results are going to be different, even on the same hardware configuration. Listing 2-2 displays the results shown in the console for the execution in the same multicore computer three times. The lines in each output that correspond to the equivalent sequential order appear highlighted.

Available for download on Wrox.com

LISTING 2-2: The results of running the same concurrent code shown in Listing 2-1 many times on the same computer

FIRST TIME

```
Ellipses converted.
Rectangles converted.
Lines converted.
Text converted.
```

SECOND TIME

```
Ellipses converted.
Lines converted.
Rectangles converted.
Text converted.
```

THIRD TIME

```
Ellipses converted.
Lines converted.
Text converted.
Rectangles converted.
```

The first time, this concurrent code produces the same output as the sequential version. However, the second and the third times, the execution order is different. For example, the third time, the rectangles output is the last one to appear, instead of being the second one. This simple example illustrates one of the differences between sequential and concurrent code.

Advantages and Trade-Offs

The key advantage of using `Parallel.Invoke` is that it's a simple way to run many methods in parallel without having to worry about tasks or threads. However, it isn't suitable for all scenarios. `Parallel.Invoke` has many trade-offs, including the following:

➤ If you use it to launch methods that need very different times to run, it will need the longest time to return control. This could lead to many logical cores staying idle for long times. Therefore, it is very important to measure the results of using this method, the speedups achieved, and the logical cores usage.

➤ It imposes a limit to the parallel scalability, because it calls a fixed number of delegates. In the previous example, if you run it in a computer with 16 logical cores, it will launch only four methods in parallel. Therefore, 12 logical cores could stay idle.

➤ Each call to this method adds an overhead before running the potentially parallel methods.

➤ As with any parallelized code, the existence of interdependencies or uncontrolled interaction between the different methods could lead to difficult-to-detect concurrency bugs and unexpected side effects. However, this trade-off applies to any concurrent code, and it isn't only a problem of using `Parallel.Invoke`. This book will help you to find mechanisms to solve most of these problems.

➤ There are no guarantees made about the order in which the methods are executed; therefore, `Parallel.Invoke` isn't suitable for running complex algorithms that require a specific execution plan of concurrent methods.

➤ Exceptions could be thrown by any of the delegates launched with different parallel execution plans; therefore, the code to catch and handle these exceptions is more complex than the traditional sequential exception-handling code.

 The aforementioned trade-offs apply to the use of `Parallel.Invoke` *as explained in the examples. However, different mechanisms can be combined to solve many of these trade-offs. You will learn about many of these mechanisms in this chapter and in the rest of this book.*

Interleaved Concurrency and Concurrency

As you saw in the previous example and as illustrated in Figure 2-5, interleaved concurrency and concurrency are different things.

Interleaved concurrency means that different parts of code can start, run, and complete in overlapping time periods. Interleaved concurrency can happen even on computers with a single logical core. When many parts of code run interleaving concurrency on a computer with a single logical core, time-slicing mechanisms and fast context switches can offer the impression of parallel execution. However, on this hardware, it requires more time to run many parts of code interleaving concurrency than running a single part of code alone, because the concurrent code is competing for hardware resources, as shown in the previous diagram. You can think of interleaved concurrency as many cars sharing a single lane. This is why interleaved concurrency is also defined as a form of virtual parallelism.

Concurrency means that different parts of code can run simultaneously, taking advantage of real parallel processing capabilities found in the underlying hardware, as explained in Chapter 1. Concurrency cannot happen on computers with a single logical core. You need at least two logical cores in order to run parallel code. You can achieve speedups when real parallelism occurs, because many parts of code running in parallel can reduce the overall time necessary to complete certain algorithms. The previous diagram offered the following potential parallelism scenarios:

➤ **Concurrency; perfect parallelism on four logical cores (four lanes)** — In this ideal situation, the instructions for each of the four methods run in a different logical core.

➤ **A combination of interleaved concurrency and concurrency; imperfect parallelism with four methods to take advantage of just two logical cores (two lanes)** — Sometimes, the instructions for each of the four methods run in parallel in a different logical core, and sometimes they have to wait for their time-slice. In such a case, there is concurrency combined with parallelism. This is the most common situation, because it is indeed very difficult to achieve perfect parallelism, even on a real-time operating system (RTOS).

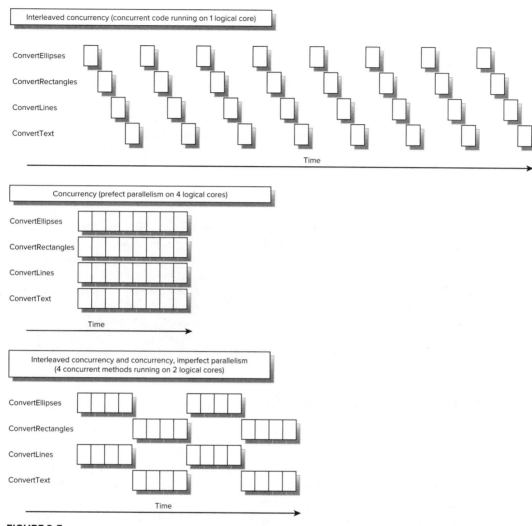

FIGURE 2-5

 When certain parts of code run at exactly the same time, new bugs may appear. Luckily, TPL offers many structures and debugging features that can help you avoid many parallelism nightmares. You will be able to combine everything you learn about imperative task parallelism in this chapter with the additional mechanisms explained in subsequent chapters to handle the challenges that parallel programming presents.

TRANSFORMING SEQUENTIAL CODE TO PARALLEL CODE

In the last decade, most C# code was written with a sequential and synchronous execution approach. Therefore, a lot of algorithms were designed with neither concurrency nor parallelism in mind. Most of the time, you won't find algorithms that can be completely converted to fully parallelized and perfectly scalable code. (It could happen, but it isn't the most common scenario.)

When you have sequential code, and you want to take advantage of potential parallelism to achieve speedups, you have to find *parallelizable hotspots*. Then, you can convert them to parallel code, measure speedups, identify potential scalability, and make sure you haven't introduced new bugs while transforming the existing sequential code to parallel code.

A hotspot is a part of the code that takes significant time to run, a bottleneck for an algorithm's performance. A parallelizable hotspot can achieve speedups if it is split in many pieces running in parallel. However, it has to be possible to split the code in different pieces (at least two) in order to take advantage of potential parallelism. If the part of code doesn't take significant time to run, the overhead introduced by TPL could reduce the speedup to 0x or even make the parallelized code run slower than the sequential version. Once you begin working with the different options offered by TPL, you'll be able to detect the parallelizable hotspots in sequential code.

Detecting Parallelizable Hotspots

Listing 2-3 is an example of a very simple console application that runs the following two sequential methods:

➤ GenerateAESKeys — This runs a `for` loop to generate the number of AES keys specified by the NUM_AES_KEYS constant. It uses the GenerateKey method provided by the System.Security.Cryptography.AesManaged class. Once the key is generated, it stores the results of converting the Byte array into a hexadecimal string representation (ConvertToHexString) in the hexString local variable.

➤ GenerateMD5Hashes — This runs a `for` loop to compute a number of hashes, using the MD5 algorithm, specified by the NUM_MD5_HASHES constant. It uses the username as a parameter to call the ComputeHash method provided by the System.Security.Cryptography .MD5 class. Once the hash is generated, it stores the results of converting the Byte array into a hexadecimal string representation (ConvertToHexString) in the hexString local variable.

LISTING 2-3: Simple serial AES keys and MD5 hash generators

```
using System;
using System.Collections.Generic;
using System.Linq;
using System.Text;
```

```
// Added for the Stopwatch
using System.Diagnostics;
// Added for the cryptography classes
using System.Security.Cryptography;
// This namespace will be used later to run code in parallel
using System.Threading.Tasks;

namespace Listing2_3
{
    class Program
    {
        private const int NUM_AES_KEYS = 800000;
        private const int NUM_MD5_HASHES = 100000;

        private static string ConvertToHexString(Byte[] byteArray)
        {
            // Convert the byte array to hexadecimal string
            var sb = new StringBuilder(byteArray.Length);

            for (int i = 0; i < byteArray.Length; i++)
            {
                sb.Append(byteArray[i].ToString("X2"));
            }

            return sb.ToString();
        }

        private static void GenerateAESKeys()
        {
            var sw = Stopwatch.StartNew();
            var aesM = new AesManaged();
            for (int i = 1; i <= NUM_AES_KEYS; i++)
            {
                aesM.GenerateKey();
                byte[] result = aesM.Key;
                string hexString = ConvertToHexString(result);
                // Console.WriteLine("AES KEY: {0} ", hexString);
            }
            Debug.WriteLine("AES: " + sw.Elapsed.ToString());
        }

        private static void GenerateMD5Hashes()
        {
            var sw = Stopwatch.StartNew();
            var md5M = MD5.Create();
            for (int i = 1; i <= NUM_MD5_HASHES; i++)
            {
                byte[] data =
                    Encoding.Unicode.GetBytes(
                    Environment.UserName + i.ToString());
                byte[] result = md5M.ComputeHash(data);
                string hexString = ConvertToHexString(result);
                // Console.WriteLine("MD5 HASH: {0}", hexString);
            }
            Debug.WriteLine("MD5: " + sw.Elapsed.ToString());
```

LISTING 2-3 *(continued)*

```
        }

        static void Main(string[] args)
        {
            var sw = Stopwatch.StartNew();

            GenerateAESKeys();
            GenerateMD5Hashes();
            Debug.WriteLine(sw.Elapsed.ToString());
            // Display the results and wait for the user to press a key
            Console.ReadLine();
        }
    }
}
```

The `for` loop in the `GenerateAESKeys` method doesn't use its controlled variable (`i`) in its code, because it just controls the number of times it generates a random AES key. However, the `for` loop in the `GenerateMD5Hashes` method uses its controlled variable (`i`) to add a number to the computer's username. Then, it uses this string as the input data to call the method that computes its hash, as shown in the following lines of code:

```
for (int i = 1; i <= NUM_MD5_HASHES; i++)
{
    byte[] data = Encoding.Unicode.GetBytes(Environment.UserName + i.ToString());
    byte[] result = md5M.ComputeHash(data);
    string hexString = ConvertToHexString(result);

    // Console.WriteLine(hexString);
}
```

code snippet is Listing2-3

The highlighted lines of code in Listing 2-3 are the ones added to measure the time it takes to run each method and the total elapsed time. It starts a new `Stopwatch`, calling its `StartNew` method at the beginning of each method, and then it writes the elapsed time to the `Debug` output.

Listing 2-3 also shows the lines that write the generated keys and hashes commented, because these operations that send strings to the console would generate a bottleneck that would distort the time measurement accuracy.

Figure 2-6 shows the sequential execution flow for this application and the time it takes to run each of the two aforementioned methods in a specific computer with a dual-core microprocessor.

`GenerateAESKeys` and `GenerateMD5Hashes` need approximately 14 seconds to run. The first one takes 8 seconds and the latter 6 seconds. Of course, these times are subject to great changes according to the underlying hardware configuration. There is no interaction between these two methods; thus, they are completely independent from each other. As the methods run sequentially, one after the other, they aren't taking advantage of the parallel processing capabilities offered by the additional cores. Therefore, these two methods represent a clear hotspot in which parallelism could help to achieve a significant speedup over sequential execution. For example, you can run both methods in parallel using `Parallel.Invoke`.

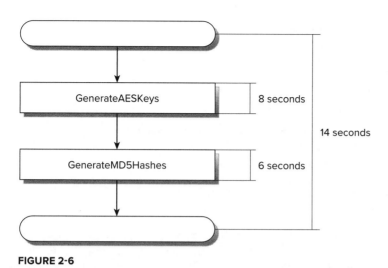

FIGURE 2-6

Measuring Speedups Achieved by Parallel Execution

Replace the `Main` method shown in Listing 2-3 with the following new version, which uses `Parallel.Invoke` to launch `GenerateAESKeys` and `GenerateMD5Hashes` in parallel:

Available for download on Wrox.com

```
static void Main(string[] args)
{
    var sw = Stopwatch.StartNew();

    Parallel.Invoke(
        () => GenerateAESKeys(),
        () => GenerateMD5Hashes());

    Debug.WriteLine(sw.Elapsed.ToString());
    //  Display the results and wait for the user to press a key
    Console.WriteLine("Finished!");
    Console.ReadLine();
}
```

code snippet is Listing2_3_withParallelInvoke

Figure 2-7 shows the parallel execution flow for the new version of this application and the time it takes to run each of the two methods in a specific computer with a dual-core microprocessor.

Now, `GenerateAESKeys` and `GenerateMD5Hashes` need approximately 9 seconds to run, because they take advantage of both cores offered by the microprocessor. Thus, you can calculate the speedup achieved using the following formula:

Speedup = (Serial execution time) / (Parallel execution time)

which, in this case, calculates to the following:

14 / 9 = 1.56x over the sequential version.

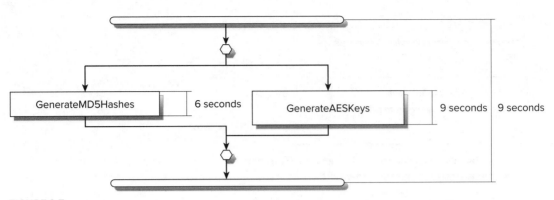

FIGURE 2-7

As you can see, `GenerateAESKeys` takes more time than `GenerateMD5Hashes` to run: 9 seconds versus 6 seconds. However, `Parallel.Invoke` doesn't go on with the next line until all the delegates finish their execution. Therefore, during 3 seconds, the application is not taking advantage of one of the cores and has a *load-imbalance* problem, as shown in Figure 2-8.

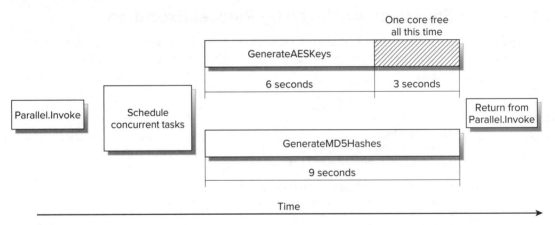

FIGURE 2-8

If this application runs on a computer with a quad-core microprocessor, its speedup over the sequential version will be nearly the same, because it won't scale to take advantage of the two additional cores found in the underlying hardware.

In this example, you detected parallelizable hotspots adding some code to measure the elapsed time to run certain methods. Then, you could achieve an interesting speedup changing just a few lines of code. You now need to know the imperative data parallelism TPL structures to achieve better results and offer improved scalability when the number of available cores increases in data-parallel scenarios.

 There is no need to initialize TPL in order to begin working with its classes and methods. TPL does a lot of work under the hood and does its best to optimize its scheduling mechanisms to take advantage of the underlying hardware at runtime. However, choosing the right structure to parallelize a hotspot is a very important task.

Understanding the Concurrent Execution

Next, you need to uncomment the lines that send output to the console in both `GenerateAESKeys` and `GenerateMD5Hashes`:

➤ `Console.WriteLine("AES KEY: {0} ", hexString);`

➤ `Console.WriteLine("MD5 HASH: {0}", hexString);`

Writing to the console will generate a bottleneck for the parallel execution. However, this time, there is no need to measure accurate times. Instead, you can visualize the output to see that both methods are running in parallel. Listing 2-4 shows a sample console output generated by this application. The shorter hexadecimal strings (highlighted in the listing) correspond to the MD5 hashes. The hexadecimal strings represent AES keys. Each AES key takes less time to generate than each MD5 hash. Remember that the code creates 800,000 AES keys (`NUM_AES_KEYS`) and 100,000 MD5 hashes (`NUM_MD5_HASHES`).

LISTING 2-4: Example output generated by keys and MD5 hash generators running in parallel

```
AES KEY: 296ADFE332D8AED2423E8CB820624900D78E79495674F1CBBBDA411CB2E23DC5
MD5 HASH: CEE3F2C283F460B668FC97A53368A9E5
MD5 HASH: BFCDA3087E249C7DE1D305870AB399CC
MD5 HASH: 164E54003C1CBD3B4AFBF45F8FBAE35C
AES KEY: A11B7FC47629C03E0A7F9B46A9C65857B4101E5E84744AAB261B58EED546556C
AES KEY: 30C4DC5168D4816F2D264EA9231C77C1EDC9BB022B673FC6F665A6B38A7316FC
AES KEY: 5898F745937BC5989515FF55E982DAA67FA445C4F60AF71BBE14B6641F8B64CB
AES KEY: F5D925B92021E5F21A943AC5CCAD89E8E929FC1A7407B789A794DFC68D63E220
AES KEY: DB6A3D03644E363A8950C69A32C724E623CB18B86BC9CB5D9D92F54891C85864
AES KEY: 41473B9A27124F4D9D50B8536F0C8E39ACF28F5A11E4DB06B80F9BBF0561549E
AES KEY: 26C2EB68720236CC15C2426378108BDAB0F6C29931930C864A692AE4D6BE62FC
AES KEY: 02FBD19C8509F9D4AF389D808FE40FEA2C1C89811C345A908EAA58AB4818A7B8
MD5 HASH: 5A041EF4132CCB7AA4EBBD6B92C80FB9
MD5 HASH: DEB81F14E7F7DD55367C15D45359D984
MD5 HASH: 1FCD39BB3BD2C1115623D51BF2C917AD
AES KEY: EE42C8B44A828BB79F11FB54D9F7202315D6BACCAEC3B413755C0C2C798B1F67
AES KEY: 862423B344622829A9CA54FE8C8619FBAD11694C849753996CD3599973C0C36C
AES KEY: 5927AFF242E24241BA1CFD2364E6B96303D8366A0AE6BE1FC6E6511819F305DA
AES KEY: D586E06A9623ADE1FD44827AE6AFAFC0274718A4EE4A98B3892879A0D7324A85
AES KEY: CF00B0268B9E1B19E9E9C0B5A9F1E5B8795F24A0FDEB862FAC886F5B6C7A5A39
AES KEY: 4ED2B64C4F34A00F7880AAF10E3CFED0CCD02D7F1BCCF18A891062C94556C7E9
AES KEY: 751206B6E98D8C7832CBEB441A8EE48AC1F5C16500DA89C93D34104B83A76FC2
AES KEY: 5865588BE6E8832EF1C8056AD3B9926456778A52FA83E355FF66F4B6295742B0
MD5 HASH: EDD39FC8108492B6BB4D9ABD806D4927
```

Now, comment the lines that send output to the console in both `GenerateAESKeys` and `GenerateMD5Hashes`, again.

PARALLELIZING LOOPS

Both `GenerateAESKeys` and `GenerateMD5Hashes` represent an opportunity to run iterations in parallel. They generate the input data to simplify the example and perform the same operation for each piece. This is an example of a *data parallelism* scenario, because you can refactor the loops to run the operations in parallel. This way, instead of running both methods in parallel, each one can take full advantage of parallelism and automatically scale according to the number of existing logical cores.

> *In this example, there are operations, the key and the hash generations, that can be applied iteration by iteration. Thus, you can apply the same task in parallel to each element. These kinds of problems are known as embarrassingly parallel, because they are easy to parallelize.*

Parallel.For

You can refactor an existing `for` loop to take advantage of parallelism by replacing a `for` with `Parallel.For` and adapting the parameters for this new method.

Listing 2-5 and Listing 2-6 show the code for the previous loops and the new code with the *refactored loops* using the imperative syntax to implement data parallelism offered by `Parallel.For`. The new methods, `ParallelGenerateAESKeys` and `ParallelGenerateMD5Hashes`, try to take advantage of all the cores available, relying on the work done under the hood by `Parallel.For` to optimize its behavior according to the existing hardware at run-time.

LISTING 2-5: The original GenerateAESKeys method with the sequential for loop and its parallelized version

ORIGINAL SEQUENTIAL FOR VERSION

```
private static void GenerateAESKeys()
{
    var sw = Stopwatch.StartNew();
    var aesM = new AesManaged();
    for (int i = 1; i <= NUM_AES_KEYS; i++)
    {
        aesM.GenerateKey();
        byte[] result = aesM.Key;
        string hexString = ConvertToHexString(result);
        // Console.WriteLine("AES KEY: {0} ", hexString);
    }
    Debug.WriteLine("AES: " + sw.Elapsed.ToString());
}
```

PARALLELIZED VERSION USING PARALLEL.FOR

```
private static void ParallelGenerateAESKeys()
{
    var sw = Stopwatch.StartNew();
    Parallel.For(1, NUM_AES_KEYS + 1, (int i) =>
    {
        var aesM = new AesManaged();
        byte[] result = aesM.Key;
```

```
        string hexString = ConvertToHexString(result);
        // Console.WriteLine("AES KEY: {0} ", hexString);
    });
    Debug.WriteLine("AES: " + sw.Elapsed.ToString());
}
```

LISTING 2-6: The original GenerateMD5Hashes method with the sequential for loop and its parallelized version

ORIGINAL SEQUENTIAL FOR VERSION

```
private static void GenerateMD5Hashes()
{
    var sw = Stopwatch.StartNew();
    var md5M = MD5.Create();
    for (int i = 1; i <= NUM_MD5_HASHES; i++)
    {
        byte[] data =
            Encoding.Unicode.GetBytes(
            Environment.UserName + i.ToString());
        byte[] result = md5M.ComputeHash(data);
        string hexString = ConvertToHexString(result);
        // Console.WriteLine("MD5 HASH: {0}", hexString);
    }
    Debug.WriteLine("MD5: " + sw.Elapsed.ToString());
}
```

PARALLELIZED VERSION USING PARALLEL.FOR

```
private static void ParallelGenerateMD5Hashes()
{
    var sw = Stopwatch.StartNew();
    Parallel.For(1, NUM_MD5_HASHES + 1, (int i) =>
    {
        var md5M = MD5.Create();
        byte[] data =
            Encoding.Unicode.GetBytes(
            Environment.UserName + i.ToString());
        byte[] result = md5M.ComputeHash(data);
        string hexString = ConvertToHexString(result);
        // Console.WriteLine("MD5 HASH: {0}", hexString);
    });
    Debug.WriteLine("MD5: " + sw.Elapsed.ToString());
}
```

The most basic version of the class function `Parallel.For` has the following parameters:

➤   fromInclusive — This is the first number for the iteration range. It can be of type `int` (`Int32`) or `long` (`Int64`).

➤   toExclusive — This is the number before which the iteration will stop, an exclusive upper bound. The type can be `int` (`Int32`) or `long` (`Int64`), and the iteration range can be from fromInclusive up to toExclusive - 1. It is very important to pay attention to this parameter, because some classic `for` loops define the iteration range using an inclusive upper bound by specifying the condition with the less than or equal operator (<=). Thus, when converting a `for` loop that uses this operator to a `Parallel.For` loop, the original upper bound has to be converted to the upper bound minus 1.

➤ `Body` — This is the delegate to be invoked, once per iteration and without a predefined execution plan. It can be of the type `Action<Int32>` or `Action<Int64>` according to the type used in the iteration range definition.

 `Parallel.For` supports neither floating-point values nor steps. However, even regular serial `for` loops over floating-point ranges can be really dangerous because of inexact additions in each round. `Parallel.For` works with `Int32` and `Int64` values, and it runs by adding 1 in each iteration. Because it runs the body in parallel, partitioning the iteration range according to the available hardware resources, there are no guarantees made about the order in which the iterations are executed. For example, in an iteration from 1 to 101 – 1 (100 inclusive), the iteration number 50 could begin running before the iteration number 2, which could also be executing in parallel, because the time it takes to run each iteration is unknown and variable. Therefore, there is no way to predict the execution order, because the loop could be split into many parallel iterations. The code has to be prepared for parallel execution, and it must avoid undesired side effects generated by parallel and concurrent executions.

`Parallel.For` can return a `ParallelLoopResult` value, because like any parallelized code, parallelized loops are more complex than sequential loops. There is no sequential execution, so you cannot access a variable to determine the number in which the loop stopped its execution. In fact, there are many chunks running in parallel.

Refactoring an Existing Sequential Loop

Listing 2-5 showed the original `GenerateAESKey` method with the sequential `for` loop. It is a good practice to create a new method with a different name when refactoring sequential code to create a parallelized version. In this case, `ParallelGenerateAESKeys` is the new method.

The original `for` loop's iteration range definition is the following:

```
for (int i = 1; i <= NUM_AES_KEYS; i++)
```

code snippet is Listing2_3

This means that it will iterate `NUM_AES_KEYS` times, from 1 (inclusive) to `NUM_AES_KEYS` (inclusive).

It is necessary to translate this definition to a `Parallel.For`, adding 1 to NUM_AES_KEYS as follows, because it is an exclusive upper bound:

```
Parallel.For(1, NUM_AES_KEYS + 1,
```

code snippet is Listing 2_7

The third parameter is the delegate. In this case, the loop doesn't use the iteration variable. However, the code uses a lambda expression to define a method with an `int` (`Int32`) parameter (`i`) as follows, which is going to work as the iteration variable to hold the current number:

```
Parallel.For(1, NUM_AES_KEYS + 1, (int i) =>
```

code snippet is Snippet2_5

The previous code was prepared to run alone, perhaps with other methods running in parallel. However, each iteration was not designed to run in parallel with other iterations of the same loop body. Using `Parallel.For` changes the rules. The code has one problem that needs to be solved. The sequential iterations shared the *aesM* local variable. The loop body has code that changes the values for this variable in each iteration. For example, consider the following lines:

```
aesM.GenerateKey();
byte[] result = aesM.Key;
string hexString = ConvertToHexString(result);
```

code snippet is Snippet2_5

The first line calls the `GenerateKey` method for an `AesManaged` instance, *aesM*. This key is going to be stored in the `aesM.Key` property. Then, the code assigns the value stored in this property to the `result` variable. Finally, the last line assigns the conversion of the key to a hexadecimal string, `hexString`. It is really difficult to imagine the results of running this code in parallel or concurrently, because it could be a really great mess. For example, one part of the code could generate a new key, which would be stored in the `aesM.Key` property that was going to be read in another part of the code running in parallel. Therefore, the value read from the `aesM.Key` property would be corrupted.

One possible solution could be using synchronization structures to protect each value and state that is changing. However, that isn't necessary in this case — it would just add more code and more synchronization overhead. There is another solution that is more scalable: refactoring the loop body and transferring these local variables as local variables inside the method acting as a delegate. In order to do this, you need to create an instance of `AesManaged` inside the loop body. This way, it is not going to be shared by all the parallel iterations. This change adds more instructions to run for each iteration, but it removes the undesirable *side effects* and creates safe and stateless parallel code. The following code shows the new body, with the *aesM* variable moved inside the delegate highlighted:

```
{
    byte[] result;
    string hexString;


    var aesM = new AesManaged();
    byte[] result = aesM.Key;
    string hexString = ConvertToHexString(result);

    // Console.WriteLine("AES KEY: {0} ", hexString);
});
```

code snippet is Snippet2_5

A very similar problem has to be solved in order to transform the original loop body found in GenerateMD5Hashes. Listing 2-6 showed the original method with the sequential for loop. In this case, ParallelGenerateMD5Hashes is the new method. It was necessary to use the same aforementioned refactoring technique, because you don't know whether the MD5 instance holds internal states that could generate problems. It is safer to create a new independent instance for each iteration. The following lines show the new body, with the *md5M* variable moved inside the delegate highlighted:

```
{

    var md5M = MD5.Create();

    byte[] data = Encoding.Unicode.GetBytes(Environment.UserName + i.ToString());
    byte[] result = md5M.ComputeHash(data);
    string hexString = ConvertToHexString(result);
    // Console.WriteLine("MD5 HASH: {0}", hexString);
});
```

code snippet is Snippet2_5

Measuring Scalability

Replace the Main method with the following new version, launching first ParallelGenerateAESKeys and then ParallelGenerateMD5Hashes:

```
static void Main(string[] args)
{
    var sw = Stopwatch.StartNew();


    ParallelGenerateAESKeys();
    ParallelGenerateMD5Hashes();


    Debug.WriteLine(sw.Elapsed.ToString());
    // Display the results and wait for the user to press a key
```

```
        Console.WriteLine("Finished!");
        Console.ReadLine();
}
```

code snippet is Snippet2_5

Now, `ParallelGenerateAESKeys` and `ParallelGenerateMD5Hashes` need approximately 7.5 seconds to run, because each one takes full advantage of both cores offered by the microprocessor. Thus, the speedup achieved is 14 / 7.5 = 1.87x over the sequential version. This is better than the previous speedup achieved using `Parallel.Invoke` (1.56x). This new version is more efficient because it runs the loops using parallel chunks. The parallel loop tries to load-balance the work done by each core. `ParallelGenerateAESKeys` takes 4.2 seconds, and `ParallelGenerateMD5Hashes` takes 3.3 seconds.

Using `Parallel.For` to parallelize this code has another advantage: the same code can scale when executed with more than two cores. The sequential version of this application running on a computer with a specific quad-core microprocessor needs approximately 11 seconds to run. The time needed to run the sequential version must be measured again, because each hardware configuration will provide different results with both sequential and parallel code. In order to measure the achieved speedup, you will always need a baseline calculated on the same hardware configuration. The version optimized using `Parallel.For` needs approximately 4.1 seconds to run. Each method takes full advantage of the four cores offered by the microprocessor. Thus, the speedup achieved is 11 / 4.1 = 2.68x over the sequential version. `ParallelGenerateAESKeys` takes 2.12 seconds, and `ParallelGenerateMD5Hashes` takes 1.98 seconds. These loops are doing a fair amount of allocation; and therefore, the default workstation garbage collection (GC) might reduce scalability. Chapter 10 explains how to activate the server GC when you need a more scalable allocator.

The parallelized code is capable of scaling as the number of cores increases, which didn't happen with the `Parallel.Invoke` *version. However, this doesn't mean that the parallelized code will offer a linear speedup. In fact, most of the time, there is a limit for the scalability. Once the parallelized code reaches a certain number of cores, the parallelized algorithms aren't going to achieve additional speedup.*

In the previous example, it was necessary to change the code for the loop's body used in each iteration. Thus, there is an additional overhead in each iteration that wasn't part of each sequential iteration, and calling delegates is more expensive than calling direct methods. Also, `Parallel.For` *and its underlying work add more overhead to distribute and coordinate the execution of different chunks with parallel iterations. This is why the speedup is not near 4x, but is approximately 2.68x when running with four cores. Most of the time, the parallelized algorithms won't offer a linear speedup. There are also bottlenecks related to serial execution and hardware architecture that can make it really difficult to scale beyond a certain number of cores.*

You should measure speedup to determine whether the performance benefits (both now and in future scalability) outweigh the overhead that results in parallelizing the code.

Figure 2-9 represents one of the possible execution flows, taking advantage of the four cores.

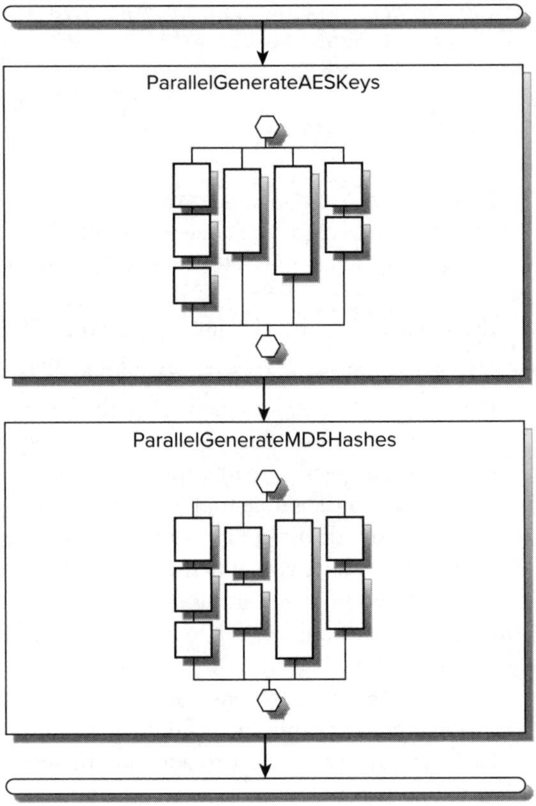

Working with Embarrassingly Parallel Problems

Not all the problems are embarrassingly parallel. However, there are many embarrassingly parallel algorithms out there, such as the previously explained examples. It is easier to understand the most important features offered by TPL working with embarrassingly parallel problems.

Embarrassingly parallel problems usually don't require complex coordination mechanisms. However, in real-life complex applications, you are going to need to add code to coordinate the communication between many concurrent tasks. Subsequent sections explain the most important structures found in TPL, and Chapter 5 covers the coordination structures, applied to the most important TPL structures.

Parallel.ForEach

Sometimes, refactoring an existing for loop as previously explained can be a complex task,

FIGURE 2-9

and the changes in the code could generate too much overhead for each iteration, thereby reducing the overall performance. One useful alternative is to partition all the data to be processed into parts that can run smaller, independent sequential loops in parallel. To do this, you use a Parallel.ForEach loop with a *custom partitioner* in order to create new versions of the sequential loops with a simpler refactoring process.

Parallel.ForEach provides a general mechanism to process a collection of data in parallel. You can take advantage of a range of integers as the set of data, and a custom partitioner to convert this range into chunks. Each chunk is processed in parallel by looping through it. Listing 2-7 shows the new code with the refactored loops using the imperative syntax to implement data parallelism offered by Parallel.ForEach. This method appears combined with a sequential for loop and a custom partitioner created with System.Collections.Concurrent.Partitioner. The new methods, ParallelPartitionGenerateAESKeys and ParallelPartitionGenerateMD5Hashes, also try to take advantage of all the cores available, relying on the work done under the hood by Parallel.ForEach and the range partitioning performed to distribute smaller sequential loops inside as many parallel loops as available cores. The code also optimizes its behavior according to the existing hardware at run-time.

LISTING 2-7: Another parallellized version of the original sequential loops using Parallel.ForEach with a custom partitioner

```
private static void ParallelPartitionGenerateAESKeys()
{
    var sw = Stopwatch.StartNew();
    Parallel.ForEach(Partitioner.Create(1, NUM_AES_KEYS + 1), range =>
        {
            var aesM = new AesManaged();
            Debug.WriteLine(
    "AES Range ({0}, {1}. TimeOfDay before inner loop starts: {2})",
                range.Item1, range.Item2,
                DateTime.Now.TimeOfDay);
            for (int i = range.Item1; i < range.Item2; i++)
            {
                aesM.GenerateKey();
                byte[] result = aesM.Key;
                string hexString = ConvertToHexString(result);
                // Console.WriteLine("AES KEY: {0} ", hexString);
            }
        });
    Debug.WriteLine("AES: " + sw.Elapsed.ToString());
}

private static void ParallelPartitionGenerateMD5Hashes()
{
    var sw = Stopwatch.StartNew();
    Parallel.ForEach(Partitioner.Create(1, NUM_MD5_HASHES + 1),
    range =>
        {
            var md5M = MD5.Create();
            Debug.WriteLine(
    "MD5 Range ({0}, {1}. TimeOfDay before inner loop starts: {2})",
                range.Item1, range.Item2,
                DateTime.Now.TimeOfDay);
            for (int i = range.Item1; i < range.Item2; i++)
            {
                byte[] data =
                    Encoding.Unicode.GetBytes(
                    Environment.UserName + i.ToString());
                byte[] result = md5M.ComputeHash(data);
                string hexString = ConvertToHexString(result);
                // Console.WriteLine("MD5 HASH: {0}", hexString);
            }
        }
    Debug.WriteLine("MD5: " + sw.Elapsed.ToString());
}
```

The code uses another important namespace for TPL, System.Collections.Concurrent, which enables you to access useful collections prepared for concurrency and custom partitioners introduced in .NET Framework 4. You can use this namespace to work with the new examples as follows:

```
using System.Collections.Concurrent;
```

code snippet is Listing2_7

The class function `Parallel.ForEach` offers 20 overrides. The definition used in Listing 2-7 has the following parameters:

➤   `source` – This is the partitioner that provides the data source split into multiple partitions.

➤   `Body` – This is the delegate to be invoked, once per iteration and without a predefined execution plan. It receives each defined partition as a parameter, which, in this case, is `Tuple<int, int>`.

In addition, `Parallel.ForEach` can return a `ParallelLoopResult` value.

Working with Partitions in a Parallel Loop

Listing 2-5 showed the original `GenerateAESKey` method with the sequential `for` loop. The highlighted lines of code shown in Listing 2-7 represent the same sequential `for` loop. The only line that changes is the `for` definition, which takes into account the lower bound and the upper bound of the partition assigned by `range.Item1` and `range.Item2` as follows:

```
for (int i = range.Item1; i < range.Item2; i++)
```

code snippet is Listing2_7

In this case, it is easier to refactor the sequential loop, because there is no need to move local variables. The only difference is that instead of working with the entire source data, `Parallel.ForEach` delegate splits the data into many independent concurrent partitions. Each partition works with a sequential inner loop.

The following code defines the partitions as the first parameter for `Parallel.ForEach`:

```
Partitioner.Create(1, NUM_AES_KEYS + 1)
```

code snippet is Listing2_7

This line splits the range from 1 (inclusive) to `NUM_AES_KEYS + 1` (exclusive) into many partitions with an upper bound and a lower bound, creating a `Tuple<int, int>` (`Tuple<Int32, Int32>`). However, it doesn't specify the number of partitions to create; and therefore, `Partitioner.Create` uses a built-in default. `ParallelPartitionGenerateAESKeys` includes the lower and upper bounds of each generated partition and the actual time (*DataTime.Now.TimeOfDay*) in which it starts to run the sequential loop for this range, as follows:

```
Debug.WriteLine("AES Range ({0}, {1}. TimeOfDay before inner loop starts: {2})",
                range.Item1, range.Item2,
                DateTime.Now.TimeOfDay);
```

code snippet is Listing2_7

Replace the `Main` method with the following new version, first launching `ParallelPartitionGenerateAESKeys` and then `ParallelParallelGenerateMD5Hashes`:

```
static void Main(string[] args)
{
    var sw = Stopwatch.StartNew();

    ParallelPartitionGenerateAESKeys();
    ParallelPartitionGenerateMD5Hashes();


    Debug.WriteLine(sw.Elapsed.ToString());
    // Display the results and wait for the user to press a key
    Console.WriteLine("Finished!");
    Console.ReadLine();
}
```

code snippet is Listing2_7

As shown in Listing 2-8, the partitioner creates 13 ranges on a particular machine. The number of ranges created by default will change based on the number of logical cores and the size of the range, among other factors. Thus, the `Parallel.ForEach` will run 13 sequential inner `for` loops with ranges. However, they don't start at the same time, because that wouldn't be a good idea with only four cores available to distribute 13 partitions. The parallelized loop tries to load-balance the execution considering the available hardware resources. The highlighted line shows the complexity added by concurrency. Taking into account the time before the inner loop starts, the first partition that reaches the sequential inner `for` loop is (66667, 133333), not (1, 66667). Remember that the upper-bound values shown in Listing 2-8 are exclusive, because the inner `for` loop uses the less than operator (<).

In addition, the order in which the data appears in the debug output is different from the order in which the `WriteLine` method is called. This change in the order happens because there are many concurrent calls to the `WriteLine` method. In fact, when measuring speedups, it is very important to comment these lines before the loop begins. Writing information to the debug output has incidence in the overall time as the method generates a bottleneck.

LISTING 2-8: Debug output for ParallelPartitionGenerateAESKeys on a quad-core microprocessor

```
AES Range (133333, 199999. TimeOfDay before inner loop starts: 15:45:38.2205775)
AES Range (66667, 133333. TimeOfDay before inner loop starts: 15:45:38.2049775)
AES Range (266665, 333331. TimeOfDay before inner loop starts: 15:45:38.2361775)
AES Range (199999, 266665. TimeOfDay before inner loop starts: 15:45:38.2205775)
AES Range (1, 66667. TimeOfDay before inner loop starts: 15:45:38.2205775)
AES Range (333331, 399997. TimeOfDay before inner loop starts: 15:45:39.0317789)
AES Range (399997, 466663. TimeOfDay before inner loop starts: 15:45:39.0317789)
AES Range (466663, 533329. TimeOfDay before inner loop starts: 15:45:39.1097790)
AES Range (533329, 599995. TimeOfDay before inner loop starts: 15:45:39.2345793)
AES Range (599995, 666661. TimeOfDay before inner loop starts: 15:45:39.3281794)
AES Range (666661, 733327. TimeOfDay before inner loop starts: 15:45:39.9365805)
AES Range (733327, 799993. TimeOfDay before inner loop starts: 15:45:40.0145806)
AES Range (799993, 800001. TimeOfDay before inner loop starts: 15:45:40.1705809)
```

This new version of using `Parallel.ForEach` with custom partitions needs approximately the same time as the previous `Parallel.For` version to run.

Optimizing the Partitions According to the Number of Cores

You can tune the generated partitions in order to match them with the number of logical cores found at run-time. The built-in default attempts to do this while also maintaining some level of load-balancing. `System.Environment.ProcessorCount` provides the number of logical cores or logical processors detected by the operating system. If you know the workload is really well balanced, you can use this value to calculate the desired range size for each partition. You can use it as a third parameter for the call to `Partitioner.Create` with the following formula:

```
((numberOfElements / numberOfLogicalCores) + 1): int or long
```

You can use the following code to create the partitions within `ParallelPartitionGenerateAESKeys`:

```
Partitioner.Create(
    1,
    NUM_AES_KEYS,
    ((int)(NUM_AES_KEYS / Environment.ProcessorCount) + 1))
```

code snippet is Listing2_9

You can use a very similar line to improve `ParallelPartitionGenerateMD5Hashes`:

```
Partitioner.Create(
    1,
    NUM_MD5_HASHES,
    ((int)( NUM_MD5_HASHES / Environment.ProcessorCount) + 1))
```

code snippet is Listing2_9

As shown in Listing 2-9, the partitioner creates four ranges, because the desired range size is ((int) (800000 / 4) + 1) = 200001. Th... e Parallel.ForEach will run four sequential inner for loops ... available logical cores.

...ated when the optimized partitions version of
...ys runs on a quad-core microprocessor

before inner loop starts: 16:32:51.3754528)
fDay before inner loop starts: 16:32:51.3754528)
fDay before inner loop starts: 16:32:51.3754528)
fDay before inner loop starts: 16:32:51.3754528)

...AESKeys and ParallelPartitionGenerateMD5Hashes need ...ecause each one generates as many partitions as cores available ...egate. Thus, the speedup achieved is 11 / 3.4 = 3.23x over the ...erhead makes it possible to reduce the time from 4.1 to 3.4

...alancing schemes used by TPL under the hood are ... know your designs, code, and algorithms better ...efore, you can analyze the algorithm's workload and ...red by modern hardware architectures. Then, you ...to use many of the features included in TPL in order ...rmance. You can reduce unnecessary overhead intro-...ation.

...ble execution flows, taking advantage of the four cores with the optimized partitioning scheme.

Listing 2-10 shows the results of the partitioner creating eight ranges in a computer with eight logical cores, because the desired range size is ((int) (800000 / 8) + 1) = 100001. In this case, the Parallel.ForEach will run eight sequential inner for loops with ranges.

LISTING 2-10: Debug output generated when the optimized partitions version of ParallelPartitionGenerateAESKeys runs on a microprocessor with eight logical cores

```
AES Range (1, 100002. TimeOfDay before inner loop starts: 00:07:21.4111496)
AES Range (500006, 600007. TimeOfDay before inner loop starts: 00:07:21.4601524)
AES Range (100002, 200003. TimeOfDay before inner loop starts: 00:07:21.4111496)
AES Range (200003, 300004. TimeOfDay before inner loop starts: 00:07:21.4111496)
AES Range (400005, 500006. TimeOfDay before inner loop starts: 00:07:21.4381511)
AES Range (300004, 400005. TimeOfDay before inner loop starts: 00:07:21.4361510)
AES Range (700008, 800000. TimeOfDay before inner loop starts: 00:07:21.5181557)
AES Range (600007, 700008. TimeOfDay before inner loop starts: 00:07:21.5181557)
```

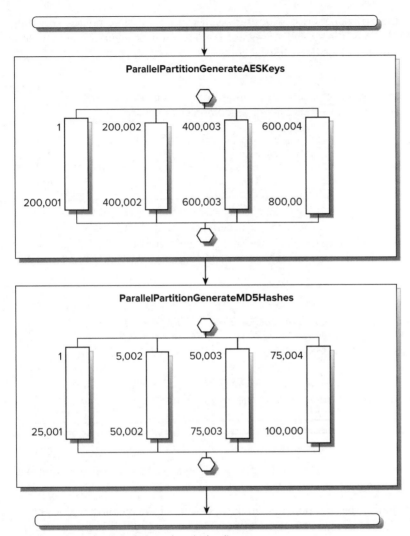

Upper bounds are inclusive values in the diagram.

FIGURE 2-10

Working with IEnumerable Sources of Data

Parallel.ForEach can also be used to refactor existing foreach loops that iterate over a collection that exposes an IEnumerable interface.

Listing 2-11 shows the code for a new GenerateMD5InputData function that returns a sequence of int numbers from 1 to NUM_AES_KEYS (inclusive). The second parameter for Enumerable.Range is the number of sequential integers to generate rather than an upper bound. Instead of using the loop to control the numbers for the iteration, the code in the ParallelForEachGenerateMD5Hashes method saves this sequence in the inputData local variable.

LISTING 2-11: A parallelized version of the GenerateMD5Hashes method using Parallel.ForEach with an IEnumerable source

```
private static IEnumerable<int> GenerateMD5InputData()
{
    // Generate a sequence of NUM_AES_KEYS integral numbers
    // The value of the first integer in the sequence (start) is 1
    // The number of sequential integers to generate (count)
    // is NUM_AES_KEYS
    return Enumerable.Range(1, NUM_AES_KEYS);
}

private static void ParallelForEachGenerateMD5Hashes()
{
    var sw = Stopwatch.StartNew();
    var inputData = GenerateMD5InputData();
    Parallel.ForEach(inputData, (int number) =>
    {
        var md5M = MD5.Create();
        byte[] data =
            Encoding.Unicode.GetBytes(
            Environment.UserName + number.ToString());
        byte[] result = md5M.ComputeHash(data);
        string hexString = ConvertToHexString(result);
        // Console.WriteLine("MD5 HASH: {0}", hexString);
    });
    Debug.WriteLine("MD5: " + sw.Elapsed.ToString());
}
```

The simplest definition of the class function `Parallel.ForEach` used in Listing 2-11 to generate a new version of the MD5 hashes generation method, `ParallelForEachGenerateMD5Hashes`, has the following parameters:

➤ `Source` – This collection exposes an IEnumerable interface and provides the data source.

➤ `Body` – This is the delegate to be invoked, once per iteration and without a predefined execution plan. It receives each element of the `source` collection, which, in this case, is an `int`.

The following line calls `Parallel.ForEach` with the source (`inputData`) and a lambda delegate method receiving the `number` for each iteration:

```
Parallel.ForEach(inputData, (int number) =>
```

code snippet is Listing2_11

The following line prepares the input data for the hash computing method and uses the value found in `number`:

```
data = Encoding.Unicode.GetBytes(Environment.UserName + number.ToString());
```

code snippet is Listing2_11

In this case, performance isn't really good compared with the other versions. The method needs almost 16 seconds to run in the same hardware configuration used for the previous examples. This isn't an optimal implementation, because the code has to iterate the 100,000 items of a sequence. It does it in parallel, but it takes more time than running loops with less overhead. It also consumes more memory. This example isn't intended to be a best practice for this case, but to help you understand the different opportunities offered by the `Parallel` class methods and evaluate them in different scenarios.

Part of the problem is that the actual iteration of the `Enumerable` happens sequentially. All the threads that support the tasks execution launched by `Parallel.ForEach` are forced to serialize while accessing the iterator. You can create a custom partitioner capable of doing a static range partition in order to avoid this serialization.

Exiting from Parallel Loops

If you want to interrupt a sequential loop, you can use the `break` sentence. However, when you're working with parallel loops, exiting the delegate body method doesn't have any effect on the parallel loop's execution, because the delegate body method is disconnected from the traditional loop structure and is called on each new iteration.

Listing 2-12 shows a new version of `ParallelForEachGenerateMD5Hashes` method, called `ParallelForEachGenerateMD5HashesBreak`.

LISTING 2-12: A new version of the ParallelForEachGenerateMD5Hashes method with the possiblity of exiting from the loop

```
private static void DisplayParallelLoopResult(ParallelLoopResult loopResult)
{
    string text;
    if (loopResult.IsCompleted)
    {
        text = "The loop ran to completion.";
    }
    else
    {
        if (loopResult.LowestBreakIteration.HasValue)
```

```
            {
                text =
                    "The loop ended by calling the Break statement.";
            }
            else
            {
                text =
                    "The loop ended prematurely with a Stop statement.";
            }
        }
        Console.WriteLine(text);
    }

    private static void ParallelForEachGenerateMD5HashesBreak()
    {
        var sw = Stopwatch.StartNew();
        var inputData = GenerateMD5InputData();
        var loopResult = Parallel.ForEach(inputData,
        (int number, ParallelLoopState loopState) =>
        {
            // There is very little value in doing this first thing
            // in the loop, since the loop itself is checking
            // the same condition prior to invoking the body delegate
            // Therefore, the following if statement appears commented
            //if (loopState.ShouldExitCurrentIteration)
            //{
            //    return;
            //}
            var md5M = MD5.Create();
            byte[] data =
                Encoding.Unicode.GetBytes(
                Environment.UserName + number.ToString());
            byte[] result = md5M.ComputeHash(data);
            string hexString = ConvertToHexString(result);
            // Console.WriteLine("MD5 HASH: {0}", hexString);
            if (sw.Elapsed.Seconds > 3)
            {
                loopState.Break();
                return;
            }
        });
        DisplayParallelLoopResult(loopResult);
        Debug.WriteLine("MD5: " + sw.Elapsed.ToString());
    }
```

Now, the `loopResult` local variable saves the result of calling the `Parallel.ForEach` class function. Moreover, the delegate body method receives a `ParallelLoopState` instance as a second parameter:

```
var loopResult = Parallel.ForEach(inputData,
(int number, ParallelLoopState loopState) =>
```

code snippet is Listing2_12

Understanding ParallelLoopState

The `loopState` instance of `ParallelLoopState` offers the following two methods to cease the execution of a `Parallel.For` or `Parallel.ForEach`:

➤ `Break` — This communicates that the parallel loop should cease the execution beyond the current iteration, as soon as possible. If iteration 100 is being processed when `Break` is called, the loop will still process all iterations < 100.

➤ `Stop` — This communicates that the parallel loop should cease the execution as soon as possible. If iteration 100 is being processed when `Stop` is called, the loop won't guarantee the processing of all iterations < 100.

 Break is more closely related to sequential semantics, where if you use break at iteration 100, you know that all iterations < 100 will have been processed.

The code shown in Listing 2-12 calls the `Break` method if the elapsed time is more than 3 seconds:

Available for download on Wrox.com

```
if (sw.Elapsed.Seconds > 3)
{

    loopState.Break();

    return;
}
```

code snippet is Listing2_12

Notice that the code in the lambda delegate body is accessing the `sw` variable defined in `ParallelForEachGenerateMD5HashesBreak`. It reads the value of the `Seconds` read-only property.

You can also check the value of the `ShouldExitCurrentIteration` read-only property in order to take decisions when there was a request to stop the parallel loop execution. This request could be made by the current or other concurrent iterations. Listing 2-12 includes the following commented lines that check whether `ShouldExitConcurrentIteration` is true:

Available for download on Wrox.com

```
if (loopState.ShouldExitCurrentIteration)
{
    return;
}
```

code snippet is Listing2_12

If the aforementioned condition is `true`, it exits the method, and avoids executing undesired iterations. The lines are commented because, in this case, an additional iteration isn't a problem; therefore, it isn't necessary to add these instructions to each iteration. You would only need to do this in the middle of a long-running iteration if you wanted to enable the loop to end earlier if another force is causing the loop to exit early.

The request to cancel a parallelized loop could also be external, in the form of cancellation. Chapter 3 explains how to work with cancellations.

Analyzing the Results of a Parallel Loop Execution

Once the `Parallel.ForEach` finishes its execution, `loopResult` offers information about the results in a `ParallelLoopResult` structure.

The `DisplayParallelLoopResult` method shown in Listing 2-12 receives a `ParallelLoopResult` structure, evaluates its read-only properties, and displays the results of executing the `Parallel.ForEach` loop in the console. Table 2-1 explains the three possible situations considered in this example.

TABLE 2-1: Read-Only Properties of ParallelLoopResult

CONDITION	EXPLANATION
`(IsCompleted)`	The loop ran to completion.
`((!IsCompleted) && (!LowestBreakIteration.HasValue))`	The loop ended prematurely with a `Stop` statement.
`((!IsCompleted) && (LowestBreakIteration.HasValue))`	The loop ended by calling the `Break` statement. The `LowestBreakIteration` property holds the value of the lowest iteration that called the `Break` statement.

It is very important to analyze the results of a parallel loop execution if the body of the loop may have called `Break` or `Stop`. The continuation with the next statement doesn't mean that it completed all the iterations after a `Break` or `Stop` was executed. Thus, it is necessary to check the values of the `ParallelLoopResult` properties or to include customized control mechanisms inside the loop bodies. In all other cases, if a parallel loop completes without throwing an exception, all iterations completed. And if it does throw an exception, there is no `ParallelLoopResult` to inspect. Again, converting sequential code to parallel and concurrent code isn't just replacing a few loops. You need to understand a very different programming paradigm and the structures prepared for this new scenario. Remember to apply all the concepts explained in Chapter 1.

Catching Exceptions that Occur Inside Parallel Loops

As many iterations run in parallel, many exceptions can occur in parallel. The classic exception-management techniques used in sequential code aren't useful with parallel loops.

When the code inside the delegate that is being called in each parallelized iteration throws an exception that isn't captured inside the delegate, it becomes part of a set of exceptions. The new `System .AggregateException` class handles this set of exceptions.

You already know how to handle exceptions in your sequential code, and you can apply almost the same techniques to your parallel code. The only difference is when an exception is thrown inside the loop body, which is a delegate. Listing 2-13 shows a new version of `ParallelForEachGenerateMD5 Hashes` method, called `ParallelForEachGenerateMD5HashesException`.

LISTING 2-13: Throwing and handling exceptions with the ParallelForEachGenerateMD5Hashes method

```csharp
private static void ParallelForEachGenerateMD5HashesException()
{
    var sw = Stopwatch.StartNew();
    var inputData = GenerateMD5InputData();
    var loopResult = new ParallelLoopResult();
    try
    {
        loopResult = Parallel.ForEach(inputData,
        (int number, ParallelLoopState loopState) =>
        {
            //if (loopState.ShouldExitCurrentIteration)
            //{
            //    return;
            //}
            var md5M = MD5.Create();
            byte[] data =
                Encoding.Unicode.GetBytes(
                Environment.UserName + number.ToString());
            byte[] result = md5M.ComputeHash(data);
            string hexString = ConvertToHexString(result);
            // Console.WriteLine("MD5 HASH: {0}", hexString);
            if (sw.Elapsed.Seconds > 3)
            {
                throw new TimeoutException(
"Parallel.ForEach is taking more than 3 seconds to complete.");
            }
        });
    }
    catch (AggregateException ex)
    {
        foreach (Exception innerEx in ex.InnerExceptions)
        {
            Debug.WriteLine(innerEx.ToString());
```

```
            // Do something considering the innerEx Exception
        }
    }
    DisplayParallelLoopResult(loopResult);
    Debug.WriteLine("MD5: " + sw.Elapsed.ToString());
}
```

Now, the body throws a `TimeOutException` if the elapsed time is more than 3 seconds:

```
if (sw.Elapsed.Seconds > 3)
{
    throw new TimeoutException(
        "Parallel.ForEach is taking more than 3 seconds to complete.");
}
```

code snippet is Listing2_13

A `try` block encloses the call to `Parallel.ForEach`. Then, instead of the classic `catch (Exception ex)` clause, the following `catch` clause catches the exception:

```
catch (AggregateException ex)
```

code snippet is Listing2_13

An `AggregateException` contains one or more exceptions that occurred during the execution of parallel and concurrent code. Therefore, once it is captured, it is possible to iterate through each individual exception contained in the `InnerExceptions` read-only collection of `Exception`. In this case, the `Parallel.ForEach` without the custom partitioner will display the contents of many exceptions. The loop result will look like it was stopped using the `Stop` keyword. However, because it is possible to catch the `AggregateException`, you can take decisions according to the problems that caused the loop to be unable to complete all the iterations. In this case, a sequential `foreach` loop retrieves all the information about each `Exception` in `InnerExceptions`.

```
catch (AggregateException ex)
{
    foreach (Exception innerEx in ex.InnerExceptions)
    {
        Debug.WriteLine(innerEx.ToString());
        // Do something considering the innerEx Exception
    }
}
```

code snippet is Listing2_13

Listing 2-14 shows the information about the first two exceptions converted to a string and sent to the debug output. The two exceptions display the same information to the debug output. However, most of the time, you will use a more sophisticated exception-management technique and provide more information about the iteration that is generating the problem.

This example is focused on the differences between an `AggregateException` and the traditional `Exception`. It doesn't promote the practice to write information about errors to the debug output as a complete exception-management technique. In fact, you will work with more complex examples in the forthcoming chapters.

LISTING 2-14: Debug output with two exceptions found in the InnerExceptions collection

```
System.TimeoutException: Parallel.ForEach is taking more than 3 seconds to complete.
    at Listing2_13.Program.<>c__DisplayClassd.
<ParallelForEachGenerateMD5HashesException>b__b
(Int32 number, ParallelLoopState loopState) in
c:\users\gaston\documents\visual studio 2010\
Projects\Listing2_13\Listing2_13\Program.cs:line 220
    at System.Threading.Tasks.Parallel.<>c__DisplayClass32`2.
<PartitionerForEachWorker>b__30()
    at System.Threading.Tasks.Task.InnerInvoke()
    at System.Threading.Tasks.Task.InnerInvokeWithArg(Task childTask)
    at System.Threading.Tasks.Task.<>c__DisplayClass7.
<ExecuteSelfReplicating>b__6(Object )
System.TimeoutException:
Parallel.ForEach is taking more than 3 seconds to complete.
    at Listing2_13.Program.<>c__DisplayClassd.
<ParallelForEachGenerateMD5HashesException>b__b
(Int32 number, ParallelLoopState loopState) in
c:\users\gaston\documents\visual studio 2010\
Projects\Listing2_13\Listing2_13\Program.cs:line 220
    at System.Threading.Tasks.Parallel.<>c__DisplayClass32`2.
<PartitionerForEachWorker>b__30()
    at System.Threading.Tasks.Task.InnerInvoke()
    at System.Threading.Tasks.Task.InnerInvokeWithArg(Task childTask)
    at System.Threading.Tasks.Task.<>c__DisplayClass7.
<ExecuteSelfReplicating>b__6(Object )
```

SPECIFYING THE DESIRED DEGREE OF PARALLELISM

Sometimes, you don't want to use all the available cores in a parallel loop, because you have specific needs and better plans for the remaining available cores. Thus, you want to specify the *maximum degree of parallelism* for a parallel loop. TPL methods always try to achieve the best results using all the available logical cores. There are unfortunately also cases where the internal heuristics of the .NET Framework result in more threads being injected and utilized than are really appropriate. In such a case, a good workaround is to specify the maximum degree of parallelism. In other cases, you want to leave one core free, because you want to create a responsive application, and this core can help you to run another part of code in parallel.

ParallelOptions

TPL allows you to specify the maximum degree of parallelism by creating an instance of the new `ParallelOptions` class and changing the value of its `MaxDegreeOfParallelism` property. Listing 2-15 shows a new version of `ParallelGenerateAESKeysMaxDegree` and `ParallelGenerateMD5HashesMaxDegree`, the two well-known methods that use `Parallel`.

LISTING 2-15: Specifying the maximum desired degree of parallelism for Parallel.For loops

```
private static void ParallelGenerateAESKeysMaxDegree(int maxDegree)
{
    var parallelOptions = new ParallelOptions();
    parallelOptions.MaxDegreeOfParallelism = maxDegree;
    var sw = Stopwatch.StartNew();
    Parallel.For(1, NUM_AES_KEYS + 1, parallelOptions, (int i) =>
    {
        var aesM = new AesManaged();
        byte[] result = aesM.Key;
        string hexString = ConvertToHexString(result);
        // Console.WriteLine("AES KEY: {0} ", hexString);
    });
    Debug.WriteLine("AES: " + sw.Elapsed.ToString());
}

private static void ParallelGenerateMD5HashesMaxDegree(int maxDegree)
{
    var parallelOptions = new ParallelOptions();
    parallelOptions.MaxDegreeOfParallelism = maxDegree;
    var sw = Stopwatch.StartNew();
    Parallel.For(1, NUM_MD5_HASHES + 1, parallelOptions, (int i) =>
    {
        var md5M = MD5.Create();
        byte[] data =
            Encoding.Unicode.GetBytes(
            Environment.UserName + i.ToString());
        byte[] result = md5M.ComputeHash(data);
        string hexString = ConvertToHexString(result);
        // Console.WriteLine("MD5 HASH: {0}", hexString);
    });
    Debug.WriteLine("MD5: " + sw.Elapsed.ToString());
}
```

Now, the `ParallelGenerateAESKeysMaxDegree` and `ParallelGenerateMD5HashesMaxDegree` methods receive an `int` with the maximum desired degree of parallelism, `maxDegree`. Each method creates a local instance of `ParallelOptions` and assigns the value received as a parameter to its `MaxDegreeOfParallelism` property, which is a new parameter for each parallel loop before the body. This way, the loop won't be optimized to take advantage of all the available cores (`MaxDegreeOfParallelism = -1`). Instead, it will be optimized as if the total number of available cores is equal to the maximum degree of parallelism specified in the property.

```
var parallelOptions = new ParallelOptions();
parallelOptions.MaxDegreeOfParallelism = maxDegree;
```

code snippet is Listing2_15

Working with static values for the desired degree of parallelism can limit the scalability when more cores are available. Therefore, you should use these options carefully and work with relative values according to the number of available logical cores, or consider this number in order to prepare the code for further scalability. It can often be advantageous to set MaxDegreeOfParallelism *to* Environment.ProcessorCount *or some value derived from it (*Environment.ProcessorCount * 2). *By default, when no* MaxDegreeOfParallelism *is specified, TPL allows a heuristic to ramp up and down the number of threads, potentially beyond* ProcessorCount. *It does this in order to better support mixed CPU and I/O-bound workloads.*

You can call both methods, `ParallelGenerateAESKeysMaxDegree` and `ParallelGenerateMD5HashesMaxDegree`, with a dynamic value based on the number of logical cores at run-time. However, this code requires a machine with at least two logical cores or an exception will be thrown.

```
// This code requires Environment.ProcessorCount > 2 to run
ParallelGenerateAESKeysMaxDegree(Environment.ProcessorCount - 1);
ParallelGenerateMD5HashesMaxDegree(Environment.ProcessorCount - 1);
```

code snippet is Listing2_15

Both `Parallel.For` loops are going to try to work with the number of logical cores − 1. If the code runs with a quad-core microprocessor, it will use just three cores.

The following is not a best practice for final code. However, sometimes you want to know whether two parallelized methods offer best performance when each is running at the same time using many cores. You can test this situation using the following:

```
Parallel.Invoke(
    () => ParallelGenerateAESKeysMaxDegree(2),
    () => ParallelGenerateMD5HashesMaxDegree(2));
```

code snippet is Snippet2_6

The two methods will be launched in parallel, and each will try to optimize its execution to use two out of four cores with a quad-core microprocessor. The obvious drawback is that this uses a static number of cores. Nonetheless, this is just for performance-testing purposes.

`ParallelOptions` also offers the following two properties to control advanced options:

➤ `CancellationToken` — This allows you to assign a new `System.Threading`
   `.CancellationToken` instance in order to propagate notification that parallel operations
   should be cancelled. Chapter 3 explains the usage of cancellations.

➤ `TaskScheduler` — This allows you to assign a customized `System.Threading.Tasks`
   `.TaskScheduler` instance. It is usually not necessary to define a customized task scheduler to

schedule parallel tasks unless you are working with very specific algorithms. For example, if you wanted a maximum degree of parallelism across multiple parallel loop invocations, you would use `ParallelOptions` for each loop. But if you wanted all of the loops in aggregate to use no more than a particular maximum degree of parallelism, you would need a `TaskScheduler` to coordinate across all of the loops. Chapter 8 explains the usage of the `TaskScheduler` class.

Counting Hardware Threads

`Environment.ProcessorCount` offers the number of logical cores. However, sometimes, the number of logical cores is different from the number of physical cores, as you learned in the previous chapter.

For example, an Intel Core i7 microprocessor with four physical cores offering Hyper-Threading Technology doubles the number to eight logical cores. In this case, `Environment.ProcessorCount` is 8 and not 4. The operating system also works with eight logical processors.

All the code created using TPL runs using multiple software *threads*. Threads are the low-level lanes to run many parts of code in parallel, taking advantage of the presence of multiple cores in the underlying hardware. However, most of the time, the code running in these lanes has some imperfections. It has the impact of latency waiting for data to be fetched from the different caches available in the microprocessor or the system memory. This means that there are idle execution units. A simple example that takes advantage of these idle units is two threads doing different kinds of math such that they can both execute almost concurrently using different resources on the chip.

Hyper-Threading Technology offers an increased instruction-level parallelism that duplicates the architectural states in order to take advantage of the imperfections of the parallel code running from a second thread when the first one is waiting. This way, it appears to be a microprocessor with two times the real number of physical cores. The logical cores are also known as *hardware threads*.

Both Windows Task Manager, shown in Figure 2-11, and the Resource Monitor, presented in Figure 2-12, display a CPU usage graph for each hardware thread. The figures show eight graphs for a quad-core microprocessor with eight hardware threads through Hyper-Threading.

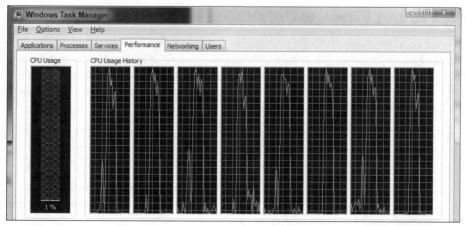

FIGURE 2-11

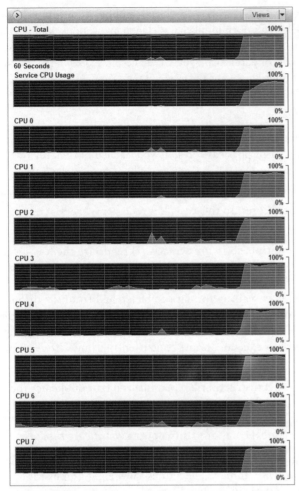

FIGURE 2-12

Logical Cores Aren't Physical Cores

It is very important to understand that logical cores are not the same as real physical cores. Sometimes, this technique improves performance through increased instruction-level parallelism when each physical core has two threads with independent instruction streams. However, if the software threads don't have too many data dependencies, the performance improvements could be less than expected. It depends on the kind of application.

By default, TPL uses the number of hardware threads or logical cores to optimize its execution and not the number of physical cores. Therefore, sometimes, you will find that certain algorithms don't offer the expected scalability as more cores appear because they aren't real physical cores.

For example, if an algorithm offered a 6.5x speedup when executed with eight physical cores, Hyper-Threading Technology would enable it to offer a more reticent 4.5x speedup on a microprocessor with four physical cores and eight logical cores.

To improve performance, you can call both methods, `ParallelGenerateAESKeysMaxDegree` and `ParallelGenerateMD5HashesMaxDegree`, with the number of physical cores and then with the number of logical cores (hardware threads), and measure the speedup achieved by using the additional logical cores. In a computer with a quad-core microprocessor and eight hardware threads, you can run these lines:

```
ParallelGenerateAESKeysMaxDegree(4);
ParallelGenerateMD5HashesMaxDegree(4);
```

code snippet is Snippet2_7

And then, run these lines:

```
ParallelGenerateAESKeysMaxDegree(8);
ParallelGenerateMD5HashesMaxDegree(8);
```

code snippet is Snippet2_8

However, it is very important to run both of the preceding code snippets under similar conditions. In some specific hardware configurations, this simple example took 5.20 seconds to run with the maximum degree of parallelism set to 4, and 4.60 seconds to do it with 8. The additional speedup is 5.20 / 4.60 = 1.13x when adding four logical cores. This example demonstrates that it is very important to understand the underlying hardware in order to test scalability and avoid drawing wrong conclusions.

USING GANTT CHARTS TO DETECT CRITICAL SECTIONS

Once you detect a parallelizable hotspot based on a loop with data parallelism, you will be able to use the previously learned TPL structures to try to take advantage of the multiple logical cores. However, as explained in Chapter 1, critical sections will always exist and can minimize the speedup achieved through parallelism.

Like traditional sequential programming, parallel programming is not just about writing code. A good design always helps. The Gantt chart is a bar chart that is typically used to illustrate a project schedule and the dependency relationship between linked tasks. Therefore, it is a useful chart to help in detecting critical sections, where parallelization is extremely difficult or nearly impossible.

You can work with Gantt charts to understand the dependency relationship between tasks and to decide which tasks can run in parallel and which ones cannot. This way, it is very easy to find the critical sections. Figure 2-13 depicts how a Gantt chart can be used for this purpose.

It is very important to consider the possibility of concurrent execution when you design your solutions. The Gantt chart is a great tool to help you find parallelization possibilities in complex algorithms.

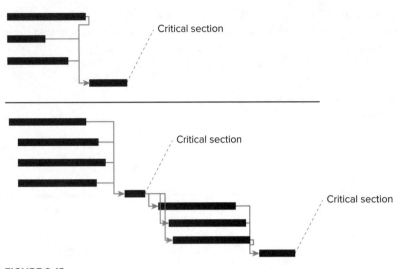

FIGURE 2-13

SUMMARY

There are many other advanced topics related to data-parallel problems. This chapter just scratched the surface of the new task-based programming model introduced with .NET Framework 4 by providing an overview of some of its classes, structures, and enumerations. This chapter also discussed the related concepts used in basic concurrent and parallel programming designs in order to tackle data-parallel problems using an imperative syntax. To summarize this chapter:

➤ You have to plan and design with concurrency and parallelism in mind. TPL offers structures that simplify the process of creating code that takes advantage of multicore and manycore architectures.

➤ You don't need to recompile your code in order to take advantage of additional cores. TPL optimizes the parallel loops and the distributions of tasks in underlying threads using load-balancing scheduling according to the available hardware resources at run-time.

➤ You can create parallelized loops.

➤ You have to take into account the lack of execution order guarantees when working with parallel loops.

➤ You can launch parallel tasks with a simple line of code. However, you also have to prepare your code for further scalability.

➤ You have to take into account critical sections and consider parallelism possibilities when you design your solutions.

➤ You must consider the number of physical cores and the number of hardware threads to measure scalability and to draw the right conclusions.

➤ You can use lambda expressions and anonymous delegates to simplify the creation of parallel code.

3

Imperative Task Parallelism

WHAT'S IN THIS CHAPTER?

➤ Understanding task parallel problems

➤ Understanding the new task-based programming model and the specific implementation of tasks offered by TPL

➤ Launching, controlling, managing, and synchronizing parallel tasks

➤ Transforming existing sequential code into parallelized code

➤ Returning values from asynchronous tasks

➤ Combining synchronous code with asynchronous code

➤ Mixing parallel and sequential code with continuations

➤ Programming complex parallel algorithms with critical sections using tasks

As explained in Chapter 2, "Imperative Data Parallelism," data parallelism isn't the only form of parallelism. Before .NET Framework 4, it was necessary to create and manage multiple threads or use the pool of threads in order to take advantage of multicore technology or multiple processors. Now, you can work with the new Task instances to solve imperative task parallelism problems and complex algorithms with simpler code. In this chapter, you will learn about this new .NET Framework 4 model.

This chapter is about the new classes, structures, and enumerations that allow you to deal with imperative task parallelism scenarios. It explains how to create parallel code using tasks instead of threads and describes the new concepts related to each scenario. By the end of the chapter, you will understand how to implement existing algorithms in parallel using basic and complex features offered by the new task-based programming model.

CREATING AND MANAGING TASKS

TPL introduced the new task-based programming model to translate multicore power into application performance without having to work with low-level, more complex, and heavyweight threads. It is very important to understand that *tasks* aren't threads. Tasks run using threads. However, it doesn't mean they replace threads. In fact, all the parallel loops used in the examples presented in Chapter 2 run creating tasks and their parallel and concurrent execution is supported by underlying threads, as shown in Figure 3-1.

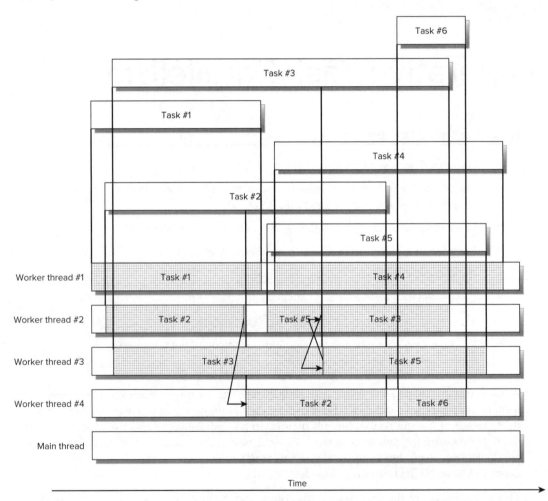

FIGURE 3-1

Task code is run using underlying threads (software threads, scheduled on certain hardware threads or logical cores). However, there isn't a 1-to-1 relationship between tasks and threads. This means you aren't creating a new thread each time you create a new task. The Common Language Runtime (CLR) creates the necessary threads to support the tasks' execution needs. Of course, this is a simplified vision of what goes on when creating tasks.

Synchronizing code running in multiple threads is indeed complex. Thus, a task-based approach offers an excellent alternative to leave some synchronization problems behind, especially those about work scheduling mechanisms. CLR uses *work-stealing queues* to reduce the locks and schedule small work chunks without adding a significant overhead. Creating a new thread introduces a big overhead, but creating a new task steals work from an existing thread, as illustrated in Figure 3-2. Therefore, tasks offer a new lightweight mechanism to create many parts of code capable of taking advantage of multiple cores.

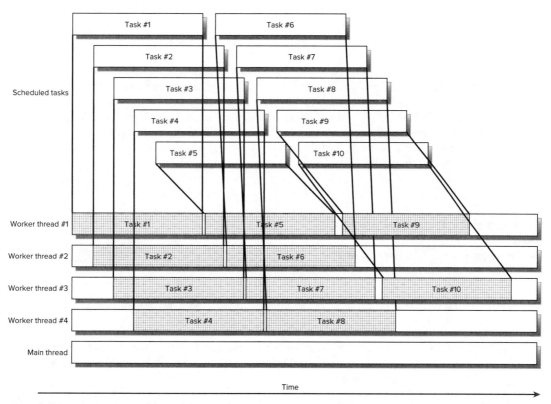

FIGURE 3-2

The default task scheduler relies on an underlying thread pool engine. Thus, when you create a new task, it uses the work-stealing queues to find the most appropriate thread to enqueue it. The code included in tasks will run in one thread; however, this will happen under the hood, and the overhead is actually smaller than manually creating a new thread.

System.Theading.Tasks.Task

TPL creates instances of System.Threading.Tasks.Task under the hood in order to support the parallel execution of the iterations explained in Chapter 2. When you call Parallel.Invoke, it also creates as many instances of Task as delegates are called.

A `Task` represents an *asynchronous operation*. It offers many methods and properties that allow you to control its execution and get information about its status. The creation of a `Task` is independent of its execution. This means that you have complete control over the execution of the associated operation. Table 3-1 explains the read-only properties for a `Task` instance.

> *When you launch many asynchronous operations as `Task` instances, the task scheduler will try to run them in parallel in order to take advantage of the available logical cores at run-time. It will try to load-balance the work of all the available cores. However, it is very important to understand that it isn't convenient to use tasks to run any piece of code, because tasks add an overhead. This overhead is smaller than the one added by a thread; however, it is still an overhead that has to be considered. For example, it doesn't make sense to create tasks to run two lines of code as two independent, asynchronous tasks that solve very simple calculations. Remember to measure the speedups achieved between the parallel execution and the sequential version to decide whether parallelism is appropriate or not. As explained in Chapter 1, "Task-Based Programming," and Chapter 2, it is also very important to consider the underlying hardware when measuring the speedups to avoid drawing wrong conclusions.*

TABLE 3-1: Task Read-Only Properties

PROPERTY	EXPLANATION
AsyncState	A state object supplied when you create the `Task` instance.
CreationOptions	The `TaskCreationOptions` value used to provide hints to the task scheduler to help it make the right scheduling actions.
CurrentId	The unique ID for the `Task` being executed. It is not equivalent to a thread ID in unmanaged code. This is a static property. You should only use it for debugging purposes.
Exception	An `AggregateException` that causes a `Task` to end prematurely. It is a null value if the `Task` finishes without throwing exceptions.
Factory	Provides access to the factory methods that allow the creation of `Task` instances with and without results. This is a static property.
Id	The unique ID for the `Task` instance.
IsCanceled	A Boolean value indicating whether the `Task` instance was canceled.
IsCompleted	A Boolean value indicating whether the `Task` has completed its execution.
IsFaulted	A Boolean value indicating whether the `Task` has aborted its execution due to an unhandled exception.
Status	The `TaskStatus` value indicating the current stage in the lifecycle of a `Task` instance.

Understanding a Task's Status and Lifecycle

It is very important to understand that each `Task` instance goes through a lifecycle. A `Task` represents concurrent code that executes based on the possibilities offered by the underlying hardware and the availability of resources at run-time. Therefore, any information about the `Task` instance could change as soon as you retrieve it, because its states are changing concurrently.

A `Task` instance completes its lifecycle just once. When it reaches one of its three possible final states, it doesn't go back to any previous state, as shown in Figure 3-3.

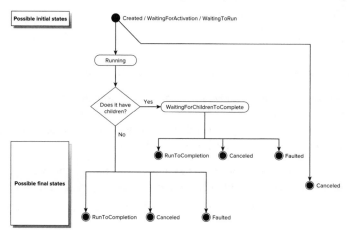

FIGURE 3-3

TaskStatus: Initial States

A `Task` instance has three possible initial states, depending on the way it was created. Table 3-2 describes the three possibilities in detail.

TABLE 3-2: Initial States for a Task Instance

VALUE	DESCRIPTION
`TaskStatus.Created`	The initial state for a `Task` instance created using the `Task` constructor. It will change once there is a call to either `Start` or `RunSynchronously`, or if the task is canceled.
`TaskStatus` `.WaitingForActivation`	The initial state for tasks that aren't scheduled until other dependent tasks finish their execution. Such tasks are created using methods that define continuations. The task really begins life in the `TaskStatus.Created` state but this state is changed to `TaskStatus.WaitingForActivation` before the reference to the `Task` instance is returned to the caller.
`TaskStatus` `.WaitingToRun`	The initial state for tasks created through `TaskFactory.StartNew`. It is waiting for the specified scheduler to pick it up and run it. The task really begins life in the `TaskStatus.Created` state, but this state is changed to `TaskStatus.WaitingToRun` before the reference to the `Task` instance is returned to the caller.

TaskStatus: Final States

Then, a `Task` instance can transition to the `TaskStatus.Running` state and finally move to a final state. If a `Task` instance has attached children, it isn't going to be considered complete, and it will transition to the `TaskStatus.WaitingForChildrenToComplete` state. Once the `Task` instance's children complete, it will move to one of the three possible final states described in detail in Table 3-3.

TABLE 3-3: Final States for a Task Instance

VALUE	DESCRIPTION
`TaskStatus .Canceled`	A cancellation request arrived before the task started its execution or during it. In the case of the request arriving during the task's execution, the task cooperatively acknowledges cancellation. The `IsCanceled` property will be `true`.
`TaskStatus .Faulted`	An unhandled exception in its body or the bodies of its attached children made the task end. The `IsFaulted` property will be `true`, and the `Exception` property will be non-null and will hold the `AggregateException` that caused the task or its attached children to end prematurely.
`TaskStatus .RanToCompletion`	The task completed its execution. It ran to the end of its body without being cancelled or throwing an unhandled exception. The `IsCompleted` property will be `true`; `IsCanceled` and `IsFaulted` will be `false`.

Using Tasks to Parallelize Code

In Chapter 2, you used `Parallel.Invoke` to launch the following two methods in parallel:

```
Parallel.Invoke(
    () => GenerateAESKeys(),
    () => GenerateMD5Hashes());
```

code snippet is Snippet 3_1

You can do the same job using two instances of `Task`, as shown in Listing 3-1.

LISTING 3-1: Working with tasks

```
var t1 = new Task(() => GenerateAESKeys());
var t2 = new Task(() => GenerateMD5Hashes());

// Start the tasks
t1.Start();
t2.Start();

// Wait for all the tasks to finish
Task.WaitAll(t1, t2);
```

The first two lines create two instances of `Task`, with a lambda expression creating a delegate for `GenerateAESKeys` and `GenerateMD5Hashes`. t1 is associated with the first method, and t2 is associated with the latter method. These methods aren't running yet, but the tasks are ready to start, so the `Status` for both `Task` instances is `TaskStatus.Created`.

> *It is also possible to use lambda expressions with multiple lines to define the action that the* `Task` *constructor receives as a parameter.*

Starting Tasks

The following line starts the *asynchronous execution* of t1:

```
t1.Start();
```

The `Start` method initiates the execution of the delegate in an independent way, and the program flow goes on with the instruction after this method, even though the delegate has not finished its execution. The code in the delegate associated with the task runs concurrently with the main program flow, also known as the *main thread*. At this point, there is a main thread and another thread or other threads supporting the execution of this new task.

The execution of the main thread is synchronous. This means that it will go on with the next instruction, the line that starts the *asynchronous execution* of t2:

```
t2.Start();
```

Now, the `Start` method initiates the execution of the delegate in another independent way, and the program flow goes on with the instruction after this method, even though this other delegate has not finished its execution. The code in the delegate associated with the task runs concurrently with the main thread and the code inside `GenerateAESKeys` that is already running. This means that at this point, there is a main thread and other threads supporting the execution of the two tasks.

> *It is easy to run asynchronous code using* `Task` *instances and the latest language improvements added to C#. With just a few lines, you can create code that runs asynchronously, control its execution flow, and take advantage of multicore microprocessors or multiple processors.*

The sequence diagram presented in Figure 3-4 shows the parallel and asynchronous execution flow for the main thread and the two tasks.

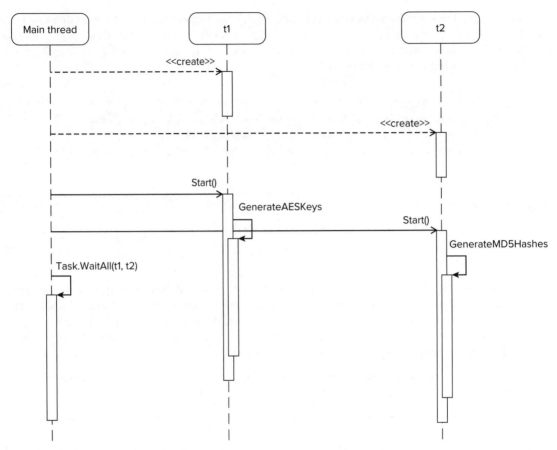

FIGURE 3-4

Visualizing Tasks Using Parallel Tasks and Parallel Stacks

The Visual C# 2010 integrated development environment (*IDE*) offers two new debugging windows: Parallel Task and Parallel Stacks. These windows display information about the tasks that are running, their status, and their relationship with the underlying threads. It is very easy to understand the relationship between the new tasks and the underlying threads that support the tasks' execution in .NET Framework 4. You can debug simple parallelized code and run it step-by-step using the new debugging windows, and they will display valuable information about tasks and threads. Parallel Tasks and Parallel Stacks allow you to monitor what is going on under the hood. By running the code step-by-step, you will be able to understand the differences between synchronous and asynchronous execution.

For example, if you insert a breakpoint in the line `Task.WaitAll(t1, t2)`, and your microprocessor has at least two cores, you will be able to see two tasks running in parallel. You just have to select Debug ➪ Windows ➪ Parallel Tasks. The IDE will display a new Parallel Tasks window with a list of all the tasks and their status (scheduled, running, waiting, waiting-deadlocked, and so on), as shown in Figure 3-5.

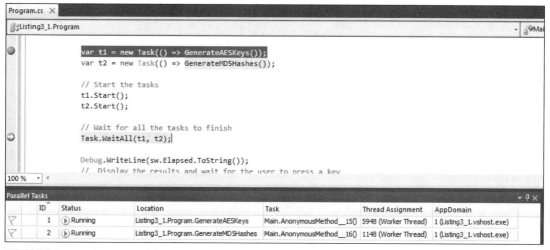

```
Program.cs ×
Listing3_1.Program                                                                        Mai

              var t1 = new Task(() => GenerateAESKeys());
              var t2 = new Task(() => GenerateMD5Hashes());

              // Start the tasks
              t1.Start();
              t2.Start();

              // Wait for all the tasks to finish
              Task.WaitAll(t1, t2);

              Debug.WriteLine(sw.Elapsed.ToString());
              // Display the results and wait for the user to press a key
100 %
```

	ID	Status	Location	Task	Thread Assignment	AppDomain
	1	▶ Running	Listing3_1.Program.GenerateAESKeys	Main.AnonymousMethod__15()	5948 (Worker Thread)	1 (Listing3_1.vshost.exe)
	2	▶ Running	Listing3_1.Program.GenerateMD5Hashes	Main.AnonymousMethod__16()	1148 (Worker Thread)	1 (Listing3_1.vshost.exe)

FIGURE 3-5

As you can see in the figure, this example has the following two tasks:

➤ Task ID 1: `Main.AnonymousMethod__15()` — This task is assigned to Worker Thread ID 5948.

➤ Task ID 2: `Main.AnonymousMethod__16()` — This task is assigned to Worker Thread ID 1148.

The status for both tasks is `Running` (`TaskStatus.Running`). Each task is identified by an auto-generated, anonymous method name and number (`Main.AnonymousMethod__15()` for the first task and `Main.AnonymousMethod__16()` for the second task in this example), as shown in Figure 3-6. This happens because the code uses lambda expressions to generate the delegates associated with each task. The compiler auto-generates the names and assigns them to those methods.

If you double-click a task name in the Parallel Tasks window, the IDE will display the next statement that is going to run for the selected task, as shown in Figure 3-7 for the first task and Figure 3-8 for the second task. Remember that the threads assigned to these tasks and the main thread are running concurrently, according to the available hardware resources and the actions taken by the CLR task scheduler and Windows scheduler.

The CLR task scheduler tries to steal work from the most appropriate thread. It can also decide to create a new thread to support the task's execution. However, this procedure doesn't guarantee that the underlying threads are going to run in parallel, even when the necessary number of logical cores is available. The operating system scheduler distributes the cores between the dozens or hundreds of threads scheduled to receive processor time from the available cores. This is why the same concurrent code can run with different parallelism levels and different concurrent times, even on the same hardware configuration.

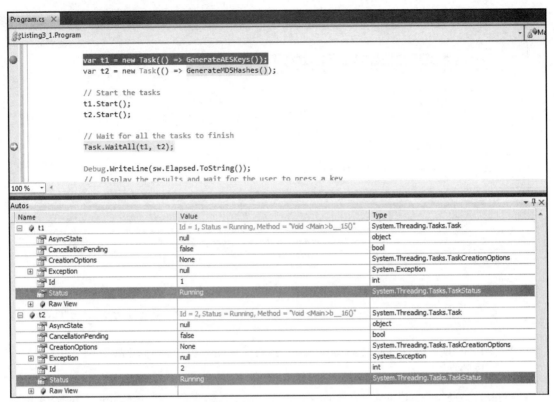

FIGURE 3-6

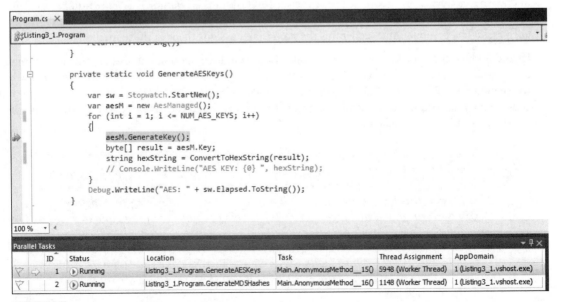

FIGURE 3-7

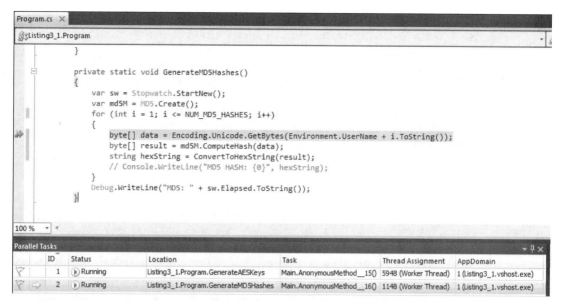

FIGURE 3-8

Similar to the way in which threads were handled in previous versions of Visual C#, you can check what is going on with each concurrent task. However, the information is better in the current IDE version, because you can check whether a task is scheduled or waiting-deadlocked. You can order and group the information shown in the windows, as you can with any other Visual C# IDE feature.

The Parallel Tasks grid includes a Thread Assignment column containing the thread ID. This ID is obtained from the Threads window, which displays a list of all threads, their categories, and their locations, as shown in Figure 3-9. You can access this window by selecting Debug ➪ Windows ➪ Threads, and use it to check which managed thread is supporting the execution of a certain task, find out what the next statement will be, and get other detailed information for each thread.

	ID	Managed ID	Category	Name	Location	Priority	
∧ Listing3_1.vshost.exe (id = 4228) : C:\Users\Gaston\Documents\Visual Studio 2010\Projects\Listing3_1\Listing3_1\bin\Debug\Listing3_1.vshost.exe							
	4652	0	Worker Thread	\<Thread Ended\>	\<not available\>	Normal	
	5784	0	Worker Thread	\<No Name\>	\<not available\>	Highest	
	6620	8	Worker Thread	\<No Name\>	\<not available\>	Normal	
	2268	9	Worker Thread	vshost.RunParkingWindow	∨ [Managed to Native Transition]	Normal	
	5520	10	Worker Thread	.NET SystemEvents	∨ [Managed to Native Transition]	Normal	
⇨	6152	11	Main Thread	Main Thread	∨ Listing3_1.Program.Main	Normal	
	5948	7	Worker Thread	Worker Thread	∨ Listing3_1.Program.GenerateAESKeys	Normal	
➡	1148	6	Worker Thread	Worker Thread	∨ Listing3_1.Program.GenerateMD5Hashes	Normal	
	5356	0	Worker Thread	\<No Name\>	∨ [Native to Managed Transition]	Normal	

FIGURE 3-9

As you can see in the figure, the Threads window uses different colors and names to distinguish between different types of threads. The thread that is usually running the user interface (UI) code or supporting the Main *method is called the* Main Thread *and is displayed with a green square next to it, and the other threads are called* Worker Threads *and have yellow squares next to them. The worker threads support the execution of tasks. Therefore, worker threads have to use delegates to update the UI in order to run code in the main thread for this purpose. In fact, updating the UI is a complex topic in the new task-based programming model, and you will learn detailed techniques in order to do so in the forthcoming chapters.*

There is a simpler way to visualize the relationship between tasks and threads. You can select Debug ➪ Windows ➪ Parallel Stacks. The IDE will show a new window (Parallel Stacks), displaying a diagram with all the tasks or threads, their status, and their relationship. The default view is Threads, as shown in Figure 3-10.

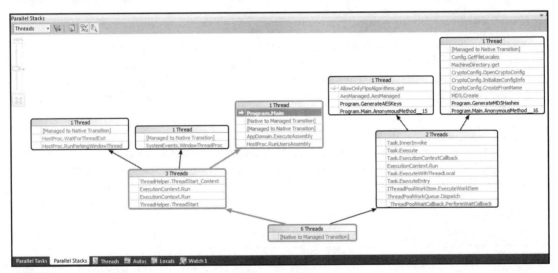

FIGURE 3-10

The two threads on the right side of the diagram are running the code scheduled by the two tasks. Each thread shows its call stack. The thread that supports `Module1.<lambda12>` is running the `GenerateAESKeys` method, specifically code inside the call to the `ConvertToHexString` method. The thread that supports `Module1.<lambda13>` is running the `GenerateMD5Hashes` method, and it shows many native-to-managed code transitions and vice versa. This diagram lets you know what each thread is doing with a great level of detail.

You can change the value for the combo box in the upper-left corner from Threads to Tasks, and the IDE will display a diagram with all the tasks, their status, relationships, and call stacks, as shown in Figure 3-11.

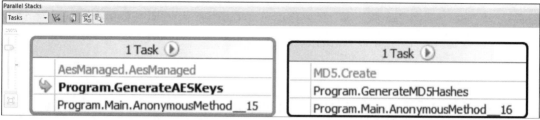

FIGURE 3-11

You can use the previously explained windows to understand the relationship between tasks and thread. You have to learn new techniques in order to debug task-based code. Chapter 7, "Visual Studio 2010 Task Debugging Capabilities," dives deep into the new features offered by the IDE to allow you to debug tasks, threads, and concurrent and parallelized code.

Waiting for Tasks to Finish

At some point, you need to wait for certain tasks, started with an asynchronous execution, to finish.

The following line calls the `Task.WaitAll` method, which will wait for the `Task` instances received as a params array of `Task` (`Task[]`), separated by commas. This method has a *synchronous execution*. This means that the main thread won't go on with the next statement until the `Task` instances received as parameters finish their execution.

```
Task.WaitAll(t1, t2);
```

In this case, *t1* and *t2* have to finish their execution. The current thread, which in this case is the main thread, will wait until both tasks finish their execution. This time spent waiting for the tasks to finish uses a lightweight mechanism to reduce the need of CPU cycles as much as possible. Once these tasks finish their execution, the next statement runs.

Forgetting About Complex Threads

As previously stated, the `Task.WaitAll` method uses synchronous execution, so if the tasks take 1 minute to run, the current thread will be waiting during this time. However, if you want to limit the number of milliseconds to wait for the tasks to finish, you can use a definition for the `Task.WaitAll` method that accepts an array of `Task` instances and the number of milliseconds to wait. The method returns a `bool` value, indicating whether the tasks were able to finish within the specified timeout. The following code waits for *t1* and *t2* to finish their execution with a 3-second timeout:

```
// Start the tasks
t1.Start();
t2.Start();

// Wait for all the tasks to finish with a 3-second timeout
if (!Task.WaitAll(new Task[] {t1, t2}, 3000))
{
```

```
    Console.WriteLine(
  "GenerateAESKeys and GenerateMD5Hashes are taking more than 3 seconds to complete.");
    Console.WriteLine(t1.Status.ToString());
    Console.WriteLine(t2.Status.ToString());
}
```

code snippet is Snippet 3_2

If *t1* and *t2* don't finish in 3 seconds, the code displays a message and the status for both tasks. If no exceptions occurred in the code for these tasks, they could be still running. The `Task.WaitAll` method with a specific timeout doesn't cancel the tasks if they take more time to run — it just returns from its synchronous execution with the `bool` result.

You can also call the `Wait` method for a `task` instance. In this case, the current thread will wait until that task finishes its execution. Of course, there is no need to send the `task` instance as a parameter, because it is an instance method. It also supports a timeout in one of its definitions. The following code waits for *t1* to finish, and if it doesn't complete its work in 3 seconds, it displays a message and its status:

Available for download on Wrox.com

```
// Start the tasks
t1.Start();
t2.Start();

// Wait for t1 to finish with a 3-second timeout
if (!t1.Wait(3000))
{
    Console.WriteLine("GenerateAESKeys is taking more than 3 seconds to complete.");
    Console.WriteLine(t1.Status.ToString());
}
```

code snippet is Snippet 3_3

The code needed to start and wait for tasks to finish is easier than the code needed to create threads. Thus, you can focus your efforts on the process of implementing a parallel algorithm instead of working with low-level and complex threads.

Cancelling Tasks Using Tokens

You can interrupt the execution of `Task` instances through the use of *cancellation tokens*. To do so, you need to add some code in the delegate in order to create a cancelable operation that is capable of terminating in a timely manner.

Listing 3-2 shows two new versions of the AES keys and MD5 hash generators. The changes made in order to support cancellation are highlighted. The new `GenerateAESKeysCancel`, which replaces the old `GenerateAESKeys`, receives a `System.Threading.CancellationToken` instance and throws an `OperationCanceledException` calling the `ThrowIfCancellationRequested` method. This way, the `Task` instance transitions to the `TaskStatus.Canceled` state, and the `IsCanceled` property will be `true`. You must press a key after the console appears and the application will create and start the two tasks.

LISTING 3-2: Cancelling tasks using tokens with changes in the AES keys and MD5 hash generators

```csharp
private static void GenerateAESKeysCancel(System.Threading.CancellationToken ct)
{
    ct.ThrowIfCancellationRequested();

    var sw = Stopwatch.StartNew();
    var aesM = new AesManaged();
    for (int i = 1; i <= NUM_AES_KEYS; i++)
    {
        aesM.GenerateKey();
        byte[] result = aesM.Key;
        string hexString = ConvertToHexString(result);
        // Console.WriteLine("AES KEY: {0} ", hexString);
        ct.ThrowIfCancellationRequested();
    }
    Debug.WriteLine("AES: " + sw.Elapsed.ToString());
}

private static void GenerateMD5HashesCancel(System.Threading.CancellationToken ct)
{
    ct.ThrowIfCancellationRequested();

    var sw = Stopwatch.StartNew();
    var md5M = MD5.Create();
    for (int i = 1; i <= NUM_MD5_HASHES; i++)
    {
        byte[] data =
            Encoding.Unicode.GetBytes(
            Environment.UserName + i.ToString());
        byte[] result = md5M.ComputeHash(data);
        string hexString = ConvertToHexString(result);
        // Console.WriteLine("MD5 HASH: {0}", hexString);
        ct.ThrowIfCancellationRequested();
    }
    Debug.WriteLine("MD5: " + sw.Elapsed.ToString());
}

static void Main(string[] args)
{
    Console.ReadLine();

    Console.WriteLine("Started");

    var cts = new System.Threading.CancellationTokenSource();
    var ct = cts.Token;

    var sw = Stopwatch.StartNew();

    var t1 = Task.Factory.StartNew(
        () => GenerateAESKeysCancel(ct), ct);
```

continues

LISTING 3-2 *(continued)*

```
        var t2 = Task.Factory.StartNew(
            () => GenerateMD5HashesCancel(ct), ct);

        // Sleep the main thread for 1 second
        System.Threading.Thread.Sleep(1000);

        cts.Cancel();

        try
        {
            // Wait for all the tasks to finish with a 1-second timeout
            if (!Task.WaitAll(new Task[] { t1, t2 }, 1000))
            {
                Console.WriteLine(
"GenerateAESKeys and GenerateMD5Hashes are taking more than 1 second to complete.");
                Console.WriteLine(t1.Status.ToString());
                Console.WriteLine(t2.Status.ToString());
            }
        }
        catch (AggregateException ex)
        {
            foreach (Exception innerEx in ex.InnerExceptions)
            {
                Debug.WriteLine(innerEx.ToString());
                // Do something based on the innerEx Exception
            }
        }
        if (t1.IsCanceled)
        {
            Console.WriteLine(
                "The task running GenerateAESKeysCancel was cancelled.");
        }
        if (t2.IsCanceled)
        {
            Console.WriteLine(
                "The task running GenerateMD5HashesCancel was cancelled.");
        }

        Debug.WriteLine(sw.Elapsed.ToString());
        //  Display the results and wait for the user to press a key
        Console.WriteLine("Finished!");
        Console.ReadLine();
    }
```

The first line of `GenerateAESKeysCancel` will throw the aforementioned exception if its cancellation was already requested at that time. This way, it won't start the loop if unnecessary at that point.

```
    ct.ThrowIfCancellationRequested();
```

In the example, the task's delegate for *t1* just calls the `GenerateAESKeysCancel` method. Thus, there is little need to do such a check first thing in the method. The task's implementation will check the token prior to invoking the delegate. However, in other cases, when a task's delegate calls many methods, you can call `ThrowIfCancellationRequested` to avoid running unnecessary loops or other instructions.

After each iteration of the loop, there is new code that calls the `ThrowIfCancellationRequested` method. The code is capable of observing an `OperationCanceledException` and compares its token to the `Task` instance's associated one. If they are the same and its `IsCancelledProperty` is true, the `Task` instance understands that there is a request for cancellation and makes the transition to the `Canceled` state, interrupting its execution. When there is code waiting for the cancelled `Task` instance, this also generates an automatic `TaskCanceledException`, which will be wrapped in an `AggregateException`.

CancellationTokenSource

In this case, the main method creates a `CancellationTokenSource` (*cts*) and a `Cancellation Token` (ct), as shown here:

```
var cts = new System.Threading.CancellationTokenSource();
var ct = cts.Token;
```

`CancellationTokenSource` is capable of initiating cancellation requests, and `CancellationToken` communicates these requests to asynchronous operations. Table 3-4 explains the read-only properties for a `CancellationTokenSource` instance.

TABLE 3-4: CancellationTokenSource Read-Only Properties

PROPERTY	EXPLANATION
IsCancellationRequested	A Boolean value indicating whether a cancellation has been requested for the `CancellationTokenSource` instance
Token	A `CancellationToken` instance associated with the `CancellationTokenSource`

CancellationToken

A `CancellationToken` must be sent as a parameter to each task delegate; therefore, the code uses one of the definitions of the `TaskFactory.StartNew` method. The following lines create and start two `Task` instances with associated actions and the same `CancellationToken` instance (ct) as parameters.

```
var t1 = Task.Factory.StartNew(
    () => GenerateAESKeysCancel(ct), ct);
var t2 = Task.Factory.StartNew(
    () => GenerateMD5HashesCancel(ct), ct);
```

A `CancellationToken` instance propagates that operations have to be canceled using a signaling mechanism. Table 3-5 explains the read-only properties for a `CancellationToken` instance.

TABLE 3-5: CancellationToken Read-Only Properties

PROPERTY	EXPLANATION
CanBeCanceled	A Boolean value indicating whether the token offers the possibility of being in the canceled state
IsCancellationRequested	A Boolean value indicating whether a cancellation has been requested for the token
WaitHandle	A WaitHandle instance associated with the CancellationToken that defines the signaling mechanism to propagate the cancellation

TaskFactory

The Main method in Listing 3-2 use the Task class's Factory property to retrieve a TaskFactory instance that can be used to create tasks with more options than the ones offered by the direct instantiation of the Task class. In this case, it uses the StartNew method, which is functionally equivalent to creating a Task using one of its constructors and then calling Start to schedule it for execution.

Then, the code calls the Sleep method to make the main thread sleep for 1 second. This following method suspends the current thread for the specified time, which in this case is an int in milliseconds:

```
Threading.Thread.Sleep(1000);
```

 The main thread is going to stay suspended for 1 second. However, the threads that are supporting the tasks' execution won't be suspended. Therefore, the tasks will be scheduled to begin their execution.

One second later, the main thread communicates a request for cancellation for both tasks through the CancellationTokenSource instance's Cancel method:

```
cts.Cancel();
```

The cancellation token is going to be evaluated in the two delegates launched by the Task instances, as previously explained.

As you can see, it is easy to cancel asynchronous actions — you just add a few lines. However, it is very important to add the necessary clean-up code. The sequence diagram presented in Figure 3-12 shows the propagation of the cancellation.

A try block encloses the call to Task.WaitAll. Because there was a request for cancellation for both tasks, there are going to be two benign exceptions of type OperationCanceledException.

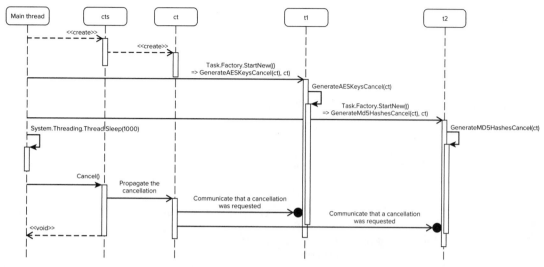

FIGURE 3-12

The IsCanceled property for both tasks is going to be true. You can check this property and add code whenever a task was cancelled.

Handling Exceptions Thrown by Tasks

When many tasks run in parallel, many exceptions can occur in parallel. Task instances also work with sets of exceptions, handled by the previously explained System.AggregateException class.

Listing 3-3 shows the highlighted lines that add an unhandled exception in the GenerateAESKeysCancel method.

LISTING 3-3: An unhandled exception in the method called by an asynchronous delegate

```
private static void GenerateAESKeysCancel(System.Threading.CancellationToken ct)
{
    ct.ThrowIfCancellationRequested();

    var sw = Stopwatch.StartNew();
    var aesM = new AesManaged();
    for (int i = 1; i <= NUM_AES_KEYS; i++)
    {
        aesM.GenerateKey();
        byte[] result = aesM.Key;
        string hexString = ConvertToHexString(result);
        // Console.WriteLine("AES KEY: {0} ", hexString);
        if (sw.Elapsed.TotalSeconds > 0.5)
        {
            throw new TimeoutException(
                "GenerateAESKeysCancel is taking more than 0.5 seconds to complete.");
        }
        ct.ThrowIfCancellationRequested();
```

continues

LISTING 3-3 *(continued)*

```
    }
    Debug.WriteLine("AES: " + sw.Elapsed.ToString());
}
```

Comment the code that requested cancellation for both tasks as follows:

```
// cts.Cancel();
```

Add the following lines to the Main method:

```
if (t1.IsFaulted)
{
    foreach (Exception innerEx in t1.Exception.InnerExceptions)
    {
        Debug.WriteLine(innerEx.ToString());
        // Do something based on the innerEx Exception
    }
}
```

code snippet is included in Listing 3_3

Because there is an unhandled exception in *t1*, its `IsFaulted` property is `true`. Therefore, `t1.Exception` (an `AggregateException`) contains one or more exceptions that occurred during the execution of its associated delegate. After checking the `IsFaulted` property, you can iterate through each individual exception contained in the `InnerExceptions` read-only collection of `Exception`. You can then perform actions based on the problems that prevented the task from completing. Listing 3-4 shows the information about the unhandled exception that was converted to a string and sent to the debug output.

LISTING 3-4: Debug output with the exceptions found in the InnerExceptions collection

```
System.TimeoutException:
    GenerateAESKeysCancel is taking more than 0.5 seconds to complete.
    at Listing3_3.Program.GenerateAESKeysCancel(CancellationToken ct)
    in c:\Projects\Listing3_4\Listing3_4\Program.cs:line 66
    at Listing3_3.Program.<>c__DisplayClass17.<Main>b__15()
    in c:\Projects\Listing3_4\Listing3_4\Program.cs:line 352
    at System.Threading.Tasks.Task.InnerInvoke()
    at System.Threading.Tasks.Task.Execute()
```

Sometimes, you need to perform important clean-up operations when you catch exceptions that occur in tasks.

Returning Values from Tasks

So far, task instances did not return values — they were delegates running void methods that did not return values. However, it is also possible to return values from tasks, invoking functions and using `Task<TResult>` instances, where *TResult* has to be replaced by the returned type.

Listing 3-5 shows the code for a new function that generates the well-known AES keys and then returns a list of the keys that begin with the character prefix received as one of the parameters (*prefix*). GenerateAESKeysWithCharPrefix returns a List of String.

LISTING 3-5: Returning a list of String instances from a task

```
private static List<String> GenerateAESKeysWithCharPrefix(
    System.Threading.CancellationToken ct, char prefix)
{
    var sw = Stopwatch.StartNew();
    var aesM = new AesManaged();
    var keysList = new List<String>();
    for (int i = 1; i <= NUM_AES_KEYS; i++)
    {
        aesM.GenerateKey();
        byte[] result = aesM.Key;
        string hexString = ConvertToHexString(result);
        if (hexString[0] == prefix)
        {
            keysList.Add(hexString);
        }
        // Console.WriteLine("AES KEY: {0} ", hexString);
        if (ct.IsCancellationRequested)
        {
            ct.ThrowIfCancellationRequested();
        }
    }
    Debug.WriteLine("AES: " + sw.Elapsed.ToString());
    return keysList;
}

static void Main(string[] args)
{
    Console.ReadLine();

    Console.WriteLine("Started");

    var cts = new System.Threading.CancellationTokenSource();
    var ct = cts.Token;

    var sw = Stopwatch.StartNew();

    // The compiler will infer t1 as Task<List<String>>
    // from the delegate's body
    var t1 = Task.Factory.StartNew(
        () => GenerateAESKeysWithCharPrefix(ct, 'A'), ct);

    try
    {
        // Wait for t1 to finish
        t1.Wait();
    }
    catch (AggregateException ex)
    {
```

continues

LISTING 3-5 *(continued)*

```
            foreach (Exception innerEx in ex.InnerExceptions)
            {
                Debug.WriteLine(innerEx.ToString());
                // Do something based on the innerEx Exception
            }
        }
        if (t1.IsCanceled)
        {
            Console.WriteLine(
                "The task running GenerateAESKeysWithCharPrefix was cancelled.");
        }
        if (t1.IsFaulted)
        {
            foreach (Exception innerEx in t1.Exception.InnerExceptions)
            {
                Debug.WriteLine(innerEx.ToString());
                // Do something based on the innerEx Exception
            }
        }
        var t2 = Task.Factory.StartNew(() => {
            for (int i = 0; i < t1.Result.Count; i++)
            {
                // Do something with the result
                // returned by the task's delegate
                Console.WriteLine(t1.Result[i]);
            }}, TaskCreationOptions.LongRunning);

        Debug.WriteLine(sw.Elapsed.ToString());
        // Display the results and wait for the user to press a key
        Console.WriteLine("Finished!");
        Console.ReadLine();
    }
```

The `Main` method uses the definition of the `TaskFactory.StartNew` method, but this time, it calls it from a `Task<TResult>` instance and not a `Task` instance. Specifically, it creates a `Task<List<String>>` instance, sending it a `CancellationToken` as a parameter to the task delegate. The compiler infers *t1* as `Task<List<String>>` from the delegate's body.

```
var t1 = Task.Factory.StartNew(
    () => GenerateAESKeysWithCharPrefix(ct, 'A'), ct);
```

code snippet is Listing3_5

You could also use the following line to create and start *t1*. However, it isn't necessary to specify `<List<String>>`.

```
var t1 = Task<List<String>>.Factory.StartNew(
    () => GenerateAESKeysWithCharPrefix(ct, 'A'), ct);
```

The delegate for *t1* is a function that returns a `List<String>`, which is going to be available in the `Task<TResult>` instance (*t1*) through its `Result` property once the associated delegate completes its execution and the function returns a value.

The main thread waits for this task to finish and then verifies that it completed its execution, checking the previously explained `Task` instance's properties.

Then, it iterates through each string in the list returned by the function called in the previous task, and displays the results on the console. It does this job running a new asynchronous task, `t2`. The code that creates and runs this `Task` is highlighted in Listing 3-5.

TaskCreationOptions

The code creates and starts the second task, `t2`, using the `StartNew` method and a lambda expression with multiple lines. However, in this case, it uses a different definition that receives a `TaskCreationOptions` parameter. This parameter specifies flags with optional behaviors for the creation, scheduling, and execution of tasks.

The `TaskCreationOptions` enumeration has the four members described in Table 3-6.

TABLE 3-6: Optional Behaviors for Tasks

VALUE	DESCRIPTION
`TaskCreationOptions .AttachedToParent`	The task is attached to a parent task. You can create tasks inside other tasks.
`TaskCreationOptions .None`	The task can use the default behavior.
`TaskCreationOptions .LongRunning`	The task will take a long time to run; therefore, the scheduler can work with it as a coarse-grained operation. You can use this option if the task is likely to take many seconds to run. Conversely, you should not use this option when a task takes less than 1 second to run.
`TaskCreationOptions .PreferFairness`	This option tells the scheduler that tasks scheduled sooner will be more likely to be run sooner and vice versa.

 You can combine multiple values using bitwise operations.

Chaining Multiple Tasks Using Continuations

The previous case is an example of *chained tasks*. Task `t1` produces a result, and `t2` needs the result as an input in order to start processing the result. In such a case, instead of adding many lines that check for the successful completion of a precedent task and then schedule a new task, TPL enables you to chain tasks using *continuations*.

You can call the `ContinueWith` method for any task instance, and create a continuation that executes when this task successfully completes its execution. This method has many definitions with diverse numbers of parameters. The most simple scenario consists of defining a simple action as done when creating `Task` instances.

Listing 3-6 shows a simplified version of the code previously used in Listing 3-5. This simplified code displays the results generated by `t1`, and chains the two tasks with a continuation.

LISTING 3-6: Chaining two tasks with a continuation

```csharp
static void Main(string[] args)
{
    Console.ReadLine();

    Console.WriteLine("Started");

    var cts = new System.Threading.CancellationTokenSource();
    var ct = cts.Token;

    var sw = Stopwatch.StartNew();

    var t1 = Task.Factory.StartNew(
        () => GenerateAESKeysWithCharPrefix(ct, 'A'), ct);

    var t2 = t1.ContinueWith((t) =>
    {
        // Do something with the result
        // returned by the task's delegate
        for (int i = 0; i < t.Result.Count; i++)
        {
            Console.WriteLine(t.Result[i]);
        }
    });

    try
    {
        // Wait for t2 to finish
        t2.Wait();
    }
...
```

You can chain many tasks and then wait for the last task (`t2` in this case) to be executed. However, you have to be careful when checking the states for all these asynchronous operations. You must consider all the potential exceptions that could be thrown.

The following line creates the new task, `t2`, chained to `t1`. The delegate receives, `t`, in this case, a `Task<List<String>>` instance. `t1` is the task that has to finish in order to enable this new task to start (`t2`).

```csharp
var t2 = t1.ContinueWith((t) =>
```

Thus, it is possible to access the `Result` property for `t`. `t` represents the precedent task, `t1`, in the delegate. The following `for` loop inside the delegate that will run `t2` accesses `t.Result`:

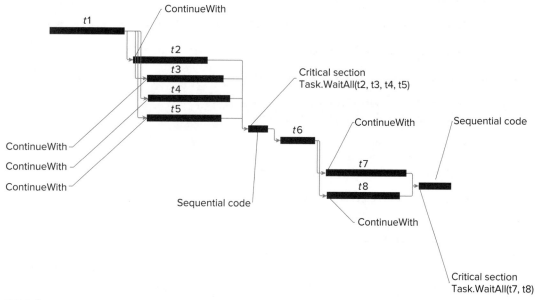

```
for (int i = 0; i < t.Result.Count; i++)
{
    Console.WriteLine(t.Result[i]);
}
```

Available for download on Wrox.com

code snippet is Listing3_6

Mixing Parallel and Sequential Code with Continuations

In Chapter 2, you learned about the possibilities offered by Gantt charts to detect critical sections and analyze task scheduling. Now you know how to create and manage tasks and chain them with continuations. Figure 3-13 shows mixed parallel and sequential code represented in a Gantt chart with the continuations and the critical sections. The critical sections have to wait for all the precedent tasks to finish in order to execute sequential code that cannot be parallelized.

FIGURE 3-13

Tasks *t2*, *t3*, *t4*, and *t5* continue when *t1* finishes. Then, there is a critical section with sequential code that has to wait for the four chained tasks to finish before running. Then, tasks *t7* and *t8* continue when the new task *t6* finishes. After this, there is another critical section with sequential code that has to wait for the two chained tasks to finish. As you can see, using a Gantt chart makes it simple to understand continuations and critical sections, including the relationship between them and the code needed to define and control the task scheduling mechanisms.

Working with Complex Continuations

The following code snippet is an example of how task continuations could be defined for the tasks and the critical sections shown in the Gantt chart in Figure 3-13. To simplify things, the code uses `TaskMethod` followed by the associated task number as the method that runs with each `Task`. For example, `TaskMethod2` runs the code for Task *t2*. The purpose of this example is to help you understand how to define multiple continuations.

```
var t1 = Task.Factory.StartNew(() => TaskMethod1());

var t2 = t1.ContinueWith((t) => TaskMethod2(t));
var t3 = t1.ContinueWith((t) => TaskMethod3(t));
var t4 = t1.ContinueWith((t) => TaskMethod4(t));
var t5 = t1.ContinueWith((t) => TaskMethod5(t));

Task.WaitAll(t2, t3, t4, t5);

// **** This code is a critical section

// Sequential code running in the main thread

var myNewList = new List<String>();

// Fill myNewList with values based on all the work done by the previous tasks

// **** End of critical section

var t6 = Task<List<String>>.Factory.StartNew(() => TaskMethod6(myNewList));

var t7 = t6.ContinueWith((t) => TaskMethod7(t));
var t8 = t6.ContinueWith((t) => TaskMethod8(t));

Task.WaitAll(t7, t8);

// **** This code is a critical section

// Sequential code running in the main thread


// **** End of critical section
```

code snippet is Snippet3_4

TaskContinuationOptions

When you add code to create and start a `Task`, you can use definitions that receive a `TaskCreationOptions` parameter. When you create a `Task` as a continuation of another `Task`, you can specify a `TaskContinuationOptions` parameter with flags to control optional behavior for the scheduling and execution of the task that has to continue after another task. For example, the following line specifies that *t10* should start after *t9* only if the latter wasn't canceled:

```
var t10 = t9.ContinueWith(
            (t) => TaskMethod10(t),
        TaskContinuationOptions.NotOnCanceled);
```

code snippet is Snippet3_5

This way, you can establish certain conditions and give the scheduler more information about the tasks that are going to continue after another one.

The `TaskContinuationOptions` enumeration has the 11 members described in Table 3-7. The default value used when this parameter isn't specified is `TaskContinuationOptions.None`.

TABLE 3-7: Optional Continuation Options for Chained Tasks

VALUE	DESCRIPTION
`TaskContinuationOptions .AttachedToParent`	The continuation task is attached to a parent task.
`TaskContinuationOptions .ExecuteSynchronously`	This option tells the scheduler that the continuation task should be executed synchronously with the precedent task. This means that it is strongly preferred that the continuation task uses the same underlying thread that transited the precedent task to its final state.
`TaskContinuationOptions .LongRunning`	The task will take a long time to run. Therefore, the scheduler can work with it as a coarse-grained operation. You can use this option if the task is likely to take many seconds to run. On the contrary, It is not convenient to use this option when a task takes less than 1 second to run.
`TaskContinuationOptions .None`	The continuation task will be scheduled when the precedent task completes its execution, regardless of its final `TaskStatus` property value. See Table 3-2 and Table 3-3 for the possible values for this property.
`TaskContinuationOptions .NotOnCanceled`	The continuation task shouldn't be scheduled if the precedent task was canceled (`TaskStatus == TaskStatus.Canceled`).
`TaskContinuationOptions .NotOnFaulted`	The continuation task shouldn't be scheduled if the precedent task threw an unhandled exception to completion (`TaskStatus == TaskStatus.Faulted`).
`TaskContinuationOptions .NotOnRanToCompletion`	The continuation task shouldn't be scheduled if the precedent task ran to completion (`TaskStatus == TaskStatus. RanToCompletion`).
`TaskContinuationOptions .OnlyOnCanceled`	The continuation task should be scheduled only if the precedent task was canceled (`TaskStatus == TaskStatus.Canceled`).
`TaskContinuationOptions .OnlyOnFaulted`	The continuation task should be scheduled only if the precedent task threw an unhandled exception to completion (`TaskStatus == TaskStatus.Faulted`).
`TaskContinuationOptions .OnlyOnRanToCompletion`	The continuation task should be scheduled only if the precedent task ran to completion (`TaskStatus == TaskStatus. RanToCompletion`).
`TaskContinuationOptions .PreferFairness`	This option tells the scheduler that tasks scheduled sooner will be more likely to be run sooner and vice versa.

You can combine multiple values using bitwise operations.

The following values aren't valid for multitask continuations:

➤ `TaskContinuationOptions.NotOnRanToCompletion`

➤ `TaskContinuationOptions.NotOnFaulted`

➤ `TaskContinuationOptions.NotOnCanceled`

➤ `TaskContinuationOptions.OnlyOnRanToCompletion`

➤ `TaskContinuationOptions.OnlyOnFaulted`

➤ `TaskContinuationOptions.OnlyOnCanceled`

If you use the default option, `TaskContinuationOptions.None`, and a precedent task is canceled, the continuation will still be scheduled and started. Therefore, you have to pay special attention to the possible options to create reliable code.

Furthermore, `TaskCreationOptions` values are duplicated in `TaskContinuationOptions`, because for continuations, you can only specify the latter enum. You can specify both a `TaskContinuationOptions` value (`TaskContinuationOptions.NotOnCanceled`) combined with a `TaskCreationOptions` equivalent value (`TaskContinuationOptions.LongRunning`) as a parameter with a bitwise OR operation, as shown here:

Available for download on Wrox.com

```
var t10 = t9.ContinueWith(
            (t) => TaskMethod10(t),
            TaskContinuationOptions.NotOnCanceled |
            TaskContinuationOptions.LongRunning);
```

code snippet is Snippet3_6

Programming Complex Parallel Algorithms with Critical Sections Using Tasks

You can write complex parallel algorithms by combining continuations with critical sections. As previously explained, TPL doesn't necessarily create a new thread when you create a new task, but it could decide to inject a new thread if it was deemed appropriate. Therefore, if you work with continuations, you are giving valuable additional information to the scheduler about the tasks that it should allocate once a precedent task finishes. However, it is very important that you create a good design to avoid undesired additional overhead that could reduce performance or generate unexpected results.

Continuations are very powerful. If you know the task or tasks that must run after a different task, it is a good practice to chain these tasks using continuations. The underlying scheduler will be able to take full advantage of the work-stealing mechanism and optimize the scheduling mechanisms based on the available resources at run-time.

Continuations simplify the code, but they are also important because they help the underlying scheduler to take the right actions based on the tasks that have to be started in the near future.

Preparing the Code for Concurrency and Parallelism

Parallel and concurrent programming, when applied to certain complex algorithms, is not as simple as what was shown in previous examples. Sometimes, the differences between a reliable and bug-free parallelized version and its sequential counterpart could reveal an initially unexpected complexity. The code can become too complex, even when taking advantage of the new features offered by TPL. In fact, a complex sequential algorithm is probably going to be a more complex parallel algorithm. Therefore, .NET 4 parallel programming support offers the following new data structures for parallel programming that simplify many complex synchronization problems:

➤ Concurrent collection classes

➤ Lightweight synchronization primitives

➤ Types for lazy initialization

These data structures were designed to avoid *locks* wherever possible and use fine-grained locking when necessary. Locks generate many potential bugs and can significantly reduce the scalability. However, writing lock-free code isn't always possible.

With these new data structures, you can forget about complex lock mechanisms in certain situations, because they already include all the necessary lightweight synchronization under the hood. Therefore, it is a good idea to use these data structures whenever possible.

In the following chapters, you will dive deep into more complex parallelized algorithms, and you will learn to master even the most complex synchronization problems.

SUMMARY

There are many other advanced topics related to creating, managing, and scheduling tasks. This chapter introduced the new .NET Framework 4 task-based programming model by providing examples of the usage of some of its classes, structures, and enumerations. This chapter also discussed the combination of sequential and parallel code, and the importance of good designs that offer predictable results and help the underlying scheduling mechanisms. To summarize this chapter:

➤ You can create tasks to run code in parallel. TPL offers the new `Task` class that allows you to schedule and start tasks with simple code.

➤ You have to check the status for a task to understand what happened with its asynchronous execution. In addition, you have to pay special attention to the possibility of leaving unhandled exceptions.

➤   You can return values from tasks and chain multiple tasks using continuations.

➤   You can use a simple signaling mechanism to cancel the execution of tasks.

➤   You can launch multiple tasks with different scheduling options and chain multiple tasks. Gantt charts can help you create task execution plans.

➤   You can use lambda expressions and anonymous delegates to specify the actions to be run asynchronously by tasks.

Concurrent Collections

Task-based programming, imperative data, and task parallelism require arrays, lists, and collections capable of supporting updates concurrently. Before .NET Framework 4, it was necessary to add complex code to synchronize the operations performed in shared arrays, lists, and collections when they were updated by multiple threads. Now, you can work with the new concurrent collections to simplify the code and to achieve the best performance. These collections allow you to solve complex algorithms with simpler code. However, because they were just introduced with .NET Framework 4, you need to learn five new classes and one new interface.

This chapter is about the new classes and the new interface that allow you to work with shared concurrent collections from multiple tasks or threads. It explains how to create parallel code that adds, removes, and updates values of different types in lists with diverse ordering schemes and structures. At the end of this chapter, you will know how to implement existing algorithms that access and update lists in parallel using basic and complex features offered by the new concurrent collections.

UNDERSTANDING THE FEATURES OFFERED BY CONCURRENT COLLECTIONS

Lists, collections, and arrays are excellent examples of when complex synchronization management is needed to access them concurrently and in parallel. If you have to write a parallel loop that adds elements in an unordered way into a shared collection, you have to add a synchronization mechanism to generate a thread-safe collection. The classic lists, collections, and arrays found in the System.Collections and System.Collections.Generic namespaces are not thread-safe, because they aren't prepared to receive concurrent instructions to add or remove elements. Therefore, creating a thread-safe collection is indeed a very complex job.

If you need to add elements to a shared System.Collections.Generic.List in a parallelized loop that creates many concurrent tasks, you cannot use its Add method without synchronizing its execution. Because many threads will be accessing it concurrently, and it isn't prepared to receive concurrent requests because it isn't thread-safe, you need to serialize the execution of the Add method.

Listing 4-1 shows a new version of the Advanced Encryption Standard (AES) key generator.

LISTING 4-1: Adding elements to a list in a critical code section

```
private static List<string> _keysList;

private static void ParallelPartitionGenerateAESKeys()
{
    var sw = Stopwatch.StartNew();
    Parallel.ForEach(Partitioner.Create(1, NUM_AES_KEYS + 1), range =>
    {
        var aesM = new AesManaged();
        Debug.WriteLine("AES Range ({0}, {1}. Time: {2})",
                        range.Item1, range.Item2,
                        DateTime.Now.TimeOfDay);
        for (int i = range.Item1; i < range.Item2; i++)
        {
            aesM.GenerateKey();
            byte[] result = aesM.Key;
            string hexString = ConvertToHexString(result);

            lock (_keysList)
            {
```

```
                // Critical code section
                // It is safe to add elements to the List
                _keysList.Add(hexString);
            }
            // Console.WriteLine("AES KEY: {0} ", hexString);
        }
    });
    Debug.WriteLine("AES: " + sw.Elapsed.ToString());
}

static void Main(string[] args)
{
    var sw = Stopwatch.StartNew();

    _keysList = new List<string>(NUM_AES_KEYS);

    ParallelPartitionGenerateAESKeys();

    Console.WriteLine("Number of keys in the list: {0}",
        _keysList.Count);
    Debug.WriteLine(sw.Elapsed.ToString());
    // Display the results and wait for the user to press a key
    Console.WriteLine("Finished!");
    Console.ReadLine();
}
```

In this case, each inner loop that processes a concurrent range adds elements to the shared
List<string> *keyList*. The code uses the lock keyword to ensure that only one thread will run the
Add method for keyList at a time. The lock keyword creates a critical code section that ensures exclusive access to *keyList*, calls the Add method to add the element to the shared list, and then releases
the lock. At the same time that one of the concurrent tasks enters this critical code section, other tasks
could be trying to acquire the lock. They will be blocked and will wait to enter this critical section
until the lock is released. The lock keyword introduces an overhead and can reduce the scalability, but
the focus of this chapter is on concurrent collections. Chapter 5, "Coordination Data Structures,"
analyzes the different problems related to locks and their possible alternatives and solutions.

If you remove the lock statement, and then you try to add elements in multiple concurrent tasks
without any kind of synchronization mechanism, the code will produce unpredictable results (in
other words, it won't offer guarantees of correctness). For example, the following code lines show
the inner loop adding elements to the _keysList without locking it:

```
for (int i = range.Item1; i < range.Item2; i++)
{
    aesM.GenerateKey();
    byte[] result = aesM.Key;
    string hexString = ConvertToHexString(result);

    // The following code will generate undpredictable results
    // It is unsafe to add elements to the List
    _keysList.Add(hexString);
    // Console.WriteLine("AES KEY: {0} ", hexString);
}
```

code snippet is Snippet 4_1

This code generates unpredictable results because the number of elements in the final List is less than the expected 800,000 defined in the NUM_AES_KEYS constant. So, if this application is executed four times in a specific computer with eight logical cores, the values for _keysList.Count will be the following:

➤   736,756

➤   731,290

➤   717,709

➤   744,123

The list's contents are corrupted, but the code doesn't throw an exception. Therefore, it is extremely dangerous if you forget to add the necessary synchronization mechanism when you work with lists, collections, and arrays that aren't prepared for concurrency.

.NET Framework 4 provides new thread-safe and scalable concurrent collections to solve this problem. Most of the time, you don't have to worry about locks and synchronization primitives while using the new concurrent collections in many tasks. The concurrent collections are already prepared to receive concurrent and parallel methods calls. They solve potential deadlocks and race conditions, and they make it easier to work with parallelized code in many advanced scenarios. In addition, they are optimized to offer the best performance in most scenarios by reducing the number of necessary locks as much as possible. Thus, they don't add unnecessary synchronization overheads that could be introduced when you try to work with unsafe arrays, collections, and lists in concurrent code. This way, the concurrent collections will offer good scalability in most cases. Concurrent collections allow you to focus on implementing your algorithm without worrying about synchronization needs.

Deadlocks and race conditions can be difficult to detect when you work with locks and other synchronization techniques. Chapter 5, "Coordination Data Structures," dives deep into these problems.

Thread safety isn't free. Concurrent collections have a higher overhead than classic lists, collections, and arrays found in the System.Collections *and* System.Collections.Generic *namespaces. Therefore, you should use concurrent collections only when you need to access collections from multiple tasks concurrently. It doesn't make sense to use them in sequential code, because they would add unnecessary overhead.*

System.Collections.Concurrent

.NET Framework 4 offers a new namespace, `System.Collections.Concurrent`, for dealing with thread-safe issues. As you previously learned, this namespace provides access to the custom partitioners for parallelized loops and PLINQ. However, it also offers access to the following collections prepared for concurrency:

➤ `BlockingCollection<T>` — Similar to the classic blocking queue data structure; in this case, prepared for producer-consumer scenarios in which many tasks add and remove data. It is a wrapper of an `IProducerConsumer<T>` instance, providing blocking and bounding capabilities.

➤ `ConcurrentBag< T>` — Offers an unordered collection of objects. It is useful when ordering doesn't matter.

➤ `ConcurrentDictionary<TKey, TValue>` — Similar to a classic dictionary with key-value pairs that can be accessed concurrently.

➤ `ConcurrentQueue< T>` — A FIFO (first in, first out) collection whereby many tasks can enqueue and dequeue elements concurrently.

➤ `ConcurrentStack<T>` — A LIFO (last in, first out) collection whereby many tasks can push and pop elements concurrently.

All these new collections employ lock-free techniques to some extent in order to achieve performance benefits. This means that they avoid the typical mutual-exclusion, heavyweight locks by using *compare-and-swap (CAS)* instructions and memory barriers. However, they also use locks in some cases. The following sections provide detailed information about the synchronization techniques used by each of the aforementioned collections.

ConcurrentQueue

`ConcurrentQueue` is completely lock-free. It never takes a lock, but when CAS operations fail and are faced with *contention*, they may end up spinning and retrying an operation. *Contention* is the condition that arises when many tasks or threads attempt to use a single resource at the same time. A `ConcurrentQueue` is the concurrent version of `System.Collections.Queue`.

As previously explained, it is difficult to use a classic shared list to add elements from many independent tasks created by the `Parallel.ForEach` method. You need to add synchronization code, which would be a great challenge without restricting the overall scalability. However, you can add strings to a queue (enqueue strings) in a shared `ConcurrentQueue` inside the parallelized code, because `ConcurrentQueue` is prepared for adding elements concurrently. Figure 4-1 shows a diagram with the three most important methods offered by a `ConcurrentQueue`, which are as follows:

➤ `Enqueue` — Adds the new element received as a parameter to the end of the queue.

➤ `TryDequeue` — Tries to remove and return the element at the beginning of the queue in the `out` parameter. It returns a `bool` value indicating whether the operation was successful, and the `out` parameter contains the object removed from the queue.

➤ `TryPeek` — Tries to return the element at the beginning of the queue in the `out` parameter without removing it from the queue. It returns a `bool` value indicating whether the operation was successful, and the out parameter contains the object at the top of the queue.

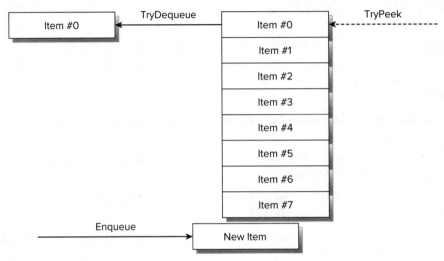

FIGURE 4-1

Listing 4-2 uses a shared `ConcurrentQueue<string>` called *_keysQueue* to hold a queue of strings that contains the AES keys generated in the parallelized loop with a custom partitioner.

LISTING 4-2: Adding elements to a ConcurrentQueue in a parallelized loop

```
private static void ParallelPartitionGenerateAESKeys()
{
    var sw = Stopwatch.StartNew();
    Parallel.ForEach(Partitioner.Create(1, NUM_AES_KEYS + 1), range =>
    {
        var aesM = new AesManaged();
        Debug.WriteLine(
"AES Range ({0}, {1}. TimeOfDay before inner loop starts: {2})",
            range.Item1, range.Item2,
            DateTime.Now.TimeOfDay);
        for (int i = range.Item1; i < range.Item2; i++)
        {
            aesM.GenerateKey();
            byte[] result = aesM.Key;
            string hexString = ConvertToHexString(result);

            _keysQueue.Enqueue(hexString);
            // Console.WriteLine("AES KEY: {0} ", hexString);
        }
    });
    Debug.WriteLine("AES: " + sw.Elapsed.ToString());
}
```

```
private static ConcurrentQueue<string> _keysQueue;

static void Main(string[] args)
{
    var sw = Stopwatch.StartNew();

    _keysQueue = new ConcurrentQueue<string>();

    ParallelPartitionGenerateAESKeys();

    Console.WriteLine("Number of keys in the list: {0}",
        _keysQueue.Count);
    Debug.WriteLine(sw.Elapsed.ToString());
    // Display the results and wait for the user to press a key
    Console.WriteLine("Finished!");
    Console.ReadLine();
}
```

All the tasks created automatically by `Parallel.ForEach` are going to call the `Enqueue` method to add elements at the end of the queue, like this:

```
_keysQueue.Enqueue(hexString)
```

code snippet is included in Listing 4_2

It is simple to work with a `ConcurrentQueue`. There is no need to worry about synchronization problems, because everything is controlled under the hood.

You can add, read, and remove elements in different tasks or threads without having to add locks or other synchronization mechanisms. For example, you could run many LINQ queries to display partial statistics while running the task *tAsync* that is adding elements to the `ConcurrentQueue`, *_keysQueue*. Listing 4-3 shows a new `Main` method that checks whether the *tAsync* task is running or waiting to run, and while this happens, it runs a LINQ query to show the number of keys that contain an F in the shared `ConcurrentQueue`, *_keysQueue*. It calls the `TryPeek` method to show the last key added to the queue at that moment.

LISTING 4-3: Reading a ConcurrentQueue and peeking elements from it

```
static void Main(string[] args)
{
    var sw = Stopwatch.StartNew();

    _keysQueue = new ConcurrentQueue<string>();

    var tAsync = Task.Factory.StartNew(
        () => ParallelPartitionGenerateAESKeys());

    string lastKey;
    while ((tAsync.Status == TaskStatus.Running) ||
           (tAsync.Status == TaskStatus.WaitingToRun))
        {
```

continues

LISTING 4-3 *(continued)*

```
                      // Display partial results
                      var countResult = _keysQueue.Count(
                          key => key.Contains("F"));

                      Console.WriteLine(
                          "So far, the number of keys that contain an F is: {0}",
                          countResult);
                      if (_keysQueue.TryPeek(out lastKey))
                      {
                          Console.WriteLine(
                              "The first key in the queue is: {0}", lastKey);
                      }
                      else
                      {
                          Console.WriteLine("No keys yet.");
                      }
                      // Sleep the main thread for 0.5 seconds
                      System.Threading.Thread.Sleep(500);
                  }

              tAsync.Wait();

              Console.WriteLine("Number of keys in the list: {0}",
                  _keysQueue.Count);
              Debug.WriteLine(sw.Elapsed.ToString());
              //  Display the results and wait for the user to press a key
              Console.WriteLine("Finished!");
              Console.ReadLine();
          }
```

The following code lines are an example of the console output, with the partial results. The first key in the queue will always be the same because the new keys are added at the bottom of the queue.

```
So far, the number of keys that contain an F is: 0
No keys yet.
So far, the number of keys that contain an F is: 83465
The first key in the queue is:
EB0C801EF5A86DF7615190A37EED18DE559A3338039342ADBDA91973ABAC9A90
So far, the number of keys that contain an F is: 214544
The first key in the queue is:
EB0C801EF5A86DF7615190A37EED18DE559A3338039342ADBDA91973ABAC9A90
So far, the number of keys that contain an F is: 349326
The first key in the queue is:
EB0C801EF5A86DF7615190A37EED18DE559A3338039342ADBDA91973ABAC9A90
So far, the number of keys that contain an F is: 542081
The first key in the queue is:
EB0C801EF5A86DF7615190A37EED18DE559A3338039342ADBDA91973ABAC9A90
So far, the number of keys that contain an F is: 743310
The first key in the queue is:
EB0C801EF5A86DF7615190A37EED18DE559A3338039342ADBDA91973ABAC9A90
Number of keys in the list: 800000
Finished!
```

If the `TryPeek` method returns `true`, it means that there are elements in the queue, and it could return the key at the beginning of the queue in the `out` parameter, *lastKey*, without removing it from the queue.

```
if (_keysQueue.TryPeek(out lastKey))
{
    Console.WriteLine(
        "The first key in the queue is: {0}", lastKey);
}
```

code snippet is included in Listing 4_3

Understanding a Parallel Producer-Consumer Pattern

`ParallelPartitionGenerateAESKeys` runs many loops in parallel to generate an AES key as an array of `Byte`, and then it calls the `ConvertToHexString` method with the array as a parameter to convert it to a string with hexadecimal values. Then, it adds the result to a `ConcurrentQueue`, *_keysQueue*. You can split this algorithm into a two-stage linear pipeline by using a *producer-consumer* pattern.

This section and the subsequent ones cover some scenarios for concurrent collections that don't represent best practices. The examples provide simple examples that must be improved. You will be able to combine everything you learned about concurrent collections in this chapter with the additional mechanisms explained in subsequent chapters to achieve both correctness and scalability.

Listing 4-4 shows the code for a two-stage linear pipeline implemented through the usage of two shared `ConcurrentQueue` instances, *_byteArraysQueue* and *_keysQueue*, as illustrated in Figure 4-2.

LISTING 4-4: One parallelized producer and one consumer working with two ConcurrentQueue instances

```
private static ConcurrentQueue<Byte[]> _byteArraysQueue;
private static ConcurrentQueue<string> _keysQueue;

private static void ParallelPartitionGenerateAESKeys(int maxDegree)
{
    var parallelOptions = new ParallelOptions();
    parallelOptions.MaxDegreeOfParallelism = maxDegree;

    var sw = Stopwatch.StartNew();
    Parallel.ForEach(
        Partitioner.Create(1, NUM_AES_KEYS + 1),
        parallelOptions, range =>
    {
        var aesM = new AesManaged();
        Debug.WriteLine("AES Range ({0}, {1}. Time: {2})",
```

continues

LISTING 4-4 *(continued)*

```
                            range.Item1, range.Item2,
                            DateTime.Now.TimeOfDay);
            for (int i = range.Item1; i < range.Item2; i++)
            {
                aesM.GenerateKey();
                byte[] result = aesM.Key;
                _byteArraysQueue.Enqueue(result);
            }
    });
    Debug.WriteLine("AES: " + sw.Elapsed.ToString());
}

private static void ConvertAESKeysToHex(Task taskProducer)
{
    var sw = Stopwatch.StartNew();
    // This condition running in a loop (spinning) is very inefficient
    // This example uses this spinning for educational purposes
    // It isn't a best practice
    // Subsequent sections and chapters explain an improved version
    while ((taskProducer.Status == TaskStatus.Running) ||
            (taskProducer.Status == TaskStatus.WaitingToRun) ||
            (_byteArraysQueue.Count > 0))
    {
        Byte[] result;
        if (_byteArraysQueue.TryDequeue(out result))
        {
            string hexString = ConvertToHexString(result);
            _keysQueue.Enqueue(hexString);
        }
    }
    Debug.WriteLine("HEX: " + sw.Elapsed.ToString());
}


static void Main(string[] args)
{
    var sw = Stopwatch.StartNew();

    _byteArraysQueue = new ConcurrentQueue<byte[]>();
    _keysQueue = new ConcurrentQueue<string>();

    var taskAESKeys = Task.Factory.StartNew(() =>
        ParallelPartitionGenerateAESKeys(
        Environment.ProcessorCount - 1));
    var taskHexStrings = Task.Factory.StartNew(() =>
        ConvertAESKeysToHex(taskAESKeys));

    string lastKey;
    // This condition running in a loop (spinning) is very inefficient
    // This example uses this spinning for educational purposes
    // It isn't a best practice
    // Subsequent sections and chapters explain an improved version
    while ((taskHexStrings.Status == TaskStatus.Running) ||
```

```
                    (taskHexStrings.Status == TaskStatus.WaitingToRun))
        {
            // Display partial results
            var countResult = _keysQueue.Count(key => key.Contains("F"));

            Console.WriteLine(
                "So far, the number of keys that contain an F is: {0}",
                countResult);
            if (_keysQueue.TryPeek(out lastKey))
            {
                Console.WriteLine("The first key in the queue is: {0}",
                    lastKey);
            }
            else
            {
                Console.WriteLine("No keys yet.");
            }
            // Sleep the main thread for 0.5 seconds
            System.Threading.Thread.Sleep(500);
        }

        Task.WaitAll(taskAESKeys, taskHexStrings);

        Console.WriteLine("Number of keys in the list: {0}",
            _keysQueue.Count);
        Debug.WriteLine(sw.Elapsed.ToString());
        //  Display the results and wait for the user to press a key
        Console.WriteLine("Finished!");
        Console.ReadLine();
    }
```

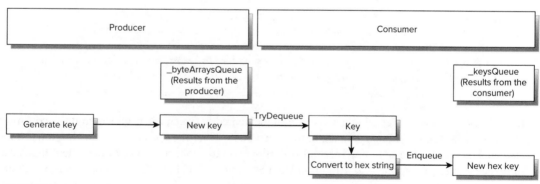

FIGURE 4-2

The new `Main` method creates and starts two asynchronous tasks: a *taskAESKeys* producer, and a *taskHexString* consumer. The former runs the `ParallelPartitionGenerateAESKeys` method with a specific maximum degree of parallelism, and the latter runs the `ConvertAESKeysToHex` method that receives the *taskAESKeys* producer task as a parameter. Now, the parallelized loop in the `ParallelPartitionGenerateAESKeys` method will run with the total number of available logical cores minus one. This way, the sequential loop that runs in the consumer can take advantage of the remaining logical core.

The producer uses a shared `ConcurrentQueue<Byte[]>`, *_byteArraysQueue*, in order to hold a queue of `Byte[]` that contains the AES keys generated in the parallelized loop with a custom partitioner. These AES keys aren't converted to hexadecimal values in a string, because this step is performed by the consumer. All the tasks created automatically by `Parallel.ForEach` are going to call the `Enqueue` method to add elements at the end of the queue.

The consumer receives the producer `Task` instance as a parameter, *taskProducer*. It checks whether this task is running or waiting to run, or if the number of elements in _byteArraysQueue is greater than zero. _byteArraysQueue is the `ConcurrentQueue` that holds the results for the producer and feeds the consumer. While the aforementioned condition is true, the consumer calls the `TryDequeue` method to remove an element from the top of the queue. If the `TryDequeue` method returns `true`, it means that there are elements in the queue and the method could remove and return the `Byte[]` at the beginning of the queue in the out parameter, *result*. Then, the consumer calls the `ConvertToHexString` method with the retrieved `Byte[]` as a parameter. Finally, the consumer adds the result at the top of the `ConcurrentQueue` that holds the results for the consumer, *_keysQueue*, as shown in the following code lines:

```
if (_byteArraysQueue.TryDequeue(out result))
{
    hexString = ConvertToHexString(result);
    _keysQueue.Enqueue(hexString);
}
```

code snippet is included in Listing 4_4

 The consumer calls the `TryDequeue` method for _keysQueue while the multiple tasks that run the producer's parallelized loop call the `Enqueue` method. When there are concurrent enqueue and dequeue operations, they are going to be a bit slower than these operations running alone. In this case, there is no synchronization code added to both the producer and the consumer, but there is a lot of synchronization in the `ConcurrentQueue` under the hood. To simplify this example, there is no exception-handling code. However, it is very important to use the exception-handling techniques explained in previous chapters.

In this case, there is no signaling mechanism implemented between the producer and the consumer. However, you should implement a signaling mechanism to let the consumer know that it has a new element to process. The signaling mechanisms allow you to avoid the usage of inefficient loops used in this example. Chapter 5, "Coordination Data Structures," includes detailed information about how to manage the communication between different tasks and threads. The `Main` method also runs the previously explained LINQ query while the producer and the consumer are working.

 The previous example implements a parallel producer-consumer pattern. You can improve its performance and reduce the overheads by using other concurrent collections and adding some coordination data structures. Because you need to learn many topics to implement more optimal producer-consumer patterns, the following sections and subsequent chapters dive deep into all the necessary topics to improve each parallelized algorithm.

Working with Multiple Producers and Consumers

It is easy to implement a parallel producer-consumer pattern or multiple-stage linear pipelines by using a ConcurrentQueue. However, it is very important to measure the overall performance and the latencies introduced by these schemes. In the previous example, the producer ran code in a parallelized loop with a desired degree of parallelism. It included many concurrent tasks that produced elements and added them to a ConcurrentQueue, as well as a consumer that removed elements from this queue and processed them.

You can also parallelize the consumer to run by using multiple tasks. You don't need to change the code in the ConvertAESKeysToHex method, because it is prepared to perform an atomic operation that removes a _byteArraysQueue_ item from the ConcurrentQueue, and adds each processed element to another ConcurrentQueue, _keysQueue_. Two or more independent concurrent tasks running the ConvertAESKeysToHex method might call the TryDequeue method at the same time for the last element in the ConcurrentQueue, _byteArraysQueue_. This situation might happen because the while condition is satisfied in all the tasks at the same time. Imagine that at this point, the consumer has finished its execution. Because the ConcurrentQueue serializes the execution of each TryDequeue method as an atomic operation, one of the tasks will receive the removed element, and the TryDequeue method will return a true value. Now, there are no more elements in the queue, because the last one was removed by the previously explained atomic operation; therefore, the TryDequeue method will return false in the other tasks. The results are predictable, and the consumer is scalable, because you can run as many consumers in parallel as needed to optimize the overall performance.

The following code lines show a new version of the Main method that uses half of the available logical cores to determine the maximum degree of parallelism for the producer's parallelized loop. This new Main method uses the remaining cores to launch many Task instances that run the ConvertAESKeysToHex consumer's method in parallel.

```
static void Main(string[] args)
{
    var sw = Stopwatch.StartNew();

    _byteArraysQueue = new ConcurrentQueue<byte[]>();
    _keysQueue = new ConcurrentQueue<string>();

    int taskAESKeysMax = Environment.ProcessorCount / 2;
    // Use the remaining logical cores
    // to create parallelized tasks to run many consumers
    int taskHexStringsMax = Environment.ProcessorCount - taskAESKeysMax;
    var taskAESKeys = Task.Factory.StartNew(() =>
        ParallelPartitionGenerateAESKeys(taskAESKeysMax));
    Task[] tasksHexStrings = new Task[taskHexStringsMax];
    for (int i = 0; i < taskHexStringsMax; i++)
    {
        tasksHexStrings[i] = Task.Factory.StartNew(() =>
            ConvertAESKeysToHex(taskAESKeys));
    }

    Task.WaitAll(tasksHexStrings);

    Console.WriteLine("Number of keys in the list: {0}", _keysQueue.Count);
```

```
        Debug.WriteLine(sw.Elapsed.ToString());
        //  Display the results and wait for the user to press a key
        Console.WriteLine("Finished!");
        Console.ReadLine();
    }
```

code snippet is Snippet 4_2

The `tasksHexStrings` array holds the instances of `Task` created by the `Task.Factory.StartNew` method. This way, there are many tasks that are producing elements as well as many tasks that are consuming elements, concurrently and potentially in parallel, as represented in the diagram in Figure 4-3.

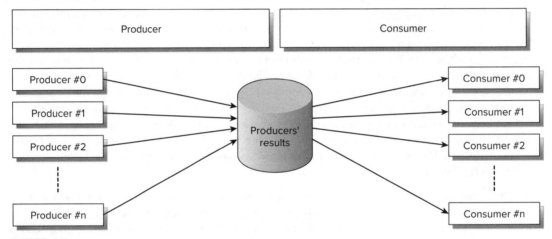

FIGURE 4-3

In this case, the multiple producers and consumers represent the configuration of a two-stage linear pipeline. You can extend this pipeline to more stages by adding another consumer to the results generated by the existing consumer. This way, the consumer for the first producer becomes a producer for the second consumer, as illustrated in Figure 4-4. You can chain many producers and consumers according to the throughput needs. However, because each new stage adds overhead and can increase the necessary memory to run the algorithms, it is very important that you test and measure different possible alternatives to organize the stages. Sometimes, an additional stage introduces too much overhead and reduces the overall performance.

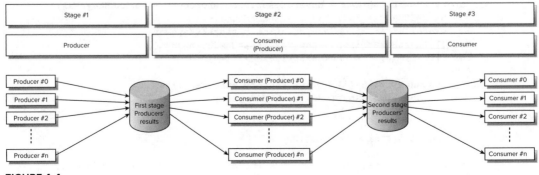

FIGURE 4-4

The code in Listing 4-5 adds another consumer that validates the hexadecimal keys retrieved from the *_keysQueue*. The code assumes that the computer has at least three logical cores to distribute the different tasks that produce and consume results for this three-stage pipeline. A new `Task` instance called *taskValidateKeys* runs the new `ValidateKeys` method. This method retrieves each hexadecimal key from *_keysQueue* and adds it to a resulting `ConcurrentCollection`, *_validKeys*, only if it doesn't contain a certain number of invalid hexadecimal values. The `IsKeyValid` method performs this individual validation.

LISTING 4-5: Another consumer to create a three-stage linear pipleine

```
private static string[] _invalidHexValues =
    {"AF", "BD", "BF", "CF", "DA", "FA", "FE", "FF" };
private static int MAX_INVALID_HEX_VALUES = 3;
private static int tasksHexStringsRunning = 0;

private static bool IsKeyValid(string key)
{
    var sw = Stopwatch.StartNew();
    int count = 0;
    for (int i = 0; i < _invalidHexValues.Length; i++)
    {
        if (key.Contains(_invalidHexValues[i]))
        {
            count++;
            if (count == MAX_INVALID_HEX_VALUES)
            {
                return true;
            }
            if (((_invalidHexValues.Length - i) + count) <
                MAX_INVALID_HEX_VALUES)
            {
                // There are no chances of being an invalid key
                return false;
            }
        }
    }
    return false;
}

private static void ValidateKeys()
{
    var sw = Stopwatch.StartNew();
    // This condition running in a loop (spinning) is very inefficient
    // This example uses this spinning for educational purposes
    // It isn't a best practice
    // Subsequent sections and chapters explain an improved version
    while ((tasksHexStringsRunning > 0) ||
            (_keysQueue.Count > 0))
    {
        string hexString;
        if (_keysQueue.TryDequeue(out hexString))
        {
            if (IsKeyValid(hexString))
```

continues

LISTING 4-5 *(continued)*

```
                {
                    _validKeys.Enqueue(hexString);
                }
            }
        }
    }
    Debug.WriteLine("VALIDATE: " + sw.Elapsed.ToString());
}


static void Main(string[] args)
{
    var sw = Stopwatch.StartNew();

    _byteArraysQueue = new ConcurrentQueue<byte[]>();
    _keysQueue = new ConcurrentQueue<string>();
    _validKeys = new ConcurrentQueue<string>();

    // This code requires at least 3 logical cores
    int taskAESKeysMax = Environment.ProcessorCount / 2;
    // Use the remaining logical cores - 1
    // to create parallelized tasks to run many consumers
    int taskHexStringsMax =
        Environment.ProcessorCount - taskAESKeysMax - 1;
    var taskAESKeys =
        Task.Factory.StartNew(
            () =>
            ParallelPartitionGenerateAESKeys(taskAESKeysMax));
    Task[] tasksHexStrings = new Task[taskHexStringsMax];
    for (int i = 0; i < taskHexStringsMax; i++)
    {
        // Increment tasksHexStringsRunning as an atomic operation
        System.Threading.Interlocked.Increment(
          ref tasksHexStringsRunning);

        tasksHexStrings[i] = Task.Factory.StartNew(() =>
        {
            try
            {
                ConvertAESKeysToHex(taskAESKeys);
            }
            finally
            {
            // Decrement tasksHexStringsRunning as an atomic operation
                System.Threading.Interlocked.Decrement(
                    ref tasksHexStringsRunning);
            }
        });
    }
    var taskValidateKeys = Task.Factory.StartNew(() =>
        ValidateKeys());
```

```
        taskValidateKeys.Wait();

        Console.WriteLine("Number of keys in the list: {0}",
            _keysQueue.Count);
        Console.WriteLine("Number of valid keys: {0}",
            _validKeys.Count);

        Debug.WriteLine(sw.Elapsed.ToString());
        //  Display the results and wait for the user to press a key
        Console.WriteLine("Finished!");
        Console.ReadLine();
    }
```

In this case, if the computer has more than three logical cores, there are going to be many `Task` instances that are adding elements to *_keysQueue* and held in the *tasksHexStrings* array. Therefore, checking the status for all these `Task` instances each time the `while` loop in the `ValidateKeys` method has to decide whether to continue or not would be a bit complex and inefficient. Thus, before a new `Task` that converts the AES keys to a string with hexadecimal values starts, the *tasksHexStringsRunning* private variable increases. Each time this `Task` instance finishes, the *tasksHexStringsRunning* private variable decreases. This way, if there aren't more elements in *_keysQueue* and *tasksHexStringsRunning* is zero, the final consumer can stop its execution. Subsequent sections explain other concurrent collections that allow you to avoid the inefficient evaluation of this condition in the consumer.

Because many tasks could start or finish concurrently or in parallel, you must make sure that both operations in this shared variable are performed as atomic operations. Before creating and starting each new Task instance, a call to the `System.Threading.Interlocked.Increment` method increases the value for the *tasksHexStringsRunning* variable as an atomic operation. The method receives *tasksHexStringsRunning* by reference. Once the task finishes, it makes sure that the value for the *tasksHexStringsRunning* variable is decremented in an atomic operation by calling the `System.Threading.Interlocked.Decrement` with the same parameter and in a `finally` block. However, you still need to add more exception handling to these multiple producers and consumers. The following code lines make sure that the value of *tasksHexStringsRunning* is representative of the real number of `Task` instances running the `ConvertAESKeysToHex` method concurrently:

```
System.Threading.Interlocked.Increment(ref tasksHexStringsRunning);
tasksHexStrings[i] = Task.Factory.StartNew(() =>
{
    try
    {
        ConvertAESKeysToHex(taskAESKeys);
    }
    finally
    {
        System.Threading.Interlocked.Decrement(ref tasksHexStringsRunning);
    }
});
```

code snippet is Listing 4_5

Sometimes, the ConcurrentQueue *isn't the most convenient concurrent collection for a specific producer-consumer scenario. In fact, it can easily become a bottleneck, because it must maintain a FIFO order. The following sections explain other useful concurrent collections that are suitable for producer-consumer scenarios and linear or nonlinear pipelines. You can also combine different concurrent collections to generate the most appropriate results and to simplify your code. Before implementing a producer-consumer scenario, be sure to read the section that covers the* BlockingCollection.

Designing Pipelines by Using Concurrent Collections

A perfect linear pipeline should have the same number of stages as the number of available logical cores, and each stage should require the same amount of work. However, this kind of pipeline isn't too common in real-life situations. Most of the time, you need to test different alternatives and group certain jobs in a specific number of stages. Also remember that the pipeline should be scalable as the number of logical cores increases, and it should provide a speedup compared with the sequential execution of the algorithm.

Imagine a pipeline that has to perform the following jobs to simulate the behavior of new universes:

➤ Generate planets.

➤ Generate satellites. The satellites require data from their related planet.

➤ Generate comets. The orbits for the simulated comets must avoid colliding with the planets and their satellites.

➤ Generate asteroids. Simulated asteroids are going to impact on the planets, but they must avoid colliding with the planets' satellites and with the comets.

➤ Generate terrains. Terrain simulation must consider the impacts of asteroids.

➤ Generate atmosphere. Atmosphere simulation must consider the effects of the asteroids when they impact on the planets' terrains.

➤ Generate weather conditions. Simulated weather conditions must consider the atmosphere, the terrains, the effects of asteroids, the satellites, and the planet's composition.

You can chain these jobs by creating a seven-stage linear pipeline with many producers and consumers. Figure 4-5 shows one of the different grouping possibilities for a four-stage linear pipeline, and the total amount of work performed in each stage represented with bars. If you launch these four stages concurrently and you have four physical cores, this combination isn't load-balanced. These seven jobs grouped in four stages waste a lot of processing resources. The generation of planets takes less time than the generation of terrains. The atmosphere and weather condition generations run lonely after the terrains generation finishes.

Figure 4-6 shows another grouping possibility that wastes a lot of processing time.

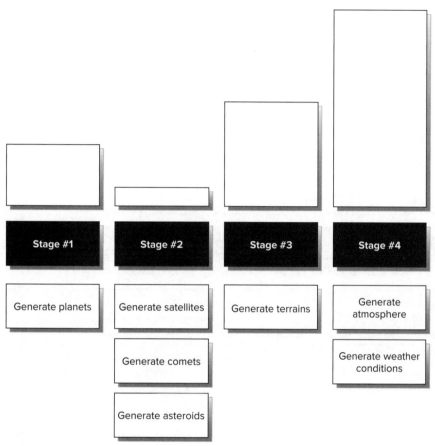

FIGURE 4-5

So, you need to test yet another grouping and try to balance the load for each stage. Figure 4-7 shows the final grouping. It runs four jobs in the first stage and one job in each of the other three stages. Most of the time, it is difficult to forecast the performance of different sequential jobs when they are executed in a pipeline, because the extra overhead added by all the synchronization mechanisms running behind the scenes can lead to unexpected final groupings.

A four-stage pipeline can take advantage of more than four logical cores. As previously explained, each stage could run parallelized to take advantage of all the available cores. However, it is also important to test different scenarios to make sure that the parallelization of each stage brings a speedup.

ConcurrentStack

ConcurrentStack is completely lock-free. It never takes a lock, but when a CAS operation fails and faces contention, it may end up spinning and retrying an operation. A ConcurrentStack is the concurrent version of System.Collections.Stack. It is very similar to the previously explained ConcurrentQueue, but it uses different method names to better represent a stack, or LIFO collection.

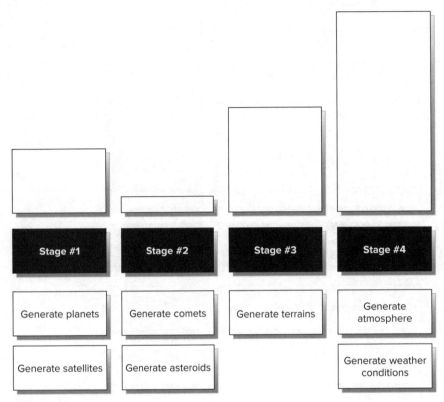

FIGURE 4-6

A `ConcurrentStack` includes the following three important methods (illustrated in the diagram in Figure 4-8):

➤ `Push` — Adds the new element received as a parameter at the top of the stack.

➤ `TryPop` — Tries to remove and return the element at the top of the stack in the `out` parameter. It returns a `bool` value indicating whether the operation was successful, and the `out` parameter contains the object removed from the stack.

➤ `TryPeek` — Tries to return the element at the top of the stack in the `out` parameter without removing it from the queue. It returns a `bool` value indicating whether the operation was successful, and the `out` parameter contains the object at the top of the queue.

In order to determine whether the stack contains any items, you can use the `IsEmpty` `bool` property instead of retrieving the number of items from the `Count` property and comparing it to 0. For example, consider the following condition:

```
if (_byteArraysStack.Count > 0)
```

You need to replace this with the following code line, because the goal is to determine whether `_byteArraysStack` is empty or not, and therefore, it isn't necessary to retrieve the number of items with the relatively expensive call to the `Count` property:

```
if (!_byteArraysStack.IsEmpty)
```

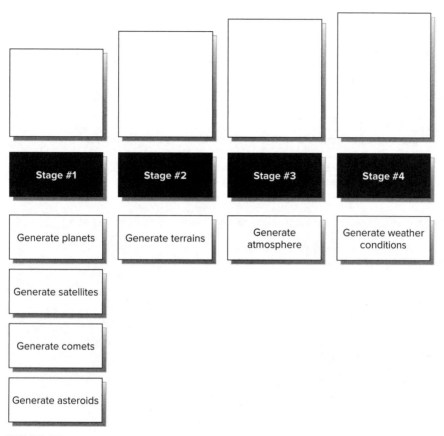

FIGURE 4-7

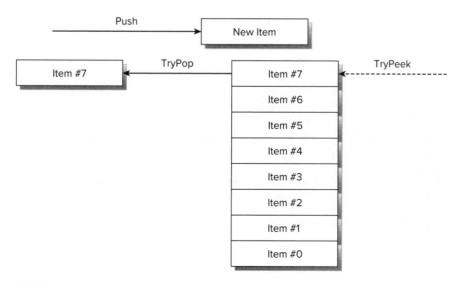

FIGURE 4-8

In *Big O notation*, IsEmpty is O(1), a constant time algorithm, whereas Count is O(n) and takes linear time for a ConcurrentStack<T>. Listing 4-6 shows a new version of the previous example. In this listing, the necessary changes have been made to use many ConcurrentStack instances instead of ConcurrentQueue ones. This version usually achieves a 1.30x speedup compared with the previous ConcurrentQueue version. However, remember that the order in which elements are added and removed is different from the queue. Sometimes, a stack is more appropriate than a queue.

LISTING 4-6: The pipeline implemented with many ConcurrentStack instances

```
private static ConcurrentStack<Byte[]> _byteArraysStack;
private static ConcurrentStack<string> _keysStack;
private static ConcurrentStack<string> _validKeys;

private static void ParallelPartitionGenerateAESKeys(int maxDegree)
{
    var parallelOptions = new ParallelOptions();
    parallelOptions.MaxDegreeOfParallelism = maxDegree;

    var sw = Stopwatch.StartNew();
    Parallel.ForEach(
        Partitioner.Create(1, NUM_AES_KEYS + 1),
        parallelOptions, range =>
        {
            var aesM = new AesManaged();
            byte[] result;
            Debug.WriteLine("AES Range ({0}, {1}. Time: {2})",
                            range.Item1, range.Item2,
                            DateTime.Now.TimeOfDay);
            for (int i = range.Item1; i < range.Item2; i++)
            {
                aesM.GenerateKey();
                result = aesM.Key;
                _byteArraysStack.Push(result);
            }
        });
    Debug.WriteLine("AES: " + sw.Elapsed.ToString());
}

private static void ConvertAESKeysToHex(Task taskProducer)
{
    var sw = Stopwatch.StartNew();
    // This condition running in a loop (spinning) is very inefficient
    // This example uses this spinning for educational purposes
    // It isn't a best practice
    // Subsequent sections and chapters explain an improved version
    while ((taskProducer.Status == TaskStatus.Running) ||
           (taskProducer.Status == TaskStatus.WaitingToRun) ||
           (!_byteArraysStack.IsEmpty))
    {
```

```
            Byte[] result;
            if (_byteArraysStack.TryPop(out result))
            {
                string hexString = ConvertToHexString(result);
                _keysStack.Push(hexString);
            }
        }
        Debug.WriteLine("HEX: " + sw.Elapsed.ToString());
    }

    private static void ValidateKeys()
    {
        var sw = Stopwatch.StartNew();
        // This condition running in a loop (spinning) is very inefficient
        // This example uses this spinning for educational purposes
        // It isn't a best practice
        // Subsequent sections and chapters explain an improved version
        while ((tasksHexStringsRunning > 0) ||
               (!_keysStack.IsEmpty))
        {
            string hexString;
            if (_keysStack.TryPop(out hexString))
            {
                if (IsKeyValid(hexString))
                {
                    _validKeys.Push(hexString);
                }
            }
        }
        Debug.WriteLine("VALIDATE: " + sw.Elapsed.ToString());
    }

    static void Main(string[] args)
    {
        var sw = Stopwatch.StartNew();

        _byteArraysStack = new ConcurrentStack<byte[]>();
        _keysStack = new ConcurrentStack<string>();
        _validKeys = new ConcurrentStack<string>();
        ...
```

A ConcurrentStack offers two methods that can insert and remove multiple elements at the top of the stack as an atomic operation: PushRange and TryPopRange. Figure 4-9 shows a diagram with their behavior. You can call these methods with an array of the same type of the elements in the ConcurrentStack. You can also use the definitions for the methods that allow you to specify the index for the item to begin inserting to or removing from the ConcurrentStack and the total number of items.

The following code shows a new version of the ValidateKeys method that calls one of the definitions for TryPopRange. This new ValidateKeys method uses a buffer to validate chunks of one hundred items, defined in bufferSize, whenever possible.

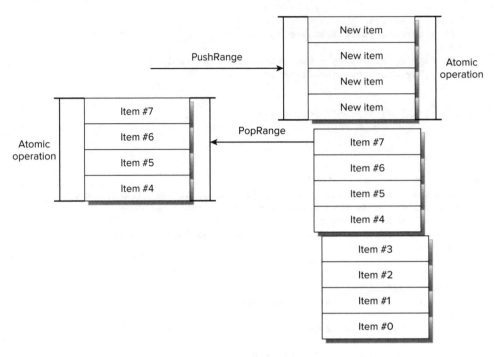

FIGURE 4-9

```
private static void ValidateKeys()
{
    var sw = Stopwatch.StartNew();
    const int bufferSize = 100;
    string[] hexStrings = new string[bufferSize];
    string[] validHexStrings = new string[bufferSize];
    // This condition running in a loop (spinning) is very inefficient
    // This example uses this spinning for educational purposes
    // It isn't a best practice
    // Subsequent sections and chapters explain an improved version
    while ((tasksHexStringsRunning > 0) ||
        (!_keysStack.IsEmpty))
    {
        int numItems = _keysStack.TryPopRange(hexStrings, 0, bufferSize);
        int numValidKeys = 0;
        for (int i = 0; i < numItems; i++)
        {
            if (IsKeyValid(hexStrings[i]))
            {
                validHexStrings[numValidKeys] = hexStrings[i];
                numValidKeys++;
            }
        }
        if (numValidKeys > 0)
        {
```

```
                _validKeys.PushRange(validHexStrings, 0, numValidKeys);
        }
    }
    Debug.WriteLine("VALIDATE: " + sw.Elapsed.ToString());
}
```

code snippet is Snippet 4_3

The `TryPopRange` method receives an array of string `hexStrings`, 0 as the initial index and `bufferSize` as the number of elements to try to remove from the top of the stack.

```
int numItems = _keysStack.TryPopRange(hexStrings, 0, bufferSize);
```

code snippet is Snippet 4_3

The method returns the number of elements successfully removed and now available in the `numItems` array received as a parameter. The number of elements could be less than the number specified, because there are not enough items in the stack at that time. Thus, it is very important that you consider the value returned by the method in order to access the right number of elements in the array. If the stack was empty, it would return 0.

Then, the code runs a sequential `for` loop that saves each validated string in the `hexStrings` array and increments a counter of valid strings, `numValidKeys`. Then, if the loop produced a number of valid strings higher than zero, it calls the `PushRange` method to insert all of them at the top of the stack in an atomic operation.

```
_validKeys.PushRange(validHexStrings, 0, numValidKeys);
```

code snippet is Snippet 4_3

The method receives the array with `validHexStrings`, 0 (the validated strings) as the initial index, and `numValidKeys` as the number of elements to push to the stack. This way, it will add the items in the `validHexStrings` array from 0 to numValidKeys - 1.

> *Sometimes, you can reduce the number of concurrent pushes and pops in a* `ConcurrentStack`. *In these cases, you can improve the performance by using the previously explained* `TryPopRange` *and* `PushRange` *methods to perform atomic operations with groups of elements. However, you have to be careful, because buffers also add overhead and consume additional memory.*

You can remove all items from the `ConcurrentStack` by calling its `Clear` method. Thus, you can also clear the stack in an atomic operation, as in the next line:

```
_keysStack.Clear()
```

Transforming Arrays and Unsafe Collections into Concurrent Collections

You can transform arrays and unsafe collections into one of the concurrent collections by creating a new instance with the unsafe collection as a parameter. The following code lines show an example that creates a `ConcurrentStack<string>` called *invalidHexValuesStack*, filling it with the values found in an existing array of `string` called *_invalidHexValues*. This way, you can remove items from the `ConcurrentStack` by using its `TryPop` method.

```
private static string[] _invalidHexValues =
    { "AF", "BD", "BF", "CF", "DA", "FA", "FE", "FF" };

static void Main(string[] args)
{
    var invalidHexValuesStack = new ConcurrentStack<string>(_invalidHexValues);

    while (!invalidHexValuesStack.IsEmpty)
    {
        string hexValue;
        invalidHexValuesStack.TryPop(out hexValue);
        Console.WriteLine(hexValue);
    }

    Console.ReadLine();
}
```

code snippet is Snippet 4_4

The previous code will generate the following output in the console. The first item was the first one in the *_invalidHexValues* string array, because its items were added to a stack, with a FIFO order.

```
FF
FE
FA
DA
CF
BF
BD
AF
```

You can use any collection that supports the `IEnumerable` interface with the same data type that the concurrent collection has defined for its elements. Thus, the previously shown code would also work if the parameter sent to the `ConcurrentStack` constructor, *_invalidHexValues*, is a `List<string>`. For example:

```
public static List<string> _invalidHexValues =
    new List<string> { "AF", "BD", "BF", "CF", "DA", "FA", "FE", "FF" };
```

Once you perform all the necessary concurrent operations with a concurrent collection, you may need to run sequential code that accesses its elements. When this happens, the extra overhead added by the thread-safety operations could make the sequential code run slower than if it was accessing an unsafe collection. In such cases, you can call one of the following methods to create an unsafe collection based on the elements in the concurrent queue:

➤ `CopyTo` — Copies the elements to an existing one-dimensional array, starting at the array index received as the second parameter. The destination array has to be dimensioned to support the number of elements in the concurrent collection. In the following example code snippet, the `invalidStrings` array is created to support the number of elements in the `invalidHexValuesStack`, and then the `CopyTo` method copies the elements starting at the array index 0:

```
string[] invalidStrings = new string[invalidHexValuesStack.Count];
invalidHexValuesStack.CopyTo(invalidStrings, 0);
```

➤ `ToArray` — Returns a new array of the same type as the elements in the concurrent collection, with all the elements added to the array. The following example code snippet shows how the `ToArray` method returns the new array of `string`, `invalidStrings`:

```
var invalidStrings = invalidHexValuesStack.ToArray();
```

You can run the aforementioned methods while other tasks or threads add and remove elements from the concurrent collection, but the new unsafe collection will be based on a snapshot of the concurrent collection at a specific time. Thus, you may receive an unsafe collection with elements that could have been removed from the concurrent collection.

 You can also use the supported `ToList`, `ToDictionary`, *and* `ToLookup` *extension methods to copy elements from a concurrent collection to other types of unsafe collections.*

ConcurrentBag

`ConcurrentBag` is a very efficient collection for certain scenarios where the same thread is adding elements (producing) and removing elements (consuming). It uses many different mechanisms to minimize the need for synchronization and its associated overhead. However, sometimes it requires locking, and it is fairly inefficient in a scenario where producer threads are completely separate from consumer threads. `ConcurrentBag` maintains a local queue for each thread that accesses the bag, and whenever possible, it accesses the local queue in a lock-free manner with little or no contention. `ConcurrentBag` represents a bag, which is an unordered collection of objects that supports duplicates. Thus, a `ConcurrentBag` is useful for storing and accessing objects when ordering doesn't matter.

The three most important methods offered by a `ConcurrentBag` are as follows:

➤ `Add` — Adds the new element received as a parameter to the bag.

➤ `TryTake` — Tries to remove and return an element from the bag in the `out` parameter. It returns a `bool` value indicating whether the operation was successful, and the `out` parameter contains the object removed from the bag.

➤ `TryPeek` — Tries to return an element from the bag in the `out` parameter without removing it from the bag. It returns a `bool` value indicating whether the operation was successful, and the `out` parameter contains the object from the bag.

These three methods are illustrated in Figure 4-10.

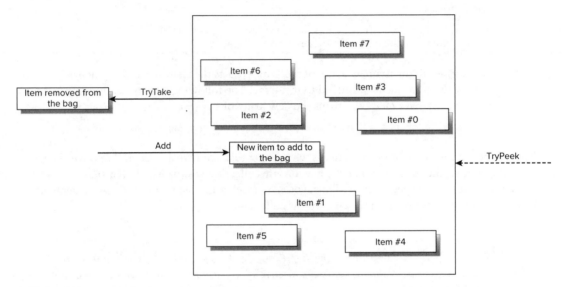

FIGURE 4-10

A `ConcurrentBag` also offers the `IsEmpty` property previously explained in the `ConcurrentStack` section.

Listing 4-7 shows the code for many producers and consumers that generates and processes two million sentences, *(NUM_SENTENCES)*, by working with the following three *ConcurrentBag* instances:

➤ *_sentencesBag*—The `ProduceSentences` method generates the two million sentences and adds them to this bag.

➤ *_capWordsInSentencesBag*—The `CapitalizeWordsInSentences` method retrieves sentences from the _sentencesBag bag and generates a new sentence with replaced delimiters and capitalized words. It adds these new sentences to this other bag, *_capWordsInSentencesBag*.

➤ *_finalSentencesBag* — The `RemoveLettersInSentences` method retrieves sentences from the *_capWordsInSentences* bag and generates a new sentence with the characters that matched certain letters removed. It adds these new sentences to this other bag, *_finalSentencesBag*.

LISTING 4-7: Producers and consumers adding and removing elements from many
ConcurrentBag instances

```
private static string RemoveLetters(char[] letters, string sentence)
{
    var sb = new StringBuilder();
    bool match = false;

    for (int i = 0; i < sentence.Length; i++)
    {
        for (int j = 0; j < letters.Length; j++)
        {
            if (sentence[i] == letters[j])
            {
                match = true;
                break;
            }
        }
        if (!match)
        {
            sb.Append(sentence[i]);
        }
        match = false;
    }
    return sb.ToString();
}

private static string CapitalizeWords(
    char[] delimiters, string sentence, char newDelimiter)
{
    string[] words = sentence.Split(delimiters);
    var sb = new StringBuilder();
    for (int i = 0; i < words.Length; i++)
    {
        if (words[i].Length > 1)
        {
            sb.Append(words[i][0].ToString().ToUpper());
            sb.Append(words[i].Substring(1).ToLower());
        }
        else
        {
            // Word with just 1 letter must be lowercase
            sb.Append(words[i].ToLower());
        }
        sb.Append(newDelimiter);
    }
    return sb.ToString();
}

private const int NUM_SENTENCES = 2000000;
private static ConcurrentBag<string> _sentencesBag;
private static ConcurrentBag<string> _capWordsInSentencesBag;
private static ConcurrentBag<string> _finalSentencesBag;
```

continues

LISTING 4-7 *(continued)*

```
private static volatile bool _producingSentences = false;
private static volatile bool _capitalizingWords = false;

private static void ProduceSentences()
{
    string[] possibleSentences =
    {
    "ConcurrentBag is included in the Systems.Concurrent.Collections namespace.",
    "Is parallelism important for cloud-computing?",
    "Parallelism is very important for cloud-computing!",
    "ConcurrentQueue is one of the new concurrent collections added in .NET Framework 4",
    "ConcurrentStack is a concurrent collection that represents a LIFO collection",
    "ConcurrentQueue is a concurrent collection that represents a FIFO collection"
    };

    try
    {
        // The Main method set productingSentences to true
        _sentencesBag = new ConcurrentBag<string>();
        var rnd = new Random();

        for (int i = 0; i < NUM_SENTENCES; i++)
        {
            var sb = new StringBuilder();
            for (int j = 0; j < possibleSentences.Length; j++)
            {
                if (rnd.Next(2) > 0)
                {
                    sb.Append(possibleSentences[
                                rnd.Next(possibleSentences.Length)]);
                    sb.Append(' ');
                }
            }
            if (rnd.Next(20) > 15)
            {
                _sentencesBag.Add(sb.ToString());
            }
            else
            {
                _sentencesBag.Add(sb.ToString().ToUpper());
            }
        }
    }
    finally
    {
        _producingSentences = false;
    }
}

private static void CapitalizeWordsInSentences()
{
    char[] delimiterChars = {
        ' ', ',', '.', ':', ';', '(', ')', '[', ']', '{', '}',
```

```
                '/', '?', '@', '\t', '"' };

        // Start after Produce sentences began working
        System.Threading.SpinWait.SpinUntil(() => _producingSentences);

        try
        {
            _capitalizingWords = true;
        // This condition running in a loop (spinning) is very inefficient
        // This example uses this spinning for educational purposes
        // It isn't a best practice
        // Subsequent sections and chapters explain an improved version
            while ((!_sentencesBag.IsEmpty) || (_producingSentences))
            {
                string sentence;
                if (_sentencesBag.TryTake(out sentence))
                {
                    _capWordsInSentencesBag.Add(
                        CapitalizeWords(delimiterChars, sentence, '\\'));
                }
            }
        }
        finally
        {
            _capitalizingWords = false;
        }
    }

    private static void RemoveLettersInSentences()
    {
        char[] letterChars = {
            'A', 'B', 'C', 'e', 'i', 'j', 'm', 'X', 'y', 'Z' };

        // Start after CapitalizedWordsInsentences began working
        System.Threading.SpinWait.SpinUntil(() => _capitalizingWords);
        // This condition running in a loop (spinning) is very inefficient
        // This example uses this spinning for educational purposes
        // It isn't a best practice
        // Subsequent sections and chapters explain an improved version
        while ((!_capWordsInSentencesBag.IsEmpty) || (_capitalizingWords))
        {
            string sentence;
            if (_capWordsInSentencesBag.TryTake(out sentence))
            {
                _finalSentencesBag.Add(
                    RemoveLetters(letterChars, sentence));
            }
        }
    }

    static void Main(string[] args)
    {
        var sw = Stopwatch.StartNew();

        _sentencesBag = new ConcurrentBag<string>();
        _capWordsInSentencesBag = new ConcurrentBag<string>();
```

continues

LISTING 4-7 *(continued)*

```
_finalSentencesBag = new ConcurrentBag<string>();

// Set _producingSentences to true before calling
// ProduceSentences concurrently with the other methods
// This way, CapitalizeWordsInSentences
// and RemoveLettersInSentences
// will see the true value for this shared variable
_producingSentences = true;

Parallel.Invoke(
    () => ProduceSentences(),
    () => CapitalizeWordsInSentences(),
    () => RemoveLettersInSentences()
    );

Console.WriteLine(
    "Number of sentences with capitalized words in the bag: {0}",
    _capWordsInSentencesBag.Count);
Console.WriteLine(
    "Number of sentences with removed letters in the bag: {0}",
    _finalSentencesBag.Count);
Debug.WriteLine(sw.Elapsed.ToString());
//  Display the results and wait for the user to press a key
Console.WriteLine("Finished!");
Console.ReadLine();
}
```

In this case, the `Main` method sets the shared `bool` variable *_producingSentences* to `true` and then launches the following three methods concurrently by calling `Parallel.Invoke`:

➤ `ProduceSentences`

➤ `CapitalizeWordsInSentences`

➤ `RemoveLettersInSentences`

Figure 4-11 shows the relationship between these methods.

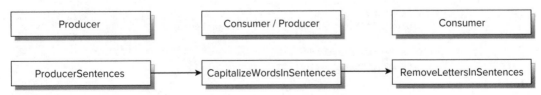

FIGURE 4-11

`ProduceSentences` is the first producer. Before it starts adding random sentences to the `ConcurrentBag` named *_sentencesBag*, the value for shared `bool` variable *_producingSentences* is set to `true`. Therefore, the consumer that checks for this value will be waiting for new items to be added to *_sentencesBag*. `ProduceSentences` makes sure that the value for *_producingSentences* will be set to `false` once the sequential loop finishes by assigning this value in the `finally` block. This way, if any exception occurs, the consumer that is checking the value for this variable in order to determine whether it has to continue waiting for new values in the shared `ConcurrentBag` won't be waiting forever if something goes wrong in the producer.

`CapitalizeWordsInSentences` is a consumer of `ProduceSentences` and a producer for `RemoveLettersInSentences`. It waits until the shared `bool` variable _producingSentences is `true` to begin working. The `Main` method sets this value before calling the producer and the two consumers with `Parallel.Invoke` because the concurrent execution might start the consumers before the main producer. The `Main` method makes sure _producingSentences is `true` before the consumers start their execution. `CapitalizeWordsInSentences` calls the `System.Threading .SpinWait.SpinUntil` method with the shared `bool` variable _producingSentences as the result for a `Func<bool>` condition. The delegate specified in the next line is going to be executed over and over until it returns `true`:

```
// This condition running in a loop (spinning) is very inefficient
// This example uses this spinning for educational purposes
// It isn't a best practice
// Subsequent sections and chapters explain an improved version

System.Threading.SpinWait.SpinUntil(() => _producingSentences);
```

The `SpinUntil` method will stop spinning once _producingSentences is `true` and will go on executing the next statements. There are many different ways to coordinate the activities performed by multiple tasks running as producers and consumers, and sometimes spinning isn't the best alternative. The example being used here shows you just one of the possibilities — you can run it and then improve on it by using other kinds of concurrent collections specially prepared to simplify the coordination needed in producer-consumer scenarios, such as the `BlockingCollection`. Chapter 5, "Coordination Data Structures," covers the `SpinUntil` method and other alternatives to coordinate work among different tasks and threads.

Before the `CapitalizeWordsInSentences` starts calling the `CapitalizeWords` method for each sentence taken from the `ConcurrentBag` named _sentencesBag, it sets the shared `bool` variable _capitalizingWords to true. It also makes sure that the value for this variable will be set to `false` once the sequential loop finishes, by assigning this value in the `finally` block. It takes an element from _sentencesBag by calling its `TryTake` method, and adds an element to _capWordsInSentencesBag by calling its `Add` method. It does this while _sentencesBag isn't empty or `ProduceSentences` is still working. It assumes that `ProduceSentences` is still working while _producingSentences is `true`. It is fairly expensive to check the value for the `IsEmpty` property on a `ConcurrentBag` because it needs to temporarily take all of the bag's locks. Thus, the condition shown in the next lines isn't the best option:

```
_capitalizingWords = true;
// This condition running in a loop (spinning) is very inefficient
// This example uses this spinning for educational purposes
// It isn't a best practice
// Subsequent sections and chapters explain an improved version
while ((!_sentencesBag.IsEmpty) || (_producingSentences))
{
    string sentence;
```

```
            if (_sentencesBag.TryTake(out sentence))
            {
                _capWordsInSentencesBag.Add(CapitalizeWords(delimiterChars, sentence, '\\'));
            }
        }
```

code snippet is Listing 4_7

The two shared `bool` variables used as flags are declared with the `volatile` keyword. These flags determine whether the consumers have to go on waiting for new values in the `ConcurrentBag` from which they are taking elements. The code doesn't use mutual exclusion locks or atomic updates to change the values for these variables declared in the following lines:

```
private static volatile bool _producingSentences = false;
private static volatile bool _capitalizingWords = false;
```

Using the `volatile` keyword ensures that the most up-to-date value will be present in the variables when they are accessed from different threads. As a result, these variables are not subject to compiler optimizations that assume they would be accessed by just a single thread. Chapter 5, "Coordination Data Structures," dives deep into volatile fields.

`RemoveLettersInSentences` is the final consumer. Its structure is similar to the previously explained `CapitalizeWordsInSentences`, and it is its consumer. However, the `RemoveLettersInSentences` method doesn't define a value for another `bool` flag. There is no need for another flag because there is no other consumer chained with the `ConcurrentBag` named *_finalSentencesBag*. `RemoveLettersInSentences` uses this `ConcurrentBag` to add the sentences with some letters removed for them.

> *The code uses* `Parallel.Invoke` *to run the previously explained three methods. It isn't prepared to take advantage of more than three logical cores, which means that the code has a limited scalability. In addition, the methods with the sequential loop could be improved to be more efficient. However, the purpose of this example is to give you an idea of some of the possibilities offered by a* `ConcurrentBag` *and introduce you to the features of the* `BlockingCollection`.

IProducerConsumerCollection

The `IProducerConsumerCollection<T>` interface defines methods to manipulate concurrent collections intended for producer-consumer scenarios. It inherits `ICollection`, `IEnumerable`, and `IEnumerable<T>`, and it exposes the following specific methods, previously explained for different concurrent collections:

- ➤ `CopyTo`
- ➤ `ToArray`
- ➤ `TryAdd`
- ➤ `TryTake`

BlockingCollection

BlockingCollection<T> is a wrapper for an IProducerConsumerCollection<T> instance. All the previously explained concurrent collection types implement IProducerConsumerCollection<T>, and therefore, they can be encapsulated in BlockingCollection<T>.

A BlockingCollection offers support for bounding and blocking. Listing 4-8 shows the code for the previous example using three BlockingCollection instances and taking advantage of some of the bound and blocking features. These features make BlockingCollection very useful for producer-consumer scenarios and for the implementation of pipelines. However, it is still possible to improve this example.

LISTING 4-8: Producers and consumers working with the bounding and blocking capabilities offered by BlockingCollection instances

```
private const int NUM_SENTENCES = 2000000;
private static BlockingCollection<string> _sentencesBC;
private static BlockingCollection<string> _capWordsInSentencesBC;
private static BlockingCollection<string> _finalSentencesBC;

private static void ProduceSentences()
{
    string[] possibleSentences =
    {
    "ConcurrentBag is included in the Systems.Concurrent.Collections namespace.",
    "Is parallelism important for cloud-computing?",
    "Parallelism is very important for cloud-computing!",
    "ConcurrentQueue is one of the new concurrent collections added in .NET Framework 4",
    "ConcurrentStack is a concurrent collection that represents a LIFO collection",
    "ConcurrentQueue is a concurrent collection that represents a FIFO collection"
    };

    var rnd = new Random();

    for (int i = 0; i < NUM_SENTENCES; i++)
    {
        var sb = new StringBuilder();
        for (int j = 0; j < possibleSentences.Length; j++)
        {
            if (rnd.Next(2) > 0)
            {
                sb.Append(possibleSentences[
                    rnd.Next(possibleSentences.Length)]);
                sb.Append(' ');
            }
        }
        if (rnd.Next(20) > 15)
        {
            _sentencesBC.Add(sb.ToString());
        }
        else
        {
            _sentencesBC.Add(sb.ToString().ToUpper());
```

continues

LISTING 4-8 *(continued)*

```
        }
    }
    // Let the consumer know the producer's work is done
    _sentencesBC.CompleteAdding();
}

private static void CapitalizeWordsInSentences()
{
    char[] delimiterChars = { ' ', ',', '.', ':', ';', '(', ')',
        '[', ']', '{', '}', '/', '?', '@', '\t', '"' };

    // This condition running in a loop (spinning) is very inefficient
    // This example uses this spinning for educational purposes
    // It isn't a best practice
    // Subsequent sections and chapters explain an improved version
    while (!_sentencesBC.IsCompleted)
    {
        string sentence;
        if (_sentencesBC.TryTake(out sentence))
        {
            _capWordsInSentencesBC.Add(
                CapitalizeWords(delimiterChars, sentence, '\\'));
        }
    }
    // Let the consumer know the producer's work is done
    _capWordsInSentencesBC.CompleteAdding();
}

private static void RemoveLettersInSentences()
{
    char[] letterChars =
        { 'A', 'B', 'C', 'e', 'i', 'j', 'm', 'X', 'y', 'Z' };

    // This condition running in a loop (spinning) is very inefficient
    // This example uses this spinning for educational purposes
    // It isn't a best practice
    // Subsequent sections and chapters explain an improved version
    while (!_capWordsInSentencesBC.IsCompleted)
    {
        string sentence;
        if (_capWordsInSentencesBC.TryTake(out sentence))
        {
            _finalSentencesBC.Add(
                RemoveLetters(letterChars, sentence));
        }
    }
    _finalSentencesBC.CompleteAdding();
}

static void Main(string[] args)
{
    var sw = Stopwatch.StartNew();

    // Set the maximum number of elements to NUM_SENTENCES
```

```
        _sentencesBC =
            new BlockingCollection<string>(NUM_SENTENCES);
        _capWordsInSentencesBC =
            new BlockingCollection<string>(NUM_SENTENCES);
        _finalSentencesBC =
            new BlockingCollection<string>(NUM_SENTENCES);

    // Exception handling should be improved to avoid potential deadlocks
        Parallel.Invoke(
            () => ProduceSentences(),
            () => CapitalizeWordsInSentences(),
            () => RemoveLettersInSentences()
            );

        Console.WriteLine(
            "Number of sentences with capitalized words in the collection: {0}",
            _capWordsInSentencesBC.Count);
        Console.WriteLine(
            "Number of sentences with removed letters in the collection: {0}",
            _finalSentencesBC.Count);
        Debug.WriteLine(sw.Elapsed.ToString());
        //  Display the results and wait for the user to press a key
        Console.WriteLine("Finished!");
        Console.ReadLine();
    }
```

The `Main` method creates the `BlockingCollection` instances, setting the maximum capacity of the collection to *NUM_SENTENCES* as shown in the following line:

```
    _sentencesBC = new BlockingCollection<string>(NUM_SENTENCES);
```

The `BoundedCapacity` property holds the specified maximum capacity for the collection. Once the collection reaches this value, if there is another request to add an item, the producing task or thread will block. It means the producing task or thread will stay waiting until an item is removed. The bounding capability is useful for controlling the maximum size of the collection in memory, especially when you need to process a huge number of elements. You don't need to use the shared `bool` flags or to add synchronization code between the producers and consumers, because the `BlockingCollection` offers specific features to help in these scenarios. Each consumer will try to remove elements from the collection until the producer's collection `IsCompleted` property is `true`. The example shown in Listing 4-8 used a condition in a `while` loop that checks the Boolean value for the `IsCompleted` property, as in the next line:

```
    // This condition running in a loop (spinning) is very inefficient
    // This example uses this spinning for educational purposes
    // It isn't a best practice
    // Subsequent sections and chapters explain an improved version
    while (!_sentencesBC.IsCompleted)
```

The `IsAddingCompleted` property is going to be set to `true` after the producer calls the `CompleteAdding` method for the `BlockingCollection` instance, as shown here:

```
    _sentencesBC.CompleteAdding();
```

The `IsCompleted` property will be set to `true` when `IsAddingCompleted` is `true` and the collection is empty. When `IsCompleted` is true, it means that the collection has been marked as complete by the producer and it has no more items to offer to the consumer. This way, when the producer calls the `CompleteAdding` method, it can let the consumer know that it has finished its work. The code is simpler, because the consumer has to check the value for just one property, `IsCompleted`, to know whether to continue. However, you can use other methods to avoid the inefficiency introduced by checking this condition in a `while` loop. The next examples will improve the code shown in Listing 4-8.

In this case, the code uses the total number of sentences to establish the bounding capacity; however, you could use a lower number to reduce the memory consumption.

The following lines of code show a definition for the three `BlockingCollection` instances, created with `NUM_SENTENCES / 20` as the bounding capacity.

```
_sentencesBC = new BlockingCollection<string>(NUM_SENTENCES / 20);
_capWordsInSentencesBC = new BlockingCollection<string>(NUM_SENTENCES / 20);
_finalSentencesBC = new BlockingCollection<string>(NUM_SENTENCES / 20);

// Exception handling should be improved to avoid potential deadlocks
Parallel.Invoke(
    () => ProduceSentences(),
    () => CapitalizeWordsInSentences(),
    () => RemoveLettersInSentences(),
    () =>
    {
        foreach(var sentence in _finalSentencesBC.GetConsumingEnumerable())
        {
            Console.WriteLine(sentence);
        }
    });
```

code snippet is Snippet 4_5

This means the `ProducingSentences` method will add no more than `NUM_SENTENCES / 20` sentences to `_sentencesBC`. Then, when it calls the `Add` method, it will wait until an item is removed. This way, the producers will require less memory, but the code can take more time to run because of the additional synchronization needs. The collection generated by the last `_finalSentencesBC` consumer requires the total capacity, because there is no consumer for it. However, the `Parallel.Invoke` adds a new consumer that removes and shows the items in the `_finalSentencesBC` collection. The `GetConsumingEnumerable` method returns the enumerator for the underlying collection and allows the use of a `foreach` to remove elements. The loop will block if the collection is empty and will wait for new elements to be added. It will end when there are no elements and the `IsAddingCompleted` property is `true`. The `RemoveLettersInSentences` method calls the `_finalSentencesBC` `.CompleteAdding` method when it finishes adding elements to the collection.

You can use the `GetConsumerEnumerable` method to replace the while loop of each consumer that removes elements from the collection until the producer's collection `IsCompleted` property is `true`. The combination of `GetConsumingEnumerable` is more efficient than the version shown in Listing 4-8. The following lines of code show the new versions of the two consumers, `CapitalizeWordsInSentences` and `RemoveLettersInSentences`:

```
private static void CapitalizeWordsInSentences()
{
    char[] delimiterChars = {
        ' ', ',', '.', ':', ';', '(', ')', '[', ']', '{', '}',
        '/', '?', '@', '\t', '"' };

    foreach (var sentence in _sentencesBC.GetConsumingEnumerable())
    {
        _capWordsInSentencesBC.Add(CapitalizeWords(delimiterChars, sentence, '\\'));
    }

    // Let the consumer know the producer's work is done
    _capWordsInSentencesBC.CompleteAdding();
}

private static void RemoveLettersInSentences()
{
    char[] letterChars = {
        'A', 'B', 'C', 'e', 'i', 'j', 'm', 'X', 'y', 'Z' };

    foreach (var sentence in _capWordsInSentencesBC.GetConsumingEnumerable())
    {
        _finalSentencesBC.Add(RemoveLetters(letterChars, sentence));
    }

    // Let the consumer know the producer's work is done
    _finalSentencesBC.CompleteAdding();
}
```

code snippet is Snippet 4_6

This new version of both consumers is simpler and more efficient. Whenever possible, you have to avoid unnecessary spinning.

By default, a `BlockingCollection` encapsulates a `ConcurrentQueue`. However, you can specify a different type of concurrent collection in its constructor. The ordering of the elements will change, but the methods used to add and remove elements will remain the same, as previously explained. The following lines show the encapsulation of a `ConcurrentStack` in the `_sentencesBC` `BlockingCollection`:

```
_sentencesBC =
    new BlockingCollection<string>(new ConcurrentStack<string>(), NUM_SENTENCES / 20);
```

code snippet is Snippet 4_7

This way, _sentenceBC will represent a LIFO concurrent collection. There is no need to change the code that adds and removes elements for this collection, because the BlockingCollection wraps the underlying concurrent collection.

Cancelling Operations on a BlockingCollection

Some producer-consumer scenarios implemented through many BlockingCollection instances can take a long time to run. Thus, it is a good idea to provide mechanisms to interrupt their execution. You can do this through the use of cancellation tokens, as you previously learned with Task instances in Chapter 3, "Imperative Task Parallelism."

As previously explained, a BlockingCollection *offers many different alternatives to consume the elements produced by a producer without the need for complex synchronization mechanisms. However, keep in mind that a wrong implementation of this concurrent collection could lead to tasks waiting forever.*

Listing 4-9 shows the code for a new version of the ProduceSentences method with support for cancellation.

Available for download on Wrox.com

LISTING 4-9: Support for cancellation added to the ProduceSentences method and the changes in the Main method to send the signal to cancel

```
private static void ProduceSentences(System.Threading.CancellationToken ct)
{
    string[] possibleSentences =
    {
    "ConcurrentBag is included in the Systems.Concurrent.Collections namespace.",
    "Is parallelism important for cloud-computing?",
    "Parallelism is very important for cloud-computing!",
    "ConcurrentQueue is one of the new concurrent collections added in .NET Framework 4",
    "ConcurrentStack is a concurrent collection that represents a LIFO collection",
    "ConcurrentQueue is a concurrent collection that represents a FIFO collection"
    };

    var rnd = new Random();

    for (int i = 0; i < NUM_SENTENCES; i++)
    {
        var sb = new StringBuilder();
        string newSentence;
        for (int j = 0; j < possibleSentences.Length; j++)
        {
            if (rnd.Next(2) > 0)
            {
                sb.Append(possibleSentences[
                    rnd.Next(possibleSentences.Length)]);
```

```
                    sb.Append(' ');
            }
        }
        if (rnd.Next(20) > 15)
        {
            newSentence = sb.ToString();
        }
        else
        {
            newSentence = sb.ToString().ToUpper();
        }
        try
        {
            if (!_sentencesBC.TryAdd(newSentence, 2000, ct))
            {
                throw new TimeoutException(
              "_sentencesBC took more than 2 seconds to add an item");
            }
        }
        catch (OperationCanceledException ex)
        {
            // The operation was cancelled
            Debug.WriteLine(ex.ToString());
            break;
            // The next statement after the loop will let
            // the consumer know the producer's work is done
        }
        catch (TimeoutException ex)
        {
            Debug.WriteLine(ex.ToString());
            break;
        }
    }
    // Let the consumer know the producer's work is done
    _sentencesBC.CompleteAdding();
}

static void Main(string[] args)
{
...
    var cts = new System.Threading.CancellationTokenSource();
    var ct = cts.Token;
    var deferredCancelTask = Task.Factory.StartNew(() =>
    {
        // Sleep the thread that runs this task for 2 seconds
        System.Threading.Thread.Sleep(2000);
        // Send the signal to cancel
        cts.Cancel();
    });

    Parallel.Invoke(
        () => ProduceSentences(ct),
        () => CapitalizeWordsInSentences(),
        () => RemoveLettersInSentences(),
        () =>
```

continues

LISTING 4-9 *(continued)*

```
        {
            foreach (var sentence in
                _finalSentencesBC.GetConsumingEnumerable(ct))
            {
                Console.WriteLine(sentence);
            }
        });
```

This method now receives a `System.Threading.CancellationToken` instance, *ct*. When it is necessary to add an item to *_sentencesBC*, it calls the `TryAdd` method with the string to add the number of milliseconds to wait for the operation to be successful and the cancellation token to observe, as shown here:

```
    if (!_sentencesBC.TryAdd(newSentence, 2000, ct)
```

If a cancellation request occurs, the call to `TryAdd` will throw an `OperationCanceledException`. If the collection takes more than 2 seconds (or `2000` milliseconds) to add the item, it will return `false`. This way, the method can support cancellation and can control the time required to perform operations if something goes wrong or an unexpected scenario occurs. The `TryTake` method also supports the milliseconds to wait and the cancellation token as parameters.

The `TryAdd` method adds a small overhead to its execution in order to be able to observe cancellation tokens. The code that catches the exception makes sure that the `CompleteAdding` method is called. However, you would need to add cancellation support for the consumers and to add exception handling in the `Parallel.Invoke` call in order to provide a complete timeout and cancellation support for all the chained producers and consumers.

`deferredCancelTask` sends the signal to cancel by calling the `cts.Cancel` method after sleeping for 2 seconds. In this case, both the loop in the `ProduceSentences` method that is removing items from *_sentencesBC* and the `foreach` loop that is consuming the results in _finalSentencesBC will cancel their execution. The latter receives the `CancellationToken` instance as a parameter, as shown in the next line:

```
    foreach (var sentence in _finalSentencesBC.GetConsumingEnumerable(ct))
```

However, the consumers will go on running until they completely remove all the elements. It is always a good idea to add cleanup code when there is a cancellation and to make sure that all the producers and consumers stop working. The technique is the same as the one explained for the `ProduceSentences` method and for `GetConsumingEnumerable`. You can establish timeouts to avoid tasks or threads to block without any kind of restrictions.

Implementing a Filtering Pipeline with Many BlockingCollection Instances

The `BlockingCollection` class offers the following static methods to add items to any of many `BlockingCollection` instances received as a parameter in an array:

➤ `AddToAny`

➤ `TryAddToAny`

In addition, it offers the following static methods to remove items from any of many `BlockingCollection` instances received as a parameter in an array:

➤ `TakeFromAny`

➤ `TryTakeFromAny`

You can use these static methods to work with many `BlockingCollection` instances as inputs or outputs. As an example, Listing 4-10 shows the code for the `PipelineFilter<TInput, TOutput>` class. It allows you to define a filter and then run it. If the filter consumes an input and produces an output, it can use the constructor that receives a `Func<TInput, TOutput>`. If it is the final consumer and it doesn't produce an output, it can use the `Action<TInput>` constructor. Each filter receives an array of `BlockingCollection<TInput>` as its input and supports cancellation through a `CancellationToken`.

Available for download on Wrox.com

LISTING 4-10: Implementation of a multiple pipeline filter with many BlockingCollection instances

```
class PipelineFilter<TInput, TOutput>
{
    private Func<TInput, TOutput> _processor = null;
    private Action<TInput> _outputProcessor = null;
    private System.Threading.CancellationToken _token;
    public BlockingCollection<TInput>[] Input;
    public BlockingCollection<TOutput>[] Output = null;
    public string Name { get; private set; }
    private const int OUT_COLLECTIONS = 5;
    private const int OUT_BOUNDING_CAPACITY = 1000;
    private const int TIMEOUT = 50;

    // Constructor for the Func<TInput, TOutput> filter
    public PipelineFilter(
        BlockingCollection<TInput>[] input,
        Func<TInput, TOutput> processor,
        System.Threading.CancellationToken token,
        string name)
    {
        Input = input;
        Output = new BlockingCollection<TOutput>[OUT_COLLECTIONS];
        // Create the output BlockingCollection instances
        for (int i = 0; i < Output.Length; i++)
        {
            Output[i] = new
                BlockingCollection<TOutput>(OUT_BOUNDING_CAPACITY);
        }
        _processor = processor;
        _token = token;
        Name = name;
    }

    // Constructor for the Action<TInput> filter
    // The final consumer
```

continues

LISTING 4-10 *(continued)*

```
    public PipelineFilter(
        BlockingCollection<TInput>[] input,
        Action<TInput> renderer,
        System.Threading.CancellationToken token,
        string name)
    {
        Input = input;
        _outputProcessor = renderer;
        _token = token;
        Name = name;
    }

    public void Run()
    {
        // Run while all the input
        // BlockingCollection instances IsCompleted is false
        // and no cancellation was requested
        while ((!Input.All(inputBC => inputBC.IsCompleted))
            && (!_token.IsCancellationRequested))
        {
            TInput item;
            int i = BlockingCollection<TInput>.TryTakeFromAny(
                Input, out item, TIMEOUT, _token);
            if (i >= 0)
            {
                if (Output != null)
                {
                    // Process the item
                    TOutput result = _processor(item);
                    // Add the result to any of the output collections
                    BlockingCollection<TOutput>.AddToAny(Output,
                        result, _token);
                }
                else
                {
                    // The code is running the last consumer
                    _outputProcessor(item);
                }
            }
        }
        if (Output != null)
        {
            // All the BlockingCollection instances finished
            foreach (var outputBC in Output)
            {
                outputBC.CompleteAdding();
            }
        }
    }
}

private const int NUM_SENTENCES = 2000000;

private static string ProduceASentence(string[] possibleSentences)
```

```
{
    var rnd = new Random();
    var sb = new StringBuilder();
    string newSentence;
    for (int j = 0; j < possibleSentences.Length; j++)
    {
        if (rnd.Next(2) > 0)
        {
            sb.Append(possibleSentences[
                rnd.Next(possibleSentences.Length)]);
            sb.Append(' ');
        }
    }
    if (rnd.Next(20) > 15)
    {
        newSentence = sb.ToString();
    }
    else
    {
        newSentence = sb.ToString().ToUpper();
    }
    return newSentence;
}

public static void Main()
{
    var cts = new System.Threading.CancellationTokenSource();
    var ct = cts.Token;
    var sw = Stopwatch.StartNew();

    BlockingCollection<string>[] sourceSentences =
        new BlockingCollection<string>[5];
    for (int i = 0; i < sourceSentences.Length; i++)
    {
        sourceSentences[i] =
            new BlockingCollection<string>(NUM_SENTENCES / 5);
    }

    string[] possibleSentences =
    {
    "ConcurrentBag is included in the Systems.Concurrent.Collections namespace.",
    "Is parallelism important for cloud-computing?",
    "Parallelism is very important for cloud-computing!",
    "ConcurrentQueue is one of the new concurrent collections added in .NET Framework 4",
    "ConcurrentStack is a concurrent collection that represents a LIFO collection",
    "ConcurrentQueue is a concurrent collection that represents a FIFO collection"
    };

    Parallel.For(0, NUM_SENTENCES, (sentenceNumber) =>
        {
            BlockingCollection<string>.TryAddToAny(
                sourceSentences,
                ProduceASentence(possibleSentences),
                50);
        });

    for (int j = 0; j < sourceSentences.Length; j++)
```

continues

LISTING 4-10 *(continued)*

```
{
    sourceSentences[j].CompleteAdding();
}

char[] delimiterChars =
    { ' ', ',', '.', ':', ';', '(', ')', '[',
      ']', '{', '}', '/', '?', '@', '\t', '"' };

var filterCapitalizeWords = new PipelineFilter<string, string>
(
    sourceSentences,
    (sentence) => CapitalizeWords(
        delimiterChars, sentence, '\\'),
    ct,
    "CapitalizeWords"
);

char[] letterChars =
    { 'A', 'B', 'C', 'e', 'i',
      'j', 'm', 'X', 'y', 'Z' };
var filterRemoveLetters = new PipelineFilter<string, string>
(
    filterCapitalizeWords.Output,
    (sentence) => RemoveLetters(letterChars, sentence),
    ct,
    "RemoveLetters"
);

var filterWriteLine = new PipelineFilter<string, string>
(
    filterRemoveLetters.Output,
    (sentence) => Console.WriteLine(sentence),
    ct,
    "WriteLine"
);

var deferredCancelTask = Task.Factory.StartNew(() =>
{
    // Sleep the thread that runs this task for 2 seconds
    System.Threading.Thread.Sleep(2000);
    // Send the signal to cancel
    cts.Cancel();
});

try
{
    Parallel.Invoke(
        () => filterCapitalizeWords.Run(),
        () => filterRemoveLetters.Run(),
        () => filterWriteLine.Run()
    );
}
```

```
    catch (AggregateException ex)
    {
        foreach (var innerEx in ex.InnerExceptions)
            Console.WriteLine(innerEx.Message);
    }

    Debug.WriteLine(sw.Elapsed.ToString());
    // Display the results and wait for the user to press a key
    Console.WriteLine("Finished!");
    Console.ReadLine();
}
```

The `Main` method creates five `BlockingCollection<string>` instances named *sourceSentences[]* to distribute the sentences. Once the sentences are distributed in the different `BlockingCollection` instances, a call to the `CompleteAdding` method makes sure that they are ready to be used in the first filter.

In this example, because a `Parallel.For` *loop fills the* `BlockingCollection` *instances by calling the* `TryAddToAny` *method, the random generator isn't going to be efficient. However, that topic will be covered in subsequent chapters.*

Then, the code defines the following three filters:

➤ `filterCapitalizeWords` — Receives a `string` and returns a `string`. Its input array is *sourceSentences[]*, and it calls the `CapitelizeWords` method for each `string` taken from these collections to produce another `string`.

➤ `filterRemoveLetters` — Receives a `string` and returns a `string`. Its input array is the output from *filterCapitalizeWords.Output*, which is an array of `BlockingCollection<string>`, and it calls the `RemoveLetters` method for each `string` taken from these collections to produce another `string`.

➤ `filterWriteLine` — This is the final consumer and doesn't generate an output. Therefore, it uses the `Action<string>` constructor as it receives a `string`. Its input array is the output from *filterRemoveLetters.Output*, which is an array of `BlockingCollection<string>`, and it calls the `Console.WriteLine` method for each `string` taken from these collections to show the resulting string on the console.

Once the three filters are defined, a new `Task` instance named *deferredCancelTask* will send the signal to cancel all the filters after 2 seconds. After starting this task, the code calls `Parallel` `.Invoke` to run the three filters in a pipeline by calling their `Run` methods concurrently and potentially in parallel.

As previously explained, the call to `Parallel.Invoke` isn't going to scale when more than three logical cores are available. However, you can use many `Task` instances, as explained in previous sections, to take advantage of additional cores in each filter. This example explained the application of different filters to a sequential stream. You can test different configurations in order to achieve the best throughput.

> *The best throughput for a pipeline is achieved when each filter runs in a different software thread. Remember that when you work with tasks, the scheduler can use different threads to support its execution. You can customize the scheduler to run each task created by a filter in a different thread. However, this is a more complex topic that will be covered in subsequent chapters.*

ConcurrentDictionary

ConcurrentDictionary is completely lock-free for read operations. It is optimized for scenarios where reading from it is the most frequent operation. When many tasks or threads add or update data in the dictionary, it uses fine-grained locking. A ConcurrentDictionary is the concurrent version of an implementation of System.Collections.IDictionary. You can define the desired concurrency level (the maximum number of tasks or threads that are going to update the dictionary), its preferred initial capacity, and an IEqualityComparer<TKey> implementation for comparing keys. You can get or set the value associated with a specified key using the Item property. This property works as the indexer for TKey and returns a TValue. The most important methods offered by a ConcurrentDictionary are the following:

➤ AddOrUpdate — If the key doesn't already exist, this method adds a new key-value pair to the dictionary. If the key already exists, this method updates a key-value. You can use functions to generate the absent key and/or update an existing key based on the key's existing value; therefore, this method returns the new value for the key. However, this method doesn't run the add or update delegates while holding a lock. Thus, you have to add the necessary synchronization code to make sure that the operations performed within the delegates are thread-safe.

➤ GetEnumerator — Returns an enumerator that iterates through the ConcurrentDictionary. You can use it concurrently to read and write to the dictionary because the enumerator's implementation is thread-safe. The enumerator exposes modifications made to the ConcurrentDictionary after you called this method because the enumerator doesn't provide a snapshot of the ConcurrentDictionary. This method returns an IEnumerator<KeyValuePair<TKey, TValue>>.

➤ GetOrAdd — If the key doesn't already exist, this method adds a new key-value pair to the dictionary. If the key already exists, this method will return its existing value without adding the new one.

➤ TryAdd — Tries to add the new key-value pair received as a parameter to the dictionary. It returns a bool value indicating whether or not the operation was successful.

➤ TryGetValue — Tries to return the value associated with the specified key. It returns a bool value indicating whether or not the operation was successful, and the out parameter contains the value retrieved from the dictionary.

➤ TryRemove — Tries to remove and return the value with the specified key in the out parameter. It returns a bool value indicating whether the operation was successful, and the out parameter contains the value removed from the dictionary.

➤ TryUpdate — Compares the value for the key received as the first parameter with a comparison value received as the third parameter. If they are equal, it updates the key with the new value received as the second parameter.

Fine-grained locking means that when ConcurrentDictionary *needs to use locks in certain operations, it locks only the portions that it really needs to lock, not the entire dictionary. In other words, multiple requests to update the dictionary could proceed in parallel, as long as they are accessing parts of the dictionary protected by different locks.*

Listing 4-11 shows the code for a Windows Presentation Foundation (WPF) application that defines a new class named RectangleInfo that implements IEqualityComparer. It defines the following properties with values related to a rectangle:

➤ Name — Used as the key in the dictionary. This property has a private set because you use it in a hash code. You don't want to be able to change its value after the hash code has been generated.

➤ Location — The rectangle's location.

➤ Size — The rectangle's size.

➤ LastUpdate — The last time this rectangle's values were updated.

➤ UpdatedTimes — Tracks the number of times the values for the instance were updated.

LISTING 4-11: Adding, comparing, and updating values in parallel for a ConcurrentDictionary

```
public partial class MainWindow : Window
{
    public MainWindow()
    {
        InitializeComponent();
    }

    private ConcurrentDictionary<string, RectangleInfo> _rectanglesDict;
    private const int MAX_RECTANGLES = 20000;
    private void GenerateRectangles()
    {
        Parallel.For(1, MAX_RECTANGLES + 1, (i) =>
        {
            for (int j = 0; j < 50; j++)
            {
                var newKey =
                    String.Format("Rectangle {0}", i % 5000);
                var newRect = new RectangleInfo(
                    String.Format("Rectangle {0}", i),
                    new Point(j, j * i),
```

continues

LISTING 4-11 *(continued)*

```
                            new Size(j * i, i / 2));
                    _rectanglesDict.AddOrUpdate(
                        newKey, newRect,
                        (key, existingRect) =>
                        {
                            // The key already exists
                            if (existingRect != newRect)
                            {
                                // The rectangles are different
                                // It is necessary
                                // to update the existing rectangle
                                // AddOrUpdate doesn't run
                                // the add or update delegates
                                // while holding a lock
                                // Lock existingRect before calling
                                // the Update method
                                lock (existingRect)
                                {
                                    // Call the Update method within
                                    // a critical section
                                    existingRect.Update(
                                        newRect.Location, newRect.Size);
                                }
                                return existingRect;
                            }
                            else
                            {
                                // The rectangles are the same
                                // No need to update the existing one
                                return existingRect;
                            }
                        });
                }
            });
    }

    private void butTest_Click(object sender, RoutedEventArgs e)
    {
        var sw = Stopwatch.StartNew();

        _rectanglesDict =
            new ConcurrentDictionary<string, RectangleInfo>();
        GenerateRectangles();

        foreach (var keyValuePair in _rectanglesDict)
        {
            listRectangles.Items.Add(
                String.Format("{0}, {1}. Updated {2} times.",
                keyValuePair.Key, keyValuePair.Value.Size,
                keyValuePair.Value.UpdatedTimes));
        }

        Debug.WriteLine(sw.Elapsed.ToString());
```

```
    }
}

class RectangleInfo : IEqualityComparer<RectangleInfo>
{
    // Name property has private set because you use it in a hash code
    // You don't want to be able to change the Name
    // If you change the name, you may never be able
    // to find the object again in the dictionary
    public string Name { get; private set; }
    public Point Location { get; set; }
    public Size Size { get; set; }
    public DateTime LastUpdate { get; set; }
    public int UpdatedTimes { get; private set; }

    public RectangleInfo(string name, Point location, Size size)
    {
        Name = name;
        Location = location;
        Size = size;
        LastUpdate = DateTime.Now;
        UpdatedTimes = 0;
    }

    public RectangleInfo(string key)
    {
        Name = key;
        Location = new Point();
        Size = new Size();
        LastUpdate = DateTime.Now;
        UpdatedTimes = 0;
    }

    public void Update(Point location, Size size)
    {
        Location = location;
        Size = size;
        UpdatedTimes++;
    }

    public bool Equals(RectangleInfo rectA, RectangleInfo rectB)
    {
        return
            ((rectA.Name == rectB.Name) &&
             (rectA.Size == rectB.Size) &&
             (rectA.Location == rectB.Location));
    }

    public int GetHashCode(RectangleInfo obj)
    {
        RectangleInfo rectInfo = (RectangleInfo)obj;
        return rectInfo.Name.GetHashCode();
    }
}
```

RectangleInfo provides two constructors: one that initializes all of the instance's properties, and one that receives just the rectangle's name as the key. The Update method allows you to assign new values for both Location and Size, and it increments the UpdatedTimes property. Then, it implements the following required IEqualityComparer methods:

➤ Equals — Returns a bool value indicating whether two objects are equal. In this case, it compares the Name, Size, and Location.

➤ GetHashCode — Returns a hash code for the object. In this case, it returns the hash code for the Name value.

The code requires adding the following using statements to run. The default values for a WPF application aren't included in this code.

```
// Added for Stopwatch
using System.Diagnostics;
// Added for Tasks
using System.Threading.Tasks;
// Added for Concurrent Collections
using System.Collections.Concurrent;
```

code snippet is Listing 4_11

The Main method creates a new ConcurrentDictionary<string, RectangleInfo> in the private variable _rectanglesDict. Then, it calls the GenerateRectangles method. This method runs Parallel .For with a sequential loop inside it. The parallelized loop runs MAX_RECTANGLES times, and the inner sequential loop runs 50 times. The code adds a new RectangleInfo instance and then updates it 199 times. It calls the AddOrUpdate method for the concurrent dictionary, _rectanglesDict. The first time it runs in the inner loop, the key doesn't exist, so the dictionary adds the new key-value pair.

However, the next 199 times, the key already exists, so the delegate code provided in the AddOrUpdte method's third parameter runs. This code compares the rectangles, and the result of this comparison will be evaluated by the Equals method defined in the RectangleInfo class. If the rectangles are different, the delegate calls the Update method for the existing rectangle, received as the second parameter for the delegate, existingRect, and returns this updated instance. However, the delegate doesn't run while holding a lock; and therefore, it is necessary to obtain an exclusive access to existingRect, execute the Update method, and then release the lock. The code uses the lock keyword to ensure that only one thread will run the Update method for the RectangleInfo instance referenced by existingRect at a time. Chapter 5, "Coordination Data Structures," analyzes locks in detail.

The AddOrUpdate method simplifies the execution of code that runs when a key already exists. Parallel.For will run many tasks to update many different keys concurrently. The Main subroutine adds the key, the size, and the number of times a RectangleInfo instance was updated to the listRectangles ListBox. Figure 4-12 shows the results of running the code shown in Listing 4-11 with all the RectangleInfo instances updated 199 times, many of them performed concurrently.

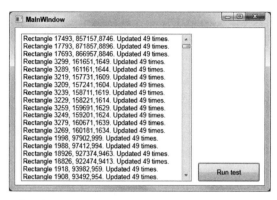

FIGURE 4-12

SUMMARY

This chapter introduced the new .NET Framework 4 concurrent collections by providing examples of the usage of the five new classes and one new interface. This chapter introduced many concurrent collections and showed some problems that appear when you work with them. Then, you improved the original examples by taking advantage of additional features found in the new concurrent collections. To summarize this chapter:

➤ You can find many new classes in the new System.Collections.Concurrent namespace.

➤ You can use the new concurrent collections when you need to insert or remove items from multiple tasks or threads.

➤ You can use BlockingCollection<T> when you need to implement producer-consumer scenarios.

➤ You can design and optimize pipelines using concurrent collections.

➤ You can avoid unnecessary spinning with the blocking and bounding features offered by BlockingCollection<T>.

➤ You can encapsulate concurrent collection types that implement IProducerConsumerCollection<T> in BlockingCollection<T>.

5

Coordination Data Structures

WHAT'S IN THIS CHAPTER?

➤ Understanding lightweight coordination data structures

➤ Working with lightweight synchronization primitives

➤ Choosing the most appropriate synchronization primitive according to your needs

➤ Synchronizing concurrent tasks with barriers

➤ Working with timeouts and cancellation tokens combined with the synchronization primitives

➤ Working with mutual-exclusion locks and critical sections

➤ Refactoring code to avoid locks

➤ Working with spin-based waiting

➤ Understanding spinning and yielding

➤ Working with lightweight manual reset events

➤ Limiting concurrency to access a resource with a semaphore

➤ Understanding and preventing synchronization-related bugs

➤ Working with atomic operations

This chapter is about synchronizing the work performed by diverse concurrent tasks. The chapter covers some classic synchronization primitives and the new lightweight coordination data structures introduced by .NET Framework 4. It is important to learn the different alternatives, so that you can choose the most appropriate one for each concurrency scenario that requires communication and/or synchronization between multiple tasks. This way, you are going to be able to implement more complex algorithms and to solve potential bugs when the designs don't consider the problems associated with heavyweight synchronization mechanisms.

USING CARS AND LANES TO UNDERSTAND THE CONCURRENCY NIGHTMARES

Figure 5-1 shows one car in a single lane. There are three black flags and two gray flags. The car must count the total number of black and gray flags found in its route. The car runs an algorithm that uses two global variables: one to hold the black flag count, and the other to hold the gray flag count. There is no concurrency, because there is just one car in a single lane.

The car in a single lane represents the typical situation of code written without concurrency in mind. What happens if you add another lane and a new car?

Undesired Side Effects

Figure 5-2 shows two cars, two lanes, and the same gray and black flags in the middle of the lanes. The cars' mission is to count the unique number of flags on the course. Both cars share the two global variables to hold the black flag count and the gray flag count. The correct counts are three black flags and two gray flags. However, because they run the previous algorithm and share the two global variables, they will yield inaccurate counts. The total values for these variables are going to be six for the black flags instead of three, and four for the gray flags instead of two.

FIGURE 5-1

The code was written for sequential execution, not concurrent execution. Because you add concurrency by using two cars instead of one, you are using code designed for a sequential execution to run it with a concurrent execution, with two cars in two separate lanes. Thus, each car increases the value for the shared global variable because the code is written without concurrency in mind. Because you add concurrency, the value for the shared global variable is incorrect. The result of running code designed for a sequential execution in two concurrent lanes with cars generates an undesired side effect. The algorithm doesn't provide correctness. When you add a new car, the results are wrong because it doesn't represent the real number of total flags for each color.

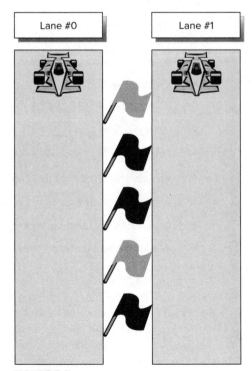

FIGURE 5-2

Race Conditions

Another algorithm that you might design but that still yields unexpected results under certain concurrency scenarios is one in which both cars share the two global variables to hold the black flag count and the gray flag count. In this scenario, each car counts, and they radio their pit bosses to come and remove the flag. Because each car now asks to remove each flag after increasing the corresponding variable, you might expect that this new algorithm wouldn't produce the undesired side effect and would lead to correctness.

However, in one of the executions, both cars reach the second black flag at the same time. Both cars increase their local counts for the black flags and radio to their pit bosses to remove the flag. Thus, there is a *race condition* that yields the wrong results. Figure 5-3 shows this situation when both cars reach the flag.

You run the application again. This time, both cars reach the second gray flag at the same time. Both cars increase their local counts for the gray flags, and they radio their pit bosses to come and remove the flag. Figure 5-4 shows this situation when both cars reach the flag. The results are different from the previous execution, and they are wrong again. You have another race condition, and the algorithm doesn't provide correctness.

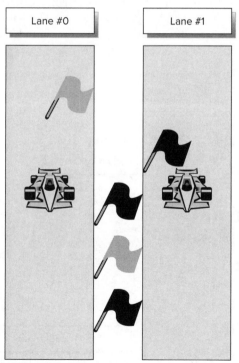

FIGURE 5-3

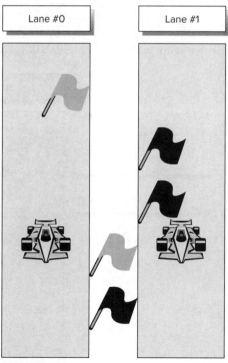

FIGURE 5-4

When many concurrent tasks read from and write to the same variable without the appropriate synchronization mechanism, a race condition *might appear. It is a correctness problem. Erroneous, parallelized code can generate wrong results under certain concurrent execution scenarios. However, when executed in some circumstances, it can generate the expected results because the race condition might not manifest. Consider the following situation: task* t1 *reads the value for public variable* A, 50, *and then it updates the value increased by one,* 51. *At the same time, task* t2 *reads the original value for public variable* A, 50, *and then it updates the value increased by one,* 51. *The final value for public variable* A *should be* 52 *instead of* 51. *The initial value was* 50, *and there were two increase operations. Later, when task* t1 *reads the value for the public variable* A, *instead of* 52, *it reads* 51, *an incorrect value.*

Deadlocks

Figure 5-5 shows two cars, two lanes, and two global variables: one to hold the black flag sum and the other to hold the gray flag sum. The new algorithm makes each car start its course in a different position. In addition, it uses locks to make sure each car has exclusive access to the variable that has to be incremented. However, this isn't the correct way to use locks because it generates an undesired situation in which the two cars will keep waiting forever.

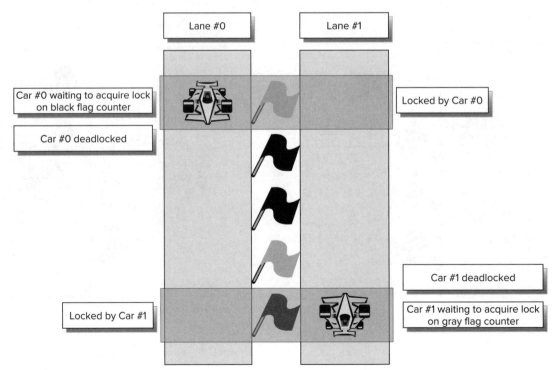

FIGURE 5-5

The new algorithm tries to solve the previously explained race condition, but it generates a *deadlock* situation. Car #0 locks the gray flag counter and it doesn't release the lock. Thus, Car #0 has exclusive access to the gray flag counter, and Car #1 cannot increase it while this variable remains locked. Car #1 locks the black flag counter and increments the value for this variable. However, it doesn't release the lock. Then, Car #0 reaches the black flag and waits to acquire a lock on the black flag counter.

Because Car #1 keeps the black flag counter locked and then waits to acquire a lock on the gray flag counter, locked by Car #0, both cars are going to wait forever. No car is willing to release its protection, so none of them make any progress, and the cars continue to wait for each other to release the lock forever.

In this example, the problem is easy to solve because each lock has to be released after the increment operation occurs, instead of keeping it locked. However, there are other possibilities that avoid locks and their related problems.

A Lock-Free Algorithm with Atomic Operations

The cars can take advantage of atomic operations to avoid both potential deadlocks and race conditions. This chapter dives deep into atomic operations in the "Working with Atomic Operations" section. However, this example introduces you to an abstract situation that doesn't use code.

A simpler and safer alternative is to distribute the flags between the two lanes and use atomic operations to increment shared variables between the lanes. Figure 5-6 shows the results of the new partition scheme for the source data, the black and gray flags.

Now, each car has assigned some flags to count. However, there are still two global variables: one to hold the black flag sum and the other to hold the gray flag sum. Each car increments the corresponding shared variable in an atomic operation — that is, everything is treated as one unit. Each car increments the corresponding variable and stores the result as a single operation that entirely succeeds or entirely fails. If it fails, the variable is left in the state it was in before the increment was attempted.

If two cars call the atomic operation to increment the same shared variable at the same time, both operations are executed as two serial increments, one after the other. Thus, there is no risk of a race condition with the new algorithm. There is no need to worry about deadlocks, because the algorithm doesn't use locks and relies on atomic operations.

Lane #0   Lane #1

FIGURE 5-6

In this example, the cars are using thread-safe atomic operations that increment variables shared by multiple threads (lanes).

A Lock-Free Algorithm with Local Storage

Another version of this algorithm can take advantage of the data partition scheme that distributes the flags in the two lanes. In this example, each lane uses two local variables to hold partial results. Then, when both cars reach the end of their lanes, a final sum that runs with a sequential execution determines the total number of flags for each color. This final sum is thread-safe because it runs in a single thread with the calculated values for each car. Figure 5-7 shows how this algorithm works with the cars and lanes.

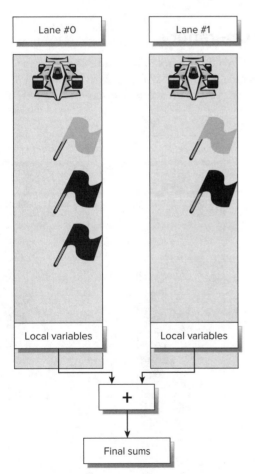

FIGURE 5-7

This lock-free algorithm partitions the source data and works with local storage for each lane. It requires more memory because it uses more variables to produce the same result. However, both cars are independent from each other until the final sum. Thus, there is no need to use locks or atomic operations to increase variables that hold the flag counters. There is no risk of a race condition and no need to worry about deadlocks.

In previous examples, when the cars used a shared variable, they used atomic operations to increment the values for this variable. In this example, they use local storage to avoid the synchronization or atomicity required to work with shared variables. However, there is serial code at the end that has to perform the final sum. This code is going to limit scalability. In fact, there is always a trade-off.

> *The goal of the preceding examples is to help you understand the essentials of some complex topics related to concurrent code and parallelized algorithms. Subsequent sections provide examples with code for the diverse alternatives to synchronize work performed by concurrent tasks and to avoid the aforementioned nightmares, undesired side effects, race conditions, and deadlocks.*

UNDERSTANDING NEW SYNCHRONIZATION MECHANISMS

.NET Framework 4 offers many new data structures for parallel programming that simplify many complex synchronization problems, including the following:

➤ Concurrent collection classes

➤ Lightweight synchronization primitives

➤ Types for lazy initialization

You already learned the features offered by the new concurrent collection classes in the previous chapter. Thus, when you need to add and/or remove elements from one of the supported type of collections in code that runs concurrently, you can avoid adding explicit synchronization code by using these specialized concurrent collections. There is still synchronization happening behind the scenes, to varying extents, depending on the collection being used.

However, sometimes you have to access variables, instances, methods, properties, or structures that aren't prepared for concurrent access. Or, you might need to execute portions of code that have to run alone, but you can't break up the tasks so that they can work independently. When tasks and threads have access to shared data and resources, you have to add explicit synchronization or use atomic operations or locks. There are many options for mutual exclusion and waiting, and you have to choose the most appropriate one for each scenario.

> *Whenever possible, try to decompose the problem in such a way that synchronization is implicit instead of explicit. If you can break up the tasks so that they can work independently, you will be able to avoid adding explicit synchronization, and your code will be more efficient and scalable. However, you also have to make sure that the code offers guarantees of correctness, as explained in Chapter 1, "Task-Based Programming." Explicit synchronization, atomic operations, and locks always add an overhead, require processor time, and can reduce scalability. If you can avoid them, you will be able to achieve better speedups. Implicit synchronization also adds overhead.*

Earlier releases of .NET Framework offered expensive locking mechanisms with its legacy multi-threading model. The new data structures enable fine-grained concurrency and parallelism, and reduce the necessary overheads. Therefore, they are known as *lightweight synchronization primitives*. They are tuned to offer faster performance for key scenarios, because they avoid expensive locking mechanisms. However, these new primitives add an unnecessary overhead when you use them in cases where wait times aren't short. Some of these new primitives have no counterparts in previous .NET Framework versions.

When you design parallelized algorithms, you are the expert who knows the explicit synchronization requirements and the most common ways in which the code is going to run. .NET Framework 4 doesn't include fortune-telling capabilities. Thus, if you need a specific order of execution, you can add explicit synchronization for this. However, whenever possible, you should take advantage of continuations, as explained in Chapter 3, "Imperative Task Parallelism."

Furthermore, you can improve performance of parallelized code, reduce its memory requirements, and avoid wasteful computation by deferring the creation of objects until they are first used. Again, because you are the one who knows the most common ways in which the code is going to run, you can combine this knowledge with the use of the new types for lazy initialization to improve your parallelized algorithms. Chapter 10, "Parallel Testing and Tuning," explains how to work with lazy initialization.

WORKING WITH SYNCHRONIZATION PRIMITIVES

.NET Framework 4 offers six new lightweight synchronization primitives in the existing `System.Threading` namespace. This namespace provides access to the legacy multithreading classes, types, and enumerations, but it also offers new ones that are closely related to the new task-based programming model and certain scenarios. The following list offers a brief introduction to the new lightweight synchronization types:

➤ `Barrier` — Allows multiple tasks to synchronize their concurrent work on multiple phases.

➤ `CountdownEvent` — Simplifies fork and join scenarios. It represents a very lightweight synchronization primitive that is signaled when its count reaches 0. The new task-based programming model offers an easier approach to express fork-join parallelism through `Task` instances, continuations, and `Parallel.Invoke`. However, `CountdownEvent` can still be useful with tasks. Using `Task.WaitAll` or the `TaskFactory.ContinueWhenAll` method requires having an array for the full set of `Task` instances to be waited on. `CountdownEvent` doesn't require the object references and can be used to track a dynamic number of tasks over time.

➤ `ManualResetEventSlim` — Allows many tasks to wait until an event handle is manually signaled by another task. When you expect wait times to be very short, it offers better performance than its heavyweight equivalent, `ManualResetEvent`.

➤ `SemaphoreSlim` — Allows you to limit the number of tasks that can concurrently access a resource or a pool of resources. When you expect wait times to be very short, it offers better performance than its heavyweight equivalent, `Semaphore`.

➤ `SpinLock` — Allows a task to *spin* until it acquires a mutual exclusion lock, which ensures that only one task at a time has access to the locked variable, object, or region. When you expect wait times for a fine-grained lock to be very short and you turn off the `SpinLock`'s debugging facility, it might offer better performance than other mutual-exclusion locks. In these scenarios, you can test replacing locks acquired by using the `System.Threading .Monitor` class methods with `SpinLock` locks. In addition, `SpinLock` is a `struct`, and therefore, its usage can reduce memory requirements and garbage collection pressure if you need a lot of locks and/or need to minimize object allocations.

> *The procedure of waiting in a loop is known as* spinning. *When a task* spins *until it acquires a mutual exclusion lock, it means that it waits in a loop, repeatedly checking until the lock becomes available. This kind of busy waiting has some advantages and disadvantages. The next section analyzes each synchronization primitive that relies on spinning.*

➤ `SpinWait` — Allows a task to perform a spin-based wait until a specified condition is satisfied. For example, a higher-level algorithm might use `SpinWait` to specify a timeout to create a *spinning-then-waiting* condition. This algorithm is known as a *two-phase wait operation*, whereby if the spin-based wait spends a certain time spinning and the condition isn't satisfied, it enters a *kernel-based wait*. This is useful for running code in tasks when certain conditions are satisfied, and the tasks aren't chained with continuations. `SpinWait` itself doesn't provide any direct support for falling back to a kernel wait; it just enables implementing that pattern.

The lightweight equivalent for the classes that have counterparts in earlier releases of .NET Framework only works inside a single process, while the heavyweight version supports both a single process and cross-process synchronization.

The following sections provide usage examples and detailed information about the most appropriate scenarios for the aforementioned lightweight synchronization types and their heavyweight equivalents that are closely related to tasks. It is very important to choose the appropriate synchronization primitive to minimize overhead.

> *Visual Studio 2010 provides new concurrency profiling features. You can use these functionalities to determine which synchronization primitive provides better performance for a specific scenario. For example, you can test a classic* Monitor *lock versus a* SpinLock *with its debugging facility turned off. In addition, you can test another version of the algorithm that uses atomic operations. Chapter 10, "Parallel Testing and Tuning," explains many tools and techniques to help you choose the most appropriate synchronization primitives among the diverse options explained in subsequent examples.*

Synchronizing Concurrent Tasks with Barriers

When you need a group of tasks to run a series of phases in parallel, but each new phase has to start after all the other tasks finish the previous phase, you can synchronize this cooperative work with an instance of the `Barrier` class. Because each phase requires synchronization between tasks, a `Barrier` object prevents individual tasks from continuing until all tasks reach the `Barrier`. Each task in the group is known as a *participant* — it signals its arrival at the `Barrier` in each given phase, and implicitly waits for all the other participants to signal their arrival before continuing. You can use the same `Barrier` instance for multiple phases.

Consider the following five phases, illustrated in Figure 5-8:

➤   `CreatePlanets`

➤   `CreateStars`

➤   `CheckCollisionsBetweenPlanets`

➤   `CheckCollisionsBetweenStars`

➤   `RenderCollisions`

You can split the work done in each phase into many tasks. For example, four tasks can run `CreatePlanets`, but the next phase, `CreateStars`, requires all the data from `CreatePlanets` to be available. Thus, these tasks cannot start running `CreateStars` until all the participants finished running the code for `CreatePlanets`.

It is possible to define task continuations and take advantage of the `Task.Factory.ContinueWhenAll` method to write a delegate that starts another four new tasks to run each new phase after the previous tasks finish their execution. However, because the five phases have to run 10 times, this technique would add a big overhead as a result of the great number of chained tasks. Each time the five phases run, the code would create four new tasks on each of the five phases, and therefore, it would create 20 `Task` instances. Because the five phases have to run 10 times, the code would be creating 200 `Task` instances. If each phase takes a short time to run, the overhead added by the creation of so many tasks would reduce the performance and the scalability for the code. You would need to measure this overhead versus the overhead introduced by a `Barrier` that enables easier expression of the synchronization required.

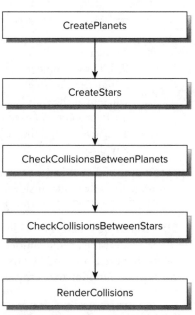

FIGURE 5-8

In this case, it is a better idea to create the four tasks and use the features offered by the `Barrier` class to define barriers before starting to run the code for each new phase. This way, the four `Task` instances are going to be able to run the five synchronized phases 10 times with less overhead.

Listing 5-1 shows an example of the usage of a `Barrier` instance to coordinate the work among a group of tasks that run the aforementioned five phases.

LISTING 5-1: Using a barrier to synchronize code in many tasks with several phases

```
private static void CreatePlanets(int participantNum)
{
    Console.WriteLine(
        "Creating planets. Participant # {0}",
```

```
            participantNum);
}

private static void CreateStars(int participantNum)
{
    Console.WriteLine(
        "Creating stars. Participant # {0}",
        participantNum);
}

private static void CheckCollisionsBetweenPlanets(int participantNum)
{
    Console.WriteLine(
        "Checking collisions between planets. Participant # {0}",
        participantNum);
}

private static void CheckCollisionsBetweenStars(int participantNum)
{
    Console.WriteLine(
        "Checking collisions between stars. Participant # {0}",
        participantNum);
}

private static void RenderCollisions(int participantNum)
{
    Console.WriteLine(
        "Rendering collisions. Participant # {0}",
        participantNum);
}

private static int _participants =
    Environment.ProcessorCount;
private static Task[] _tasks;
private static Barrier _barrier;

static void Main(string[] args)
{
    _tasks = new Task[_participants];
    _barrier = new Barrier(_participants, (barrier) =>
    {
        Console.WriteLine("Current phase: {0}",
            barrier.CurrentPhaseNumber);
    });

    for (int i = 0; i < _participants; i++)
    {
        _tasks[i] = Task.Factory.StartNew((num) =>
        {
            var participantNumber = (int)num;
            for (int j = 0; j < 10; j++)
            {
                CreatePlanets(participantNumber);
                _barrier.SignalAndWait();
                CreateStars(participantNumber);
                _barrier.SignalAndWait();
```

continues

LISTING 5-1 *(continued)*

```
                CheckCollisionsBetweenPlanets(participantNumber);
                _barrier.SignalAndWait();
                CheckCollisionsBetweenStars(participantNumber);
                _barrier.SignalAndWait();
                RenderCollisions(participantNumber);
                _barrier.SignalAndWait();
            }
        }, i);
    }

    var finalTask = Task.Factory.ContinueWhenAll(_tasks, (tasks) =>
    {
        // Wait for all the tasks to ensure
        // the propagation of any exception occurred
        // in any of the _tasks
        Task.WaitAll(_tasks);
        Console.WriteLine(
            "All the phases were executed.");
        // Dispose the Barrier instance
        _barrier.Dispose();
    });

    // Wait for finalTask to finish
    finalTask.Wait();

    Console.ReadLine();
}
```

The number of participants stored in the *_participants* private variable is equal to the number of available logical cores. Listing 5-1 and the examples in the following sections assume that the following two `using` statements are included:

Available for
download on
Wrox.com

```
using System.Threading;
using System.Threading.Tasks;
```

code snippet from Listing5_1

The *_barrier* private variable stores an instance of `Barrier`. The code uses its *_participants* constructor to receive the number of initial participants, and a `System.Action<Barrier>` to be executed after each phase. Each time the barrier receives signals from all the participants, it increments its phase number, runs the action specified in its constructor, and unblocks each participant's `Task` instance. This way, the participants are going to be able to continue executing code. The number of the barrier's current phase is available in its `CurrentPhaseNumber` read-only property. Thus, when each phase advances, the action specified as the second parameter in the barrier's constructor will display the phase number. After the post-phase action runs, `CurrentPhaseNumber` increments its value to represent the new phase that is going to run. The delegate receives the `Barrier` instance in its *barrier* parameter as follows:

```
_barrier = new Barrier(_participants, (barrier) =>
{
    Console.WriteLine("Current phase: {0}", barrier.CurrentPhaseNumber);
});
```

The code shown in Listing 5-1 for the five methods that represent each phase just displays text on the console to keep things simple and to focus on the effects of the barrier. However, the time needed by each participant to run the code for each phase might be different. Figure 5-9 shows an example of the effect of having four participants that require diverse times to run each phase. Many participants will have to wait for the other participants to signal their arrival. This diagram also shows when the post-phase action is going to run and the values for the CurrentPhaseNumber read-only property.

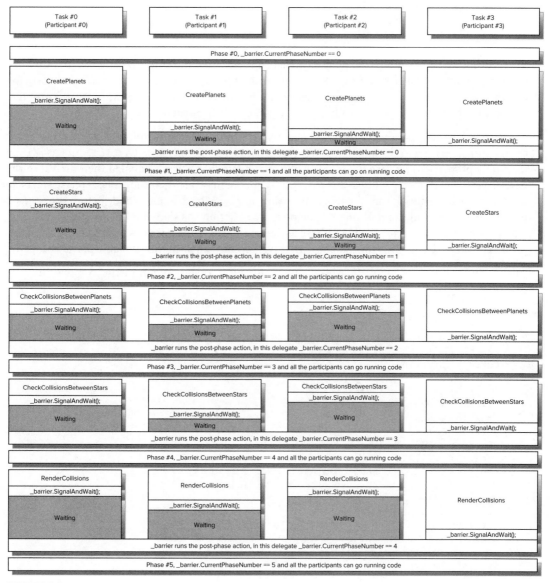

FIGURE 5-9

Each participant runs a loop that executes the five phases 10 times. After each method that represents a phase runs, it calls the _barrier.SignalAndWait method as follows:

```
CreatePlanets(participantNumber);
_barrier.SignalAndWait();
CreateStars(participantNumber);
_barrier.SignalAndWait();
CheckCollisionsBetweenPlanets(participantNumber);
_barrier.SignalAndWait();
CheckCollisionsBetweenStars(participantNumber);
_barrier.SignalAndWait();
RenderCollisions(participantNumber);
_barrier.SignalAndWait();
```

This method signals that a participant has reached the barrier and starts waiting for all other participants to reach the barrier as well. The current task will stay waiting until all the other participants call the SignalAndWait method for this barrier. It isn't necessary to add extra synchronization to call this method, because it is already prepared to be called concurrently.

The barrier's ParticipantCount read-only property stores the number of participants that have to signal their arrival to the barrier. Moreover, other tasks can access its ParticipantsRemaining read-only property to retrieve the number of participants that haven't signaled their arrival to the barrier yet. This property will have the ParticipantCount value each time a new phase starts and will decrease by one each time a participant calls the SignalAndWait method. Before starting a new phase, the barrier will run the code for the post-phase action. As shown previously in Figure 5-9, when the delegate that runs the post-phase action is executed, the barrier's CurrentPhaseNumber property will have the value for the phase that has recently finished, not the new phase number.

The following lines display the first results of running the code shown in Listing 5-1 with four logical cores:

```
Creating planets. Participant # 1
Creating planets. Participant # 2
Creating planets. Participant # 0
Creating planets. Participant # 3
Current phase: 0
Creating stars. Participant # 3
Creating stars. Participant # 1
Creating stars. Participant # 0
Creating stars. Participant # 2
Current phase: 1
Checking collisions between planets. Participant # 2
Checking collisions between planets. Participant # 3
Checking collisions between planets. Participant # 0
Checking collisions between planets. Participant # 1
Current phase: 2
Checking collisions between stars. Participant # 1
Checking collisions between stars. Participant # 2
Checking collisions between stars. Participant # 0
Checking collisions between stars. Participant # 3
Current phase: 3
```

```
Rendering collisions. Participant # 3
Rendering collisions. Participant # 0
Rendering collisions. Participant # 2
Rendering collisions. Participant # 1
Current phase: 4
Creating planets. Participant # 1
Creating planets. Participant # 0
Creating planets. Participant # 3
Creating planets. Participant # 2
Current phase: 5
```

The code written in the barrier's post-phase shows a line that displays the value for the barrier's CurrentPhaseNumber property. At that moment, this value is indicating the phase number that has already been completed by the four participants. As previously explained for tasks and threads, the execution for the participants can be different for each phase. For example, in the previously shown output, the fourth participant, Participant #3, is the last one to start running the code in the CreatePlanets method for the first phase, Phase #0, but it is the first one to start running the code in the CreateStars method for the second phase, Phase #1.

Barrier and ContinueWhenAll

A final task, *finalTask*, uses a special task-continuation method called ContinueWhenAll that's provided by Task.Factory. One of the definitions for this method receives an array of Task instances and the action that has to be scheduled to run after all the Task instances finish their execution, in a new task. This new task indicates that the phases were executed and calls the Dispose method for the barrier as follows:

```
var finalTask = Task.Factory.ContinueWhenAll(_tasks, (tasks) =>
{
    // Wait for all the tasks to ensure
    // the propagation of any exception occurred
    // in any of the _tasks
    Task.WaitAll(_tasks);
    Console.WriteLine(
        "All the phases were executed.");
    // Dispose the Barrier instance
    _barrier.Dispose();
});
```

 You should always dispose a barrier when you have finished with it.

In fact, the ContinueWhenAll method is an interesting alternative when you need to run code after many tasks finish their work. If you need two or three phases that run a group of tasks just once, it can be more convenient to use the ContinueWhenAll method instead of working with a barrier. However, when you need to run many phases in a loop, the barrier usually provides the best alternative.

In this example, because the `Main` method waits for `finalTask` to finish in the main thread, you can also do a `Task.WaitAll(tasks)` followed by the `WriteLine` and `_barrier.Dispose`. The following lines produce the same effect without creating a new `Task` instance:

```
Task.WaitAll(_tasks);
Console.WriteLine(
    "All the phases were executed.");
// Dispose the Barrier instance
// This line will run after all _tasks finished
_barrier.Dispose();
Console.ReadLine();
```

Catching Exceptions in all Participating Tasks

If the code in the barrier's post-phase action throws an exception, it will be wrapped in a `BarrierPostPhaseException`, and all the participant tasks or threads will be able to catch it. The original exception will be available in the `BarrierPostPhaseException` instance's `InnerException` property.

The following lines show a new version of the first part of the `Main` method presented in Listing 5-1 that throws an `InvalidOperationException` when the barrier has finished phase number 10. A call to the `SignalAndWait` method that runs for phase number 10 is included in a `try...catch` block. This block captures a `BarrierPostPhaseException` in bppex. This way, when all the participants send their signals indicating that a phase has been completed, and the post-phase action runs and determines that the phase number is 10, the code displays the value for the original exception's message, `bppex.InnerException.Message`, and exits the `for` loop. Thus, the participants won't go on running the code for the additional phases in the barrier.

```
static void Main(string[] args)
{
    _tasks = new Task[_participants];
    _barrier = new Barrier(_participants, (barrier) =>
    {
        Console.WriteLine("Current phase: {0}",
            barrier.CurrentPhaseNumber);
        if (barrier.CurrentPhaseNumber == 10)
        {
            throw new InvalidOperationException(
                "No more phases allowed.");
        }
    });

    for (int i = 0; i < _participants; i++)
    {
        _tasks[i] = Task.Factory.StartNew((num) =>
        {
            var participantNumber = (int)num;
            for (int j = 0; j < 10; j++)
            {
                CreatePlanets(participantNumber);
                try
                {
```

```
                           _barrier.SignalAndWait();
                       }
                       catch (BarrierPostPhaseException bppex)
                       {
                           Console.WriteLine(
                               "{0}", bppex.InnerException.Message);
                           // Exit the for loop
                           break;
                       }
                       CreateStars(participantNumber);
                       _barrier.SignalAndWait();
                       CheckCollisionsBetweenPlanets(participantNumber);
                       _barrier.SignalAndWait();
                       CheckCollisionsBetweenStars(participantNumber);
                       _barrier.SignalAndWait();
                       RenderCollisions(participantNumber);
                       _barrier.SignalAndWait();
                   }
               }, i);
           }
       ...
```

code snippet from Snippet5_1

You can use this method of throwing an exception in a post-phase action to communicate something to all the participants that can capture this exception. The participants can then determine the exception type by checking its InnerException *property and make a decision based on this. However, remember that throwing an exception is expensive; therefore, if you need frequent communications, you may want to use other coordination structures explained in the next sections.*

Working with Timeouts

One of the problems with barriers is that there are many tasks waiting for the other participants to signal their arrival to the barrier, and if one or more participants don't signal their arrival, the other tasks will keep waiting forever. To better understand this situation, try changing the code for the CreatePlanets method shown in Listing 5-1 with the following lines:

Available for download on Wrox.com

```
private static void CreatePlanets(int participantNum)
{
    Console.WriteLine(
        "Creating planets. Participant # {0}",
        participantNum);
    if (participantNum == 0)
    {
        // Spin until there aren't remaining participants
        // for the current phase
        // This condition running in a loop (spinning) is very inefficient
        // This example uses this spinning for educational purposes
```

```
        // It isn't a best practice
        SpinWait.SpinUntil(() => (_barrier.ParticipantsRemaining == 0));
    }
}
```

code snippet from Snippet5_2

The first task, `Participant #0`, that runs the first phase will keep waiting until the `ParticipantsRemaining` property for the barrier reaches 0. `CreatePlanets` uses the `SpinWait` `.SpinUntil` method to spin until the condition is true. However, this condition will never be true, because the participant that is waiting for `ParticipantsRemaining` to reach 0 will never finish the execution of the `CreatePlanets` method; therefore, its task won't reach the code that signals its arrival to the barrier. The following lines display the results of running the code with four logical cores:

```
Creating planets. Participant # 2
Creating planets. Participant # 3
Creating planets. Participant # 0
Creating planets. Participant # 1
```

The application doesn't run the post-phase action, because it never finishes the first barrier's phase. If you use the Break All command to stop the execution and display the Parallel Tasks window by selecting Debug ⇨ Windows ⇨ Parallel Tasks, the status for all the tasks that are participating in the barrier will be `Waiting`, as shown in Figure 5-10. The problem with this is that they are going to keep waiting forever. Under certain circumstances, you might see the task that runs the `CreatePlanets` method with its `participantNum` parameter equal to 0 in the `SpinWait` `.SpinUntil` line, showing the task's status of `Running` rather than `Waiting`. The status shown depends on whether you happen to catch the spinning in sleep or wait state due to the yielding and sleeping used internally, or whether you catch it running code.

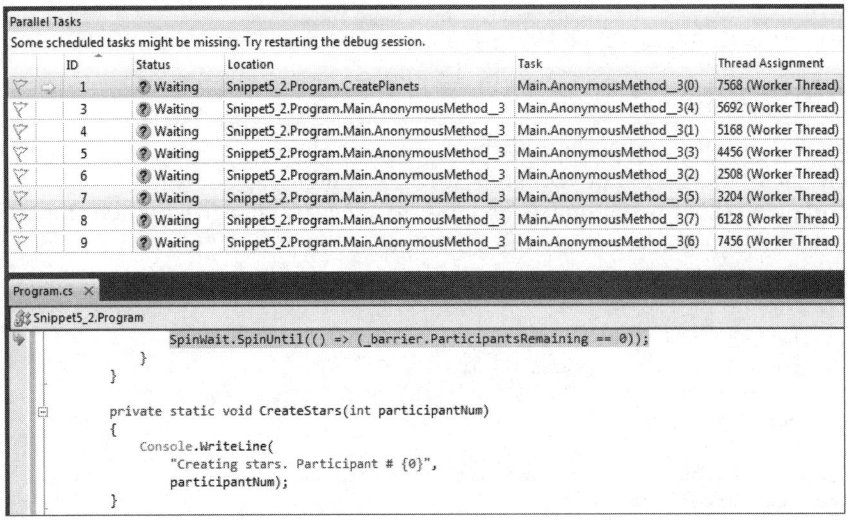

Parallel Tasks
Some scheduled tasks might be missing. Try restarting the debug session.

	ID	Status	Location	Task	Thread Assignment
	1	? Waiting	Snippet5_2.Program.CreatePlanets	Main.AnonymousMethod__3(0)	7568 (Worker Thread)
	3	? Waiting	Snippet5_2.Program.Main.AnonymousMethod__3	Main.AnonymousMethod__3(4)	5692 (Worker Thread)
	4	? Waiting	Snippet5_2.Program.Main.AnonymousMethod__3	Main.AnonymousMethod__3(1)	5168 (Worker Thread)
	5	? Waiting	Snippet5_2.Program.Main.AnonymousMethod__3	Main.AnonymousMethod__3(3)	4456 (Worker Thread)
	6	? Waiting	Snippet5_2.Program.Main.AnonymousMethod__3	Main.AnonymousMethod__3(2)	2508 (Worker Thread)
	7	? Waiting	Snippet5_2.Program.Main.AnonymousMethod__3	Main.AnonymousMethod__3(5)	3204 (Worker Thread)
	8	? Waiting	Snippet5_2.Program.Main.AnonymousMethod__3	Main.AnonymousMethod__3(7)	6128 (Worker Thread)
	9	? Waiting	Snippet5_2.Program.Main.AnonymousMethod__3	Main.AnonymousMethod__3(6)	7456 (Worker Thread)

Program.cs

Snippet5_2.Program

```
        SpinWait.SpinUntil(() => (_barrier.ParticipantsRemaining == 0));
    }
}

private static void CreateStars(int participantNum)
{
    Console.WriteLine(
        "Creating stars. Participant # {0}",
        participantNum);
}
```

FIGURE 5-10

As explained in previous examples, establishing a timeout is very important to prevent tasks or threads from blocking without any kind of restrictions. Thus, you can use a definition for the SignalAndWait method that accepts the number of milliseconds to wait. The method returns a bool value that indicates whether all participants reached the barrier within the specified time. The following code shows a new version of the Main method that uses a timeout and a CancellationToken to be able to fault and cancel the tasks when something goes wrong with one or more participants:

```
// 2,000 milliseconds = 2 seconds timeout
private const int TIMEOUT = 2000;

private static void CreatePlanets(int participantNum)
{
    Console.WriteLine(
        "Creating planets. Participant # {0}",
        participantNum);
    if (participantNum == 0)
    {
        // Spin until there aren't remaining participants
        // for the current phase, with a TIMEOUT * 3 timeout
        // This condition running in a loop (spinning) is very inefficient
        // This example uses this spinning for educational purposes
        // It isn't a best practice
        SpinWait.SpinUntil(() =>
            (_barrier.ParticipantsRemaining == 0), TIMEOUT * 3);
    }
}

static void Main(string[] args)
{
    var cts =
        new System.Threading.CancellationTokenSource();
    var ct = cts.Token;

    _tasks = new Task[_participants];
    _barrier = new Barrier(_participants, (barrier) =>
    {
        Console.WriteLine("Current phase: {0}", barrier.CurrentPhaseNumber);
    });

    for (int i = 0; i < _participants; i++)
    {
        _tasks[i] = Task.Factory.StartNew((num) =>
        {
            var participantNumber = (int)num;
            for (int j = 0; j < 10; j++)
            {
                CreatePlanets(participantNumber);
                if (!_barrier.SignalAndWait(TIMEOUT))
                {
                    Console.WriteLine(
"Participants are requiring more than {0} seconds
to reach the barrier.",
                        TIMEOUT);
```

```
                           throw new OperationCanceledException(
                               String.Format(
    "Participants are requiring more than {0} seconds
    to reach the barrier at the Phase # {1}.",
                               TIMEOUT,
                               _barrier.CurrentPhaseNumber), ct);
                   }
                   CreateStars(participantNumber);
                   _barrier.SignalAndWait();
                   CheckCollisionsBetweenPlanets(participantNumber);
                   _barrier.SignalAndWait();
                   CheckCollisionsBetweenStars(participantNumber);
                   _barrier.SignalAndWait();
                   RenderCollisions(participantNumber);
                   _barrier.SignalAndWait();
               }
           }, i, ct);
       }

       var finalTask = Task.Factory.ContinueWhenAll(_tasks, (tasks) =>
       {
           // Wait for all the tasks to ensure
           // the propagation of any exception occurred
           // in any of the _tasks
           Task.WaitAll(_tasks);
           Console.WriteLine(
               "All the phases were executed.");
       }, ct);

       // Wait for finalTask to finish
       try
       {
           // Use a timeout
           if (!finalTask.Wait(TIMEOUT * 2))
           {
               bool faulted = false;
               for (int t = 0; t < _participants; t++)
               {
                   if (_tasks[t].Status != TaskStatus.RanToCompletion)
                   {
                       faulted = true;
                       if (_tasks[t].Status == TaskStatus.Faulted)
                       {
                           foreach (var innerEx
                                   in _tasks[t].Exception.InnerExceptions)
                               Console.WriteLine(innerEx.Message);
                       }
                   }
               }
               if (faulted)
               {
                   Console.WriteLine(
                       "The phases failed their execution.");
               }
               else
```

```
            {
                Console.WriteLine(
                    "All the phases were executed.");
            }
        }
    }
    catch (AggregateException ex)
    {
        foreach (var innerEx in ex.InnerExceptions)
            Console.WriteLine(innerEx.Message);
        Console.WriteLine(
            "The phases failed their execution.");
    }
    finally
    {
        // Dispose the Barrier instance
        _barrier.Dispose();
    }

    Console.ReadLine();
}
```

code snippet from Snippet5_3

In this case, the same *ct* (`CancellationToken`) instance is associated to the participants' tasks and *finalTask* scheduled with the `ContinueWhenAll` method. After the `CreatePlanets` method finishes its execution, the participants call the `_barrier.SignalAndWait` method and wait for `TIMEOUT` seconds. After that time, which is 2 seconds, the `SignalAndWait` method returns `false` because there is one participant that requires more than 2 seconds to signal its arrival to the barrier. Thus, all the participants, except the one that hasn't signaled its arrival, throw a new `OperationCanceledException` with the *ct* (`CancellationToken`) instance as one of the parameters. The corresponding `Task` instances are faulted because there is an unhandled exception.

The code that waits for *finalTask* to finish also sends a timeout in milliseconds as a parameter to the `Wait` method. In this case, the timeout is twice the milliseconds specified for the `_barrier.SignalAndWait` method. Because one of the participants is going to stay in the `SpinWait.SpinUntil` line for three times the milliseconds specified for `_barrier.SignalAndWait`, the `Wait` method is going to return `false`. When this happens, the code checks the value of the `Status` property for each `Task` instance that was a participant in the barrier. The code will iterate through the `InnerExceptions` property for the `Task` instances that hold the `TaskStatus.Faulted` value in their `Status` property, and will display the messages associated with the exceptions. Because there is at least one `Task` instance that holds the `TaskStatus.Faulted` value in its `Status` property, `faulted == true`, the code writes a message explaining that the phases failed their execution. The code that disposes the `Barrier` instance is included in the `finally` section of a try...catch...finally block.

 It is very important to include timeouts and cancellations when working with barriers and other synchronization mechanisms because an error in the code or an unpredictable situation can generate a task or a thread that will be waiting forever.

If you insert a breakpoint in the line that sets `faulted = true` in the `Main` method, and you activate the Parallel Tasks window, you will notice that there is just one task, as shown in Figure 5-11. The other tasks aren't waiting, because all of them threw an exception. The task that is waiting is running the `SpinWait.SpinUntil` method, and it is going to be canceled when the `Cancel` method for `cts` is called. Remember that the status shown might be `Waiting` or `Running`, depending on whether you happen to catch the spinning in sleep or wait state.

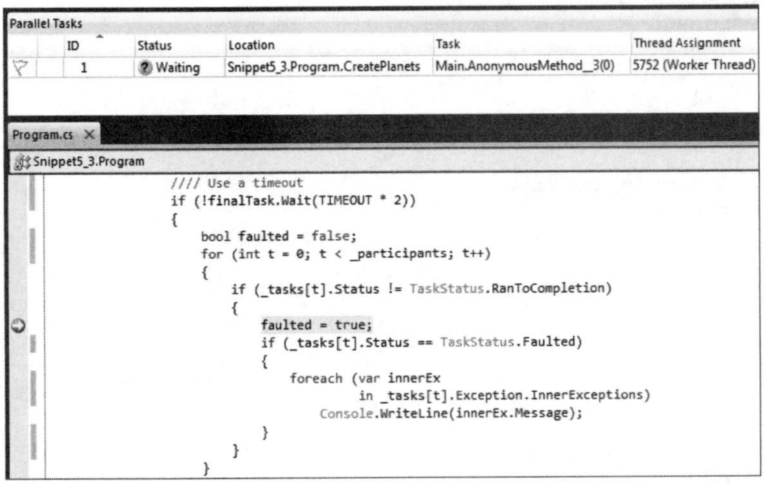

Parallel Tasks					
	ID	Status	Location	Task	Thread Assignment
▽	1	ⓘ Waiting	Snippet5_3.Program.CreatePlanets	Main.AnonymousMethod_3(0)	5752 (Worker Thread)

Program.cs ✕

Snippet5_3.Program

```
                //// Use a timeout
                if (!finalTask.Wait(TIMEOUT * 2))
                {
                    bool faulted = false;
                    for (int t = 0; t < _participants; t++)
                    {
                        if (_tasks[t].Status != TaskStatus.RanToCompletion)
                        {
                            faulted = true;
                            if (_tasks[t].Status == TaskStatus.Faulted)
                            {
                                foreach (var innerEx
                                        in _tasks[t].Exception.InnerExceptions)
                                    Console.WriteLine(innerEx.Message);
                            }
                        }
                    }
                }
```

FIGURE 5-11

Working with a Dynamic Number of Participants

The `Barrier` class provides four methods that allow you to add and remove participants on the fly for a `Barrier` instance. However, you must be very careful when you use these methods, because they change the number of signals that the barrier is going to expect from the participants before unblocking the tasks that are waiting and advancing to the next phase.

The following methods allow you to control the number of participants, and they can't be invoked within a post-phase action. It is possible to call them concurrently and in parallel, because they are thread-safe methods.

➤ `AddParticipant` — Adds just one participant to the `Barrier` instance.

➤ `AddParticipants` — Adds the number of participants received as an `int` parameter to the `Barrier` instance.

➤ `RemoveParticipant` — Removes just one participant from the `Barrier` instance.

➤ `RemoveParticipants` — Removes the number of participants received as an `int` parameter from the `Barrier` instance.

WORKING WITH MUTUAL-EXCLUSION LOCKS

When you have a critical section that only one task has to access at a time but that has to be called by many tasks or in loops, and using task continuations isn't a good option, one alternative is to use a mutual-exclusion lock primitive. The `lock` keyword obtains a mutual-exclusion lock for an object, executes a statement block as a critical section, and then releases the lock for the object. The following code shows the typical usage of the `lock` keyword to run a block of statements with exclusive access to the _myObject_ private object:

```
lock (_myObject)
{
    // Beginning of critical code section
    // These statements run with an exclusive access to myObject
    _myObject.Add(myNewMessage1);
    _myObject.Add(myNewMessage2);
    // End of critical code section
}
```

The `lock` keyword calls `System.Threading.Monitor.Enter` with the object as a parameter to acquire the exclusive lock on this object before executing the statement block. Then, if it actually acquires the lock, it executes the code as a critical section, `lock` calls `System.Threading.Monitor.Exit` to release the previously acquired exclusive lock on the object and leave the critical section. Thus, the previously shown code snippet is equivalent to the following code that uses `Monitor.Enter` and `Monitor.Exit` instead of the `lock` keyword:

```
bool lockTaken = false;
try
{
    Monitor.Enter(_myObject, ref lockTaken);
    // Monitor acquired a lock on myObject
    // Beginning of critical code section
    // These statements run with an exclusive access to myObject
    _myObject.Add(myNewMessage1);
    _myObject.Add(myNewMessage2);
    // End of critical code section
}
finally
{
    // You need to make sure that you release the lock on myObject
    if (lockTaken)
        Monitor.Exit(_myObject);
}
```

 The previous code snippet is the compiler-generated code for `lock` *in .NET Framework 4 and the recommended pattern. Prior to .NET Framework 4, there was a different recommended pattern.*

The System.Threading.Monitor class provides the mechanism that synchronizes access to objects by using mutual-exclusion locks. The equivalent code that uses the lock keyword is simpler to use because you don't need to write a try...finally block to ensure that you release the previously acquired lock. However, the Monitor class provides additional methods that allow you to have more control over the lock acquisition process and to work with timeouts. If the object passed to the Monitor.Exit method is different from the object used for Monitor.Enter, Monitor will throw a SynchronizationLockException.

> *The* lock *keyword and the* Monitor *class are still the preferred methods to pro-vide mutual exclusion. However, in certain scenarios, you might find that other mutual-exclusion lock primitives, such as* SpinLock, *offer better performance or less overhead.*

> *The* lock *keyword and the* Monitor *class allow you to lock objects, that is, refer-ence types. Don't use* lock *or* Monitor *with value types. If you need to synchro-nize access to value types, you must use a separate synchronization object and lock it when you need to run code as a critical section.*

The following lines show a new version of the first part of the Main method presented in Listing 5-1. This new version uses the lock keyword to acquire a lock and run code in a critical section, and adds information to a log string by using a StringBuilder named *sb* in all the bar-rier's participants.

```csharp
static void Main(string[] args)
{
    _tasks = new Task[_participants];
    _barrier = new Barrier(_participants, (barrier) =>
    {
        Console.WriteLine("Current phase: {0}",
            barrier.CurrentPhaseNumber);
    });

    var sb = new StringBuilder();

    for (int i = 0; i < _participants; i++)
    {
        _tasks[i] = Task.Factory.StartNew((num) =>
        {
            var participantNumber = (int)num;
            for (int j = 0; j < 10; j++)
            {
                CreatePlanets(participantNumber);
                _barrier.SignalAndWait();
                CreateStars(participantNumber);
                _barrier.SignalAndWait();
                CheckCollisionsBetweenPlanets(participantNumber);
                _barrier.SignalAndWait();
```

```csharp
                    CheckCollisionsBetweenStars(participantNumber);
                    _barrier.SignalAndWait();
                    RenderCollisions(participantNumber);
                    _barrier.SignalAndWait();

                    var logLine =
                        String.Format(
"Time: {0}, Phase: {1}, Participant: {2}, Phase completed OK\n",
                            DateTime.Now.TimeOfDay,
                            _barrier.CurrentPhaseNumber,
                            participantNumber);
                    lock (sb)
                    {
                        // Critical section
                        sb.Append(logLine);
                        // End of critical section
                    }
                }
            }, i);
    }

    var finalTask = Task.Factory.ContinueWhenAll(_tasks, (tasks) =>
    {
        // Wait for all the tasks to ensure
        // the propagation of any exception occurred
        // in any of the _tasks
        Task.WaitAll(_tasks);
        Console.WriteLine(
            "All the phases were executed.");
        Console.WriteLine(sb);
        // Dispose the Barrier instance
        _barrier.Dispose();
    });

    // Wait for finalTask to finish
    finalTask.Wait();

    Console.ReadLine();
}
```

code snippet from Snippet5_4

The following lines are the results of displaying the final contents of the StringBuilder *sb* instance that added information from all the participants in the critical section:

```
Time: 16:22:03.5449965, Phase: 5, Participant: 2, Phase completed OK
Time: 16:22:03.5605965, Phase: 5, Participant: 1, Phase completed OK
Time: 16:22:03.5761965, Phase: 5, Participant: 3, Phase completed OK
Time: 16:22:03.5917965, Phase: 5, Participant: 0, Phase completed OK
Time: 16:22:03.5917965, Phase: 10, Participant: 1, Phase completed OK
Time: 16:22:03.5917965, Phase: 10, Participant: 3, Phase completed OK
Time: 16:22:03.5917965, Phase: 10, Participant: 2, Phase completed OK
Time: 16:22:03.5917965, Phase: 10, Participant: 0, Phase completed OK
Time: 16:22:03.6073966, Phase: 15, Participant: 2, Phase completed OK
```

```
Time: 16:22:03.6073966, Phase: 15, Participant: 3, Phase completed OK
Time: 16:22:03.6073966, Phase: 15, Participant: 1, Phase completed OK
Time: 16:22:03.6073966, Phase: 15, Participant: 0, Phase completed OK
Time: 16:22:03.6229966, Phase: 20, Participant: 1, Phase completed OK
Time: 16:22:03.6229966, Phase: 20, Participant: 3, Phase completed OK
Time: 16:22:03.6229966, Phase: 20, Participant: 0, Phase completed OK
Time: 16:22:03.6229966, Phase: 20, Participant: 2, Phase completed OK
Time: 16:22:03.6385966, Phase: 25, Participant: 0, Phase completed OK
Time: 16:22:03.6385966, Phase: 25, Participant: 2, Phase completed OK
Time: 16:22:03.6385966, Phase: 25, Participant: 3, Phase completed OK
Time: 16:22:03.6385966, Phase: 25, Participant: 1, Phase completed OK
Time: 16:22:03.6541967, Phase: 30, Participant: 0, Phase completed OK
Time: 16:22:03.6541967, Phase: 30, Participant: 1, Phase completed OK
Time: 16:22:03.6541967, Phase: 30, Participant: 2, Phase completed OK
Time: 16:22:03.6541967, Phase: 30, Participant: 3, Phase completed OK
Time: 16:22:03.6697967, Phase: 35, Participant: 1, Phase completed OK
Time: 16:22:03.6697967, Phase: 35, Participant: 3, Phase completed OK
Time: 16:22:03.6697967, Phase: 35, Participant: 2, Phase completed OK
Time: 16:22:03.6697967, Phase: 35, Participant: 0, Phase completed OK
Time: 16:22:03.6853967, Phase: 40, Participant: 3, Phase completed OK
Time: 16:22:03.6853967, Phase: 40, Participant: 1, Phase completed OK
Time: 16:22:03.6853967, Phase: 40, Participant: 0, Phase completed OK
Time: 16:22:03.7009967, Phase: 40, Participant: 2, Phase completed OK
Time: 16:22:03.7009967, Phase: 45, Participant: 0, Phase completed OK
Time: 16:22:03.7009967, Phase: 45, Participant: 1, Phase completed OK
Time: 16:22:03.7009967, Phase: 45, Participant: 2, Phase completed OK
Time: 16:22:03.7009967, Phase: 45, Participant: 3, Phase completed OK
Time: 16:22:03.7165968, Phase: 50, Participant: 2, Phase completed OK
Time: 16:22:03.7165968, Phase: 50, Participant: 1, Phase completed OK
Time: 16:22:03.7165968, Phase: 50, Participant: 3, Phase completed OK
Time: 16:22:03.7165968, Phase: 50, Participant: 0, Phase completed OK
```

The critical section runs a single line of code that calls the `Append` method for the `StringBuilder` `sb` instance, and adds information about the time, phase number, and participant number to a log string. Because the critical section is going to be serialized, it is safe to call the `Append` method. Notice that the critical section just calls the `Append` method with the previously formatted `logLine` string. The `String.Format` method returns a formatted string outside of the critical section to avoid keeping a lock for more time than absolutely necessary. You need the lock to add the new string, but you don't need a lock to format a string to be added.

When the code uses the `lock` keyword, the `Monitor.Enter` method is going to try to acquire the lock on `sb`, and if it can't, the task will block until it can acquire the lock. Once it acquires the lock, the line after `// Critical section` will run. If other tasks call the `Monitor.Enter` method at this time, they will block until the task that is running the critical section calls the `Monitor.Exit` method for `sb` in order to release the lock. Remember that the code calls `Monitor.Exit` in a try...`finally` block after the last sentence block because it uses the `lock` keyword. After the code has exited this critical section block, one of the other tasks will be able to acquire a lock and perform the same sequence.

Working with Monitor

The following code shows the compiler-generated code that previous .NET Framework versions would have used to replace the `lock` keyword to run the critical section block with a mutual-exclusion lock. As you can see, the code uses `Monitor.Enter` and `Monitor.Exit` instead of the `lock` keyword:

```
Monitor.Enter(sb);
try
{
    // Monitor acquired a lock on sb
    // Critical section
    sb.Append(logLine);
    // End of critical section
}
finally
{
    // You need to make sure that
    // you release the lock on sb
    Monitor.Exit(sb);
}
```

code snippet from Snippet5_5

.NET Framework 4 adds a new overload for the `Monitor.Enter` method that receives a `bool` variable by reference as an additional parameter. In fact, .NET Framework 4 uses this parameter in the compiler-generated code that replaces the `lock` keyword. Once `Monitor` acquires the lock, it automatically sets the reference `bool` variable to `true`. The following code shows how you can use this parameter:

```
bool lockTaken = false;
try
{
    Monitor.Enter(sb, ref lockTaken);
    // Monitor acquired a lock on sb
    // Critical section
    sb.Append(logLine);
    // End of critical section
}
finally
{
    // You need to make sure that
    // you release the lock on sb
    if (lockTaken)
    {
        // Gives up the lock if it actually acquired it
        Monitor.Exit(sb);
    }
}
```

code snippet from Snippet5_6

Each participant sets the *lockTaken* `bool` variable to `false` and then calls the `Monitor.Enter` method to acquire the lock on *sb*. The second parameter for `Monitor.Enter` is *lockTaken*, sent by reference. Once `Monitor` acquires the lock, `lockTaken` will change to `true`, and the line after `// Critical section` will run. The code in the `finally` section checks whether `lockTaken` is true in order to release the lock by calling the `Monitor.Exit` method only if it actually acquired it. If `Monitor.Enter` can't acquire the lock because an exception was thrown, the `lockTaken` variable will be `false`, and as a result, the code in the `finally` section won't call `Monitor.Exit`.

You should avoid locking on external objects, because this might result in difficult-to-solve deadlocks. In addition, avoid acquiring a lock and releasing it across members and/or class boundaries. For similar reasons, avoid calling unknown code while holding a lock. If you are unable to do so, the developer that writes this unknown code should know that a lock will be held while the code is invoked. Keep the code in the critical section as simple as possible. The critical section must have code that has to be serialized.

Working with Timeouts for Locks

As happened with the barrier, because there are going to be many tasks trying to acquire the lock to enter the critical section, if one participant doesn't release the lock, the other tasks will stay blocked forever in the `Monitor.Enter` method. To see an example of this, change the following lines in the critical section code:

Available for download on Wrox.com

```
bool lockTaken = false;
try
{
    Monitor.Enter(sb, ref lockTaken);
    // Monitor acquired a lock on sb
    // Critical section
    sb.Append(logLine);

    // Spin until there aren't remaining participants
    // for the current phase
    // This should never be used inside a critical region
    SpinWait.SpinUntil(() => (_barrier.ParticipantsRemaining == 0));
    // End of critical section
}
finally
{
    // You need to make sure that
    // you release the lock on sb
    if (lockTaken)
    {
        // Gives up the lock if it actually acquired it
        Monitor.Exit(sb);
    }
}
```

code snippet from Snippet5_7

The first task that acquires the lock on `sb` and reaches the critical section will remain blocked until the `ParticipantsRemaining` property for the barrier reaches `0`. That condition will never be true, and therefore, the end of the critical section won't arrive and `Monitor.Exit` won't run to release the lock. All the other tasks will stay in the `Monitor.Enter` method, blocked and waiting forever for the lock on `sb` to be released.

If you use the `Break All` command to stop the execution and display the Parallel Tasks window by selecting Debug ➪ Windows ➪ Parallel Tasks, the status for all the tasks that are participating in the barrier will be `Waiting`, as shown in Figure 5-12. The problem with this is that they are going to keep waiting forever. Under certain circumstances, a status of `Running` rather than `Waiting` might be displayed for the task that is running the `SpinWait.SpinUntil` line in the critical section.

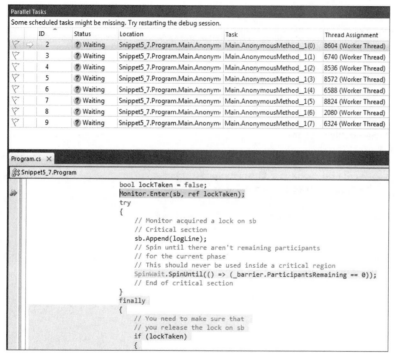

FIGURE 5-12

 The previous example called the `SpinWait.SpinUntil` *method inside the critical section merely to illustrate a* deadlock *situation — this is one of the most undesired problems in parallel programming, and you should not actually write this type of code. While holding a lock, you should avoid blocking or calling anything that itself may block.*

You can establish a timeout by using the `Monitor.TryEnter` method instead of `Monitor.Enter`. One of its definitions accepts the number of milliseconds to wait as the first parameter and the `bool` variable as the second parameter. Unlike `Monitor.Enter`, `Monitor.TryEnter` won't block indefinitely while waiting for the lock to be available. It will block until either the lock is available or the specified timeout has expired. Therefore, it is necessary to check the value for the `bool` variable after calling `Monitor.TryEnter`, because a false value will mean that the lock hasn't been acquired due to an expired timeout.

The following lines show a new version of the code that tries to acquire the lock with a timeout and runs the critical section. The next line after the call to the `Monitor.TryEnter` method checks whether `lockTaken` is `false`, and if so, it throws a `TimeoutException`. In this case, the exception isn't caught, so each task that cannot acquire the lock will be faulted and will stop its execution.

```csharp
bool lockTaken = false;
try
{
    Monitor.TryEnter(sb, 2000, ref lockTaken);
    if (!lockTaken)
    {
        // It was not possible to acquire the lock
        // within the 2000 milliseconds timeout
        Console.WriteLine(
            "Lock timeout for participant: {0}",
            participantNumber);
        throw new TimeoutException(
            String.Format(
                "Participants are requiring more than {0} seconds " +
                "to acquire the lock at the Phase # {1}.",
                2000, _barrier.CurrentPhaseNumber));
    }
    // Monitor acquired a lock on sb
    // Critical section
    sb.Append(logLine);
    // Spin until there aren't remaining participants
    // for the current phase
    // This should never be used inside a critical region
    SpinWait.SpinUntil(() => (_barrier.ParticipantsRemaining == 0));
    // End of critical section
}
finally
{
    // You need to make sure that
    // you release the lock on sb
    if (lockTaken)
    {
        // Gives up the lock if it actually acquired it
        Monitor.Exit(sb);
    }
}
```

code snippet from Snippet5_8

This example leaves the task that executes the `SpinWait.SpinUntil` method running forever. In fact, this task runs forever to make it possible to test the timeout in the other tasks that want to acquire the lock that the task that is spinning and waiting never does leave. You already know how to add code to cancel tasks when something goes wrong and how to add cleanup code.

> *Whenever possible, you should use a timeout to avoid a difficult-to-detect dead-lock situation. When it isn't possible to acquire a lock in a specified timeout, you can use a `CancellationToken` instance to cancel the task that causes the problems. It is also important to add the necessary cleanup code.*

The `Monitor` class provides the following three additional methods that allow you to send notifications about locks to other threads and block threads until they reacquire a lock. However, you must be very careful when you use these methods, because an error on a notification can lead to a task or thread blocked forever.

➤ `Pulse` — Notifies a change in the state for the object with the lock received as a parameter to a thread in the waiting queue that called `Monitor.Wait` with the object as a parameter.

➤ `PulseAll` — Notifies a change in the state for the object with the lock received as a parameter to all the threads in the waiting queue that called `Monitor.Wait` with the object as a parameter.

➤ `Wait` — Releases the lock on the object received as a parameter and blocks the current thread until it reacquires this lock. This will only happen after the wait has been pulsed. The `Wait` method has many overrides that allow you to define a timeout in order to avoid having the thread waiting forever to reacquire the lock.

Refactoring Code to Avoid Locks

You can avoid using locks by refactoring the previous example to generate the log string without creating a critical section. The following lines show a new version of the code that creates an independent string log for each participant and returns it as a result of each `Task` instance. Now, each task is a `Task<string>` instance, which calls the `AppendFormat` method for a local `StringBuilder` instance named *localsb*. This way, each task returns its own string log, making it unnecessary to acquire a lock to access a shared `StringBuilder` instance. The *finalTask* generates the final string log by appending the individual string logs held in the `Result` property for each `Task` instance that finished its execution.

Available for download on Wrox.com

```
// Each participant must return its log string
private static Task<string>[] _tasks;

static void Main(string[] args)
{
    _tasks = new Task<string>[_participants];
    _barrier = new Barrier(_participants, (barrier) =>
    {
        Console.WriteLine("Current phase: {0}",
            barrier.CurrentPhaseNumber);
    });

    for (int i = 0; i < _participants; i++)
```

```csharp
            {
                _tasks[i] = Task<string>.Factory.StartNew((num) =>
                {
                    var localsb = new StringBuilder();
                    var participantNumber = (int)num;
                    for (int j = 0; j < 10; j++)
                    {
                        CreatePlanets(participantNumber);
                        _barrier.SignalAndWait();
                        CreateStars(participantNumber);
                        _barrier.SignalAndWait();
                        CheckCollisionsBetweenPlanets(participantNumber);
                        _barrier.SignalAndWait();
                        CheckCollisionsBetweenStars(participantNumber);
                        _barrier.SignalAndWait();
                        RenderCollisions(participantNumber);
                        _barrier.SignalAndWait();

                        localsb.AppendFormat(
"Time: {0}, Phase: {1}, Participant: {2}, Phase completed OK\n",
                            DateTime.Now.TimeOfDay,
                            _barrier.CurrentPhaseNumber,
                            participantNumber);
                    }
                    return localsb.ToString();
                }, i);
            }

        var finalTask = Task.Factory.ContinueWhenAll(_tasks, (tasks) =>
        {
            // Wait for all the tasks to ensure
            // the propagation of any exception occurred
            // in any of the _tasks
            // The code should observe potential exceptions
            // This example doesn't observe exceptions for simplicity
            Task.WaitAll(_tasks);
            Console.WriteLine(
                "All the phases were executed.");

            // Collect the results
            var finalsb = new StringBuilder();
            for (int t = 0; t < _participants; t++)
            {
                if ((!_tasks[t].IsFaulted) && (!_tasks[t].IsCanceled))
                {
                    finalsb.Append(_tasks[t].Result);
                }
            }
            // Display the final string
            Console.WriteLine(finalsb);

            // Dispose the Barrier instance
            _barrier.Dispose();
```

```
    });

    // Wait for finalTask to finish
    finalTask.Wait();

    Console.ReadLine();
}
```

code snippet from Snippet5_9

The following lines are the results of displaying the contents of the StringBuilder *finalsb* instance that appended the information from all the participants in the *finalTask*:

```
Time: 18:58:23.0931808, Phase: 5, Participant: 0, Phase completed OK
Time: 18:58:23.1087808, Phase: 10, Participant: 0, Phase completed OK
Time: 18:58:23.1243809, Phase: 15, Participant: 0, Phase completed OK
Time: 18:58:23.1399809, Phase: 20, Participant: 0, Phase completed OK
Time: 18:58:23.1555809, Phase: 25, Participant: 0, Phase completed OK
Time: 18:58:23.1711810, Phase: 30, Participant: 0, Phase completed OK
Time: 18:58:23.1867810, Phase: 35, Participant: 0, Phase completed OK
Time: 18:58:23.2023810, Phase: 40, Participant: 0, Phase completed OK
Time: 18:58:23.2023810, Phase: 45, Participant: 0, Phase completed OK
Time: 18:58:23.2179810, Phase: 50, Participant: 0, Phase completed OK
Time: 18:58:23.0775808, Phase: 5, Participant: 1, Phase completed OK
Time: 18:58:23.1087808, Phase: 10, Participant: 1, Phase completed OK
Time: 18:58:23.1243809, Phase: 15, Participant: 1, Phase completed OK
Time: 18:58:23.1399809, Phase: 20, Participant: 1, Phase completed OK
Time: 18:58:23.1555809, Phase: 25, Participant: 1, Phase completed OK
Time: 18:58:23.1711810, Phase: 30, Participant: 1, Phase completed OK
Time: 18:58:23.1867810, Phase: 35, Participant: 1, Phase completed OK
Time: 18:58:23.2023810, Phase: 40, Participant: 1, Phase completed OK
Time: 18:58:23.2023810, Phase: 45, Participant: 1, Phase completed OK
Time: 18:58:23.2179810, Phase: 50, Participant: 1, Phase completed OK
Time: 18:58:23.0775808, Phase: 5, Participant: 2, Phase completed OK
Time: 18:58:23.1087808, Phase: 10, Participant: 2, Phase completed OK
Time: 18:58:23.1243809, Phase: 15, Participant: 2, Phase completed OK
Time: 18:58:23.1399809, Phase: 20, Participant: 2, Phase completed OK
Time: 18:58:23.1555809, Phase: 25, Participant: 2, Phase completed OK
Time: 18:58:23.1711810, Phase: 30, Participant: 2, Phase completed OK
Time: 18:58:23.1867810, Phase: 35, Participant: 2, Phase completed OK
Time: 18:58:23.2023810, Phase: 40, Participant: 2, Phase completed OK
Time: 18:58:23.2023810, Phase: 45, Participant: 2, Phase completed OK
Time: 18:58:23.2179810, Phase: 50, Participant: 2, Phase completed OK
Time: 18:58:23.0775808, Phase: 5, Participant: 3, Phase completed OK
Time: 18:58:23.1087808, Phase: 10, Participant: 3, Phase completed OK
Time: 18:58:23.1243809, Phase: 15, Participant: 3, Phase completed OK
Time: 18:58:23.1399809, Phase: 20, Participant: 3, Phase completed OK
Time: 18:58:23.1555809, Phase: 25, Participant: 3, Phase completed OK
Time: 18:58:23.1711810, Phase: 30, Participant: 3, Phase completed OK
Time: 18:58:23.1867810, Phase: 35, Participant: 3, Phase completed OK
Time: 18:58:23.2023810, Phase: 40, Participant: 3, Phase completed OK
Time: 18:58:23.2023810, Phase: 45, Participant: 3, Phase completed OK
Time: 18:58:23.2179810, Phase: 50, Participant: 3, Phase completed OK
```

In this case, the strings aren't going to be ordered by time as they were in the previous example. However, you can order them in an additional operation. The new code without locks has the following advantages over the previous version:

➤ It is simpler, because there is no need to create a critical section. This way, the code is less error-prone.

➤ It is more scalable, because there is no need to spin and wait for locks to be acquired, and there is no serialization of the code that builds each string log.

However, the code without locks has the following disadvantages:

➤ It requires more memory, because instead of using a single `StringBuilder` instance to create the string log, it uses one per participant plus one final `StringBuilder` instance to collect the results.

➤ It adds overhead to collect the results from each task and to produce the final string log. This overhead runs with a serial execution.

➤ It generates an unordered string log. If you want it to be ordered, you need to add another operation, a sort.

 This example demonstrated that, in some cases, locks may be avoidable. To choose the most convenient alternative, you need to analyze the aforementioned advantages and disadvantages. Sometimes, it is convenient to avoid locks, but in certain situations, the additional memory consumption and the new overhead required by the lock-free alternative can be prohibitive. Remember to use profiling features to help you choose the most convenient option.

In this case, there is another alternative: You can use one of the new concurrent collections that you learned about in the previous chapter in order to add each new string for the log. A concurrent collection eliminates the need to add your explicit synchronization, because it is already prepared for concurrent addition and removal of elements.

USING SPIN LOCKS AS MUTUAL-EXCLUSION LOCK PRIMITIVES

When lock hold times are always extremely short and locks are fine-grained, a spin lock can offer better performance than other locking mechanisms. Sometimes, profiling and other performance monitoring demonstrates that the `Monitor` mutual-exclusion locks are too expensive. In such cases, you can test the results of replacing the `Monitor` locks with spin locks.

The following lines show a new version of the first part of the `Main` method presented in Listing 5-1. This new version uses a `SpinLock` instance named `sl` to acquire a lock and run code in a critical section, and adds information to a log string by using a `StringBuilder` named `sb` in all the barrier's participants. The `SpinLock` instance and its methods replace the `Monitor` methods to acquire and release the lock. However, this doesn't mean that `SpinLock` is a better alternative than `Monitor` — it depends on the situation. In fact, `StringBuilder` requires memory allocation, and therefore, it may take an unknown amount of time, potentially including paging that can require a lot of CPU cycles. It isn't a good idea to use the `StringBuilder`'s `Append` method in a critical section with `SpinLock`. The following lines show you how to modify the code to change from `Monitor` to `SpinLock`.

```csharp
static void Main(string[] args)
{
    _tasks = new Task[_participants];
    _barrier = new Barrier(_participants, (barrier) =>
    {
        Console.WriteLine("Current phase: {0}",
            barrier.CurrentPhaseNumber);
    });

    // You pass false for enableThreadOwnerTracking
    // because you want the best performance out of SpinLock
    var sl = new SpinLock(false);
    var sb = new StringBuilder();

    for (int i = 0; i < _participants; i++)
    {
        _tasks[i] = Task.Factory.StartNew((num) =>
        {
            var participantNumber = (int)num;
            for (int j = 0; j < 10; j++)
            {
                CreatePlanets(participantNumber);
                _barrier.SignalAndWait();
                CreateStars(participantNumber);
                _barrier.SignalAndWait();
                CheckCollisionsBetweenPlanets(participantNumber);
                _barrier.SignalAndWait();
                CheckCollisionsBetweenStars(participantNumber);
                _barrier.SignalAndWait();
                RenderCollisions(participantNumber);
                _barrier.SignalAndWait();

                var logLine =
                    String.Format(
"Time: {0}, Phase: {1}, Participant: {2}, Phase completed OK\n",
                        DateTime.Now.TimeOfDay,
                        _barrier.CurrentPhaseNumber,
                        participantNumber);

                bool lockTaken = false;
                try
                {
                    sl.Enter(ref lockTaken);
                    // SpinLock acquired a lock
                    // Critical section
                    sb.Append(logLine);
                    // End of critical section
                }
                finally
                {
```

```
                        // You need to make sure that
                        // you release the lock
                        if (lockTaken)
                        {
                            // Gives up the lock if it actually acquired it
                            // You want performance at the expense of fairness
                            // Therefore, you pass false for useMemoryBarrier
                            sl.Exit(false);
                        }
                    }
                }
        }, i);
    }

    var finalTask = Task.Factory.ContinueWhenAll(_tasks, (tasks) =>
    {
        // Wait for all the tasks to ensure
        // the propagation of any exception occurred
        // in any of the _tasks
        Task.WaitAll(_tasks);
        Console.WriteLine(
            "All the phases were executed.");
        Console.WriteLine(sb);
        // Dispose the Barrier instance
        _barrier.Dispose();
    });

    // Wait for finalTask to finish
    finalTask.Wait();

    Console.ReadLine();
}
```

code snippet from Snippet5_10

The output will be equivalent to the results displayed by the example that uses Monitor to acquire and release locks instead of SpinLock. The final contents of the StringBuilder *sb* instance contain the information from all the participants in the critical section.

The code passes false as a parameter to the constructor for the SpinLock structure and stores this instance in the *sl* local variable that is going to be shared by all the participant tasks. The false value disables the option that tracks thread IDs for debugging purposes. When you want the best performance out of SpinLock, you can pass false to the constructor, as in the previous example.

SpinLock makes sure that the critical section is going to be serialized, and therefore, it is safe to call the Append method after SpinLock acquires a mutual-exclusion lock. Each participant sets the *lockTaken* bool variable to false and then calls the Enter method for the SpinLock *sl* instance with lockTaken by reference as its parameter. A try…finally block makes sure that the lock is released if something goes wrong. At this point, the Enter method is going to try to acquire the lock, and if it can't, the task will wait in a loop and repeatedly check for the lock to become available. It will spin until it can acquire the lock. Once it acquires the lock, lockTaken will change to true, and the line after // Critical section will run. If other tasks call the Enter method at this time, they will start spinning until the task that is running the critical section calls the `Exit` method for the `SpinLock` `sl` instance in order to release the lock. Therefore, it is very important to make sure that this method is always called, even if an exception occurs in the critical section. The code in the `finally` section checks whether `lockTaken` is `true` to release the lock by calling the `Exit` method only if it actually acquired it. After this line is executed, one of the other tasks will be able to acquire a lock and perform the same sequence. In order to immediately publish the exit operation to other threads, the code passes `false` to a parameter to the `Exit` method to indicate that a memory fence should not be issued. Because `SpinLock` doesn't use the memory barrier, you gain performance at the expense of fairness.

Available for download on Wrox.com

```
bool lockTaken = false;
try
{
    sl.Enter(ref lockTaken);
    // SpinLock acquired a lock
    // Critical section
    sb.Append(logLine);
    // End of critical section
}
finally
{
    // You need to make sure that
    // you release the lock
    if (lockTaken)
    {
        // Gives up the lock if it actually acquired it
        // You want performance at the expense of fairness
        // Therefore, you pass false for useMemoryBarrier
        sl.Exit(false);
    }
}
```

code snippet from Snippet5_11

 Don't declare a `SpinLock` as a `readonly` field because doing so can cause every call to the field to return a new copy of the `SpinLock` instead of the original one. All the calls to the `Enter` method succeed in acquiring the lock, and the protected critical sections aren't serialized as expected.

Working with Timeouts

As you previously learned with `Monitor` locks, `SpinLock` provides methods to try to acquire a lock within a specified timeout. You can establish a timeout using the `TryEnter` method instead of `Enter` for the `SpinLock` `sl` instance. One of its definitions accepts the number of milliseconds to wait as its first parameter and the `bool` variable as the second parameter. Unlike `Enter`, `TryEnter` won't block indefinitely while waiting for the lock to be available. It will block until either the lock is available or the specified timeout has expired. Therefore, it is necessary to check the value for the `bool` variable after calling `TryEnter`, because a false value will mean that the lock hasn't been acquired due to an expired timeout.

The following lines show a new version of the code that tries to acquire the lock within a 2000 millisecond timeout and runs the critical section. The next line after the call to the `TryEnter` method checks whether `lockTaken` is `false`, and if so, it throws a `TimeoutException`. In this case, the exception isn't caught, so the task will be faulted and will stop its execution.

```
bool lockTaken = false;
try
{
    sl.TryEnter(2000, ref lockTaken);
    if (!lockTaken)
    {
        // It was not possible to acquire the lock
        Console.WriteLine(
            "Lock timeout for participant: {0}",
            participantNumber);
        throw new TimeoutException(
            String.Format(
"Participants are requiring more than {0} seconds " +
"to acquire the lock at the Phase # {1}.",
            2000, _barrier.CurrentPhaseNumber));
    }
    // SpinLock acquired a lock
    // Critical section
    sb.Append(logLine);
    // End of critical section
}
finally
{
    // You need to make sure that
    // you release the lock
    if (lockTaken)
    {
        // Gives up the lock if it actually acquired it
        // SpinLock doesn't
        // You want performance at the expense of fairness
        // Therefore, you pass false for useMemoryBarrier
        sl.Exit(false);
    }
}
```

code snippet from Snippet5_12

Working with Spin-Based Waiting

When you have to wait for a short time until a specified condition is satisfied and you don't want an expensive context-switch to happen, spin-based waiting can be a good alternative. The `SpinWait` type offers basic spinning functionality and provides the `SpinUntil` method to spin until a specified condition is satisfied. In addition, `SpinWait` is a `struct` and just a single `Int32` in size. It doesn't generate unnecessary allocation overheads. Its usage is cheap from a memory perspective.

Spinning for a long time isn't a good idea, because it blocks higher-priority threads and their related tasks or the garbage collector. Instead, `SpinWait` will yield the time slice of the underlying thread and initiate context switches when spinning is long enough. This synchronization type is designed to provide correct spinning behavior for most cases, without getting confused with a simple loop behavior. It offers a smart behavior that will decide when to stop spinning and initiate a context switch. This context switch is expensive, but it is more expensive to continue spinning for a long time. SpinWait usually stops spinning after it has been doing it for the length of time required for a kernel transition. SpinLock is just a thin wrapper around SpinWait.

When a thread is spinning, it puts one of the cores into a tight loop, and it doesn't yield the rest of its current time slice of processor time. However, as previously explained, the smart logic included in the SpinWait structure stops spinning and yields when spinning is long enough. When a task or a thread calls the Thread.Sleep method, the underlying thread might yield the rest of its current slice of processor time, which is expensive. Thus, in most cases, you don't call Thread.Sleep inside a loop to wait until a specified condition is satisfied. However, it is important to notice that if you pass 0 to Thread.Sleep, the current thread might be suspended to allow other waiting threads to execute.

Chapter 4, "Concurrent Collections," introduced ConcurrentBag and presented an example that launched three methods concurrently, representing producers and consumers. CapitalizeWordsInSentences is a consumer of ProduceSentences and a producer for RemoveLettersInSentences. It uses the SpinWait.SpinUntil method to wait until the shared bool variable _producingSententes is true to begin working, as shown here:

```
private static void CapitalizeWordsInSentences()
{
    char[] delimiterChars = {
        ' ', ',', '.', ':', ';', '(', ')', '[', ']', '{', '}',
        '/', '?', '@', '\t', '"' };

    // Start after Produce sentences began working
    System.Threading.SpinWait.SpinUntil(() => _producingSentences);

    try
    {
        _capitalizingWords = true;
        // This condition running in a loop (spinning) is very inefficient
        // This example uses this spinning for educational purposes
        // It isn't a best practice, as explained in Chapter 4
        // Chapter 4 explained an improved version
        while ((!_sentencesBag.IsEmpty) || (_producingSentences))
        {
            string sentence;
            if (_sentencesBag.TryTake(out sentence))
            {
                _capWordsInSentencesBag.Add(
                    CapitalizeWords(delimiterChars, sentence, '\\'));
            }
        }
    }
    finally
    {
        _capitalizingWords = false;
    }
}
```

code snippet from Snippet5_13

If _producingSentences never becomes true, the task that runs the CapitalizeWordsInSentences will stay blocked forever. It is simple to understand this situation by commenting the line of code for the ProduceSentences method that assigns the true value for that variable:

```
private static void ProduceSentences()
{

    string[] possibleSentences =
    {
"ConcurrentBag is included in the System.Concurrent.Collections namespace.",
"Is parallelism important for cloud-computing?",
"Parallelism is very important for cloud-computing!",
"ConcurrentQueue is one of the new concurrent collections added in .NET
Framework 4",
"ConcurrentStack is a concurrent collection that represents a LIFO collection",
"ConcurrentQueue is a concurrent collection that represents a FIFO collection"
    };

    try
    {
        //_producingSentences = true;
    ...
```

code snippet from Snippet5_14

The tasks that run the two consumers, CapitalizeWordsInSentences and RemoveLettersInSentences, wait forever. The delegate specified in the SpinWait.SpinUntil method never returns true. If you use the Break All command to stop the execution and display the Parallel Tasks window by selecting Debug ⇨ Windows ⇨ Parallel Tasks, the status will be one task running the ProduceSentences method, and the other two tasks will be Waiting, as shown in Figure 5-13. The problem with this is that they are going to keep waiting forever, and the main thread is also going to stay waiting for the Parallel.Invoke method to finish — therefore, the application will never end its execution.

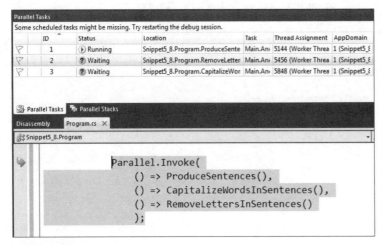

FIGURE 5-13

You can use another definition for the SpinWait.SpinUntil method that accepts the number of milliseconds to wait as the second parameter. The method returns a bool value that indicates whether the delegate returned true within the specified time. The following code shows a new version of the CapitalizeWordsInSentences method that uses a timeout to be able to stop waiting after 5 seconds:

Available for download on Wrox.com

```
// 5,000 milliseconds = 5 seconds timeout
private const int TIMEOUT = 5000;

private static void CapitalizeWordsInSentences()
{
    char[] delimiterChars = {
        ' ', ',', '.', ':', ';', '(', ')', '[', ']', '{', '}',
        '/', '?', '@', '\t', '"' };

    // Start after Produce sentences began working
    // use a 5 seconds timeout
    if (!System.Threading.SpinWait.SpinUntil(
        () => _producingSentences, TIMEOUT))
    {
        throw new TimeoutException(
            String.Format(
                "CapitalizeWordsInSentences has been waiting " +
                "for {0} seconds to access sentences.",
                TIMEOUT));
    }
    ...
```

code snippet from Snippet5_15

In this case, the SpinWait.SpinUntil method will wait 5 seconds for *_producingSentences* to become true, and after this time, the method will return false. The code throws a TimeoutException, and the task that called it is going to be faulted. The code needs a cancellation mechanism, and the Main method should check the status for the tasks and catch the AggregateException, as explained in previous examples.

Spinning and Yielding

The previous example used the SpinWait.SpinUntil method. You can create a SpinWait instance and use its methods and properties to provide basic spinning functionality and determine whether a new spin will yield the time slice of the underlying thread and initiate a context switch. A SpinWait instance offers the following two additional methods:

➤ Reset — Resets the spin counter. This way, the Count property will be 0, and it will start counting spins again as though no calls to SpinOnce had been issued on the SpinWait instance.

➤ SpinOnce — Performs a single spin. However, after a certain number of spins performed by the SpinWait instance, it will yield the time slice of the underlying thread and initiate a context switch if necessary. So, its behavior changes according to the number of times it has been executed.

A `SpinWait` instance exposes the following two read-only properties:

➤   `Count` — Provides the number of times the `SpinWait` instance performed a single spin through the `SpinOnce` method.

➤   `NextSpinWillYield` — Offers a `bool` value indicating whether the next spin through the `SpinOnce` method will yield the time slice of the underlying thread and initiate a context switch.

> `SpinWait` *isn't designed to be used with multiple tasks or threads concurrently. Therefore, if multiple tasks or threads have to use its methods to spin, each one should use its own instance of* `SpinWait`*. However, you don't want to use it from multiple threads because of its back-off spinning logic.*

The following lines show the first part of a new version of the `ProduceSentences` method. It runs a loop that calls the `SpinOnce` method for a local `SpinWait` instance, *spinW*, 150 times to waste some time before assigning `true` to the *_producingSentences* variable. This way, the underlying thread is going to spin and yield.

```
private static void ProduceSentences()
{

    string[] possibleSentences =
    {
"ConcurrentBag is included in the System.Concurrent.Collections namespace.",
"Is parallelism important for cloud-computing?",
"Parallelism is very important for cloud-computing!",
"ConcurrentQueue is one of the new concurrent collections added in .NET
Framework 4",
"ConcurrentStack is a concurrent collection that represents a LIFO collection",
"ConcurrentQueue is a concurrent collection that represents a FIFO collection"
    };

    try
    {
        Console.WriteLine("ProduceSentences is going to run {0} times",
NUM_SENTENCES);
        var spinW = new SpinWait();
        // Spin 150 times
        for (int w = 0; w < 150; w++)
        {
            spinW.SpinOnce();
        }

        _producingSentences = true;
...
```

code snippet from Snippet5_16

The following lines show the first part of a new version of the `CapitalizeWordsInSentences` method. It calls the `SpinOnce` method for a local `SpinWait` instance, *spinW*, while *_producingSentences* is `false`. It checks the value of the `NextSpinWillYield` property to determine whether the next spin is going to yield or not. If the spin yields, the method increments the value for *contextSwitches*. It uses a `Stopwatch` instance to establish a timeout in order to prevent the `while` block from running forever if *_producingSentences* doesn't become `true`.

```
// 5,000 milliseconds = 5 seconds timeout
private const int TIMEOUT = 5000;

private static void CapitalizeWordsInSentences()
{
    char[] delimiterChars = {
        ' ', ',', '.', ':', ';', '(', ')', '[', ']', '{', '}',
        '/', '?', '@', '\t', '"' };

    var spinW = new SpinWait();
    // The number of times the SpinOnce method yields
    int contextSwitches = 0;
    var sw = Stopwatch.StartNew();
    // This example uses this spinning for educational purposes
    // It isn't a best practice
    while (!_producingSentences)
    {
        if (spinW.NextSpinWillYield)
        {
            // The SpinWait instance
            // is ready to initiate a context-switch
            contextSwitches++;
        }
        spinW.SpinOnce();
        if (sw.ElapsedMilliseconds >= TIMEOUT)
        {
            throw new TimeoutException(
                String.Format(
                    "CapitalizeWordsInSentences has been waiting " +
                    "for {0} seconds to access sentences.",
                    TIMEOUT));
        }
    }
    Console.WriteLine(
        "CapitalizeWordsInSentences has called SpinOnce {0} times.",
        spinW.Count);
    Console.WriteLine(
        "It yielded the time slice {0} times.", contextSwitches);
    ...
```

code snippet from Snippet5_17

This sample code doesn't try to show an efficient way of spinning until a condition is satisfied, because the `SpinWait.SpinUntil` method you learned about previously is usually more convenient.

Instead, it demonstrates the spinning behavior of a `SpinWait` instance and its methods and properties.

When *_producingSentences* becomes `true`, the method displays the number of times it called the `SpinOnce` method and the number of times the underlying thread yielded. You need to make changes to other methods for this application because if a `TimeoutException` is thrown, this method will never set *_capitalizingWords* to `true`. However, the purpose of this example is to help you understand spinning and yielding.

The results will vary according to the underlying hardware and the application running on the operating system. The only fixed variable is the timeout, established in 5 seconds. However, spinning and yielding depends on the CPU processing capabilities. The following lines display the first results of running the code shown in the previous snippets. In this case, `SpinOnce` ran 134 times and yielded 123 times.

```
ProduceSentences is going to run 2000000 times
CapitalizeWordsInSentences has called SpinOnce 134 times.
It yielded the time slice 123 times.
```

If you run the code many times, the results might be different. In fact, on some computers, it could even be necessary to spin more times in the `ProduceSentences` method in order to make `CapitalizeWordsInSentences` spin if *_producingSentences* is `false`.

`SpinWait` will always yield when it runs on a single-core computer. Spinning is typically useless in single-core computers, because there is just one core, and that core is occupied with the thread that calls `SpinWait`'s methods. There is no other core capable of running concurrent code to change the condition that the spinning is monitoring. Remember the differences between interleaved concurrency and concurrency that were explained in Chapter 1, "Task-Based Programming."

In most cases, you can decide to stop spinning before yielding, and you can use a lightweight manual reset event to notify other tasks or threads that an event has occurred by signaling. Signaling is more expensive than spinning. However, you can use a combination of spinning until it is time to yield and signal. Yielding is expensive and it wouldn't make sense to continue spinning and yielding all the time because of the expense. Remember that the `SpinWait.SpinUntil` method provides a smart behavior that offers good results when wait times are extremely short.

 Whenever possible, try to use the synchronization primitives offered by the framework. Create your own customized mechanisms only if you believe that the default behavior isn't suitable for your needs and you know what you are doing. Appendix C, "Parallel Extensions Extras," provides information about additional coordination data structures. Check this appendix before creating your own mechanisms.

Using the Volatile Modifier

In the previous spinning and yielding examples, there is a task that monitors the value for the *_producingSentences* variable, and another concurrent task modifies its `bool` value. Each of these tasks runs in a different concurrent thread. The thread that runs the `ProduceSentences` method changes the value for _producingSentences_. The code doesn't use mutual-exclusion locks or atomic updates to serialize the update of the `bool` value for this shared variable.

The code that declares this variable uses the `volatile` keyword as a modifier in order to avoid compiler optimizations that assume that the field is going to be accessed by a single thread:

```
private static volatile bool _producingSentences = false;
```

The volatile keyword ensures that the most up-to-date value will be present in the shared variable at all times when accessed from different threads and updated without locks or atomic operations. In this example, the thread that is consuming the produced sentences will be able to read the change for the `bool` variable faster than the same code subject to the default compiler optimizations.

 You can apply this modifier to fields for classes or structs. You can't declare local variables with the `volatile` *keyword.*

You can apply the `volatile` modifier to `bool`, integral types, enum types with an integral base type, reference types, generic type parameters known to be reference types, pointer types in unsafe contexts, and platform-specific types that represent a pointer or a handle such as `IntPtr` and `UIntPtr`. A volatile pointer only affects the pointer — not the object that it points to. The same happens with volatile references.

WORKING WITH LIGHTWEIGHT MANUAL RESET EVENTS

If you expect wait times to be very short, the new lightweight manual reset event, `ManualResetEventSlim`, allows you to signal and wait for *event handles*. Because its heavyweight counterpart, `ManualResetEvent`, is more expensive, you can use the combination of spinning and kernel-based wait provided by this new slimmed-down version when wait times aren't long. This version is also more appropriate for a task-based programming model.

A *manual reset event* is an event object with two possible states: set/signaled (`true`) or unset/nonsignaled (`false`). This object allows one task to send a signal to another task, indicating that an event has occurred. This signaling mechanism happens at the underlying threads' level; however, you already know that each task needs a thread to run its concurrent code. While one task sends a signal, another task can use `Wait` functions to wait for the state of an event object to be signaled. The `Wait` functions block the task and its underlying thread until the event object is signaled or a specified timeout expires.

Working with ManualResetEventSlim to Spin and Wait

`ManualResetEventSlim` offers a combination of spinning and kernel-based waiting with event wait handles that encapsulate a manual reset event. You can use an instance of this class to send signals between tasks and to wait for them to occur. Listing 5-2 shows a new version of the previous `SpinWait.SpinUntil` example that replaces the usage of this method and a shared `bool volatile` variable with the usage of `ManualResetEventSlim` instances. The new code uses signaling mechanisms to let tasks know that they can start their work. Remember that this code should also catch the potential `AggregateException` that could be thrown by the `Parallel.Invoke` method.

LISTING 5-2: Using ManualResetEventSlim instances to send signals and wait

```
// This code has references to two methods presented in
// Listing 4-7: RemoveLetters and CapitalizeWords

private const int NUM_SENTENCES = 2000000;
private static ConcurrentBag<string> _sentencesBag;
private static ConcurrentBag<string> _capWordsInSentencesBag;
private static ConcurrentBag<string> _finalSentencesBag;

private static ManualResetEventSlim _mresProduceSentences;
private static ManualResetEventSlim _mresCapitalizeWords;

private static void ProduceSentences()
{

    string[] possibleSentences =
    {
"ConcurrentBag is included in the System.Collections.Conncurrent namespace.",
"Is parallelism important for cloud-computing?",
"Parallelism is very important for cloud-computing!",
"ConcurrentQueue is one of the new concurrent collections added in .NET Framework 4",
"ConcurrentStack is a concurrent collection that represents a LIFO collection",
"ConcurrentQueue is a concurrent collection that represents a FIFO collection"
    };

    try
    {
        // Signal/Set
        _mresProduceSentences.Set();

        var rnd = new Random();

        for (int i = 0; i < NUM_SENTENCES; i++)
        {
            var sb = new StringBuilder();
            for (int j = 0; j < possibleSentences.Length; j++)
            {
                if (rnd.Next(2) > 0)
                {
                    sb.Append(possibleSentences[
                        rnd.Next(possibleSentences.Length)]);
                    sb.Append(' ');
                }
            }
            if (rnd.Next(20) > 15)
            {
                _sentencesBag.Add(sb.ToString());
            }
```

```csharp
                else
                {
                    _sentencesBag.Add(sb.ToString().ToUpper());
                }
            }
        }
        finally
        {
            // Switch to nonsignaled/unset
            _mresProduceSentences.Reset();
        }
    }

    // 5,000 milliseconds = 5 seconds timeout
    private const int TIMEOUT = 5000;

    private static void CapitalizeWordsInSentences()
    {
        char[] delimiterChars = { ' ', ',', '.', ':', ';', '(', ')',
            '[', ']', '{', '}', '/', '?', '@', '\t', '"' };

        // Start after ProduceSentences began working
        // Wait for _mresProduceSentences to become signaled
        _mresProduceSentences.Wait();

        try
        {
            // Signal/Set
            _mresCapitalizeWords.Set();
            // This condition running in a loop (spinning)
            // is very inefficient
            // This example uses this spinning for educational purposes
            // It isn't a best practice, as explained in Chapter 4
            // Chapter 4 explained an improved version
            while ((!_sentencesBag.IsEmpty) ||
                    (_mresProduceSentences.IsSet))
            {
                string sentence;
                if (_sentencesBag.TryTake(out sentence))
                {
                    _capWordsInSentencesBag.Add(
                        CapitalizeWords(
                            delimiterChars, sentence, '\\'));
                }
            }
        }
        finally
        {
            // Switch to nonsignaled/unset
            _mresCapitalizeWords.Reset();
        }
    }

    private static void RemoveLettersInSentences()
    {
```

continues

LISTING 5-2 *(continued)*

```
    char[] letterChars =
        { 'A', 'B', 'C', 'e', 'i', 'j', 'm', 'X', 'y', 'Z' };

    // Start after CapitalizeWordsInSentences began working
    // Wait for _mresCapitalizeWords to become signaled
    _mresCapitalizeWords.Wait();

    // This condition running in a loop (spinning)
    // is very inefficient
    // This example uses this spinning for educational purposes
    // It isn't a best practice, as explained in Chapter 4
    // Chapter 4 explained an improved version
    while ((!_capWordsInSentencesBag.IsEmpty) ||
           (_mresCapitalizeWords.IsSet))
    {
        string sentence;
        if (_capWordsInSentencesBag.TryTake(out sentence))
        {
            _finalSentencesBag.Add(
                RemoveLetters(letterChars, sentence));
        }
    }
}

static void Main(string[] args)
{
    var sw = Stopwatch.StartNew();

    _sentencesBag = new ConcurrentBag<string>();
    _capWordsInSentencesBag = new ConcurrentBag<string>();
    _finalSentencesBag = new ConcurrentBag<string>();

    // Construct the two ManualResetEventSlim instances
    // with a spincount of 100, it will spin-wait 100 times before
    // switching to a kernel-based wait
    _mresProduceSentences = new ManualResetEventSlim(false, 100);
    _mresCapitalizeWords = new ManualResetEventSlim(false, 100);

    try
    {
        Parallel.Invoke(
            () => ProduceSentences(),
            () => CapitalizeWordsInSentences(),
            () => RemoveLettersInSentences()
            );
    }
    finally
    {
        // Dispose the two ManualResetEventSlim instances
        _mresProduceSentences.Dispose();
        _mresCapitalizeWords.Dispose();
    }
```

```
            Console.WriteLine(
                "Number of sentences with capitalized words in the bag: {0}",
                _capWordsInSentencesBag.Count);
            Console.WriteLine(
                "Number of sentences with removed letters in the bag: {0}",
                _finalSentencesBag.Count);

            Debug.WriteLine(sw.Elapsed.ToString());
            //  Display the results and wait for the user to press a key
            Console.WriteLine("Finished!");
            Console.ReadLine();
        }
```

One of the `ManualResetEventSlim` constructors receives a `bool` value that represents the initial state as follows:

➤   `true` means set/signaled.

➤   `false` means unset/nonsignaled.

Another constructor receives the aforementioned value and a second `int` parameter indicating the number of spin waits that will occur before falling back to a kernel-based wait. The `Main` method uses this constructor to initialize the two `ManualResetEventSlim` instances, _mresProduceSentences_ and _mresCapitalizeWords_, with an initial unset/nonsignaled state and a spin count of 100 times, as shown in the next lines:

```
            _mresProduceSentences = new ManualResetEventSlim(false, 100);
            _mresCapitalizeWords = new ManualResetEventSlim(false, 100);
```

code snippet from Listing5_18

This way, when a task calls each instance's `Wait` method, it will perform up to 100 spins and, if the state doesn't change during this spin-wait process, it will start the kernel-based wait. The task that calls the `Wait` method will stay blocked until the state changes.

A `ManualResetEventSlim` instance offers the following methods:

➤   `Reset` — Sets the event to `false` (unset/nonsignaled).

➤   `Set` — Sets the event to `true` (set/signaled). If tasks called the `Wait` method, they will unblock once this method is called.

➤   `Wait` — Blocks the current task or thread until another task or thread sets the event for this `ManualResetEventSlim` instance to `true` (set/signaled) by calling its `Set` method. If the event is already set/signaled, it will return immediately. It will always perform a spin-wait process and then a kernel-based wait, even if no `spincount` was specified in the constructor. The `spincount` value in the constructor provides more control over how much spinning is employed so that you can tune your own usage based on performance profiling. The `Wait` method offers many definitions that allow you to send it a `CancellationToken` instance and/ or a timeout as an `int` or a `TimeSpan`.

A `ManualResetEventSlim` instance exposes the following three read-only properties:

➤ `IsSet` — Offers a `bool` value indicating whether the event is `true` (set/signaled).

➤ `SpinCount` — Provides the number of spin waits that will be performed before starting a kernel-based wait. It is the value specified in the constructor.

➤ `WaitHandle` — Provides the `WaitHandle` object that encapsulates the operating-system object. This object allows waiting for exclusive access to a shared resource.

Before the `ProduceSentences` method starts adding elements to the `_sentencesBag` ConcurrentBag, it sets/signals the initially nonsignaled/unset `_mresProduceSentences` ManualResetEventSlim by calling its `Set` method. The `CapitalizeWordsInSentences` method that runs in another task calls the `_mresProduceSentences.Wait` method, and the task will stay blocked until `_mresProduceSentences` is set/signaled. When `_mresProduceSentences` is set/signaled, the `CapitalizeWordsInSentences` method sets/signals the initially unset/nonsignaled `_mresCapitalizeWords` ManualResetEventSlim by calling its `Set` method, before the task starts adding elements to the `_capWordsInSentencesBag` ConcurrentBag. Then, the `CapitalizeWordsInSentences` method continues running the `while` block while `_sentencesBag` isn't empty or `_mresProduceSentences` is signaled.

There is no need to add a shared variable to use as a flag, because the `_mresProduceSentences.IsSet` property will be `true` while the `ManualResetEventSlim` is signaled. When the `ProduceSentences` method finishes adding elements to the `_sentencesBag` ConcurrentBag, it sets the event to nonsignaled in `_mresProduceSentences` ManualResetEventSlim by calling its `Reset` method. This way, the other task that is running the `while` block will get `false` when it checks the `_mresProduceSentences.IsSet` property. The call to the `Reset` method appears in the `finally` block — it is important to make sure that this method is called to avoid blocking other waiting tasks forever.

 You should always dispose a `ManualResetEventSlim` *instance when you have finished with it.*

Working with Timeouts and Cancellations

As previously mentioned, you should use timeouts and cancellations to avoid the problems caused by tasks blocked forever. Because there are many tasks waiting for `ManualResetEventSlim` instances to get signaled, if one task doesn't call the `Set` method, the other tasks will stay blocked forever. Initially, these tasks will start spinning, and then, they will stay in a kernel-wait forever. The following lines show a situation in which an exception occurs in the task that calls the `ProduceSentences` method. Because the code doesn't catch this exception, the next statement after the line that causes the exception doesn't run. This is the statement that calls the `_mresProduceSentences.Set` method and, as it doesn't run, the other two tasks will stay in the `Wait` method forever.

```
private static void ProduceSentences()
{

    string[] possibleSentences =
    {
"ConcurrentBag is included in the System.Concurrent.Collections namespace.",
```

```
"Is parallelism important for cloud-computing?",
"Parallelism is very important for cloud-computing!",
"ConcurrentQueue is one of the new concurrent collections added in .NET
Framework 4",
"ConcurrentStack is a concurrent collection that represents a LIFO collection",
"ConcurrentQueue is a concurrent collection that represents a FIFO collection"
    };

    // Wrong code that will produce an exception
    // It is difficult to detect this error at design-time
    Console.WriteLine("This is wrong {0} {1}", 1);
    // The next lines will never run because
    // an exception will occur in the previous one
    try
    {
        // Signal
        _mresProduceSentences.Set();
...
```

code snippet from Snippet5_19

The task that runs `ProduceSentences` will be faulted and will stop running. All the other tasks will stay in the `Wait` method, spinning and then waiting forever for the `ManualResetEventSlim` to be signaled. If you use the `Break All` command to stop the execution and display the Parallel Tasks window by selecting Debug ⇨ Windows ⇨ Parallel Tasks, the status for the two remaining tasks out of the three that were started by the `Parallel.Invoke` method will be `Waiting`, as shown in Figure 5-14. The problem is that they are going to keep waiting forever.

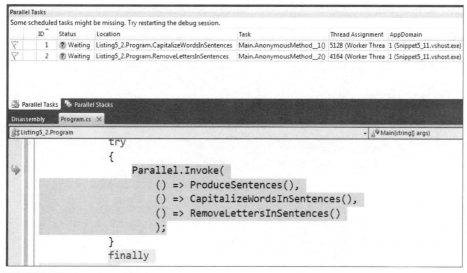

FIGURE 5-14

You can establish a timeout by sending the number of milliseconds as a parameter to the `Wait` method for each `ManualResetEventSlim` instance. This way, `Wait` won't block indefinitely waiting for the state of an event object to be signaled. Instead, it will block until either the state is signaled or the specified timeout has expired. However, you need to check the `bool` value returned by this method — a `false` value means that the timeout has been reached, and the state wasn't signaled.

The following lines show a new version of the code that produces an exception in the `ProduceSentences` method, but it sends a timeout in milliseconds as a parameter for both consumers, `CapitalizeWordsInSentences` and `RemoveLettersInSentences`. Thus, these methods call the `Wait` method for the corresponding `ManualResetEventSlim` instance with the timeout value received as a parameter, and if they return `false`, throw a `TimeoutException`. Because the exception isn't caught, the task will be faulted and will stop its execution. Now, the `Main` method has code that catches the three `InnerException` instances contained in the `AggregateException` as a result of calling `Parallel.Invoke` with the three actions that generate faulted tasks.

```
private static void CapitalizeWordsInSentences(int millisecondsTimeout)
{
    char[] delimiterChars = {
        ' ', ',', '.', ':', ';', '(', ')', '[', ']', '{',
        '}', '/', '?', '@', '\t', '"' };

    // Start after ProduceSentences began working
    // Wait for _mresProduceSentences to become signaled
    if (!_mresProduceSentences.Wait(millisecondsTimeout))
    {
        throw new TimeoutException(
            String.Format(
                "CapitalizeWordsInSentences has been waiting " +
                "for {0} seconds to access sentences.",
                millisecondsTimeout));
    }

    try
    {
        // Signal
        _mresCapitalizeWords.Set();
        while ((!_sentencesBag.IsEmpty) || (_mresProduceSentences.IsSet))
        {
            string sentence;
            if (_sentencesBag.TryTake(out sentence))
            {
                _capWordsInSentencesBag.Add(
                    CapitalizeWords(
                        delimiterChars, sentence, '\\'));
            }
        }
    }
    finally
    {
        // Switch to nonsignaled
        _mresCapitalizeWords.Reset();
    }
}

private static void RemoveLettersInSentences(int millisecondsTimeout)
{
    char[] letterChars =
```

```
            { 'A', 'B', 'C', 'e', 'i', 'j', 'm', 'X', 'y', 'Z' };

        // Start after CapitalizeWordsInSentences began working
        // Wait for _mresCapitalizeWords to become signaled
        if (!_mresCapitalizeWords.Wait(millisecondsTimeout))
        {
            throw new TimeoutException(
                String.Format(
                    " RemoveLettersInSentences has been waiting " +
                    "for {0} seconds to access sentences.",
                    millisecondsTimeout));
        }

        while ((!_capWordsInSentencesBag.IsEmpty) || (_mresCapitalizeWords.IsSet))
        {
            string sentence;
            if (_capWordsInSentencesBag.TryTake(out sentence))
            {
                _finalSentencesBag.Add(RemoveLetters(letterChars, sentence));
            }
        }
    }
}

private static ManualResetEventSlim _mresProduceSentences;
private static ManualResetEventSlim _mresCapitalizeWords;

// 5,000 milliseconds = 5 seconds timeout
private const int TIMEOUT = 5000;

static void Main(string[] args)
{
    var sw = Stopwatch.StartNew();

    _sentencesBag = new ConcurrentBag<string>();
    _capWordsInSentencesBag = new ConcurrentBag<string>();
    _finalSentencesBag = new ConcurrentBag<string>();

    // Construct the two ManualResetEventSlim instances
    // with a spincount of 100, it will spin-wait 100 times before
    // switching to a kernel-based wait
    _mresProduceSentences = new ManualResetEventSlim(false, 100);
    _mresCapitalizeWords = new ManualResetEventSlim(false, 100);

    try
    {
        Parallel.Invoke(
            () => ProduceSentences(),
            () => CapitalizeWordsInSentences(TIMEOUT),
            () => RemoveLettersInSentences(TIMEOUT)
            );
    }
    catch (AggregateException ex)
    {
        foreach (var innerEx in ex.InnerExceptions)
            Console.WriteLine(innerEx.Message);
```

```
            Console.WriteLine(
                "The producers/consumers failed their execution.");
        }
        finally
        {
            // Dispose the two ManualResetEventSlim instances
            _mresProduceSentences.Dispose();
            _mresCapitalizeWords.Dispose();
        }

        Console.WriteLine(
            "Number of sentences with capitalized words in the bag: {0}",
            _capWordsInSentencesBag.Count);
        Console.WriteLine(
            "Number of sentences with removed letters in the bag: {0}",
            _finalSentencesBag.Count);

        Debug.WriteLine(sw.Elapsed.ToString());
        // Display the results and wait for the user to press a key
        Console.WriteLine("Finished!");
        Console.ReadLine();
    }
```

code snippet from Snippet5_20

In this case, the first task that has to signal the state of an event object throws an exception; therefore, this code isn't executed. However, in other cases, the code that calls the `Set` method for a `ManualResetEventSlim` instance can't be executed because the task stays blocked for some other reason before this line. In order to avoid these complex problems, you can use the other definitions of the `Wait` method that accept both a timeout and a `CancellationToken` instance as parameters. Moreover, remember that creating `Task` instances instead of calling `Parallel.Invoke` would give you more control over the propagation of the cancellation to `Task` instances when something goes wrong.

For example, if a consumer task reached the timeout, it would send a signal to cancel the producer task. If you didn't cancel the producer, it would go on working when there were no active consumers in the next stages for the data being produced. You can use the techniques learned in the previous sections if you need to cancel the `Wait` method in `ManualResetEventSlim` instances.

Working with ManualResetEvent

When you need to do cross-process or cross-AppDomain synchronization, you must work with `ManualResetEvent` instead of `ManualResetEventSlim`. `ManualResetEvent` doesn't have the same members as `ManualResetEventSlim` — for example, it doesn't have the `IsSet` property to check whether the event is `true` (set/signaled), and it doesn't work with cancellation tokens. A `ManualResetEvent` instance offers the following methods that are equivalent to the methods explained for `ManualResetEventSlim`:

➤ `Reset` — Sets the event to `false` (nonsignaled).

➤ `Set` — Sets the event to `true` (signaled). If tasks called the `WaitOne` method, they will unblock once this method is called.

➤ `WaitOne` — Equivalent to the `Wait` method for `ManualResetEventSlim`. This method blocks the current task or thread until another task or thread sets the `EventWaitHandle` event for this `ManualResetEvent` instance by calling its `Set` method. If the event is already signaled, it will return immediately. It will always perform a kernel-based wait. The `WaitOne` method offers many definitions that allow you to send it a timeout as an `int` or a `TimeSpan`.

`ManualResetEvent` *provides more methods. However, the preceding list explains the most common methods that you will use when you just need to signal and wait for events in tasks.*

A `ManualResetEvent` instance exposes the `SafeWaitHandle` property that allows you to get or set the native operating system handle.

LIMITING CONCURRENCY TO ACCESS A RESOURCE

Sometimes, you need to limit the number of concurrent tasks or threads that can access a resource or a pool of resources. In these cases, the `System.Threading.Semaphore` class that represents a *counting semaphore* is usually helpful. It represents a Windows kernel semaphore object. However, when you expect wait times to be very short, the new `SemaphoreSlim` adds less overhead and is more appropriate to work with tasks, because it provides a counting semaphore that doesn't use a Windows kernel semaphore object.

A counting semaphore, known as *semaphore* in .NET Framework, coordinates the access to resources by tracking the tasks or threads that enter and leave. The semaphore needs to know the maximum number of tasks that will be able to access the shared resource through its coordination features. Then, it uses a count that it decrements and increments according to the tasks that enter and leave the zone controlled by the semaphore.

Each time a task enters the semaphore, its count is decremented. This way, when the count reaches 0, new requests that arrive will block until other tasks leave the semaphore. Each time a task leaves the resource coordinated by the semaphore, the task must release the semaphore and the semaphore's count is incremented. At this point, one of the tasks that is blocked and waiting for the semaphore to enable it to access the shared resource will be able to enter the semaphore, and its count will be decremented.

A semaphore reduces scalability, and it is meant to do so. Therefore, you must use it very carefully and only when necessary. Leaving resources controlled by a semaphore will limit the scalability of the code that accesses these resources. As with any other synchronization technique, use semaphores when you are sure that they are the best option.

Figure 5-15 illustrates the way a semaphore controls access to resources by counting enters and releases, and blocking when necessary. There are four tasks that request to enter a semaphore whose maximum number of concurrent tasks is set to 3 and whose initial count is also 3. The first three tasks that request to enter the semaphore are able to access the shared resource, and the semaphore's count is decremented to 0 as a result. At this point, a fourth task, Task #3, requests to enter the semaphore. This task is blocked until one of the other three tasks releases the semaphore. Then, Task #0 releases the semaphore, its count is incremented to 1, and the semaphore grants access to Task #3. The semaphore's count is decremented to 0 again.

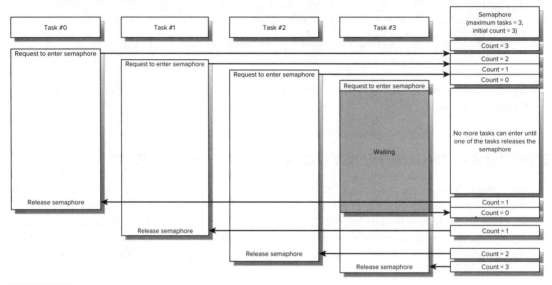

FIGURE 5-15

Working with SemaphoreSlim

A SemaphoreSlim instance allows you to control access to shared resources. Each task has to use its methods to enter and release the semaphore. One of the SemaphoreSlim constructors receives an int value with the initial number of concurrent requests that can be granted. This value is the initial value for the count, and it is also used to set the maximum number of concurrent requests that the semaphore is going to allow. Another constructor receives two int parameters: the initial and the maximum number of requests. You can use this constructor when you want to specify an initial value for the count that differs from the maximum number of requests.

Listing 5-3 shows the code for an application that simulates concurrent attacks to machines. In order to keep the example simple, the code simulates the workload for the attacks by using a Thread.Sleep method to block the task for a few random seconds. Remember that random-number generation should be improved in order to generate real random numbers in concurrent tasks. Appendix C, "Parallel Extensions Extras," provides information about the ThreadSafeRandom class. However, the example code uses the standard Random class to keep things simple.

LISTING 5-3: Using SemaphoreSlim to simulate a maximum number of concurrent attacks

```
private static SemaphoreSlim _semaphore;

private static Task[] _tasks;

private const int MAX_MACHINES = 3;
private static int _attackers =
    Environment.ProcessorCount;

private static void SimulateAttacks(int attackerNumber)
{
    // Simulate workload
    var sw = Stopwatch.StartNew();
    // Generate a Random number of milliseconds to wait for
    var rnd = new Random();
    Thread.Sleep(rnd.Next(2000,5000));
    // At this point, the method has the necessary data
    // to simulate the attack
    // Needs to enter the semaphore
    // Wait for _semaphore to grant access

    Console.WriteLine(
"WAIT #### Attacker {0} requested to enter the semaphore.",
        attackerNumber);
    _semaphore.Wait();

    // This code runs when it entered the semaphore
    try
    {
        Console.WriteLine(
"ENTER ---> Attacker {0} entered the semaphore.",
            attackerNumber);

        // Simulate the attack
        // Simulate workload
        sw.Restart();
        Thread.Sleep(rnd.Next(2000,5000));
    }
    finally
    {
        // Exit the semaphore
        _semaphore.Release();
        Console.WriteLine(
"RELEASE <--- Attacker {0} released the semaphore.",
            attackerNumber);
    }
}

static void Main(string[] args)
{
    _tasks = new Task[_attackers];
    // Create the SemaphoreSlim instance
    // with its initial count set to MAX_MACHINES
```

continues

LISTING 5-3 *(continued)*

```
        // Its maximum concurrent accesses
        // is also going to be set to MAX_MACHINES
        _semaphore = new SemaphoreSlim(MAX_MACHINES);
        Console.WriteLine(
   "{0} attackers are going to be able to enter the semaphore.",
            _semaphore.CurrentCount);

        for (int i = 0; i < _attackers; i++)
        {
            _tasks[i] = Task.Factory.StartNew((num) =>
            {
                var attackerNumber = (int)num;
                for (int j = 0; j < 10; j++)
                {
                    SimulateAttacks(attackerNumber);
                }
            }, i);
        }

        var finalTask =
            Task.Factory.ContinueWhenAll(_tasks, (tasks) =>
        {
            // Wait for all the tasks to ensure
            // the propagation of any exception occurred
            // in any of the _tasks
            Task.WaitAll(_tasks);
            Console.WriteLine(
                "The simulation was executed.");
            // Dispose the SemaphoreSlim instance
            _semaphore.Dispose();
        });

        // Wait for finalTask to finish
        finalTask.Wait();

        Console.ReadLine();
    }
```

The `Main` method creates a `SemaphoreSlim` instance named *_semaphore*, with the initial count of `MAX_MACHINES` set to the maximum concurrent accesses that the semaphore is going to grant. It creates as many `Task` instances as the logical number of cores available. The code in the `SimulateAttacks` method assumes that an attack simulation requires processing a lot of complex data before running the code that is limited by the semaphore. Thus, this code could take advantage of all the available logical cores. In fact, when the instructions needed to prepare the data for each attack are very different, the code can benefit from the additional parallelism.

When each task needs to access the code that requires limited concurrency, it calls the `_semaphore` `.Wait` method. As soon as it finishes, it calls the `_semaphore.Release` method. The `SimulateAttacks` method includes this call in the `finally` section of a `try…finally` block. It is very important that you ensure that the `Release` method is called, even if an exception occurs.

(You already learned about the headaches caused by blocked tasks in the previous sections.) It is also a good practice to dispose a `SemaphoreSlim` instance when you have finished with it.

A `SemaphoreSlim` instance offers the following methods:

➤ `Release` — Exits the semaphore and increments its count. The method returns the previous count of the `SemaphoreSlim`. You can also call this method with the number of times to exit the semaphore as an `int` parameter.

➤ `Wait` — Blocks the current task or thread until its count is greater than 0 and it can enter the semaphore. If the semaphore's count is greater than 0, this method will decrement its count and will return immediately after performing this operation. It offers many definitions that allow you to send it a `CancellationToken` instance and/or a timeout as an `int` or a `TimeSpan`.

A `SemaphoreSlim` instance exposes the following two read-only properties:

➤ `CurrentCount` — Gets the number of tasks or threads that will be granted access to enter the semaphore. Because this value is always changing, when the semaphore executes concurrent `Release` and `Wait` methods, a `CurrentCount > 0` at one time doesn't mean that it will remain `true` in the next instruction in a task or thread. Therefore, it is very important that you use the `Wait` and `Release` methods to enter and leave the resources protected by the semaphore.

➤ `AvailableWaitHandle` — Provides the `WaitHandle` object that encapsulates the operating-system object. This object allows waiting on the semaphore, but it doesn't change the semaphore's count. This behavior is different from `Semaphore`, where calling `WaitOne` for the `WaitHandle` object will change its count. If you need this behavior, you need to use `Semaphore` instead of `SemaphoreSlim`.

The following lines are an example of what happens when you execute the code in Listing 5-3 on a computer with four logical cores, and four attackers request to enter the semaphore. Three of them are granted access, and after one of them releases the semaphore, the fourth attacker, `Attacker 3`, can enter the semaphore.

```
3 attackers are going to be able to enter the semaphore.
WAIT #### Attacker 1 requested to enter the semaphore.
WAIT #### Attacker 0 requested to enter the semaphore.
WAIT #### Attacker 2 requested to enter the semaphore.
WAIT #### Attacker 3 requested to enter the semaphore.
ENTER ---> Attacker 2 entered the semaphore.
ENTER ---> Attacker 0 entered the semaphore.
ENTER ---> Attacker 1 entered the semaphore.
RELEASE <--- Attacker 1 released the semaphore.
RELEASE <--- Attacker 0 released the semaphore.
RELEASE <--- Attacker 2 released the semaphore.
ENTER ---> Attacker 3 entered the semaphore.
RELEASE <--- Attacker 3 released the semaphore.
```

Figure 5-16 shows the line that requests to enter the semaphore by calling the `Wait` method, and the Autos window that displays `Current Count = 0` for _semaphore.

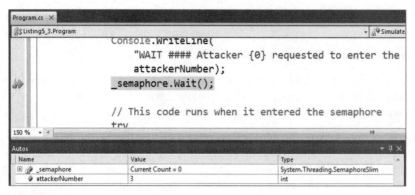

FIGURE 5-16

A SemaphoreSlim *instance doesn't guarantee an order for the tasks or threads that are waiting to enter the semaphore. There are no LIFO or FIFO queues.*

Working with Timeouts and Cancellations

As with the coordination structures you learned about previously, a semaphore could block a task or thread forever. If one or more tasks don't call the Release method, other tasks could never enter the semaphore. In order to keep the previous example simple, it didn't include the necessary code to handle exceptions for the Task instances.

You can establish a timeout by sending the number of milliseconds as a paramter to the Wait method for a SemaphoreSlim instance, and you can also send a CancellationToken instance. The previous sections offered detailed examples to work with timeouts and cancellations for other coordination structures. The same techniques can be used with a SemaphoreSlim instance.

Working with Semaphore

When you need to do cross-process or cross-AppDomain synchronization, or you need WaitHandle operations to decrement the semaphore's count, you must work with Semaphore instead of SemaphoreSlim. Semaphore doesn't have the same members as SemaphoreSlim — for example, it doesn't have the CurrentCount property to retrieve the number of tasks or threads that will be granted access to enter the semaphore, and it doesn't work with cancellation tokens. A Semaphore instance offers the following methods that are equivalent to the methods explained for SemaphoreSlim:

➤ Release — Exits the semaphore and increments its count. The method returns the previous count of the Semaphore. You can also call this method with the number of times to exit the semaphore as an int parameter.

➤ WaitOne — Equivalent to the Wait method for SemaphoreSlim. This method blocks the current task or thread until its count is greater than 0 and it can enter the semaphore. This happens when the `WaitHandle` receives a signal. If the semaphore's count is greater than 0, this method will decrement its count and will return immediately after performing this operation. It offers many definitions that allow you to send it a timeout as an `int` or a `TimeSpan`.

Semaphore provides more methods. However, the preceding list explains the most common methods that you will use when you need the basic features of a counting semaphore.

A `Semaphore` instance exposes the `SafeWaitHandle` property that allows you to get or set the native operating system handle.

Listing 5-4 shows the code for an application that simulates attackers attempting to grant access to machines. This new code uses `Semaphore` instead of `SemaphoreSlim` to grant access to a maximum number of concurrent attacker tasks.

LISTING 5-4: Using Semaphore to simulate a maximum number of concurrent attacks

Available for download on Wrox.com

```
private static Semaphore _semaphore;

private static Task[] _tasks;

private const int MAX_MACHINES = 3;
private static int _attackers =
    Environment.ProcessorCount;

private static void SimulateAttacks(int attackerNumber)
{
    // Simulate workload
    var sw = Stopwatch.StartNew();
    // Generate a Random number of milliseconds to wait for
    var rnd = new Random();
    Thread.Sleep(rnd.Next(2000,5000));
    // At this point, the method has the necessary data
    // to simulate the attack
    // Needs to enter the semaphore
    // Wait for _semaphore to grant access

    Console.WriteLine(
"WAIT #### Attacker {0} requested to enter the semaphore.",
        attackerNumber);
    _semaphore.WaitOne();

    // This code runs when it entered the semaphore
    try
    {
        Console.WriteLine(
"ENTER ---> Attacker {0} entered the semaphore.",
            attackerNumber);
```

continues

LISTING 5-4 *(continued)*

```
        // Simulate the attack
        // Simulate workload
        sw.Restart();
        Thread.Sleep(rnd.Next(2000,5000));
    }
    finally
    {
        // Exit the semaphore
        _semaphore.Release();
        Console.WriteLine(
"RELEASE <--- Attacker {0} released the semaphore.",
            attackerNumber);
    }
}

static void Main(string[] args)
{
    _tasks = new Task[_attackers];
    // Create the Semaphore instance
    // with its initial count set to MAX_MACHINES
    // and its maximum concurrent accesses
    // also set to MAX_MACHINES
    _semaphore = new Semaphore(MAX_MACHINES, MAX_MACHINES);
    Console.WriteLine(
"{0} attackers are going to be able to enter the semaphore.",
        MAX_MACHINES);

    for (int i = 0; i < _attackers; i++)
    {
        _tasks[i] = Task.Factory.StartNew((num) =>
        {
            var attackerNumber = (int)num;
            for (int j = 0; j < 10; j++)
            {
                SimulateAttacks(attackerNumber);
            }
        }, i);
    }

    var finalTask =
        Task.Factory.ContinueWhenAll(_tasks, (tasks) =>
    {
        // Wait for all the tasks to ensure
        // the propagation of any exception occurred
        // in any of the _tasks
        Task.WaitAll(_tasks);
        Console.WriteLine(
            "The simulation was executed.");
        // Dispose the Semaphore instance
        _semaphore.Dispose();
    });

    // Wait for finalTask to finish
```

```
        finalTask.Wait();

        Console.ReadLine();
    }
```

The simplest constructor for `Semaphore` requires two `Int32` parameters: the initial number of concurrent requests and the maximum number of concurrent entries. In Listing 5-4, the `Semaphore` instance doesn't reserve entries, and therefore, the code calls the constructor passing `MAX_MACHINES` for both parameters, as shown in the next line:

```
    _semaphore = new Semaphore(MAX_MACHINES, MAX_MACHINES);
```

SIMPLIFYING DYNAMIC FORK AND JOIN SCENARIOS WITH COUNTDOWNEVENT

Sometimes, you need to track a dynamic number of tasks over time. `CountdownEvent` is a very lightweight synchronization primitive that can be less expensive than using `Task.WaitAll` or `TaskFactory.ContinueWhenAll` to run code when other tasks finish their execution.

A `CountdownEvent` instance has an initial signal count. In a typical fork/join scenario, each time a task completes its work, it signals the `CountdownEvent` instance and decrements the signal count by one. The task that calls the `Wait` method for the `CountdownEvent` instance will block until the signal count reaches `0`. You can reuse a `CountdownEvent` instance by resetting it with the new desired signal count. The `CountdownEvent` constructor receives an `int` value with the initial signal count.

Listing 5-5 shows the code for an application that launches a dynamic number of concurrent tasks to simulate paths. In order to keep the example simple, the code simulates the workload for the path simulation by using a `Thread.Sleep` method to block the task for a few random seconds.

LISTING 5-5: Using CountdownEvent to simulate a dynamic number of paths with concurrent tasks

Available for download on Wrox.com

```
private static CountdownEvent _countdown;

private static int MIN_PATHS =
    Environment.ProcessorCount;
private static int MAX_PATHS =
    Environment.ProcessorCount * 3;

private static void SimulatePaths(int pathCount)
{
    for (int i =0; i < pathCount; i++)
    {
        Task.Factory.StartNew((num) =>
        {
            try
            {
                var pathNumber = (int)num;
                // Simulate workload
                var sw = Stopwatch.StartNew();
                // Generate a Random number
```

continues

LISTING 5-5 *(continued)*

```
                    // of milliseconds to wait for
                    var rnd = new Random();
                    Thread.Sleep(rnd.Next(2000,5000));
                    Console.WriteLine(
                        "Path {0} simulated.",
                        pathNumber);
                }
                finally
                {
                    // Signal the CountdownEvent
                    // to decrement the count
                    _countdown.Signal();
                }
            }, i);
        }
    }

    static void Main(string[] args)
    {
        _countdown = new CountdownEvent(MIN_PATHS);

        var t1 = Task.Factory.StartNew(() =>
            {
                for (int i = MIN_PATHS; i <= MAX_PATHS; i++)
                {
                    Console.WriteLine(
                        ">>>> {0} Concurrent paths start.",
                        i);
                    // Reset the count to i
                    _countdown.Reset(i);
                    SimulatePaths(i);
                    // Join
                    _countdown.Wait();
                    Console.WriteLine(
                        "<<<< {0} Concurrent paths end.",
                        i);
                }
            });

        try
        {
            t1.Wait();
            Console.WriteLine(
                "The simulation was executed.");
        }
        finally
        {
            _countdown.Dispose();
        }

        Console.ReadLine();
    }
```

The `Main` method creates a `CountdownEvent` instance named _countdown, with the initial signal count of `MIN_PATHS` set to the number of logical cores. The method creates and starts a new *t1* `Task` instance. This task runs a loop that calls the `SimulatePaths` method to launch a number of independent tasks that are going to signal _countdown when they finish their work. The loop runs from `MIN_PATHS` to `MAX_PATHS`, where `MAX_PATHS` is set to three times the number of logical cores. The loop reuses the _countdown `CountdownEvent` instance. The loop performs the following actions to run a dynamic fork/join scenario:

1. It writes a line indicating the number of paths that are going to be simulated.

2. It calls the `Reset` method for _countdown, passing the i loop variable as a parameter. This way, the number of signals that _countdown needs to unblock the task that calls its `Wait` method is equal to i.

3. It calls the `SimulatePaths` method with the i loop variable as a parameter. `SimulatePaths` creates and starts the number of tasks received as a parameter. The method returns immediately after creating and starting the tasks — it doesn't wait for the tasks to finish their execution. Each time a task finishes its work, it calls the `Signal` method for _countdown and the signal count decrements by one.

4. It calls the `Wait` method for _countdown to join. The task will block until the signal count reaches 0. The signal count will reach 0 when all the tasks launched by `SimulatePaths`, in the current iteration of the loop, signal _countdown.

5. After all the tasks signal _countdown, the task unblocks and writes a line indicating the number of paths that were simulated.

The following lines display the first results of running the code shown in Listing 5-5 with eight logical cores:

```
>>>> 8 Concurrent paths start.
Path 1 simulated.
Path 2 simulated.
Path 3 simulated.
Path 5 simulated.
Path 4 simulated.
Path 6 simulated.
Path 0 simulated.
Path 7 simulated.
<<<< 8 Concurrent paths end.
>>>> 9 Concurrent paths start.
Path 0 simulated.
Path 1 simulated.
Path 3 simulated.
Path 8 simulated.
Path 7 simulated.
Path 6 simulated.
Path 4 simulated.
Path 5 simulated.
Path 2 simulated.
<<<< 9 Concurrent paths end.
>>>> 10 Concurrent paths start.
```

```
Path 5 simulated.
Path 4 simulated.
Path 8 simulated.
Path 0 simulated.
Path 6 simulated.
Path 2 simulated.
Path 7 simulated.
Path 9 simulated.
Path 3 simulated.
Path 1 simulated.
<<<< 10 Concurrent paths end.
>>>> 11 Concurrent paths start.
…
…
```

When each task created and started by `SimulatePaths` finishes its work, it calls the `_countdown` `.Signal` method. The `SimulatePaths` method includes this call in the `finally` section of a try... finally block. It is very important that you ensure that the `Signal` method is called, even if an exception occurs. (You already learned about the headaches caused by blocked tasks in the previous sections.) It is also a good practice to dispose a `CountdownEvent` instance when you have finished with it.

A `CountdownEvent` instance offers the following methods:

➤ `AddCount` — Increments the current count by one or by the value specified as an `int` parameter.

➤ `Reset` — Resets the number of remaining signals required to unblock the task or thread that called the `Wait` method to the initial count or to the value specified as an `int` parameter. You should only call this method when no other tasks or threads are accessing the `CountdownEvent`.

➤ `Signal` — Registers one signal and decreases the remaining signals required to unblock the task or thread that called the `Wait` method. By default, the method decrements the current count by one. However, there is another definition of this method that allows you to specify an `int` parameter with the number of signals to register in a single call and decrements the count by the specified amount.

➤ `TryAddCount` — Tries to increment the current count by one or by the value specified as an `int` parameter. Returns a `bool` value indicating whether the increment succeeded.

➤ `Wait` — Blocks the current task or thread until the `CountdownEvent` is set; that is, until the signal count reaches 0. If the signal count is already 0, the method will return immediately. The `Wait` method offers many definitions that allow you to send it a `CancellationToken` instance and/or a timeout as an `int` or a `TimeSpan`.

A `CountdownEvent` instance exposes the following four read-only properties:

➤ `CurrentCount` — Gets the number of remaining signals required to unblock the task or thread that called the `Wait` method.

➤ `InitialCount` — Gets the number of signals initially required to unblock the task or thread that called the `Wait` method.

➤ IsSet — Offers a `bool` value indicating whether the event is `true` (set).

➤ WaitHandle — Provides the `WaitHandle` object that encapsulates the operating-system object. This operating-system object allows you to wait for the event to be set.

As with the coordination structures you learned about previously, a `CountdownEvent` could block a task or thread that joins forever. If one or more tasks don't call the `Signal` method, the task that called the `Wait` method will stay blocked. In order to keep things simple, the previous example did not include the necessary code to handle exceptions for the `Task` instances or timeouts.

You can establish a timeout by sending the number of milliseconds as a parameter to the `Wait` method for a `CountdownEvent` instance. You can also send a `CancellationToken` instance. The previous sections offered detailed examples of how to work with timeouts and cancellations for other coordination structures. The same techniques can be used with a `CountdownEvent` instance.

WORKING WITH ATOMIC OPERATIONS

Listing 5-1 presented an example of many concurrent tasks that ran diverse coordinated phases to render a scene. You have many alternatives for counting the number of times that these tasks run the necessary methods. Think about an algorithm that must use a shared variable. Many concurrent tasks run the group of methods that render a scene. You cannot increment a shared variable with the traditional increment operations, because they aren't thread-safe.

You can't use the `lock` keyword or `Monitor` with integral types. Therefore, if you want to serialize the increment operation on a shared `int` variable, you have to obtain a mutual exclusion lock on an object and perform the increment in the critical section. In fact, it is a common practice to use a separate synchronization object.

An increment operation is really cheap, and therefore, you might be thinking that a `SpinLock` is a great alternative to serialize the increment operation. Although it isn't the best alternative, the following lines show a new version of the first part of the `Main` method presented in Listing 5-1. This new version uses a `SpinLock` instance named `s1` to acquire a lock and run code in a critical section, and increments the `int` variable named `totalRenders` shared by all the barrier's participants. It was also necessary to add a few lines of code to increment the value of a shared `int` variable in a task-safe and thread-safe way.

Available for download on Wrox.com

```
static void Main(string[] args)
{
    _tasks = new Task[_participants];
    _barrier = new Barrier(_participants, (barrier) =>
    {
        Console.WriteLine("Current phase: {0}",
            barrier.CurrentPhaseNumber);
    });

    // You pass false for enableThreadOwnerTracking
    // because you want the best performance out of SpinLock
    var sl = new SpinLock(false);

    int totalRenders = 0;
```

```csharp
for (int i = 0; i < _participants; i++)
{
    _tasks[i] = Task.Factory.StartNew((num) =>
    {
        var participantNumber = (int)num;
        for (int j = 0; j < 10; j++)
        {
            CreatePlanets(participantNumber);
            _barrier.SignalAndWait();
            CreateStars(participantNumber);
            _barrier.SignalAndWait();
            CheckCollisionsBetweenPlanets(participantNumber);
            _barrier.SignalAndWait();
            CheckCollisionsBetweenStars(participantNumber);
            _barrier.SignalAndWait();
            RenderCollisions(participantNumber);
            _barrier.SignalAndWait();

            bool lockTaken = false;
            try
            {
                sl.Enter(ref lockTaken);
                // SpinLock acquired a lock
                // Critical section
                // This is not a best practice
                // Use atomic operations instead
                totalRenders++;
                // End of critical section
            }
            finally
            {
                // You need to make sure that
                // you release the lock
                if (lockTaken)
                {
                    // Gives up the lock if it actually acquired it
                    // You want performance at the expense of fairness
                    // Therefore, you pass false for useMemoryBarrier
                    sl.Exit(false);
                }
            }
        }
    }, i);
}

var finalTask = Task.Factory.ContinueWhenAll(_tasks, (tasks) =>
{
    // Wait for all the tasks to ensure
    // the propagation of any exception occurred
    // in any of the _tasks
    Task.WaitAll(_tasks);
    Console.WriteLine(
        "{0} renders were executed.",
```

```
            totalRenders);
        // Dispose the Barrier instance
        _barrier.Dispose();
    });

    // Wait for finalTask to finish
    finalTask.Wait();

    Console.ReadLine();
}
```

code snippet from Snippet5_21

When all the barrier's participants finish their work, `finalTask` runs code that displays the final value for `totalRenders`. The code works fine because the increment operation is serialized. However, instead of using mutual-exclusion locks to perform simple operations on shared variables, you can use simpler atomic operations. You already learned about the simplicity of atomic operations with the example of the cars, lanes, and flags at the beginning of this chapter. Now, it is time to write the code to perform atomic operations.

The `System.Threading.Interlocked` class provides atomic operations for variables shared by multiple tasks and threads. This class provides methods that perform operations on shared variables as a single operation that entirely succeeds or entirely fails. The key advantages of using the atomic operations provided by the `Interlocked` class is that they are cheap, efficient, and thread-safe.

You already know the problems with concurrent code running on different cores. Incrementing the value for a shared instance variable usually requires the following low-level steps:

1. Load the shared instance variable's value into a register.

2. Increment the register's value.

3. Store the new value in the shared instance variable.

If two or more threads increment the value by following the aforementioned steps without a serialized execution, the final value for the variable will be unpredictable.

The `Interlocked.Increment` method increments an integral variable and stores its new result as an atomic and thread-safe operation. The following lines show a new version of the previous code, without locks. This new version uses the `Interlocked.Increment` method to increment `totalRenders` in an atomic operation.

Available for download on Wrox.com

```
static void Main(string[] args)
{
    _tasks = new Task[_participants];
    _barrier = new Barrier(_participants, (barrier) =>
    {
        Console.WriteLine("Current phase: {0}",
            barrier.CurrentPhaseNumber);
    });

    int totalRenders = 0;
```

```
for (int i = 0; i < _participants; i++)
{
    _tasks[i] = Task.Factory.StartNew((num) =>
    {
        var participantNumber = (int)num;
        for (int j = 0; j < 10; j++)
        {
            CreatePlanets(participantNumber);
            _barrier.SignalAndWait();
            CreateStars(participantNumber);
            _barrier.SignalAndWait();
            CheckCollisionsBetweenPlanets(participantNumber);
            _barrier.SignalAndWait();
            CheckCollisionsBetweenStars(participantNumber);
            _barrier.SignalAndWait();
            RenderCollisions(participantNumber);
            _barrier.SignalAndWait();

            // Increment totalRenders with an atomic operation
            Interlocked.Increment(ref totalRenders);
        }
    }, i);
}

var finalTask = Task.Factory.ContinueWhenAll(_tasks, (tasks) =>
{
    // Wait for all the tasks to ensure
    // the propagation of any exception occurred
    // in any of the _tasks
    Task.WaitAll(_tasks);
    Console.WriteLine(
        "{0} renders were executed.",
        totalRenders);
    // Dispose the Barrier instance
    _barrier.Dispose();
});

// Wait for finalTask to finish
finalTask.Wait();

Console.ReadLine();
}
```

code snippet from Snippet5_22

This code is simpler and more efficient, because there is no need to acquire a mutual-exclusion lock. The atomic operation is safe and cheap. The following single line of code that passes the totalRenders variable to increment by reference performs the operation in a task-safe and thread-safe way. The result of running this line is totalRenders + 1 stored in totalRenders as an atomic operation:

```
Interlocked.Increment(ref totalRenders);
```

The Increment method returns the incremented value.

The `Interlocked` class provides many atomic operations and supports diverse types. Table 5-1 provides a brief summary of the methods, the atomic operations that they perform, and the supported types. Subsequent chapters use many of these operations in code examples.

TABLE 5-1: System.Threading.Interlocked Methods

NAME	ATOMIC OPERATION DESCRIPTION	SUPPORTED TYPES
Add	Adds two integers and replaces the first integer with the sum	Int32 and Int64
CompareExchange	Compares two values for equality and, if they are equal, replaces the first value received as a parameter with the second one	Double, Int32, Int64, IntPtr, Object, and Single
CompareExchange<T>(T, T, T)	Compares two instances of the specified type T for equality and, if they are equal, replaces the first instance received as a parameter with the second one	T is the specified type
Decrement	Decrements the variable and stores the result	Int32 and Int64
Exchange	Sets the first parameter to the value passed as the second parameter and returns the original value	Double, Int32, Int64, IntPtr, Object, and Single
Exchange<T>(T, T)	Sets the first parameter of the specified type T to the value passed as the second parameter and returns the original value	T is the specified type
Increment	Increments the variable and stores the result	Int32 and Int64
Read	Returns a 64-bit value	Int64

If you run atomic operations on 32-bit systems with 64-bit types, you have to access 64-bit values through the members of the Interlocked *class. The 64-bit overloads of the* Interlocked.Increment, Interlocked.Decrement, *and* Interlocked.Add *methods are truly atomic only on 64-bit systems. Thus, on 32-bit systems, read operations for 64-bit values are atomic if you use* Interlocked.Read *to read the values. For example, if you call* Interlocked .Increment *for a 64-bit type in a 32-bit system, you should use* Interlocked .Read *to read the actual value in an atomic operation.* Interlocked.Read *isn't necessary on 64-bit systems, because read operations of the relevant sized data are atomic.*

SUMMARY

There are many other advanced topics related to coordinating and synchronizing the work done by concurrent tasks. This chapter described many of the new lightweight coordination data structures introduced with .NET Framework 4, some of the most common synchronization primitives, and examples of how to use its classes and structures. This chapter also discussed how you can use timeouts and cancellations to create code that doesn't continue to wait forever. To summarize this chapter:

➤ You should use the coordination data structures that are most appropriate to your needs.

➤ You can use the new lightweight synchronization primitives unless, from a functionality perspective, the corresponding heavyweight primitives are necessary, such as if you need cross-process synchronization.

➤ You can use timeouts and cancellation tokens to avoid having tasks blocked forever without notice.

➤ You should take advantage of the new possibilities offered by the new Task class whenever possible. However, remember to use profiling tools to determine the most convenient option for each scenario.

➤ When wait times are short, you can spin to avoid undesired context-switches.

➤ For efficiency and maximum scalability, avoid locks whenever possible. However, for ease of coding, use locks and don't try to write lock-free code all the time. Writing lock-free code is inherently very difficult and very error-prone if you don't have the necessary experience.

➤ Whenever possible, use atomic operations instead of locks. However, remember that correctness is even more important than good performance. Use atomic operations when you know what you are doing and you are sure that you don't need locks.

PLINQ: Declarative Data Parallelism

WHAT'S IN THIS CHAPTER?

➤ Transforming LINQ into parallelized LINQ

➤ Understanding partitioning in PLINQ

➤ Performing reduction operations with PLINQ

➤ Creating custom PLINQ aggregate functions

➤ Working with concurrent PLINQ tasks

➤ Cancelling PLINQ and measuring its scalability

➤ Specifying the desired degree of parallelism

➤ Working with `ForAll` and understanding how it differs from `foreach`

➤ Configuring how PLINQ results are returned by using WithMergeOptions

➤ Handling exceptions thrown by PLINQ

➤ Using PLINQ to execute Map Reduce algorithms

This chapter explains how to work with declarative data parallelism and a mix of task and data decomposition using Parallel Language Integrated Query (PLINQ). It is very important to understand all the things explained in the previous chapters before reading this one, because this chapter combines many of the topics studied before.

This chapter explains how to transform a LINQ query into a PLINQ query and the different techniques to tune its parallel execution according to different scenarios. In addition, it explains the execution of the classic parallel Map Reduce algorithms using PLINQ and its aggregate functions. Sometimes, PLINQ doesn't offer the results that developers expected. Therefore, it is also important to understand the potential performance bottlenecks and the different ways to solve them.

TRANSFORMING LINQ INTO PLINQ

You already know that *Language Integrated Query (LINQ)* is very useful to query and process different data sources. If you are using *LINQ to Objects*, now you can take advantage of parallelism using its parallel implementation, *Parallel LINQ (PLINQ)*.

> *PLINQ implements the full set of LINQ operators and adds new operators for parallel execution. PLINQ can achieve significant speedups over its LINQ counterpart, but it depends on the scenario, as is always the case with parallelism. If the query involves an appreciable number of calculations and memory-intensive operations, and ordering doesn't matter, the speedups could be significant. However, when ordering matters, the speedups could be reduced.*

As you might have expected, LINQ and PLINQ can work with the new concurrent collections explained in Chapter 4, "Concurrent Collections." The following code defines a simple but intensive method to count and return the number of letters in a string received as a parameter:

```
static int CountLetters(String key)
{
    int letters = 0;
    for (int i = 0; i < key.Length; i++)
    {
        if (Char.IsLetter(key, i))
        {
            letters++;
        }
    }
    return letters;
}
```

code snippet from Snippet6_1

A simple LINQ expression to return all the AES keys with at least 10 letters containing an *A*, an *F*, and a *9*, but not a *B*, would look like the following:

```
var keysWith10Letters = from key in Keys
            where (CountLetters(key) >= 10)
                && (key.Contains('A'))
                && (key.Contains('F'))
                && (key.Contains('9'))
                && (!key.Contains('B'))
            select key;
```

In order to transform the aforementioned LINQ expression into a PLINQ expression that can take advantage of parallelism, it is necessary to use the `AsParallel` method, as shown here:

```
var keysWith10Letters = from key in Keys.AsParallel()
            where (CountLetters(key) >= 10)
                && (key.Contains('A'))
                && (key.Contains('F'))
                && (key.Contains('9'))
                && (!key.Contains('B'))
            select key;
```

This way, when the query is executed, it will try to take advantage of all the available logical cores at run-time in order to run faster than its sequential version.

You can add code at the end of the `main` method of the example that filled a `ConcurrentQueue` (*Keys*) with AES keys using the `ParallelPartitionGenerateAESKeysWCP` method defined in Chapter 4, "Concurrent Collections," in order to return some results according to the PLINQ query. The following code shows the new `main` method:

```
static void Main(string[] args)
{
    Console.ReadLine();
    Console.WriteLine("Started");

    var cts = new System.Threading.CancellationTokenSource();
    var ct = cts.Token;

    var sw = Stopwatch.StartNew();

    Keys = new ConcurrentQueue<String>();

    var tAsync = new Task(() => ParallelPartitionGenerateAESKeysWCP(ct, 'A'));
    tAsync.Start();

    // Do something else
    // Wait for tAsync to finish
    tAsync.Wait();

    // Define the query indicating that it should run in parallel
    var keysWith10Letters = from key in Keys.AsParallel()
                where (CountLetters(key) >= 10)
                    && (key.Contains('A'))
                    && (key.Contains('F'))
                    && (key.Contains('9'))
                    && (!key.Contains('B'))
                select key;

    // Write some of the results of executing the query
    // Remember that the PLINQ query is going to be executed at this point
    // when the code requires results
    var keysList = keysWith10Letters.ToList();
    Console.WriteLine("The code generated {0} keys with at least ten letters, A, F and 9
but no B in the hexadecimal code.",
        keysList.Count());
```

```
Console.WriteLine("First key: {0} ",
    keysList.ElementAt(0));
Console.WriteLine("Last key: {0} ",
    keysList.ElementAt(keysWith10Letters.Count() - 1));

Console.WriteLine("Finished in {0}", sw.Elapsed.ToString());

Console.ReadLine();
}
```

code snippet from Snippet6_1

This code shows the number of keys that comply with the conditions, the first one and the last one, stored in the results of the PLINQ query that worked against *Keys*, the ConcurrentQueue<String>. The following code lines represent an example of the console output:

```
Started
The code generated 834 keys with at least ten letters, A, F and 9 but no B in
the hexadecimal code.
First key ACAEFE9D07EE894E03D62D87A65D18A6F9F01C6458D41A00168F4290CE1097D9:
Last key A3DF422312C02E8F4079648071E1C8C8CE82C3C01103DEE3207F57495C7A39F9:
Finished in 00:00:02.9270689
```

 It is easy to transform a LINQ query into a PLINQ query. However, when you're transforming sequential queries to parallelized queries, you must consider new scenarios brought by the parallel execution of the original sequential query, as explained in the following sections.

ParallelEnumerable and Its AsParallel Method

The System.Linq.ParallelEnumerable class is responsible for exposing most of PLINQ's additional functionality, including its most important one: the AsParallel method. Table 6-1 summarizes the PLINQ-specific methods.

TABLE 6-1: PLINQ Operators Exposed by ParallelEnumerable

VALUE	DESCRIPTION
AsOrdered()	PLINQ must preserve the ordering of the source sequence for the rest of the query, until it changes using an orderby clause or until it is turned off with AsUnordered.
AsParallel()	The rest of the query should be parallelized, whenever possible.
AsSequential()	The rest of the query should run sequentially, as in traditional LINQ.
AsUnordered()	PLINQ doesn't have to preserve the ordering of the source sequence for the rest of the query.

VALUE	DESCRIPTION
`ForAll()`	This enumeration method enables the results to be processed in parallel, using multiple tasks.
`WithCancellation`	This works with a cancellation token to permit cancelation of the query execution, as you learned with parallelized loops and tasks in previous chapters.
`WithDegreeOfParallelism`	PLINQ will be optimized as if the total number of available cores were equal to the degree of parallelism specified as a parameter for this method.
`WithExecutionMode`	This can force parallel execution when the default behavior would be to run it sequentially as traditional LINQ.
`WithMergeOptions`	This can provide hints about the way PLINQ should merge the parallel pieces of the result on the thread that is consuming the query.

AsOrdered and the orderby Clause

The previous example showed the first and last keys as a result of executing a query without a specific order. This means that there are no guarantees that the first key in the result is the first key in the data source, the *Keys* `ConcurrentCollection<String>`, because the results are added in parallel.

In order to show the real first key that matches the query definition in the source collection, you need to tell PLINQ to preserve the ordering of the source. You do this by adding the `AsOrdered()` operator, as shown in the following code lines:

```
var keysWith10Letters = from key in Keys.AsParallel().AsOrdered()
        where (CountLetters(key) >= 10)
           && (key.Contains('A'))
           && (key.Contains('F'))
           && (key.Contains('9'))
           && (!key.Contains('B'))
        select key;
```

code snippet from Snippet6_2

Another alternative is to show the first key according to the resulting keys sorted in ascending order. You do this by adding an `orderby` clause and removing the `AsOrdered()` operator, as shown in the following code lines:

```
var keysWith10Letters = from key in Keys.AsParallel()
        where (CountLetters(key) >= 10)
           && (key.Contains('A'))
           && (key.Contains('F'))
           && (key.Contains('9'))
```

```
              && (!key.Contains('B'))
       orderby key
       select key;
```

code snippet from Snippet6_3

The `AsOrdered()` operator isn't necessary anymore, because the results are going to be sorted by the alphanumerical values of each key in ascending order. It isn't necessary to tell PLINQ to preserve the ordering of the source. This way, PLINQ can optimize its execution by running its efficient algorithms in order to sort the resulting data. It is convenient to add operators and clauses only when they are necessary. If they aren't needed, remove them and let PLINQ decide the best way to take advantage of parallelism.

The simple example shown in Listing 6-1 can help you understand the differences between PLINQ and LINQ in the order of the source data and the query results. The code defines an array with nine unsorted words (strings). A simple PLINQ query filters the words that contain the a character. Then, the code writes the words that match the query definition to the console output. The example won't offer a significant speedup by executing the simple PLINQ on nine strings. In this case, the focus is on understanding the importance of the results and their order.

LISTING 6-1: Simple PLINQ query that demonstrates the different ordering possibilities

```
using System;
using System.Collections.Generic;
using System.Linq;
using System.Text;

namespace Listing6_1
{
    class Program
    {
        static string[] words = {
            "Day",
            "Car",
            "Land",
            "Road",
            "Mountain",
            "River",
            "Sea",
            "Shore",
            "Mouse" };

        static void Main(string[] args)
        {
            var query = from word in words.AsParallel()
                        where (word.Contains("a"))
                        select word;

            foreach (var result in query)
            {
```

```
            Console.WriteLine(result);
        }
        Console.ReadLine();
    }
  }
}
```

The initial order for the source data is as follows:

1. Day
2. Car
3. Land
4. Road
5. Mountain
6. River
7. Sea
8. Shore
9. Mouse

Because the PLINQ definition doesn't specify a required order, one of the executions in parallel of this simple query will show the following results:

1. Day
2. Car
3. Road
4. Mountain
5. Sea
6. Land

If the query had to preserve the order of the data source, `Land` should be the third word and not the last one. A second execution of the same application produces the following results:

1. Day
2. Land
3. Road
4. Mountain
5. Sea
6. Car

This time, `Land` is the second word, but it should be the third one. If you add the `AsOrdered()` operator, as shown in the following code lines, the results will preserve the order of the data source.

```
var query = from word in words.AsParallel().AsOrdered()
            where (word.Contains("a"))
            select word;
```

code snippet from Snippet6_4

The results will be in the following order, regardless of the number of times you run the application:

1. Day
2. Car
3. Land
4. Road
5. Mountain
6. Sea

Finally, if you remove the `AsOrdered()` operator from the PLINQ query and add the `orderby` and `descending` clauses, as shown in the following code lines, the results will be sorted by the contents of each string in a descending order.

```
var query = from word in words.AsParallel()
            where (word.Contains("a"))
            orderby word descending
            select word;
```

code snippet from Snippet6_5

The results will be in the following order, regardless of the number of times you run the application:

1. Sea
2. Road
3. Mountain
4. Land
5. Day
6. Car

Because using `AsOrdered` and the `orderby` clause in PLINQ queries can reduce any speed gains, it is very important that you compare the speedup achieved against the sequential version before requesting ordered results when they aren't essential.

If a PLINQ query that requires ordered results doesn't achieve significant performance improvements, you have another interesting option to take advantage of parallelism: running many LINQ queries in independent tasks or using `Parallel.Invoke`.

SPECIFYING THE EXECUTION MODE

You already know that in order to parallelize sequential code, it is necessary to add some overhead. The same happens with the work done by PLINQ to parallelize the execution of the query. In fact, PLINQ uses tasks and threads that support the parallel execution of different parts of the query.

By default, when a PLINQ query has to be executed, .NET will try to avoid parallelizing algorithms with high overheads that would be likely to slow down the performance compared to a sequential execution. This analysis is applied to many parts of a complex query. .NET makes the decision based on the query shape. It does not consider either the data set size or the delegates' execution time. However, you can force the parallel implementation regardless of the results of the analysis made by the execution engine. You can do this by adding a call to the `WithExecutionMode` method with `ParallelExecutionMode.ForceParallelism`, as shown in the following PLINQ query:

```
var query =
          from word in
          words.AsParallel().WithExecutionMode(ParallelExecutionMode.ForceParallelism)
          where (word.Contains("a"))
          orderby word descending
          select word;
```

code snippet from Snippet6_6

The `ParallelExecutionMode` enumeration offers another value, `ParallelExecutionMode.Default`. If you add a call to the `WithExecutionMode` method with this value as a parameter, the PLINQ query will be executed with the previously explained default behavior.

UNDERSTANDING PARTITIONING IN PLINQ

The following code lines show a PLINQ query that calculates the total number of letters in words that contain an `a`. It uses the `sum` aggregate function and calls the `CountLetters` method for each word.

```
static void Main(string[] args)
{
    var query = (from word in words.AsParallel()
                where (word.Contains('a'))
                select CountLetters(word)).Sum();

    Console.WriteLine(
        "The total number of letters for the words that contain an 'a' is {0}", query);
    Console.ReadLine();
}
```

code snippet from Snippet6_7

When .NET decides that it is convenient to run the PLINQ query in parallel, its first step is to partition the data source. However, it is very important that you understand that complex queries could be repartitioned during its execution. PLINQ takes the input data source and splits it into multiple pieces according to the number of available logical cores. It uses tasks to process each part in a different core. For example, if you run the previously shown PLINQ query with eight thousand words in a computer with four logical cores, PLINQ could break the eight thousand words into four partitions of two thousand words. Each partition could be consumed in one of the four tasks, processing the data and performing a partial sum over the results of each partition. Finally, the four partial sums must be added together to offer a final result, as shown in Figure 6-1.

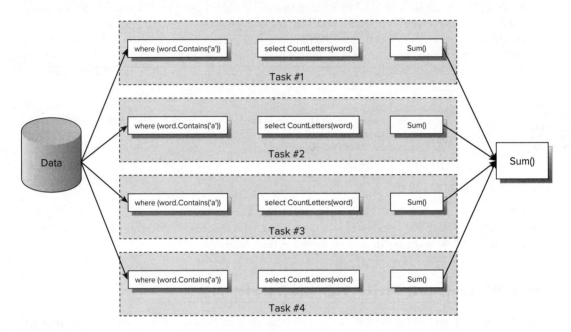

FIGURE 6-1

The PLINQ execution engine has to make very important decisions in a short period of time to avoid adding a great overhead to the query execution. Thus, according to the query shape, it uses the following four primary algorithms for partitioning the data:

➤ **Range partitioning** — This works with indexable data sources as lists and arrays. When PLINQ works against an `IEnumerable` or `IEnumerable<T>`, it queries for the `IList<T>` interface. If it finds this interface, it will use its implementation with range partitioning, splitting the data in as many ranges as logical cores found, as illustrated in Figure 6-2. In these cases, PLINQ knows the exact length of the data source, and it can directly access any of the elements in the list or array. As you learned in previous chapters, this partitioning mechanism offers interesting performance benefits in most cases. This default partitioning scheme can be overridden using one of the `Partitioner.Create` overloads that accepts an `IList<TSource>` and a `Boolean` as parameters. A `true` value for the `Boolean` parameter indicates that the created partitioner should dynamically load balance between partitions rather than statically partition.

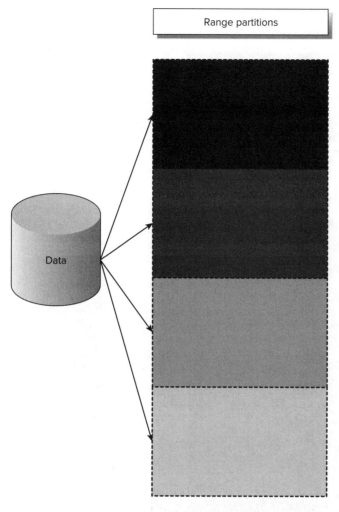

FIGURE 6-2

➤ **Chunk partitioning** — This works for any data source. When PLINQ works against non-indexable data sources, the different tasks request data, which is served in chunks with probable different sizes, as illustrated in Figure 6-3. When an `IEnumerable` or `IEnumerable<T>` doesn't offer a fixed number of elements, chunk partitioning balances the load among cores. The tasks dynamically request more work as needed. The size for the delegates is adjusted dynamically.

➤ **Striped partitioning** — This is optimized for processing items at the top of the data source. Thus, PLINQ uses this scheme when the query includes `SkipWhile` or `TakeWhile`. It is a special case of the previously explained range partitioning, and it can be applied to arrays and types that implement the `IList<T>` interface. Each task works with a small number of items (typically just one) as illustrated in Figure 6-4. This set of items is known as a *stripe*. Each task can determine its data corresponding to each stripe via simple arithmetic; therefore, this scheme doesn't require inter-thread synchronization mechanisms.

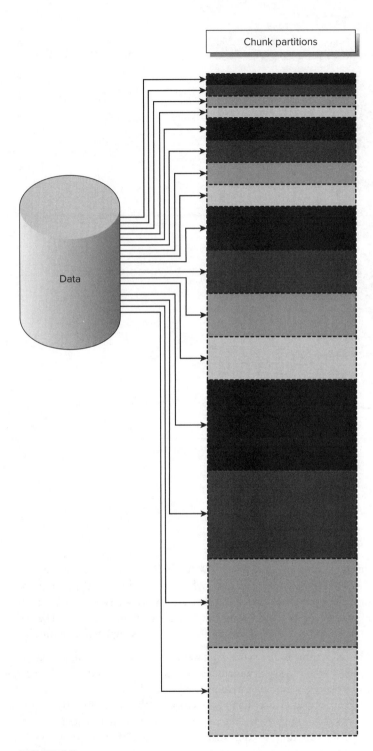

FIGURE 6-3

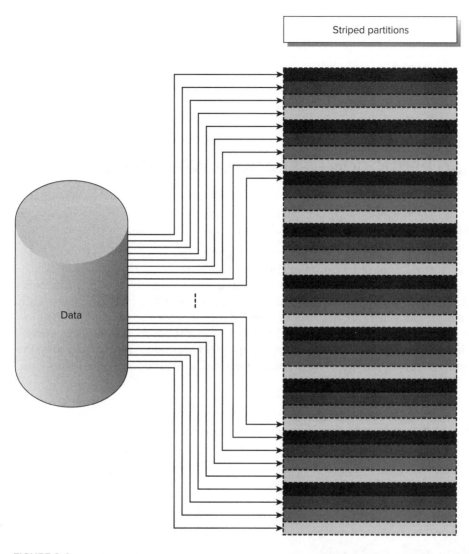

FIGURE 6-4

➤ **Hash partitioning** — This is optimized to compare data elements. The data is channeled to tasks in order to send items with identical hash codes to the same task. PLINQ has to compute a hash for each element's key and assign it to the corresponding output partition according to the computed hash. This way, all possible matches end up in the same partition, simplifying the processing of the comparison operators and reducing the shared data between different tasks, as illustrated in Figure 6-5. Of course, this distribution requires an important overhead. However, the comparison processes can be executed without further synchronization requirements. PLINQ uses this special type of partitioning for processing the following query operators that have to compare data elements:

   ➤ `distinct`

   ➤ `except`

➤ groupjoin

➤ groupby

➤ intersect

➤ join

➤ union

PERFORMING REDUCTION OPERATIONS WITH PLINQ

PLINQ simplifies the procedure of applying a function across all the members of a sequence or group, known as *reduction operation*. You can take advantage of parallelism here by using aggregate functions as Average, Max, Min, and Sum in PLINQ queries. In fact, the previous example performed a reduction in parallel, a Sum.

A reduction performed in parallel can offer different results than a serial reduction can because of rounding when the operation isn't both commutative and associative. The distribution of the sequence or group elements in diverse parallel tasks can be dissimilar in each execution, and this can generate differences in the final results for this kind of operations. Therefore, it is very important that you use the parallel equivalents to define the original data source in order to help PLINQ to achieve an optimal execution. Listing 6-2 shows the code for a reduction operation, an average, performed in LINQ, and Listing 6-3 shows its PLINQ version.

LISTING 6-2: A LINQ query that demonstrates a reduction operation, an average

```
static int NUM_INTS = 50000000;

static IEnumerable<int> GenerateInputData()
{
    return Enumerable.Range(1, NUM_INTS);
}

static void Main(string[] args)
{
    var inputIntegers = GenerateInputData();

    var seqReductionQuery = (from intNum in inputIntegers
                             where ((intNum % 5) == 0)
                             select (intNum / Math.PI)).Average();

    Console.WriteLine("Average {0}", seqReductionQuery);
    Console.ReadLine();
}
```

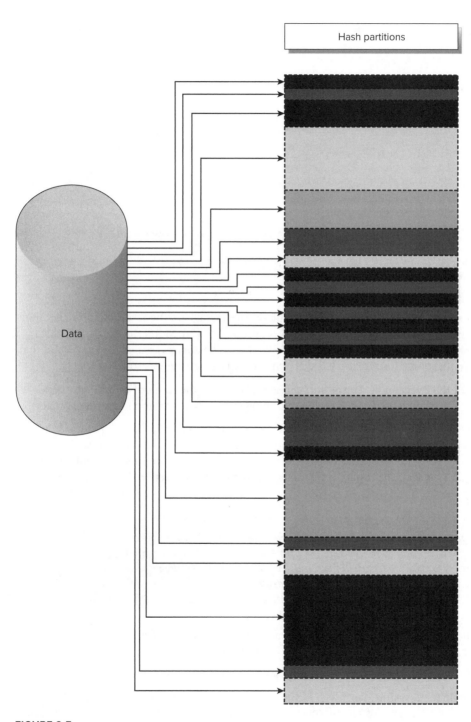

FIGURE 6-5

LISTING 6-3: A PLINQ query that demonstrates a reduction operation, an average

```
static int NUM_INTS = 50000000;

static ParallelQuery<int> GenerateInputData()
{
    return ParallelEnumerable.Range(1, NUM_INTS);
}

static void Main(string[] args)
{
    var inputIntegers = GenerateInputData();

    var parReductionQuery = (from intNum in inputIntegers.AsParallel()
                             where ((intNum % 5) == 0)
                             select (intNum / Math.PI)).Average();

    Console.WriteLine("Average {0}", parReductionQuery);
    Console.ReadLine();
}
```

seqReductionQuery is a LINQ query that calculates the average on the result of an integer number divided by π for each of the numbers from 1 to 50000000 (NUM_INTS) that is divisible by 5. parReductionQuery defines the same query as a PLINQ. The GenerateInputData method that generates the data source for the query is different in the two versions, as follows:

➤ In the LINQ version, it returns an IEnumerable<int>, the result of calling the Enumerable .Range method to generate a sequence of integral numbers within the specified range.

In the PLINQ version, it returns a ParallelQuery<int>, the result of using the parallel equivalent of System.Linq.Enumerable, System.Linq.ParallelEnumerable, and calling the ParallelEnumerable.Range method to generate a *parallel sequence* of integral numbers within the specified range. This way, the result represents a parallel sequence, prepared to run in parallel with PLINQ.

It is possible to run the PLINQ query, parReductionQuery, *using the same* GenerateInputData *method defined for the LINQ version presented in Listing 6-2. However, it will need more time to run. Thus, the code shown in Listing 6-3 is going to offer the best results.*

If you want to define a LINQ query that works against a data source of the Customer type, and store it in the *seqCustomerQuery* variable, you usually define it as follows:

```
private IEnumerable<Customer> seqCustomerQuery;
```

If you want to define the same query as a PLINQ query, you will have to use ParallelQuery<Customer> instead of IEnumerable<Customer>, as shown in the following line:

```
private ParallelQuery<Customer> parCustomerQuery;
```

CREATING CUSTOM PLINQ AGGREGATE FUNCTIONS

PLINQ offers an `Aggregate` overload that enables the implementation of customized parallel reduction algorithms. One of its overrides applies in parallel an accumulator function over a sequence. This override enables intermediate aggregation on each parallelized partition of the query and a final aggregation function to combine the results generated in the partitions. Listing 6-4 shows an example of calculating the following three statistical functions over a sequence by using custom PLINQ `Aggregate` functions:

➤ **Standard deviation** — This is a measure of how widely values are dispersed from the mean (the average value).

➤ **Skewness** — This characterizes the degree of asymmetry of a distribution around its mean. A positive skewness indicates a distribution with an asymmetric tail extending toward more positive values. A negative skewness indicates a distribution with an asymmetric tail extending toward more negative values.

➤ **Kurtosis** — This characterizes the relative peakedness or flatness of a distribution compared with the normal distribution. A positive kurtosis indicates a relatively peaked distribution. A negative kurtosis indicates a relatively flat distribution.

LISTING 6-4: Using PLINQ Aggregate functions to calculate standard deviation, skewness, and kurtosis for parallel sequence

```
static void Main(string[] args)
{
    int[] inputIntegers =
        {0, 3, 4, 8, 15, 22, 34, 57, 68, 32, 21, 30};

    var mean = inputIntegers.AsParallel().Average();

    var standardDeviation = inputIntegers.AsParallel().Aggregate(
        // Seed
        0d,
        // Update accumulator function
        (subTotal, thisNumber) => subTotal +
            Math.Pow((thisNumber - mean), 2),
        // Combine accumulators function
        (total, thisTask) => total + thisTask,
        // Result selector
        (finalSum) => Math.Sqrt((finalSum /
            (inputIntegers.Count() - 1))));

    var skewness = inputIntegers.AsParallel().Aggregate(
        // Seed
        0d,
        // Update accumulator function
        (subTotal, thisNumber) => subTotal +
            Math.Pow(((thisNumber - mean) / standardDeviation), 3),
        // Combine accumulators function
        (total, thisTask) => total + thisTask,
```

continues

LISTING 6-4 *(continued)*

```
            // Result selector
            (finalSum) =>
                ((finalSum * inputIntegers.Count()) /
                ((inputIntegers.Count() - 1) *
                (inputIntegers.Count() - 2)))));

    var kurtosis = inputIntegers.AsParallel().Aggregate(
            // Seed
            0d,
            // Update accumulator function
            (subTotal, thisNumber) => subTotal +
                Math.Pow(((thisNumber - mean) /
                standardDeviation), 4),
            // Combine accumulators function
            (total, thisTask) => total + thisTask,
            // Result selector
            (finalSum) =>
                ((finalSum * inputIntegers.Count() *
                  (inputIntegers.Count() + 1)) /
                ((inputIntegers.Count() - 1) *
                (inputIntegers.Count() - 2) *
                (inputIntegers.Count() - 3))) -
                ((3 *
                  Math.Pow((inputIntegers.Count() - 1), 2)) /
                ((inputIntegers.Count() - 2) *
                (inputIntegers.Count() - 3)))));

    Console.WriteLine("Mean: {0}", mean);
    Console.WriteLine("Standard deviation: {0}", standardDeviation);
    Console.WriteLine("Skewness: {0}", skewness);
    Console.WriteLine("Kurtosis: {0}", kurtosis);

    Console.ReadLine();
}
```

The code calculates the standard deviation, the skewness, and the kurtosis for the integer data source, *inputIntegers*, in parallel. It would likely be more efficient to do all of the operations as part of one `Aggregate` call rather than one for each. However, the purpose of this example is to help you understand how to define multiple PLINQ aggregate functions. There are many different alternatives for calculating the skewness and the kurtosis, but this code uses the formulas of the equivalent Microsoft Office Excel statistical functions: STDEV, SKEW, and KURT. Figure 6-6 shows the three formulas, where:

➤ x_i is each element in the sample

➤ *s* is the sample standard deviation

➤ *n* is the sample size

➤ $\bar{x}$ is the sample mean (average)

Standard deviation

$$\sqrt{\frac{\Sigma(x - \bar{x})^2}{(n - 1)}}$$

Skewness

$$\frac{n}{(n - 1)(n - 2)} \Sigma \left(\frac{x_i - \bar{x}}{s} \right)^3$$

Kurtosis

$$\left\{ \frac{n(n + 1)}{(n - 1)(n - 2)(n - 3)} \Sigma \left(\frac{x_i - \bar{x}}{s} \right)^4 \right\}$$
$$- \frac{3(n - 2)^2}{(n - 2)(n - 3)}$$

FIGURE 6-6

Because the three calculations require the sample mean, the first thing that the code does is calculate the mean (an average for the data set) in parallel, stored in mean:

```
var mean = inputIntegers.AsParallel().Average();
```

Then, it calculates the standard deviation by defining a custom parallel reduction algorithm to implement its formula in PLINQ. The parameters for the Aggregate extension are illustrated in Figure 6-7.

As you can see in the figure, Aggregate uses the following four parameters to calculate the standard deviation:

➤ **Initial value for the accumulator function** — In this case, it's 0 typified as a double:

```
0d
```

➤ **Update accumulator function** — This is invoked on each element in a partition. In this case, it sums the difference between the element, thisNumber, and the previously calculated mean value, mean. Then, it raises this result to the power of 2 and adds it to the actual value stored in the subTotal variable. The code runs for each element in each different partition.

```
(subTotal, thisNumber) => subTotal + Math.Pow((thisNumber - mean), 2)
```

➤ **Combine accumulators function** — This is invoked to compute values based on the final results for each partition. In this case, it sums the yielded element from each partition, thisTask, and accumulates the result in the total variable. The code runs after the results for each partition have been calculated, once per partition.

```
(total, thisTask) => total + thisTask
```

➤ **Result selector** — After the accumulated value for all the partitions is calculated, this transforms it into the desired final result. In this case, the code calculates the square root of the result of dividing the final sum, *finalSum*, by the total number of elements minus 1.

```
(finalSum) => Math.Sqrt((finalSum / (inputIntegers.Count() - 1))));
```

This code runs once before returning the result of the customized aggregate operation, as illustrated in Figure 6-8.

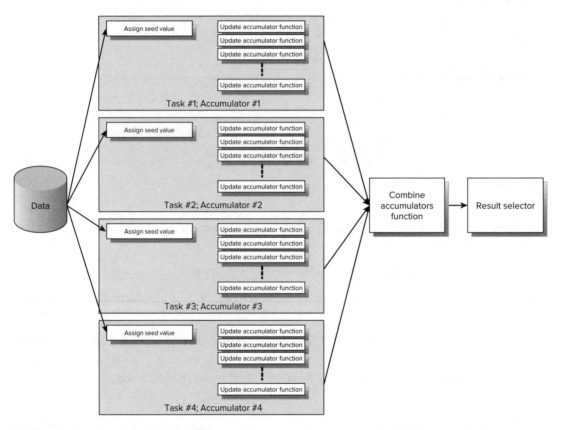

FIGURE 6-7

You can use a similar approach to calculate more complex parallel reduction algorithms. However, it would likely be more efficient to do all of the operations as part of one `Aggregate` call rather than one for each. In fact, the skewness and the kurtosis calculations call the `Aggregate` extension with the same four parameters, performing different calculations to represent their formulas. The code shown in Listing 6-4 may seem too complex; however, if you take a look at the formula while reading the code, you will see that it is very easy to transform formulas like these into a PLINQ parallel reduction algorithm.

The code defines an array with 12 integral numbers as follows:

```
int[] inputIntegers = {0, 3, 4, 8, 15, 22, 34, 57, 68, 32, 21, 30};
```

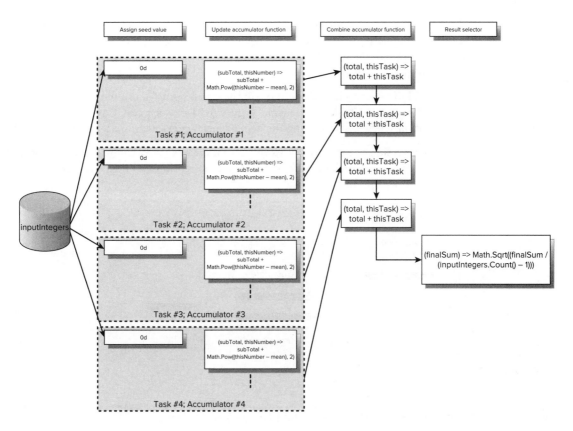

FIGURE 6-8

To generate a parallel sequence of one hundred million integral numbers, you would just replace that line with the following line that calls the `ParallelEnumerable.Range` method:

```
var inputIntegers = ParallelEnumerable.Range(1, 100000000);
```

CONCURRENT PLINQ TASKS

Listing 6-4 performs many calculations using many PLINQ queries. However, these parallelized queries run in a synchronous way, one after the other and in the main thread. Figure 6-9 shows a Gantt diagram with the representation of the different PLINQ queries as executed in Listing 6-4 and the dependencies between them.

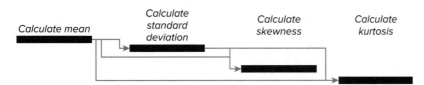

FIGURE 6-9

The standard deviation calculation requires the mean. Both the skewness and the kurtosis calculations need the results of the mean and the standard deviation. If the scalability for the skewness and the kurtosis calculations in parallel were limited, it would be possible to run them in parallel, limiting the number of cores for each PLINQ query.

You can also include PLINQ queries in tasks and chain these tasks with continuations, as you learned in Chapter 3, "Imperative Task Parallelism." Figure 6-10 shows a new Gantt diagram with the possible new execution scheme, considering the dependencies previously analyzed in Figure 6-9.

Listing 6-5 shows a new version of the previous example that creates many chained tasks according to the diagram shown in Figure 6-10. The code will throw an exception and the next section will explain the reason for this exception.

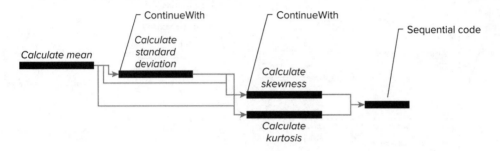

FIGURE 6-10

LISTING 6-5: Combining PLINQ queries with tasks and continuations

```
private static ParallelQuery<int> inputIntegers =
    ParallelEnumerable.Range(1, 100000000);

private static double CalculateMean(
    System.Threading.CancellationToken ct)
{
    return inputIntegers.AsParallel().WithCancellation(ct).Average();
}

private static double CalculateStandardDeviation(
    System.Threading.CancellationToken ct, double mean)
{
    return inputIntegers.AsParallel().WithCancellation(ct).Aggregate(
        // Seed
      0d,
        // Update accumulator function
      (subTotal, thisNumber) => subTotal +
         Math.Pow((thisNumber - mean), 2),
        // Combine accumulators function
      (total, thisTask) => total + thisTask,
        // Result selector
      (finalSum) => Math.Sqrt((finalSum /
         (inputIntegers.Count() - 1))));
```

```csharp
}

private static double CalculateSkewness(
    System.Threading.CancellationToken ct,
    double mean, double standardDeviation)
{
    return inputIntegers.AsParallel().WithCancellation(ct).Aggregate(
        // Seed
      0d,
        // Update accumulator function
        (subTotal, thisNumber) => subTotal +
            Math.Pow(((thisNumber - mean) / standardDeviation), 3),
        // Combine accumulators function
        (total, thisTask) => total + thisTask,
        // Result selector
        (finalSum) =>
            ((finalSum * inputIntegers.Count()) /
             ((inputIntegers.Count() - 1) *
             (inputIntegers.Count() - 2))));
}

private static double CalculateKurtosis(
    System.Threading.CancellationToken ct,
    double mean, double standardDeviation)
{
    return inputIntegers.AsParallel().WithCancellation(ct).Aggregate(
        // Seed
        0d,
        // Update accumulator function
        (subTotal, thisNumber) => subTotal +
            Math.Pow(((thisNumber - mean) /
              standardDeviation), 4),
        // Combine accumulators function
        (total, thisTask) => total + thisTask,
        // Result selector
        (finalSum) =>
            ((finalSum * inputIntegers.Count() *
              (inputIntegers.Count() + 1)) /
             ((inputIntegers.Count() - 1) *
             (inputIntegers.Count() - 2) *
             (inputIntegers.Count() - 3))) -
            ((3 *
              Math.Pow((inputIntegers.Count() - 1), 2)) /
             ((inputIntegers.Count() - 2) *
             (inputIntegers.Count() - 3))));
}

static void Main(string[] args)
{
    Console.ReadLine();

    Console.WriteLine("Started");

    var cts = new System.Threading.CancellationTokenSource();
```

continues

LISTING 6-5 *(continued)*

```csharp
var ct = cts.Token;

var sw = Stopwatch.StartNew();

var taskMean = new Task<double>(() => CalculateMean(ct), ct);

var taskSTDev = taskMean.ContinueWith<double>((t) =>
    {
        // At this point
        // t.Result = mean
        return CalculateStandardDeviation(ct, t.Result);
    }, TaskContinuationOptions.OnlyOnRanToCompletion);

var taskSkewness = taskSTDev.ContinueWith<double>((t) =>
    {
        // At this point
        // t.Result = standard deviation
        return CalculateSkewness(ct, taskMean.Result, t.Result);
    }, TaskContinuationOptions.OnlyOnRanToCompletion);

var taskKurtosis = taskSTDev.ContinueWith<double>((t) =>
    {
        // At this point
        // t.Result = standard deviation
        return CalculateKurtosis(ct, taskMean.Result, t.Result);
    }, TaskContinuationOptions.OnlyOnRanToCompletion);

var deferredCancelTask = Task.Factory.StartNew(() =>
{
    // Sleep the thread that runs this task for 5 seconds
    System.Threading.Thread.Sleep(5000);
    // Send the signal to cancel
    cts.Cancel();
});

try
{
    // Start taskMean and then all the chained tasks
    taskMean.Start();

    // Wait for both taskSkewness and taskKurtosis to finish
    Task.WaitAll(taskSkewness, taskKurtosis);

    Console.WriteLine("Mean: {0}", taskMean.Result);
    Console.WriteLine("Standard deviation: {0}", taskSTDev.Result);
    Console.WriteLine("Skewness: {0}", taskSkewness.Result);
    Console.WriteLine("Kurtosis: {0}", taskKurtosis.Result);

    Console.ReadLine();
}
catch (AggregateException ex)
{
```

```
        foreach (Exception innerEx in ex.InnerExceptions)
        {
            Debug.WriteLine(innerEx.ToString());
            // Do something considering the innerEx Exception
            if (ex.InnerException is OperationCanceledException)
            {
                // A task was cancelled
                // Write each task status to the console
                Console.WriteLine("Mean task: {0}",
                    taskMean.Status);
                Console.WriteLine("Standard deviation task: {0}",
                    taskSTDev.Status);
                Console.WriteLine("Skewness task: {0}",
                    taskSkewness.Status);
                Console.WriteLine("Kurtosis task: {0}",
                    taskKurtosis.Status);
                Console.ReadLine();
            }
        }
    }
}
```

Each of the following tasks runs a PLINQ query and generates a `double` result:

➤ **taskMean** — Calculates the mean.

➤ **taskSTDev** — Calculates the standard deviation after the mean is computed.

➤ **taskSkewness** — Calculates the skewness after both the mean and the standard deviation are computed.

➤ **taskKurtosis** — Calculates the kurtosis after both the mean and the standard deviation are computed.

In this case, each chained task requires a result from its precedent task. Thus, the `TaskContinuationOptions.OnlyOnRanToCompletion` option is specified as a parameter. This way, each chained task will run only if the precedent task ran to completion. Because both `taskSkewness` and `taskKurtosis` are scheduled to start after `taskSTDev` finishes its execution, their PLINQ queries could run in parallel and will try to take full advantage of the number of logical cores. You can optimize the parallel execution for this new schedule by specifying the degree of parallelism for each task that runs concurrently with other tasks (`taskSkewness` and `taskKurtosis`).

CANCELLING PLINQ

Some PLINQ queries can take a long time to run. Thus, it is a good idea to provide mechanisms to interrupt their execution. You can do this through the use of cancellation tokens, as you learned with `Task` instances in Chapter 3, "Imperative Task Parallelism."

Listing 6-5 showed the code for many PLINQ queries, with the necessary changes made in order to support cancellation. Each method that runs a PLINQ query receives a `System.Threading .CancellationToken` instance, `ct`, and throws an `OperationCanceledException`. The cancellation request could occur after the PLINQ query started its execution. Therefore, each PLINQ query receives this `CancellationToken` instance, *ct*, by using the `WithCancellation` method defined in `ParallelEnumerable`.

```
return inputIntegers.AsParallel().WithCancellation(ct).Aggregate(…
```

This way, the PLINQ query adds a small overhead to its execution in order to observe an `OperationCanceledException` and compares its token to the one received as a parameter in the `WithCancellation` method. If both tokens are the same and the `IsCancellationRequested` property is true, the PLINQ execution engine understands that there is a request for cancellation and interrupts its execution. Because there is no code catching this exception inside the `Task` instance delegate, the exception is raised and will be wrapped in an `AggregateException`. As a result, the `Task` instance that runs this query transitions to the `TaskStatus.Faulted` state and the `IsFaulted` property will be `true`.

If you run the example with Visual Studio 2010 default options, a message indicating that an `OperationCanceledException` was unhandled by user code will appear, as shown in Figure 6-11. You just have to select Tools ⇨ Options ⇨ Debugging ⇨ General and deactivate the Enable Just My Code check box. This way, the IDE won't catch exceptions thrown from user code through PLINQ. You can also just select Debug ⇨ Continue or press F5.

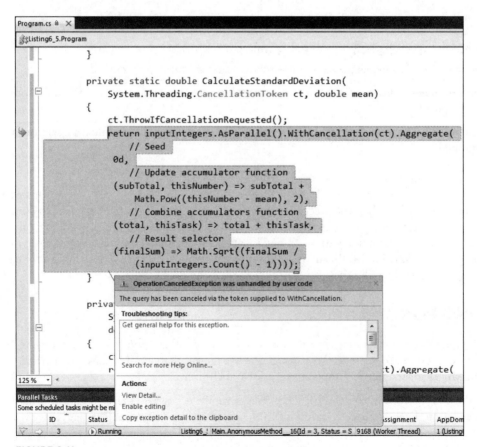

FIGURE 6-11

Depending on the hardware on which you run this example, the results could vary. In some cases, when the *deferredCancelTask* task sends the signal to cancel by calling the `cts.Cancel` method after sleeping for 5 seconds, both the skewness and the kurtosis PLINQ queries will get canceled and their associated `Task` instances, *taskSkewness* and *taskKurtosis*, will become faulted, as shown in the following console output:

```
Started
Mean task: RanToCompletion
Standard deviation task: RanToCompletion
Skewness task: Faulted
Kurtosis task: Faulted
```

If you replace the code that defines and starts the *deferredCancelTask* with the following code lines, it will send the signal to cancel after sleeping for 2 seconds:

```
var deferredCancelTask = Task.Factory.StartNew(() =>
{
    // Sleep the thread that runs this task for 2 seconds
    System.Threading.Thread.Sleep(2000);
    // Send the signal to cancel
    cts.Cancel();
});
```

code snippet from Snippet6_8

The standard deviation PLINQ query that is currently running will get canceled, and its associated `Task` instance, *taskSTDev*, will become faulted. Because *taskSkewness* and *taskKurtosis* are chained to *taskSTDev* with a continuation option defined to `TaskContinuationOptions.OnlyOnRanToCompletion`, and *taskSTDev* is faulted (didn't run to completion), the two chained tasks will be canceled by the scheduling engine, as shown in the following console output:

```
Started
Mean task: RanToCompletion
Standard deviation task: Faulted
Skewness task: Canceled
Kurtosis task: Canceled
```

SPECIFYING THE DESIRED DEGREE OF PARALLELISM

By default, PLINQ always tries to achieve the best results using all the available logical cores. However, you can specify a different maximum degree of parallelism with the `WithDegreeOfParallelism` method.

WithDegreeOfParallelism

The following code runs the two PLINQ queries that calculate the skewness and kurtosis, specifying that they use a maximum of half the number of logical cores as concurrent tasks. Because both queries are launched in tasks that start at the same time, each one is going to take advantage of half of the cores.

```csharp
// Environment.ProcessorCount requires a Platform Invoke (P/Invoke)
// This variable caches its value
// However, the number of logical cores might change in some specific hardware
private static int processorCount = Environment.ProcessorCount;

private static double CalculateSkewness(
    System.Threading.CancellationToken ct,
    double mean, double standardDeviation)
{
    return inputIntegers.AsParallel().WithCancellation(ct)
     .WithDegreeOfParallelism(processorCount / 2)
     .Aggregate(
        // Seed
       0d,
        // Update accumulator function
       (subTotal, thisNumber) => subTotal +
          Math.Pow(((thisNumber - mean) / standardDeviation), 3),
        // Combine accumulators function
       (total, thisTask) => total + thisTask,
        // Result selector
       (finalSum) =>
          ((finalSum * inputIntegers.Count()) /
            ((inputIntegers.Count() - 1) *
             (inputIntegers.Count() - 2))));
}

private static double CalculateKurtosis(
    System.Threading.CancellationToken ct,
    double mean, double standardDeviation)
{
    return inputIntegers.AsParallel().WithCancellation(ct)
        .WithDegreeOfParallelism(processorCount / 2)
        .Aggregate(
        // Seed
        0d,
        // Update accumulator function
        (subTotal, thisNumber) => subTotal +
            Math.Pow(((thisNumber - mean) /
            standardDeviation), 4),
        // Combine accumulators function
        (total, thisTask) => total + thisTask,
        // Result selector
        (finalSum) =>
            ((finalSum * inputIntegers.Count() *
              (inputIntegers.Count() + 1)) /
             ((inputIntegers.Count() - 1) *
              (inputIntegers.Count() - 2) *
              (inputIntegers.Count() - 3))) -
             ((3 *
               Math.Pow((inputIntegers.Count() - 1), 2)) /
```

```
            ((inputIntegers.Count() - 2) *
            (inputIntegers.Count() - 3)))));
}
```

code snippet from Snippet6_9

`Environment.ProcessorCount` requires a Platform Invoke (P/Invoke); and therefore, it isn't so cheap to call it. The private static *processorCount* variable caches the result for `Environment.ProcessorCount`. The number of logical cores might change in some specific hardware, most likely on servers. Thus, you should retrieve the value for `Environment.ProcessorCount` before running a long-running parallelized algorithm. Then, you can refresh this value before running another algorithm.

If the code runs with a microprocessor with eight logical cores, each PLINQ query is going to run with a maximum of four concurrent tasks. You can also launch many PLINQ queries with different maximum degrees of parallelism using `Parallel.Invoke`. Some PLINQ queries have a limited scalability, so these options allow you to take advantage of additional cores.

You shouldn't work with half the number of logical cores, because for some computers, this number could be odd (for example, three logical cores). When you make scheduling decisions like the previous example, you should always use dynamic values suitable for both even and odd numbers of cores. The following line shows an example that evaluates whether the number of logical cores is even or odd and assigns one core more if it is odd:

```
int maxDegree =
    (processorCount % 2 == 0) ? (processorCount / 2) :
    ((processorCount / 2) + 1)
```

code snippet from Snippet6_9_Enhanced

Besides, sometimes you may want to leave one core free in order to create a responsive application. This core can help you to run another part of code in parallel, bringing a more responsive UI while computing intensive and long-running queries. To do this, you can add the following line:

```
.WithDegreeOfParallelism(processorCount - 1)
```

Measuring Scalability

As you previously learned for parallel loops, sometimes it's useful to run a PLINQ query with many different degrees of parallelism in order to measure its scalability. Table 6-2 summarizes the results of running a PLINQ query that calculates the mean with two data sources. The query ran with eight different maximum degrees of parallelism in a computer with four physical cores and eight logical cores.

TABLE 6-2: PLINQ Query Results for Calculating a Mean with Multiple Data Sources

DEGREE OF PARALLELISM EXECUTION TIME (SECONDS)	DATA SOURCE = 800,000,000 INTEGRAL NUMBERS	DATA SOURCE = 1,600,000,000 INTEGRAL NUMBERS
1	7.80	15.60
2	4.83	10.30
3	4.27	8.41
4	3.60	7.09
5	3.55	6.95
6	3.55	6.58
7	3.14	6.25
8	3.14	5.97

Figure 6-12 shows a line chart with the time needed to run each query, and Figure 6-13 shows another line chart with the speedups achieved.

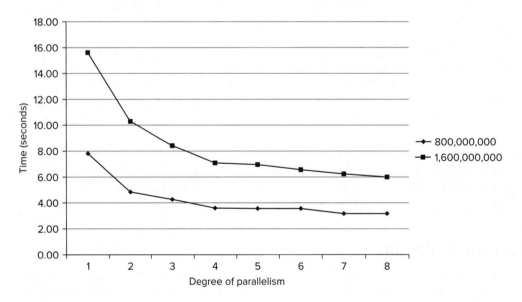

FIGURE 6-12

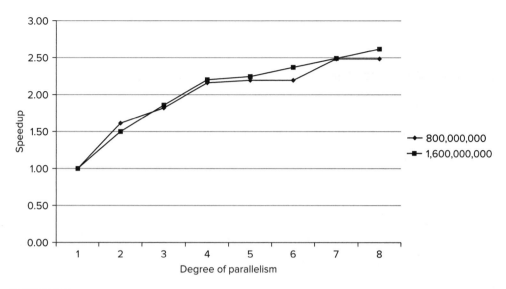

FIGURE 6-13

The computer has four physical cores; and therefore, the parallelized query offers an important scalability up to four cores. Beyond four cores, the additional tasks run in the Hyperthreaded cores that share the same physical core. You can expect really smaller speedups once the degree of parallelism goes beyond the number of physical cores, as happens in this example. Chapter 1 explained the difference between physical cores and logical cores.

According to the results offered by running the PLINQ query with different degrees of parallelism, you can decide to combine it with other queries or try other alternatives to run the algorithms. In this example, the query just calculates an average and it scales pretty well when it distributes the work on additional physical cores.

WORKING WITH FORALL

As you learned in Chapter 4, "Concurrent Collections," `Systems.Collections.Concurrent.ConcurrentBag` is one of the concurrent collections that allows many elements to be added by multiple tasks running in parallel. The `ForAll` extension method exposed by `ParallelEnumerable` is very useful for processing the results of a query in parallel without requiring you to write a parallel loop. It receives an action as a parameter, offering the same possibilities as the corresponding parameter received by the `Task` constructors described in Chapter 3, "Imperative Task Parallelism." Thus, using lambda expressions, you can combine parallelized processing actions from the results of a PLINQ query.

Listing 6-6 shows the code of the well-known MD5 hash generator. The `GenerateMD5InputData` method returns a `ParallelQuery<int>` by calling `ParallelEnumerable.Range`. Then, a simple call to `ForAll` processes a sequence of integral numbers in parallel and adds the result of calling the `GenerateMD5Hash` method with the number as a parameter.

LISTING 6-6: Generating MD5 hashes using ForAll and a ConcurrentBag

```csharp
private const int NUM_MD5_HASHES = 100000;

private static ParallelQuery<int> GenerateMD5InputData()
{
    return ParallelEnumerable.Range(1, NUM_MD5_HASHES);
}

private static string ConvertToHexString(Byte[] byteArray)
{
    // Convert the byte array to hexadecimal string
    var sb = new StringBuilder(byteArray.Length);

    for (int i = 0; i < byteArray.Length; i++)
    {
        sb.Append(byteArray[i].ToString("X2"));
    }

    return sb.ToString();
}

private static string GenerateMD5Hash(int number)
{
    var md5M = MD5.Create();
    byte[] data =
        Encoding.Unicode.GetBytes(
        Environment.UserName + number.ToString());
    byte[] result = md5M.ComputeHash(data);
    string hexString = ConvertToHexString(result);

    return hexString;
}

static void Main(string[] args)
{
    Console.ReadLine();
    Console.WriteLine("Started");

    var sw = Stopwatch.StartNew();

    var inputIntegers = GenerateMD5InputData();
    var hashesBag = new ConcurrentBag<string>();
    inputIntegers.ForAll((i) => hashesBag.Add(GenerateMD5Hash(i)));

    Console.WriteLine("Finished in {0}", sw.Elapsed);
    Console.WriteLine("{0} MD5 hashes generated in {1}",
        hashesBag.Count(), sw.Elapsed.ToString());
    Console.WriteLine("First MD5 hash: {0}", hashesBag.First());
```

```
        Console.WriteLine("Last MD5 hash: {0}", hashesBag.Last());
        Console.ReadLine();
    }
```

Then, the `Main` method shows the elapsed time, the number of MD5 hashes generated, and the first and last items in the `ConcurrentBag`. The following line of code adds elements in parallel to the new `ConcurrentBag`, `hashesBag`, an unordered collection of `string`:

```
inputIntegers.ForAll((i) => hashesBag.Add(GenerateMD5Hash(i)));
```

code snippet from Listing6_6

 inputIntegers is a `ParallelQuery<int>` *and hashesBag is going to store all the MD5 hashes generated in parallel. This* `ConcurrentBag` *will allow most additions to end up being lock-free. There are other more efficient ways to produce similar results. The purpose of this example is to help you understand how to store items in a concurrent data structure from* `ForAll`*.*

 It is not necessary to add `.AsParallel()`*, because the* `ForAll` *extension method is already prepared to run in parallel.*

Differences Between foreach and ForAll

When you define a PLINQ query and then use either a `foreach` or `for` loop to execute it and iterate through the results, that part of the code doesn't run in parallel. In fact, it requires the PLINQ query output merged into the thread that is running the loop, as shown in Figure 6-14. The same happens when you invoke methods to generate a specific output such as `ToArray`, `ToDictionary`, or `ToList`.

When you need to process data with a specific sequential order, you have to use the aforementioned sequential loops or methods. However, if you don't need a specific order, you can achieve the best performance by using `ForAll` as previously explained. `ForAll` processes the results in parallel as shown in Figure 6-15, and it doesn't need to perform the final merge step.

Measuring Scalability

You can combine the `ForAll` extension method applied to the `ParallelQuery<int>`, *inputIntegers*, with the `WithDegreeOfParallelism` method in order to measure its scalability. The following line shows an example of defining a degree of parallelism of 4:

```
inputIntegers.WithDegreeOfParallelism(4).ForAll((i) =>
    hashesBag.Add(GenerateMD5Hash(i)));
```

code snippet from Listing6_6_Speedup

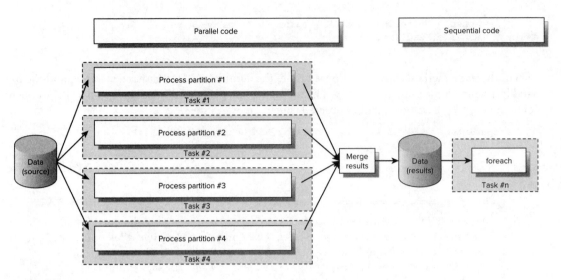

FIGURE 6-14

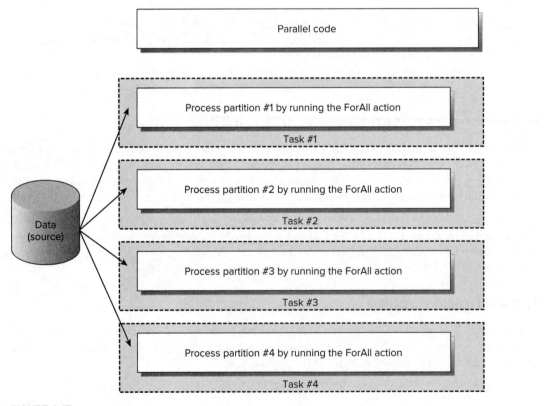

FIGURE 6-15

In this case, because the amount of work done for each element is higher than in the mean calculation PLINQ query, the scalability is better. Table 6-3 summarizes the results of running the code that generates the MD5 hashes using `ForAll` and the `ConcurrentBag`. The test ran with eight different maximum degrees of parallelism in a computer with four physical cores and eight logical cores.

TABLE 6-3: Results of Running the ForAll Extension Method to Calculate MD5 Hashes

DEGREE OF PARALLELISM	EXECUTION TIME (SECONDS)	SPEEDUP
1	19.26	1.00x
2	7.32	2.63x
3	2.70	7.13x
4	2.36	8.16x
5	2.10	9.17x
6	2.00	9.63x
7	1.93	9.98x
8	1.88	10.24x

Figure 6-16 shows a line chart with the time needed to run each query, and Figure 6-17 shows a line chart with the speedups achieved. As happened in the previous example, the computer has four physical cores; and therefore, the parallelized MD5 hashes generation offers an outstanding scalability up to four cores. Beyond four cores, the additional tasks run in the Hyperthreaded cores that share the same physical core. Thus, the speedups are really smaller once the degree of parallelism goes beyond the number of physical cores.

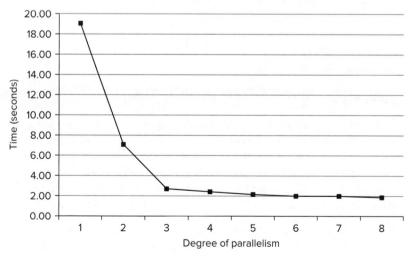

FIGURE 6-16

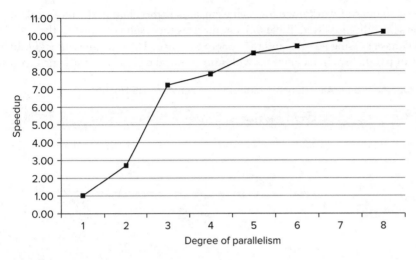

FIGURE 6-17

CONFIGURING HOW RESULTS ARE RETURNED BY USING WITHMERGEOPTIONS

PLINQ splits the data source into many parallel pieces, and then it has to merge the resulting pieces on the thread that is consuming the query. The execution is done in parallel, but the results must be streamed back to the consumer serially, introducing an overhead and the need for synchronization, performed by the execution engine under the hood.

You can give PLINQ hints about the preferred way it should merge the parallel pieces of the result by using the `WithMergeOptions` extension method. This method receives a `ParallelMergeOptions` parameter. Table 6-4 summarizes this parameter's four possible values and their effect on the PLINQ query.

TABLE 6-4: ParallelMergeOptions Members

VALUE	DESCRIPTION
AutoBuffered	PLINQ uses an output buffer to accumulate the results before they are available to the consumer. PLINQ determines the most appropriate buffer's size in order to provide reasonably fast access to the results while offering a good overall throughput. It returns the results in chunks, and keeps a balance between latency for the first results and the synchronization needed to add the results in chunks.
Default	PLINQ uses the default merge type, `ParallelMergeOptions` `.AutoBuffered`. This is the default option when the PLINQ query doesn't have a `ParallelMergeOptions` extension method.

VALUE	DESCRIPTION
NotBuffered	PLINQ doesn't use an output buffer to accumulate the results. Thus, the calling thread would have access to the data as soon as results are available, reducing the latency between beginning the query execution and elements being yielded. Every item added to the results introduces synchronization overhead, because each item has to be merged individually, without an output buffer. Therefore, this approach could increase the overall execution time. If the query is going to be consumed and output as a stream, this option could reduce the latency to show the first elements.
FullyBuffered	PLINQ uses a full output buffer to accumulate the results before they are available to the consumer. Thus, the calling thread would have access to the data after all the results are available. This option increases the latency between beginning the query execution and elements being yielded. However, the `FullyBuffered` option reduces the synchronization overhead and offers the best performance when there is no need for partial results.

Even when the `ParallelMergeOptions` extension method offers a hint to PLINQ, it isn't going to be respected by the execution engine all the time. When a PLINQ query requires sorting the data, it will ignore hints advising it to run without buffers. The following code lines illustrate how to use this extension method. The code snippet offers a different version of the first example for this chapter to provide PLINQ a hint to run a query without output buffers and show the first results as soon as possible. Because the consumer wants to see the first element that matches the query definition, the `ParallelMergeOptions.NotBuffered` option reduces the time needed to show this partial result. This option runs the PLINQ query without output buffers.

```
static void Main(string[] args)
{
    Console.ReadLine();
    Console.WriteLine("Started");

    var cts = new System.Threading.CancellationTokenSource();
    var ct = cts.Token;

    var sw = Stopwatch.StartNew();

    Keys = new ConcurrentQueue<String>();

    var tAsync = new Task(() => ParallelPartitionGenerateAESKeysWCP(ct, 'A'));
    tAsync.Start();

    // Do something else
    // Wait for tAsync to finish
    tAsync.Wait();

    // Define the query indicating that it should run in parallel
    var keysWith10Letters = from key in Keys.AsParallel()
                            .WithMergeOptions(ParallelMergeOptions.NotBuffered)
                        where (CountLetters(key) >= 10)
```

```
                                      && (key.Contains('A'))
                                      && (key.Contains('F'))
                                      && (key.Contains('9'))
                                      && (!key.Contains('B'))
                             select key;

    // Write some of the results of executing the query
    // Remember that the PLINQ query is going to be executed at this point
    // when the code requires results
    Console.WriteLine("First key: {0} ",
        keysWith10Letters.ElementAt(0));
    Console.WriteLine("First result shown in {0}", sw.Elapsed.ToString());

    Console.ReadLine();
}
```

code snippet from Snippet6_10

> *Each option has its advantages and disadvantages, so it is very important that you measure the time to show the first results and the overall time required to complete the query.*

HANDLING EXCEPTIONS THROWN BY PLINQ

Just as many tasks run in parallel to support the parallel execution of a PLINQ query, many exceptions can also occur in parallel. PLINQ queries work with set of exceptions, handled by the previously explained System.AggregateException class. Listing 6-7 shows the highlighted lines that add an unhandled InvalidOperationException exception in the GenerateMD5Hash method.

LISTING 6-7: Handling exceptions in a PLINQ query and its consumer code

```
private static string GenerateMD5Hash(int number)
{
    if ((number % 10000) == 0)
    {
        throw new InvalidOperationException(
            String.Format(
            "The MD5 hash generator doesn't work with input numbers divisible by {0}.
Number received {1}",
            10000, number));
    }
    var md5M = MD5.Create();
    byte[] data = Encoding.Unicode.GetBytes(Environment.UserName + number.ToString());
    byte[] result = md5M.ComputeHash(data);
    string hexString = ConvertToHexString(result);

    return hexString;
```

```
    }

    static void Main(string[] args)
    {
        Console.ReadLine();
        Console.WriteLine("Started");

        var sw = Stopwatch.StartNew();

        var inputIntegers = GenerateMD5InputData();

        var hashesBag = new ConcurrentBag<string>();

        try
        {
            inputIntegers.ForAll((i) =>
                hashesBag.Add(GenerateMD5Hash(i)));

            Console.WriteLine("First MD5 hash: {0}", hashesBag.First());
            Console.WriteLine("Started to show results in {0}",
                sw.Elapsed);
            Console.WriteLine("Last MD5 hash: {0}", hashesBag.Last());
            Console.WriteLine("{0} MD5 hashes generated in {1}",
                hashesBag.Count(), sw.Elapsed.ToString());
        }
        catch (AggregateException ex)
        {
            foreach (Exception innerEx in ex.InnerExceptions)
            {
                Debug.WriteLine(innerEx.ToString());
                // Do something considering the innerEx Exception
                if (innerEx is InvalidOperationException)
                {
                    Console.WriteLine(
                        String.Format(
                        "The MD5 generator failed. Exception details: {0}",
                        innerEx.Message));
                }
            }
            // Something went wrong
            // Create a new empty ConcurrentBag with no results
            hashesBag = new ConcurrentBag<string>();
        }

        Console.ReadLine();
    }
```

Because the PLINQ queries have deferred execution, it is very important to catch exceptions that can happen when the data generated by the query is consumed. Also, because there is no execution order, when you run the code many times, the first exception isn't the same in the InnerExceptions read-only collection of Exception.

The execution of the PLINQ query will try to stop as soon as there is one unhandled exception. However, because there could be many tasks running different parts in parallel, there may be more than one exception in `InnerExceptions`. A `try` block encloses the PLINQ query definition and the code that consumes this query.

There are many numbers that are divisible by 10,000, so there may be more than one exception before the PLINQ query stops its execution. Listing 6-8 shows the results of executing the same code four times.

LISTING 6-8: Results of running the code shown in Listing 6-7 four times

FIRST TIME

```
Started
The MD5 generator failed. Exception details: The MD5 hash generator doesn't work
 with input numbers divisible by 10000. Number received 40000
```

SECOND TIME

```
Started
The MD5 generator failed. Exception details: The MD5 hash generator doesn't work
 with input numbers divisible by 10000. Number received 90000
```

THIRD TIME

```
Started
The MD5 generator failed. Exception details: The MD5 hash generator doesn't work
 with input numbers divisible by 10000. Number received 40000
The MD5 generator failed. Exception details: The MD5 hash generator doesn't work
 with input numbers divisible by 10000. Number received 90000
```

FOURTH TIME

```
Started
The MD5 generator failed. Exception details: The MD5 hash generator doesn't work
 with input numbers divisible by 10000. Number received 30000
```

In one of the executions, the `try` block catches two `Exception` instances in `InnerExceptions`. This might happen because many parts are running in parallel, and the exceptions occur almost at the same time. The exceptions occur in the underlying parallel tasks that support the parallelization for the query before the PLINQ engine finishes communicating the need to cancel the execution to all these tasks.

USING PLINQ TO EXECUTE MAPREDUCE ALGORITHMS

MapReduce, also known as *Map/Reduce* or *Map & Reduce*, is a very popular algorithmic framework that can take advantage of parallelism for processing huge datasets. Its basic idea is very simple and consists of splitting a data processing problem into the following two independent and parallelizable operations:

➤ **Map** — Takes the data source and computes a key-value pair for each item. The result is a collection of key-value pairs, grouped by key.

➤ **Reduce** — Takes all the key-value pairs grouped by key resulting from the map operation and performs a reduction computation for each group. It can return one or many values.

Figure 6-18 shows a diagram with the Map and Reduce operations and their results.

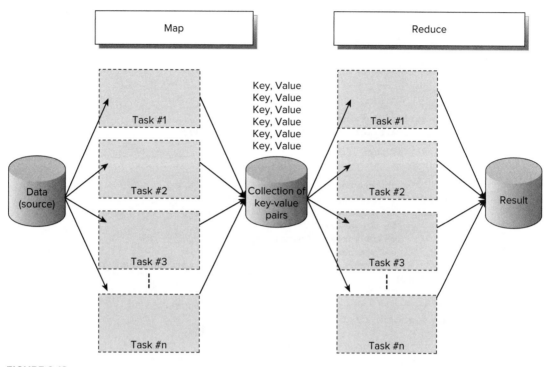

FIGURE 6-18

 The aforementioned definition is the simplest implementation of MapReduce. Some implementations can define additional stages, distribute each of them into smaller sub-problems, and run them in different computers (worker nodes).

The code shown in Listing 6-9 defines a List<string>, *words*, with 28 words. Then it uses two PLINQ queries to split an algorithm that counts the number of times each word appears in a map operation and a reduce operation.

LISTING 6-9: A simple MapReduce algorithm implementation using two PLINQ queries

```
public static List<string> words = new List<string>
    { "there", "is", "a",
        "great", "house", "and",
        "an", "amazing", "lake",
        "there", "is", "a",
        "computer", "running", "a",
        "new", "query", "there",
        "is", "a", "great",
        "server", "ready", "to",
```

continues

LISTING 6-9 *(continued)*

```
            "process",
            "map", "and", "reduce" };

static void Main(string[] args)
{
    // Map
    // Generate a (word, 1) key, value pair
    ILookup<string, int> map =
        words.AsParallel().ToLookup(p => p, k => 1);
    // End of Map

    // Reduce
    // Calculate the number of times a word appears and
    // select the words that appear more than once
    var reduce = from IGrouping<string, int> wordMap
                 in map.AsParallel()
                 where wordMap.Count() > 1
                 select new
                     { Word = wordMap.Key, Count = wordMap.Count() };
    // End of Reduce

    // Show each word and the number of times it appears
    foreach (var word in reduce)
        Console.WriteLine("Word: '{0}'; Count: {1}",
            word.Word, word.Count);

    Console.ReadLine();
}
```

The map operation generates key-value pairs composed of a word and a 1. This means that the code will add each word as a key with 1 as a value. It creates an ILookup<string, int> in parallel, *map*, that maps the keys (in this case, the words) to the enumerable sequence of values.

```
ILookup<string, int> map = words.AsParallel().ToLookup(p => p, k => 1);
```

code snippet from Listing6_9

The reduce operation calculates the number of times a word appears, and filters the words that emerge more than once. The PLINQ query uses IGrouping<string, int> to select from a collection of elements that have a common key. This way, it can access the Key property and the Count extension method.

```
var reduce = from IGrouping<string, int> wordMap
             in map.AsParallel()
             where wordMap.Count() > 1
             select new
                 { Word = wordMap.Key, Count = wordMap.Count() };
```

code snippet from Listing6_9

Then, a sequential `foreach` iterates through the results of the reduce operation and displays each word with the number of times that it appears. Here are the results of running the example shown in Listing 6-9:

```
Word: 'a'; Count: 4
Word: 'great'; Count: 2
Word: 'there'; Count: 3
Word: 'and'; Count: 2
Word: 'is'; Count: 3
```

Because of the deferred execution of PLINQ queries, the code shown in Listing 6-9 doesn't represent a pure implementation of a MapReduce algorithm. You can solve this problem by using different kinds of PLINQ queries. However, because MapReduce is very popular, it is a good idea to learn the options offered by PLINQ to implement some variations of its algorithmic framework. You can also solve this problem using parallelized loops.

DESIGNING SERIAL STAGES USING PLINQ

You can use what you've learned thus far about PLINQ to execute a set of serial stages in parallel with data flowing through it. Consider the following jobs:

➤ **CreatePoints** — Create four points considering a center location received as a parameter.

➤ **CreateLines** — Use the four points to create two lines.

➤ **CreateEllipse** — Use the two lines to calculate an ellipse based on one line as the semi-major axe and the other as the semi-minor axe.

➤ **CreateCircle** — Create a circle in the middle of the ellipse.

➤ **CreateBoundingBox** — Create a bounding box for the ellipse.

➤ **FillBoundingBox** — Fill the bounding box with a gradient.

Figure 6-19 shows the work done by the aforementioned jobs as in an assembly line. If each job is represented by different classes and methods that receive parameters from the previous stage, and you have to perform this work many times based on a data source, you can design the set of stages based on the parallelization possibilities offered by PLINQ.

You can create a class or a method capable of managing the data flow between all these jobs, and run it using the `ForAll` extension method or inside a PLINQ query. The following code lines show an example of a method that processes each set of stages with different jobs:

```
public static ComplexGeometry ExecuteStages(Point centerLocation)
{
    var finalGeometry = new List<Geometry>();

    List<Point> pointsList = GeomPoint.CreatePoints();
    finalGeometry.Add(pointsList);
    List<Line> linesList = GeomLine.CreateLines(pointsList);
    finalGeometry.Add(linesList);
    Ellipse ellipse = GeomEllipse.CreateEllipse(linesList);
    finalGeometry.Add(ellipse);
```

```
        Circle circle = GeomCircle.CreateCircle(ellipse);
        finalGeometry.Add(circle);
        BoundingBox boundingBox = GeomBoundingBox.CreateBoundingBox(ellipse);
        finalGeometry.Add(boundingBox);

        return finalGeometry;
    }
```

code snippet from Snippet6_10

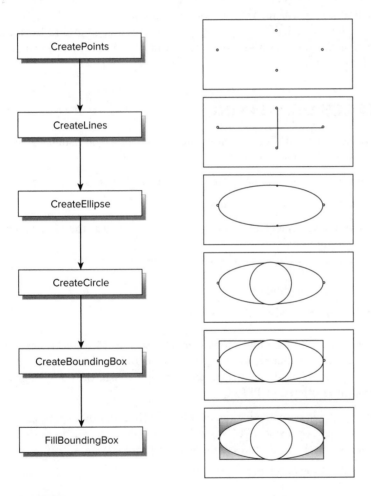

FIGURE 6-19

The following code line processes the serial stages in parallel, considering that *centerLocations* is a List<Point> and the data source to run the ExecuteStages method. The results are stored in a ConcurrentBag<ComplexGeometry>, and each element is a List<Geometry>.

```
var centerLocations = GenerateCenterLocations();
var complexGeometryBag = new ConcurrentBag<ComplexGeometry>();
centerLocations.ForAll((e) => complexGeometryBag.Add(ExecuteStages(e)));
```

code snippet from Snippet6_11

Locating Processing Bottlenecks

It is very important that you measure the speedups achieved by PLINQ queries and analyze other alternatives as parallelized loops to make sure that PLINQ is the most convenient option. If the PLINQ query isn't offering the desired performance, it helps to locate its potential processing bottlenecks.

Visual Studio 2010 offers many new tools that enable you to locate processing bottlenecks in parallelized code, including PLINQ queries. Chapter 7, "Visual Studio 2010 Task Debugging Capabilities," and Chapter 10, "Parallel Testing and Tuning," contain detailed information and techniques that will help you analyze the behavior of PLINQ queries.

SUMMARY

This chapter explained the details about the new and powerful PLINQ and its execution engine. It provided examples of the usage of its extension methods and enumerations. This chapter also discussed the combination of Task instances and concurrent collections with PLINQ, and the importance of good designs in order to offer predictable results and help the underlying scheduling mechanisms. To summarize this chapter:

➤ You can transform existing LINQ queries to run them in parallel by introducing many small changes in the code.

➤ You have to consider everything learned so far about parallel execution when writing PLINQ queries.

➤ You can tune the performance benefits offered by PLINQ using many of its extension methods.

➤ You can combine Task instances with PLINQ queries in order to create more responsive applications.

➤ You can use simple signaling mechanisms to cancel the execution of PLINQ.

➤ You can launch multiple PLINQ queries with different scheduling options when they don't scale as expected. Gantt charts can help you create execution plans.

➤ You can apply MapReduce algorithms by using PLINQ.

7

Visual Studio 2010 Task Debugging Capabilities

This chapter is about the new task debugging features introduced in Visual Studio 2010. It describes how the new windows display important information about the tasks and their relationships with the source code and the threads assigned to support their execution. These new windows enable you to detect and solve potential bugs when working with parallelized code in .NET Framework 4, which you'll learn about in this chapter as well.

TAKING ADVANTAGE OF MULTI-MONITOR SUPPORT

Visual Studio 2010 offers many different user interface (UI) elements and windows. Debugging a parallelized application requires more information on the screen than debugging sequential code does. Sometimes, even the resolution offered by Full HD monitors isn't enough to display all the necessary windows at the same time. Figure 7-1 shows the integrated development environment (IDE) of a typical debugging session. It displays information about multiple tasks, their underlying threads, and the code that is being executed. There are too many windows to display all of them on one screen, so it is usually necessary to move and resize these windows every 5 seconds.

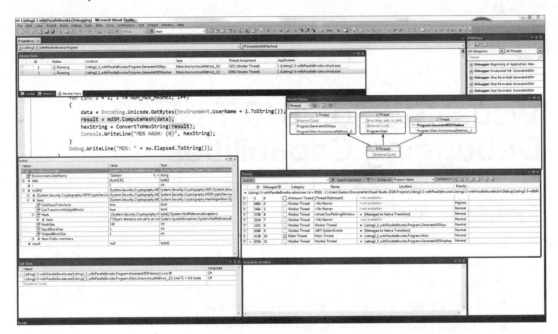

FIGURE 7-1

When you work with parallel code for many hours using one monitor, you will find yourself moving many windows to organize the information on your screen while debugging. You will want to watch status information for the active and scheduled tasks, and their related threads. At the same time, you will want to use the classic windows for debugging code, including Watch, Locals, and IntelliTrace Events windows. You need to view the code that is running in each task as well.

Visual Studio 2010 adds a very interesting feature: the ability to distribute its different UI elements and windows across more than one monitor. When the IDE detects that a computer has more than one monitor connected to it, it allows you to take advantage of the extended desktop. You can use multiple monitors to display more information simultaneously without having to scroll or redistribute the different UI elements and windows many times in a few hours. Figure 7-2 and Figure 7-3 show the IDE displaying the typical debugging session distributed in two monitors, as follows:

- ➤ Figure 7-2 shows the information displayed on the left screen: the code, the menu, the toolbars, IntelliTrace, Solution Explorer, and Autos windows.

- ➤ Figure 7-3 shows the information displayed on the right screen: Parallel Tasks, Parallel Stacks, Object Browser, Threads, and Locals windows.

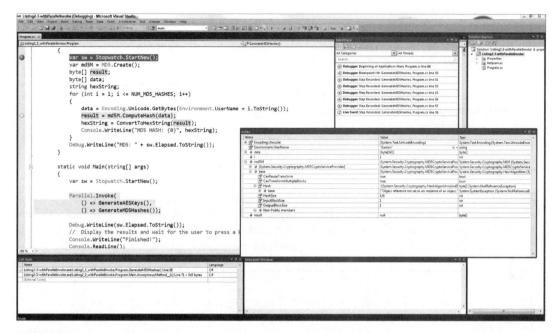

FIGURE 7-2

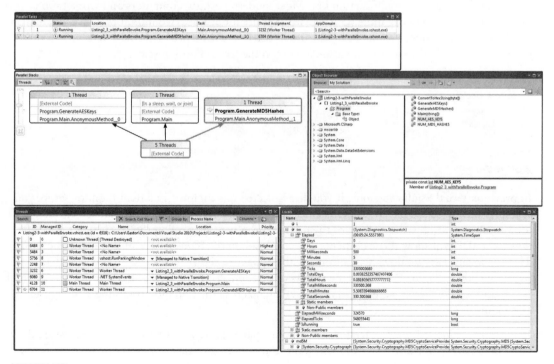

FIGURE 7-3

It is easier to debug parallel code when you can see all the necessary information without having to move and resize your windows every 5 seconds.

Visual Studio 2010 adds another interesting feature: the capability to maximize floating tool windows. You can right-click a window's title and select Float in the context menu to convert a tool window from docked to floating. Figure 7-4 shows the context menu and the Float option for the Parallel Tasks window.

Parallel Tasks		
	ID	**Float**
	1	Dock
	2	Dock as Tabbed Document
	3	Auto Hide
	4	Hide
	5	

FIGURE 7-4

When the window floats, a Maximize button appears on the right side of the title bar. Figure 7-5 shows the Maximize button for the Parallel Tasks window. You can drag a floating tool window to the desired monitor, maximize it to take advantage of the Full Screen mode, and when you finish working with this window, restore it and return it to the original screen.

Parallel Tasks					
	ID	Status	Location	Task	Thread Assignment	AppDomain
	1	ⓘ Waiting	Snippet6	Main.An	8400 (Worker Threa 1	Maximize

FIGURE 7-5

You usually have to switch to multi-monitor mode and extend the desktop in many laptops by pressing a shortcut or a dedicated function key. Most modern desktop computers and workstations also include graphics processing units (GPUs) with support for at least two monitors. Once you activate the dual-monitor mode, Visual Studio 2010 will detect the presence of the new screen. Figure 7-6 shows a laptop's dual-monitor activation icon with the Extend option selected.

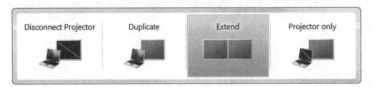

| Disconnect Projector | Duplicate | Extend | Projector only |

FIGURE 7-6

In previous Visual Studio versions, if you disconnected one monitor in a dual-monitor setup, you wouldn't be able to see the UI elements and windows that were displayed on that screen. In Visual Studio 2010, if you disconnect one of the monitors that was displaying the UI elements and windows, the IDE will show those elements and windows on the remaining visible desktop monitor. Those elements and windows will automatically appear in the visible screen, but you will have to reorganize them. Figure 7-7 shows the results of disconnecting the second monitor for all the UI elements and windows that were originally distributed across the two monitors shown in Figure 7-2 and Figure 7-3.

In the next sections, you will learn to work with new debugging windows that offer extensive information about parallelized code, and you will want to watch most of them on your screens simultaneously.

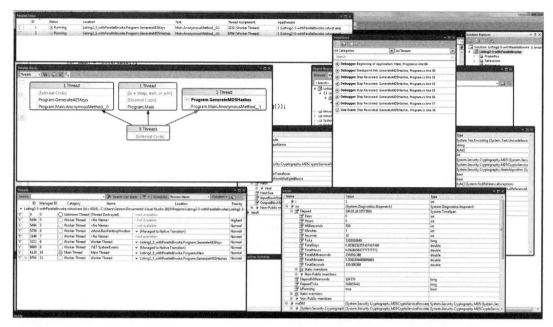

FIGURE 7-7

UNDERSTANDING THE PARALLEL TASKS DEBUGGER WINDOW

In Chapter 3, "Imperative Task Parallelism," you worked with two new debugging windows introduced in Visual Studio 2010: Parallel Tasks and Parallel Stacks. Now it's time to learn more about how you can use these windows to debug applications that run concurrent code by launching many tasks.

Follow these steps to use the Parallel Tasks window to debug the example you created in Chapter 6, "PLINQ: Declarative Data Parallelism:"

1. Open the project Snippet6_1.

2. Replace all the occurrences of ParallelPartitionGenerateAESKeysWCP with ParGenAES. The ParallelPartitionGenerateAESKeysWCP method name is too long to have a clear view in the debugger windows. The new, shorter ParGenAES name will make it easier to understand the new debugging features.

3. In the Main method, insert three breakpoints in each of the highlighted lines shown in the following code snippet:

```
static void Main(string[] args)
{
    Console.ReadLine();
    Console.WriteLine("Started");

    var cts = new System.Threading.CancellationTokenSource();
    var ct = cts.Token;
```

```
var sw = Stopwatch.StartNew();

Keys = new ConcurrentQueue<String>();

var tAsync = new Task(() => ParGenAES(ct, 'A'));
tAsync.Start();

// Do something else
// Wait for tAsync to finish
tAsync.Wait();

// Define the query indicating that it should run in parallel
var keysWith10Letters = from key in Keys.AsParallel()
            where (CountLetters(key) >= 10)
                && (key.Contains('A'))
                && (key.Contains('F'))
                && (key.Contains('9'))
                && (!key.Contains('B'))
            select key;

// Write some of the results of executing the query
// Remember that the PLINQ query is going to be executed at this point
// when the code requires results
var keysList = keysWith10Letters.ToList();
Console.WriteLine(
    "The code generated {0} keys with at least ten letters, " +
    "A, F and 9 but no B in the hexadecimal code.",
    keysList.Count());
Console.WriteLine("First key: {0} ",
    keysList.ElementAt(0));
Console.WriteLine("Last key: {0} ",
    keysList.ElementAt(keysList.Count() - 1));

Console.WriteLine("Finished in {0}", sw.Elapsed.ToString());

Console.ReadLine();
}
```

code snippet from Snippet7_1

4.   In the `ParGenAES` method, insert two breakpoints in each of the highlighted lines shown in the following code snippet:

```
private static void ParGenAES(
    System.Threading.CancellationToken ct,
    char prefix)
{
    var sw = Stopwatch.StartNew();
    var parallelOptions = new ParallelOptions();
    // Set the CancellationToken for the ParallelOptions instance
    parallelOptions.CancellationToken = ct;
```

```
    Parallel.ForEach(Partitioner.Create(1, NUM_AES_KEYS + 1), parallelOptions,
range =>
    {
        var aesM = new AesManaged();
        Debug.WriteLine("AES Range ({0}, {1}. TimeOfDay before inner loop starts:
{2})",
                        range.Item1, range.Item2,
                        DateTime.Now.TimeOfDay);
        for (int i = range.Item1; i < range.Item2; i++)
        {
            aesM.GenerateKey();
            byte[] result = aesM.Key;
            string hexString = ConvertToHexString(result);
            // Console.WriteLine("AES KEY: {0} ", hexString);
            if (hexString[0] == prefix)
            {
                Keys.Enqueue(hexString);
            }
            parallelOptions.CancellationToken.ThrowIfCancellationRequested();
        }
    });
    Debug.WriteLine("AES: " + sw.Elapsed.ToString());
}
```

code snippet from Snippet7_1

5. Select Debug ➪ Start Debugging or press F5. Then, press any key when the Console window for the application appears, and wait for the first breakpoint to be hit.

6. Select Debug ➪ Windows ➪ Parallel Tasks (Ctrl+D, K). The IDE will display a new window, Parallel Tasks. At this point, this window shows "No task to display," because there aren't any running or waiting Task instances currently scheduled. Figure 7-8 shows the line that is going to create a new Task instance, *tAsync*, as the next statement, and the Parallel Tasks window with no tasks.

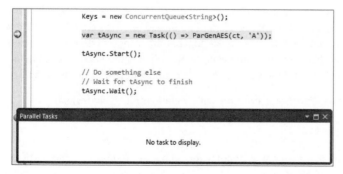

FIGURE 7-8

7. Select Debug ➪ Step Over or press F10. The following line will run, and *tAsync* will be created:

```
var tAsync = new Task(() => ParGenAES(ct, 'A'));
```

8.   Step over again. The following line will run, and *tAsync* will be scheduled to start its execution as soon as possible:

```
tAsync.Start();
```

If you are lucky, you will be able to see the new task listed in the Parallel Tasks window, with the scheduled value displayed in its Status column. Figure 7-9 shows the task in the scheduled state that hasn't been run and doesn't have an assigned thread. Table 7-1 explains the four possible values for the Status column in the Parallel Stacks window.

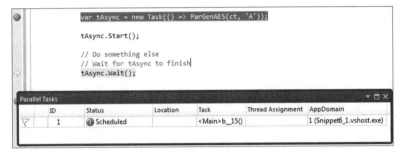

FIGURE 7-9

TABLE 7-1: Possible Values for the Status Column in the Parallel Tasks Window

VALUE	DESCRIPTION
Scheduled	A task that hasn't been run. It doesn't have an assigned thread, a call stack, or current location information.
Running	A task that was executing code before breaking in the debugger. It has been assigned a thread, it has a call stack, and the window displays its current location information.
Waiting (thread assignment column is not empty)	A blocked task that is waiting for another task to finish its execution, an event to be signaled, or a lock to be released. This status is a specialization of a `Running` task. The task is assigned a thread and was executing, but the debugger detected that it was blocked when the program entered the break state. Blocked is defined as any wait, sleep, or join state such as waiting for a lock to be released. Any wait, sleep, or join state could trigger this condition.
Waiting (thread assignment column is empty)	A task that has run, but is now implicitly waiting for its child tasks to complete.
Waiting-Deadlocked	A blocked task that became deadlocked with another task or thread. This status is a specialization of a `Waiting` task. A number of tasks were found to be in the waiting state in a circular fashion, such that if they remain like that, none of them will make progress.

Sometimes, when you step over the previous line, the task can get scheduled and then start its execution, instead of just getting scheduled. In this case, the Parallel Tasks window will list the new task with the running value displayed in its Status column. Figure 7-10 shows the task in the running state that has an assigned thread, 8868 (Worker Thread). However, there is no current location shown in the Location column, because the task didn't start running the managed code — instead, it is running external code.

If you hover the mouse pointer over the cell for this task in the Location column, a tooltip with the [External code] label will appear. In order to see the actual stack frames, select Tools ➪ Options ➪ Debugging ➪ General and deactivate the Enable Just My Code check box. After you deactivate this option, hover the mouse pointer over the cell for the task in the Location column to display a tooltip with the external code that is running.

When you step over after the Start method for a Task instance, the external code displayed will depend on the external code method that is running at that time. For example, the label might display the value shown in Figure 7-10, mscorlib.dll!System.Threading.Tasks .Task.Execute() +0x43 bytes, because the current location is in the Execute method. However, you can repeat the preceding Steps 5–8 many times, and you might see different values for this tooltip.

Table 7-2 explains all the columns that you can view in the Parallel Tasks window to obtain information about the tasks. You can select the columns that you want to be visible by right-clicking on the column header and checking the desired column title in the context menu.

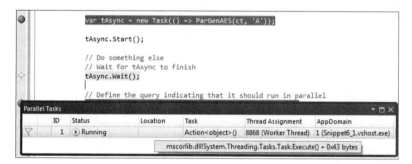

FIGURE 7-10

TABLE 7-2: Columns in the Parallel Tasks Window

COLUMN TITLE	DESCRIPTION
ID	The number provided by the system to this task. This is its unique identifier, and it remains the same during the task's lifecycle.
Status	The task's state before breaking in the debugger. Each possible state is explained in Table 7-1.
Location	The task's current location in its call stack.
Task	The initial method and its arguments, passed to the task during its creation.

continues

TABLE 7-2 *(continued)*

COLUMN TITLE	DESCRIPTION
Parent	The parent task's ID that created the task as a child. This is blank when a task doesn't have a parent task. Don't confuse Parent task with Thread Assignment. By default, the Parent column is hidden. In order to display this column, right-click the column header within the Parallel Tasks window and select Parent in the context menu.
Thread Assignment	The unique identifier, ID, and the name of the thread that is assigned to support this task's execution. The name of the threads that support the execution of tasks is usually `Worker Thread`, unless it gets inlined on the `Main Thread`. However, you can rename it during the debugging process. Remember that the thread that is assigned to support a task's execution doesn't change during a task's lifecycle. After a thread gets assigned to support a task, it stays assigned until the task dies. However, the same thread can be assigned to multiple tasks with only the topmost task on the thread's stack making progress.
AppDomain	The application domain in which the task is executing. It is the process.

9. Step over again. The following line will run, and the main thread will block until *tAsync* finishes its execution:

```
tAsync.Wait();
```

The debugger will hit the first breakpoint inserted in the `ParGenAES` method. The anonymous method that defined the action for the new `Task` instance, *tAsync*, and sent as an argument to its constructor, calls this method once the task starts its execution. Now, the debugger is showing you the code that is running in the *tAsync* task and in a worker thread. The worker thread, specified in the Thread Assignment column, is independent from the main thread. The Parallel Tasks window shows the initial method name in the Task column, `Main.AnonymousMethod__15()`. The auto-generated anonymous method name and number are displayed, because the code uses a lambda expression to generate the delegate associated with the task.

The Location column indicates `Snippet6_1.ParGenAES`, because this is the current method in the task's call stack. Figure 7-11 shows the information displayed by the Parallel Tasks window, as well as the entire call stack, known as the *stack tip*, for the task at the bottom of the Location cell as a result of the mouse being hovered over it. The stack tip enables you to see how the execution flow for the task arrived at the current location, and the same execution flow appears in the Threads window. If you want to switch to a specific stack frame, you can double-click on it in the stack tip list.

10. Select Debug ➪ Windows ➪ Call Stack (Ctrl+D, C). The IDE will display the Call Stack window that includes the method calls that are currently on the stack for the current task or thread. It is the same information shown in the Parallel Tasks window in Figure 7-11, but in this case, it displays a grid, and you can double-click on each method call to see the related code. Figure 7-12 shows the Call Stack window that displays the call stack for the *tAsync* task.

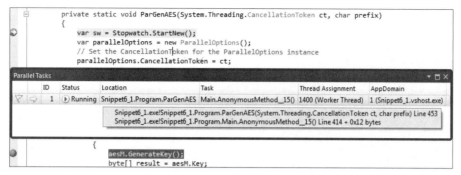

FIGURE 7-11

```
Call Stack
  Name                                                                                                            Language
⊙ Snippet6_1.exe!Snippet6_1.Program.ParGenAES(System.Threading.CancellationToken ct, char prefix) Line 453        C#
  Snippet6_1.exe!Snippet6_1.Program.Main.AnonymousMethod__15() Line 414 + 0x12 bytes                              C#
  mscorlib.dll!System.Threading.Tasks.Task.InnerInvoke() + 0x27 bytes
  mscorlib.dll!System.Threading.Tasks.Task.Execute() + 0x43 bytes
  mscorlib.dll!System.Threading.Tasks.Task.ExecutionContextCallback(object obj) + 0x27 bytes
  mscorlib.dll!System.Threading.ExecutionContext.Run(System.Threading.ExecutionContext executionContext, System.Threading.Cont
  mscorlib.dll!System.Threading.Tasks.Task.ExecuteWithThreadLocal(ref System.Threading.Tasks.Task currentTaskSlot) + 0x154 bytes
  mscorlib.dll!System.Threading.Tasks.Task.ExecuteEntry(bool bPreventDoubleExecution) + 0x8b bytes
  mscorlib.dll!System.Threading.Tasks.Task.System.Threading.IThreadPoolWorkItem.ExecuteWorkItem() + 0x7 bytes
  mscorlib.dll!System.Threading.ThreadPoolWorkQueue.Dispatch() + 0x147 bytes
  mscorlib.dll!System.Threading._ThreadPoolWaitCallback.PerformWaitCallback() + 0x2d bytes
  [Native to Managed Transition]



  ⟲ Call Stack   ▦ Immediate Window   ▦ Autos   ▦ Locals   ▦ Output
```

FIGURE 7-12

You can right-click the headers or the grid within the Call Stack window and use the context menu to configure the level of detail shown for a stack frame. Figure 7-13 shows the context menu with the default options checked. You can select whether to show the module names, parameter types, names and values, line numbers, and byte offsets. The stack tip in the Parallel Tasks window and the tooltips in the Parallel Stacks window also use this configuration to display the information.

The Parallel Tasks window displays a column with icons, located at the left of the ID column. This icon column also appears on the Threads window. The three possible icons that can appear in this column are as follows:

➤ **White arrow** — This indicates the task that was current when the debugger was invoked. This task is known as the *breaking task*.

➤ **Yellow arrow** — This indicates the current task that is running the code. The current task is the topmost task of the current thread.

➤ **Pause icon** — The thread assigned to the task was frozen (paused its execution), and it is not going to run code until it is unfrozen. You'll learn how to freeze and thaw tasks and their related threads later in this chapter.

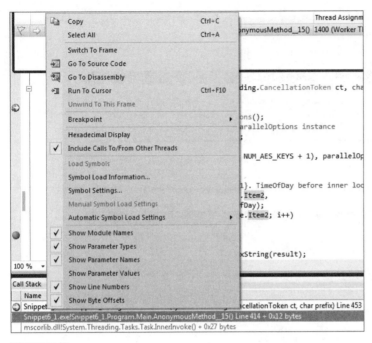

FIGURE 7-13

VIEWING THE PARALLEL STACKS DIAGRAM

Follow these steps to use the Parallel Stacks window to understand the call paths for tasks and threads:

1. Select Debug ⇨ Windows ⇨ Parallel Stacks (Ctrl+D, K). The IDE will display a new window, Parallel Stacks. The default view, selected in the drop-down list located at the upper-left corner, is Threads and shows a diagram with the call stacks for all the threads. At this point, the ParGenAES method didn't call the Parallel.ForEach method, and therefore, the *tAsync* task that called this method is assigned to one thread. Figure 7-14 shows the diagram with the call stack for the thread that is assigned to support *tAsync* at the left and the call stack for the main thread at the right. The diagram indicates that the main thread is running Program.Main and is in a sleep, wait, or join state. In fact, it is waiting for *tAsync* to finish because it called this Task instance Wait method. The external code appears with a gray font color. Because you deactivated the Enable Just My Code check box, each node includes the details for the external code.

2. Select Tasks in the drop-down list located at the upper-left corner of the Parallel Stacks window. This way, the window will switch to the diagram with the call stacks for the tasks. Figure 7-15 shows the diagram of the call stack for just one task, *tAsync*, with its call stack.

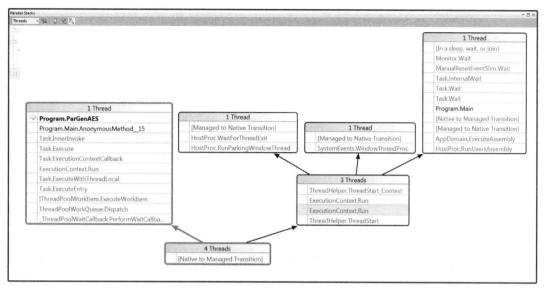

FIGURE 7-14

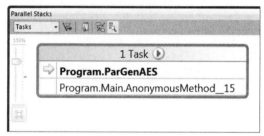

FIGURE 7-15

 Remember that the main thread isn't a task, and therefore, it doesn't appear in any tasks list or diagram. The main thread appears in all the views and windows that display information about threads; for example, the Parallel Stacks window with the Threads option selected and the Threads window.

3. Select Debug ➪ Continue or press F5, and wait for the next breakpoint within the ParGenAES method to be hit. The debugger will break in the first line within the for loop inside the call to Parallel.ForEach. The following code snippet highlights the line where the debugger breaks:

```
Parallel.ForEach(Partitioner.Create(1, NUM_AES_KEYS + 1), parallelOptions, range =>
{
    var aesM = new AesManaged();
```

```
        Debug.WriteLine("AES Range ({0}, {1}. TimeOfDay before inner loop starts:
    {2})",
                        range.Item1, range.Item2,
                        DateTime.Now.TimeOfDay);
        for (int i = range.Item1; i < range.Item2; i++)
        {
            aesM.GenerateKey();
```

4. Look at the new contents for the Parallel Tasks window. Right-click on the Location column header, and select Group By Location in the context menu. Figure 7-16 shows all the tasks grouped by their current location. In this case, as a result of debugging the application in a computer with eight logical cores, the `Parallel.ForEach` method with the custom partitioner launched eight tasks. These eight tasks appear below `Snippet6_1.Program.ParGenAES.AnonymousMethod__1a`. There is an anonymous method because the `Parallel.ForEach` executes delegates.

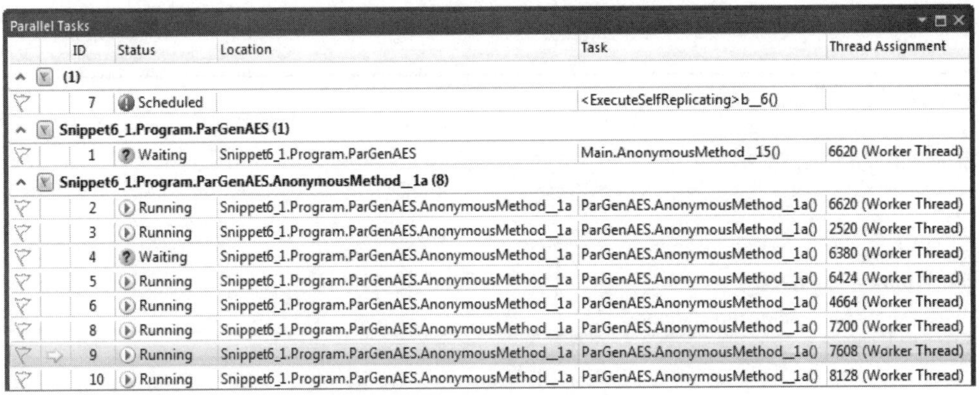

	ID	Status	Location	Task	Thread Assignment
(1)					
	7	Scheduled		<ExecuteSelfReplicating>b__6()	
Snippet6_1.Program.ParGenAES (1)					
	1	Waiting	Snippet6_1.Program.ParGenAES	Main.AnonymousMethod__15()	6620 (Worker Thread)
Snippet6_1.Program.ParGenAES.AnonymousMethod__1a (8)					
	2	Running	Snippet6_1.Program.ParGenAES.AnonymousMethod__1a	ParGenAES.AnonymousMethod__1a()	6620 (Worker Thread)
	3	Running	Snippet6_1.Program.ParGenAES.AnonymousMethod__1a	ParGenAES.AnonymousMethod__1a()	2520 (Worker Thread)
	4	Waiting	Snippet6_1.Program.ParGenAES.AnonymousMethod__1a	ParGenAES.AnonymousMethod__1a()	6380 (Worker Thread)
	5	Running	Snippet6_1.Program.ParGenAES.AnonymousMethod__1a	ParGenAES.AnonymousMethod__1a()	6424 (Worker Thread)
	6	Running	Snippet6_1.Program.ParGenAES.AnonymousMethod__1a	ParGenAES.AnonymousMethod__1a()	4664 (Worker Thread)
	8	Running	Snippet6_1.Program.ParGenAES.AnonymousMethod__1a	ParGenAES.AnonymousMethod__1a()	7200 (Worker Thread)
	9	Running	Snippet6_1.Program.ParGenAES.AnonymousMethod__1a	ParGenAES.AnonymousMethod__1a()	7608 (Worker Thread)
	10	Running	Snippet6_1.Program.ParGenAES.AnonymousMethod__1a	ParGenAES.AnonymousMethod__1a()	8128 (Worker Thread)

FIGURE 7-16

5. Look at the new contents for the Parallel Stacks window in the Tasks view. Figure 7-17 shows the diagrams that display the call stack segments for the tasks in nodes. The node located at the left shows the call stack for the *tAsync* task, and the node at the right offers information for the eight tasks created by the `Parallel.ForEach` method to parallelize the execution. Figure 7-17 also shows the status information for the eight tasks: 1 Waiting Tasks and 7 Running Tasks. This additional information appears in a tooltip when you hover the mouse pointer over the node header located at the top of the stack frame.

This Tasks view of the Parallel Stacks window shows the external code (selected with the Show External Code option from the context menu), which enables you to see the real estate that each task is taking up, and Figure 7-18 is the Tasks view with the external code hidden and doesn't show the additional nodes for the six tasks that are running external code. Sometimes, when the Threads view shows external code, the additional information that appears might confuse you. If this happens, you can hide the external code and enable it again when necessary.

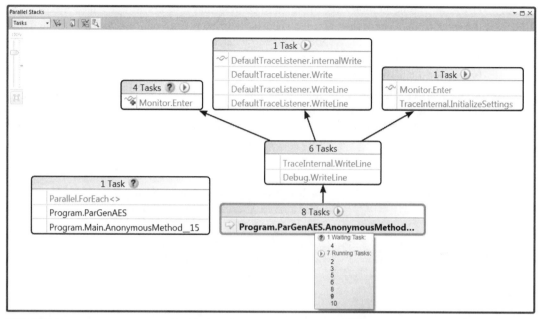

FIGURE 7-17

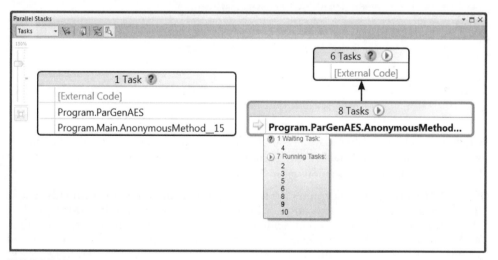

FIGURE 7-18

 The arrow lines connect nodes to make up the entire call path for the tasks or threads, according to the selected view for the Parallel Stacks window. The blue highlight indicates the path of the current task or thread, according to the selected view.

6. Hover the mouse pointer over the method context that appears with a yellow arrow icon in the stack frame. The yellow arrow indicates that the method context contains the active stack frame of the current task. A tooltip will show details of all the stack frames that the method context represents. The data for the current task will appear in bold. Figure 7-19 shows this tooltip for the Tasks view, and the Task ID appears as a prefix for each line.

Remember that the tooltip includes the same level of detail for each stack frame as is currently configured in the Call Stack window, and thus can take up a lot of screen real estate. You can help make the tooltip less wide by turning off the Show Module Names option. Figure 7-20 shows the new tooltip without the module names.

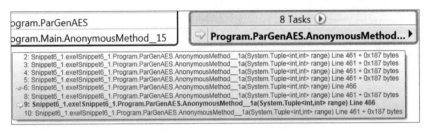

FIGURE 7-19

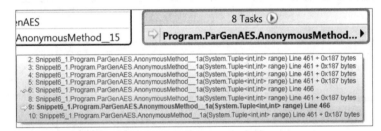

FIGURE 7-20

7. Select Threads from the drop-down list located in the upper-left corner of the Parallel Stacks window to switch to the Threads view. Then select Debug ➪ Windows ➪ Threads (Ctrl+D, T). The IDE now shows a new window called Threads.

Figure 7-21 shows the stack frames for the main thread and the worker threads that are assigned to support the execution of the tasks. The main thread is waiting for the *tAsync* task to finish, and it is represented by the stack frame in middle of the Parallel Stacks window that shows `Program.Main` at the bottom. The thread that was assigned to support the execution of the *tAsync* task appears in the node at the left, and shows `Program.Main.AnonymousMethod__15` at the bottom. When the code in the delegate executed by this task called the `Parallel.ForEach` method, it created eight tasks, and one of these tasks uses the same thread. Thus, the call stack segment shows the following tooltip for the last method context in black before the three lines that represent external code in gray:

```
6620: Snippet6_1.Program.ParGenAES.AnonymousMethod__1a(System.Tuple<int,int> range)
Line 461 + 0x187 bytes
```

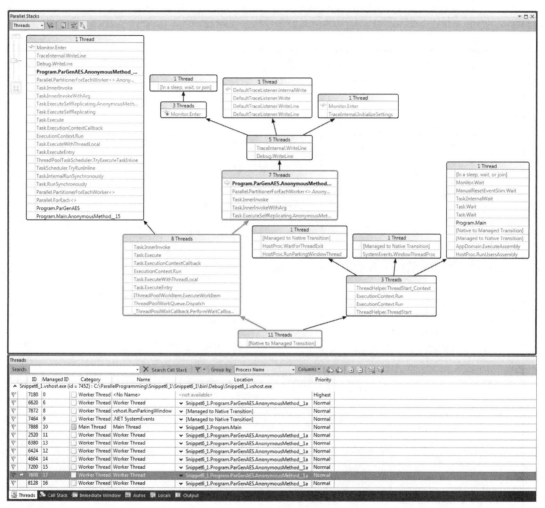

FIGURE 7-21

If you only want to see the threads applicable to your program and have a clearer picture, you can turn off the *Visual Studio Hosting Process*. In order to do so, right-click on the project name in Solution Explorer and select Properties. Then, click on the Debug page and deactivate the Enable the Visual Studio Hosting Process check box. Figure 7-22 shows the Threads view of the Parallel Stacks window with the hosting process turned off. There are fewer threads than the view shown in Figure 7-21. However, remember that the hosting process improves debugging performance, allows you to evaluate design time expressions and enables partial trust debugging. If you turn off the hosting process, you won't be able to take advantage of these features.

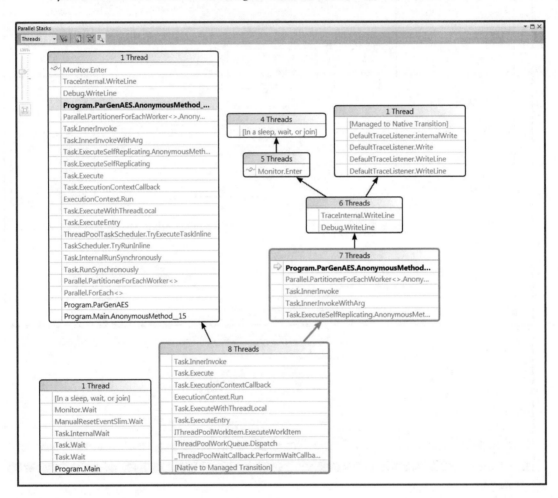

FIGURE 7-22

8. Locate the stack frame at the left side of Figure 7-21. Then, double-click the last method context in black before the gray lines that represent external code. The debugger displays the next statement to execute when this thread returns from the current method. Figure 7-23 shows the statement for this thread. The thread is assigned to support the execution of code for one task.

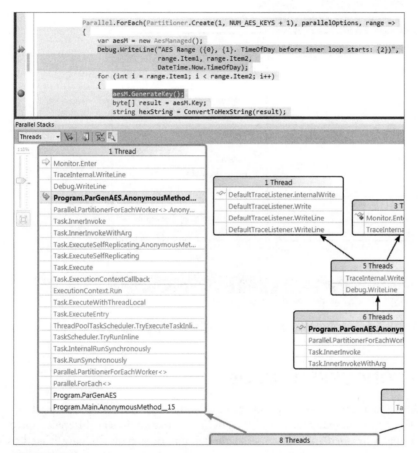

FIGURE 7-23

9. Double-click on `Program.Main` within the node on the right side of the window, and the debugger will display the next statement to execute when this thread returns from the current function. Figure 7-24 shows that the main thread is waiting for *tAsync* to finish. You can also check the current and the next statement for a thread by double-clicking on its row in the Threads window.

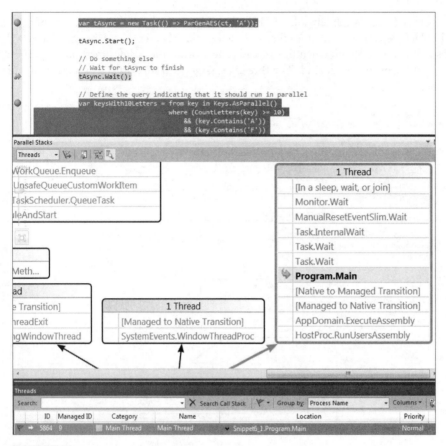

FIGURE 7-24

FOLLOWING THE CONCURRENT CODE

Each time you run code in a debugging session for an application that runs parallelized code, the debugger can execute instructions in many tasks and threads. This situation is very different from a debugging session for a single-threaded application. A single step into or step over in parallelized code can imply the execution of many statements in different tasks or threads. The debugger will step into or step over the current statement, but the other active tasks or threads will resume their executions during the time needed for the step into or step over. When the debugger comes back from the execution, many active tasks or threads could change their current statement and their call stacks. This situation could be very confusing if you are used to working with only single-threaded applications.

 By default, when you step into or step over in an application that has multiple tasks running or threads, the current task or thread can change from one step to the other. Thus, you have to pay special attention to the yellow arrow shown in the Parallel Tasks window on each step in order to determine your current task. When you are working with threads instead of tasks, you must check the yellow arrow shown in the Threads window.

Follow these steps to see how the information in the Parallel Tasks, Parallel Stacks, and Threads windows changes while you debug parallelized code:

1. Step into the code many times until you enter into the `ConvertToHexString` method. You will notice that each time you step into the code, the debugger can switch from one task to the other, and the program flow doesn't advance from one statement to the next one in a sequential order. This happens because the debugger can show the next statement for different tasks in each step into the code.

> When you step, the debugger places a hidden breakpoint on the next line, and after your program hits it, the hidden breakpoint is removed. When you initiate the step command, all the threads in your application resume their execution. Whichever thread happens to hit a breakpoint first is the one that will be current when the program enters the break state.
>
> Figure 7-25 shows the next step for the current task and the Parallel Tasks and Parallel Stacks windows. The Parallel Tasks window is displaying two tasks that entered into the `ConvertToHexString` method. The other six tasks created by the `Parallel.ForEach` method are running code in the delegate, but they haven't entered into the `ConvertToHexString` method. It is very easy to understand the call path with the new stack frames shown in the Threads view of the Parallel Stacks window. Two threads that are assigned to support the execution of two tasks are running the `Program.ConvertToHexString` method, including the current task, whose next statement is displayed in the code window with the yellow arrow.

2. Switch to the Tasks view in the Parallel Stacks window. Figure 7-26 shows the stack frames and the call path for eight tasks that split their paths. Without considering external code, two tasks are running the `Program.ConvertToHexString` method.

As the call stack for each task grows deeper, the stack frames and the call paths become more complex. The Parallel Stacks window offers a toolbar with a Toggle Zoom Control button that displays a zoom slider at the left. You can also activate the Auto Scroll To Current Stack Frame option button, and the window will automatically display the current stack frame in its visible viewport. In addition, when the diagram requires more space than the window's available viewport and there are scrollbars present, the space between the scrollbars reveals a button that provides a bird's-eye view. When you click this button, it shows a thumbnail view of the whole diagram, and you can use it to quickly scroll around the picture. Figure 7-27 shows the bird's-eye view for the Tasks view of the Parallel Stacks window.

3. These options are useful, but when the number of tasks also increases, it is a better idea to simplify the diagram so it displays only the information that you need. Go to the Parallel Tasks window and click on the flag outline that appears in the first column for each task that shows `ParGenAES.AnonymousMethod__1a()` in its Task cell. You can also achieve the same effect by right-clicking on the corresponding row and selecting Flag in the context menu. The flag's color will change to blue, indicating that the task is flagged. This way, all the tasks created by the `Parallel.ForEach` that are running the anonymous method will

be flagged. Right-click the Location column header, and select Group By Location in the context menu. You can click the flag button in the group header to flag or unflag all tasks with the desired actions. For example, Figure 7-28 shows two flagged tasks that are running the `ConvertToHexString` method grouped under a header. These two tasks are part of the eight tasks launched by `Parallel.ForEach`. After you have flagged the desired tasks, click the Show Only Flagged option button on the Parallel Tasks window (the blue flag icon with a blue arrow), and it will display the diagram with the stack frames and the call paths for these eight tasks. Now, you can focus on the tasks related to the `Parallel.ForEach` method.

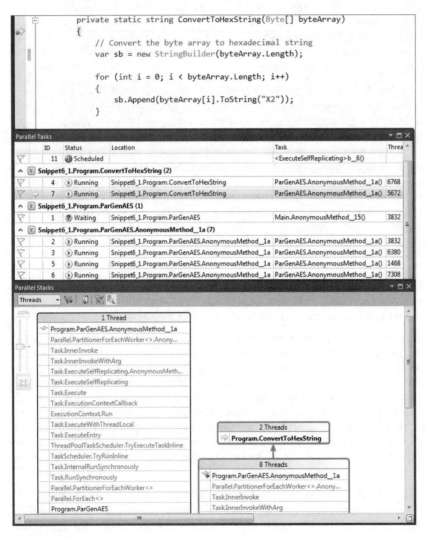

FIGURE 7-25

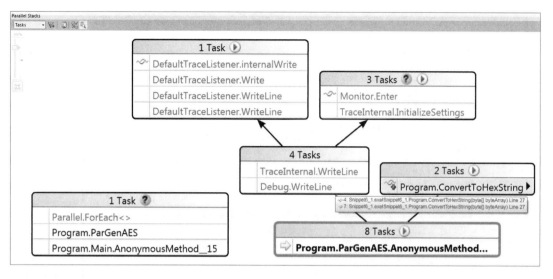

FIGURE 7-26

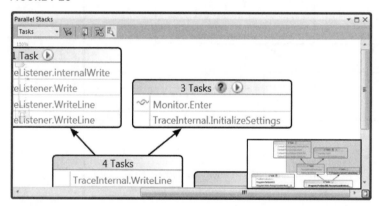

FIGURE 7-27

4. Similarly, the Threads view of the Parallel Stacks window can be filtered to show flagged threads only. Go to the Threads window and click the white flag that appears in the first column for each thread that shows Snippet6_1.Program.ParGenAES .AnonymousMethod__1a() or Snippet6_1.Program.ConvertToHexString in its Location cell. The flag's color will change to red, indicating that the thread is flagged. This way, all the threads that are assigned to support the execution of tasks created by the Parallel .ForEach will be flagged. Select Flag Indicator in the Group By drop-down list located at the top of the Threads window, and the flagged threads will appear together. Now, the Parallel Stacks window will show the diagram with the stack frames and the call paths for these eight threads, so you can also focus on the threads that are assigned to support the execution of tasks related to the Parallel.ForEach method. Figure 7-29 shows the flagged tasks grouped in the Threads window and the new Parallel Stacks diagram in the Threads view.

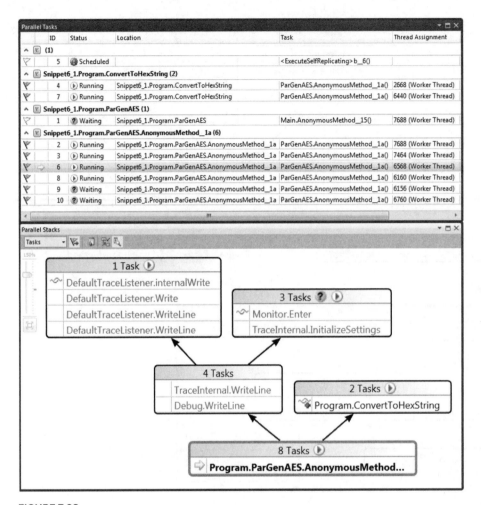

FIGURE 7-28

5. Parallel Stacks, Parallel Tasks, and the Threads windows offer a very useful snapshot of the situation of all the tasks and threads when you break the execution. You can double-click on the desired task in the Parallel Tasks window or thread in the Threads window and view its next statement. Many tasks or threads can have the same lines as their next statements. However, the values for their local variables are going to be independent for each task or thread. You can inspect the values for variables, watch their values, and use the Locals window to display variables local to the current context or scope. When you change the task or thread, these inspections are in the context for the selected task or thread. Figure 7-30 shows the Locals window with the values of the local variables for Task ID 2. For example, the range parameter has {(1, 33334)} as its value. Figure 7-31 shows the Locals window for Task ID 5. The next statement is the same as the one shown for Task ID 2, but the values for the local variables are different because they are independent from the other task. For example, the range parameter has {(100000, 133333)} as its value. Visual Studio 2010 enables you to view multiple thread call stacks in the same window. It would be great in a future

version of Visual Studio to be able to view the values of variables across multiple thread stack frames in the same method context.

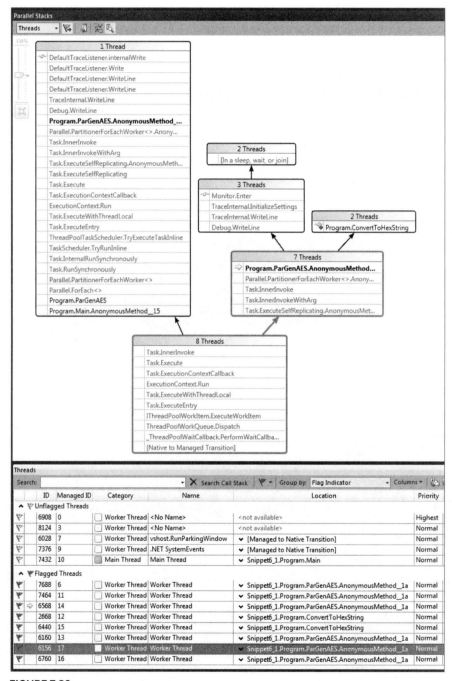

FIGURE 7-29

```
                Parallel.ForEach(Partitioner.Create(1, NUM_AES_KEYS + 1), parallelOptions, range =>
                {
                    var aesM = new AesManaged();
                    Debug.WriteLine("AES Range ({0}, {1}. TimeOfDay before inner loop starts: {2})",
                                range.Item1, range.Item2,
                                    DateTime.Now.TimeOfDay);
                    for (int i = range.Item1; i < range.Item2; i++)
                    {
                        aesM.GenerateKey();
                        byte[] result = aesM.Key;
                        string hexString = ConvertToHexString(result);
                        // Console.WriteLine("AES KEY: {0} ", hexString);
                        if (hexString[0] == prefix)
```

Locals

Name	Value	Type
⊞ �`range	{(1, 33334)}	System.Tuple<int,int>
⊞ �`result	{byte[32]}	byte[]
�`hexString	"700D3231218F3B79A80D67FA7A32CE858A9B2C4CF6038CFA5D147AB5609C2B7F" 🔍▾	string
�`i	3	int
⊞ �`aesM	{System.Security.Cryptography.AesManaged}	System.Security.Cryptography.AesManaged
⊞ �`parallelOptions	{System.Threading.Tasks.ParallelOptions}	System.Threading.Tasks.ParallelOptions
�`prefix	65 'A'	char

Parallel Tasks

	ID	Status	Location	Task	Thread Assignment	App
▽	11	🕓 Scheduled		<ExecuteSelfReplicating> b__6()		1 (S
▽	4	▶ Running	Snippet6_1.Program.ConvertToHexString	ParGenAES.AnonymousMethod__1a()	6048 (Worker Thread)	1 (S
▽	1	❓ Waiting	Snippet6_1.Program.ParGenAES	Main.AnonymousMethod__15()	4532 (Worker Thread)	1 (S
➡	2	▶ Running	Snippet6_1.Program.ParGenAES.AnonymousMethod__1a	ParGenAES.AnonymousMethod__1a()	4532 (Worker Thread)	1 (S
▽	3	▶ Running	Snippet6_1.Program.ParGenAES.AnonymousMethod__1a	ParGenAES.AnonymousMethod__1a()	3924 (Worker Thread)	1 (S
▽	5	▶ Running	Snippet6_1.Program.ParGenAES.AnonymousMethod__1a	ParGenAES.AnonymousMethod__1a()	296 (Worker Thread)	1 (S
▽	6	▶ Running	Snippet6_1.Program.ParGenAES.AnonymousMethod__1a	ParGenAES.AnonymousMethod__1a()	7956 (Worker Thread)	1 (S
▽	7	▶ Running	Snippet6_1.Program.ParGenAES.AnonymousMethod__1a	ParGenAES.AnonymousMethod__1a()	7244 (Worker Thread)	1 (S
▽	8	▶ Running	Snippet6_1.Program.ParGenAES.AnonymousMethod__1a	ParGenAES.AnonymousMethod__1a()	7020 (Worker Thread)	1 (S
▽	9	▶ Running	Snippet6_1.Program.ParGenAES.AnonymousMethod__1a	ParGenAES.AnonymousMethod__1a()	8132 (Worker Thread)	1 (S
▽	10	▶ Running	Snippet6_1.Program.ParGenAES.AnonymousMethod__1a	ParGenAES.AnonymousMethod__1a()	7584 (Worker Thread)	1 (S

FIGURE 7-30

```
                Parallel.ForEach(Partitioner.Create(1, NUM_AES_KEYS + 1), parallelOptions, range =>
                {
                    var aesM = new AesManaged();
                    Debug.WriteLine("AES Range ({0}, {1}. TimeOfDay before inner loop starts: {2})",
                                range.Item1, range.Item2,
                                    DateTime.Now.TimeOfDay);
                    for (int i = range.Item1; i < range.Item2; i++)
                    {
                        aesM.GenerateKey();
                        byte[] result = aesM.Key;
                        string hexString = ConvertToHexString(result);
                        // Console.WriteLine("AES KEY: {0} ", hexString);
                        if (hexString[0] == prefix)
```

Locals

Name	Value	Type
⊞ �`range	{(100000, 133333)}	System.Tuple<int,int>
⊞ �`result	{byte[32]}	byte[]
�`hexString	"BF00498F3D5F761E1B4296E6327E1B482299A5BACBC5A4D723606F1187BF5CE9" 🔍▾	string
�`i	100001	int
⊞ �`aesM	{System.Security.Cryptography.AesManaged}	System.Security.Cryptography.AesManaged
⊞ �`parallelOptions	{System.Threading.Tasks.ParallelOptions}	System.Threading.Tasks.ParallelOptions
�`prefix	65 'A'	char

Parallel Tasks

	ID	Status	Location	Task	Thread Assignment	Ap
▽	11	🕓 Scheduled		<ExecuteSelfReplicating> b__6()		1 (S
▽	4	▶ Running	Snippet6_1.Program.ConvertToHexString	ParGenAES.AnonymousMethod__1a()	6048 (Worker Thread)	1 (S
▽	1	❓ Waiting	Snippet6_1.Program.ParGenAES	Main.AnonymousMethod__15()	4532 (Worker Thread)	1 (S
▽ ⇨	2	▶ Running	Snippet6_1.Program.ParGenAES.AnonymousMethod__1a	ParGenAES.AnonymousMethod__1a()	4532 (Worker Thread)	1 (S
▽	3	▶ Running	Snippet6_1.Program.ParGenAES.AnonymousMethod__1a	ParGenAES.AnonymousMethod__1a()	3924 (Worker Thread)	1 (S
▽ ⇨	5	▶ Running	Snippet6_1.Program.ParGenAES.AnonymousMethod__1a	ParGenAES.AnonymousMethod__1a()	296 (Worker Thread)	1 (S

FIGURE 7-31

6. Right-click on a method context in either the Threads or Tasks view within one of the stack frames shown in the Parallel Stacks window. A context menu will appear with many options, described in Table 7-3. Select the Switch To Frame option, and a submenu will list the specific stack frames for the method context. Click on one of the stack frames, and the debugger will switch to the corresponding task and thread, and it will display the next statement.

TABLE 7-3: Context Menu Options in the Threads or Tasks View within a Stack Frame

OPTION	DESCRIPTION
Go To Disassembly	Shows the assembler code that corresponds to the stack frame in the Disassembly window.
Go To Source Code	Shows the code that corresponds to the stack frame in the source code editor.
Go To Task	Switches to the Tasks view and keeps the same stack frame highlighted in the new diagram (if that stack frame appears there already).
Go To Thread	Switches to the Threads view and keeps the same stack frame highlighted in the new diagram.
Hexadecimal Display	Toggles between decimal and hexadecimal display for the numbers. It affects all the debugging windows that show numbers.
Show External Code	Shows or hides external code. By default, external code is hidden and appears as [External Code] in all relevant debugger windows.
Switch To Frame	Displays a submenu that allows you to select the desired stack frame that corresponds to one method context. When you select an item from this submenu, the code that corresponds to the stack frame will appear in the source code editor.
Symbol Load Information	Displays a dialog box with a list of locations where the debugger will look for symbol files.
Symbol Settings	Displays the Options dialog box located on the Debugging ⇨ Symbols page.

Figure 7-32 shows the submenu for Switch To Frame that displays the eight stack frames for a method context. The eight method contexts show the values for the `range` parameter. This enables you to locate the code that is running a specific partition of the `Parallel.ForEach` in a task.

When you need to debug the `for` loop called by each of the parallel tasks created by the `Parallel.ForEach` method, you want to execute the code one step after the other. However, this is difficult to accomplish if the debugger switches from one task to the other after each step into or step over. You can suspend the execution of one or many concurrent tasks in order to focus one part of your debugging session on one or more tasks. Follow these steps to pause all the threads that are assigned to support the execution of some tasks:

1. Go to the Parallel Tasks window and select one of the tasks created by the `Parallel.ForEach` method. Right-click on it and select the Freeze All Threads But This option in the context menu. This option suspends the execution of all threads assigned to tasks that are different from the selected task. The tasks that are assigned to frozen threads will appear with a blue pause icon in the second column in the Parallel Tasks window. The Threads window shows the frozen threads that are assigned to support the execution for these tasks with the same blue pause icon in the second column. Figure 7-33 shows the Parallel Tasks and the Threads windows with the blue pause icons in many rows as a result of freezing threads.

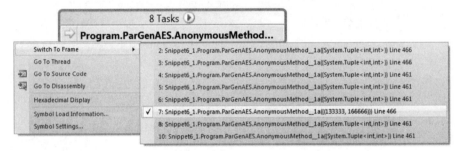

FIGURE 7-32

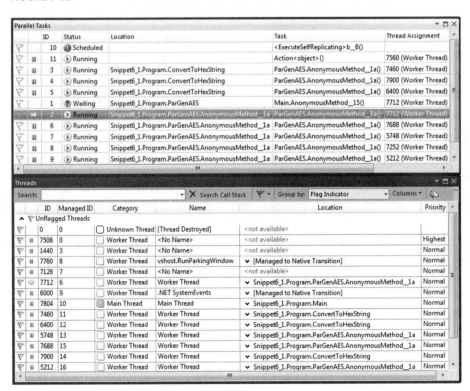

FIGURE 7-33

2. Double-click on the task that isn't frozen in the Parallel Tasks window, and the code window will display its next statement.

3. Step over. The current statement will run, and the next statement will move to the next line with a sequential execution, because the current task is the only one that is running. The other tasks are suspended until you thaw the threads that are assigned to support their execution. This enables you to debug the method running alone and step-by-step. The method runs with a sequential execution as in single-threaded code.

> *When you debug code by leaving just one task running and freezing the threads that are assigned to support the other tasks' execution, you have to consider that the results of running the code could differ when the other tasks run concurrently. When you freeze threads, you are limiting the code that is running concurrently.*

4. Step over many times to check the execution step-by-step.

5. Go to the Parallel Tasks window and select one of the tasks created by the `Parallel .ForEach` method that appears frozen with the blue pause icon. Switch to this task by double-clicking on it, and then right-click and select Thaw Assigned Thread. The blue pause icon will disappear for this task. Right-click on this task again and select the Freeze All Threads But This option in the context menu. The thread that was assigned to support the execution of the active task that you were debugging will be frozen, and the thread that is assigned to support the execution of the new selected task will resume its execution. Figure 7-34 shows the next statement for the new current task and the Parallel Tasks window with the blue pause icons in many rows as a result of the freezing threads.

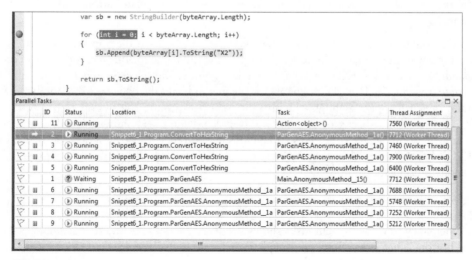

FIGURE 7-34

To resume the execution for a single task, right-click on it in the Parallel Tasks window and select Thaw Assigned Thread in the context menu. To suspend the execution of a single task, right-click on it in the Parallel Tasks window and select Freeze Assigned Thread in the context menu. You can perform these operations on many tasks at the same time by selecting multiple rows in the Parallel Tasks window before right-clicking.

You can also freeze and thaw threads in the Threads window, but you will need to check the information in the Thread Assignment column for a task when you want to suspend or resume the execution of a thread assigned to a task. When you right-click on a thread in the Threads window, a context menu offers the Freeze and Thaw options according to the thread's current state.

Debugging Anonymous Methods

When you work with parallelized code, you need to define actions and delegates. Lambda expressions and their anonymous methods simplify the code but add greater complexity to the debugging process. When the code uses lambda expressions, the auto-generated anonymous method names and numbers appear in the stack frames, in the Location and Task columns in the Parallel Tasks window, and in the Location column in the Threads window. However, you won't find these auto-generated anonymous method names in the source code, because there is no code that defines them.

Follow these steps to track anonymous methods while debugging parallelized code:

1. Go to the Parallel Tasks window, select all the tasks, right-click, and select Thaw Assigned Threads in the context menu. Right-click again and select Unflag All Tasks.

2. Go to the Threads window, select all the threads, right-click, and select Unflag All Threads.

3. Go to the Parallel Stacks window, deactivate the Show Only Flagged button, and switch to the Tasks view.

4. One stack frame shows `Program.Main.AnonymousMethod__15` at the bottom, but there is no method with this name in the code. To display the full name for this method and its corresponding line number, right-click on the method context and select Switch To Frame in the context menu. Click on the full name for the method, and the code that this anonymous method runs will appear highlighted with a different background color in the source code editor. By default, the background color will be green. Figure 7-35 shows the code that represents `AnonymousMethod__15`. This anonymous method represents the action for the *tAsync* task. The following code line appears highlighted inside the lambda expression that defines the anonymous method:

```
var tAsync = new Task(() => ParGenAES(ct, 'A'));
```

5. The other stack frame with eight tasks shows `Program.ParGenAES.AnonymousMethod__1a` at the bottom. This is the anonymous method that represents the delegate defined for the `Parallel.ForEach` method, but there is no method with this name in the code. To display the code that represents this method, right-click on this method context, select Switch To

Frame in the context menu, and then select one of the method context options that appear. This is a multi-line anonymous method, and the lines of code that it runs will appear highlighted with a different background color in the source code editor. This code represents `ParGenAES.AnonymousMethod__1a`, which means `AnonymousMethod__1a` within the `ParGenAES` method.

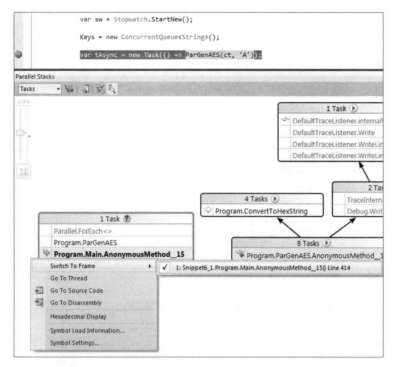

FIGURE 7-35

Viewing Methods

The Parallel Stacks window allows you to switch to a simplified diagram that shows all the methods on all tasks and threads that either call or are called by the selected method. It is useful to switch from the Stacks view to this Method view when you want to focus on a more specific call path graph for a method.

Follow these steps to work with the Method view in both the Tasks view and the Threads view:

1. Go to the Parallel Stacks window and switch to the Tasks view. Double-click on the anonymous method name called by the *tAsync* task: `Program.Main.AnonymousMethod__15`. Figure 7-36 shows the Parallel Stacks window with the selected method context.

2. Click the Toggle Method View option button, located at the top of the Parallel Stacks window. The Method view will display the anonymous method with a call path to the `ParGenAES` method. Figure 7-37 shows the Method view for the Parallel Stacks window previously shown in Figure 7-30.

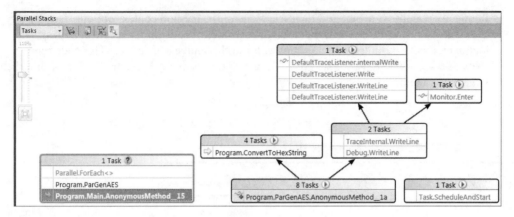

FIGURE 7-36

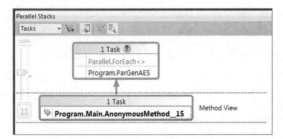

FIGURE 7-37

You can use all the functions offered by the Parallel Stacks window in the Method view. The diagram shown in the Method view is also going to be updated as in the Stack view when you continue executing instructions in the debugging session.

3. Click the Toggle Method View option button again to switch back to the complete stacks frames diagram.

4. Switch to the Threads view. Double-click on the `Program.ConvertToHexString` method name called by one of the threads. Figure 7-38 shows the Parallel Stacks window in the Threads view with the selected method context.

5. Click the Toggle Method View option button. The Method view will display the anonymous method context for `ParallelPartitionGenerateAESKeys.AnonymousMethod__1a`, which is running one of the partitions defined for the `Parallel.ForEach` execution. This anonymous method has a call path to the `ConvertToHexString` method. Figure 7-39 shows the Method view for the Parallel Stacks window previously shown in Figure 7-38. The simplified view allows you to focus on a particular method and its immediate relationship with other tasks and threads.

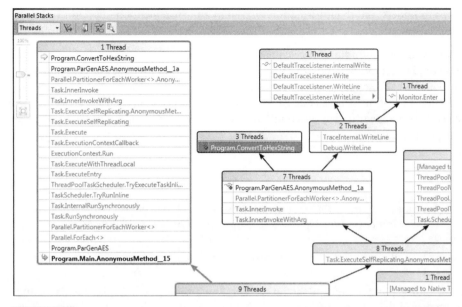

FIGURE 7-38

6. Go back to the full diagram.

This example introduced the Method view feature. You will see its full value when detecting deadlocks in a subsequent section.

Viewing Threads in the Source Code

When you are debugging concurrent code, it is important that you know the next code statements that are going to be executed in each task or thread. This can help you understand what the multiple concurrent tasks and threads are doing. You can use the windows that were introduced in the previous sections to get a clear snapshot of the situation when the debugger breaks. However, you have to select each method context to check the next statement for each thread and the task that it is assigned to support. Sometimes, it helps to know whether other threads are running code in the same method in which you are focused. The Show Threads In Source option provides this information in the source code editor during debugging.

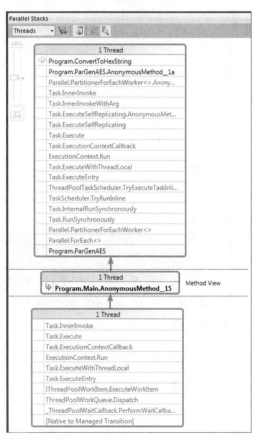

FIGURE 7-39

Follow these steps to understand the information offered by the aforementioned option and its effect in the source code editor:

1. Go to the `Main` method in the source code editor. Click the Show Threads In Source option button in the Debug toolbar. You can also activate this option by right-clicking on the Threads window and selecting the option with the same name in the context menu. The gutter on the left side of the source code editor will display a thread marker in the following line, and the code will appear with a different background color (the default background color for a running code thread is gray):

```
tAsync.Wait();
```

 The thread marker is an icon that resembles two cloth threads: a blue thread and a red thread. It indicates that there is a thread stopped at the highlighted line at this time.

2. Hover the mouse pointer over the thread marker, and a tooltip will display the name and ID for the thread that is stopped at this line. Figure 7-40 shows the thread marker and the tooltip that display `[7804] Main Thread` as the only thread at the `tAsync.Wait` line.

```
        static void Main(string[] args)
        {
            Console.ReadLine();
            Console.WriteLine("Started");

            var cts = new System.Threading.CancellationTokenSource();
            var ct = cts.Token;

            var sw = Stopwatch.StartNew();

            Keys = new ConcurrentQueue<String>();

            var tAsync = new Task(() => ParGenAES(ct, 'A'));

            tAsync.Start();

            // Do something else
            // Wait for tAsync to finish
            tAsync.Wait();
Thread(s) at Location:
  [7804] Main Thread  Define the query indicating that it should run in parallel
            var keysWith10Letters = from key in Keys.AsParallel()
                            where (CountLetters(key) >= 10)
                                && (key.Contains('A'))
                                && (key.Contains('F'))
                                && (key.Contains('9'))
                                && (!key.Contains('B'))
                            select key;
```

FIGURE 7-40

3. Go to the `ParGenAES` method in the source code editor. The gutter on the left side of the source code editor will display thread markers in many lines, and these lines will appear with a different background color, as shown here:

```
Debug.WriteLine("AES Range ({0}, {1}. TimeOfDay before inner loop starts: {2})",
                range.Item1, range.Item2,
```

```
                    DateTime.Now.TimeOfDay);
for (int i = range.Item1; i < range.Item2; i++)
{
    aesM.GenerateKey();
    byte[] result = aesM.Key;
    string hexString = ConvertToHexString(result);
```

4. Figure 7-41 shows two thread markers that have a + sign. This additional sign means that there is more than one thread at this location. Hover the mouse pointer over one of the thread markers and a tooltip will display the names and ID numbers for the threads that are stopped at the line. Figure 7-41 shows two threads at the `aesM.GenerateKey()` line: [5748] `Worker Thread`, and [5212] `Worker Thread`.

```
private static void ParGenAES(System.Threading.CancellationToken ct, char prefix)
{
    var sw = Stopwatch.StartNew();
    var parallelOptions = new ParallelOptions();
    // Set the CancellationToken for the ParallelOptions instance
    parallelOptions.CancellationToken = ct;

    Parallel.ForEach(Partitioner.Create(1, NUM_AES_KEYS + 1), parallelOptions, range =>
    {
        var aesM = new AesManaged();
        Debug.WriteLine("AES Range ({0}, {1}. TimeOfDay before inner loop starts: {2})",
                        range.Item1, range.Item2,
                        DateTime.Now.TimeOfDay);
        for (int i = range.Item1; i < range.Item2; i++)
        {
            aesM.GenerateKey();
            byte[] result = aesM.Key;
            string hexString = ConvertToHexString(result);
            // Console.WriteLine("AES KEY: {0} ", hexString);
            if (hexString[0] == prefix)
            {
                Keys.Enqueue(hexString);
            }
            parallelOptions.CancellationToken.ThrowIfCancellationRequested();
        }
    });
    Debug.WriteLine("AES: " + sw.Elapsed.ToString());
}
```

Thread(s) at Location:
[5748] Worker Thread
[5212] Worker Thread

FIGURE 7-41

5. Right-click on the thread marker, and a context menu is displayed with two submenus: Switch To and Flag. These two submenus will display the names and ID numbers for the threads that are stopped at the line as items. You can use these submenus to switch one of the threads or to flag it. Figure 7-42 shows the items displayed in the Switch To submenu for the thread marker at the `aesM.GenerateKey()` line.

```
        Debug.WriteLine("AES Range ({0}, {1}. TimeOfDay before inner loop starts: {2})",
                        range.Item1, range.Item2,
                        DateTime.Now.TimeOfDay);
        for (int i = range.Item1; i < range.Item2; i++)
        {
            aesM.GenerateKey();
```

Switch To   ▶   [5748] Worker Thread
Flag   ▶   [5212] Worker Thread

```
                                             oHexString(result);
                                         KEY: {0} ", hexString);
            if (hexString[0] == prefix)
            {
                Keys.Enqueue(hexString);
```

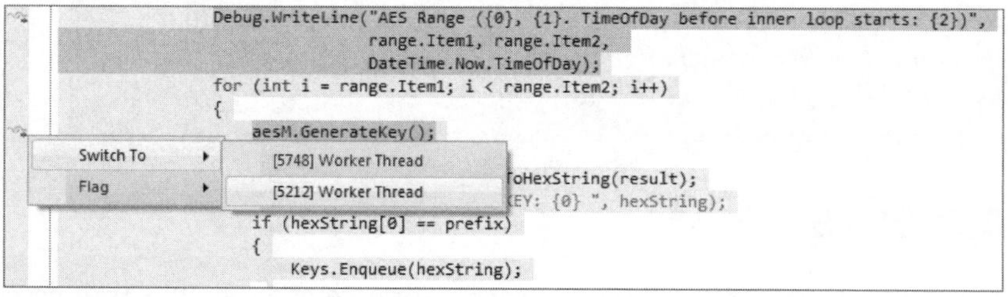

FIGURE 7-42

6. The thread markers shown in the source code editor are representing threads. However, it is easy to find out what task a thread in a thread marker is assigned to. You can use the aforementioned context menu to switch to one of the threads stopped at the thread marker, which causes the Parallel Tasks window to switch to its assigned task. Figure 7-43 shows the result of switching to the [5212] Worker Thread. Task ID number 9 becomes the current task at the Parallel Tasks window, because it is assigned to the active thread.

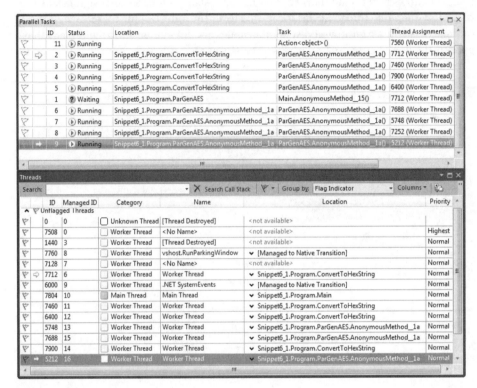

FIGURE 7-43

7. Finish the execution of the application, and then analyze the changes in the different windows you learned about in the previous sections.

 When you switch to a different thread by using one of the options provided by the debugger, the current task will also switch to match the topmost task that is assigned to the thread. When you change the current task, the thread that is assigned to this task will be the current thread.

DETECTING DEADLOCKS

A deadlock is a situation in which at least two tasks are waiting for each other, but the wait never ends, because one task won't continue with its instructions until the other task releases the protection held over certain resources. The other task is also waiting for resources held by its counterpart to resume its execution. Because no task is willing to release its protection, none of the tasks make any progress, and they continue to wait for each other forever.

Consider the following situation: task *t1* holds a protection over resource A and is waiting to gain exclusive access over resource B. At the same time, task *t2* holds a protection over resource B and is waiting to gain exclusive access over resource A. This is one of the most horrible bugs.

Listing 7-1 shows the code for a very simple application that generates a deadlock. The code doesn't represent a good practice because it does many things that you should never do. The Main method creates two tasks, *t1* and *t2*, and then calls the Start method for both and waits for them to finish their execution. *t1* runs the CountTasks1 method, and *t2* calls CountTasks2.

LISTING 7-1: An application with horrible code that generates a deadlock

```csharp
using System;
using System.Collections.Generic;
using System.Linq;
using System.Text;
using System.Threading;
using System.Threading.Tasks;

namespace DeadlockTest
{
    class Program
    {
        private static Object _sharedVariable1 = new Object();
        private static Object _sharedVariable2 = new Object();

        private static int _tasksCounter1;
        private static int _tasksCounter2;

        private static void CountTasks1()
        {
            lock (_sharedVariable1)
            {
                _tasksCounter1++;
                Thread.Sleep(5000);
                lock (_sharedVariable2)
                {
                    _tasksCounter2++;
                }
            }
        }

        private static void CountTasks2()
        {
            lock (_sharedVariable2)
            {
                _tasksCounter2++;
                Thread.Sleep(5000);
                lock (_sharedVariable1)
                {
```

continues

LISTING 7-1 *(continued)*

```
                    _tasksCounter1++;
                }
            }
        }

        static void Main(string[] args)
        {

            _tasksCounter1 = 0;
            _tasksCounter2 = 0;

            var t1 = new Task(() => CountTasks1());
            var t2 = new Task(() => CountTasks2());

            t1.Start();
            t2.Start();

            Task.WaitAll(t1, t2);
        }
    }
}
```

`CountTasks1` locks *_sharedVariable1*. When it acquires the lock, it increments *_tasksCounter1* and puts the underlying thread to sleep for 5000 milliseconds (5 seconds). During those 5 seconds, *_sharedVariable1* is going to stack locked and, without releasing this lock, it locks *_sharedVariable2*. When it acquires this second lock, it increments *_tasksCounter2*, as shown here:

Available for download on Wrox.com

```
lock (_sharedVariable1)
{
    _tasksCounter1++;
    Thread.Sleep(5000);
    lock (_sharedVariable2)
    {
        _tasksCounter2++;
    }
}
```

Again, the goal for this example is to explain the features offered by the new debugger windows to detect a deadlock, but it doesn't represent a good practice. `CountTasks2` performs a similar procedure, but with the locks in an inverted sequence. First, it locks *_sharedVariable2*. When it acquires the lock, it increments *_tasksCounter2* and puts the underlying thread to sleep for 5000 milliseconds (5 seconds). During those 5 seconds, *_sharedVariable2* is going to stack locked and, without releasing this lock, it tries to acquire a lock for *_sharedVariable1*. When it acquires this second lock, it increments *_tasksCounter1*. However, because `CountTasks1` is going to run concurrently, when `CountTasks1` tries to acquire a lock on *_sharedVariable2*, it will be locked by the first lock in `CountTasks2`. When `CountTasks2` tries to acquire a lock on *_sharedVariable1*, it will be locked by the first lock in `CountTasks1`. The locks don't have a timeout; therefore, the code will wait forever to acquire each lock. Because the threads will sleep for 5 seconds with a lock, there will be several seconds of a deadlock between tasks *t1* and *t2*.

Follow these steps to understand the information offered by the Parallel Stacks and Parallel Tasks windows when they detect a deadlock:

1. Select Debug ➪ Start Debugging or press F5.

2. Wait 2 seconds and select Debug ➪ Break All or click the pause button in the Debug toolbar. Instead of following this step, you could modify the code shown in Listing 7-1 to create a task that sleeps for 2 seconds and then calls `Debugger.Break`. However, this example represents the most common scenario that you will face when an application stops responding. There is a deadlock behind the scenes, and you have to discover what's going on.

3. View the Parallel Stacks and Parallel Tasks windows. Both tasks will appear with Waiting as their status, because they are running the `Thread.Sleep` instruction. Figure 7-44 shows the two stack frames for the two tasks in the Parallel Stacks window, and the Parallel Tasks window displaying the Waiting status for both tasks.

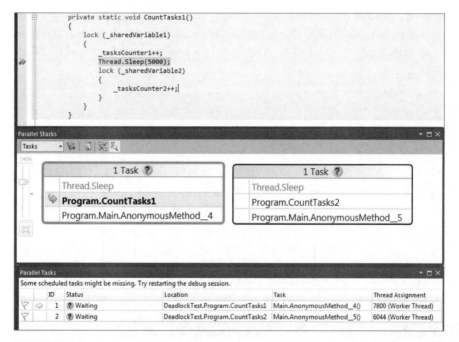

FIGURE 7-44

4. Select Debug ➪ Continue or press F5.

5. Wait 3 seconds and select Debug ➪ Break All or click the pause button in the Debug toolbar. View the Parallel Stacks and Parallel Tasks windows. Both tasks will appear with Waiting-Deadlocked as their status, because `CountTasks1`, called by *t1*, is trying to acquire a lock on *_sharedVariable2*, and, at the same time, `CountTasks2`, called by *t2*, is trying to acquire a lock on *_sharedVariable1*. A deadlock occurs because *_sharedVariable1* is locked by `CountTasks1` and *_sharedVariable2* is locked by `CountTasks2`. Figure 7-45 shows the two stack frames for the two deadlock tasks in

the Parallel Stacks window, and the Parallel Tasks window displaying the Waiting-
Deadlocked status for both tasks. Hover the mouse pointer over the Status cell for task
ID number 2, and a tooltip will display additional information about the causes of the
deadlock. Figure 7-45 shows the information displayed by the tooltip for task ID number
2. Because the Parallel Stacks window displays the external code, you can see that both
tasks are running the `Monitor.Enter` method. This means that they are trying to acquire
a lock. In Chapter 5, "Coordination Data Structures," you learned the `Monitor` methods
that the `lock` keyword calls. Thus, when you detect a deadlock, you must enable external
code for the debugging windows. The following list shows the information that appears as
a tooltip for each task and an explanation:

➤ Task ID number 1 displays this tooltip: "'Task 1' is waiting on object: Object of type
'System.Object' (Owned by thread 6044)." It means that task ID number 1 is waiting
on an object of type `System.Object` whose lock was acquired by thread ID 6044.

➤ Task ID number 2 displays this tooltip: "'Task 2' is waiting on object: Object of type
'System.Object' (Owned by thread 7800)." It means that task ID number 2 is waiting
on an object of type `System.Object` whose lock was acquired by thread ID 7800.

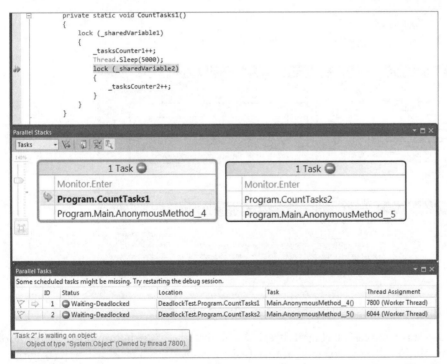

FIGURE 7-45

 *Each tooltip lets you know the thread that is keeping an object locked and is
generating a deadlocked task. Thus, you can switch to this thread, go to its supported task, and check the code that is keeping an object locked.*

6. Go to the Parallel Stacks window in the Tasks View. Double-click on the anonymous method name called by the *t1* task: `Program.Main.AnonymousMethod__4`. The following part of this line in the `Main` method will appear highlighted with a different background:

```
var t1 = new Task(() => CountTasks1());
```

7. Click the Toggle Method View option button, located at the top of the Parallel Stacks window. The Method view will display the anonymous method with a call path to the `CountTasks1` method and an icon that defines the task's status as Waiting-DeadLocked. Figure 7-46 shows the Method view for the Parallel Stacks window previously shown in Figure 7-35. It is very clear that `CountTasks1` is calling `Monitor.Enter`.

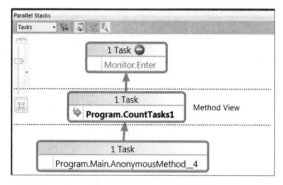

FIGURE 7-46

8. Switch to the `Monitor.Enter` enter method. Now, the Method view will display two tasks that have called `Monitor.Enter`. The full value for the Method view appears, because the method selected (`Monitor.Enter`) has two divergent paths below it. Figure 7-47 shows the Method view for the Parallel Stacks window with the two tasks calling `Monitor.Enter`.

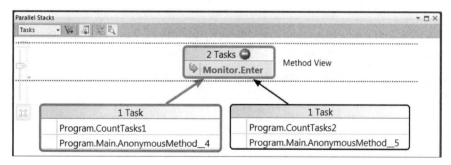

FIGURE 7-47

9. Right-click the method context for `Monitor.Enter` and select Switch To Frame in the context menu. Click the full name for one of the calls to `Monitor.Enter`, and the code that has the `lock` keyword will appear highlighted with a different background color in the source code editor. Figure 7-48 shows the line that tries to lock `_sharedVariable2` in `CountTasks1`. This line is one of the causes of the deadlock.

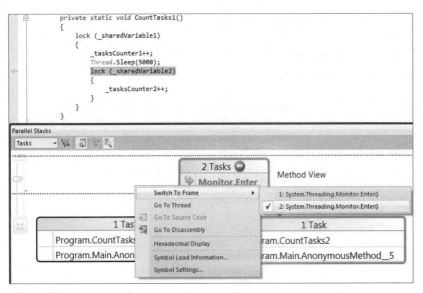

```
        private static void CountTasks1()
        {
            lock (_sharedVariable1)
            {
                _tasksCounter1++;
                Thread.Sleep(5000);
                lock (_sharedVariable2)
                {
                    _tasksCounter2++;
                }
            }
        }
```

FIGURE 7-48

SUMMARY

This chapter explained the details about many of the new debugging features introduced by Visual Studio 2010. There are many other advanced topics related to debugging parallel tasks and the threads that support their execution, but this chapter provided simple examples of the usage of the most important windows and their features. To summarize this chapter:

➤ You can use more than one monitor to enhance your debugging experience.

➤ You can combine breakpoints with the Parallel Tasks and Parallel Stacks windows to debug concurrent code.

➤ You can understand the relationship between tasks and the threads that support their execution by watching the Parallel Tasks, Parallel Stacks, and Threads windows.

➤ You can navigate through stack frames with the interactive diagrams shown in the Parallel Stacks window.

➤ You can freeze and thaw threads that support the execution of tasks to reduce concurrency and debug code with a sequential execution.

➤ You have to pay attention to the information for anonymous methods shown in the Parallel Tasks and Parallel Stacks windows.

➤ You can use the Parallel Tasks and Parallel Stacks windows to detect the causes of a deadlock.

Thread Pools

➤ Understanding the improved thread pool engine

➤ Requesting work items to run in threads in the thread pool

➤ Using lightweight synchronization primitives with threads

➤ Coordinating worker threads

➤ Using tasks instead of threads to queue jobs

➤ Understanding local queues, work-stealing mechanisms, and fine-grained parallelism

➤ Specifying a custom task scheduler

This chapter is about the changes in the Common Language Runtime (CLR) thread pool engine introduced by .NET Framework 4. It is important to understand the differences between using tasks and directly requesting work items to run in threads in the thread pool. If you have worked with the thread pool, you can take advantage of the new improvements and move your code to a task-based programming model. This chapter also provides an example of a customized task scheduler.

GOING DOWNSTAIRS FROM THE TASKS FLOOR

In previous chapters, you created tasks to parallelize the execution of code. In some cases, you didn't write statements to create `Task` instances; instead, you used .NET Framework 4's new classes and methods that created the necessary tasks to parallelize the execution. For example, `Parallel.Invoke`, `Parallel.For`, `Parallel.ForEach`, and `PLINQ` (among others) create tasks under the hood.

Figure 8-1 shows a simple staircase with three floors, Tasks, Threads, and CLR thread pool engine. The Tasks floor typically has some tasks assigned to threads and other tasks waiting to be assigned to threads. If you go downstairs from the tasks floor, you will usually find threads assigned to these tasks and other threads that aren't assigned to tasks, apart from the main

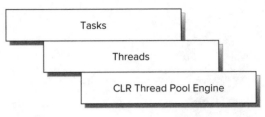

FIGURE 8-1

thread. If you go downstairs from the threads floor, you will find the CLR thread pool engine.

The CLR thread pool engine manages a pool of threads that can process work items. Instead of creating a new thread for each work item that has to be executed, the work items get queued and then picked up by diverse worker threads. The CLR thread pool engine creates and manages the necessary worker threads to support the execution of the work items and can reuse existing threads to avoid the expensive process of creating new, unnecessary threads.

The creation of a new managed thread requires thousands of CPU cycles and consumes memory. There are also significant costs to switching between threads, and therefore, you want a pool as a concurrency throttling mechanism. Thus, the CLR thread pool engine uses efficient and fine-tuned algorithms that allow you to queue work items in multiple threads without having to worry about either the creation or the destruction of the necessary threads. The CLR thread pool engine maintains a minimum number of idle worker threads that is typically equal to the number of logical cores. However, the number of idle worker threads can drop below this level. In effect, there are at least n worker threads in the thread pool, where n is the minimum of the number of logical cores and the number of queued work items. For example, if the number of logical cores is eight and the number of queued work items is two, the minimum number of idle worker threads will be two.

.NET Framework 4 uses this pool of worker threads for the following purposes:

➤ Assign tasks to threads

➤ Process the asynchronous I/O completion

➤ Process the callback functions for the timer defined in the `System.Threading.Timer` class

> *Don't confuse the timer defined in the* `System.Threading.Timer` *class with the timer component defined in the* `System.Windows.Forms.Timer` *class. The former runs the callback function in a different worker thread than the UI thread that creates the timer, and the latter just raises an event in the UI thread in a Windows Forms application. If a thread-pool thread creates the* `System.Threading.Timer` *instance, it is certainly possible that the same thread which created the timer also executes its callbacks.*

➤ Run asynchronous method calls using delegates

➤ Process registered wait operations

UNDERSTANDING THE NEW CLR 4 THREAD POOL ENGINE

While working with tasks, you have indirectly used the services provided by this engine. You can also directly request a work item to run in a thread in the thread pool by using the methods provided by the `System.Threading.ThreadPool` class. However, if you do so, you won't have access to a `Task` instance and its features.

The only advantage of requesting a work item to run in a thread in the thread pool is that you avoid the extra overhead required to create and manage the `Task` instance. If you don't need the features provided by a `Task` instance, in some specific cases, you might improve overall performance at the expense of more complex code. However, the new CLR 4 thread pool engine has been improved from its previous version to provide optimal performance when assigning work to tasks. In addition, the new thread pool engine is prepared for further scalability and optimized to take advantage of the newest multicore microprocessor architectures. Thus, whenever possible, try to work with the new tasks instead of directly requesting a work item to run in a thread in the thread pool — unless you are sure that this will significantly improve performance. Subsequent sections in this chapter provide examples that use tasks instead of threads to queue jobs in the thread pool.

Understanding Global Queues

Listing 8-1 shows the XAML code for the main window of a Windows Presentation Foundation (WPF) application that displays two `Button` controls and one `Label` on a window. You can see the design view for this window in Figure 8-2. Listing 8-1 also shows the C# code for the main window, with the code that defines the `Click` event handlers for the two buttons.

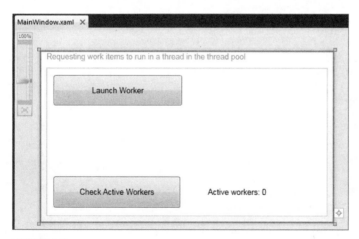

FIGURE 8-2

LISTING 8-1: Requesting work items to run in a thread in the thread pool

MAINWINDOW.XAML

```
<Window x:Class="Listing8_1.MainWindow"
  xmlns="http://schemas.microsoft.com/winfx/2006/xaml/presentation"
```

continues

LISTING 8-1 *(continued)*

```
xmlns:x="http://schemas.microsoft.com/winfx/2006/xaml"
Title="Requesting work items to run in a thread in the thread pool"
Height="283" Width="498">
<Grid>
    <Button Content="Launch Worker" Height="50"
      HorizontalAlignment="Left" Margin="12,12,0,0"
      Name="butLaunchWorker" VerticalAlignment="Top"
      Width="218" Click="butLaunchWorker_Click" />
    <Button Content="Check Active Workers" Height="51"
      HorizontalAlignment="Left" Margin="12,179,0,0"
      Name="butCheckActive" VerticalAlignment="Top"
      Width="215" Click="butCheckActive_Click" />
    <Label Content="Active workers: 0" Height="32"
      HorizontalAlignment="Left" Margin="269,192,0,0"
      Name="lblActiveWorkers" VerticalAlignment="Top"
      Width="165" />
</Grid>
</Window>
```

MAINWINDOW.XAML.CS

```csharp
using System;
using System.Collections.Generic;
using System.Linq;
using System.Text;
using System.Windows;
using System.Windows.Controls;
using System.Windows.Data;
using System.Windows.Documents;
using System.Windows.Input;
using System.Windows.Media;
using System.Windows.Media.Imaging;
using System.Windows.Navigation;
using System.Windows.Shapes;
// Added
using System.Diagnostics;
using System.Threading;

namespace Listing8_1
{
    /// <summary>
    /// Interaction logic for MainWindow.xaml
    /// </summary>
    public partial class MainWindow : Window
    {
        public MainWindow()
        {
            InitializeComponent();
        }

        // The total number of workers
        private int _workerCount = 0;
```

```csharp
        // The number of active workers
        private int _activeWorkers = 0;

        private void DoSomeWork(int workerNum)
        {
            // Simulate some work
            // between 7 and 12 seconds
            var milliSecs =
                new Random().Next(7000, 12000);
            Debug.WriteLine(
"Worker #{0} will simulate work for {1} milliseconds ",
                workerNum,
                milliSecs);
            var sw = Stopwatch.StartNew();
            // Simulate some CPU-bound work
            while (sw.Elapsed.TotalMilliseconds < milliSecs)
            {
                // Go on simulating CPU-bound work
                double calc = Math.Pow(
                    Math.PI *
                    sw.Elapsed.TotalMilliseconds, 2);
            }
        }

        private void butLaunchWorker_Click(
            object sender, RoutedEventArgs e)
        {
            // Increment the worker count
            // There is no need for an atomic operation here
            // because this code runs always on the UI thread
            _workerCount++;
            // Request ThreadPool to queue
            // a work item (a WaitCallback)
            // and send _workerCount as a
            // parameter to the WaitCallback
            ThreadPool.QueueUserWorkItem(
                (state) =>
                {
                    // Retrieve the workerNum received
                    // as a parameter in object state
                    int workerNum = (int)state;
                    // Increment the number of active workers
                    // with an atomic operation
                    Interlocked.Increment(
                        ref _activeWorkers);
                    try
                    {
                        Debug.WriteLine(
                            "Worker #{0} started ", workerNum);

                        DoSomeWork(workerNum);

                        Debug.WriteLine(
                            "Worker #{0} finished ", workerNum);
```

continues

LISTING 8-1 *(continued)*

```
                }
                finally
                {
                    // Decrement the number of active workers
                    // with an atomic operation
                    Interlocked.Decrement(
                        ref _activeWorkers);
                }
            }, _workerCount);
        }

        private void butCheckActive_Click(
            object sender, RoutedEventArgs e)
        {
            lblActiveWorkers.Content =
                String.Format(
                    "Active workers: {0}",
                    _activeWorkers);
        }
    }
}
```

When you click the Launch Worker button, the code in the butLaunchWorker_Click event handler increments the value for the _workerCount private integer variable. This variable holds the total number of workers — that is, the number of times the user pressed the button. Because the code for this event handler always runs with a serialized execution in the main thread, there is no need to use an atomic operation or to enclose the increment operation with a mutual-exclusion lock. The only thread that accesses _workerCount is the main thread.

> *When you work with WPF or Windows Forms applications, the code programmed in event handlers for controls typically runs in the User Interface (UI) thread. By default, the UI thread creates these controls and is the main thread for the application. It is possible to create controls in other threads and run message loops in them. However, it isn't the most common scenario.*

Then, the code for the event handler calls the QueueUserWorkItem method for the ThreadPool class. This method requests a work item to run in a thread in the thread pool. When you call QueueUserWorkItem, the WaitCallback delegate sent as a parameter specifies the callback method that has to run in a thread in the thread pool. This delegate gets queued on a *global queue*, and therefore runs with an asynchronous execution. The QueueUserWorkItem method returns immediately; therefore, the main thread continues with the next statement in the event handler's code. At this point, the callback method hasn't run yet, and the user can work with the UI controls because the main thread is free of work items. The thread pool doesn't use the main thread to schedule the execution of work items. Figure 8-3 shows the global queue for the thread pool and its first work item added to this queue and waiting to be executed.

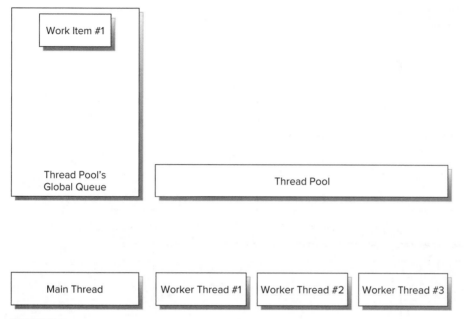

FIGURE 8-3

When the code calls the `ThreadPool.QueueUserWorkItem` method, it uses one of its definitions that allows you to pass a parameter to the `WaitCallback` delegate. The event handler passes the current value for `_workerCount` as a parameter that the delegate will receive as the `state object`.

Each time you click the Launch Worker button, a new work item is going to be added to the global queue for the thread pool. Each callback method will run with a different value for the `state` parameter. Figure 8-4 shows the global queue for the thread pool with two work items added to this queue and waiting to be executed.

The CLR thread pool injects many idle worker threads that dequeue and start the execution of each worker item waiting in the queue in FIFO (first in, first out) order. Figure 8-5 shows two work items running in two different threads of the thread pool that has an idle worker thread.

When all the available worker threads for the thread pool are already executing work items, the new work items added to the global queue for the thread pool will wait until a worker thread becomes available. Figure 8-6 shows three work items running in three different threads of the thread pool and four work items waiting in the global queue. Figure 8-7 shows how the global queue changes when `Worker thread #1` finishes executing `Work item #1` and picks out the first worker item in the queue for its execution, `Worker item #4`.

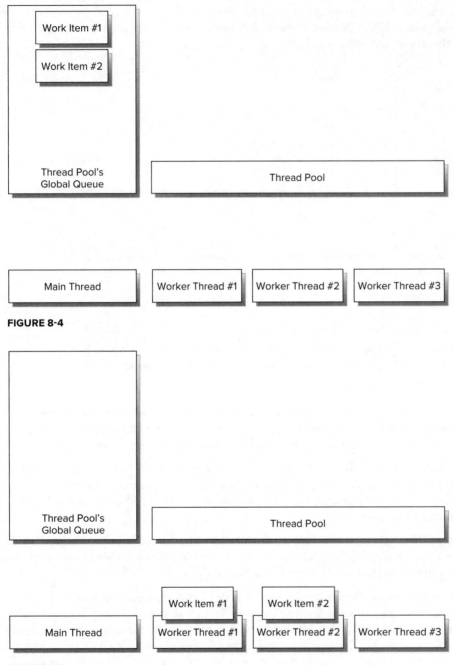

FIGURE 8-4

FIGURE 8-5

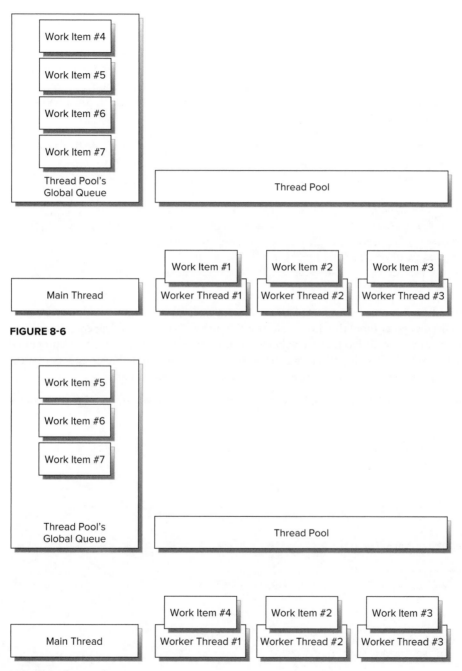

FIGURE 8-6

FIGURE 8-7

One of the improvements introduced in .NET Framework 4 is the implementation of a lock-free algorithm to queue and dequeue work items. The CLR 4 thread pool engine uses an algorithm that is similar to the `ConcurrentQueue` class, which you learned about in Chapter 4. This lock-free algorithm reduces the time needed to queue and dequeue work items; therefore, it improves both performance and scalability for the thread pool. In addition, this algorithm eliminates, or at least significantly reduces, the bottleneck generated by the locks on the global queue in the previous version of the thread-pool engine.

> *The thread-pool engine can create additional idle threads at intervals in order to pick out work items that are waiting in the global queue and execute them. You should avoid changing the default maximum worker threads and completion port threads parameters unless you have an application that requires specific tuning and you are sure that the new maximum values provide a benefit for your specific needs. The static* `ThreadPool.SetMaxThread` *method allows you to specify new values for the previously mentioned parameters.*

The CLR 4 thread-pool engine uses a *hill-climbing algorithm*. This algorithm monitors throughput and determines whether more threads would result in more work items being completed. The algorithm predicates on the notion that work items require some kind of resource to be processed, whether it is CPU, network bandwidth, or whatever. In addition, the algorithm considers that there is a saturation point where more threads would actually decrease throughput.

In the WPF application used as an example, when a worker thread from the thread pool becomes available, it runs the following code:

```
int workerNum = (int)state;
Interlocked.Increment(
    ref _activeWorkers);
try
{
    Debug.WriteLine(
        "Worker #{0} started ", workerNum);

    DoSomeWork(workerNum);

    Debug.WriteLine(
        "Worker #{0} finished ", workerNum);
}
finally
{
    Interlocked.Decrement(
        ref _activeWorkers);
}
```

code snippet from Listing8_1

The delegate receives the `state object` as a parameter. The code must cast this object to an `int` to retrieve the worker number and store it in the `workerNum` local variable. Then, the code calls the

`Interlocked.Increment` method to increment the number of active workers stored in the `_activeWorkers` variable, declared as a private variable for the `MainWindow` class. The main thread can access this variable to display the number of active workers that are running code in a thread in the thread pool. A try...`finally` block makes sure that the code calls the `Interlocked.Decrement` method to decrement the number of active workers after it performs the necessary work. Even if an exception occurs, the number of active workers will be decremented.

After incrementing the _activeWorkers variable, the code that runs within the try block does the following:

1. It writes information about the worker number that started executing code.

2. It calls the DoSomeWork method and passes workerNum as a parameter. (Remember that workerNum has the value retrieved from the state parameter.)

3. It writes information about the worker number that finished executing code.

The following lines show the code for the DoSomeWork method that receives an int workerNum parameter and simulates some work in order to keep the sample application easy to understand. The method generates a random number of milliseconds between 7,000 and 12,000, and holds it in the milliSecs local variable. Then, the method writes information about the number of milliseconds that this worker is going to spend simulating CPU-bound work by performing some math operations as follows:

Available for download on Wrox.com

```
private void DoSomeWork(int workerNum)
{
    var milliSecs =
        new Random().Next(7000, 12000);
    Debug.WriteLine(
        "Worker #{0} will simulate work for {1} milliseconds",
        workerNum,
        milliSecs);
    var sw = Stopwatch.StartNew();
    // Simulate some CPU-bound work
    while (sw.Elapsed.TotalMilliseconds < milliSecs)
    {
        // Go on simulating CPU-bound work
        double calc = Math.Pow(
            Math.PI *
            sw.Elapsed.TotalMilliseconds, 2);
    }
}
```

code snippet from Listing8_1

The following lines appear in the Output window as the result of clicking the Launch Worker button five times:

```
Worker #1 started
Worker #1 will simulate work for 10436 milliseconds
Worker #2 started
Worker #2 will simulate work for 11919 milliseconds
Worker #3 started
```

```
Worker #3 will simulate work for 8560 milliseconds
Worker #4 started
Worker #4 will simulate work for 11836 milliseconds
Worker #5 started
Worker #5 will simulate work for 11787 milliseconds
```

You can click the Launch Worker button many times without restrictions, because its click event handler that runs code in the UI thread just runs a few statements and calls the `ThreadPool` `.QueueUserWorkItem`. As previously explained, the UI thread doesn't wait until the work item completes its execution. Each worker will announce that it has finished its work after performing some math operations for the specified number of milliseconds. The following lines will start appearing in the Output window as each worker finishes its work:

```
Worker #3 finished
Worker #1 finished
Worker #2 finished
Worker #4 finished
Worker #5 finished
```

`Worker #3` is the first one to finish its work because its thread spent 8,560 milliseconds performing math operations. The work simulation time for this thread was the lowest time.

Click the Launch Worker button five times, wait 1 second, and then use the Break All command to stop the execution. Because you wait 1 second, many work items will be running in worker threads managed by the thread-pool engine. The results will vary according to the number of logical cores available in your computer. Display the Threads window by selecting Debug ⇨ Windows ⇨ Threads, and the grid will display many threads with `Worker Thread` as their `Name` and the `DoSomeWork` method in the `Location` column. These worker threads are running the code for the `DoSomeWork` method that was called by the callback delegate scheduled to run in a thread in the thread pool. Figure 8-8 shows five worker threads that are running the `DoSomeWork` method.

Display the Parallel Stacks window by selecting Debug ⇨ Windows ⇨ Parallel Stacks and switch to the Threads view. Figure 8-9 shows the stack frame for the five worker threads that are running the `while` block in the `DoSomeWork` method. The main thread is the one that is waiting for new messages from the UI controls, located at the `App.Main` method.

When you click the Check Active Workers button at any time, the code in the `butCheckActive_` `Click` event handler displays the number of active workers in a label. This code runs in the UI thread and formats the value held in the private `_activeWorkers` variable as a string that indicates the number of active workers. Remember that the worker threads increase and decrease the value for the private `_activeWorkers` variable by using atomic operations. Because the UI thread is free to run code, you can click the Check Active Workers button many times to see the effect of the worker threads finishing their execution and decreasing the value for the `_activeWorkers` variable as a result. Figure 8-10 shows the label indicating that there are nine active workers.

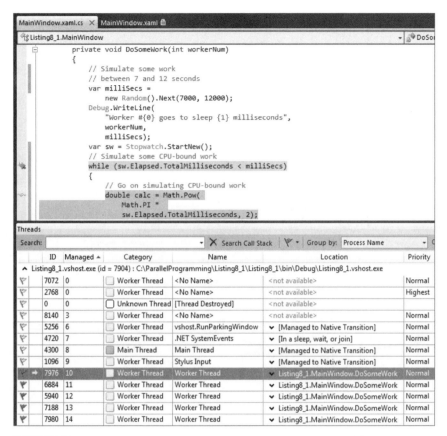

FIGURE 8-8

Waiting for Worker Threads to Finish Their Work

If you close the application's window while there are worker threads running code, all these threads will stop their execution and the main process will quit. This happens because the threads managed by the thread pool are *background threads* that don't keep an application running if all the *foreground threads* exited. When you close the application's window, all of the foreground threads exit; therefore, the background threads also stop executing their code and get destroyed.

When you use the `ThreadPool.QueueUserWorkItem` method to run code in threads in the thread pool, you don't get an identity for each work item that has to be executed. Thus, if you want to wait for all the work items to finish, you have to use coordination data structures and their signaling mechanisms.

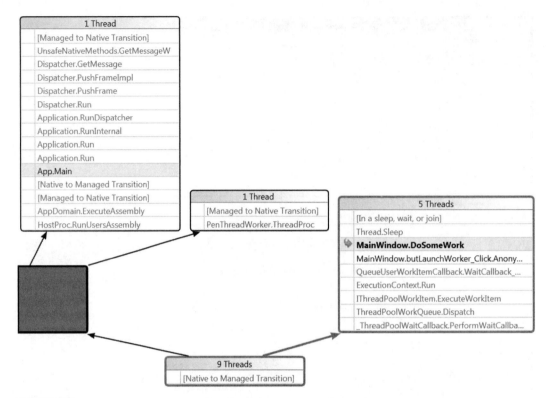

FIGURE 8-9

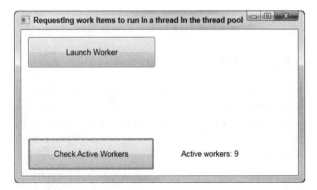

FIGURE 8-10

Listing 8-2 shows the XAML code for a new version of the main window of the WPF application that displays an additional `Button` control named `butWaitAll`. Listing 8-2 also shows the C# code for the main window, with the new lines of code highlighted.

LISTING 8-2: Using a concurrent collection of ManualResetEvent to wait for work items to finish

MAINWINDOW.XAML

```xml
<Window x:Class="Listing8_2.MainWindow"
 xmlns="http://schemas.microsoft.com/winfx/2006/xaml/presentation"
 xmlns:x="http://schemas.microsoft.com/winfx/2006/xaml"
 Title="Requesting work items to run in a thread in the thread pool"
 Height="283" Width="498">
 <Grid>
     <Button Content="Launch Worker" Height="50"
       HorizontalAlignment="Left" Margin="12,12,0,0"
       Name="butLaunchWorker" VerticalAlignment="Top"
       Width="218" Click="butLaunchWorker_Click" />
     <Button Content="Check Active Workers" Height="51"
       HorizontalAlignment="Left" Margin="12,179,0,0"
       Name="butCheckActive" VerticalAlignment="Top"
       Width="215" Click="butCheckActive_Click" />
     <Label Content="Active workers: 0" Height="32"
       HorizontalAlignment="Left" Margin="269,192,0,0"
       Name="lblActiveWorkers" VerticalAlignment="Top"
       Width="165" />
     <Button Content="Wait for All Workers to Finish"
       Height="54" HorizontalAlignment="Left"
       Margin="281,12,0,0"
       Name="butWaitAll" VerticalAlignment="Top"
       Width="183" Click="butWaitAll_Click"
       Visibility="Visible" />
 </Grid>
</Window>
```

MAINWINDOW.XAML.CS

```csharp
using System;
using System.Collections.Generic;
using System.Linq;
using System.Text;
using System.Windows;
using System.Windows.Controls;
using System.Windows.Data;
using System.Windows.Documents;
using System.Windows.Input;
using System.Windows.Media;
using System.Windows.Media.Imaging;
using System.Windows.Navigation;
using System.Windows.Shapes;
// Added
using System.Diagnostics;
using System.Threading;
using System.Threading.Tasks;
using System.Collections.Concurrent;
```

continues

LISTING 8-2 *(continued)*

```
// Don't consider this code as a best practice
namespace Listing8_2
{
    /// <summary>
    /// Interaction logic for MainWindow.xaml
    /// </summary>
    public partial class MainWindow : Window
    {
        public MainWindow()
        {
            InitializeComponent();
        }

        // The total number of workers
        private int _workerCount = 0;

        // The number of active workers
        private int _activeWorkers = 0;

        // The concurrent collection of ManualResetEvent
        private ConcurrentQueue<ManualResetEvent> _handlesQueue =
            new ConcurrentQueue<ManualResetEvent>();

        private void DoSomeWork(int workerNum)
        {
            // Simulate some work
            // between 7 and 12 seconds
            var milliSecs =
                new Random().Next(7000, 12000);
            Debug.WriteLine(
    "Worker #{0} will simulate work for {1} milliseconds ",
                workerNum,
                milliSecs);
            var sw = Stopwatch.StartNew();
            // Simulate some CPU-bound work
            while (sw.Elapsed.TotalMilliseconds < milliSecs)
            {
                // Go on simulating CPU-bound work
                double calc = Math.Pow(
                    Math.PI *
                    sw.Elapsed.TotalMilliseconds, 2);
            }
        }

        private void butLaunchWorker_Click(
            object sender, RoutedEventArgs e)
        {
            // Increment the worker count
            // There is no need for an atomic operation here
            // because this code runs always on the UI thread
            _workerCount++;
            // Request ThreadPool to queue
```

```csharp
        // a work item (a WaitCallback)
        // and send _workerCount as a
        // parameter to the WaitCallback
        ThreadPool.QueueUserWorkItem(
            (state) =>
            {
                // Retrieve the workerNum received
                // as a parameter in object state
                int workerNum = (int)state;
                // Increment the number of active workers
                // with an atomic operation
                Interlocked.Increment(
                    ref _activeWorkers);
                // Create a new unsignaled ManualResetEvent
                // and add it to
                // the _handlesQueue ConcurrentQueue
                var handle = new ManualResetEvent(false);
                _handlesQueue.Enqueue(handle);
                try
                {
                    Debug.WriteLine(
                        "Worker #{0} started ", workerNum);

                    DoSomeWork(workerNum);

                    Debug.WriteLine(
                        "Worker #{0} finished ", workerNum);

                    // Signal (set) the ManualResetEvent
                    handle.Set();
                }
                finally
                {
                    // Decrement the number of active workers
                    // with an atomic operation
                    Interlocked.Decrement(
                        ref _activeWorkers);
                }
            }, _workerCount);
}

private void butCheckActive_Click(
    object sender, RoutedEventArgs e)
{
    lblActiveWorkers.Content =
        String.Format(
            "Active workers: {0}",
            _activeWorkers);
}

private void butWaitAll_Click(
    object sender, RoutedEventArgs e)
{
    // Create and start a new task that waits
    // for all the events to be set
```

continues

LISTING 8-2 *(continued)*

```
        var t1 = Task.Factory.StartNew(
            () =>
            {
                if (_handlesQueue.Count > 0)
                {
                    // Wait for all the events to be set
                    WaitHandle.WaitAll(
                        _handlesQueue.ToArray());
                }
            });

        // Block this thread - the UI thread - until
        // the t1 task finishes
        // It is obviously a very bad practice
        // to block the UI thread like this
        // This is done just for example purposes
        t1.Wait();

        // Update the Button's title
        butWaitAll.Content = "Done!";
    }
  }
}
```

Now, if you launch many workers and then click the Wait For All Workers To Finish button, the UI thread will block until all the workers finish. This happens because the application uses a `ManualResetEvent` instance for each worker item. Figure 8-11 shows how the UI gets frozen and the Wait For All Workers To Finish button remains pressed because the UI thread is blocked and doesn't release the button until all the workers are finished.

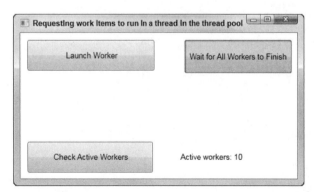

FIGURE 8-11

When a worker thread from the thread pool becomes available, the following lines of code create a new, unsignaled `ManualResetEvent` and add it to the `_handlesQueue ConcurrentQueue`:

```
var handle = new ManualResetEvent(false);
_handlesQueue.Enqueue(handle);
```

code snippet from Listing8_2

_handlesQueue is declared as a private variable for the MainWindow class. Because many threads from the thread pool can create and add ManualResetEvent instances concurrently, the code uses a ConcurrentQueue.

When the code that runs in a thread in the thread pool returns from the DoSomeWork method, it sets the state of the ManualResetEvent to signaled by calling the Set method, as in the next line:

```
handle.Set();
```

code snippet from Listing8_2

When you click the Wait For All Workers To Finish button, the code in the butWaitAll_Click event handler creates and starts a new task named *t1*. This new task calls the WaitHandle.WaitAll method and passes an array of ManualResetEvent — that is, _handlesQueue is converted to an array. The WaitHandle.WaitAll method blocks until all the events in the array are set to the signaled state. Thus, *t1* will wait for all the work items to set their ManualResetEvent.

The code in the event handler blocks the UI thread until *t1* finishes its work by calling t1.Wait. Thus, the UI thread will stop processing events until all the work items set their ManualResetEvent. When this happens, the button's title is going to change to Done!

The code in the event handler creates and starts a new task, because the UI thread in a WPF application is a *single-threaded apartment* (STA) thread. If you run the WaitHandle.WaitAll method in the UI thread, passing an array of more than one handle as a parameter, a NotSupportedException will be raised. The WaitHandle.WaitAll method doesn't support a wait on multiple handles on an STA thread. Because the code in the event handler runs in the UI thread, it creates a new task that is assigned and runs in a *multithreaded apartment* (MTA) thread from the thread pool. Therefore, you can use the WaitHandle.WaitAll method to block the task until all the workers finish in the new task.

> *The UI thread for both WPF and Windows Forms applications is an STA thread.*
> *Therefore, the code that you write in the event handlers runs in an STA thread.*
> *However, the thread pool creates MTA threads.*

The code uses ManualResetEvent, because it has to wait for many events to be set to the signaled state. For example, the WaitHandle.WaitAll method requires an array of WaitHandle, and ManualResetEvent is a subclass of WaitHandle; thus, you can call the WaitHandle.WaitAll method with an array of ManualResetEvent. In this scenario, you can't use ManualResetEventSlim to replace ManualResetEvent, because ManualResetEventSlim isn't a subclass of WaitHandle.

Because the new example creates a ManualResetEvent instance for each work item, the code introduces an overhead. Thus, when you need to have more control over the work items that run in threads in the thread pool, the code becomes more complex and consumes additional resources. As a result of this new scenario, the benefits of using the thread pool with direct requests instead of creating Task instances become less attractive. This chapter describes another version of this example — one in which you work with tasks instead of using the ThreadPool.QueueUserWorkItem method combined with ManualResetEvent instances.

Tracking a Dynamic Number of Worker Threads

The previous example was a typical fork/join scenario. Thus, you can simplify the synchronization code by using a CountdownEvent to track the dynamic number of worker threads.

Listing 8-3 shows the C# code for a new version of the WPF application's main window that uses a CountdownEvent to wait for all the work items to finish. The new lines of code are highlighted.

LISTING 8-3: Using a CountdownEvent to wait for work Items to finish

MAINWINDOW.XAML.CS

```csharp
using System;
using System.Collections.Generic;
using System.Linq;
using System.Text;
using System.Windows;
using System.Windows.Controls;
using System.Windows.Data;
using System.Windows.Documents;
using System.Windows.Input;
using System.Windows.Media;
using System.Windows.Media.Imaging;
using System.Windows.Navigation;
using System.Windows.Shapes;
// Added
using System.Diagnostics;
using System.Threading;

namespace Listing8_3
{
    /// <summary>
    /// Interaction logic for MainWindow.xaml
    /// </summary>
    public partial class MainWindow : Window
    {
        public MainWindow()
        {
            InitializeComponent();
        }

        // The total number of workers
        private int _workerCount = 0;

        // The number of active workers
        private int _activeWorkers = 0;


        // A CountdownEvent
        // with its initial count set to 1
        private CountdownEvent _countdown =
            new CountdownEvent(1);
```

```csharp
        private void DoSomeWork(int workerNum)
        {
            // Simulate some work
            // between 7 and 12 seconds
            var milliSecs =
                new Random().Next(7000, 12000);
            Debug.WriteLine(
"Worker #{0} will simulate work for {1} milliseconds ",
                workerNum,
                milliSecs);
            var sw = Stopwatch.StartNew();
            // Simulate some CPU-bound work
            while (sw.Elapsed.TotalMilliseconds < milliSecs)
            {
                // Go on simulating CPU-bound work
                double calc = Math.Pow(
                    Math.PI *
                    sw.Elapsed.TotalMilliseconds, 2);
            }
        }

        private void butLaunchWorker_Click(
            object sender, RoutedEventArgs e)
        {
            // Increment the worker count
            // There is no need for an atomic operation here
            // because this code runs always on the UI thread
            _workerCount++;
            // Request ThreadPool to queue
            // a work item (a WaitCallback)
            // and send _workerCount as a
            // parameter to the WaitCallback
            ThreadPool.QueueUserWorkItem(
                (state) =>
                {
                    // Retrieve the workerNum received
                    // as a parameter in object state
                    int workerNum = (int)state;
                    // Increment the number of active workers
                    // with an atomic operation
                    Interlocked.Increment(
                        ref _activeWorkers);
                    // Increment the current count
                    // for the shared CountdownEvent
                    _countdown.AddCount(1);
                    try
                    {
                        Debug.WriteLine(
                            "Worker #{0} started ", workerNum);

                        DoSomeWork(workerNum);

                        Debug.WriteLine(
                            "Worker #{0} finished ", workerNum);
```

continues

LISTING 8-3 *(continued)*

```
                        // Register one signal
                        // for the shared CountdownEvent
                        // and decrease the remaining signals
                        // required to unblock the thread
                        // that called the Wait method
                        _countdown.Signal();
                }
                finally
                {
                        // Decrement the number of active workers
                        // with an atomic operation
                        Interlocked.Decrement(
                            ref _activeWorkers);
                }
            }, _workerCount);
        }

        private void butCheckActive_Click(
            object sender, RoutedEventArgs e)
        {
            lblActiveWorkers.Content =
                String.Format(
                    "Active workers: {0}",
                    _activeWorkers);
        }

        private void butWaitAll_Click(
            object sender, RoutedEventArgs e)
        {
            // Signal once to equal the number of workers
            _countdown.Signal();
            // Block the UI thread until
            // the signal count for the
            // CountdownEvent reaches 0
            // It is obviously a very bad practice
            // to block the UI thread like this
            // This is done just for example purposes
            _countdown.Wait();
            // Reset the number of remaining signals
            // to 1
            _countdown.Reset(1);
            butWaitAll.Content = "Done!";
        }
    }
}
```

You have to change the namespace specified in the MainWindow.xaml file from Listing8_2 to
Listing8_3 in order to run the new application. The first line of MainWindow.xaml should be as follows:

```
<Window x:Class="Listing8_3.MainWindow"
```

code snippet from Listing8_3

If you launch many workers, and then click the Wait For All Workers To Finish button, the UI thread blocks until all the workers finish. The result is the same as in the previous example. However, this new version doesn't use a `ManualResetEvent` instance for each worker item. The new code uses a single `CountdownEvent` instance that is lightweight and reduces the overhead introduced by `ManualResetEvent`.

The initial count for the shared `CountdownEvent` (_countdown) is 1 to avoid it being signaled. Because _countdown has the initial count of 1, the worker threads can increment its current count. _countdown is declared as a private variable for the `MainWindow` class. When a worker thread from the thread pool becomes available, the following line of code increments the current count for the _countdown `CountdownEvent`:

```
_countdown.AddCount(1);
```

code snippet from Listing8_3

When the code that runs as a thread in the thread pool returns from the `DoSomeWork` method, it decreases the remaining signals required to unblock the thread that called the `Wait` method for the _countdown `CountdownEvent`. The following line calls the `Signal` method:

```
_countdown.Signal();
```

code snippet from Listing8_3

When you click the Wait For All Workers To Finish button, the code in the `butWaitAll_Click` event handler signals the _countdown `CountdownEvent` once. Because _countdown's initial count was 1, it must be signaled to reach 0. Then, the code calls the _countdown.`Wait` method, and the UI thread blocks until _countdown's count reaches 0. Thus, the UI thread waits for all the work items to signal the _countdown `CountdownEvent`. It isn't necessary to create a new task to call the _countdown.`Wait` method, because you can call this method from an STA thread; therefore, the code is simpler than in the previous example. After the UI thread unblocks, the code calls the _countdown.`Reset` method to reset the number of remaining signals for the `CountdownEvent` to 1. This way, you can click the button again to wait for all the workers to finish. The following lines show the code that runs in the `butWaitAll_Click` event handler:

```
_countdown.Signal();
_countdown.Wait();
_countdown.Reset(1);
butWaitAll.Content = "Done!";
```

code snippet from Listing8_3

The new code is simpler and takes advantage of one of the new lightweight synchronization primitives introduced in .NET Framework 4. Chapter 5 provides a detailed explanation of the different synchronization techniques that you can use when you have to work with worker threads from the thread pool.

Using Tasks Instead of Threads to Queue Jobs

You can work with the well-known tasks to queue jobs instead of working with the `ThreadPool` class. The creation of a `Task` instance for each work item adds overhead, but it also provides each work item with an identity. You already learned the benefits of working with the new task-based programming model in previous chapters. For example, one of the great benefits of using `Task` instances instead of the `ThreadPool` class is that you can take advantage of the cancellation tokens. This chapter explains other important advantages related to fine-grained parallelism scenarios.

Listing 8-4 shows the C# code for a new version of the WPF application's main window that uses tasks instead of the `ThreadPool` class to queue worker items. The new version also uses the `CountdownEvent` to wait for all the work items to finish.

LISTING 8-4: Using tasks to queue work items and a CountdownEvent to wait for them to finish

MAINWINDOW.XAML.CS

```csharp
using System;
using System.Collections.Generic;
using System.Linq;
using System.Text;
using System.Windows;
using System.Windows.Controls;
using System.Windows.Data;
using System.Windows.Documents;
using System.Windows.Input;
using System.Windows.Media;
using System.Windows.Media.Imaging;
using System.Windows.Navigation;
using System.Windows.Shapes;
// Added
using System.Diagnostics;
using System.Threading;
using System.Threading.Tasks;

namespace Listing8_4
{
    /// <summary>
    /// Interaction logic for MainWindow.xaml
    /// </summary>
    public partial class MainWindow : Window
    {
        public MainWindow()
        {
            InitializeComponent();
        }

        // The total number of workers
        private int _workerCount = 0;

        // The number of active workers
        private int _activeWorkers = 0;
```

```csharp
    // A CountdownEvent
    // with its initial count set to 1
    private CountdownEvent _countdown =
        new CountdownEvent(1);

    private void DoSomeWork(int workerNum)
    {
        // Simulate some work
        // between 7 and 12 seconds
        var milliSecs =
            new Random().Next(7000, 12000);
        Debug.WriteLine(
"Worker #{0} will simulate work for {1} milliseconds ",
            workerNum,
            milliSecs);
        var sw = Stopwatch.StartNew();
        // Simulate some CPU-bound work
        while (sw.Elapsed.TotalMilliseconds < milliSecs)
        {
            // Go on simulating CPU-bound work
            double calc = Math.Pow(
                Math.PI *
                sw.Elapsed.TotalMilliseconds, 2);
        }
    }

    private void butLaunchWorker_Click(
        object sender, RoutedEventArgs e)
    {
        // Increment the worker count
        // There is no need for an atomic operation here
        // because this code runs always on the UI thread
        _workerCount++;
        // Create and start a new Task
        // and send _workerCount as a
        // parameter to the action delegate
        var workerTask =
            Task.Factory.StartNew((num) =>
            {
                // Retrieve the workerNum received
                // as a parameter in object num
                int workerNum = (int)num;
                // Increment the number of active workers
                // with an atomic operation
                Interlocked.Increment(
                    ref _activeWorkers);
                // Increment the current count
                // for the shared CountdownEvent
                _countdown.AddCount(1);
                try
                {
                    Debug.WriteLine(
                        "Worker #{0} started ", workerNum);
```

continues

LISTING 8-4 *(continued)*

```
                DoSomeWork(workerNum);

                Debug.WriteLine(
                    "Worker #{0} finished ", workerNum);

                // Register one signal
                // for the shared CountdownEvent
                // and decreases the remaining signals
                // required to unblock the thread
                // that called the Wait method
                _countdown.Signal();                        }
            finally
            {
                // Decrement the number of active workers
                // with an atomic operation
                Interlocked.Decrement(
                    ref _activeWorkers);
            }
        }, _workerCount);
    }

    private void butCheckActive_Click(
        object sender, RoutedEventArgs e)
    {
        lblActiveWorkers.Content =
            String.Format(
                "Active workers: {0}",
                _activeWorkers);
    }

    private void butWaitAll_Click(
        object sender, RoutedEventArgs e)
    {
        // Signal once to equal the number of workers
        _countdown.Signal();
        // Block the UI thread until
        // the signal count for the
        // CountdownEvent reaches 0
        // It is obviously a very bad practice
        // to block the UI thread like this
        // This is done just for example purposes
        _countdown.Wait();
        // Reset the number of remaining signals
        // to 1
        _countdown.Reset(1);
        butWaitAll.Content = "Done!";
    }
  }
}
```

You have to change the namespace specified in the `MainWindow.xaml` file from `Listing8_3` to `Listing8_4` to run the new application. The first line of `MainWindow.xaml` should be as follows:

```
<Window x:Class="Listing8_4.MainWindow"
```

code snippet from Listing8_4

The new code uses `Task.Factory.StartNew` to create and start a new `Task` instance. This call replaced the call to the `ThreadPool.QueueUserWorkItem` in the previous version. It is easy to switch from threads to tasks to queue jobs.

This new example a very lightweight synchronization primitive to wait for the tasks to finish: a `CountdownEvent`. This chapter shows another version of the application that uses the `Task.WaitAll` method instead of `CountdownEvent`. You can choose the most appropriate mechanism to coordinate the work items according to your needs and your performance goals.

Understanding the Relationship Between Tasks and the Thread Pool

When you click the Launch Worker button, the code for the event handler calls the `Task.Factory.StartNew` method. This method creates and starts a new `Task` instance. Creating and starting a `Task` is the equivalent of calling `QueueUserWorkItem` for the `ThreadPool` class, but it generates a different result on the underlying thread-pool engine.

When you create and start a new task, you use the CLR thread pool through Task Parallel Library (TPL). The action delegate sent as a parameter specifies the method that has to run in a task, and this task is assigned to a thread in the thread pool. This task gets queued on the global queue and runs with an asynchronous execution. However, each thread assigned to a task in the thread pool has its own *local queue* in addition to the single global queue. This chapter explains the benefits of these local queues. Figure 8-12 shows the global queue for the thread pool, with the first task added to this queue and waiting to be assigned to a thread and executed. Notice that each worker thread has its own local queue.

Each time you click the Launch Worker button, a new task is added to the global queue for the thread pool. Each action delegate will run with a different value for the `num` parameter. Figure 8-13 shows the global queue for the thread pool, with two tasks added to this queue and waiting to be executed. The code created these tasks in the context of the UI thread — that is, the main thread.

The CLR thread pool injects many idle worker threads that grab and start the execution of each task waiting in the queue. This typically happens in FIFO order, but there are no guarantees about a specific order. Figure 8-14 shows two tasks running in two different threads of the thread pool that has an idle worker thread. The local queues for the two threads that grabbed tasks for their execution are free, because there aren't new tasks created in the context of these running tasks. Each time you click the Launch Worker button, the code creates a new task in the context of the UI thread, and this task becomes part of the global queue.

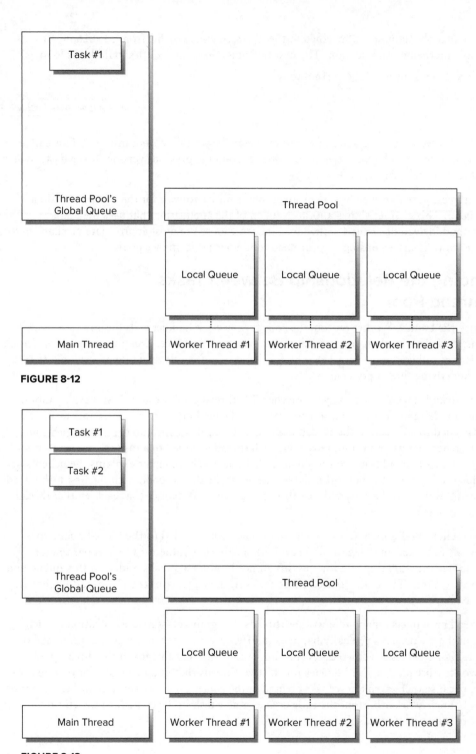

FIGURE 8-12

FIGURE 8-13

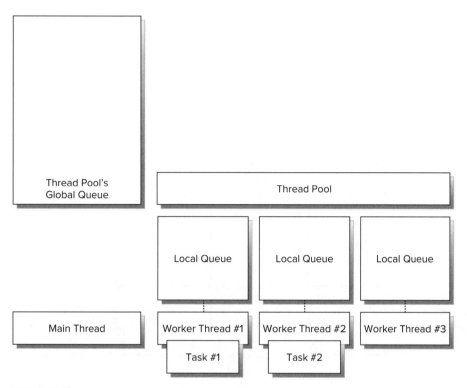

FIGURE 8-14

When all available worker threads for the thread pool are already assigned to tasks, the new tasks added to the global queue for the thread pool will wait until a worker thread becomes available. Figure 8-15 shows three tasks assigned to three different threads of the thread pool and four tasks waiting in the global queue. Figure 8-16 shows how the global queue changes when `Worker thread #1` finishes executing `Task #1` and grabs the first task in the queue for its execution: `Task #4`.

Click the Launch Worker button five times, wait 1 second, and then use the Break All command to stop the execution. Because you wait 1 second, many tasks will be assigned to worker threads managed by the thread-pool engine. The results will vary according to the number of logical cores available in your computer. Display the Threads window by selecting Debug ⇨ Windows ⇨ Threads, and the grid will display many threads with `Worker Thread` as their `Name` and the `DoSomeWork` method in the `Location` column. These worker threads are running the code for the `DoSomeWork` method that was called by the action delegate passed as a parameter to the `Task.Factory.StartNew` method. Figure 8-17 shows five worker threads that are running the `DoSomeWork` method. At the thread-pool level, the results are similar to the example that used the `ThreadPool.QueueUserWorkItem` method.

When you create and start tasks in the context of the main thread or another thread that isn't assigned to a specific task, these tasks are going to compete for work items in the global queue. These tasks are known as *top-level tasks*.

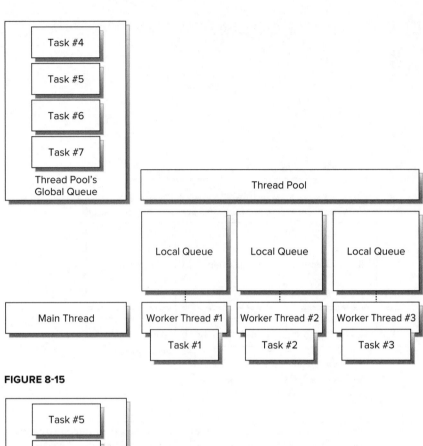

FIGURE 8-15

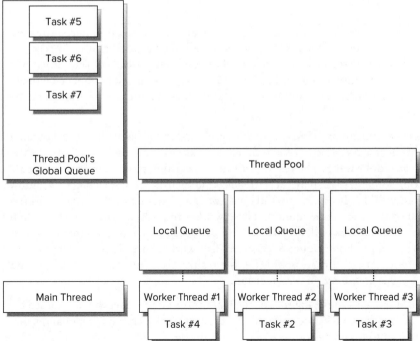

FIGURE 8-16

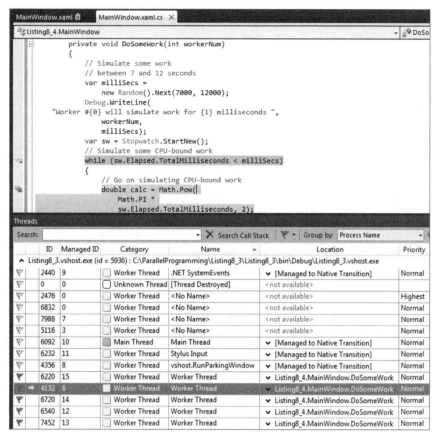

FIGURE 8-17

However, things change when you create tasks in the context of other tasks, because you can take advantage of the improvements introduced by the local queues.

Understanding Local Queues and the Work-Stealing Algorithm

The previous examples represented scenarios of *coarse-grained parallelism*, where the code created many long-running top-level tasks. Listing 8-5 shows a new version of the DoSomeWork method that creates three nested tasks in the context of the top-level task that runs this method. This is an example of *fine-grained parallelism*.

LISTING 8-5: Launching nested tasks that use the local queue

```
private void DoSomeWorkAtZone(
    int workerNum,
    string zone)
{
    // Simulate some work
    // between 1 and 3 seconds
```

continues

LISTING 8-5 *(continued)*

```
        var milliSecs =
            new Random(
                Thread.CurrentThread.ManagedThreadId).Next(
                    1000, 3000);
        Debug.WriteLine(
            "Worker #{0} works at the {1} {2} seconds",
            workerNum,
            zone,
            milliSecs);
        var sw = Stopwatch.StartNew();
        // Simulate some CPU-bound work
        while (sw.Elapsed.TotalMilliseconds < milliSecs)
        {
            // Go on simulating CPU-bound work
            double calc = Math.Pow(
                Math.PI *
                sw.Elapsed.TotalMilliseconds, 2);
        }
    }
}


    private void DoSomeWork(int workerNum)
    {
        var taskLeft =
            new Task(() =>
                {
                    DoSomeWorkAtZone(
                        workerNum,
                        "left");
                });

        var taskCenter =
            new Task(() =>
            {
                DoSomeWorkAtZone(
                    workerNum,
                    "center");
            });

        var taskRight =
            new Task(() =>
            {
                DoSomeWorkAtZone(
                    workerNum,
                    "right");
            });

        taskLeft.Start();
        taskCenter.Start();
```

```
        taskRight.Start();
        Task.WaitAll(
            new[] { taskLeft,
                    taskCenter,
                    taskRight });
    }
```

Take the previous WFP application solution. Add the code for the new `DoSomeWorkAtZone` method and replace the existing `DoSomeWork` method with the code shown in Listing 8-5.

The new `DoSomeWork` method creates the following three tasks that finish fairly quickly:

- ➤ `taskLeft`
- ➤ `taskCenter`
- ➤ `taskRight`

Then, it starts each of the aforementioned tasks and waits for them to finish their work by calling the `Task.WaitAll` method. Each task calls the `DoSomeWorkAtZone` method with different values for its `zone` parameter. This method simulates some work in order to keep the sample application easy to understand. The method generates a random number of milliseconds between 1,000 and 3,000, and holds it in the `milliSecs` local variable. Then, the method writes information about the received `zone` string and the number of milliseconds that this subworker is going to work, and simulates CPU-bound work by performing some math operations.

The `DoSomeWork` method simulates a scenario in which each task that represents a work item has to create many subworkers. Because each subworker finishes fairly quickly, the need to queue and dequeue from the global queue would be frequent, and it would easily become a bottleneck. For this reason, the thread-pool engine introduced a local queue per thread to reduce contention on the global queue and favor performance in fine-grained parallelism scenarios.

When you click the Launch Worker button, the code for the event handler calls the `Task.Factory.StartNew` method. This method creates and starts a new topmost `Task` instance. The `DoSomeWork` method creates three new `Task` instances that call the `DoSomeWorkAtZone` method. At this moment, the three nested tasks end up on the local queue for the thread assigned to their parent task, as shown in Figure 8-18.

The parent task (`Task #1` in Figure 8-18) stays blocked, waiting for the three nested tasks to finish. Because the existing thread is blocked, one of the tasks in the local queue can be assigned to this thread. At that point, the task assigned to that thread performs the wait operation and can be used to run code from another task. This technique is known as *task inlining*, which usually enhances performance because it reduces the need for an additional thread.

The local queue typically grabs tasks for execution in LIFO (last in, first out) order, instead of the FIFO order explained for the global queue. The LIFO order usually benefits *data locality* and improves performance at the expense of some level of *fairness*. This means that the LIFO order is unfair with the order in which tasks arrive but usually provides a performance benefit. Data locality means that the necessary data to run the last arrive task is cheap to access. Most of the time, the data for the last task sent to the local queue is still available in any of the CPU cache memory levels. Because the data is still hot in the cache, executing the last task immediately might provide a performance benefit. In the example, `taskRight` typically starts its execution before `taskCenter`. The following lines appear in the Output window as the result of clicking the Launch Worker button:

```
Worker #1 started
Worker #1 works at the right 2990 seconds
Worker #1 works at the left 2035 seconds
Worker #1 works at the center 1080 seconds
Worker #1 finished
```

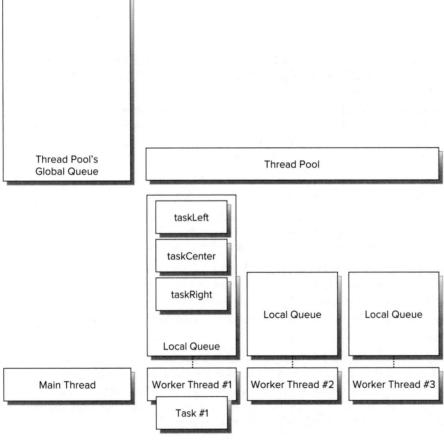

FIGURE 8-18

In this case, `taskRight` was the first of the three nested tasks to start its execution, which is an example of the LIFO order. However, remember that although LIFO order is the typical choice for local queues, there are no guarantees that this order will be used by the thread-pool engine.

To help you understand the work-stealing algorithm, Figure 8-19 illustrates an interesting scenario. First, Worker thread #1 completes the execution of its assigned task. Then, Worker thread #1 goes to its local queue, but finds it empty. So, Worker thread #1 goes to the global queue, but finds it empty, too.

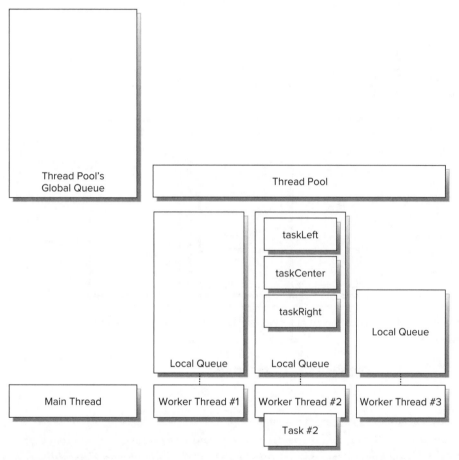

FIGURE 8-19

It isn't a good idea to keep an idle thread when another worker thread has many items waiting in its local queue. In this scenario, Worker thread #1 goes to the local queue of another thread (Worker thread #2), steals a task that is waiting in this queue, and executes it. Figure 8-20 shows how taskLeft was grabbed by Worker thread #1.

This algorithm typically steals tasks from other local queues in FIFO order. The data required for the stolen task is usually cold in the cache or completely out of the cache. Thus, stealing the older task leaves the younger tasks with their data still hot in the cache in the queue to be grabbed by the most appropriate worker thread that can take advantage of this data locality.

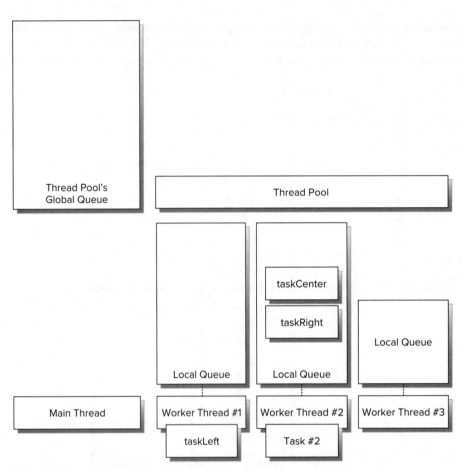

FIGURE 8-20

 When the required data is still in the cache but expensive to access, it is said that the data is "cold in the cache." On the other hand, when the required data is still in the cache and cheap to access, it is said that the data is "hot in the cache."

The way most typical divide-and-conquer scenarios work represents another reason for the typical FIFO order used by the aforementioned work-stealing mechanism. In these scenarios, the older tasks have more opportunities to generate more subworkers — that is, nested or child tasks. When this happens, the additional threads end up in the local queue for the worker thread that has stolen the task, which reduces the need for further stealing and favors data locality.

Local queues and work-stealing usually make it possible to load-balance work in fine-grained parallelism scenarios. Therefore, you should use the services provided by TPL instead of the `ThreadPool` methods whenever possible.

 Both child tasks and nested tasks use the local queue and work-stealing algorithms. If you don't want a specific task to be put on a local queue, you can specify `TaskCreationOptions.PreferFairness` *or* `TaskContinuationOptions.PreferFairness`*.*

Specifying a Custom Task Scheduler

The default `TaskFactory` creates and schedules tasks with the previously explained scheduling techniques. This default scheduler is based on the CLR 4 thread-pool engine. The scheduler injects and retires threads as necessary to achieve the maximum throughput in many heterogeneous scenarios. The work-stealing algorithms provide a smart load-balancing scheme, as well as overall good performance for most scenarios. However, when you find a specific scenario that would benefit from a special way of scheduling tasks, you can create and use a custom task scheduler for certain tasks or parallel loops.

You can create a customized task scheduler by creating a subclass of `System.Threading.Tasks.TaskScheduler` and overriding many of its methods. A `TaskScheduler` instance represents an object that manages the low-level work of queuing tasks onto threads. A `TaskScheduler`'s job isn't easy; therefore, you should not create a customized scheduler unless you are really sure about the benefits that it will provide to your specific scenario.

 Appendix C introduces 13 implementations of `TaskScheduler` *that provide diverse types of task schedulers. These task schedulers aren't production-quality, but they have been developed by Microsoft and are part of the parallel programming samples for .NET Framework 4. If you have specific needs, you should first find out if one of these sample task schedulers is suitable before trying to create your own scheduler from scratch.*

Sometimes, you need to make sure that each task runs in a different dedicated thread. An example of an algorithm that typically benefits from this scheduling mechanism is a *pipeline*. In a pipeline, each task that represents a stage running in a different thread can provide a performance benefit. However, remember to measure the results for a specific scenario before making your own scheduling decisions.

Listing 8-6 shows the code for the `ThreadPerTaskScheduler` class, a subclass of `TaskScheduler`. The code defines the `ThreadPerTaskScheduler` class within the `System.Threading.Tasks.Schedulers` namespace. This code is part of the task schedulers included in the .NET Framework 4 parallel programming samples.

LISTING 8-6: ThreadPerTaskScheduler.cs

```
// This code is part of the
// Parallel Programming Samples for .NET Framework 4
// Copyright (c) Microsoft Corporation. All rights reserved.
//
// File: ThreadPerTaskScheduler.cs
using System.Collections.Generic;
using System.Linq;

namespace System.Threading.Tasks.Schedulers
{
    public class ThreadPerTaskScheduler : TaskScheduler
    {
        protected override IEnumerable<Task> GetScheduledTasks()
        {
            return Enumerable.Empty<Task>();
        }

        protected override void QueueTask(Task task)
        {
            new Thread(
                () => TryExecuteTask(task))
                { IsBackground = true }.Start();
        }

        protected override bool TryExecuteTaskInline(
            Task task, bool taskWasPreviouslyQueued)
        {
            return TryExecuteTask(task);
        }
    }
}
```

`ThreadPerTaskScheduler` starts a new thread each time that a task has to be processed. This way, the scheduler algorithm makes sure that each task runs in a different thread. The scheduler uses neither the local queues nor the work-stealing techniques. The `ThreadPerTaskScheduler` class overrides the following three protected methods inherited from `TaskScheduler`:

➤ `GetScheduledTasks` — Returns the tasks currently scheduled to the scheduler. Because this scheduler launches tasks as soon as they are queued by creating a new thread for each new task, the method will always return an empty enumerable.

➤ `QueueTask` — Queues the `Task` instance received as a parameter to the scheduler. Because this scheduler doesn't use queues, the implementation of this method creates a new background thread that executes the `Task` instance received as a parameter. The method calls the `TryExecuteTask` method inherited from `TaskScheduler` in the new thread. The `TryExecuteTask` method receives the `Task` instance as a parameter and attempts to execute this `Task` instance on this scheduler in the new thread context. The new thread is a background thread and gets started immediately after its creation.

➤ `TryExecuteTaskInLine` — Determines whether the `Task` instance received as a parameter can be executed synchronously in this call, and if so, the method executes this `Task` instance. This method receives a Boolean value as a second parameter, indicating whether or not the `Task` instance was previously queued. Because this scheduler doesn't use queues, the implementation of this method ignores the second parameter and returns the Boolean value received from calling the `TryExecuteTask` method inherited from `TaskScheduler` in the current thread. The `TryExecuteTask` method receives the `Task` instance as a parameter and returns a Boolean value indicating whether it was possible to execute this `Task` instance on this scheduler in the current thread context.

Listing 8-7 shows the code for a new version of the WPF application that uses the `ThreadPerTaskScheduler` customized scheduler to run each work item in a different thread. In order to keep the example simple, the new code uses the previous version of the `DoSomeWork` method that spends a few seconds simulating CPU-bound work by performing some math operations. This version doesn't create additional nested tasks.

LISTING 8-7: Using a Customized Scheduler

MAINWINDOW.XAML.CS

```
using System;
using System.Collections.Generic;
using System.Linq;
using System.Text;
using System.Windows;
using System.Windows.Controls;
using System.Windows.Data;
using System.Windows.Documents;
using System.Windows.Input;
using System.Windows.Media;
using System.Windows.Media.Imaging;
using System.Windows.Navigation;
using System.Windows.Shapes;
// Added
using System.Diagnostics;
using System.Threading;
using System.Threading.Tasks;
using System.Threading.Tasks.Schedulers;

namespace Listing8_7
{
    /// <summary>
    /// Interaction logic for MainWindow.xaml
    /// </summary>
    public partial class MainWindow : Window
```

continues

LISTING 8-7 *(continued)*

```
{
    // The total number of workers
    private int _workerCount = 0;

    // The number of active workers
    private int _activeWorkers = 0;

    // The list of worker tasks
    private List<Task> _workerTasks = new List<Task>();

    // The TaskFactory instance
    // that uses the ThreadPerTaskScheduler
    private TaskFactory _threadFactory;

    // The thread per task scheduler
    private ThreadPerTaskScheduler _taskScheduler;

    public MainWindow()
    {
        InitializeComponent();

        _taskScheduler = new ThreadPerTaskScheduler();

        _threadFactory = new TaskFactory(_taskScheduler);
    }

    private void DoSomeWork(int workerNum)
    {
        // Simulate some work
        // between 7 and 12 seconds
        var seconds =
            new Random().Next(7000, 12000);
        Debug.WriteLine(
    "Worker {0} will simulate work for {1} seconds",
            workerNum,
            seconds);
        var sw = Stopwatch.StartNew();
        // Simulate some CPU-bound work
        while (sw.Elapsed.TotalMilliseconds < milliSecs)
        {
            // Go on simulating CPU-bound work
            double calc = Math.Pow(
                Math.PI *
                sw.Elapsed.TotalMilliseconds, 2);
        }
    }

    private void butLaunchWorker_Click(
        object sender, RoutedEventArgs e)
    {
        // Increment the worker count
        // There is no need for an atomic operation here
```

```csharp
    // because this code runs always on the UI thread
    _workerCount++;
    // Create and start a new Task
    // and send _workerCount as a
    // parameter to the action delegate
    // Uses _threadFactory instead of Task.Factory
    var workerTask =
        _threadFactory.StartNew((num) =>
    {
        // Retrieve the workerNum received
        // as a parameter in object num
        int workerNum = (int)num;
        // Increment the number of active workers
        // with an atomic operation
        Interlocked.Increment(
            ref _activeWorkers);
        try
        {
            Debug.WriteLine(
                "Worker {0} started ", workerNum);

            DoSomeWork(workerNum);

            Debug.WriteLine(
                "Worker {0} finished ", workerNum);
        }
        finally
        {
            // Increment the number of active workers
            // with an atomic operation
            Interlocked.Decrement(
                ref _activeWorkers);
        }
    }, _workerCount);

    // Add the new Task instance
    // to the _workerTasks list
    _workerTasks.Add(workerTask);
}

private void butCheckActive_Click(
    object sender, RoutedEventArgs e)
{
    lblActiveWorkers.Content =
        String.Format(
            "Active workers: {0}",
            _activeWorkers);
}

private void butWaitAll_Click(
    object sender, RoutedEventArgs e)
{
    // Wait for all the tasks in _workerTasks
    // to finish their work
    // It is obviously a very bad practice
```

continues

LISTING 8-7 *(continued)*

```
        // to block the UI thread like this
        // This is done just for example purposes
        Task.WaitAll(_workerTasks.ToArray());
        butWaitAll.Content = "Done!";
    }
  }
}
```

Take the previous WFP application solution. Add the code for the `ThreadPerTaskScheduler` class in the `ThreadPerTaskScheduler.cs` class, as shown in Listing 8-6. Then, replace the code for the `MainWindow.xaml.cs` file with the lines shown in Listing 8-7. Finally, change the namespace specified in the `MainWindow.xaml` file from `Listing8_4` to `Listing8_7` to run the new application. The first line of `MainWindow.xaml` should be as follows:

```
<Window x:Class="Listing8_7.MainWindow"
```

code snippet from Listing8_7

The `MainWindow`'s constructor creates a new instance of `ThreadPerTaskScheduler` and saves it into the `_taskScheduler` private variable. In this case, the constructor for `ThreadPerTaskScheduler` doesn't require parameters. However, other specialized schedulers might require the specification of parameters during their construction to define their behavior.

Then, the `MainWindow`'s constructor creates a new instance of `TaskFactory` and sends `_taskScheduler` as a parameter. This way, `_threadFactory` is going to use `_taskScheduler` to schedule the tasks that this factory creates.

When you click the Launch Worker button, the code in the `butLaunchWorker_Click` event handler creates and starts a new `Task` instance and saves it in the `workerTask` local variable.

The following line would create and start the new task using the default `TaskFactory`:

```
var workerTask = Task.Factory.StartNew((num) =>
```

However, the code uses this line to create and start the new task using `_threadFactory`. Thus, the new task uses the scheduler specified for `_threadFactory` in its constructor: `_taskScheduler`.

```
var workerTask = _threadFactory.StartNew((num) =>
```

To test the results of using a customized scheduler, you just need to change a few lines of code, as in the predecing example.

The code keeps a list of worker tasks in the `_workerTasks` private variable. `_workerTasks` is a `List<Task>`, and the UI thread is the only thread that makes changes to this list. Thus, there is no need to use a concurrent collection or to add locks when the code creates and starts a new task and then adds it to _workerTasks.

When you click the Wait For All Workers To Finish button, the code in the butWaitAll_Click event handler calls the Task.WaitAll method and passes an array of Task — that is, _workerTasks converted to an array. When you use tasks and give them an identity, the code is usually easier than the equivalent version that calls methods from the ThreadPool class.

SUMMARY

There are many other advanced topics related to the low-level work of queuing tasks onto threads. This chapter explained the relationship between the thread-pool engine and TPL. Because the chapter is focused on the advantages of the new task-based programming model, it doesn't pretend to be a reference of the ThreadPool class. The main focus of the chapter was to discuss the usage of the new features found in .NET Framework 4 in favor of TPL. To summarize this chapter:

➤ If you go downstairs from the tasks floor, you will find threads and the CLR thread pool.

➤ You can use tasks instead of threads to simplify the code that uses services from the ThreadPool class.

➤ When you use tasks, you take advantage of local queues and work-stealing mechanisms.

➤ You should use tasks when you face fine-grained parallelism scenarios.

➤ You can test different task schedulers when you think that the default scheduler isn't appropriate for a specific algorithm.

Asynchronous Programming Model

This chapter is about the advantages of mixing existing asynchronous programming models with tasks. The asynchronous programming models aren't new and they've been included as part of .NET since the first version. However, the task-based programming model is completely new. Therefore, mixing the old models with the new one is a bit complex. This chapter provides real-life examples that take advantage of the simplicity of Task instances and their task continuation features to perform concurrent asynchronous jobs related to the existing asynchronous programming models.

In addition, this chapter teaches one of the most complex topics related to concurrent programming: the process of updating the user interface (UI) from diverse tasks and threads. The chapter explains patterns to update the UI in both Windows Forms and Windows Presentation Foundation (WPF) applications.

MIXING ASYNCHRONOUS PROGRAMMING WITH TASKS

A `Task` represents an asynchronous operation, as explained in Chapter 2, "Imperative Data Parallelism." Therefore, if you want to perform many computationally intensive asynchronous operations, I/O-bound asynchronous operations, or a combination of both, you can use the simplicity and power provided by the Task Parallel Library (TPL).

I/O-bound workflows typically leave one thread waiting until the I/O operations finish. When you use tasks instead of threads, you can take advantage of the task-scheduling algorithms explained in Chapter 8, "Thread Pools," to support many concurrent I/O operations without requiring a large number of threads. However, if you use a task to call a synchronous I/O operation, the operation will block the assigned thread for the duration of this I/O operation.

Threads are expensive, and you don't want to create a new thread for each asynchronous I/O operation. A thread blocked waiting for the I/O operation to finish wastes valuable resources, because it isn't doing real work. You can use the `Task.Factory.FromAsync` method to run as many concurrent asynchronous I/O operations as necessary to take full advantage of parallelism and finish the work in less time. No threads are going to be used at all while an asynchronous I/O operation is in flight. It is necessary to use threading resources when the I/O operation completes because the results must be processed.

Your code is going to scale better and consume fewer resources if you call asynchronous operations with `Task.Factory.FromAsync` instead of working with threads. The task scheduler assigns tasks to threads that are blocked waiting and avoids creating additional threads when they aren't necessary. This way, you can write your code to perform concurrent asynchronous I/O operations and leave the complex work for the CLR 4 thread-pool engine. Chapter 8 explains how the thread-pool engine injects and retires threads as necessary to achieve the maximum throughput in many heterogeneous scenarios. `Task.Factory.FromAsync` enable you to create responsive and scalable applications that perform concurrent asynchronous I/O operations.

In addition, you can provide the user with a responsive UI by unblocking the UI thread while the concurrent I/O operations run in diverse tasks. If you have to create a new application from scratch, you can work with tasks, their continuation features, and wait operations. This way, the code is easy to understand, and you are able to achieve the desired scalability according to the maximum I/O performance.

However, sometimes, you need to interact with one of the following two standard patterns for performing asynchronous operations introduced in previous .NET versions:

➤ **Asynchronous Programming Model (APM)** — .NET Framework 1 introduced this pattern, also known as the *Begin/End Pattern*, for asynchronous operations. A method with the `Begin` prefix launches the asynchronous execution and returns a `System.IAsyncResult` that represents the status for this asynchronous operation. This method usually receives additional parameters related to the asynchronous operation and a `System.AsyncCallback` that specifies the method that must be called when the asynchronous operation completes its execution. Then, you can call the method with the `End` prefix and pass the `System.IAsyncResult` that represents the status for the pending asynchronous operation. This method with the End prefix allows you to wait for the asynchronous operation received as a parameter to complete. The method with the `End` prefix joins and blocks the current task or thread until the

I/O operation has completed. In addition, this method typically returns information related to the results of the asynchronous operation. For example, the `Begin`/`End` pair of methods for the `System.IO.FileStream` class that performs an asynchronous read is composed of the `BeginRead` and `EndRead` methods. The `EndRead` method returns the number of bytes read from the stream.

➤ **Event-based Asynchronous Pattern (EAP)** — .NET Framework 2 introduced this pattern for asynchronous operations. A method with the `Async` suffix launches the asynchronous execution. When the execution completes or is canceled, the asynchronous operation raises an event, typically with the `Completed` suffix. A delegate provides the callback method that is invoked when this event is raised. For example, the method/event pair for the `System.Net.NetworkInformation.Ping` class is composed of the `SendAsync` method and the `PingCompleted` event.

You can use tasks to implement either the APM or the EAP pattern in a class. In addition, you can expose either APM or EAP operations found in existing classes as tasks to simplify your code and make it compatible with the new task-based programming model.

Appendix C, "Parallel Extensions Extras," introduces classes that provide new extension methods for existing classes. These extension methods add new asynchronous counterparts that use and return tasks. These returned tasks represent the asynchronous operations and contain their results. The new extension methods take advantage of tasks to interact with classes that implement either the APM or the EPA patterns. These extension methods aren't production-quality, but they have been developed by Microsoft and are part of the parallel programming samples for .NET Framework 4. If you have specific needs, be sure to check if one of these extension methods is suitable before trying to create your own methods from scratch.

Working with TaskFactory.FromAsync

Listing 9-1 shows the XAML code for the main window of a WPF application that displays a `Button` control on a window. You can see the design view for this window in Figure 9-1. Listing 9-1 also shows the C# code for the main window, with the code that defines the `Click` event handler for the button.

LISTING 9-1: Encapsulating many asynchronous read operations in tasks

MAINWINDOW.XAML

```xml
<Window x:Class="Listing9_1.MainWindow"
    xmlns="http://schemas.microsoft.com/winfx/2006/xaml/presentation"
    xmlns:x="http://schemas.microsoft.com/winfx/2006/xaml"
    Title="Performing Concurrent Read Operations"
    Height="350" Width="525">
    <Grid>
```

continues

LISTING 9-1 *(continued)*

```
        <Button Content="Concatenate Text Files" Height="43"
            HorizontalAlignment="Left" Margin="12,12,0,0"
            Name="butConcatTextFiles" VerticalAlignment="Top"
            Width="190" Click="butConcatTextFiles_Click" />
    </Grid>
</Window>
```

MAINWINDOW.XAML.CS

```csharp
using System;
using System.Collections.Generic;
using System.Linq;
using System.Text;
using System.Windows;
using System.Windows.Controls;
using System.Windows.Data;
using System.Windows.Documents;
using System.Windows.Input;
using System.Windows.Media;
using System.Windows.Media.Imaging;
using System.Windows.Navigation;
using System.Windows.Shapes;
// Added
using System.Threading.Tasks;
using System.IO;

namespace Listing9_1
{
    /// <summary>
    /// Interaction logic for MainWindow.xaml
    /// </summary>
    public partial class MainWindow : Window
    {
        public MainWindow()
        {
            InitializeComponent();
        }

        // The file names to read
        private string[] fileNames = {
            "file01.txt",
            "file02.txt",
            "file03.txt",
            "file04.txt",
            "file05.txt",
            "file06.txt",
            "file07.txt",
            "file08.txt",
            "file09.txt",
            "file10.txt",
            "file11.txt",
            "file12.txt",
            "file13.txt",
            "file14.txt",
```

```
        "file15.txt",
        "file16.txt"
};

// The list of tasks
// Each Task instance returns a string
// and reads a file with an APM operation
private List<Task<string>> fileTasks;

// The buffer size for the stream reader
private const int BUFFER_SIZE = 0x2000;

private Task<string> ReadAllTextAsync(string path)
{
    // Get information for the file
    FileInfo info = new FileInfo(path);
    if (!info.Exists)
    {
        // The file doesn't exist
        throw new FileNotFoundException(
            String.Format("{0} does not exist.", path),
            path);
    }

    // This array will hold the data
    // read from the file
    byte[] data = new byte[info.Length];

    // Create the new FileStream
    // to read from the file with
    // useAsync set to true
    // in order to use asynchronous input
    FileStream stream =
        new FileStream(path, FileMode.Open,
            FileAccess.Read, FileShare.Read,
            BUFFER_SIZE, true);

    // Wrap the APM read operation in a Task
    // Encapsulate the APM stream.BeginRead and
    // stream.EndRead methods in task
    Task<int> task =
        Task<int>.Factory.FromAsync(
        stream.BeginRead, stream.EndRead,
        data, 0, data.Length, null,
        TaskCreationOptions.None);

    // The Task will hold the number of bytes
    // read as a result
    // Add a continuation to task
    // and return it
    return task.ContinueWith((t) =>
        {
            stream.Close();
            Console.WriteLine(
              "One task has read {0} bytes from {1}.",
              t.Result, stream.Name);
```

continues

LISTING 9-1 *(continued)*

```
                        // This continuation Task returns
                        // the data read from the file
                        // as a string with UTF8 encoding
                        return (t.Result > 0) ?
                            new UTF8Encoding().GetString(data) : "";
                    },
                    TaskContinuationOptions.ExecuteSynchronously);
        }

        private void butConcatTextFiles_Click
        (object sender, RoutedEventArgs e)
        {
            fileTasks =
                new List<Task<string>>(fileNames.Length);
            foreach (string fileName in fileNames)
            {
                // Launch a Task<string>
                // that will hold all the data
                // read from the file in a string
                // as the task's result
                var readTask =
                    ReadAllTextAsync(
                        @"C:\MYFILES\" + fileName);
                // Add the new Task<string> to fileTasks
                // There is no need to call the Start method
                // because the task was created
                // with the FromAsync method
                fileTasks.Add(readTask);
            }
            // Block this thread waiting
            // until all the tasks finish their work
            Task.WaitAll(fileTasks.ToArray());

            // Write all the data read from the files
            foreach (Task<string> fileTask in fileTasks)
            {
                Console.WriteLine(fileTask.Result);
            }
        }
    }
}
```

To run the code shown in Listing 9-1, you have to create many text files specified in the `fileNames` private array of `string`. The default location for these text files is the `C:\MYFILES` folder. However, you can replace this path with your preference.

When you click the Concatenate Text Files button, the code in the `butConcatTextFiles_Click` event handler launches a new `Task<string>` for each file in the *fileNames* array of `string`. A `foreach` loop calls the `ReadAllTextAsync` method for each file name and then adds the `Task<string>` returned by this method to *fileTasks*. Each `Task<string>` reads all the data from a file and stores the resulting `string` in its `Result` property.

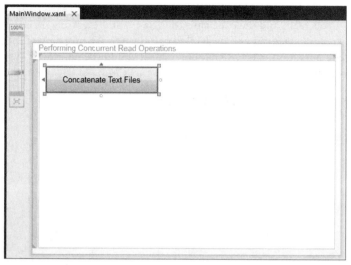

FIGURE 9-1

Many of these read operations will run in parallel according to the available hardware resources and the I/O speed. Then, the code blocks the UI thread, waiting until all the tasks finish their work by calling the `Task.WaitAll` method. Because each file read operation has its associated `Task` instance, it is easy to write code that waits for all the necessary concurrent read operations to complete their executions.

Finally, the code writes the text read from all the files to the output. In this example, the focus is on the `ReadAllTextAsync` method that wraps an APM operation in a `Task<string>`. It is not a best practice to block the UI thread until multiple concurrent tasks finish. This chapter shows you other versions of this simple example that won't block the UI thread and update UI controls with the results of these asynchronous and concurrent I/O operations.

The `ReadAllTextAsync` method receives a full path of the file to read as a parameter and returns a `Task<string>`. The method checks for the file to exist and defines an array of `byte`, called *data*, to hold all the data read from this file. Then, the method creates a new `System.IO.FileStream` instance, called *stream*, to read the file. The last parameter for the `FileStream` constructor, *useAsync*, is set to `true` to use asynchronous input. The following code snippet shows the lines that encapsulate the APM read operation in a `Task<int>`:

```
Task<int> task =
    Task<int>.Factory.FromAsync(
    stream.BeginRead, stream.EndRead,
    data, 0, data.Length, null,
    TaskCreationOptions.None);
```

code snippet from Listing9_1

The `TaskFactory.FromAsync` and `TaskFactory<TResult>.FromAsync` methods provide many definitions that return a `Task` or `Task<TResult>`. The preceding code snippet uses an overload to create a `Task<int>` that represents a pair of `Begin`/`End` methods. This pair of methods conforms to the previously introduced APM pattern. The code encapsulates the APM `stream.BeginRead` and `stream.EndRead` methods in a `Task<int>`, which is the *task* local variable. Then, `stream.EndRead` returns an `int` with the number of bytes read, and the code calls the `Task<int>.Factory.FromAsync` method. The result of the `stream.EndRead` method will be available in the `Result` property of the `Task<int>` that is wrapping the APM operation, *task*. The following list shows the parameter types and names, followed by the value that the code passes to the `FromAsync` method:

➤ `Func<byte[], int, AsyncCallBack, object, IAsyncResult>` *beginMethod* — `stream.BeginRead`

➤ `Func<IAsyncResult, int>` *endMethod* — `stream.EndRead`

➤ `byte[]` *arg1* — *data*

➤ `int` *arg2* — 0

➤ `int` *arg3* — `data.Length`

➤ `object` *state* — `null`

➤ `TaskCreationOptions` *creationOptions* — `TaskCreationOptions.None`

The `FromAsync` method sends the previously mentioned parameters to the `stream.BeginRead` method and then uses the `IAsyncResult` returned by `BeginRead` to call the `EndRead` method. The following list shows the parameter types and names followed by the variable names and the actual values that the `stream.BeginRead` method receives from the previous list:

➤ `byte[]` *array* — *arg1*, the `data` local variable. This variable will be used as a buffer to read data into.

➤ `int` *offset* — *arg2*, 0. The code will begin reading from byte offset 0.

➤ `int` *numBytes* — *arg3*, `data.Length`. The code will read the whole file.

➤ `Object` *stateObject* — *state*, `null`. The code won't distinguish this asynchronous request from other requests.

There is no need to call the `Start` method for the new `Task<int>`, because no task is being scheduled. The `FromAsync` method calls the begin method and, when the operation completes, it calls the end method and uses its result to complete the task. In fact, if you call the `Start` method for a `Task` instance created with the `FromAsync` method, the code will raise an exception. The `Task<int>` begins life in the `TaskStatus.Created` state, but this state is changed to `TaskStatus.WaitingForActivation` before the reference to the `Task<int>` instance is returned to the `FromAsync` method caller. This happens when you create tasks with the `FromAsync` method.

Because there aren't special needs for this new `Task<int>`, the `TaskCreationOptions.None` value is the last parameter for the `FromAsync` method. However, you can use another value when necessary for this parameter.

Programming Continuations After Asynchronous Methods End

The `ReadAllTextAsync` method adds a continuation to the `Task<int>` (*task*) created with the `FromAsync` method. In fact, the method returns the new `Task<string>` chained with the

ContinueWith method to *task*. The following code snippet shows the lines that define the continuation that returns a string with the file contents:

```
return task.ContinueWith((t) =>
    {
        stream.Close();
        Console.WriteLine(
            "One task has read {0} bytes from {1}.",
            t.Result, stream Name) ;

        // This continuation Task returns
        // the data read from the file
        // as a string with UTF8 encoding
        return (t.Result > 0) ?
            new UTF8Encoding().GetString(data) : "";
    },
    TaskContinuationOptions.ExecuteSynchronously);
```

code snippet from Listing9_1

The ContinueWith method specifies the TaskContinuationOptions.ExecuteSynchronously value to tell the scheduler that the continuation task should be executed synchronously with the precedent task (*task*). You should specify this value whenever possible to make sure that this continuation task uses the same underlying thread that transited the precedent task to its final state, because it will use the data read from the file by the precedent task (*task*). If the data is still hot in the cache, you want to prevent the scheduler from assigning this continuation task to a different thread. In addition, you want to avoid the unnecessary overhead of having to schedule this continuation.

The continuation task closes the FileStream (*stream*), writes information to the console about the file that has been read, and returns the data read from the file as a string with UTF8 encoding. The Result property of the precedent task that is referred to as *t* in the delegate holds the number of bytes read from the file.

The ReadAllTextAsync method returns a Task<string> continuation task that starts after the FileStream (*stream*) finishes reading the file. The code uses a Task<string> for each file to be read and runs concurrent asynchronous operations, taking advantage of the task-based programming model.

Combining Results from Multiple Concurrent Asynchronous Operations

The previous example blocked the UI thread, waiting until the I/O operations finish. You can use the TaskFactory.ContinueWhenAll method in conjunction with the tasks created with the FromAsync method to launch asynchronous code that has to run after the operations complete their executions. Because each asynchronous operation is a Task<string>, you can program a continuation with the TaskFactory.ContinueWhenAll method, as explained in Chapter 5, "Coordination Data Structures."

The following code snippet shows a new version of the code that runs when you click Concatenate Text Files but doesn't keep the UI thread blocked:

```
private void butConcatTextFiles_Click(
    object sender,
    RoutedEventArgs e)
{
    fileTasks =
        new List<Task<string>>(fileNames.Length);
    foreach (string fileName in fileNames)
    {
        // Launch a Task<string>
        // that will hold all the data
        // read from the file in a string
        // as the task's result
        var readTask =
            ReadAllTextAsync(
                @"C:\MYFILES\" + fileName);
        // Add the new Task<string> to fileTasks
        // There is no need to call the Start method
        // because the task was created
        // with the FromAsync method
        fileTasks.Add(readTask);
    }

    // Program a continuation
    // to start after all the asynchronous
    // operations finish
    Task.Factory.ContinueWhenAll(
        fileTasks.ToArray(),
        (antecedentTasks) =>
        {
            // Wait for all the antecedent
            // tasks to ensure the propagation
            // of any exception occurred
            // in any of the antecedent tasks
            Task.WaitAll(antecedentTasks);

            var sb = new StringBuilder();
            // Write all the data read from the files
            foreach (Task<string> fileTask
                in antecedentTasks)
            {
                sb.Append(fileTask.Result);
            }
            Console.WriteLine(sb);
        });
}
```

code snippet from Snippet9_1

The new code in the butConcatTextFiles_Click event handler launches a new Task<string> for each file in the *fileNames* array of string. It calls the previously explained ReadAllTextAsync method that uses `FromAsync`. When the `foreach` loop creates and schedules all the tasks, the code uses `Task.Factory.ContinueWhenAll` to program a continuation after all these tasks finish the execution of the asynchronous read operations. The action specified for `ContinueWhenAll` will run in a new task as another asynchronous piece of code that doesn't block the UI thread. The code in the event handler doesn't wait for this new continuation task to finish; therefore, there is no more code running in the UI thread and the user can use the UI controls while all these asynchronous operations and the continuations run.

Now, the continuation task creates a new `StringBuilder` instance, *sb*, and uses it to concatenate the text from all the files. Then, the code writes all the text to the console output. While this happens, the user can interact with the UI controls because the WPF application can run code in the UI thread and process the corresponding events. The code calls the `Console.WriteLine` method; therefore, the text read from the files appears in the IDE's Output window. Figure 9-2 shows the WPF application's window with a textbox control and the user writing in it while the Output window displays the text read from all the files.

> *The code written in the UI controls' events performs many actions that should be placed in independent classes to decouple one or more layers from the UI. However, these examples are kept as simple as possible and focused on the possibilities offered by TPL and .NET Framework 4. In real-life applications, you can combine these possibilities with your decoupling techniques and your object-oriented programming skills.*

The `FromAsync` method enables you to wrap APM operations in a `Task`. By using this method, you can perform many concurrent asynchronous operations with tasks that aren't going to consume an excessive number of threads.

Performing Asynchronous WPF UI Updates

When you declare controls in the XAML code for a WPF window, the UI thread creates these controls at run-time. Only the thread that creates the controls can update these controls. Thus, by default, you have to write code in the UI thread to change the values for the properties of these controls. You already know that the task scheduler assigns new tasks to diverse worker threads. When the tasks run in these worker threads, they cannot update the controls created in the UI thread.

In a real-life WPF application, you aren't going to write output to the console. Instead, you have to update controls, and you have to provide the user with a responsive UI. Therefore, you need to run some code in the UI thread and some code in other worker threads.

Listing 9-2 shows the XAML code for a new version of the main window of the WPF application that displays two new controls: a `TextBox` (*txtAllText*) and a `ProgressBar` (*pgbFiles*). You can see the design view for this window in Figure 9-3.

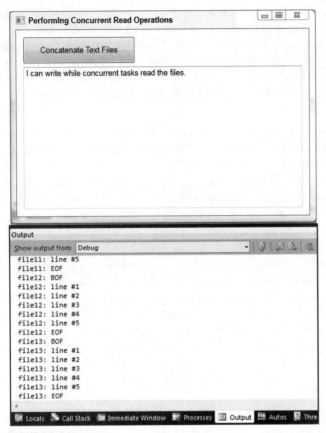

FIGURE 9-2

LISTING 9-2: New controls to provide feedback to the UI

MAINWINDOW.XAML

```xml
<Window x:Class="Listing9_2.MainWindow"
    xmlns="http://schemas.microsoft.com/winfx/2006/xaml/presentation"
    xmlns:x="http://schemas.microsoft.com/winfx/2006/xaml"
    Title="Performing Concurrent Read Operations"
    Height="350" Width="525">
    <Grid>
        <Button Content="Concatenate Text Files" Height="43"
            HorizontalAlignment="Left" Margin="12,12,0,0"
            Name="butConcatTextFiles" VerticalAlignment="Top"
            Width="190" Click="butConcatTextFiles_Click" />
        <TextBox Margin="12,61,12,0" Name="txtAllText"
            AcceptsReturn="True" Height="205"
            VerticalAlignment="Top" />
        <ProgressBar Height="27" HorizontalAlignment="Left"
```

```
            Margin="12,272,0,0" Name="pgbFiles"
            VerticalAlignment="Top" Width="479" />
        </Grid>
    </Window>
```

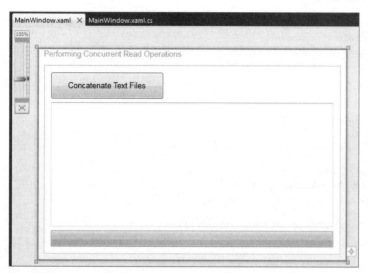

FIGURE 9-3

When you have code running in worker threads and you want to update a control created in the UI thread, you can use the UI thread `Dispatcher`. If you want to marshal the work that updates the UI back to the UI thread so that you can access the control safely, you can call the `Invoke` or `BeginInvoke` method for the `Dispatcher` as follows:

➤ The `Invoke` method executes a delegate synchronously. This method calls the `Send` method for the `SynchronizationContext` to synchronously invoke the delegate.

➤ The `BeginInvoke` method executes a delegate asynchronously and lets you specify a priority for this delegate on the queue. This method calls the `Post` method for the `SynchronizationContext` to asynchronously invoke the delegate.

For example, you can call `pgbFiles.Dispatcher.BeginInvoke` with an asynchronous execution to marshal the work to the thread that created the `pgbFiles` control. The method will return immediately after adding the delegate to the `SynchronizationContext` queue by calling its `Post` method. The method won't wait for the delegate to finish its execution.

The `TaskScheduler` class provides the `FromCurrentSynchronizationContext` static method, which makes it simple to create a `TaskScheduler` instance associated with the current `SynchronizationContext`. Thus, you can create a specific `TaskScheduler` to run the tasks that perform asynchronous updates to the UI controls, and you don't have to work with the `Dispatcher`. You can simplify your code and take advantage of task continuations, scheduled to run in the appropriate synchronization context.

The following code snippet shows a new version of the code that runs when you click the Concatenate Text Files button. This code creates a new `TaskScheduler` instance that schedules task continuations that update the UI controls:

```csharp
private void AdvanceProgressBar()
{
    // This code runs in the UI thread
    // There is no possible concurrency
    // Neither a lock nor an atomic operation
    // is necessary
    pgbFiles.Value++;
}

private void butConcatTextFiles_Click(
    object sender,
    RoutedEventArgs e)
{
    // This scheduler will execute tasks
    // on the current SynchronizationContext
    // That is, it will access UI controls safely
    var uiScheduler =
        TaskScheduler.FromCurrentSynchronizationContext();

    fileTasks =
        new List<Task<string>>(fileNames.Length);

    // Reset the progress bar
    pgbFiles.Value = 0;
    // Set the maximum value for the progress bar
    pgbFiles.Maximum = fileNames.Length;

    foreach (string fileName in fileNames)
    {
        // Launch a Task<string>
        // that will hold all the data
        // read from the file in a string
        // as the task's result
        var readTask =
            ReadAllTextAsync(
                @"C:\MYFILES\" + fileName);

        readTask.ContinueWith(
            (t) =>
            {
                // This code runs
                // in the UI thread
                AdvanceProgressBar();
            }, uiScheduler);

        // Add the new Task<string> to fileTasks
        // There is no need to call the Start method
        // because the task was created
```

```
        // with the FromAsync method
        fileTasks.Add(readTask);
    }

    // Program a continuation
    // to start after all the asynchronous
    // operations finish

    var builderTask =
        Task.Factory.ContinueWhenAll(
        fileTasks.ToArray(),
        (antecedentTasks) =>
        {
            // Wait for all the antecedent
            // tasks to ensure the propagation
            // of any exception occurred
            // in any of the antecedent tasks
            Task.WaitAll(antecedentTasks);

            var sb = new StringBuilder();
            // Write all the data read from the files
            foreach (Task<string> fileTask
                in antecedentTasks)
            {
                sb.Append(fileTask.Result);
            }

            return sb.ToString();
        });

    builderTask.ContinueWith(
        (antecedentTask) =>
        {
            // This code runs
            // in the UI thread
            txtAllText.Text =
                antecedentTask.Result;
        }, uiScheduler);
}
```

code snippet from Snippet9_2

The new code calls the `TaskScheduler.FromCurrentSynchronizationContext` to create a new scheduler capable of marshaling work to the appropriate `SynchronizationContext` to update UI controls safely. The *uiScheduler* local variable holds this new `TaskScheduler`.

Before launching the tasks that read the files, the code resets the *pgbFiles* ProgressBar and sets its maximum value. Then, the code uses the `ContinueWith` method to schedule a continuation task to the *readTask* Task. This continuation task advances the *pgbFiles* ProgressBar, because the task that read one file finished its work. This continuation task runs in the UI thread that created the `pgbFiles` control, because the call to the `ContinueWith` method specifies *uiScheduler* as the `TaskScheduler` to use to schedule the execution of this action, as follows:

```
readTask.ContinueWith(
    (t) =>
    {
        AdvanceProgressBar();
    }, uiScheduler);
```

code snippet from Snippet9_3

The continuation task calls the `AdvanceProgressBar` method that increases the value for the `pgbFiles.Value` property. Because the code that updates this control always has to run in the UI thread, there is no possible concurrency. This means that there aren't going to be many tasks or threads changing the value for the `pgbFiles.Value` property. The code that updates the control is always serialized; therefore, it isn't necessary to use locks or atomic operations.

After the `foreach` loop creates and schedules all the tasks, the code uses `Task.Factory .ContinueWhenAll` to program a continuation after all these tasks finish the execution of the asynchronous read operations. The new code holds this continuation task in the *builderTask* local variable. *builderTask* is a `Task<string>` that concatenates all the text read from the files in a single `string` and returns it. `builderTask` doesn't block the UI thread while it concatenates all the text read from the files.

Finally, the code uses the `ContinueWith` method to schedule a continuation task to the *builderTask* Task. This continuation task displays the `string` that contains the text read from all the files in the *txtAllText* TextBox. This string is the result of the antecedent task; therefore, it is available in the `antecedentTask.Result` property. This continuation task runs in the UI thread that created the `txtAllText` control, because the call to the `ContinueWith` method specifies *uiScheduler* as the `TaskScheduler` to use to schedule the execution of this action, as follows:

```
builderTask.ContinueWith(
    (antecedentTask) =>
    {
        txtAllText.Text =
            antecedentTask.Result;
    }, uiScheduler);
```

code snippet from Snippet9_4

Figure 9-4 shows the WPF application's window with the progress bar that is displaying the current status for background asynchronous operations without blocking the UI responsiveness.

Because most of the code runs in worker threads assigned to tasks and the UI thread isn't blocked, the user can close the window at any time. If the user closes the window, all the tasks are destroyed. The effect of interrupting the execution of the code that runs in tasks depends on the application. When you unblock the UI thread, make sure that you wait for the necessary tasks to finish their work before closing the window, as explained in Chapter 3, "Imperative Task Parallelism."

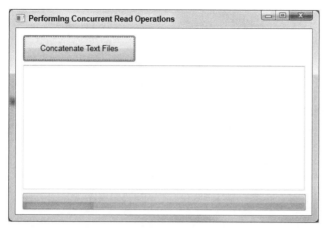

FIGURE 9-4

When you click the Concatenate Text Files button, the event handler runs many sentences of the ReadAllTextAsync method in the UI thread for each file to read. Thus, the button stays pressed for 1 or 2 seconds, keeping an unresponsive UI.

The following code snippet shows a refactored version of the code that minimizes the number of statements processed in the UI thread when you click the Concatenate Text Files button. This code creates the scheduler, resets the progress bar, and then calls Task.Factory.StartNew to create and start a new task that runs the rest of the code without blocking the UI thread.

Available for download on Wrox.com

```
private void butConcatTextFiles_Click(
    object sender,
    RoutedEventArgs e)
{
    // This scheduler will execute tasks
    // on the current SynchronizationContext
    // That is, it will access UI controls safely
    var uiScheduler =
        TaskScheduler.FromCurrentSynchronizationContext();

    // Reset the progress bar
    pgbFiles.Value = 0;
    // Set the maximum value for the progress bar
    pgbFiles.Maximum = fileNames.Length;

    Task.Factory.StartNew(() =>
    {
        fileTasks =
            new List<Task<string>>(fileNames.Length);

        foreach (string fileName in fileNames)
        {
            // Launch a Task<string>
            // that will hold all the data
            // read from the file in a string
            // as the task's result
            var readTask =
                ReadAllTextAsync(
```

continues

```
                         @"C:\MYFILES\" + fileName);

        readTask.ContinueWith(
            (t) =>
            {
                // This code runs
                // in the UI thread
                AdvanceProgressBar();
            }, uiScheduler);

        // Add the new Task<string> to fileTasks
        // There is no need to call the Start method
        // because the task was created
        // with the FromAsync method
        fileTasks.Add(readTask);
    }

    // Program a continuation
    // to start after all the asynchronous
    // operations finish

    var builderTask =
        Task.Factory.ContinueWhenAll(
        fileTasks.ToArray(),
        (antecedentTasks) =>
        {
            // Wait for all the antecedent
            // tasks to ensure the propagation
            // of any exception occurred
            // in any of the antecedent tasks
            Task.WaitAll(antecedentTasks);

            var sb = new StringBuilder();
            // Write all the data read from the files
            foreach (Task<string> fileTask
                in antecedentTasks)
            {
                sb.Append(fileTask.Result);
            }

            return sb.ToString();
        });

    builderTask.ContinueWith(
            (antecedentTask) =>
            {
                // This code runs
                // in the UI thread
                txtAllText.Text =
                    antecedentTask.Result;
            }, uiScheduler);
    });
}
```

code snippet from Snippet9_5

Now, when the user clicks the Concatenate Text Files button, the UI thread remains responsive, because most of the code runs in worker threads assigned to tasks. The refactored code adds a small overhead, because it creates and starts another task. However, it provides a responsive UI.

 To keep the example as simple as possible, the code listings and snippets don't include all the necessary exception handling mechanisms. You already learned how to handle exceptions in tasks with multiple continuations in Chapter 3, "Imperative Task Parallelism."

Performing Asynchronous Windows Forms UI Updates

When you add controls in the Windows Forms designer, the UI thread creates these controls at runtime. As happens with WPF windows, only the thread that creates the controls can update these controls. However, the Windows Forms UI framework doesn't provide the `Dispatcher` explained for WPF and uses a different model to marshal the work to a particular synchronization context.

If you want to marshal the work that updates the UI back to the UI thread so that you can access the control safely, you can call the `Invoke` or `BeginInvoke` method of the target control. You can also call these methods for a different control that was created in the same thread, which created the control you want to update. The two methods are similar to the methods provided by the WPF `Dispatcher` and work as follows:

1. The `Invoke` method executes a delegate synchronously.

2. The `BeginInvoke` method executes a delegate asynchronously.

You can call `pgbFiles.BeginInvoke` with an asynchronous execution to marshal the work to the thread that created the `pgbFiles` control. The method will return immediately after adding the delegate to the appropriate synchronization context queue, without waiting for the delegate to finish its execution.

You can take advantage of the `TaskScheduler.FromCurrentSynchronizationContext` static method to perform asynchronous updates to the UI controls without having to worry about the marshaling model of each UI framework. This means that you can use the same code that creates continuation tasks to update UI controls in the WPF example in a new Windows Forms application.

Listing 9-3 shows the code for a new version of the previous WPF application as a Windows Forms application. This Windows Forms application has a main window (`MainForm.cs`) that displays three controls: a `Button` (*butConcatTextFiles*), a `TextBox` (*txtAllText*), and a `ProgressBar` (*pgbFiles*). You can see the design view for this window in Figure 9-5. Listing 9-3 also shows the C# code for the main window, with the code that defines the `Click` event handler for the button.

LISTING 9-3: Performing asynchronous Windows Forms UI updates

MAINFORM.DESIGNER.CS

```
namespace Listing9_3
{
```

continues

LISTING 9-3 *(continued)*

```csharp
partial class MainForm
{
    private System.ComponentModel.IContainer components = null;

    protected override void Dispose(bool disposing)
    {
        if (disposing && (components != null))
        {
            components.Dispose();
        }
        base.Dispose(disposing);
    }

    #region Windows Forms Designer generated code

    private void InitializeComponent()
    {
        this.butConcatTextFiles =
            new System.Windows.Forms.Button();
        this.pgbFiles = new System.Windows.Forms.ProgressBar();
        this.txtAllText = new System.Windows.Forms.TextBox();
        this.SuspendLayout();
        //
        // butConcatTextFiles
        //
        this.butConcatTextFiles.Location =
            new System.Drawing.Point(13, 13);
        this.butConcatTextFiles.Name = "butConcatTextFiles";
        this.butConcatTextFiles.Size =
            new System.Drawing.Size(162, 38);
        this.butConcatTextFiles.TabIndex = 0;
        this.butConcatTextFiles.Text = "Concatenate Text Files";
        this.butConcatTextFiles.UseVisualStyleBackColor = true;
        this.butConcatTextFiles.Click +=
            new System.EventHandler(
                this.butConcatTextFiles_Click);
        //
        // pgbFiles
        //
        this.pgbFiles.Location =
            new System.Drawing.Point(12, 293);
        this.pgbFiles.Name = "pgbFiles";
        this.pgbFiles.Size = new System.Drawing.Size(495, 20);
        this.pgbFiles.TabIndex = 1;
        //
        // txtAllText
        //
        this.txtAllText.Location =
            new System.Drawing.Point(12, 57);
        this.txtAllText.Multiline = true;
        this.txtAllText.Name = "txtAllText";
        this.txtAllText.Size =
```

```
            new System.Drawing.Size(495, 230);
        this.txtAllText.TabIndex = 2;
        //
        // MainForm
        //
        this.AutoScaleDimensions =
            new System.Drawing.SizeF(6F, 13F);
        this.AutoScaleMode =
            System.Windows.Forms.AutoScaleMode.Font;
        this.ClientSize = new System.Drawing.Size(519, 325);
        this.Controls.Add(this.txtAllText);
        this.Controls.Add(this.pgbFiles);
        this.Controls.Add(this.butConcatTextFiles);
        this.Name = "MainForm";
        this.Text = "Performing Concurrent Read Operations";
        this.ResumeLayout(false);
        this.PerformLayout();

    }

    #endregion

    private System.Windows.Forms.Button butConcatTextFiles;
    private System.Windows.Forms.ProgressBar pgbFiles;
    private System.Windows.Forms.TextBox txtAllText;
    }
}
```

MAINFORM. CS

```
using System;
using System.Collections.Generic;
using System.ComponentModel;
using System.Data;
using System.Drawing;
using System.Linq;
using System.Text;
using System.Windows.Forms;
// Added
using System.Threading.Tasks;
using System.IO;

namespace Listing9_3
{
    public partial class MainForm : Form
    {
        public MainForm()
        {
            InitializeComponent();
        }

        // The file names to read
        private string[] fileNames = {
            "file01.txt",
```

continues

LISTING 9-3 *(continued)*

```
                    "file02.txt",
                    "file03.txt",
                    "file04.txt",
                    "file05.txt",
                    "file06.txt",
                    "file07.txt",
                    "file08.txt",
                    "file09.txt",
                    "file10.txt",
                    "file11.txt",
                    "file12.txt",
                    "file13.txt",
                    "file14.txt",
                    "file15.txt",
                    "file16.txt"
        };

        // The list of tasks
        // Each Task instance returns a string
        // and reads a file with an APM operation
        private List<Task<string>> fileTasks;

        // The buffer size for the stream reader
        private const int BUFFER_SIZE = 0x2000;

        private Task<string> ReadAllTextAsync(string path)
        {
            // Get information for the file
            FileInfo info = new FileInfo(path);
            if (!info.Exists)
            {
                // The file doesn't exist
                throw new FileNotFoundException(
                    String.Format("{0} does not exist.", path),
                    path);
            }

            // This array will hold the data
            // read from the file
            byte[] data = new byte[info.Length];

            // Create the new FileStream
            // to read from the file with
            // useAsync set to true
            // in order to use asynchronous input
            FileStream stream =
                new FileStream(path, FileMode.Open,
                    FileAccess.Read, FileShare.Read,
                    BUFFER_SIZE, true);

            // Wrap the APM read operation in a Task
            // Encapsulate the APM stream.BeginRead and
```

```csharp
    // stream.EndRead methods in task
    Task<int> task =
        Task<int>.Factory.FromAsync(
        stream.BeginRead, stream.EndRead,
        data, 0, data.Length, null,
        TaskCreationOptions.None);

    // The task Task will hold the number of bytes
    // read as a result
    // Add a continuation to task
    // and return it
    return task.ContinueWith((t) =>
    {
        stream.Close();
        Console.WriteLine(
          "One task has read {0} bytes from {1}.",
          t.Result, stream.Name);

        // This continuation Task returns
        // the data read from the file
        // as a string with UTF8 encoding
        return (t.Result > 0) ?
            new UTF8Encoding().GetString(data) : "";
    },
        TaskContinuationOptions.ExecuteSynchronously);
}

private void AdvanceProgressBar()
{
    // This code runs in the UI thread
    // There is no possible concurrency
    // Neither a lock nor an atomic operation
    // is necessary
    pgbFiles.Value++;
}

private void butConcatTextFiles_Click(
    object sender, EventArgs e)
{
    // This scheduler will execute tasks
    // on the current SynchronizationContext
    // That is, it will access UI controls safely
    var uiScheduler =
        TaskScheduler.FromCurrentSynchronizationContext();

    // Reset the progress bar
    pgbFiles.Value = 0;
    // Set the maximum value for the progress bar
    pgbFiles.Maximum = fileNames.Length;

    Task.Factory.StartNew(() =>
    {
        fileTasks =
            new List<Task<string>>(fileNames.Length);
```

continues

LISTING 9-3 *(continued)*

```
foreach (string fileName in fileNames)
{
    // Launch a Task<string>
    // that will hold all the data
    // read from the file in a string
    // as the task's result
    var readTask =
        ReadAllTextAsync(
            @"C:\MYFILES\" + fileName);

    readTask.ContinueWith(
        (t) =>
        {
            // This code runs
            // in the UI thread
            AdvanceProgressBar();
        }, uiScheduler);

    // Add the new Task<string> to fileTasks
    // There is no need to call the Start method
    // because the task was created
    // with the FromAsync method
    fileTasks.Add(readTask);
}

// Program a continuation
// to start after all the asynchronous
// operations finish

var builderTask =
    Task.Factory.ContinueWhenAll(
    fileTasks.ToArray(),
    (antecedentTasks) =>
    {
        // Wait for all the antecedent
        // tasks to ensure the propagation
        // of any exception occurred
        // in any of the antecedent tasks
        Task.WaitAll(antecedentTasks);

        var sb = new StringBuilder();
        // Write all the data read from the files
        foreach (Task<string> fileTask
            in antecedentTasks)
        {
            sb.Append(fileTask.Result);
        }

        return sb.ToString();
    });
```

```
builderTask.ContinueWith(
    (antecedentTask) =>
    {
        // This code runs
        // in the UI thread
        txtAllText.Text =
            antecedentTask.Result;
    }, uiScheduler);
        });
    }
}
}
```

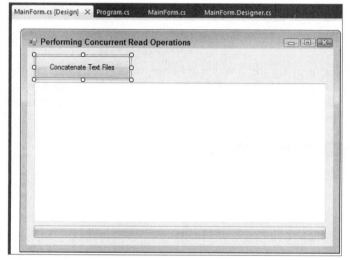

FIGURE 9-5

When the user clicks the Concatenate Text Files button, the UI thread remains responsive, because most of the code runs in worker threads assigned to tasks, as previously explained for the WPF application. The tasks that have to update the UI controls run in the UI thread, because they specify uiScheduler as their TaskScheduler. Figure 9-6 shows the Windows Forms application's window with the progress bar that is displaying the current status for background asynchronous operations without blocking the UI responsiveness.

If you write code for both WPF and Windows Forms applications, you can work with the TaskScheduler for the appropriate synchronization context. Thus, you can use the same code for both WPF and Windows Forms applications, taking advantage of the task-based programming model.

Creating Tasks that Perform EAP Operations

You cannot use the FromAsync method to expose EAP operations found in existing classes as tasks. However, you can use a System.Threading.Task.TaskCompletionSource<TResult> instance to represent EAP operations as a Task<TResult>.

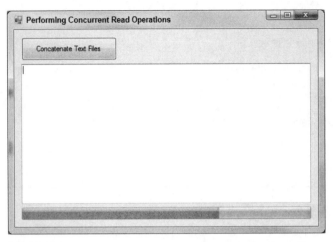

FIGURE 9-6

Listing 9-4 shows the XAML code for the main window of a WPF application that displays two `Button` controls and a `ListBox` on a window. You can see the design view for this window in Figure 9-7. Listing 9-4 also shows the C# code for the main window, with the code that defines the `Click` event handler for the two buttons.

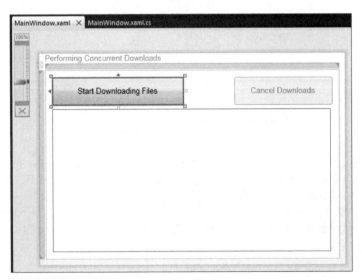

FIGURE 9-7

LISTING 9-4: Downloading files with AEP operations in tasks

MAINWINDOW.XAML

```
<Window x:Class="Listing9_4.MainWindow"
  xmlns="http://schemas.microsoft.com/winfx/2006/xaml/presentation"
  xmlns:x="http://schemas.microsoft.com/winfx/2006/xaml"
```

```
    Title="Performing Concurrent Downloads" Height="350" Width="525">
    <Grid>
        <Button Content="Start Downloading Files"
                Height="46" HorizontalAlignment="Left"
                Margin="12,12,0,0" Name="butDownloadFiles"
                VerticalAlignment="Top" Width="225"
                Click="butDownloadFiles_Click" />
        <ListBox Margin="12,64,15,12" Name="lstStatus" />
        <Button Content="Cancel Downloads" Height="46"
                HorizontalAlignment="Left" Margin="325,12,0,0"
                Name="butCancel" VerticalAlignment="Top"
                Width="166" Click="butCancel_Click"
                IsEnabled="False" />
    </Grid>
</Window>
```

MAINWINDOW.XAML.CS

```csharp
using System;
using System.Collections.Generic;
using System.Linq;
using System.Text;
using System.Windows;
using System.Windows.Controls;
using System.Windows.Data;
using System.Windows.Documents;
using System.Windows.Input;
using System.Windows.Media;
using System.Windows.Media.Imaging;
using System.Windows.Navigation;
using System.Windows.Shapes;
// Added
using System.Threading;
using System.Threading.Tasks;
using System.ComponentModel;
using System.IO;
using System.Net;

namespace Listing9_4
{
    /// <summary>
    /// Interaction logic for MainWindow.xaml
    /// </summary>
    public partial class MainWindow : Window
    {
        public MainWindow()
        {
            InitializeComponent();
        }

        // The addresses for the
        // files to download
        private string[] fileAddresses = {
@"http://media.wiley.com/product_data/
  excerpt/4X/04705022/047050224X.pdf",
```

continues

LISTING 9-4 *(continued)*

```
@"http://media.wiley.com/product_data/
  excerpt/4X/04705022/047050224X-1.pdf",
@"http://media.wiley.com/product_data/
  excerpt/4X/04705022/047050224X-2.pdf"
        };

        // The list of tasks
        // Each Task instance returns a string
        // with the file name downloaded
        // and downloads a file with an EAP operation
        private List<Task<string>> _downloadTasks;

        private CancellationTokenSource _cts;
        private CancellationToken _ct;

        private void CreateToken()
        {
            _cts =
                new System.Threading.CancellationTokenSource();
            _ct = _cts.Token;
        }

        private Task<string> DownloadFileInTask(
            Uri address, CancellationToken ct)
        {
            // This is the task that the method
            // is going to return
            var tcs =
                new TaskCompletionSource<string>(address);

            // Get the file name
            // from the last part of the URI
            string fileName =
                @"C:\MYFILES\" +
                address.Segments[address.Segments.Length - 1];

            // Get information for the file
            FileInfo info = new FileInfo(fileName);
            if (info.Exists)
            {
                // The file already exists
                tcs.TrySetException(
                    new  InvalidOperationException(
                    String.Format("{0} already exists.",
                    fileName)));

                // Return the Task<string>
                // created by the
                // TaskCompletionSource<string>
                return tcs.Task;
            }

            var wc = new WebClient();
```

```csharp
            // If there is a request to cancel
            // the ct CancellationToken
            // the CancelAsync method cancels
            // the WebClient's async operation
    ct.Register(
        () =>
        {
            if (wc != null)
            {
                // wc wasn't disposed
                // and it is possible
                // to cancel the async
                // download
                wc.CancelAsync();
                // Set the canceled status
                tcs.TrySetCanceled();
            }
        });

    // Declare handler as null
    // to be able to use it
    // within the delegate's code
    AsyncCompletedEventHandler handler = null;

    // Now, define the delegate that handles
    // the completion of the asynchronous operation
    handler =
        (hSender, hE) =>
        {
            if (hE.Error != null)
            {
                // An error occurred
                // Set an exception
                tcs.TrySetException(hE.Error);
            }
            else if (hE.Cancelled)
            {
                // The async operation
                // was cancelled
                // Set the canceled status
                tcs.TrySetCanceled();
            }
            else
            {
                // It worked!
                // Set the result
                tcs.TrySetResult(fileName);
            }

            // Unregister the callback
            wc.DownloadFileCompleted -= handler;
        };

wc.DownloadFileCompleted += handler;
```

continues

LISTING 9-4 *(continued)*

```
        try
        {
            wc.DownloadFileAsync(address, fileName);
        }
        catch (Exception ex)
        {
            // Something went wrong when the async operation
            // was trying to start

            // Unregister the callback
            wc.DownloadFileCompleted -= handler;

            // Set an exception
            tcs.TrySetException(ex);
        }

    // Return the Task<string>
    // created by the
    // TaskCompletionSource<string>
    return tcs.Task;
}

private void butDownloadFiles_Click(
    object sender, RoutedEventArgs e)
{
    CreateToken();

    // This scheduler will execute tasks
    // on the current SynchronizationContext
    // That is, it will access UI controls safely
    var uiScheduler =
        TaskScheduler.FromCurrentSynchronizationContext();

    // Clear the ListBox
    lstStatus.Items.Clear();

    // Enable butCancel
    butCancel.IsEnabled = true;

    Task.Factory.StartNew(() =>
    {
        _downloadTasks =
            new List<Task<string>>(fileAddresses.Length);

        foreach (string address in fileAddresses)
        {
            // Launch a Task<string>
            // that will download the file
            var downloadTask =
                DownloadFileInTask(new Uri(address), _ct);

            downloadTask.ContinueWith(
```

```
                        (t) =>
                        {
                            string line = "";

                            if (t.IsCanceled)
                            {
                                line = "Canceled.";
                            }
                            else if (t.IsFaulted)
                            {
                                foreach (Exception innerEx
                                    in t.Exception.InnerExceptions)
                                {
                                    // Just one exception
                                    // No need to worry
                                    // about the usage
                                    // of a StringBuilder
                                    // instead of +=
                                    line += innerEx.Message;
                                }
                            }
                            else
                            {
                                line = t.Result;
                            }
                            // This code runs
                            // in the UI thread
                            lstStatus.Items.Add(line);
                        }, uiScheduler);

            // Add the new Task<string>
            // to _downloadTasks
            // There is no need
            // to call the Start method
            // because the Task comes
            // from TaskCompletionSource
            _downloadTasks.Add(downloadTask);
    }

    var uiTF = new TaskFactory(uiScheduler);
    uiTF.ContinueWhenAll(
        _downloadTasks.ToArray(),
        (antecedentTasks) =>
        {
            // Disable butCancel
            butCancel.IsEnabled = false;

            // Runs in the UI thread
            var completed =
                (from task in antecedentTasks
                 where !(task.IsCanceled ||
                        task.IsFaulted)
                 select task).Count();
```

continues

LISTING 9-4 *(continued)*

```
                            if (completed ==
                                antecedentTasks.Length)
                            {
                                lstStatus.Items.Add(
                                    "All downloads completed!");
                            }
                            _downloadTasks.Clear();
                        });
                });
        }

        private void butCancel_Click(
            object sender, RoutedEventArgs e)
        {
            // Communicate a request for cancellation
            _cts.Cancel();
        }
    }
}
```

The code shown in Listing 9-4 specifies the URLs of files to download in the *fileAddresses* private array of string. In addition, the application uses a default hardcoded location, the C:\MYFILES folder, to save these files. To run this code, you have to replace the addresses for the files to download with the URLs of files you have access to download, and then specify your desired download folder.

When you click the Start Downloading Files button, the code in the butDownloadFiles_Click event handler calls the CreateToken method. This method creates a new CancellationTokenSource (_cts) and then assigns its token to the _ct private CancellationToken. This CancellationToken enables the user to cancel the asynchronous download operations with a combination of the task cancellation capabilities and the EAP operation's cancellation feature. The code uses the previously explained *uiScheduler* TaskScheduler to run the tasks that must update controls in the appropriate synchronization context.

The code clears the *lstStatus* ListBox that provides status information about the downloaded files and enables the *butCancel* Button. Then, the code creates and executes a new Task that starts the multiple concurrent downloads outside of the UI thread.

This task launches a new Task<string> for each address in the *fileAddresses* array of string. A foreach loop calls the DownLoadFileInTask method for each file address and then adds the Task<string> returned by this method to *_downloadTasks*. Each Task<string> decodes the file name from the address, downloads the file with an asynchronous execution, and saves it in a local path. The code passes a new Uri and the *_ct* private CancellationToken to the DownLoadFileInTask method. This method can access *_ct*, because it is a private variable. However, the example shows how to implement a cancellation feature with this method that might run in a different scope; therefore, the method receives the CancellationToken as a parameter.

If the download was successful, the DownLoadFileInTask method stores the resulting file name string in its Result property. If something went wrong, the Task<string> will hold the appropriate status. The code manipulates the `Task<string>` to represent the work done by the wrapped EAP implementation.

Then, the code uses the `ContinueWith` method to schedule a continuation task that analyzes the status of the precedent *downloadTask*, received as *t* in the action delegate. This continuation task runs in the UI thread that created the `lstStatus` control, because the call to the `ContinueWith` method specifies *uiScheduler* as the `TaskScheduler` to use to schedule the execution of this action as follows:

```
downloadTask.ContinueWith(
    (t) =>
    {
        string line = "";

        if (t.IsCanceled)
        {
            line = "Canceled.";
        }
        else if (t.IsFaulted)
        {
            foreach (Exception innerEx
                in t.Exception.InnerExceptions)
            {
                line += innerEx.Message;
            }
        }
        else
        {
            line = t.Result;
        }
        lstStatus.Items.Add(line);
    }, uiScheduler);
```

code snippet from Snippet9_6

The `DownloadFileInTask` method uses the methods provided by `TaskCompletionSource` to transition the `Task<string>` that the method returns to its real state. Therefore, this continuation task can analyze the values of the `IsCanceled` and `IsFaulted` properties for its precedent `Task` to write status information about the related download to the *lstStatus* ListBox.

Finally, the code in the event handler creates a new `TaskFactory` (*uiTF*) that uses `uiScheduler` as its `TaskScheduler`:

```
var uiTF = new TaskFactory(uiScheduler);
```

Thus, the `Task` instances created with *uiTF* will run in the UI thread that created the controls that have to be updated. When the `foreach` loop creates and schedules all the tasks that download files, the code uses `uiTF.ContinueWhenAll` to program a continuation after all these tasks finish the execution of the asynchronous download operations. The action specified for `ContinueWhenAll` will run in a new task, but in the UI thread. The code in the event handler doesn't wait for this new continuation task to finish; therefore, there is no more code running in the UI thread, and the user can use the UI controls while all these asynchronous downloads and the continuations run.

This final continuation disables the *butCancel* Button and uses a LINQ query to determine whether the total number of file downloads completed successfully or not, as shown here:

```
uiTF.ContinueWhenAll(
    _downloadTasks.ToArray(),
    (antecedentTasks) =>
    {
        butCancel.IsEnabled = false;

        var completed =
            (from task in antecedentTasks
                where !(task.IsCanceled || task.IsFaulted)
                select task).Count();

        if (completed == antecedentTasks.Length)
        {
            lstStatus.Items.Add(
                "All downloads completed!");
        }
        _downloadTasks.Clear();
    });
```

code snippet from Snippet9_7

The LINQ query counts the number of tasks that aren't canceled or faulted from the array of antecedent Task<string> instances. If this count is equal to the total number of tasks, the code adds a message to the *lstStatus* ListBox.

Working with TaskCompletionSource

The DownloadFileInTask method receives an Uri (*address*) and a CancellationToken (*ct*). This method creates a TaskCompletionSource<string> instance (*tcs*) that represents the producer side of a Task<string>.

The code retrieves the file name from the last part of the Uri received as a parameter and checks whether this file exists. If the file exists, the code calls the TrySetException method for *tcs* and returns the underlying faulted Task as follows:

```
FileInfo info = new FileInfo(fileName);
if (info.Exists)
{
    tcs.TrySetException(
        new InvalidOperationException(
        String.Format("{0} already exists.",
        fileName)));

    return tcs.Task;
}
```

code snippet from Snippet9_8

`TaskCompletionSource<TResult>` provides the following methods to attempt to transition the underlying `Task<TResult>` into a specific state:

➤ `TrySetCanceled` — Transitions to `TaskStatus.Canceled`.

➤ `TrySetException` — Transitions to `TaskStatus.Faulted` and binds one `Exception` or an `IEnumerable<Exception>` to the task's `AggregateException`.

➤ `TrySetResult` — Transitions to `TaskStatus.RanToCompletion` and binds the result received as a parameter to the task's `Result` property.

The aforementioned methods return a Boolean value that indicates whether the attempt was successful or not. You can control the consumer side of a `Task<TResult>` by using these methods, and simplify the code that has to wrap many operations as part of a `Task<TResult>`.

If the file doesn't exist, the code creates a new `System.Net.WebClient` instance (*wc*) and registers a delegate that will be called when the *ct* is canceled. When *ct* is canceled, this delegate calls the `CancelAsync` method for *wc* (if it has not already been destroyed). This enables a task cancellation mechanism to be propagated to an EAP asynchronous operation. Then, the delegate calls the `TrySetCanceled` method for *tcs* to attempt to set the `TaskStatus.Canceled` to the underlying `Task<string>` as follows:

Available for download on Wrox.com

```
ct.Register(
    () =>
    {
        if (wc != null)
        {
            wc.CancelAsync();
            tcs.TrySetCanceled();
        }
    });
```

code snippet from Snippet9_9

Then, the code declares an `AsyncCompletedEventHandler` (*handler*) and initializes it as `null`. This enables the code to reference *handler* within the delegate to handle the completion of the asynchronous download operation. The code will call the `DownloadFileAsync` method that implements the previously explained EAP pattern.

The following code snippet defines the *handler* delegate that will run when the asynchronous download completes:

Available for download on Wrox.com

```
handler =
    (hSender, hE) =>
    {
        if (hE.Error != null)
        {
            tcs.TrySetException(hE.Error);
        }
        else if (hE.Cancelled)
        {
            tcs.TrySetCanceled();
```

continues

```
        }
        else
        {
            tcs.TrySetResult(fileName);
        }

        // Unregister the callback
        wc.DownloadFileCompleted -= handler;
    };
```

code snippet from Snippet9_10

The delegate receives the well-known object *sender* and *AsyncCompletedEventArgs e* parameters. Because the code is written in another event, the delegate uses *hSender* and *hE* as the names for these parameters instead of the classic names. The code analyzes the results of the asynchronous download and calls the corresponding methods for *tcs* to transfer the real status of the operation to the underlying Task<string>. Finally, the code unregisters itself as the callback for the DownloadFileCompleted event. Remember to unregister the callback to avoid unwanted leaks.

When the code defines the delegate that handles the completion of the asynchronous download, *handler* must be attached to the DownloadFileCompleted event for *wc*, as follows:

```
    wc.DownloadFileCompleted += handler;
```

Then, the code calls the DownloadFileAsync method to start the asynchronous download. This method returns immediately, because it has an asynchronous execution, and the previously attached callback will run when the download completes. However, something might go wrong when the code calls the DownloadFileAsync method; therefore, the call to this method is included within a try...catch block. If an exception is raised, the catch block unregisters the callback for the DownloadFileCompleted event and then calls the TrySetException method for *tcs* to bind the exception to the underlying Task<string>, as follows:

Available for
download on
Wrox.com

```
try
{
    wc.DownloadFileAsync(address, fileName);
}
catch (Exception ex)
{
    wc.DownloadFileCompleted -= handler;
    tcs.TrySetException(ex);
}
```

code snippet from Snippet9_11

Regardless of whether an exception occurred or not, the code returns the underlying Task<string> that is associated with the TaskCompletionSource<string> *tcs* and is accessible through its Task property:

```
    return tcs.Task;
```

This Task<string> represents the EAP asynchronous download, with the additional behavior that sets the status information to this Task<string> instance. The results of the asynchronous download are propagated to the underlying Task<string>.

There is no need to call the Start *method for the new* Task<string> *returned by the* DownloadFileAsync *method, because the* TaskCompletionSource<string> *instance starts the underlying* Task<string>.*In fact, if you call the* Start *method for the underlying* Task *instance associated with a* TaskCompletionSource<TResult> *instance, the code will raise an exception.*

When you run the application for the first time and you click the Start Downloading Files button, the asynchronous downloads add the file names to the *lstStatus* ListBox. If all downloads are successful, "All downloads completed!" displays in the ListBox. Figure 9-8 shows the result of three successful downloads.

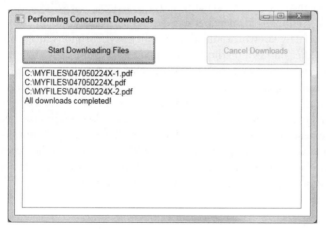

FIGURE 9-8

If you try to download files that already exist in the destination folder, the code stops the execution of the tasks and displays an error message for each file. Figure 9-9 shows the result of three attempts to download files that were already downloaded.

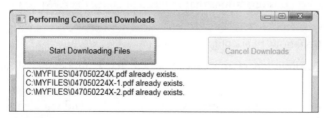

FIGURE 9-9

While the application is completing asynchronous downloads, you can click the Cancel Downloads button. This button communicates a request for cancellation that stops the execution of the asynchronous downloads and their related tasks. Figure 9-10 shows one file downloaded and two files whose download operations were canceled.

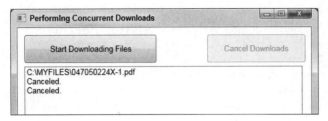

FIGURE 9-10

In October 2010, Microsoft launched the Microsoft Visual Studio Async Community Technology Preview (CTP). You can download the Visual Studio Async CTP at **http://msdn.com/vstudio/async** and install it for Visual Studio 2010. However, you must remember that it is a CTP and you shouldn't use it in production unless you are sure about the risks of doing so. This CTP introduces the new Task-based Asynchronous Pattern (TAP) and many new asynchronous operations that will be available in future C# and .NET Framework versions. This new pattern defines simple rules to create methods that are compatible with the two new keywords added to simplify asynchronous programming: **async** and **await**. The **async** modifier marks a method or a lambda expression as asynchronous. It is necessary to add the async keyword to a method's signature when you make asynchronous calls by using the **await** operator. The **await** operator yields control until an asynchronous operation completes. By using this modifier, you don't have to create callback functions anymore. The compiler does the necessary work to transform your code into an asynchronous call and also handles the necessary conversion to return TResult, instead of Task<TResult>. These new keywords will allow you to write simpler and easier-to-understand code. You can start working with the Visual Studio Async CTP or you can wait for its final implementation. All the techniques you learned through this chapter are going to be useful to use the forthcoming .NET Framework asynchronous features.

SUMMARY

Parallel programming is useful when you have to perform I/O-bound workloads. The new task-based programming model makes it easy to run multiple concurrent asynchronous operations and perform asynchronous updates to the UI controls. To summarize this chapter:

➤ You can use tasks to wrap asynchronous operations that implement either the APM or EAP standard pattern.

➤ You can take advantage of continuations to simplify your code.

➤ You can update the UI controls without having to worry about the marshaling model of each particular UI framework.

➤ When you use Task.Factory.FromAsync to perform asynchronous I/O-bound workloads, threading resources are only going to be used to process the results.

➤ You can propagate the results of complex asynchronous operations to underlying tasks by working with a TaskCompletionSource<TResult> instance.

10

Parallel Testing and Tuning

WHAT'S IN THIS CHAPTER?

➤ Preparing parallel tests

➤ Working with Visual Studio 2010 performance profiling features

➤ Measuring and visualizing concurrency

➤ Identifying common parallel performance problems

➤ Detecting serialized execution problems

➤ Identifying diverse lock contention scenarios

➤ Working with concurrent garbage-collection mechanisms

This chapter is about the new profiling features introduced in Visual Studio 2010 Premium and Ultimate editions. In this chapter, you will learn to detect common problems related to parallelized code with .NET Framework 4 by using these new profiling features. A profiling session provides you with valuable feedback to optimize your code. The chapter explains the different techniques used to profile parallelized code, and teaches you how to refactor an existing application according to the results of each profiling session.

PREPARING PARALLEL TESTS

When you add parallelism to an existing serial application or create a new parallelized algorithm from scratch, you must run the necessary tests to make sure that your application provides the following:

➤ **Correctness** — The parallelized application's execution should always lead to the correct result. Chapter 1, "Task-Based Programming," introduced the importance of correctness when different pieces of code run with a concurrent code.

➤ **Desired speedup** — The parallelized application should run faster than its serial counterpart on certain hardware capable of running code with a real concurrent execution. You should test whether the parallelized application achieves the desired speedup on specific multicore hardware.

➤ **Scalability as the number of cores increase** — The parallelized application should be prepared to take advantage of additional cores as they become available. Chapter 2, "Imperative Data Parallelism," explained how to measure speedups and the scalability offered by parallelized code. However, there are situations where the algorithm has a built-in ceiling.

➤ **Compatibility with single-core hardware** — If the requirements specify that the application can run on single-core computers, the parallelized application should run when the number of logical cores is equal to one. In addition, the parallelized application shouldn't add unnecessary overhead when it runs on single-core computers. In general, this is an important requirement.

If you decide that a parallelized application must run on computers with a minimum number of logical cores, you must specify this requirement. In addition, you can add code to test this requirement when the application launches. You don't want an application to raise an exception when it tries to run code in parallel because it assumes that a minimum number of cores are available.

When you test a parallelized application, you have to make sure that it provides correctness to the diverse target hardware configurations. You should follow your traditional test procedures on environments with a diverse number of cores. However, you usually don't have access to all the possible hardware configurations in which the application should run.

For example, if your application is capable of providing a reasonable scalability in computers from 1 logical core to 20 logical cores, an optimal test would require you to run the application on dozens of hardware configurations. However, unless you have a huge budget to work with, you won't be able to run your application on so many different computers. Thus, a combination of different computers with virtualization usually provides the necessary number of environments to make sure that an application will meet the requirements previously listed.

Imagine that you have the following three different hardware configurations to test your application:

➤ Dual-core CPU with 2 logical cores

➤ Quad-core CPU with 8 logical cores

➤ 10-core CPU with 20 logical cores

Imagine that your main interest is to check the behavior of your application with one, two, three, four, six, and eight cores. However, you also want to test the application with other random configurations with more than eight cores. You can use virtualization to create the following additional environments to test your application:

➤ 1 logical core virtualized on the dual-core CPU

➤ 3 logical cores virtualized on the quad-core CPU

➤ 6 logical cores virtualized on the 10-core CPU

➤ 10 logical cores virtualized on the 10-core CPU

➤ 16 logical cores virtualized on the 10-core CPU

Some virtualization tools aren't capable of generating the aforementioned environments. These environments are based on VirtualBox 3.2.x, which allows you to create virtual machines with up to 32 logical cores. If you consider both the real environments and the virtualized ones, you will be able to test your application in the real and virtualized environments listed in Table 10-1. This table shows a random subset of all the possibilities.

TABLE 10-1: Environments to Test the Parallelized Application

ENVIRONMENT TYPE	NUMBER OF LOGICAL CORES FOR THE APPLICATION	UNDERLYING PHYSICAL CPU
Virtualized	1	Dual-core CPU with 2 logical cores
Real physical cores	2	Dual-core CPU with 2 logical cores
Virtualized	3	Quad-core CPU with 8 logical cores
Real physical cores	4	Quad-core CPU with 8 logical cores
Virtualized	6	10-core CPU with 20 logical cores
Real logical cores	8	Quad-core CPU with 8 logical cores
Real physical cores	10	10-core CPU with 20 logical cores
Virtualized on an insufficient number of physical cores	16	10-core CPU with 20 logical cores
Real logical cores	20	10-core CPU with 20 logical cores

By running tests on this mix of nine environments, you will have a good idea of both the application's scalability and correctness. However, the architectures of the different multicore microprocessors used in those computers can be different. For example, imagine that the dual-core CPU has 2 megabytes of shared L3 cache memory, but the 10-core CPU has 10 megabytes of shared L3 cache memory. The additional 8 megabytes of L3 cache memory has a huge impact on the application's performance when you run the tests on the 10-core CPU. Therefore, if you want to test scalability, it is a good idea to use the same hardware with a different number of virtualized cores. However, this won't necessarily provide you with accurate scalability numbers because some algorithms have built-in ceilings.

For example, you can use the 10-core CPU to run the same application with a number of cores from 1 to 10 in the virtual machine. Modern virtualization software enables you to specify the number of cores to assign to a virtual machine, and you can generate scripts to change this virtual machine setting and automate tests. Because you have 10 physical cores, when you have the results for the 10 tests, you will have a good idea of the real scalability for the application. In addition, you can run tests with a number of cores from 11 to 20, but you have to take into account that these additional cores aren't going to represent real physical ones. Chapter 2 explained the difference between logical cores and physical cores in the section "Logical Cores Aren't Physical Cores." First, check the application's performance on real physical cores and then measure the benefits of the additional logical cores provided by the CPUs.

Then, you can test on diverse computers to check the results on different architectures. By performing these tests, you will have a good idea of the application's performance. One or more of these tests should provide you with a *baseline*.

 After you have a measurable and reproducible baseline, you can optimize your application and test the new performance offered by each new version. The baseline is the performance metric you can use as a basis to compare the different versions of the same application. Remember to use release builds *to define a baseline and to generate each new version. Release builds include all the optimizations.*

After you have a baseline, you can analyze and tune your application to optimize performance. However, don't forget that your application must provide correctness with each new optimized version. Therefore, you must run the correctness tests for each new version.

Because the baseline should be measurable and reproducible, it is a good idea to disable turbo modes offered by certain microprocessors when testing performance. For example, Intel Turbo Boost Technology makes it difficult to measure speedups in parallelized code. Sometimes, parallelized code can run slower than its sequential version because Intel Turbo Boost Technology can make the latter run at faster clock frequencies than the former. Therefore, if you work with a microprocessor with Intel Turbo Boost Technology enabled, you will have to pay attention to the changes introduced by this technology.

Chapter 1 explained modern shared-memory multicore architectures in the section "Working with Shared-Memory Multicore." Turbo modes can distort your speedup measurements. Thus, you can run all the tests with the turbo mode disabled and then you can enable this mode to check its benefits.

There is an easy way to enable and disable turbo modes, such as Intel Turbo Boost Technology, in both 32-bit and 64-bit versions of Windows. You can use TMonitor, a free utility developed by CPUID. You just have to download the appropriate version from www.cpuid.com and run the compressed executable file, TMonitor32.exe or TMonitor64.exe. Then, right-click on the TMonitor window, select Turbo from the context menu that displays, and click Disable. Figure 10-1 shows the TMonitor context menu that enables you to control Intel Turbo Boost Technology in a microprocessor that supports this turbo mode. When you want to enable the turbo mode again, you can repeat this step and click Enable.

 If you run tests on virtualized environments, you must disable and enable turbo modes in the host operating system. The host operating system can control the underlying hardware.

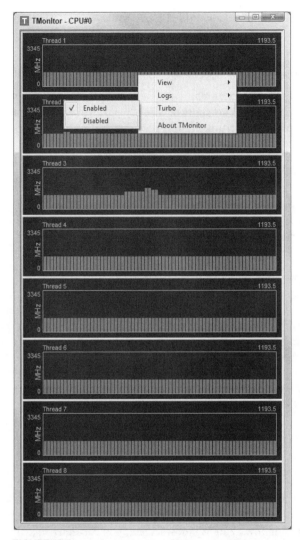

FIGURE 10-1

You can test your concurrent code in many hardware configurations, but this doesn't mean that it will provide correctness in all the possible concurrent execution paths. Chapter 5, "Coordination Data Structures," explained the race conditions. You might spend months running a complex parallelized algorithm in many hardware configurations providing correctness. However, the complex algorithm could still yield unexpected results under certain concurrency scenarios due to race conditions. Race conditions are very complex to detect.

There are race detectors that analyze your code to forecast potential race conditions. These race detectors use diverse algorithms that analyze the diverse concurrent execution paths and the synchronization primitives used in the code.

Unfortunately, at the time of this writing, there is no race detector based on code analysis for C# with support for the new coordination data structures introduced by .NET Framework 4. However, you can expect improvements in future Visual Studio versions, third-party tools, and add-ins that will provide static and/or dynamic analysis for concurrent code in the forthcoming months.

Working with Performance Profiling Features

Visual Studio 2010 Premium and Ultimate editions support many performance profiling features. Some of these features are useful to detect parallelizable hotspots or already parallelized functions that require further optimizations. For example, the instrumentation profiling method allows you to measure function call counts and timing.

The instrumentation profiling method is useful when you need to know where your application is spending most of its time and find frequently called functions that impact your application's performance.

Subsequent sections cover some of the new profiling methods that are very useful to analyze the behavior of parallelized applications. You can use these methods when you have an application that runs concurrent code and you want to know what's happening under the hood. However, you must understand that each profiling method adds an overhead to your existing application. Thus, if you just want to measure the time required to run a specific algorithm, you should run the release version of your application without a profiling method.

The profiling methods provided by the concurrency visualizer require Windows Vista, Windows 7, Windows Server 2008, or Windows Server 2008 R2.

Before using the profiling methods, you must follow these prerequisites:

➤   You must start Visual Studio 2010 as a system administrator user. In Windows Server 2008 R2 or 2008, if you are already logged in as Administrator on the machine, you can simply run Visual Studio 2010. However, in Windows 7 or Windows Vista, you can start Visual Studio 2010 as a system administrator user by right-clicking the Visual Studio 2010 shortcut and selecting Run As Administrator in the context menu. If you try to run the profiling methods without starting Visual Studio 2010 as a system administrator user, a dialog box will ask you to restart the IDE with the necessary privileges.

➤   Because parallel code based on .NET Framework 4 calls Windows functions, you must have access to Windows .pdb symbol files to get the best results. The simplest configuration for the Windows symbol files uses Microsoft Symbol Servers and caches the .pdb files in a local folder. Select Tools ➪ Options ➪ Debugging ➪ Symbols in Visual Studio's main menu and the IDE will display the options for Symbols. Activate the Microsoft Symbol Servers check box. Then, create a new folder in your local drive to cache these symbol files, and specify this folder in Cache Symbols In This Directory. Figure 10-2 shows the Options dialog box with the Symbols options configured to download the .pdb files from Microsoft Symbol

Servers and cache these files in the C:\Symbols folder. Before running the examples in subsequent sections, select the All Modules, Unless Excluded option under Automatically Load Symbols For, and then click OK.

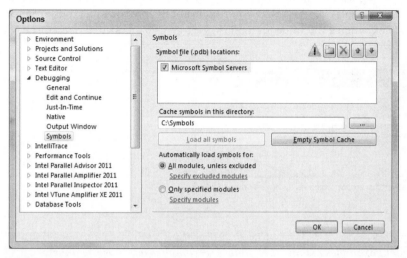

FIGURE 10-2

The IDE requires an Internet connection to download the necessary symbol files from Microsoft Symbol Servers. After you have these files in the cache folder, you can run the profiling methods without the Internet connection. However, an Internet connection makes sure that you always have the latest version of the necessary symbol files. If you don't have the necessary configuration for the symbol files when you try to run one of the profiling methods, the IDE will show the dialog box shown in Figure 10-3, suggesting that you verify the previously explained options.

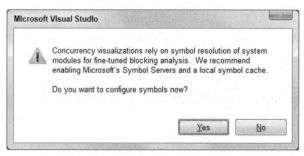

FIGURE 10-3

➤ Because debug builds insert some diagnostic code into an application and don't include certain optimizations, you shouldn't use these builds to profile and tune your application. Release builds provide more accurate information about your real application's performance; therefore, you should change the active configuration to Release before running a profiling method.

If you run Visual Studio 2010 on a 64-bit Windows version, the IDE will probably display the dialog box shown in Figure 10-4 the first time you try to run one of the profiling methods. If this happens, click Yes, and the IDE will disable *executive paging* and reboot your computer. When executive paging is disabled, kernel-mode drivers and system code always remain in physical memory and cannot be paged to disk. This setting prevents disk reads from getting code or data that is critical for the profiling session because all the code and data always resides in physical memory. The dialog box won't display the next time you run one of the profiling methods. You can enable executive paging by changing the value for a registry entry, as explained at `http://go.microsoft.com/fwlink/?LinkId=157265`.

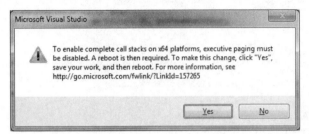

FIGURE 10-4

 Subsequent examples assume that your IDE complies with the previously explained prerequisites and that you work with release builds. The next examples include several references to specific colors that you can see on your screen. However, the snapshots included in the book display shades of gray instead of color. You can download the code and run the examples on your computer to check the real colors on your screen.

Measuring Concurrency

Listing 10-1 shows the code for a console application that runs a simple Parallel Language Integrated Query (PLINQ) expression to filter numbers and calculate an average with a parallel execution. This simple application provides a great opportunity to learn one of the profiling methods introduced in Visual Studio 2010.

LISTING 10-1: An application that runs a simple PLINQ query with unnecessary locks

```
using System;
using System.Collections.Generic;
using System.Linq;
using System.Text;
using System.Diagnostics;
using System.Threading.Tasks;
// This code has performance problems
// Don't consider this code as a best practice
namespace Listing10_1
{
    class Program
    {
```

```
        // 500,000,000 ints
        private static int NUM_INTS = 500000000;

        private static ParallelQuery<int> GenerateInputData()
        {
            return ParallelEnumerable.Range(1, NUM_INTS);
        }

        private static object _syncCalc = new Object();

        private static double CalculateX(int intNum)
        {
            // This code has an unnecessary lock
            double result;
            lock (_syncCalc)
            {
                result =
                    Math.Pow(Math.Sqrt(intNum / Math.PI), 3);
            }
            return result;
        }

        static void Main(string[] args)
        {
            var sw = Stopwatch.StartNew();

            var inputIntegers = GenerateInputData();

            var parReductionQuery =
                (from intNum in inputIntegers.AsParallel()
                 where ((intNum % 5) == 0) ||
                       ((intNum % 7) == 0) ||
                       ((intNum % 9) == 0)
                 select (CalculateX(intNum))).Average();

            Console.WriteLine("Average {0}", parReductionQuery);

            // Comment the next two lines
            // while profiling
            Console.WriteLine("Elapsed time {0}",
                sw.Elapsed.TotalSeconds.ToString());
            Console.ReadLine();
        }
    }
}
```

The GenerateInputData method returns a parallel sequence with 500 million integer numbers — that is, a populated ParallelQuery<int>. The Main method calls the GenerateInputData method and holds the 500 million integer numbers in *inputIntegers*. Then, the code performs a reduction operation, an average, by declaring a PLINQ query that calls the CalculateX method for each filtered integer number. The CalculateX method receives an integer, *intNum*, and returns the result of some mathematical operations to consume some CPU time-crunching numbers. However, this method uses an unnecessary lock to perform the mathematical operation in a critical section.

This wrong piece of code will enable you to understand very important concepts related to profiling parallelized algorithms.

Follow these steps to visualize the behavior of the application shown in Listing 10-1 by collecting detailed information about its multiple threads:

1. You want the application to finish as soon as the query runs and to analyze its behavior, without waiting for a key to be pressed. To do this, comment the last two lines of the `Main` method as follows:

```
// Console.WriteLine("Elapsed time {0}", sw.Elapsed.TotalSeconds.ToString());
// Console.ReadLine();
```

code snippet from Snippet10_1

2. Select Analyze ⇨ Launch Performance Wizard. A dialog box with the available profiling methods and options displays. Select the Concurrency radio button and then select the Visualize the Behavior of a Multithreaded Application check box. Then, click Next.

3. The Performance Wizard dialog box displays the collected information to create a new performance session. Check the information shown, make sure that the Launch Profiling After the Wizard Finishes check box is selected, and click Finish.

4. The IDE launches the console application and collects the necessary data to generate a report based on the specified profiling method. The IDE displays a message as shown in Figure 10-5 while it collects data from the application that runs. After the application finishes its execution, the Output window indicates that the collected data has been written to a trace file, and the profiler starts processing this file. While processing the trace file, the profiler loads the previously explained symbol files. After the trace analysis finishes, the Concurrency Visualization window displays a report with the behavior of the multithreaded application.

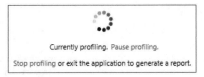

Currently profiling. Pause profiling.
Stop profiling or exit the application to generate a report.

FIGURE 10-5

Figure 10-6 shows the Summary view of the Concurrency Visualization report.

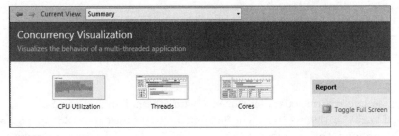

FIGURE 10-6

Click the CPU Utilization button, and the IDE will display the average CPU utilization for the analyzed process on a graph, considering the available hardware threads — that is, the number of logical cores. In this case, the average CPU utilization was 79 percent, as shown in Figure 10-7. The green area in the graph represents the CPU utilization for the analyzed process. The X-axis of the graph shows the elapsed time in milliseconds.

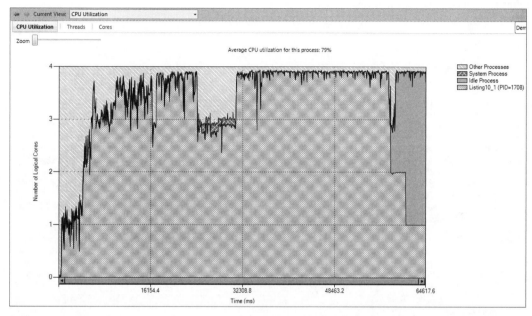

FIGURE 10-7

The application has a high CPU utilization percentage. However, it isn't an efficient code, because it uses an excessive number of unnecessary locks that consume needless CPU cycles. This is one of the problems of the CPU utilization analysis: it can lead to incorrect assumptions about a parallelized algorithm. The application consumes CPU cycles from the four logical cores most of the time. However, you want a parallelized algorithm to provide both performance and correctness. Parallel optimization is about taking advantage of the parallel processing power to reduce the overall time required to run an algorithm. Your main goal is to reduce the time required to run an algorithm. Thus, you have to be careful when you analyze the CPU utilization graph. Your main goal is to not consume unnecessary CPU cycles to generate a nice CPU utilization graph. In this case, you already know that this application has unnecessary locks.

 Visual Studio and the profiler itself are consuming CPU cycles. If you want to minimize this overhead, you can use the command-line profiling tools instead of the full IDE. You can check their usage at `http://msdn.microsoft.com/en-us/library/bb385768.aspx`.

Click the Threads button, and the IDE will display visual timelines for the disks activities, the main thread, and all the worker threads. This is a useful visualization, because it helps you to measure execution and synchronization times. Visual Studio uses different colors to represent the activities in the visual timelines. Figure 10-8 shows the graph and the visible timeline profile for the current profiling session. However, you have to take into account that these timelines show the activities of the different threads. Therefore, the timelines show the threads that the tasks were assigned to, not what happened at the tasks level.

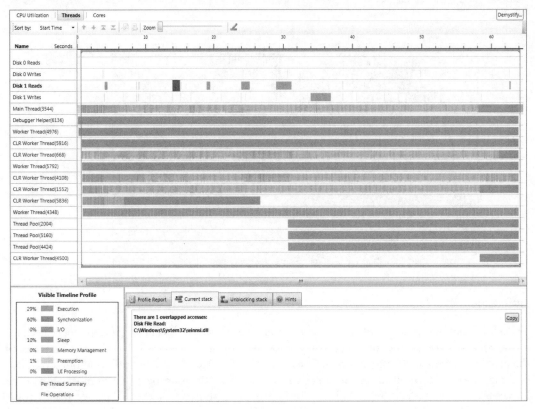

FIGURE 10-8

The default view shows the threads sorted by their start times. If you take a look at the graph shown in Figure 10-8, you will notice that the following four threads executed the tasks created by the PLINQ query:

➤ Main Thread (3544)

➤ CLR Worker Thread (668)

➤ CLR Worker Thread (4108)

➤ CLR Worker Thread (1552)

You can use the Zoom slider to zoom in and click some of the green bars that represent execution time for each of the aforementioned threads. If you click one of the bars and then click the Current Stack tab, the IDE will display the stack for this thread at that time. Figures 10-9 through 10-12 show the stack for each of the threads that executed the tasks created by the PLINQ query. Notice that the four figures show the following information related to the execution of the methods run by the PLINQ query:

➤ **Main Thread** (3544) — See Figure 10-9.

➤ **CLR Worker Thread** (668) — See Figure 10-10.

➤ **CLR Worker Thread** (4108) — See Figure 10-11.

➤ **CLR Worker Thread** (1552) — See Figure 10-12.

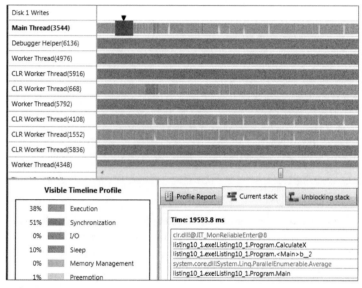

FIGURE 10-9

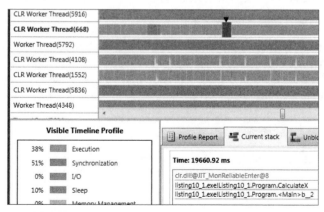

FIGURE 10-10

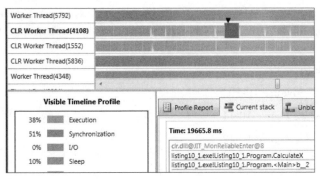

FIGURE 10-11

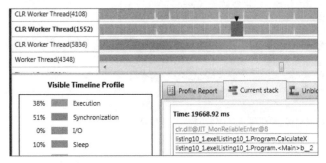

FIGURE 10-12

Use the Zoom slider to zoom out, and use the mouse to select an area where you see the graphs for the aforementioned threads with green, yellow, and red colors. Now, you are working on a new visible time period to analyze it with further detail. The information shown in the Visible Timeline Profile changes according to this visible time period.

Click the Synchronization label in the Visible Timeline Profile. Then, click on the Profile Report tab and activate the Just My Code check box. The IDE will display the Synchronization Blocking Profile report and will filter the call stack to show only your code plus one level of called functions. Expand all the names of the functions for each level of the call stack shown in the grid. In this case, the unnecessary lock is responsible for an important amount of exclusive blocking time. Figure 10-13 shows the Synchronization Blocking Profile displaying `System.Threading.Monitor.Enter` as the method responsible for the exclusive blocking time. Chapter 5 explained how the `lock` statement calls the `Monitor.Enter` method.

Profile Report	Current stack	Unblocking stack	Hints			
Synchronization Blocking Profile		Noise reduction at 2 %		☑ Just My Code		
Name		Instances	Inclusive Blocking Time (ms)	Exclusive Blocking Time (ms)	API / Wait Categ
◢ listing10_1.exe		314	12577.6715	0	
◢ Listing10_1.Program.<Main>b__2		195	11321.5614	0	
◢ Listing10_1.Program.CalculateX		190	11319.6521	0	
System.Threading.Monitor.Enter		190	11319.6521	11319.6521	Monitor.Enter
◢ Listing10_1.Program.Main		119	1256.1101	0	
◢ System.Linq.ParallelEnumerable.Average		119	1256.1101	0	
◢ Listing10_1.Program.<Main>b__2		119	1256.1101	0	
◢ Listing10_1.Program.CalculateX		114	1253.3091	0	
System.Threading.Monitor.Enter		114	1253.3091	1253.3091	Monitor.Enter

FIGURE 10-13

If you right-click the line that displays `System.Threading.Monitor.Enter` and select View Call Sites from the context menu, the IDE will show the code that ends up in this call. You can check whether you can improve the code to avoid unnecessary blocks that decrease overall performance.

Click the Cores button, and the IDE will display a graph with visual timelines that show how each thread was mapped to the available logical processor cores. This information is useful when you write code that controls *thread affinity*. Thread affinity suggests the operating system scheduler to assign a thread to a specific logical core. However, when you work with .NET Framework 4 and C#, you don't have an easy access to thread-affinity settings. In addition, in these examples, you are working with task-based programming and you don't work at the thread level.

This graph with visual timelines shows how the managed thread scheduler and the operating system distribute the diverse threads during their lifetime. When threads move from one core to the other, a cross-core context switch occurs, and the legends for the graph provide summary information about the total number of these cross-core context switches. Figure 10-14 shows how the different threads created by the application run on the four logical cores.

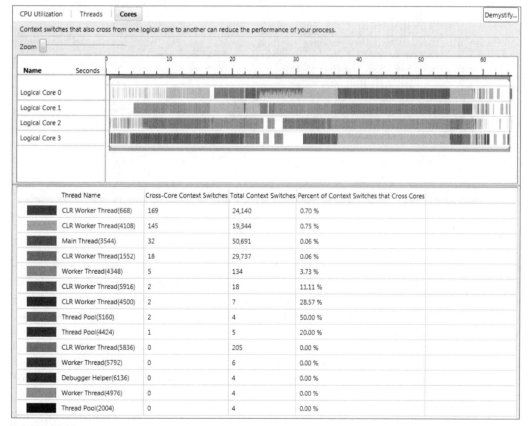

FIGURE 10-14

The application with the unnecessary locks required 64,617 milliseconds to run with the profiler in the background, with an average CPU utilization of 79 percent. Listing 10-2 shows a new version of the `CalculateX` method without the unnecessary locks.

LISTING 10-2: A new version of the CalculateX method without locks

```
private static double CalculateX(int intNum)
{
    return Math.Pow(Math.Sqrt(intNum / Math.PI), 3);
}
```

Follow the previously explained steps to visualize the behavior of the application with the new version of the CalculateX method shown in Listing 10-2. When the Summary view of the Concurrency Visualization report appears, click the CPU Utilization button. The IDE will display the average CPU utilization, which, in this case, was 58 percent, as shown in Figure 10-15. Remember that the green area in the graph represents the CPU utilization for the analyzed process.

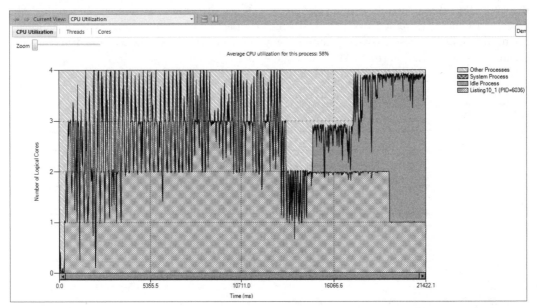

FIGURE 10-15

The average CPU utilization is lower than in the previous version of the application. However, this application takes less time to run. The new application without the unnecessary locks required 21,422 milliseconds to run with the profiler in the background. The new application has more efficient code, because it requires less time with the same available hardware resources. The speedup achieved with the profiler running in the background is 64,617 / 21,422 = 3.01x more than the previous version. The profiler adds an overhead because it consumes CPU cycles in the background. If you run the applications without the profiler running in the background, the new version requires just 12,500 milliseconds, whereas the older version needs more than 60,000 milliseconds.

Click the Threads button, and the IDE will switch to the previously explained visual timelines for the disks activities, the main thread, and all the worker threads. Figure 10-16 shows the graph and the visible timeline profile for the current profiling session. Because the time required to run the application is less than the previous version, you will notice that the timelines have bigger blocks with the different colors on your screen. When you compare the results of different profiling sessions, it is very important for you to use the appropriate zoom levels to compare the same behavior of the application.

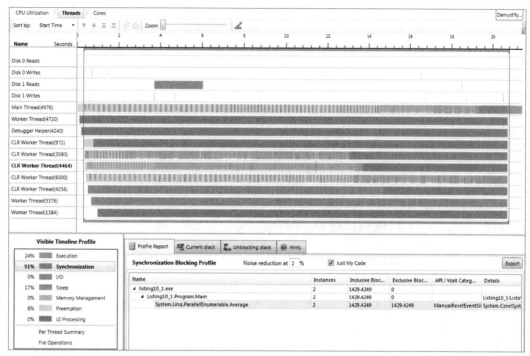

FIGURE 10-16

The default view shows the threads sorted by their start time. If you take a look at the graph shown in Figure 10-16, you will notice that the following four threads executed the tasks created by the PLINQ query:

➤ Main Thread (4976)

➤ CLR Worker Thread (3580)

➤ CLR Worker Thread (4464)

➤ CLR Worker Thread (6000)

Remember that you can check the Current Stack of each of these threads by using the Zoom slider to zoom in and clicking on the green bar that represents the execution time for the thread.

Click the Cores button, and the IDE will display visual timelines that show how each thread was mapped to the available logical processor cores. Figure 10-17 shows this information — note that the aforementioned threads were assigned to the tasks created by the PLINQ query.

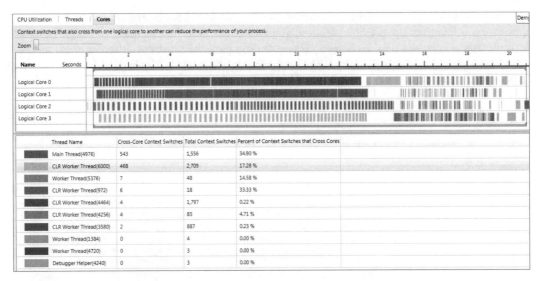

FIGURE 10-17

SOLUTIONS TO COMMON PATTERNS

You can use the different graphs that provide information about the behavior of a multithreaded application to detect common problematic patterns in parallelized applications. However, it is a good idea to isolate the suspicious algorithm in a console application to simplify its detailed analysis. If you try to profile a complex application, it will require more time and effort to detect certain problems.

Subsequent sections use simple examples that provide an easy-to-recognize visual pattern in some of the views offered by the previously explained concurrency profiling method. However, you should analyze each pattern to make sure it relates to your particular problems.

Serialized Execution

Listing 10-3 shows the code for a new version of the console application introduced in Listing 10-1. This application runs the PLINQ query that creates many tasks to run with a parallelized execution. However, the application runs with a serialized execution and doesn't take advantage of the available cores. The application launches the necessary threads, but only one thread is usually executing at a given time. Serial execution is used because a critical section defined in the CalculateX method takes a long time to run. The PLINQ query calls this method for each filtered integer number; therefore, the query runs with a very slow performance.

LISTING 10-3: An application that runs a simple PLINQ query with serialized execution

```
using System;
using System.Collections.Generic;
using System.Linq;
using System.Text;
using System.Diagnostics;
```

```
using System.Threading.Tasks;

// This code has performance problems
// Don't consider this code as a best practice
namespace Listing10_3
{
    class Program
    {
        private static int NUM_INTS = 5000;

        private static ParallelQuery<int> GenerateInputData()
        {
            return ParallelEnumerable.Range(1, NUM_INTS);
        }

        private static object _syncCalc = new Object();

        private static double CalculateX(int intNum)
        {
            double result = 0;

            lock (_syncCalc)
            {
                for (int i = 0; i < 50000; i++)
                {
                    double newResult =
                        Math.Pow(
                          Math.Sqrt(intNum / Math.PI), 3) * i;
                    if (newResult > result)
                    {
                        result = newResult;
                    }
                }
            }

            return result;
        }

        static void Main(string[] args)
        {
            var sw = Stopwatch.StartNew();

            var inputIntegers = GenerateInputData();

            var parReductionQuery =
                (from intNum in inputIntegers.AsParallel()
                 where ((intNum % 5) == 0) ||
                       ((intNum % 7) == 0) ||
                       ((intNum % 9) == 0)
                 select (CalculateX(intNum))).Average();

            Console.WriteLine("Average {0}", parReductionQuery);

            // Comment the next two lines
            // while profiling
```

continues

LISTING 10-3 *(continued)*

```
                    // Console.WriteLine("Elapsed time {0}",
                    //    sw.Elapsed.TotalSeconds.ToString());
                    // Console.ReadLine();
                }
            }
        }
```

Figure 10-18 shows the CPU Utilization view for this application. The average CPU utilization for the process is 26 percent, and it is easy to see that the application is using just one of the four cores. This is one of the first symptoms of a serialized execution.

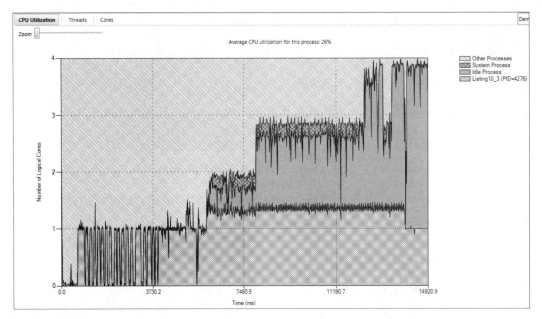

FIGURE 10-18

Figure 10-19 shows the Threads view for the four threads that run the PLINQ query. If you zoom in on the timeline graphs for these threads, you will notice a typical visual pattern for a serialized execution. The green bars that represent chunks of execution time move from one thread to the other, signifying that there is just one thread executing code at a time. Figure 10-20 shows the typical visual pattern that indicates a serialized execution between multiple threads.

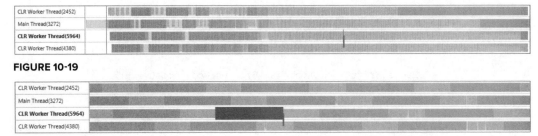

FIGURE 10-19

FIGURE 10-20

Lock Contention

The previous serialized execution problem was caused by excessive synchronization and lock contention. The threads are competing to acquire a lock that allows them to enter a critical section. Because the code that runs in the critical sections needs some milliseconds to run, the threads that are waiting for this lock to be acquired will be blocked during this time. In the profiling session for Listing 10-1, you learned how to detect the code responsible for exclusive blocking time. You can also use other features when you face a lock contention scenario.

Click one of the red bars that represent synchronization segments. The IDE will display the call stack for the blocked thread in the Current Stack tab. Figure 10-21 shows that the method call that blocked the thread was a `Monitor.Enter`, which is a lock statement in the code that's trying to enter the long-running critical section. You can also check the thread that removed the blocking condition by clicking Unblocking Stack. Figure 10-22 shows the *Thread Ready connector*, which appears when you click the synchronization segment, because the unblocking event occurred in another thread in the application's process. The execution segment identified by this connector enabled the blocked thread to resume its execution. You can right-click the methods shown in Current Stack or Unblocking Stack and select View Source to show the code that blocked or unblocked the thread.

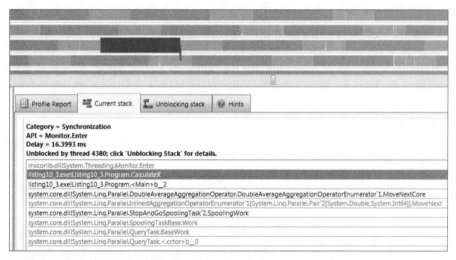

FIGURE 10-21

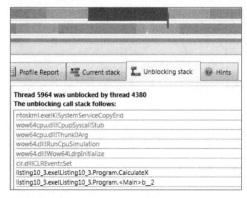

FIGURE 10-22

> *Unnecessary critical sections should be removed, and critical sections should run only the code that requires a serialized execution.*

Lock Convoys

The code in Listing 10-3 uses the `lock` keyword to define the critical section. The `lock` keyword calls `Monitor.Enter` to acquire an unfair mutual-exclusion lock. It is an unfair mutual-exclusion lock because the first thread that tries to acquire the lock doesn't necessarily end up being the first one to acquire it. `Monitor` doesn't enforce a first in, first out (FIFO) order on threads waiting for the lock. Thus, the first thread that finds the lock free can acquire it even if there were other threads waiting for it. The lock isn't fair, but it usually provides faster performance than fair locks because it allows threads that don't have to wake up to acquire locks. Unfair locks help to mitigate *lock convoy* scenarios.

> *Fair locks enforce a FIFO order and can lead to a lock convoy scenario.*

If many threads try to acquire a lock and the critical section requires some time to run, many of the threads fail to acquire the lock. When this situation is combined with the usage of a fair lock that enforces a FIFO order, it leads to threads that progress but require frequent context switches. A lock convoy scenario is similar to the previously explained lock contention, but it provides worse performance because of the fairness.

Listing 10-4 shows the code for a new version of the console application with the lock contention problem presented in Listing 10-3. This application uses a local `System.Threading.Mutex` instance to control access to the critical section instead of the `lock` keyword. A `Mutex` provides a synchronization primitive that grants exclusive access to a shared resource for a single thread or task at a time.

LISTING 10-4: An application that generates a lock convoy scenario

```
using System;
using System.Collections.Generic;
using System.Linq;
using System.Text;
using System.Diagnostics;
using System.Threading;
using System.Threading.Tasks;

namespace Listing10_4
{
    class Program
    {
        private static int NUM_INTS = 5000;

        private static ParallelQuery<int> GenerateInputData()
        {
            return ParallelEnumerable.Range(1, NUM_INTS);
```

```csharp
}

private static Mutex _mut = new Mutex();

private static double CalculateX(int intNum)
{
    double result = 0;

    // Wait until it is safe to enter
    // the critical section protected by a Mutex
    _mut.WaitOne();
    try
    {
        for (int i = 0; i < 50000; i++)
        {
            double newResult =
                Math.Pow(Math.Sqrt(intNum / Math.PI), 3) * i;
            if (newResult > result)
            {
                result = newResult;
            }
        }
    }
    finally
    {
        // Release the Mutex
        _mut.ReleaseMutex();
    }

    return result;
}

static void Main(string[] args)
{
    var sw = Stopwatch.StartNew();

    var inputIntegers = GenerateInputData();

    var parReductionQuery =
        (from intNum in inputIntegers.AsParallel()
         where ((intNum % 5) == 0) ||
               ((intNum % 7) == 0) ||
               ((intNum % 9) == 0)
         select (CalculateX(intNum))).Average();

    Console.WriteLine("Average {0}", parReductionQuery);

    // Comment the next two lines
    // while profiling
    //Console.WriteLine("Elapsed time {0}",
    //    sw.Elapsed.TotalSeconds.ToString());
    //Console.ReadLine();
    }
    }
}
```

Before entering the critical section that takes a long time to run, the `CalculateX` method calls the `WaitOne` method for the shared `Mutex` instance, `_mut`. This method blocks the current thread until it is safe to enter the critical section protected by `_mut`. Then, after the code in the critical section is executed, a call to the `ReleaseMutex` method releases `_mut` and allows the first thread that tried to acquire the `Mutex` to enter the critical section. Because the critical section takes a long time to run, that thread has to wake up, which implies an expensive context-switch. Remember that in these examples, the code is unnecessarily protected in a critical section. The purpose of the examples is to help you understand common problems with the code.

Figure 10-23 shows the CPU Utilization view for this application. The average CPU utilization for the process is 22 percent, and it is easy to realize that the application uses just one of the four cores. This is one of the first symptoms of a serialized execution. In this case, the serialized execution is combined with a lock convoy.

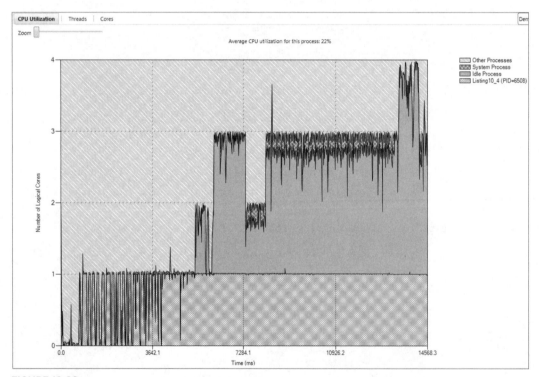

FIGURE 10-23

If you zoom in on the timeline graphs for the Threads view for the four threads that run the PLINQ query, you will notice a typical visual pattern for a lock convoy. The green bars that represent chunks of execution time move from one thread to the other, following a repetitive pattern. There is just one thread executing code at a time. Figure 10-24 shows the typical visual pattern that indicates a lock convoy scenario.

Figure 10-25 shows the Cores view that also provides an easy-to-understand visual pattern, where each logical core executes one thread at a time.

CLR Worker Thread(6796)	
CLR Worker Thread(6728)	
Main Thread(6504)	
CLR Worker Thread(4972)	

FIGURE 10-24

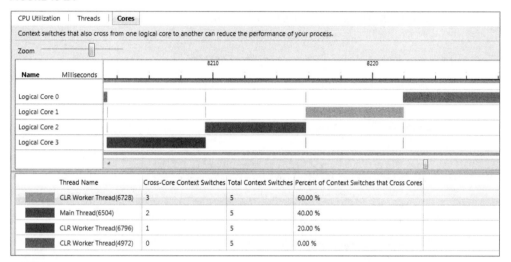

FIGURE 10-25

Oversubscription

When an application runs code in more concurrent threads than the available number of logical cores, there is an oversubscription problem. Chapter 1 explained the difference between concurrency and interleaved concurrency. In an oversubscription scenario, all the threads cannot run concurrently because there aren't enough cores.

Listing 10-5 shows the code for a new version of the console application that launches many tasks to run the same sequential LINQ query. Because the application launches a number of concurrent tasks that is three times the number of logical cores, and the queries take some time to run, the CLR usually injects more threads than the number of logical cores.

LISTING 10-5: An application that generates an oversubscription scenario

```
using System;
using System.Collections.Generic;
using System.Linq;
using System.Text;
using System.Diagnostics;
using System.Threading.Tasks;

namespace Listing10_5
{
    class Program
    {
```

continues

LISTING 10-5 *(continued)*

```
private static int NUM_INTS = 100000000;

private static IEnumerable<int> GenerateInputData()
{
    return Enumerable.Range(1, NUM_INTS);
}

private static double CalculateX(int intNum)
{
    return Math.Pow(Math.Sqrt(intNum / Math.PI), 3);
}

static void Main(string[] args)
{
    var sw = Stopwatch.StartNew();
    var inputIntegers = GenerateInputData();
    var numTasks = Environment.ProcessorCount * 3;
    var tasks = new List<Task>(numTasks);

    for (int i = 0; i < numTasks; i++)
    {
        var t = Task.Factory.StartNew(
          () =>
          {
              var seqReductionQuery =
                  (from intNum
                      in inputIntegers
                   where ((intNum % 5) == 0) ||
                         ((intNum % 7) == 0) ||
                         ((intNum % 9) == 0)
                   select (CalculateX(intNum)))
                      .Average();

              Console.WriteLine("Average {0}",
                  seqReductionQuery);
          });
        tasks.Add(t);
    }

    Task.WaitAll(tasks.ToArray());

    // Comment the next two lines
    // while profiling
    // Console.WriteLine("Elapsed time {0}",
    //    sw.Elapsed.TotalSeconds.ToString());
    // Console.ReadLine();
    }
  }
}
```

Figure 10-26 shows the CPU Utilization view for this application. The average CPU utilization for the process is 79 percent. However, the code isn't efficient, because it creates too many long-running tasks.

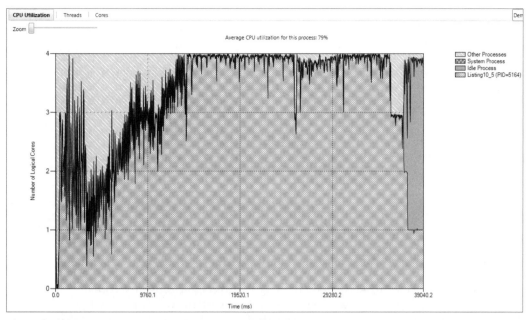

FIGURE 10-26

If you switch to the Threads view and click the Per Thread Summary label in the Visible Timeline Profile, you will notice that there is an important area of the worker threads in yellow. Figure 10-27 shows the Per Thread Summary with the following Thread IDs that represent the worker threads: 6364, 2388, 5732, 6328, 6764, and 6448. In fact, the application used six threads to support the execution of the tasks, which are two threads more than the number of available logical cores. These additional active and concurrent threads generate a large percentage in preemption. This means that one thread is preempted by another one.

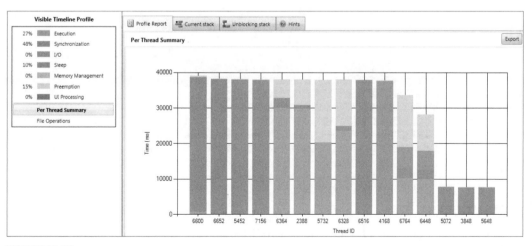

FIGURE 10-27

You will also notice that there are too many yellow blocks in the timeline graphs for the six threads that run the tasks. Because the main thread stays blocked until all the tasks finish their concurrent work, this thread appears in red most of the time. Figure 10-28 shows the timeline graphs.

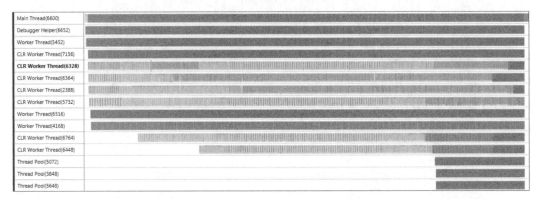

FIGURE 10-28

It is easier to analyze the threads that are running the tasks by selecting Execution in the Sort By drop-down list. Figure 10-29 shows the timeline graphs with the yellow bars that represent preemptions. If you hover the mouse over one of these blocks, a tooltip displays the thread that preempted the thread represented by the timeline.

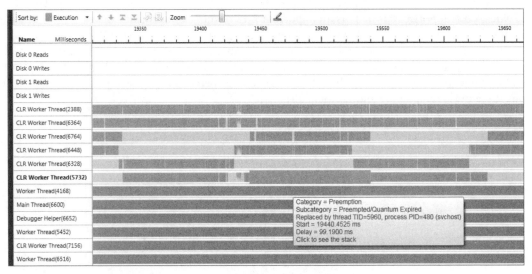

FIGURE 10-29

Undersubscription

When you want to take full advantage of the parallel execution possibilities offered by the underlying hardware, but the application runs code in fewer concurrent threads than the available number of logical cores, there is an undersubscription problem.

Listing 10-6 shows a new version of the Main method code for the console application shown in Listing 10-5. The new code launches many tasks to run the same sequential LINQ query. Because the application launches a number of concurrent tasks that is half the number of logical cores, and the queries take some time to run, the CLR injects fewer threads than the number of logical cores, and the application generates an undersubscription problem.

LISTING 10-6: The Main method for an application that generates an undersubscription scenario

```csharp
static void Main(string[] args)
{
    var sw = Stopwatch.StartNew();
    var inputIntegers = GenerateInputData();
    var numTasks = Environment.ProcessorCount / 2;
    var tasks = new List<Task>(numTasks);

    for (int i = 0; i < numTasks; i++)
    {
        var t = Task.Factory.StartNew(
            () =>
            {
                var seqReductionQuery =
                    (from intNum
                        in inputIntegers
                     where ((intNum % 5) == 0) ||
                           ((intNum % 7) == 0) ||
                           ((intNum % 9) == 0)
                     select (CalculateX(intNum)))
                        .Average();

                Console.WriteLine("Average {0}",
                    seqReductionQuery);
            });
        tasks.Add(t);
    }

    Task.WaitAll(tasks.ToArray());

    // Comment the next two lines
    // while profiling
    // Console.WriteLine("Elapsed time {0}",
    //     sw.Elapsed.TotalSeconds.ToString());
    // Console.ReadLine();
}
```

Figure 10-30 shows the CPU Utilization view for this application. The average CPU utilization for the process is 38 percent.

Figure 10-31 shows the Threads view with just two worker threads that use green blocks to represent the active execution of code. When you have an undersubscription scenario, you can schedule more work in parallel, or you can redesign your algorithms to be more scalable as the number of available cores increase.

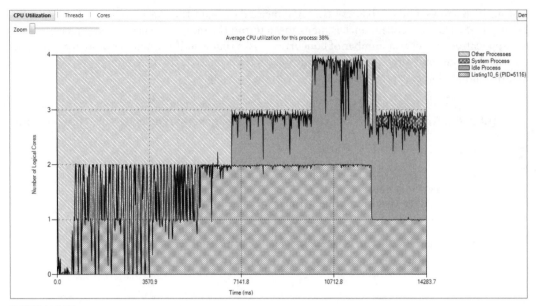

FIGURE 10-30

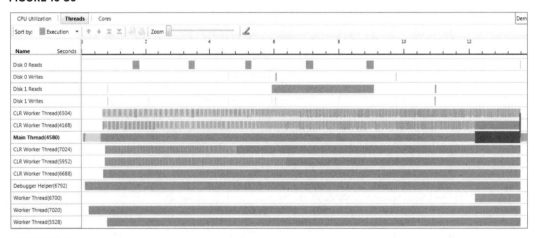

FIGURE 10-31

Partitioning Problems

Sometimes, an application launches many tasks and each concurrent task has an uneven workload. For example, if you launch the following four tasks, you have four logical cores, and the code waits for all these tasks to finish before running additional workloads:

➤ **Task t0** — Finishes in 10 seconds

➤ **Task t1** — Finishes in 20 seconds

➤ **Task t2** — Finishes in 30 seconds

➤ **Task t3** — Finishes in 40 seconds

Because task t3 requires 40 seconds but the other tasks require less time to complete their work, there is a potential partitioning problem, typically referred to as a *load imbalance*. If it were possible, some of the work done by t3 should be done by other tasks to improve the parallel execution and reduce the overall time required to complete the algorithm.

Listing 10-7 shows a new version of the Main method code for the console application shown in Listing 10-5. The new code launches many tasks to run the same sequential LINQ query a certain number of times. Each task runs the sequential LINQ query a different number of times to represent an uneven workload.

LISTING 10-7: The Main method for an application that generates an uneven workload

```csharp
static void Main(string[] args)
{
    var sw = Stopwatch.StartNew();
    var inputIntegers = GenerateInputData();
    var numTasks = Environment.ProcessorCount;
    var tasks = new List<Task>(numTasks);

    for (int i = 0; i < numTasks; i++)
    {
        var t = Task.Factory.StartNew(
            (taskNum) =>
            {
                for (int j = 0;
                    j < (((((int)taskNum) + 1) * 2);
                    j++)
                {
                    var seqReductionQuery =
                        (from intNum
                            in inputIntegers
                            where ((intNum % 5) == 0) ||
                                ((intNum % 7) == 0) ||
                                ((intNum % 9) == 0)
                            select (CalculateX(intNum)))
                            .Average();

                    Console.WriteLine("Average {0}",
                        seqReductionQuery);
                }
            }, i);
        tasks.Add(t);
    }

    Task.WaitAll(tasks.ToArray());

    // Comment the next two lines
    // while profiling
    // Console.WriteLine("Elapsed time {0}",
    //     sw.Elapsed.TotalSeconds.ToString());
    // Console.ReadLine();
}
```

Figure 10-32 shows a clear step-down in the CPU Utilization view for this application. The average CPU utilization for the process is 59 percent. However, there is a lack of load-balancing in this application.

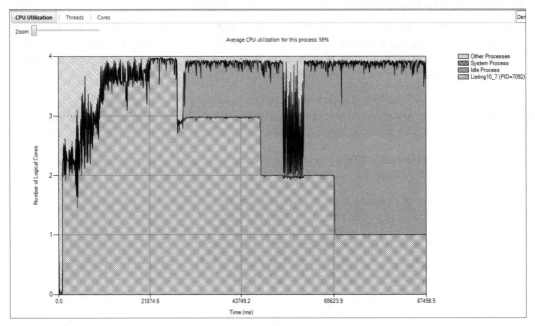

FIGURE 10-32

Figure 10-33 shows the Threads view, where you can see that each worker thread stops executing code and is free to receive additional workload. The first thread that finishes its work is CLR Worker Thread (3272), then CLR Worker Thread (6552).

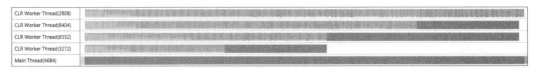

FIGURE 10-33

It is also interesting to check the Cores view, because it is easy to determine that the application ends up using just one logical core. Figure 10-34 shows how the number of threads mapped to logical cores gets reduced.

FIGURE 10-34

Workstation Garbage-Collection Overhead

When a loop or a parallelized query creates too many temporary objects that are then discarded, the application might face a workstation garbage-collection overhead scenario.

Listing 10-8 shows the code for a console application with horrible code that creates too many temporary strings. This code isn't a best practice, but it's being shown here to demonstrate a common patter when you have frequent garbage collections that block all the threads until it completes the collection. Of course, you should avoid creating unnecessary temporary objects in loops or queries.

LISTING 10-8: An application that generates a garbage-collection overhead scenario

```
using System;
using System.Collections.Generic;
using System.Linq;
using System.Text;
using System.Diagnostics;
using System.Threading.Tasks;

// This code has performance problems
// Don't consider this code as a best practice
namespace Listing10_8
{
    class Program
    {
        private static int NUM_INTS = 100000000;

        private static string ConvertToHexString(
            char[] charArray)
        {
            // Convert the byte array to hexadecimal string
            var sb = new StringBuilder(charArray.Length);

            for (int i = 0; i < charArray.Length; i++)
            {
                sb.Append(((int) charArray[i]).ToString("X2"));
            }
            // This is horrible code that
            // creates too many temporary strings
            var tempString = sb.ToString();
            var tempString2 = tempString.ToLower();
            var tempString3 =
                tempString2.Substring(
                    0, tempString2.Length - 1);
            return tempString3.ToUpper();
        }

        private static ParallelQuery<int> GenerateInputData()
        {
            return ParallelEnumerable.Range(1, NUM_INTS);
        }

        private static string CreateString(int intNum)
```

continues

LISTING 10-8 *(continued)*

```
            {
                return ConvertToHexString(
                    (Math.Pow(Math.Sqrt(intNum / Math.PI), 3)).
                    ToString().ToCharArray());
            }

            static void Main(string[] args)
            {
                var sw = Stopwatch.StartNew();

                var inputIntegers = GenerateInputData();

                var parReductionQuery =
                    (from intNum
                        in inputIntegers
                        .AsParallel()
                    where ((intNum % 5) == 0) ||
                        ((intNum % 7) == 0) ||
                        ((intNum % 9) == 0)
                    select (CreateString(intNum))).Max();

                Console.WriteLine("Max: {0}", parReductionQuery);

                // Comment the next two lines
                // while profiling
                //Console.WriteLine("Elapsed time {0}",
                //    sw.Elapsed.TotalSeconds.ToString());
                //Console.ReadLine();
            }
        }
    }
```

Figure 10-35 shows the Threads view with many red blocks that leave just one thread running and the other threads waiting for the garbage collection to finish. If you click one of these red areas, the Current Stack provides detailed information that shows the thread is waiting for the garbage collection to finish.

The following lines indicate that the thread is waiting for the garbage collection:

```
Category = Synchronization
API = CLREvent::Wait
Delay = 0.3248 ms
Unblocked by thread 7012; click 'Unblocking Stack' for details.
clr.dll!CLREvent::Wait
clr.dll!WKS::gc_heap::wait_for_gc_done
clr.dll!WKS::gc_heap::try_allocate_more_space
clr.dll!WKS::gc_heap::allocate_more_space
clr.dll!WKS::GCHeap::Alloc
clr.dll!Alloc
clr.dll!SlowAllocateString
clr.dll!FramedAllocateString
mscorlib.dll!System.Text.StringBuilder.ToString
```

```
listing10_8.exe!Listing10_8.Program.ConvertToHexString
listing10_8.exe!Listing10_8.Program.CreateString
listing10_8.exe!Listing10_8.Program.<Main>b__1
```

FIGURE 10-35

If you click the green block that indicates that the thread is running while the other threads are waiting for the garbage collection to finish, you will find the following line in the Current Stack:

```
Clr.dll!WKS::GCHeap::GarbageCollectGeneration
```

This means that this thread is running the garbage collection and the other threads will stay blocked until the collection finishes. This happens because the application is running with the default single-threaded workstation garbage collection. If you cannot reduce the memory pressure in your algorithms, you will usually achieve a speedup by enabling the server garbage collection, also known as Server GC.

The Server GC maximizes throughput because it creates a managed heap and a thread per logical core. Each Server GC dedicated thread has its appropriate thread-affinity setting assigned to each available logical core. The Server GC still blocks the active threads when a collection is required or triggered. However, the Server GC requires less time to complete the collection process and improves scalability as the number of cores increases.

Working with the Server Garbage Collector

If you want to enable the Server GC for an application, follow these steps:

1.   If your solution already has an App.config file, go to step 5.

2.   Right-click the solution's name in Solution Explorer.

3.   Select Add ⇨ New Item in the context menu.

4.   Select General within Installed Templates, select Application Configuration File, and then click Add. Visual Studio adds an `App.config` file to the solution.

5.   Open the `App.config` file and add the following highlighted lines that enable the Server GC (the parameters are case-sensitive). You just need to add the relevant `configuration/runtime/gcServer` value to your existing `App.Config` file:

```xml
<?xml version="1.0" encoding="utf-8" ?>
<configuration>
  <runtime>
    <gcServer enabled="true" />
  </runtime>
</configuration>
```

code snippet from Snippet10_2

6.   Rebuild your application.

> *To return to the default workstation GC, just change the value for the* `gcServer` `enabled` *runtime parameter from* `true` *to* `false`.

If you switch to the Server GC in the sample application shown in Listing 10-8, you will notice the difference in the Threads view. The application will require less time to complete its execution. Figure 10-36 shows the Threads view that shows the four threads that have tasks assigned to them. These threads are waiting for the four concurrent garbage collections that are running in the other four threads. The four threads that have a green block run garbage collection for each heap. The Thread Ready connector indicates that the thread that performs the garbage collection for CLR Worker Thread (5320) is Worker Thread (6940).

I/O Bottlenecks

Chapter 9, "Asynchronous Programming Model," explained how to take advantage of the simplicity of tasks and continuations to perform concurrent asynchronous jobs related to the existing asynchronous programming models. When you visualize the behavior of a multithreaded application, you can locate threads that wait for I/O operations to complete.

Figure 10-37 shows the results of profiling the sample application Snippet9_5, explained in Chapter 9. The segments in the timeline associated with I/O blocking time appear in magenta. When you suspect I/O bottlenecks, you can zoom in on the timelines to check the Current Stack and the source code that originates each I/O block.

Main Thread Overload

Chapter 9 explained how to create a responsive UI. However, it is important to avoid an excessive load on the main UI thread.

Listing 10-9 shows the XAML code for the main window of a WPF application that displays one

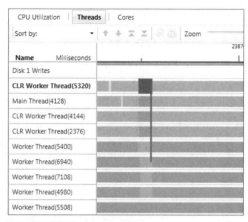

FIGURE 10-36

Button control, a TextBox, and a ProgressBar. The application represents an anti-pattern, which is code that you should never write. The C# code includes the Click event handler definition for the button.

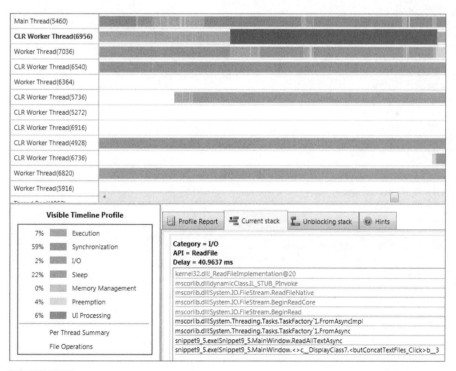

FIGURE 10-37

LISTING 10-9: An application with wrong code that generates a main thread overhead

MAINWINDOW.XAML

```xml
<Window x:Class="Listing10_9.MainWindow"
    xmlns="http://schemas.microsoft.com/winfx/2006/xaml/presentation"
    xmlns:x="http://schemas.microsoft.com/winfx/2006/xaml"
    Title="Main Thread Overload"
    Height="350" Width="525">
    <Grid>
        <Button Content="Run Query" Height="43"
            HorizontalAlignment="Left" Margin="12,12,0,0"
            Name="butConcatTextFiles" VerticalAlignment="Top"
            Width="190" Click="butRunQuery_Click" />
        <TextBox Margin="12,61,12,0" Name="txtResult"
         AcceptsReturn="True" Height="205"
         VerticalAlignment="Top" />
        <ProgressBar Height="27" HorizontalAlignment="Left"
         Margin="12,272,0,0" Name="pgbProgress"
         VerticalAlignment="Top" Width="479" />
    </Grid>
</Window>
```

MAINWINDOW.XAML.CS

```csharp
using System;
using System.Collections.Generic;
using System.Linq;
using System.Text;
using System.Windows;
using System.Windows.Controls;
using System.Windows.Data;
using System.Windows.Documents;
using System.Windows.Input;
using System.Windows.Media;
using System.Windows.Media.Imaging;
using System.Windows.Navigation;
using System.Windows.Shapes;
using System.Threading.Tasks;
using System.IO;

// This code has performance problems
// Don't consider this code as a best practice
namespace Listing10_9
{
    public partial class MainWindow : Window
    {
        public MainWindow()
        {
            InitializeComponent();
        }

        private TaskFactory _uiTF;
        private static int NUM_INTS = 50000;

        private static ParallelQuery<int> GenerateInputData()
        {
```

```
            return ParallelEnumerable.Range(1, NUM_INTS);
    }

    private void AdvanceProgressBar()
    {
        // This code runs in the UI thread
        // there is no possible concurrency
        pgbProgress.Value++;
    }

    private double CalculateX(int intNum)
    {
        // Horrible code that updates
        // the UI thousands of times
        var uiTask = _uiTF.StartNew(
            () =>
            {
                AdvanceProgressBar();
            });
        return Math.Pow(Math.Sqrt(intNum / Math.PI), 3);
    }

    private void butRunQuery_Click(
        object sender, RoutedEventArgs e)
    {
        var uiScheduler =
            TaskScheduler.FromCurrentSynchronizationContext();

        _uiTF = new TaskFactory(uiScheduler);

        var inputIntegers = GenerateInputData();

        // Reset the progress bar
        pgbProgress.Value = 0;
        // Set the maximum value for the progress bar
        pgbProgress.Maximum = inputIntegers.Count();

        var taskQ = Task<double>.Factory.StartNew(
            () =>
            {
                var parReductionQuery =
                    (from intNum in inputIntegers.AsParallel()
                     select (CalculateX(intNum))).Average();

                return parReductionQuery;
            });

        taskQ.ContinueWith(
            (t) =>
            {
                // This code runs
                // in the UI thread
                txtResult.Text = String.Format("Average: {0}",
                    t.Result);
            }, uiScheduler);
    }
}
}
```

When you click the Run Query button, the code tries to update the progress bar for each call that the PLINQ query makes to the `CalculateX` method. The problem is that the PLINQ query calls this method 50,000 times; therefore, the code tries to update the UI 50,000 times. The code generates a nonresponsive UI thread because it is overloaded with requests from the dispatcher.

Run only the necessary code in the UI thread, and remember to decouple the UI.

UNDERSTANDING FALSE SHARING

Chapter 1 explained some details about modern multicore microprocessors. These microprocessors have many levels of cache memory. These cache memories group data in *cache lines* to transport data to and from the main memory. Cache lines usually have a 64-byte size or more. This means that the minimum amount of data that can travel from the main memory to one of the cache memories is the cache line size. This grouping can cause unexpected problems in your parallelized algorithms.

If multiple threads running in different cores have to make changes to data contained in a contiguous address space that shares the same cache line, the cache coherency mechanism can invalidate the whole line on each write operation. This cache line invalidation that happens at the hardware level causes a performance problem known as *false sharing*. This problem is also known as *cache line ping-ponging*. This problem isn't just a write-write conflict, but also a write-read conflict. The impact on an application is similar to a serialized execution generated by a critical section with a mutual exclusion lock. However, the performance penalty only appears when the need for exclusive access shares the small cache line.

Listing 10-10 shows the code for a console application that uses a simple `NumberGenerator` class to generate new numbers. The `_lastNumber` private variable is an internal state for this class. Thus, it is possible to reproduce a false sharing scenario when it is combined with arrays updated in parallel.

LISTING 10-10: An application that shares the cache line

```csharp
using System;
using System.Collections.Generic;
using System.Linq;
using System.Text;
using System.Threading.Tasks;
using System.Diagnostics;

namespace Listing10_10
{
    class NumberGenerator
    {
        private int _lastNumber = 0;

        public int GenerateNext()
        {
            _lastNumber++;
```

```
                return _lastNumber;
        }
    }

    class Program
    {
        private static int NUM_INTS = 50000000;

        private static void GenerateNumbersSharedLine()
        {
            NumberGenerator ng1 = new NumberGenerator();
            NumberGenerator ng2 = new NumberGenerator();
            int[] numbers1 = new int[NUM_INTS];
            int[] numbers2 = new int[NUM_INTS];

            // Generate numbers in parallel
            // with a high probability
            // of sharing the cache line
            Parallel.Invoke(
                () =>
                {
                    for (int i = 0; i < NUM_INTS; i++)
                    {
                        numbers1[i] = ng1.GenerateNext();
                    }
                },
                () =>
                {
                    for (int i = 0; i < NUM_INTS; i++)
                    {
                        numbers2[i] = ng2.GenerateNext();
                    }
                });

            Console.WriteLine("numbers1: {0}",
                numbers1.Max());
            Console.WriteLine("numbers2: {0}",
                numbers2.Max());
        }

        static void Main(string[] args)
        {
            var sw = Stopwatch.StartNew();
            GenerateNumbersSharedLine();
            Console.WriteLine(sw.Elapsed.TotalSeconds);
            Console.ReadLine();
        }
    }
}
```

The application measures the time required to run the GenerateNumbersSharedLine method. This method declares and creates two NumberGenerator instances and two arrays of int with a NUM_INTS capacity. This is where the problem starts, because each NumberGenerator instance has an internal state, and the arrays are going to share the cache line when the code has to update their values.

Then, the code launches two parallel tasks to populate the two previously created arrays with the numbers generated by the two `NumberGenerator` instances.

You won't notice the performance problem until you run a similar version of this application that avoids sharing the cache line. Listing 10-11 shows this new version, which just changes the place in which the arrays and the `NumberGenerator` instances are declared and created. Because the new code creates each instance of `NumberGenerator` inside the delegate that defines the action that runs in parallel, the internal state update is much less likely to generate problems with the cache line. In addition, the code initializes each array within the delegate to avoid the false sharing problem. It is still possible that the two-number generator instances can end up next to each other on the heap, but this is less likely to happen with the new code.

LISTING 10-11: An application that avoids sharing the cache line

```csharp
using System;
using System.Collections.Generic;
using System.Linq;
using System.Text;
using System.Threading.Tasks;
using System.Diagnostics;

namespace Listing10_11
{
    class NumberGenerator
    {
        private int _lastNumber = 0;

        public int GenerateNext()
        {
            _lastNumber++;
            return _lastNumber;
        }
    }

    class Program
    {
        private static int NUM_INTS = 50000000;

        private static void GenerateNumbersExcLine()
        {
            int[] numbers1;
            int[] numbers2;

            Parallel.Invoke(
                () =>
                {
                    NumberGenerator ng1 = new NumberGenerator();
                    numbers1 = new int[NUM_INTS];
                    for (int i = 0; i < NUM_INTS; i++)
                    {
                        numbers1[i] = ng1.GenerateNext();
                    }
```

```
                    Console.WriteLine("numbers1: {0}",
                        numbers1.Max());
                },
                () =>
                {
                    NumberGenerator ng2 = new NumberGenerator();
                    numbers2 = new int[NUM_INTS];
                    for (int i = 0; i < NUM_INTS; i++)
                    {
                        numbers2[i] = ng2.GenerateNext();
                    }
                    Console.WriteLine("numbers2: {0}",
                        numbers2.Max());
                });
        }

        static void Main(string[] args)
        {
            var sw = Stopwatch.StartNew();
            GenerateNumbersExcLine();
            Console.WriteLine(sw.Elapsed.TotalSeconds);
            Console.ReadLine();
        }
    }
}
```

If you run both this application and the one shown in Listing 10-10 on a computer with at least two physical cores, you will notice an important speedup in the code shown in Listing 10-11.

SUMMARY

This chapter explained some of the most common problems found in parallelized code with .NET Framework 4. The chapter also introduced the usage of the profiling features to identify these problems and to improve both the performance and scalability for your parallelized applications. To summarize this chapter:

➤ You must run the necessary tests to make sure that your application provides correctness, the desired speedup achievement, and scalability.

➤ Sometimes, your parallelized application should be compatible with single-core computers. If it isn't, be sure to specify the appropriate requirements.

➤ You can use the appropriate profiling methods to detect common problems related to parallelized code.

➤ You can isolate parallelized algorithms to simplify your profiling sessions.

11

Vectorization, SIMD Instructions, and Additional Parallel Libraries

WHAT'S IN THIS CHAPTER?

➤ Understanding SIMD and vectorization

➤ Understanding extended instruction sets

➤ Working with Intel Math Kernel Library

➤ Working with multicore-ready, highly optimized software functions

➤ Mixing task-based programming with external optimized libraries

➤ Generating pseudo-random numbers in parallel

➤ Working with the `ThreadLocal<T>` class

➤ Using Intel Integrated Performance Primitives

In the previous 10 chapters, you learned to create and coordinate code that runs many tasks in parallel to improve performance. If you want to improve throughput even further, you can take advantage of other possibilities offered by modern hardware related to parallelism. This chapter is about the usage of additional performance libraries and includes examples of their integration with .NET Framework 4 and the new task-based programming model. In addition, the chapter provides examples of the usage of the new thread-local storage classes and the lazy-initialization capabilities provided by these classes.

UNDERSTANDING SIMD AND VECTORIZATION

The "Parallel Programming and Multicore Programming" section of Chapter 1, "Task-Based Programming," introduced the different kinds of parallel architectures. This section also explained that most modern microprocessors can execute Single Instruction, Multiple Data

(SIMD) instructions. Because the execution units for SIMD instructions usually belong to a physical core, it is possible to run as many SIMD instructions in parallel as available physical cores. The usage of these vector-processing capabilities in parallel can provide important speedups in certain algorithms.

Here's a simple example that will help you understand the power of SIMD instructions. Figure 11-1 shows a diagram that represents the PABSD instruction. This instruction is part of the Supplemental Streaming SIMD Extensions 3 (SSSE 3) introduced with the Intel Core 2 architecture.

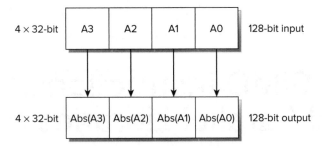

FIGURE 11-1

The PABSD mnemonic means *packed absolute value for double-word*. This assembly instruction receives a 128-bit input parameter that contains four 32-bit signed integers. The instruction returns a 128-bit output that contains the absolute value for each of the four 32-bit signed integers, packed in the 128-bit output.

You can calculate the absolute values for four 32-bit signed integers with a single call to the PABSD instruction. If you have to calculate the absolute values for 1,000 32-bit signed integers, you can do it with 250 calls to this instruction instead of using a single instruction for each 32-bit signed integer. You can achieve very important speedups. However, because it is necessary to pack the data before calling the SIMD instruction and then unpack the output, it is also important to measure this overhead that adds some code.

If you have to calculate the absolute values for four 32-bit signed integers, the additional overhead will reduce the overall speedup. However, if you have to calculate the absolute values for 100 32-bit signed integers, you will usually benefit from the usage of this kind of SIMD instruction.

If you have to calculate the absolute values for 1,000 32-bit signed integers and you are running the code on a CPU with two physical cores that support the SSSE3 extended instruction set, you can run PABSD instructions in parallel to increase throughput. You can calculate these values with 125 calls to this instruction in each physical core and achieve a speedup through parallelism combined with the execution of SIMD instructions. The absolute value calculation would be as follows:

125 calls x 2 physical cores x 4 integers per PABSD instruction call = 1,000 32-bit signed integers

Figure 11-2 shows a diagram that represents the execution of the PABSD in parallel on two physical cores.

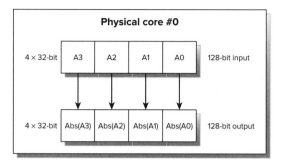
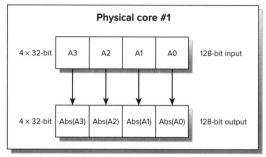

FIGURE 11-2

Each SIMD instruction can typically work with different packed data types. For example, the SSSE3 extended instruction set includes three assembly SIMD instructions that calculate packed absolute values for the following data types:

➤ PABSB — Calculates the absolute value for 16 signed bytes

➤ PABSW — Calculates the absolute value for eight 16-bit signed integers (words)

➤ PABSD — Calculates the absolute value for four 32-bit signed integers (double-words)

The aforementioned SIMD instructions can also calculate the absolute values for a lower number of packed values. For example, PABSB can calculate the absolute value for 8 signed bytes instead of 16.

Many applications written in C and C++ take advantage of these instruction sets to work on vectors and matrixes. They are very useful to improve performance in algorithms that need to perform multiple calculations on many data blocks. Most modern C and C++ compilers optimize loops to take advantage of SIMD instruction sets. Therefore, they are able to perform an auto-vectorization when you follow certain guidelines for writing the loops that perform operations on arrays.

.NET Framework 4 does not provide direct support for SIMD or auto-vectorization. This means that your C# code cannot call SIMD instructions, and the C# compiler doesn't provide an option to enable the usage of SIMD instructions when you perform operations on arrays. However, you can use libraries that are optimized to take advantage of the performance improvements offered by SIMD instructions. You can call the functions provided by these libraries, and you can combine them with the advantages of task-based programming. Subsequent sections provide examples of two performance libraries that take advantage of both parallelism and SIMD instructions, targeting several application domains. These libraries are Intel Math Kernel Library (MKL) and Intel Integrated Performance Primitives (IPP).

FROM MMX TO SSE4.X AND AVX

Most modern microprocessors can execute SIMD instructions. However, these instructions are part of different extended instruction sets. Because the need for greater computing performance continues to grow across industry segments, many microprocessor manufacturers have incorporated extended instruction sets in their new CPU models. At the time of this writing, the most advanced Intel CPU includes support for the following SIMD instruction sets:

➤ MMX — MultiMedia eXtensions

➤ SSE — Streaming SIMD Extensions

➤ SSE2 — Streaming SIMD Extensions 2

➤ SSE3 — Streaming SIMD Extensions 3

➤ SSSE3 — Supplemental Streaming SIMD Extensions 3

➤ SSE4.1 — Streaming SIMD Extensions 4.1

➤ SSE4.2 — Streaming SIMD Extensions 4.2

➤ AES-NI — Advanced Encryption Standard New Instructions

➤ AVX — Advanced Vector eXtensions

The previously mentioned MKL and IPP performance libraries detect the available extended instruction sets and optimize their execution according to the possibilities offered by the underlying hardware. Thus, if you run the same code in two similar dual-core microprocessors, but they support diverse extended instruction sets, you might achieve very different performance results. For example, if a CPU supports Advanced Vector eXtensions (AVX), it can perform certain operations on 256-bit packed types with a single instruction.

There is a very easy way to check the instruction set supported by a CPU in both 32-bit and 64-bit versions of Windows. You can use CPU-Z, a free utility developed by CPUID. You just have to download the appropriate version from www.cpuid.com and install it or run the compressed executable file, cpuz.exe. Then, select the CPU tab and check the list of values listed in the Instructions field. Figure 11-3 shows an example of a CPU tab and the values it displays.

The Instructions field in this example contains the following values:

```
MMX, SSE(1, 2, 3, 3S, 4.1, 4.2), EM64T, VT-x
```

This means that the Intel Core i7 Q820 CPU supports the following SIMD instruction sets:

➤ MMX

➤ SSE (indicated as 1 after SSE)

➤ SSE2

➤ SSE3

➤ SSSE3 (indicated as 3S after SSE)

➤ SSE4.1

➤ SSE4.2

FIGURE 11-3

The Intel Core i7 Q820 CPU does not support the AES instruction set or the AVX instruction set.

USING THE INTEL MATH KERNEL LIBRARY

Intel MKL is a library of highly optimized math routines for science, engineering, and financial applications. The math routines use multiple threads and SIMD instructions to achieve the best performance according to the underlying hardware. MKL 10.3 introduced a simple DLL named `mkl_rt.dll`, which you can call within your C# code through Platform Invokes (P/Invokes).

Listing 11-1 shows the XAML code for the main window of a WPF application that displays a `Button` control and a `ListBox` on a window. You can see the design view for this window in Figure 11-4. In addition, Listing 11-1 shows the C# code for the main window, with the code that defines the `Click` event handler for the button, and the code that defines the wrappers for MKL in the `MKL_dtfi.cs` file.

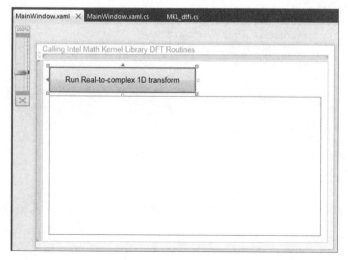

FIGURE 11-4

Listing 11-1 shows an example of calculating a discrete Fourier transform. The Fourier transform converts a signal indexed by time into a signal indexed by frequency. The Fourier transform is a linear function and provides reciprocity, and therefore, you can reconstruct the original signal from the information in the Fourier coefficients. A discrete Fourier transform, also known as DFT, is a specific type of a Fourier transform that is applied to a finite sequence of discrete values. A fast Fourier transform, also known as FFT, represents an algorithm to perform a discrete Fourier transform in an optimized manner. This algorithm reduces the necessary number of computations for N points from $2N^2$ to $2 \times N \times \log_2(N)$. Discrete Fourier transforms are very useful in signal processing and digital filtering. The discrete Fourier Transforms routines included in MKL use the FFT algorithm.

LISTING 11-1: Running an MKL forward discrete Fourier transform

MAINWINDOW.XAML

```
<Window x:Class="Listing11_1.MainWindow"
 xmlns="http://schemas.microsoft.com/winfx/2006/xaml/presentation"
 xmlns:x="http://schemas.microsoft.com/winfx/2006/xaml"
 Title="Calling Intel Math Kernel Library DFT Routines"
 Height="350" Width="525">
    <Grid>
        <Button Content="Run Real-to-complex 1D transform"
            Height="43" HorizontalAlignment="Left"
            Margin="12,12,0,0"
            Name="butRun" VerticalAlignment="Top"
            Width="258" Click="butRun_Click" />
        <ListBox Height="238" HorizontalAlignment="Left"
            Margin="12,61,0,0" Name="lstOutput"
            VerticalAlignment="Top" Width="479" />
    </Grid>
</Window>
```

MAINWINDOW.XAML.CS

```
using System;
using System.Collections.Generic;
using System.Linq;
using System.Text;
using System.Windows;
using System.Windows.Controls;
using System.Windows.Data;
using System.Windows.Documents;
using System.Windows.Input;
using System.Windows.Media;
using System.Windows.Media.Imaging;
using System.Windows.Navigation;
```

```csharp
using System.Windows.Shapes;
// Added for tasks
using System.Threading.Tasks;
// Added for MKL
using mkl;

namespace Listing11_1
{
    public partial class MainWindow : Window
    {
        public MainWindow()
        {
            InitializeComponent();
        }

        // The size of the input array of double
        private const int INPUT_SIZE = 30000;

        private double[] Generate1DInput()
        {
            double[] data = new double[INPUT_SIZE];
            for (int i = 0; i < INPUT_SIZE; i++)
            {
                data[i] =
                    Math.Sin(i + 1) *
                    Math.Sqrt(3d) / 2d;
            }

            return data;
        }

        private double[] DFT1DRealToComplex()
        {
            /* Real-to-complex 1D transform
             * for double precision data
             * not inplace with pack format
             * Configuration parameters for MKL DFTI
             * DFTI.FORWARD_DOMAIN = DFTI.REAL
             * DFTI.PRECISION      = DFTI.DOUBLE
             * DFTI.DIMENSION      = 1
             * DFTI.LENGTHS        = INPUT_SIZE (n)
             * DFTI.PLACEMENT      = DFTI.NOT_INPLACE
             * DFTI.BACKWARD_SCALE = (1.0 / n) (backwardScale)
             * Default values:
             * DFTI.PACKED_FORMAT  = DFTI.PACK_FORMAT
             * DFTI.FORWARD_SCALE  = 1.0
             */
            IntPtr descriptor = new IntPtr();
            int precision = DFTI.DOUBLE;
            int forwardDomain = DFTI.REAL;
            int dimension = 1;
            int n = INPUT_SIZE;

            // The input data to be transformed
            double[] input = Generate1DInput();
```

continues

LISTING 11-1 *(continued)*

```csharp
            // Create a new DFTI descriptor
            DFTI.DftiCreateDescriptor(ref descriptor,
                precision, forwardDomain, dimension, n);
            // Configure DFTI.BACKWARD_SCALE
            double backwardScale = 1.0 / n;
            DFTI.DftiSetValue(descriptor,
                DFTI.BACKWARD_SCALE, backwardScale);
            // Configure DFTI.PLACEMENT
            DFTI.DftiSetValue(descriptor,
                DFTI.PLACEMENT, DFTI.NOT_INPLACE);
            // Configure DFTI.PACKET_FORMAT
            DFTI.DftiSetValue(descriptor,
                DFTI.PACKED_FORMAT, DFTI.PACK_FORMAT);
            // Commit the descriptor with the configuration
            DFTI.DftiCommitDescriptor(descriptor);
            // This is the output array
            double[] output = new double[n];

            // Compute the forward transform
            var err = DFTI.DftiComputeForward(descriptor,
                input, output);

            // Free the descriptor
            DFTI.DftiFreeDescriptor(ref descriptor);

            if (err == DFTI.NO_ERROR)
            {
                return output;
            }
            else
            {
                throw new MKLException(
                    String.Format("DFTI returned error code {0}",
                    err));
            }
        }

        // The output of the Forward Fast Fourier Transform
        private double[] _output;

        private void butRun_Click(
            object sender, RoutedEventArgs e)
        {
            butRun.IsEnabled = false;

            // This scheduler will execute tasks
            // on the current SynchronizationContext
            // That is, it will access UI controls safely
            var uiScheduler =
                TaskScheduler.FromCurrentSynchronizationContext();

            var fourierTask = Task.Factory.StartNew<double[]>(
```

```
                    () =>
                    {
                        return DFT1DRealToComplex();
                    });

            fourierTask.ContinueWith(
                (antecedentTask) =>
                {
                    // This code runs in the UI thread
                    try
                    {
                        _output = antecedentTask.Result;
                        // Show the results
                        // in the lstOutput ListBox
                        lstOutput.ItemsSource = _output;
                    }
                    catch (AggregateException ex)
                    {
                        lstOutput.Items.Clear();
                        foreach (Exception innerEx
                            in ex.InnerExceptions)
                        {
                            // Show the error message
                            lstOutput.Items.Add(
                                innerEx.Message);
                        }
                    }
                    butRun.IsEnabled = true;
                }, uiScheduler);
        }
    }
}
```

MKL_DTFI.CS

```csharp
using System;
// Added for Intel MKL interop
using System.Security;
using System.Runtime.InteropServices;

namespace mkl
{
    [Serializable()]
    public class MKLException : System.Exception
    {
        public MKLException()
          : base() { }
        public MKLException(string message)
          : base(message) { }
        public MKLException(string message, System.Exception inner)
          : base(message, inner) { }
        protected MKLException(
          System.Runtime.Serialization.SerializationInfo info,
          System.Runtime.Serialization.StreamingContext context) { }
```

continues

LISTING 11-1 *(continued)*

```
    }

public sealed class DFTI
{
    private DFTI() { }

    /* These are just the necessary constants
     * for DFTI for this example
     * Based on the mkl_dfti.h file
     * mkl_dfti.h and DFTI
     * Copyright (C) 2010 Intel Corporation.
     * All Rights Reserved.
     */
    // Configuration parameters for DFTI
    public static int BACKWARD_SCALE = 5;
    public static int PLACEMENT = 11;
    public static int PACKED_FORMAT = 21;
    // Configuration values for DFTI
    public static int DOUBLE = 36;
    public static int REAL = 33;
    public static int NOT_INPLACE = 44;
    public static int PACK_FORMAT = 55;
    // Predefined errors for DFTI and their values
    public static int NO_ERROR = 0;
    public static int MEMORY_ERROR = 1;
    public static int INVALID_CONFIGURATION = 2;
    public static int INCONSISTENT_CONFIGURATION = 3;
    public static int NUMBER_OF_THREADS_ERROR = 8;
    public static int MULTITHREADED_ERROR = 4;
    public static int BAD_DESCRIPTOR = 5;
    public static int UNIMPLEMENTED = 6;
    public static int MKL_INTERNAL_ERROR = 7;
    public static int LENGTH_EXCEEDS_INT32 = 9;

    // Wrappers to native DFTI native calls
    public static int DftiCreateDescriptor(ref IntPtr desc,
        int precision, int domain, int dimension, int length)
    {
        return DFTINative.DftiCreateDescriptor(ref desc,
            precision, domain, dimension, length);
    }

    public static int DftiFreeDescriptor(ref IntPtr desc)
    {
        return DFTINative.DftiFreeDescriptor(ref desc);
    }

    public static int DftiSetValue(IntPtr desc,
        int config_param, int config_val)
    {
        return DFTINative.DftiSetValue(desc,
```

```
                    config_param, __arglist(config_val));
        }

        public static int DftiSetValue(IntPtr desc,
            int config_param, double config_val)
        {
            return DFTINative.DftiSetValue(desc,
                config_param, __arglist(config_val));
        }

        public static int DftiGetValue(IntPtr desc,
            int config_param, ref double config_val)
        {
            return DFTINative.DftiGetValue(desc,
                config_param, __arglist(ref config_val));
        }

        public static int DftiCommitDescriptor(IntPtr desc)
        {
            return DFTINative.DftiCommitDescriptor(desc);
        }

        public static int DftiComputeForward(IntPtr desc,
            [In] double[] x_in, [Out] double[] x_out)
        {
            return DFTINative.DftiComputeForward(
                desc, x_in, x_out);
        }

        public static int DftiComputeBackward(IntPtr desc,
            [In] double[] x_in, [Out] double[] x_out)
        {
            return DFTINative.DftiComputeBackward(
                desc, x_in, x_out);
        }
    }

// Native declarations that call the
// mkl_rt DLL functions
// They require Intel Math Kernel Library 10.3 or higher
// installed on the developer computer
/* Intel Math Kernel Library 10.3
 * Copyright (C) 2010 Intel Corporation.
 * All Rights Reserved.
 */
[SuppressUnmanagedCodeSecurity]
internal sealed class DFTINative
{
    [DllImport("mkl_rt", CallingConvention = CallingConvention.Cdecl,
        ExactSpelling = true, SetLastError = false)]
    internal static extern int DftiCreateDescriptor(ref IntPtr desc,
        int precision, int domain, int dimension, int length);
    [DllImport("mkl_rt", CallingConvention = CallingConvention.Cdecl,
        ExactSpelling = true, SetLastError = false)]
```

continues

LISTING 11-1 *(continued)*

```
        internal static extern int DftiCommitDescriptor(IntPtr desc);
        [DllImport("mkl_rt", CallingConvention = CallingConvention.Cdecl,
            ExactSpelling = true, SetLastError = false)]
        internal static extern int DftiFreeDescriptor(ref IntPtr desc);
        [DllImport("mkl_rt", CallingConvention = CallingConvention.Cdecl,
            ExactSpelling = true, SetLastError = false)]
        internal static extern int DftiSetValue(IntPtr desc,
            int config_param, __arglist);
        [DllImport("mkl_rt", CallingConvention = CallingConvention.Cdecl,
            ExactSpelling = true, SetLastError = false)]
        internal static extern int DftiGetValue(IntPtr desc,
            int config_param, __arglist);
        [DllImport("mkl_rt", CallingConvention = CallingConvention.Cdecl,
            ExactSpelling = true, SetLastError = false)]
        internal static extern int DftiComputeForward(IntPtr desc,
            [In] double[] x_in, [Out] double[] x_out);
        [DllImport("mkl_rt", CallingConvention = CallingConvention.Cdecl,
            ExactSpelling = true, SetLastError = false)]
        internal static extern int DftiComputeBackward(IntPtr desc,
            [In] double[] x_in, [Out] double[] x_out);
    }
}
```

To run the code shown in Listing 11-1, you must have Intel MKL 10.3 or higher installed on your computer. Intel MKL is a commercial product, but you can download a free trial version from `http://software.intel.com/en-us/intel-mkl/`.

When you click the Run Real-to-Complex 1D Transform button, the code in the `butRun_Click` event handler launches *fourierTask*, which is a `Task<double[]>` that calls the `DFT1DRealToComplex` method. Then, the code programs a continuation for *fourierTask* that shows the results of the discrete Fourier transform in the *lstOutput* ListBox or an error if the transform was not completed. The code uses tasks and continuations to run the discrete Fourier transform with an asynchronous execution and keep the UI thread unblocked until it is necessary to display the results.

The `DFT1DRealToComplex` method runs a real-to-complex 1D discrete Fourier transform for the double-precision data generated by the `Generate1DInput` method. The `Generate1DInput` method returns an array of `double` with an `INPUT_SIZE` number of elements.

The `DFT1DRealToComplex` method calls the static methods defined in the `DFTI` class to configure the parameters for the discrete Fourier transform. First, it creates a `DFTI` descriptor (*descriptor*), and then, it calls some methods to set the values for the `DFTI.BACKWARD_SCALE`, `DFTI.PLACEMENT`, and `DFTI.PACKED_FORMAT` parameters. When the required parameters associated with the `DFTI` descriptor are defined, the code calls the `DFTI.DftiCommitDescriptor` method to commit the descriptor with the defined configuration. The code uses the wrappers defined in the `DFTI` class, which are included in the `MKL_dfti.cs` file. This class defines constants based on the `mkl_dfti.h` file and calls the `mkl_rt.dll` native methods as declared in the `DFTINative` class. Each call to a `DFTINative` method requires a Platform Invoke (P/Invoke), which introduces an overhead.

Then, the `DFT1DRealToComplex` method calls the `DFTI.DftiComputeForward` method, which, in turn, calls the corresponding `mkl_rt.dll` function to compute the forward discrete Fourier transform for the `input` array and stores the results in the `output` array.

```
var err = DFTI.DftiComputeForward(descriptor, input, output);
```

code snippet from Listing11_1

Then, regardless of the results of the computation, the code calls the `DFTI.DftiFreeDescriptor` method to free the resources used by *descriptor*. If the `DFTI.DftiComputeForward` method returns `DFTI.NO_ERROR`, it means that the computation was successful and the output array will have the discrete Fourier transform results as specified in the *descriptor* configuration. The `DFT1DRealToComplex` method returns `output`. However, if something goes wrong, the method throws a `MKLException`.

The *fourierTask* task was defined as a `Task<double[]>`, and it returns the result of calling the `DFT1DRealToComplex` method. The continuation task chained to *fourierTask* task receives this task as *antecedentTask*. If an exception occurs, the code catches it and shows it in the *lstOutput* ListBox. If the computation of the discrete Fourier transform runs without problems, the code that runs in the same thread that created the UI controls shows the results as items in the *lstOutput* ListBox:

```
fourierTask.ContinueWith(
    (antecedentTask) =>
    {
        // This code runs in the UI thread
        try
        {
            _output = antecedentTask.Result;
            lstOutput.ItemsSource = _output;
        }
```

code snippet from Listing11_1

Figure 11-5 shows the WPF application's window with the contents of the discrete Fourier transform computation's output array displayed in the list box.

Working with Multicore-Ready, Highly Optimized Software Functions

When the code in Listing 11-1 calls the `DFTI.DftiComputeForward` method, the defined P/Invoke method allows you to run the unmanaged `DftiComputeForward` function for the MKL DLL (`mkl_rt.dll`). This function uses multiple threads and SIMD instructions to optimize the computation.

Because the example works with a multicore-ready optimized software function, it creates threads outside of the scope of managed code. Therefore, it is important to check the documentation for these optimized software functions. If they are already optimized for multicore, you should not call them from multiple threads because that might cause an oversubscription problem and reduce the overall performance.

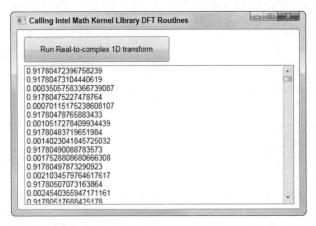

FIGURE 11-5

For example, suppose that you call the DftiComputeForward function from managed code for a huge data set, and the MKL DLL creates four threads to optimize the execution to take advantage of the four logical cores. If you have to compute four discrete Fourier transforms on four independent huge data sets, and you don't know that this function is already optimized for multicore and is thread-safe, you might decide to run four calls to the DftiComputeForward function from four independent tasks to optimize your application. However, because each DftiComputeForward function uses four threads to optimize its execution, you would have 4 x 4 = 16 threads with heavy computation requirements, which would create an oversubscription problem.

If, however, you read the documentation as recommended, you will discover that the function is optimized for multicore and it uses multiple threads; therefore, you should call one DftiComputeForward function after the other. Each execution of the DftiComputeForward function takes advantage of multicore by using the necessary threads. Appendix B, "Concurrent UML Models," explains how to add concurrency documentation to UML diagrams.

Mixing Task-Based Programming with External Optimized Libraries

Listing 11-1 shows an example of how to combine the advantages of task-based programming with the execution of functions from external libraries that are already optimized for multicore. The code creates a new task that configures the parameters for the external library and calls the function with an asynchronous execution. The code encapsulates the external call in a Task<TResult>, where TResult is the output from the external function.

Instead of keeping the UI thread blocked, the code uses tasks and continuations to run just the necessary code in the UI thread. You can perform P/Invokes from tasks; therefore, you can call the MKL functions within the action delegate that a task executes.

In this example, the optimized library enables you to take advantage of SIMD instructions in a C# application, and task-based programming enables you to create a responsive UI with simple code.

Generating Pseudo-Random Numbers in Parallel

The System.Random class represents a pseudo-random number generator. However, if you need to generate a sequence of pseudo-random numbers in parallel, you should avoid using a shared Random instance. Because the System.Random class holds an internal state, it isn't thread-safe — meaning that if you call the methods that return pseudo-random numbers concurrently, this state will get corrupted.

You can solve the problem by using a mutual-exclusion lock before calling the method that returns each pseudo-random number, but that would serialize the generation of the numbers and would provide a really poor performance.

You can create a new System.Random instance each time that you have to generate a pseudo-random number, but again, the creation of a new instance for each number would provide a poor performance. However, there is a worse problem: the quality of the pseudo-random numbers won't be as good as expected compared with the results of the serial execution of this pseudo-random number generation. By default, when you create a new Random instance by using its parameterless constructor, the class uses a time-related value as the seed. When you run code on a multicore microprocessor, the creation of multiple Random instances with a real concurrent execution and the aforementioned behavior are big problems. Multiple instances might share the same seed; therefore, they might produce exactly the same pseudo-random numbers.

The Random class uses Environment.TickCount (the number of ticks) as the default seed. This number is continuously changing, but it takes several milliseconds to increase its count. If you write the previously explained parallelized code, there is a very high probability of having many Random classes with the same seed if you run the code on a computer with a multicore microprocessor. If you want decent pseudo-random numbers, you need to find a better alternative.

Appendix C, "Parallel Extensions Extras," provides information about useful classes and structures that complement Parallel Extensions. One of these classes is the System.Threading .ThreadSafeRandom class. This class provides a simple thread-safe implementation of Random that allows you to generate pseudo-random numbers concurrently.

Listing 11-2 shows the code for the ThreadSafeRandom class, a subclass of Random. The code defines the ThreadSafeRandom class within the System.Threading namespace. This code is part of the coordination data structures included in the parallel programming samples for .NET Framework 4.

LISTING 11-2: A pseudo-random number generator prepared for concurrency

```
//  This code is part of the
//  Parallel Programming Samples for .NET Framework 4
//  Copyright (c) Microsoft Corporation. All rights reserved.
//
//  File: ThreadSafeRandom.cs
//  The comments aren't part of the original file
using System;
using System.Security.Cryptography;

namespace System.Threading
```

continues

LISTING 11-2 *(continued)*

```
{
    public class ThreadSafeRandom : Random
    {
        // This is the seed provider
        private static readonly RNGCryptoServiceProvider _global
            = new RNGCryptoServiceProvider();

        // This is the provider of randomness
        // There is going to be
        // one instance of Random per thread
        // because it is declared as ThreadLocal<Random>
        private ThreadLocal<Random> _local =
            new ThreadLocal<Random>(() =>
            {
                // This is the valueFactory function
                // This code will run for each thread
                // to initialize each independent instance
                // of Random
                var buffer = new byte[4];
                // Calls the GetBytes method for
                // RNGCryptoServiceProvider because
                // this class is thread-safe for this usage
                _global.GetBytes(buffer);
                // Return the new thread-local Random instance
                // initialized with the generated seed
                return new Random(
                    BitConverter.ToInt32(buffer, 0));
            });

        public override int Next()
        {
            return _local.Value.Next();
        }

        public override int Next(int maxValue)
        {
            return _local.Value.Next(maxValue);
        }

        public override int Next(int minValue, int maxValue)
        {
            return _local.Value.Next(minValue, maxValue);
        }

        public override double NextDouble()
        {
            return _local.Value.NextDouble();
        }

        public override void NextBytes(byte[] buffer)
        {
            _local.Value.NextBytes(buffer);
        }
    }
}
```

The `ThreadSafeRandom` class uses the `System.Threading.ThreadLocal<T>` class introduced in .NET Framework 4 to initialize one independent `Random` instance per thread. The `ThreadLocal<T>` class provides thread-local storage of data in an efficient way and enables you to specify a `Func<T>` to be invoked to produce a lazy-initialized value. This means that when you specify this `Func<T>` and there is an attempt to retrieve the value of the instance for the current thread, if this instance wasn't initialized, the initialization function is invoked. This way, the code specified as `Func<T>` returns the value on demand, as each new thread requires accessing it. This mechanism is known as *lazy initialization*.

The following lines define the `private ThreadLocal<Random> _local` variable:

```
private ThreadLocal<Random> _local = new ThreadLocal<Random>(() =>
    {
        var buffer = new byte[4];
        _global.GetBytes(buffer);
        return new Random(BitConverter.ToInt32(buffer, 0));
    });
```

code snippet from Listing11_2

If you create a new instance of `ThreadSafeRandom` in a task that is assigned to `Thread #0`, and this instance accesses `_local`, the `Func<Random>` specified as a parameter of the `ThreadLocal<Random>` runs. The code creates a new `Random` instance with a seed and returns it as the value for `_local`. If the same task assigned to `Thread #0` calls one of the methods of the `ThreadSafeRandom` instance that accesses `_local`, the initialization code won't run again, and the `ThreadLocal<Random>` instance that controls the value for the `_local` variable will provide access to the previously created `Random` instance. The lazy-initialization code doesn't run again because there is an instance already created for the current thread, `Thread #0`.

If you access the previously created instance of `ThreadSafeRandom` in a different task that is assigned to `Thread #1`, and you call a method that accesses `_local`, the `Func<Random>` specified as a parameter of the `ThreadLocal<Random>` will run. This happens because `ThreadLocal` is responsible for initializing an independent value for each different thread. The code creates a new `Random` instance with a seed and returns it as the value for `_local`. If the same task assigned to `Thread #1` calls one of the methods of the `ThreadSafeRandom` instance that accesses `_local`, the initialization code won't run again, and the `ThreadLocal<Random>` instance that controls the value for the `_local` variable will provide access to the `Random` instance created for `Thread #1`. `ThreadLocal` makes sure that each thread has its `Random` instance initialized on demand.

 `ThreadLocal<T>` *provides an efficient implementation of thread-local storage. However, there is an overhead to access its value. Thus, you should be careful when using this class for supporting isolation.*

The usage of `ThreadLocal<Random>` solves the problem of independent `Random` instances per thread. However, as you might recall, there is still the problem of using equal seeds with a concurrent execution. The `ThreadSafeRandom` class solves this problem by using a shared `System .Security.Cryptography.RNGCryptoServiceProvider` instance (`_global`) as an efficient seed provider. Each time that the lazy-initialization code for the shared Random instance runs, it calls the GetBytes method to fill an array of byte (*buffer*) with a cryptographically strong sequence of random values. The lazy-initialization function returns a new Random instance with this array of byte converted to an integer as the initial seed. This way, each thread has an independent Random instance with a completely different initial seed. Therefore, multiple tasks that are assigned to diverse threads can share the same ThreadSafeRandom instance to generate pseudo-random numbers with a concurrent execution.

The ThreadSafeRandom class overrides the methods that generate and return the pseudo-random values: Next, NextDouble, and NextBytes. The new overridden methods use the Random instance controlled by ThreadLocal and returned when they access _*local*, to generate and return the corresponding pseudo-random values.

Listing 11-3 shows a new version of the Generate1DInput method that uses a ThreadSafeRandom instance to generate pseudo-random double values for the discrete Fourier transform with a parallelized loop.

> **LISTING 11-3:** A new version of the Generate1DInput method that creates pseudo-random numbers

```
// This code requires the default using statements
// for an XAML Window, as shown in Listing 11-1, MainWindow.xaml.cs
// Added for tasks
using System.Threading.Tasks;
// Added for MKL
using mkl;
// Added for ConcurrentBag
using System.Collections.Concurrent;
// Added for ThreadSafeRandom
using System.Threading;

namespace Listing11_3
{
    public partial class MainWindow : Window
    {
        public MainWindow()
        {
            InitializeComponent();
        }

        // The size of the input array of double
        private const int INPUT_SIZE = 30000;

        private double[] Generate1DInput()
        {
            var randomNumbers =
                new ConcurrentBag<double>();
            var tsRandom =
                new ThreadSafeRandom();

            Parallel.For(0, INPUT_SIZE,
                (int i) =>
                {
                    // Each thread has its own
```

```
                    // independent instance
                    // of Random because it
                    // uses ThreadLocalStorage<Random>
                    randomNumbers.Add(
                        tsRandom.NextDouble());
            });

        return randomNumbers.ToArray<double>();
    }
```

The new `Generate1DInput` method creates a new `ThreadSafeRandom` instance (*tsRandom*) and then runs a `Parallel.For` loop to populate a `ConcurrentBag` (*randomNumbers*) with the results of the `tsRandom.NextDouble` method. The diverse tasks created by the `Parallel.For` loop will run on different threads, and each thread will have its underlying `Random` instance initialized with a very different seed value that's not related to the number of ticks. Then, the code converts the `ConcurrentBag` to an array of `double` and returns the pseudo-random numbers generated in parallel.

USING INTEL INTEGRATED PERFORMANCE PRIMITIVES

Intel IPP is a library of highly optimized math software functions for digital media and data-processing applications. The functions use multiple threads and SIMD instructions to achieve the best performance according to the underlying hardware. IPP includes multiple DLLs, and you can call its functions from your C# code through Platform Invokes (P/Invokes).

Listing 11-4 shows the XAML code for the main window of a WPF application that displays a `Button` control and an `Image` on a window. You can see the design view for this window in Figure 11-6. In addition, Listing 11-4 shows the C# code for the main window, with the code that defines the `Click` event handler for the button.

FIGURE 11-6

LISTING 11-4: Running an IPP Image filter

MAINWINDOW.XAML

```
<Window x:Class="Listing11_4.MainWindow"
 xmlns="http://schemas.microsoft.com/winfx/2006/xaml/presentation"
 xmlns:x="http://schemas.microsoft.com/winfx/2006/xaml"
 Title="Calling Intel Performance Primitives Routines"
 Height="436" Width="574">
    <Grid>
        <Button Content="Apply Sobel Filter Vertical"
                Height="41" HorizontalAlignment="Left"
                Margin="12,12,0,0" Name="butProcessImage"
                VerticalAlignment="Top" Width="218"
                Click="butProcessImage_Click" />
        <Image Margin="12,59,12,12"
                Name="imgProcessedImage" Stretch="Fill" />
    </Grid>
</Window>
```

MAINWINDOW.XAML.CS

```
// This code requires the default using statements
// for an XAML Window, as shown in Listing 11-1, MainWindow.xaml.cs
// Added
using System.Drawing;
using System.Drawing.Imaging;
using System.Threading.Tasks;
using System.Windows.Interop;
using ipp;

namespace Listing11_4
{
    public partial class MainWindow : Window
    {
        public MainWindow()
        {
            InitializeComponent();
        }

        private BitmapData GetBitmapData(
            Bitmap bitmap, ImageLockMode lockMode)
        {
            return bitmap.LockBits(
                new System.Drawing.Rectangle(0, 0,
                    bitmap.Width, bitmap.Height),
                lockMode,
                System.Drawing.Imaging.PixelFormat.Format24bppRgb);
        }

        unsafe private Bitmap ApplyFilterSobelVert()
        {
            // This is the file name to process
            string fileName =
```

```
                    @"C:\Pictures\Test.jpg";
        var originalImage = new Bitmap(fileName);
        var srcBitmapData = GetBitmapData(
            originalImage, ImageLockMode.ReadOnly);

        var destinationImage = new Bitmap(
            originalImage.Width, originalImage.Height);
        var dstBitmapData = GetBitmapData(
            destinationImage, ImageLockMode.ReadWrite);

        IppiSize roi = new IppiSize(
                originalImage.Width - 3,
                originalImage.Height - 3);
        const int ksize = 5;
        const int half = ksize / 2;
        byte* pSrc = (byte*)srcBitmapData.Scan0 +
            (srcBitmapData.Stride + 3) * half;
        byte* pDst = (byte*)dstBitmapData.Scan0 +
            (dstBitmapData.Stride + 3) * half;

        IppStatus status =
            ipp.ip.ippiFilterSobelVert_8u_C3R(
                pSrc, srcBitmapData.Stride,
                pDst, dstBitmapData.Stride,
                roi);

        // Unlock bits for both source and destination
        originalImage.UnlockBits(srcBitmapData);
        destinationImage.UnlockBits(dstBitmapData);

        return destinationImage;
    }

    private void butProcessImage_Click(
        object sender, RoutedEventArgs e)
    {
        butProcessImage.IsEnabled = false;

        // This scheduler will execute tasks
        // on the current SynchronizationContext
        // That is, it will access UI controls safely
        var uiScheduler =
            TaskScheduler.
            FromCurrentSynchronizationContext();

        var filterTask =
            Task.Factory.StartNew<Bitmap>(
            () =>
            {
                return ApplyFilterSobelVert();
            });

        filterTask.ContinueWith(
            (antecedentTask) =>
            {
```

continues

LISTING 11-4 *(continued)*

```
                    // This code runs in the UI thread
                    try
                    {
                        var outBitmap = antecedentTask.Result;
                        // Show the results
                        // in the Image control
                        imgProcessedImage.Source = Imaging.
                            CreateBitmapSourceFromHBitmap(
                            outBitmap.GetHbitmap(),
                            IntPtr.Zero,
                            System.Windows.Int32Rect.Empty,
                            BitmapSizeOptions.FromWidthAndHeight(
                                outBitmap.Width, outBitmap.Height));
                    }
                    catch (AggregateException ex)
                    {
                        foreach (Exception innerEx
                            in ex.InnerExceptions)
                        {
                            // Add code
                            // to display the error messages
                            // found in innerEx.Message);
                        }
                    }
                    butProcessImage.IsEnabled = true;
                }, uiScheduler);
            }
        }
    }
```

To run the code shown in Listing 11-4, you must have Intel IPP 8.0 or higher installed on your computer. Intel IPP is a commercial product, but you can download a free trial version from `http://software.intel.com/en-us/intel-ipp/`.

Before running the example shown in Listing 11-4, you must perform the following steps:

1. Right-click the project's name in Solution Explorer and select Properties. Click the Build page and activate the Allow Unsafe Code check box. You need to activate this option because the example uses unsafe pointers to prepare the necessary data for the IPP filter.

2. Right-click References in Solution Explorer and select Add Reference. Click the .NET tab, select `System.Drawing`, and then click OK. You need to add this reference because this is a WPF application that uses the `System.Drawing.Bitmap` class to manipulate the pixels of a bitmap image.

3. Decompress the language-related samples for IPP in a new folder. These samples are usually compressed into a file called `ipp-samples-language.zip` file and located in the IPP subfolder of the Intel product that includes IPP. If you have problems locating this file, you can just search for it in the `Intel` folder found in `Program Files`. For example, Intel Parallel

Composer 2011 includes the IPP samples in `Program Files\Intel\Parallel Studio 2011\Composer\Samples\en_US\IPP`.

4. Right-click the project's name in Solution Explorer and select Add Existing ⇨ Item. Go to the folder that contains the results of decompressing the `ipp-samples-language.zip` file, and locate the subfolder `ipp-samples-language\ipp-samples\language-interface\ csharp\interface`. Add all `.cs` files found in this folder (`*.cs`). This way, you will have the necessary wrappers to call the IPP functions from C#.

5. Choose an RGB (Red Green Blue) JPEG image, copy it in a new folder, and change the image path for filename in the `ApplyFilterSobelVert` method. You can use any photo taken with a digital camera and saved with the JPEG format for this example, because the photo uses three channels — red, green, and blue. The example applies a Sobel vertical filter to the image and displays the results on the screen. The default image is `C:\Pictures\Test.jpg`.

When you click the Apply Sobel Filter Vertical button, the code in the `butProcessImage_Click` event handler launches *filterTask*, which is a `Task<Bitmap>` that calls the `ApplyFilterSobelVert` method. Then, the code programs a continuation for *filterTask* that shows the results of the Sobel vertical filter applied to a JPEG image in the *imgProcessedImage* Image. To keep this example simple, the code doesn't check for errors that could occur. Instead, the code uses tasks and continuations to run the Sobel vertical filter with an asynchronous execution and to keep the UI thread unblocked until it is necessary to display the resulting image.

The `ApplyFilterSobelVert` unsafe method runs a Sobel vertical filter for the `C:\Pictures\Test .jpg` bitmap. This method prepares the source and destination data and pointers to call the image-processing IPP method that applies the filter `ipp.ip.ippiFilterSobelVert_8u_C3R`.

First, the method creates a new `Bitmap` (*originalImage*) by reading the path specified in the *fileName* local variable and locks the bits into system memory by calling the `GetBitmapData` method. The read-only bits are available through *srcBitmapData*.

Because you need to have a destination `bitmap`, the method creates a new `Bitmap` called *destinationImage*, with the same width and height as the original bitmap. Then, the code locks the bits into system memory by calling the `GetBitmapData` method. These bits are available for reading and writing through *dstBitmapData*.

The new *roi* `IppiSize` structure specifies the region of interest (ROI) for the image. Then, the code defines the byte pointers *pSrc* and *pDst*, which access the pixel data for the source and destination bitmaps. At this point, all the necessary parameters for the Sobel filter are available; therefore, the code calls the `ipp.ip.ippiFilterSobelVert_8u_C3R` method as follows:

```
IppStatus status = ipp.ip.ippiFilterSobelVert_8u_C3R(pSrc, srcBitmapData.Stride,
        pDst, dstBitmapData.Stride, roi);
```

code snippet from Listing11_4

This method applies the filter and stores the resulting pixels in the destination bitmap. Then, regardless of the results of the IPP filter, the code unlocks the bits for both source and destination bitmaps and returns *destinationImage*. However, if something went wrong, the method should check the value for the *status* variable and throw the necessary exceptions. You already know how to handle exceptions in tasks with continuations.

The *filterTask* task was defined as a Task<Bitmap>, and it returns the result of calling the ApplyFilterSobelVert method. The continuation task chained to the *filterTask* task receives this task as *antecedentTask*. If an exception occurs, the code just catches it. If the image-processing filter ran without problems, the code that runs in the same thread that created the UI controls shows the resulting bitmap in the *imgProcessedImage* control as follows:

```
filterTask.ContinueWith(
    (antecedentTask) =>
    {
        try
        {
            var outBitmap = antecedentTask.Result;
            imgProcessedImage.Source = Imaging.CreateBitmapSourceFromHBitmap(
                outBitmap.GetHbitmap(), IntPtr.Zero, System.Windows.Int32Rect.Empty,
                BitmapSizeOptions.FromWidthAndHeight(outBitmap.Width, outBitmap.Height));
        }
        catch (AggregateException ex)
        {
            foreach
                (Exception innerEx in ex.InnerExceptions)
            {
            }
        }
        butProcessImage.IsEnabled = true;
    }, uiScheduler);
```

code snippet from Listing11_4

Because this is a WPF application, you need to use the System.Windows.Interop.Imaging .CreateBitmapSourceFromHBitmap method to create a BitmapSource from a GDI+ System .Drawing.Bitmap instance.

Figure 11-7 shows an original image, and Figure 11-8 shows the WPF application's window with the same image after the Sobel vertical filter in the Image control has been applied to it.

In this example, the optimized IPP library allows you to take advantage of SIMD instructions in a C# application, and task-based programming enables you to create a responsive UI with simple code.

When the code in Listing 11-4 calls the ipp.ip.ippiFilterSobelVert_8u_C3R method, the defined P/Invoke method allows you to run the unmanaged ippiFilterSobelVert_8u_C3R function for the IPP DLL (ippi-8.0.dll). This function uses multiple threads and SIMD instructions to optimize the computation. When calling IPP routines, you should take into account the multicore-read and highly optimized software functions explained in the previous sections of this chapter.

FIGURE 11-7

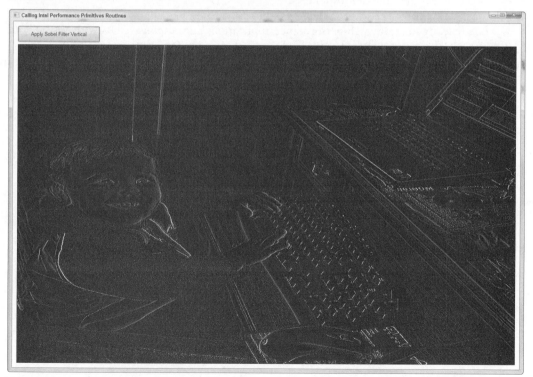

FIGURE 11-8

SUMMARY

There are many multicore-ready libraries that take advantage of SIMD instructions. Intel Math Kernel Library and Intel Integrated Performance Primitives are just two examples of how you can combine the new task-based programming model introduced in .NET Framework 4 with high-performance libraries.

To summarize this chapter:

➤ You can call routines from multicore-ready libraries.

➤ You can use libraries to take advantage of SIMD instructions from C#.

➤ You can use the `ThreadLocal<T>` class when you need simple and fast access to thread-local instances.

➤ You can use the lazy-initialization capabilities offered by the `ThreadLocal<T>` class.

➤ You can use the `ThreadSafeRandom` class to generate pseudo-random numbers from a shared instance of this class in concurrent code.

➤ You should check the documentation for optimized software functions before running them in your concurrent code.

➤ You can call IPP routines from tasks.

Now, you are ready to create high-performance applications and responsive UIs with Visual Studio 2010, C#, .NET Framework 4, and optimized external libraries. Don't forget to read the appendixes, which include additional information about useful examples, patterns, classes, and structures.

.NET 4 Parallelism Class Diagrams

This appendix includes diagrams for the classes, interfaces, structures, delegates, enumerations, and exceptions that support parallelism with the new lightweight concurrency model and the underlying threading model. There are also references to the chapters that explain the contents of these diagrams in more detail.

TASK PARALLEL LIBRARY

Figure A-1 shows a diagram of the relationship between PLINQ, the Task Parallel Library (TPL), data structures for coordination in parallel programming, threads that support the lightweight concurrency model, and layers of the underlying hardware.

This section includes diagrams for classes, structures, enumerations, and exceptions closely related to the TPL. It is divided into the following topics:

➤ System.Threading.Tasks.Parallel classes and structures

➤ Task classes, enumerations, and exceptions

System.Threading.Tasks.Parallel Classes and Structures

Figure A-2 shows the diagram for the following classes and structures within the System .Threading.Tasks namespace:

➤ Parallel

➤ ParallelLoopResult

➤ ParallelOptions

➤ ParallelLoopState

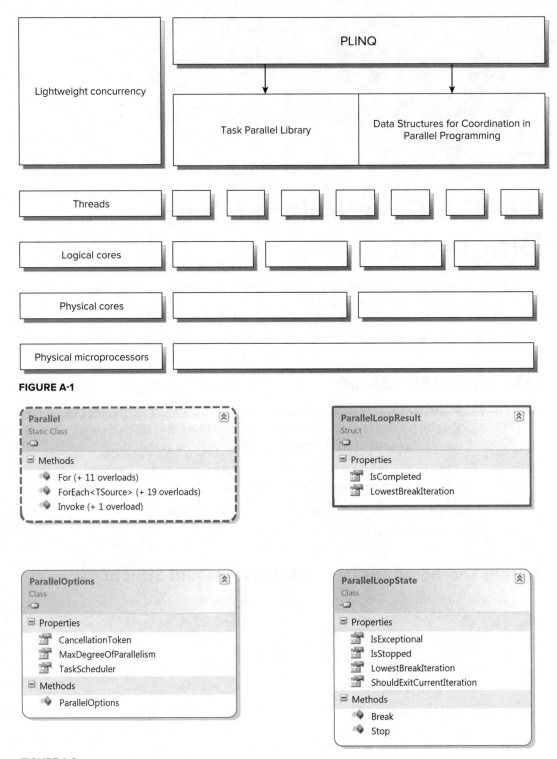

FIGURE A-1

FIGURE A-2

For more information about these classes, read Chapter 2, "Imperative Data Parallelism."

Task Classes, Enumerations, and Exceptions

Figure A-3 shows the diagram for the following classes within the System.Threading.Tasks namespace that are related to task parallelism:

➤ Task

➤ Task<TResult>

➤ TaskFactory

➤ TaskScheduler

➤ TaskFactory<TResult>

➤ TaskCompletionSource<TResult>

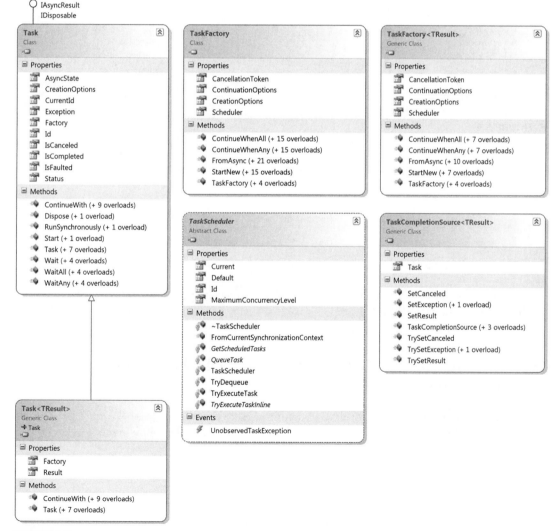

FIGURE A-3

Figure A-4 shows the diagram for the following enumerations related to `Task` creation and instances:

➤ `TaskContinuationOptions`

➤ `TaskCreationOptions`

➤ `TaskStatus`

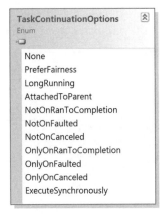

FIGURE A-4

Figure A-5 shows the diagram for the following exceptions related to task parallelism:

➤ `TaskSchedulerException`

➤ `UnobservedTaskExceptionEventArgs`

➤ `OperationCanceledException`

➤ `TaskCanceledException`

For more information about many of these classes, enumerations, and exceptions, read Chapter 3, "Imperative Task Parallelism."

DATA STRUCTURES FOR COORDINATION IN PARALLEL PROGRAMMING

This section includes diagrams for data structures used to coordinate parallel programming in the new lightweight concurrency model. It is organized according to the following topics:

➤ Concurrent collection classes: `System.Collections.Concurrent`

➤ Lightweight synchronization primitives

➤ Lazy initialization classes

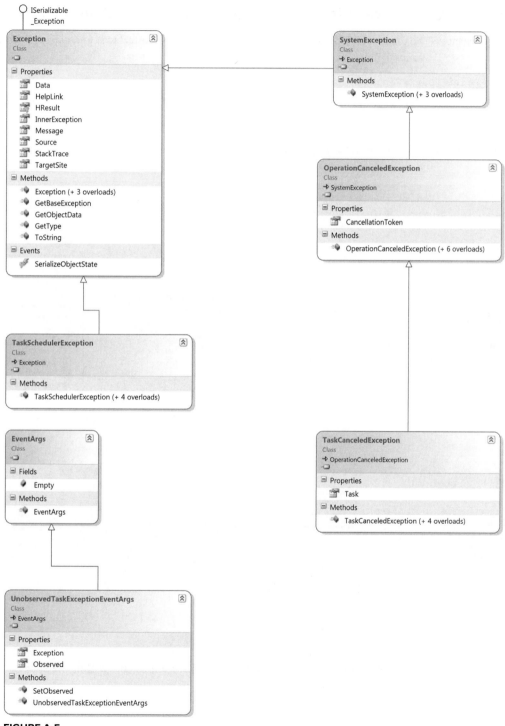

FIGURE A-5

Concurrent Collection Classes: **System.Collections.Concurrent**

Figure A-6 shows the diagram for the following concurrent collection interfaces and classes within the System.Collections.Concurrent namespace:

➤   Partitioner<TSource>

➤   OrderablePartitioner<TSource>

➤   Partitioner

➤   IProducerConsumerCollection<T>

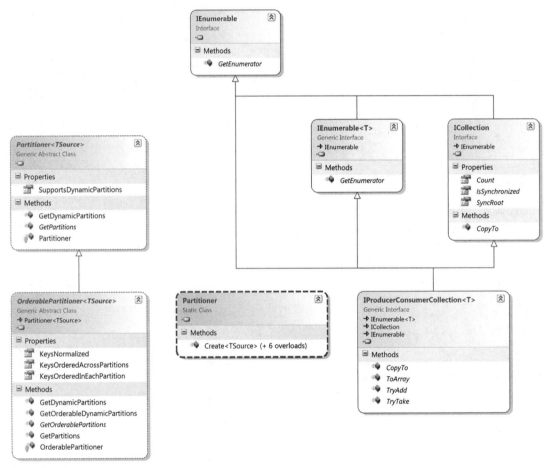

FIGURE A-6

Figure A-7 shows the diagram for the following concurrent collection classes within the System .Collections.Concurrent namespace:

➤   BlockingCollection<T>

➤   ConcurrentBag<T>

➤   `ConcurrentDictionary<TKey, TValue>`

➤   `ConcurrentQueue<T>`

➤   `ConcurrentStack<T>`

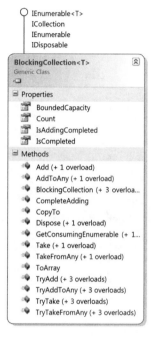

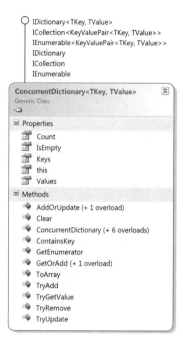

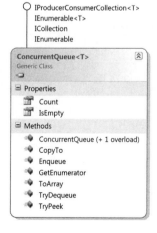

FIGURE A-7

For more information about these interfaces and classes, read Chapter 4, "Concurrent Collections."

Lightweight Synchronization Primitives

Figure A-8 shows the diagram for the following classes within the System.Threading namespace:

➤ Barrier

➤ CountdownEvent

➤ ManualResetEventSlim

➤ SemaphoreSlim

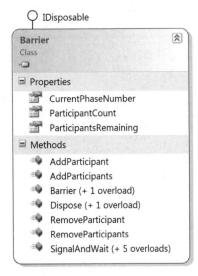

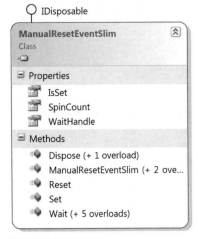

FIGURE A-8

Figure A-9 shows the diagram for the following structures within the `System.Threading` namespace:

➤   SpinLock

➤   SpinWait

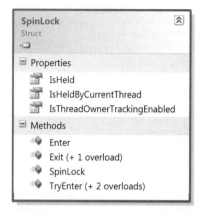

FIGURE A-9

For more information about these classes and structures, read Chapter 5, "Coordination Data Structures."

Lazy Initialization Classes

Figure A-10 shows the diagram for the following classes:

➤   System.Lazy<T>

➤   System.Threading.ThreadLocal<T>

➤   System.Threading.LazyInitializer

For more information about these classes, read Chapter 10, "Parallel Testing and Tuning."

PLINQ

Figure A-11 shows the diagram for the `System.Linq.ParallelEnumerable` static class.

For more information about this class, read Chapter 6, "PLINQ: Declarative Data Parallelism."

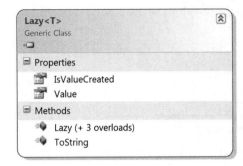

Lazy<T>
Generic Class

Properties
- IsValueCreated
- Value

Methods
- Lazy (+ 3 overloads)
- ToString

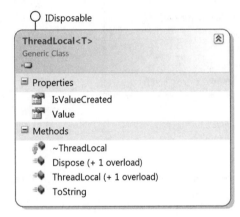

○ IDisposable

ThreadLocal<T>
Generic Class

Properties
- IsValueCreated
- Value

Methods
- ~ThreadLocal
- Dispose (+ 1 overload)
- ThreadLocal (+ 1 overload)
- ToString

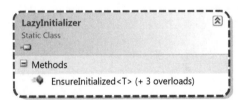

LazyInitializer
Static Class

Methods
- EnsureInitialized<T> (+ 3 overloads)

FIGURE A-10

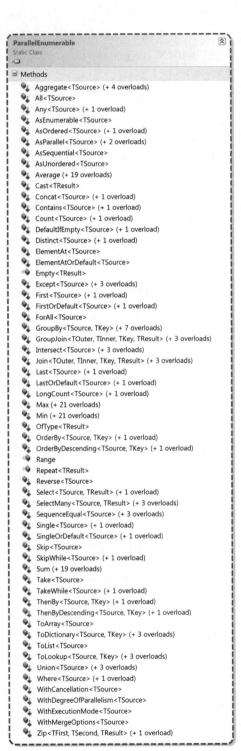

ParallelEnumerable
Static Class

Methods
- Aggregate<TSource> (+ 4 overloads)
- All<TSource>
- Any<TSource> (+ 1 overload)
- AsEnumerable<TSource>
- AsOrdered<TSource> (+ 1 overload)
- AsParallel<TSource> (+ 2 overloads)
- AsSequential<TSource>
- AsUnordered<TSource>
- Average (+ 19 overloads)
- Cast<TResult>
- Concat<TSource> (+ 1 overload)
- Contains<TSource> (+ 1 overload)
- Count<TSource> (+ 1 overload)
- DefaultIfEmpty<TSource> (+ 1 overload)
- Distinct<TSource> (+ 1 overload)
- ElementAt<TSource>
- ElementAtOrDefault<TSource>
- Empty<TResult>
- Except<TSource> (+ 3 overloads)
- First<TSource> (+ 1 overload)
- FirstOrDefault<TSource> (+ 1 overload)
- ForAll<TSource>
- GroupBy<TSource, TKey> (+ 7 overloads)
- GroupJoin<TOuter, TInner, TKey, TResult> (+ 3 overloads)
- Intersect<TSource> (+ 3 overloads)
- Join<TOuter, TInner, TKey, TResult> (+ 3 overloads)
- Last<TSource> (+ 1 overload)
- LastOrDefault<TSource> (+ 1 overload)
- LongCount<TSource> (+ 1 overload)
- Max (+ 21 overloads)
- Min (+ 21 overloads)
- OfType<TResult>
- OrderBy<TSource, TKey> (+ 1 overload)
- OrderByDescending<TSource, TKey> (+ 1 overload)
- Range
- Repeat<TResult>
- Reverse<TSource>
- Select<TSource, TResult> (+ 1 overload)
- SelectMany<TSource, TResult> (+ 3 overloads)
- SequenceEqual<TSource> (+ 3 overloads)
- Single<TSource> (+ 1 overload)
- SingleOrDefault<TSource> (+ 1 overload)
- Skip<TSource>
- SkipWhile<TSource> (+ 1 overload)
- Sum (+ 19 overloads)
- Take<TSource>
- TakeWhile<TSource> (+ 1 overload)
- ThenBy<TSource, TKey> (+ 1 overload)
- ThenByDescending<TSource, TKey> (+ 1 overload)
- ToArray<TSource>
- ToDictionary<TSource, TKey> (+ 3 overloads)
- ToList<TSource>
- ToLookup<TSource, TKey> (+ 3 overloads)
- Union<TSource> (+ 3 overloads)
- Where<TSource> (+ 1 overload)
- WithCancellation<TSource>
- WithDegreeOfParallelism<TSource>
- WithExecutionMode<TSource>
- WithMergeOptions<TSource>
- Zip<TFirst, TSecond, TResult> (+ 1 overload)

FIGURE A-11

THREADING

This section includes diagrams for classes, structures, delegates, exceptions, and components related to the threading model. It is divided into the following topics:

➤ Thread and ThreadPool classes and their exceptions

➤ Signaling classes

➤ Structures, delegates, and enumerations for threading

➤ BackgroundWorker component

Thread and ThreadPool Classes and Their Exceptions

Figure A-12 shows the diagram for the following classes and exceptions closely related to Thread and ThreadPool within the System.Threading namespace:

➤ Thread

➤ ThreadPool

➤ ThreadAbortException

➤ ThreadInterruptedException

➤ ThreadStartException

➤ ThreadStateException

For more information about these classes and exceptions, read Chapter 8, "Thread Pools."

Signaling Classes

Figure A-13 shows the diagram for the following signaling classes within the System.Threading namespace:

➤ WaitHandle

➤ EventWaitHandle

➤ AutoResetEvent

➤ ManualResetEvent

➤ Mutex

Figure A-14 shows the diagram for the following classes and exceptions within the System .Threading namespace:

➤ AbandonedMutexException

➤ CancellationTokenSource

➤ CompressedStack

- ➤ CountdownEvent

- ➤ ExecutionContext

- ➤ HostExecutionContext

- ➤ HostExecutionContextManager

- ➤ Interlocked

- ➤ LockRecursionException

- ➤ Monitor

- ➤ Overlapped

- ➤ ReaderWriterLock

- ➤ RegisteredWaitHandle

- ➤ SemaphoreFullException

- ➤ SynchronizationContext

- ➤ SynchronizationLockException

- ➤ Timeout

- ➤ Timer

- ➤ WaitHandleCannotBeOpenedException

For more information about some of these classes and exceptions, read Chapter 5, "Coordination Data Structures", Chapter 8, "Thread Pools" and Chapter 10, "Parallel Testing and Tuning."

Threading Structures, Delegates, and Enumerations

Figure A-15 shows the diagram for the following structures within the System.Threading namespace:

- ➤ AsyncFlowControl

- ➤ CancellationToken

- ➤ CancellationTokenRegistration

- ➤ LockCookie

- ➤ NativeOverlapped

_Thread
Interface

Methods
- GetIDsOfNames
- GetTypeInfo
- GetTypeInfoCount
- Invoke

ThreadPool
Static Class

Methods
- BindHandle (+ 1 overload)
- GetAvailableThreads
- GetMaxThreads
- GetMinThreads
- QueueUserWorkItem (+ 1 overload)
- RegisterWaitForSingleObject (+ 3 overloads)
- SetMaxThreads
- SetMinThreads
- UnsafeQueueNativeOverlapped
- UnsafeQueueUserWorkItem
- UnsafeRegisterWaitForSingleObject (+ 3 overloads)

○ _Thread

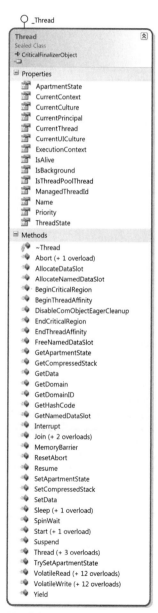

Thread
Sealed Class
→ CriticalFinalizerObject

Properties
- ApartmentState
- CurrentContext
- CurrentCulture
- CurrentPrincipal
- CurrentThread
- CurrentUICulture
- ExecutionContext
- IsAlive
- IsBackground
- IsThreadPoolThread
- ManagedThreadId
- Name
- Priority
- ThreadState

Methods
- ~Thread
- Abort (+ 1 overload)
- AllocateDataSlot
- AllocateNamedDataSlot
- BeginCriticalRegion
- BeginThreadAffinity
- DisableComObjectEagerCleanup
- EndCriticalRegion
- EndThreadAffinity
- FreeNamedDataSlot
- GetApartmentState
- GetCompressedStack
- GetData
- GetDomain
- GetDomainID
- GetHashCode
- GetNamedDataSlot
- Interrupt
- Join (+ 2 overloads)
- MemoryBarrier
- ResetAbort
- Resume
- SetApartmentState
- SetCompressedStack
- SetData
- Sleep (+ 1 overload)
- SpinWait
- Start (+ 1 overload)
- Suspend
- Thread (+ 3 overloads)
- TrySetApartmentState
- VolatileRead (+ 12 overloads)
- VolatileWrite (+ 12 overloads)
- Yield

ThreadAbortException
Sealed Class
→ SystemException

Properties
- ExceptionState

ThreadInterruptedException
Class
→ SystemException

Methods
- ThreadInterruptedException (+ 3 overloads)

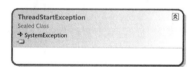

ThreadStartException
Sealed Class
→ SystemException

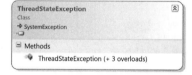

ThreadStateException
Class
→ SystemException

Methods
- ThreadStateException (+ 3 overloads)

FIGURE A-12

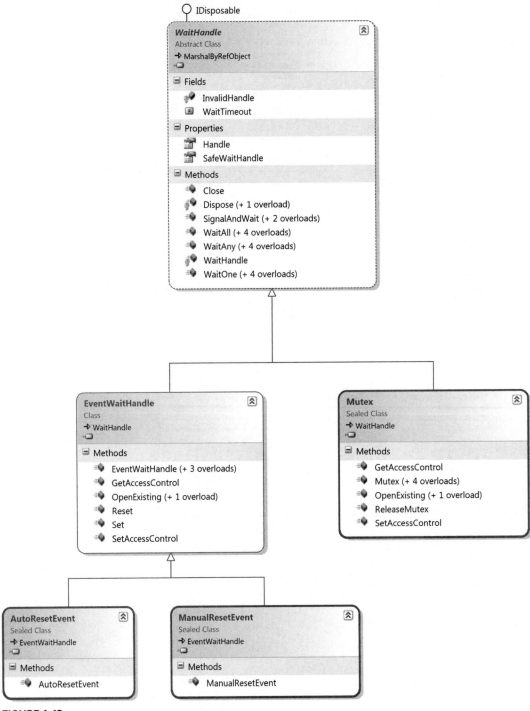

FIGURE A-13

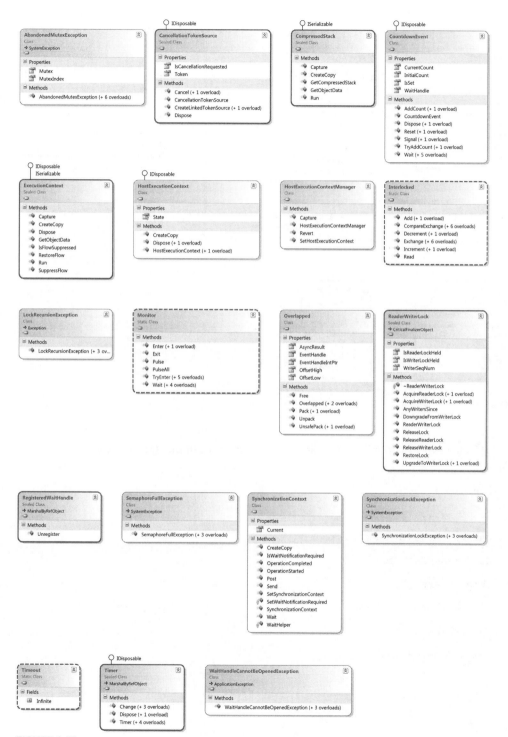

FIGURE A-14

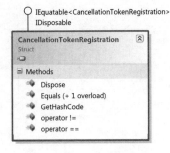

FIGURE A-15

Figure A-16 shows the diagram for the following delegates within the System.Threading namespace:

➤ ContextCallback

➤ IOCompletionCallback

➤ ParameterizedThreadStart

➤ SendOrPostCallback

➤ ThreadStart

➤ TimerCallback

➤ WaitCallback

➤ WaitOrTimerCallback

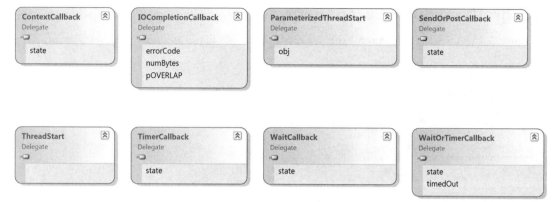

FIGURE A-16

Figure A-17 shows the diagram for the following enumerations within the System.Threading namespace:

- ➤ ApartmentState
- ➤ EventResetMode
- ➤ ThreadPriority
- ➤ ThreadState

FIGURE A-17

For more information about some of these structures, delegates, and enumerations, read Chapter 8, "Thread Pools."

BackgroundWorker Component

Figure A-18 shows the diagram for the System.ComponentModel.BackgroundWorker component.

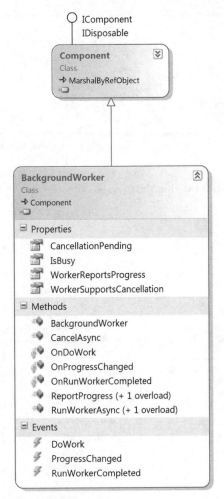

FIGURE A-18

B

Concurrent UML Models

Version 2.2 of the *Unified Modeling Language* (UML) infrastructure specification doesn't define many specific features related to concurrency. You can extend UML definitions to provide some visual guidelines and additional notations in models that consider concurrency. The new definitions can help both architects and developers to understand designs prepared for concurrency.

This appendix gives you some examples of how you can use UML models to represent designs and code prepared for both concurrency and parallelism. You can extend the classic models by adding a few simple and standardized visual elements. However, some models don't need changes; therefore, this appendix doesn't include them.

Visual Studio 2010 Ultimate supports some of the modeling diagrams, based on UML infrastructure specification 2.1.2. This appendix explains how Visual Studio 2010 Ultimate modeling features support a specific diagram, if at all.

STRUCTURE DIAGRAMS

Structure diagrams describe the structure of a system from different points of view. The following four structure diagrams would benefit from additional notations related to concurrency and parallelism:

- ➤ Class diagram
- ➤ Component diagram
- ➤ Deployment diagram
- ➤ Package diagram

Class Diagram

Visual Studio 2010 Ultimate modeling features support UML class diagrams. However, you need to specify new stereotypes, as described in Table B-1.

TABLE B-1: New Stereotypes for a Class Diagram

DESCRIPTION	STEREOTYPE
Immutable data types	`immutable`
Immutable classes	`immutable`
Optimized operations (methods that run using many tasks or threads). These operations use techniques to take advantage of multiple cores. Therefore, it isn't necessary to parallelize the execution of these operations, because it is already parallelized under the hood.	`parallelized`
Thread-safe types	`thread-safe`
Thread-safe classes	`thread-safe`
Stateless classes	`stateless`

Thread-safe also means task-safe. In other words, a thread-safe type or class is prepared for concurrency.

Visual Studio Ultimate provides the `Concurrency` property for an operation in a class or interface on a UML class diagram. The three possible values for this property are the following:

➤ **`Sequential`** — The operation isn't prepared for concurrency. Calling this operation concurrently might result in failures.

➤ **`Guarded`** — The operation will wait for another instance to complete before starting its execution.

➤ **`Concurrent`** — Multiple calls to this operation can run concurrently without problems. The operation is thread-safe and was designed with concurrency in mind.

The problem is that assigning any of the aforementioned values to the `Concurrency` property doesn't change the visual representation of the operation. However, if you use stereotypes like the ones shown in Table B-1, they display labels on modeled classes to help you visualize the concurrency behavior of these classes. Figure B-1 shows a diagram for the

«thread-safe» **Statistical**
«parallelized» +CalculateStandardDeviation() : double «parallelized» +CalculateKutosis() : double «parallelized» +CalculateSkewness() : double

FIGURE B-1

thread-safe `Statistical` class that provides three methods: `CalculateStandardDeviation`, `CalculateKurtosis`, and `CalculateSkewness`. These methods are already optimized to take advantage of the available logical cores, as indicated by the `parallelized` stereotype.

Component Diagram

Visual Studio 2010 Ultimate modeling features support UML class diagrams. However, you need to specify a new stereotype, `parallelized`, to indicate that all the services provided by a specific component must run optimized to take full advantage of multiple cores in the machine or machines in which the component is executed. This way, you can detect components that should be optimized according to the deployment plans and the performance requirements for the software system. Additional notes can provide details about the parallelization level achieved by the

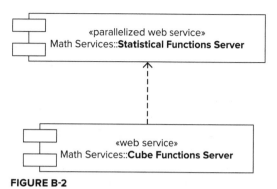

FIGURE B-2

component. Figure B-2 shows a component diagram with two Web Services: `Statistical Functions Server` and `Cube Functions Server`. The former takes advantage of parallelism, and the latter runs without special optimizations.

Deployment Diagram

You can use constraints and notes to include information regarding the number of minimum hardware threads that certain nodes require. This information must consider the minimum requirements to offer reasonable performance improvements through parallelization.

Figure B-3 shows a simple deployment diagram with three nodes: `Client`, `ApplicationServer`, and `DatabaseServer`. These nodes include constraints that provide information about the minimum number of hardware threads for the hardware that is going to support it and the recommended operating system version.

Package Diagram

You must specify a new stereotype with the parallelized prefix (such as `parallelized services`) to indicate that the package contains a group of services optimized to take full advantage of multiple cores. The package diagram helps you identify the packages that could be optimized to improve the overall performance. Figure B-4 shows a package diagram with a `Business Intelligence` system that has access to the parallelized services contained in the `Math Services` package.

BEHAVIOR DIAGRAMS

Behavior diagrams describe what happens in the system being modeled from different points of view. The following two behavior diagrams would benefit from additional notations related to concurrency and parallelism:

➤ Activity diagram

➤ Use case diagram

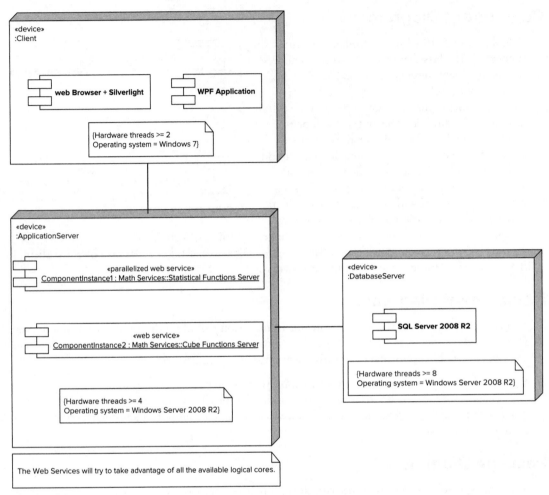

FIGURE B-3

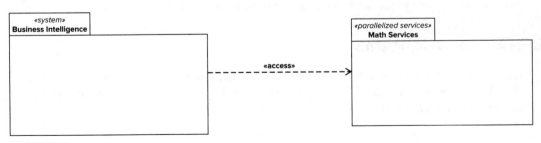

FIGURE B-4

Activity Diagram

Visual Studio 2010 Ultimate modeling features support UML activity diagrams. An activity diagram provides the following four symbols related to multiple threads, shown in Figure B-5, and one optional zone representation rectangle:

➤ **Accept event action** — Defines an action that can wait for a signal or event. This is useful for modeling when a task or a thread has to wait for certain signals, such as a request for cancellation.

➤ **Send signal to action** — Defines an action that sends a signal to another task, thread, system, or event.

➤ **Fork node** — Defines a fork node where each incoming task or thread splits into many concurrent tasks or threads. Because the original definition is only related to threads, you can add a note indicating that the design splits an incoming task into multiple tasks.

➤ **Join node** — Defines a join node that brings together several threads, waiting for them to finish before continuing with the next actions. Because the original definition is only related to threads, you can add a note indicating that the design allows a single task to emerge from the outgoing flow. This single task is going to be supported by a thread.

➤ **Swim lane** — Defines a horizontal or vertical zone that allows grouping elements of the activity diagram according to the subprocesses that compose it. It can also be used to represent different threads or tasks, but Visual Studio 2010 Ultimate modeling features don't support swim lanes. Therefore, you have to add a rectangle and a comment to build a swim lane. It is also known as *swimlane* (one word).

Figure B-6 shows an activity diagram with a fork node that starts four tasks that run concurrent actions: `ConvertEllipses`, `ConvertRectangles`, `ConvertLines`, and `ConvertText`. In addition, there is a join node that waits for these four tasks to finish and then continues with the `MergeConversions` action. Two notes add information to the model, indicating that the fork and join nodes are related to tasks instead of threads.

Use Case Diagram

Visual Studio 2010 Ultimate modeling features support UML use case diagrams. A use case diagram provides you with a great opportunity to start thinking about potential scenarios that could occur in parallel and that would benefit from parallelism.

The classic definition for a use case is that it describes a sequence of actions that provide something of measurable value to an actor. However, it can also describe sequences of parallel actions if it

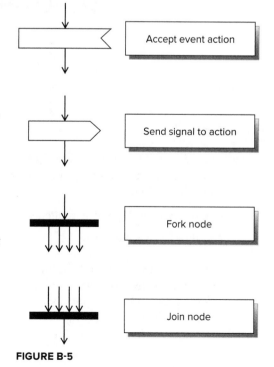

FIGURE B-5

is implemented with parallelism in mind. Also, many use cases could be executed concurrently. Of course, the use case diagram doesn't need to include details about the technical implementation, but it is a good idea to use this diagram to plan for parallelism.

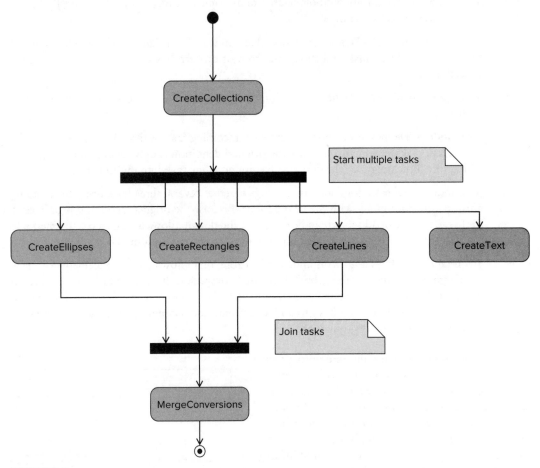

FIGURE B-6

Figure B-7 shows a simple use case diagram with many use cases related to an order processing system. The note indicates that a Customer, the actor, should be able to perform the following two use cases in parallel:

➤ Browse catalog and select items

➤ Preview a 3D model

This use case diagram provides useful information about the possibilities to consider parallelism to implement the two use cases. A user might need to perform both use cases at the same time; and therefore, there is a great opportunity to run these two use cases in parallel. A use case diagram is also particularly useful to prioritize the use cases that must take advantage of parallelism to offer the best response time.

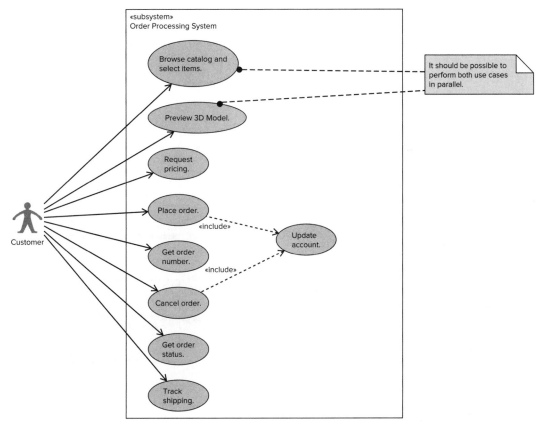

FIGURE B-7

INTERACTION DIAGRAMS

Interaction diagrams describe the flow of data and control operations among the diverse elements in the system being modeled from different points of view. They are a subset of the previously explained behavior diagrams. The following two behavior diagrams would benefit from additional notations related to concurrency and parallelism:

➤ Interaction overview diagram

➤ Sequence diagram

Interaction Overview Diagram

This diagram is similar to the activity diagram; therefore, all the additions explained for the activity diagram also apply to this diagram. An interaction overview diagram emphasizes the high-level control flow and can include nodes with references to other diagrams. It is useful to include comments explaining whether these nodes have a sequential or a parallel execution.

Figure B-8 shows a simple interaction overview diagram with three nodes that include references to sequence diagrams: `CreateCollections`, `ConvertCollections`, and `MergeConversions`. These nodes include comments that provide information about the kind of execution implemented. The `ConvertCollections` node runs parallelized using multiple tasks.

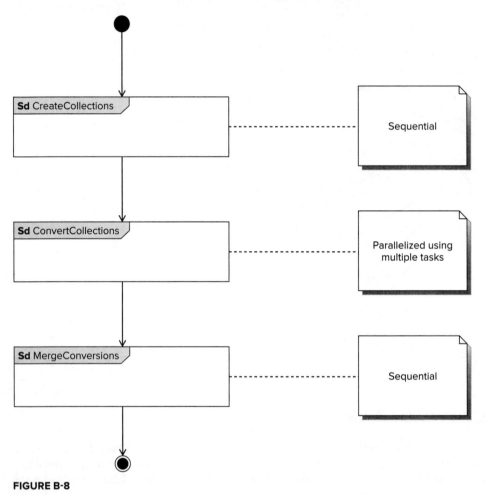

FIGURE B-8

Sequence Diagram

Visual Studio 2010 Ultimate modeling features support UML sequence diagrams. A sequence diagram is very important to depict the interaction between instances and methods running in different tasks and threads. Therefore, it is very important that you add information about the task or thread that the object lifeline is representing for the object. In fact, thread-safe instances can run code in many different tasks or threads at the same time. Thus, sometimes, you need to add many lifelines for a single object, each one representing a different task or thread. This way, the sequence diagram can represent parallel sequences.

For example, Figure B-9 shows a simple sequence diagram in which there are many calls to methods for the `OptimizedMath` object in the main thread (the UI thread) and in two other tasks (*t1* and *t2*).

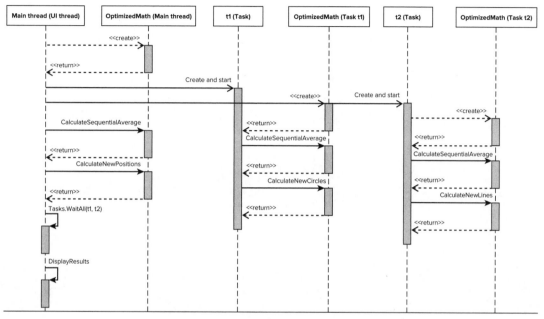

FIGURE B-9

In the figure, the `OptimizedMath` object appears in the following three lifelines:

➤ **OptimizedMath (Main thread)** — This instance runs in the main thread.

➤ **OptimizedMath (Task t1)** — This instance runs in a different task, *t1*, which is supported by a thread.

➤ **OptimizedMath (Task t2)** — This instance runs in a different task, *t2*, which is supported by a thread.

It is very easy to visualize the concurrent tasks and the potential parallelism that can happen with these sequences, because parallelism is represented with different instances for the `OptimizedMath` object.

Parallel Extensions Extras

Parallel Extensions Extras is a complementary project that isn't part of the .NET Framework 4 classes, but it has been developed by Microsoft and is part of the parallel programming samples for .NET Framework 4. These extras aren't production quality because they are neither fully tested nor stable code bases. However, they include the source code, and you can tailor them for your specific needs. This appendix includes diagrams and brief descriptions for the classes and structures that compose the Parallel Extensions Extras.

INSPECTING PARALLEL EXTENSIONS EXTRAS

The Parallel Extensions Extras are a bit hidden because they are included in one of the projects in the Parallel Extensions Samples. The direct link to download the latest Samples version is `http://code.msdn.microsoft.com/ParExtSamples/Release/ProjectReleases.aspx`. So, if you download these samples for parallel programming with .NET 4, you can find and inspect the `ParallelExtensionsExtras` project that contains all the extras organized in many folders. Figure C-1 displays the contents for this project in Visual Studio 2010 Solution Explorer.

The Parallel Extensions Extras project contains seven folders at the time of this writing. These folders and their subfolders contain classes, and these classes belong to diverse namespaces. Table C-1 provides a brief summary of each class and its related namespace and folder.

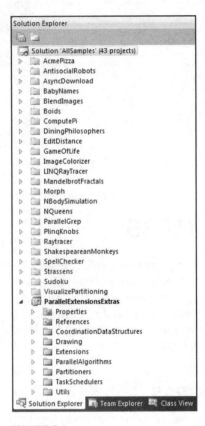

FIGURE C-1

TABLE C-1: Parallel Extensions Extras Project Folders, Namespaces, and Classes

FOLDER	NAMESPACE	CLASS NAME
Coordination DataStructures	System.Threading	ActionCountdownEvent
Coordination DataStructures	System.Collections .Concurrent	ConcurrentPriorityQueue<TKey, TValue>
Coordination DataStructures	System.Collections .Concurrent	ObjectPool<T>
Coordination DataStructures	System.Collections .Concurrent	ObservableConcurrentCollection <T>
Coordination DataStructures	System.Collections .Concurrent	ObservableConcurrentDictionary <TKey, TValue>
Coordination DataStructures	System.Threading	Pipeline

FOLDER	NAMESPACE	CLASS NAME
Coordination DataStructures	System.Threading	Pipeline<TInput, TOutput>
Coordination DataStructures	System.Collections .Concurrent	ProducerConsumerCollectionBase <T>
Coordination DataStructures	System.Threading	Reduction Variable<T>
Coordination DataStructures	System.Threading.Tasks	SerialTaskQueue
Coordination DataStructures	System.Threading	SpinLockClass
Coordination DataStructures	System.Threading	ThreadSafeRandom
Coordination DataStructures	System.Threading	TransferStream
Coordination DataStructures\ AsyncCoordination	System.Threading.Async	AsyncBarrier
Coordination DataStructures\ AsyncCoordination	System.Threading	AsyncCache<TKey, TValue>
Coordination DataStructures\ AsyncCoordination	System.Threading.Tasks	AsyncCall
Coordination DataStructures\ AsyncCoordination	System.Threading.Tasks	AsyncCall<T>
Coordination DataStructures\ AsyncCoordination	System.Threading.Async	AsyncProducerConsumer Collection<T>
Coordination DataStructures\ AsyncCoordination	System.Threading.Async	AsyncReaderWriter
Coordination DataStructures\ AsyncCoordination	System.Threading.Async	AsyncSemaphore

continues

TABLE C-1 *(continued)*

FOLDER	NAMESPACE	CLASS NAME
Coordination DataStructures\ AsyncCoordination	System.Threading.Async	HtmlAsyncCache
Drawing	Microsoft.Drawing	FastBitmap
Extensions	System	AggregateExceptionExtensions
Extensions	System.Collections .Concurrent	BlockingCollectionExtensions
Extensions	System.Threading	CancellationTokenExtensions
Extensions	System.Threading.Tasks	CompletedTask
Extensions	System	DelegateBasedObserver<T>
Extensions	System	DelegateExtensions
Extensions	System.Collections .Concurrent	IProducerConsumerCollection Extensions
Extensions	System	LazyExtensions
Extensions	System.Linq	LinqToTasks
Extensions	System.Linq	ParallelLinqOptions
Extensions	System.Threading.Tasks	ParallelOptionsExtensions
Extensions	System.Linq	PlinqExtensions
Extensions	System.Threading.Tasks	TaskCompletionSourceExtensions
Extensions	System.Threading.Tasks	TaskExtrasExtensions
Extensions	System.Threading.Tasks	TaskSchedulerExtensions
Extensions\APM	System.IO	FileAsync
Extensions\APM	System.IO	StreamExtensions
Extensions\APM	System.Net	WebRequestExtensions
Extensions\EAP	System.Threading.Tasks	EAPCommon
Extensions\EAP	System.Net .NetworkInformation	PingExtensions
Extensions\EAP	System.Net .NetworkInformation	SmtpClientExtensions
Extensions\EAP	System.Net	WebClientExtensions

FOLDER	NAMESPACE	CLASS NAME
Extensions\TaskFactoryExtensions	System.Threading.Tasks	TaskFactoryExtensions
ParallelAlgorithms	System.Threading.Algorithms	ParallelAlgorithms
Partitioners	System.Collections.Concurrent.Partitioners	ChunkPartitioner
Partitioners	System.Collections.Concurrent.Partitioners	SingleItemPartitioner
TaskSchedulers	System.Threading.Tasks.Schedulers	ConcurrentExclusiveInterleave
TaskSchedulers	System.Threading.Tasks.Schedulers	CurrentThreadTaskScheduler
TaskSchedulers	System.Threading.Tasks.Schedulers	IOCompletionPortTaskScheduler
TaskSchedulers	System.Threading.Tasks.Schedulers	IOTaskScheduler
TaskSchedulers	System.Threading.Tasks.Schedulers	LimitedConcurrencyLevelTaskScheduler
TaskSchedulers	System.Threading.Tasks.Schedulers	OrderedTaskScheduler
TaskSchedulers	System.Threading.Tasks.Schedulers	QueuedTaskScheduler
TaskSchedulers	System.Threading.Tasks.Schedulers	ReprioritizableTaskScheduler
TaskSchedulers	System.Threading.Tasks.Schedulers	RoundRobinTaskSchedulerQueue
TaskSchedulers	System.Threading.Tasks.Schedulers	RoundRobinSchedulerGroup
TaskSchedulers	System.Threading.Tasks.Schedulers	StaTaskScheduler

continues

TABLE C-1 *(continued)*

FOLDER	NAMESPACE	CLASS NAME
TaskSchedulers	System.Threading .Tasks.Schedulers	SynchronizationContext TaskScheduler
TaskSchedulers	System.Threading .Tasks.Schedulers	ThreadPer TaskScheduler
TaskSchedulers	System.Threading .Tasks.Schedulers	WorkStealing TaskScheduler
Utils	System.Linq	SortedTopN<TKey, TValue>

This appendix describes the Parallel Extensions Extras project's structure — including its most relevant classes, folders, and subfolders — in more detail.

COORDINATION DATA STRUCTURES

The CoordinationDataStructures folder includes classes that provide new synchronous and asynchronous coordination data structures, concurrent collections, and data processing features. Figure C-2 shows the diagram for the following classes within the CoordinationDataStructures folder:

➤ ProducerConsumerCollectionBase<*T*> — Provides a base implementation for producer-consumer collections that wrap other producer-consumer collections. It is an abstract class. *T* specifies the type of the elements stored in the collection.

➤ ObjectPool<*T*> — Provides a thread-safe object pool. *T* specifies the type of the elements stored in the pool.

➤ ObservableConcurrentCollection<*T*> — Provides a thread-safe, concurrent collection for use with data binding. *T* specifies the type of elements in the collection.

➤ TransferStream — Implements a writeable stream for using a separate task in a producer-consumer scenario.

Figure C-3 shows the diagram for the following classes within the CoordinationDataStructures folder:

➤ ActionCountdownEvent — Runs an action specified by a delegate when a CountdownEvent reaches zero.

➤ ConcurrentPriorityQueue<*TKey*, *TValue*> — Provides a thread-safe priority queue data structure. *TKey* specifies the type of keys used to prioritize values, and *TValue* determines the type of elements in the queue.

➤ ObservableConcurrentDictionary<*TKey*, *TValue*> — Provides a thread-safe, concurrent dictionary for use with data binding. *TKey* specifies the type of keys in the dictionary, and *TValue* determines the type of the values.

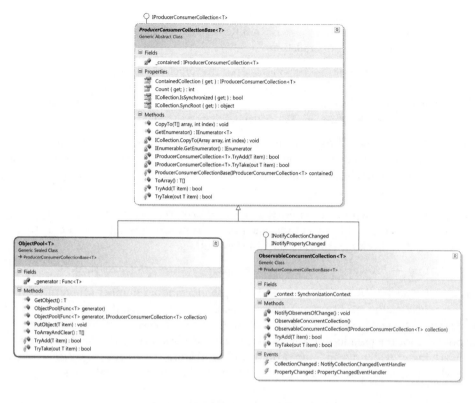

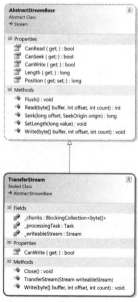

FIGURE C-2

➤ `Pipeline` — Provides support for pipelined data processing. It uses `ThreadPerTaskScheduler` so that each task that represents a stage uses a different thread whenever possible. This class supports customized degrees of parallelism.

➤ `Pipeline<TInput, TOutput>` — Provides support for pipelined data processing. `TInput` specifies the type of the input data to the pipeline, and `TOutput` determines the output data from the pipeline's stage. This class supports cancellation and customized degrees of parallelism. It uses the `ThreadPerTaskScheduler` defined in the `Pipeline` class.

➤ `ReductionVariable<T>` — Provides a reduction variable for aggregating data across multiple threads involved in a computation. `T` specifies the type for the data aggregated and the accumulated value. This class uses thread-local storage for each thread's value. The class is useful for performing the reduction computations in Map Reduce algorithms.

➤ `SerialTaskQueue` — Represents an ordered queue of tasks that has to be started and executed serially. This class allows you to queue tasks to be processed serially according to a LIFO order and to check the status of the tasks' executions.

➤ `SpinLockClass` — Provides a reference type wrapper for the `SpinLock` structure.

➤ `ThreadSafeRandom` — Represents a thread-safe pseudo-random number generator. This class is a subclass of `Random` and overrides its `Next`, `NextDouble`, and `NextBytes` methods. The class uses `System.Security.Cryptography.RNGCryptoServiceProvider` as the seed provider for the pseudo-number generator, and one instance of the `Random` class as the underlying provider of randomness in thread-local storage for each thread. This class is useful when you need to generate pseudo-random numbers in different threads.

Figure C-4 shows the diagram for the following classes within the `CoordinationDataStructures\` `AsyncCoordination` subfolder:

➤ `AsyncCache<TKey, TValue>` — Caches asynchronously received data. `TKey` specifies the type of the cache's keys, and `TValue` determines the type of the cache's values. This class uses tasks to asynchronously produce each cache's value. The class offers an enumerator to access the contents of the cache.

➤ `HtmlAsyncCache` — Provides an asynchronous cache for downloaded HTML. It is a subclass of `AsyncCache<Uri, string>`, and it uses the `DownloadStringTask` method defined in the `WebClientExtensions` class. The `WebClientExtensions` class is included in the `Extensions\EAP` subfolder.

➤ `AsyncBarrier` — Provides an asynchronous barrier. When a round completes, it signals a task.

➤ `AsyncCall<T>` — Allows you to asynchronously invoke a handler for every posted item. `T` specifies the type of data posted by the instance. This class is a subclass of `MarshalByRefObject`.

➤ `AsyncCall` — Provides static factory methods for creating instances of `AsyncCall<T>`.

➤ `AsyncProducerConsumerCollection<T>` — Provides an asynchronous producer-consumer collection. `T` specifies the type of the elements stored in the collection. This class uses an `AsyncSemaphore` to keep track of asynchronous work.

➤ `AsyncReaderWriter` — Provides asynchronous execution of exclusive and concurrent readers, and exclusive writers. You can specify the desired `TaskFactory` to initialize the `AsyncReaderWriter` instance.

➤ `AsyncSemaphore` — Provides an asynchronous semaphore.

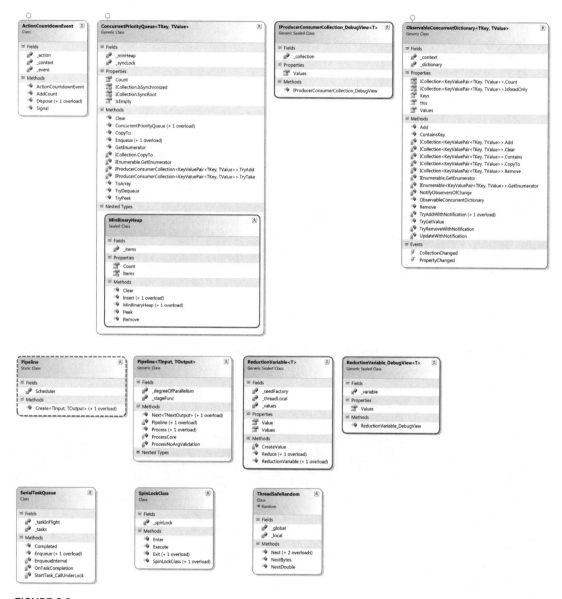

FIGURE C-3

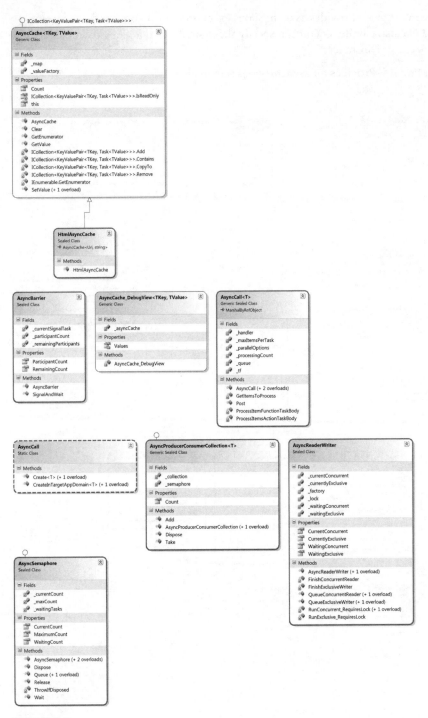

FIGURE C-4

EXTENSIONS

The Extensions folder includes classes that provide new extension methods to add features to existing classes and interfaces. Figure C-5 shows the diagram for the following classes within the Extensions folder:

➤ AggregateExceptionExtensions — Adds extension methods for AggregateException.

➤ BlockingCollectionExtensions — Adds extension methods for BlockingCollection.

➤ CancellationTokenExtensions — Adds extension methods for CancellationToken.

➤ CompletedTask — Provides access to a Task instance that has already completed its execution. You can access a completed task to use ContinueWith overloads when you can't work with StartNew.

➤ CompletedTask<TResult> — Provides access to a Task<TResult> instance that has already completed its execution.

➤ DelegateBasedObserver<T> — This internal class implements IObserver<T> and allows you to define three actions: OnCompleted, OnError, and OnNext.

➤ DelegateExtensions — Adds the parallel extensions for delegates: ParallelDynamicInvoke for Delegate, WithFailFast for Action, and WithFailFast<T> for Func<T>.

➤ LazyExtensions — Adds extension methods related to Lazy for Lazy<T> and Task<T>.

➤ LinqToTasks — Implements the primary standard query operators to tasks. This class provides LINQ support for Task instances.

➤ ParallelLinqExtensions — Adds the following public extension methods to PLINQ:

  ➤ AsParallel<TSource> — Enables you to define a ParallelLinqOptions instance to define the PLINQ options. TSource specifies the type of the input elements.

  ➤ MapReduce<TSource, TMapped, TKey, TResult> — Implements a Map Reduce operation. TSource specifies the type of the source elements. TMapped indicates the type of the mapped elements, TKey specifies the type of the element keys, and TResult defines the type of the result.

  ➤ OutputToProducerConsumerCollection<TSource> — Executes the query and outputs its results into a target collection that implements IProducerConsumerCollection <TSource>. TSource specifies the type of the source and target elements.

  ➤ TakeTop<TSource, TKey> — Takes a top number of elements as if they were sorted. This method uses a specified function to extract a key from each element in the source. The method uses SortedTopN<TKey, TValue>, included within the Utils folder, to keep a sorted list per thread in order to keep track of the best N elements for each thread. TSource specifies the type of the source elements. TKey specifies the type of the element keys.

➤ ParallelLinqOptions — Provides groups with common PLINQ options.

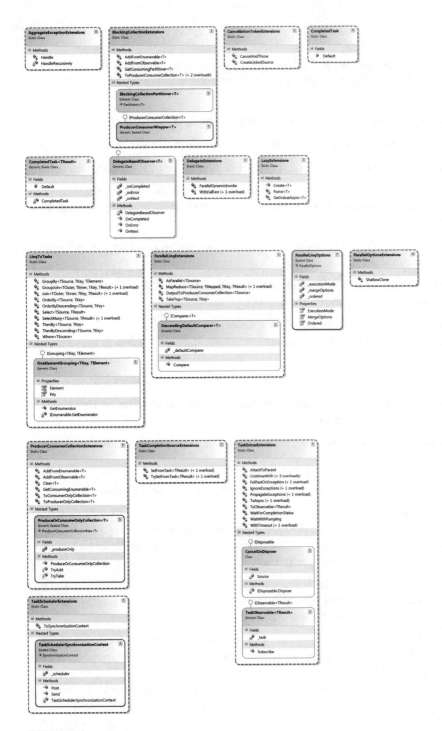

FIGURE C-5

➤ ParallelOptionsExtensions — Provides the ShallowClone extension method for ParallelOptions. This method returns a shallow clone from the ParallelOptions instance.

➤ ProducerConsumerCollectionExtensions — Adds extension methods for IProducerConsumerCollection.

➤ TaskCompletionSourceExtensions — Adds the following public extension methods for TaskCompletionSource:

 ➤ SetFromTask<*TResult*> — The two definitions for this method transfer the result of a Task or Task<*TResult*> to the TaskCompletionSource. *TResult* specifies the type of the result.

 ➤ TrySetFromTask<*TResult*> — The two definitions for this method provide the aforementioned functionality, but they return a Boolean value indicating whether the transfer could be completed.

➤ TaskExtrasExtensions — Adds the following public extension methods for Task:

 ➤ AttachToParent — This method ensures that a parent task can't transition to TaskStatus.RanToCompletion state until the Task instance that calls this method has also completed. The method ensures this condition even if the Task instance that calls this method isn't already a child task.

 ➤ ContinueWith — The four definitions for this method create a continuation task using the TaskFactory instance specified as a parameter.

 ➤ FailFastOnException — The two definitions for this method fail immediately when an exception is encountered in the Task instance. These methods create a continuation for the task that runs only if the task is faulted, and call the Environment .FailFast method to immediately terminate the process after writing a message to the Windows Application event log.

 ➤ IgnoreExceptions — The two definitions for this method suppress the default exception handling of the Task instance. These methods create a continuation for the task that runs only if the task is faulted. They prevent the exception from rising to the finalizer thread.

 ➤ PropagateExceptions — The two definitions for this method propagate any exceptions that occurred on the Task instance or on the array of Task instances.

 ➤ ToAsync — The two definitions for this method create and return a new Task or Task<*TResult*> instance that represents the completion of the Task instance that calls ToAsync. The methods schedule a specified AsyncCallback to run upon completion of the Task instance that calls ToAsync.

 ➤ ToObservable<*TResult*> — This method creates and returns an IObservable<*TResult*> that represents the completion of the Task instance that calls this method.

 ➤ WaitForCompletionStatus — This method waits for the Task instance to complete its execution, and returns the TaskStatus value for this Task instance's Status property. This method is useful to write code that considers a task's completion status in order to perform appropriate follow-up processing. You can use this method if you want to wait for a task, but you don't want the `Wait` method to raise an exception.

➤ `WaitWithPumping` — This method is designed to help testing procedures with WPF applications. The method enters a message loop that exits when the `Task` instance completes its execution. The method adds a continuation to exit the message loop. You can use this method to wait for a task to complete in the UI thread of a WPF application without blocking this thread. This method allows you to maintain a responsive application during the time the task is being executed.

➤ `WithTimeout` — The two definitions for this method create and return a new `Task` or `Task<TResult>` instance that clones the `Task` or `Task<TResult>` instance that calls `WithTimeout`. The new task will be canceled after the timeout specified as a parameter.

➤ `TaskSchedulerExtensions` — Adds a new extension method for `TaskScheduler`. The new `ToSynchronizationContext` extension method gets and returns a `SynchronizationContext` that targets the `TaskScheduler` instance.

Figure C-6 shows the diagram for the following classes within the `CoordinationDataStructures\` `APM` subfolder:

➤ `FileAsync` — This class provides asynchronous counterparts to the members of the `File` class.

➤ `StreamExtensions` — This class defines extension methods for working with asynchronous streams. The extension methods work for the `Stream` class.

➤ `WebRequestExtensions` — This class defines extension methods for working with asynchronous Web requests. The extension methods work for the `WebRequest` class.

Figure C-7 shows the diagram for the following classes within the `CoordinationDataStructures\` `EAP` subfolder:

➤ `PingExtensions` — This class defines extension methods for working with the `Ping` class asynchronously.

➤ `SmtpClientExtensions` — This class defines extension methods for working with the `SmtpClient` class asynchronously.

➤ `WebClientExtensions` — This class defines extension methods for working with the `WebClient` class asynchronously.

The `CoordinationDataStructures\TaskFactoryExtensions` subfolder includes many files that add methods to the `TaskFactoryExtensions` class. Because this class is defined as a partial class, each file adds one or more static methods with extension methods for the `TaskFactory` class. Figure C-8 shows the diagram for the following public static methods:

➤ `Create` — Defined in `TaskFactoryExtensions_Create.cs`. The 12 definitions for this method create a new `Task` instance using the `TaskFactory`. The diverse definitions allow you to create tasks with the `TaskFactory` with different options.

➤ `FromAsync` — Defined in `TaskFactoryExtensions_FromAsync.cs`. This method creates a new `Task` instance that will be completed when a specified `WaitHandle` is signaled.

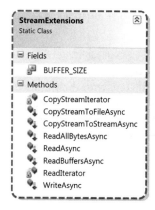

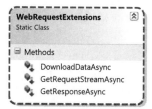

FIGURE C-6

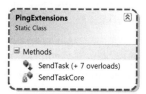

FIGURE C-7

➤ FromException — Defined in TaskFactoryExtensions_From.cs. The three definitions for this method create a new Task or Task<*TResult*> instance that has completed in the TaskStatus.Faulted final state with the specified Exception. These extension methods are useful for testing purposes when you need to simulate exceptions in `Task` instances. *TResult* defines the type of the result.

➤ `FromResult<TResult>` — Defined in `TaskFactoryExtensions_From.cs`. The two definitions for this method create a new `Task` or `Task<TResult>` instance that has completed in the `TaskStatus.RanToCompletion` final state with the specified `TResult`. These extension methods are useful for testing purposes when you need to simulate certain results in `Task` instances. They are also useful when you already have the result but you need to return the data in the form of a `Task` instance. *TResult* defines the type of the result.

➤ `GetTargetScheduler` — Defined in `TaskFactoryExtensions_Common.cs`. The two definitions for this method get and return the `TaskScheduler` instance that should be used to schedule tasks.

➤ `Iterate` — Defined in `TaskFactoryExtensions_Iterate.cs`. The 10 definitions for this method allow asynchronous iteration through enumerable `Task` instances, with diverse options. You can use these methods with iterators where you can write an iterate that is executed as an asynchronous method.

➤ `StartNewDelayed` — Defined in `TaskFactoryExtensions_Delayed.cs`. The 18 definitions for this method create a new `Task` or `Task<TResult>` instance that will complete in the `TaskStatus.RanToCompletion` final state after a specified delay. These extension methods are useful for testing purposes when you need to simulate certain behaviors of `Task` instances that require some time to complete their execution. *TResult* defines the type of the result.

➤ `ToGeneric<TResult>` — Defined in `TaskFactoryExtensions_Common.cs`. This method creates and returns a generic `TaskFactory<TResult>` instance from a non-generic one. *TResult* defines the type of the result.

➤ `ToNonGeneric<TResult>` — Defined in `TaskFactoryExtensions_Common.cs`. This method creates and returns a non-generic `TaskFactory` instance from a generic one. *TResult* defines the type of the result.

➤ `TrackedSequence` — Defined in `TaskFactoryExtensions_TrackedSequence.cs`. This method asynchronously executes a sequence of `Task` instances and maintains a list of all the processed `Task` instances.

➤ `WhenAll` — Defined in `TaskFactoryExtensions_ContinueWhenAllAny.cs`. The two definitions for this method create a continuation `Task` instance that will run upon the completion of a set of specified tasks. When all the tasks in the set complete their execution, the continuation will run.

➤ `WhenAny` — Defined in `TaskFactoryExtensions_ContinueWhenAllAny.cs`. The two definitions for this method create a continuation `Task` instance that will run upon the completion of any one of a set of specified tasks. If at least one of the set of specified tasks completes, the continuation will run.

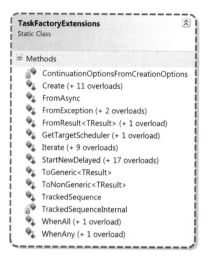

FIGURE C-8

PARALLEL ALGORITHMS

The `ParallelAlgorithms` folder includes many files that add methods to the `ParallelAlgorithms` class. Because this class is defined as a partial class, each file adds one or more static methods with parallelized algorithms of common operations. Figure C-9 shows the diagram with the following relevant public static methods:

➤ `Filter<T>` — Defined in `ParallelAlgorithms_Filter.cs`. The two definitions for this method filter an input list running a predicate over each element of the input. The methods return a new list with all those elements from the input list that passed the filter. `T` specifies the type of the elements stored in the input list.

➤ `For` — Defined in `ParallelAlgorithms_For.cs`. The two definitions for this method execute a `for` loop in which iterations can run in parallel. These methods allow you to run a parallelized `for` with `BigInteger` values for both the start index (inclusive) and the end index (exclusive).

➤ `ForRange` — Defined in `ParallelAlgorithms_ForRange.cs`. The 12 definitions for this method execute a loop over ranges in which iterations may run in parallel. All these definitions return a `ParallelLoopResult` structure.

➤ `InclusiveScanInPlaceParallel<T>` — Defined in `ParallelAlgorithms_Scan.cs`. Computes a parallel inclusive prefix scan over the array using a specified function. This method overwrites the data received as a parameter with the results. `T` specifies the type of the elements stored in the array.

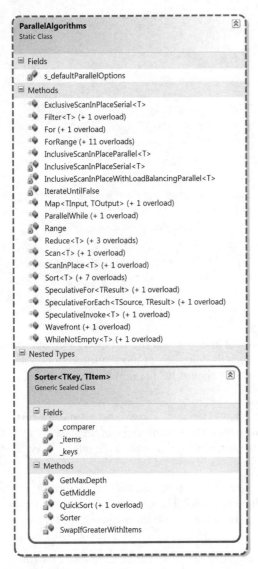

FIGURE C-9

➤ `Map<TInput, TOutput>` — Defined in `ParallelAlgorithms_Map.cs`. The two definitions for this method execute a map operation in parallel. The map operation consists of converting an input list into an output list by invoking a specified transform function for each element. `TInput` specifies the type of the input data, and `TOutput` determines the output data. These methods are useful to perform the mapping operations in Map Reduce algorithms.

➤ `ParallelWhile` — Defined in `ParallelAlgorithms_While.cs`. The two definitions for this method repeatedly execute an action in parallel while a specified condition evaluates to `true`.

➤ `Reduce<T>` — Defined in `ParallelAlgorithms_Reduce.cs`. The four definitions for this method reduce the input data using a specified aggregation operation and return the reduced value. The reduction operation must be associative and commutative. T specifies the type for the aggregated data and the accumulated value. These methods are useful to perform the reduction computations in Map Reduce algorithms.

➤ Scan<T> — Defined in `ParallelAlgorithms_Scan.cs`. The two definitions for this method compute a parallel prefix scan over the source enumerable using a specified function and return the results of the scan operation. T specifies the type of the elements stored in the source enumerable. These methods define a generalized implementation. Most of the time, when you work with very small functions, such as addition, a specialized version that targets a specific type and operation will offer better performance than this generic prefix-scan implementation.

➤ ScanInPlace<T> — Defined in `ParallelAlgorithms_Scan.cs`. The two definitions for this method compute a parallel prefix scan on the array using a specified function. These methods overwrite the data received as a parameter with the results. T specifies the type of the elements stored in the array. These methods define a generalized implementation for a parallel prefix scan. Most of the time, when you work with very small functions, such as addition, a specialized version that targets a specific type and operation will offer better performance than this generic prefix scan implementation.

➤ Sort<T> and Sort<$TKey$, $TValue$> — Defined in `ParallelAlgorithms_Sort.cs`. The eight definitions for these methods sort an array in parallel. These definitions allow you to specify a customized comparer, the index at which to start the sort, and the number of elements to be sorted. In Sort<T>, T specifies the type of data in the array. In Sort<$TKey$, $TValue$>, $TKey$ specifies the type of the keys array, and $TValue$ determines the type of the items array.

➤ SpeculativeFor<$TResult$> — Defined in `ParallelAlgorithms_SpeculativeFor.cs`. The two definitions for this method execute a function for each value in a range, return the first result achieved, and cease the execution. $TResult$ specifies the type of data returned.

➤ SpeculativeForEach<$TSource$, $TResult$> — Defined in `ParallelAlgorithms_SpeculativeForEach.cs`. The two definitions for this method execute a function for each element in a source enumerable, return the first result achieved, and cease the execution. $TSource$ specifies the type of the input elements to be processed, and $TResult$ indicates the type of data returned.

➤ SpeculativeInvoke<T> — Defined in `ParallelAlgorithms_SpeculativeInvoke.cs`. The two definitions for this method invoke the specified functions (potentially in parallel), cancel the invocations that remain executing once one completes its execution, and return the result from the function that completed. T specifies the type of data returned.

➤ Wavefront — Defined in `ParallelAlgorithms_Wavefront.cs`. The two definitions for this method process a matrix in parallel where every cell has a dependency on the cell above it and to its left. One of its definitions requires the definition of blocks of cells to partition the original matrix, and invokes a specified action based on those blocks. The other definition invokes a specified action for every cell.

➤ WhileNotEmpty<T> — Defined in `ParallelAlgorithms_ WhileNotEmpty.cs`. The two definitions for this method process source enumerable data in parallel by calling an action for each item. These methods allow the processing function to add more data to be processed. These methods use two `ConcurrentStack` instances to manage thread-safe source and destination stacks.

PARTITIONERS

The `Partitioners` folder includes two public classes that provide static methods to create customized partitions. Figure C-10 shows the diagram for the following two public classes within the `Partitioners` folder and their related private and internal classes:

➤ `ChunkPartitioner` — Provides three public static methods to partition an enumerable into chunks based on user-supplied criteria. Each implementation of the `Create<TSource>` method returns a `ChunkPartitioner<TSource>`, included in Figure C-10 as `ChunkPartitioner<T>`. `TSource` is the type of the data being partitioned.

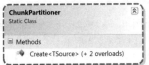
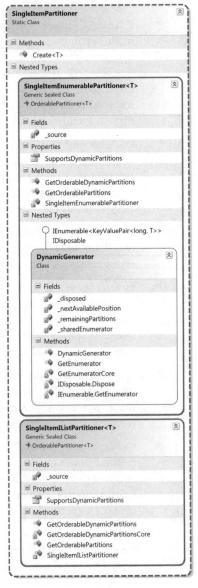

FIGURE C-10

➤ SingleItemPartitioner — Provides a public static method to partition a data source one item at a time. The Create<*T*> method returns an OrderablePartitioner<*T*>. *T* is the type of data contained in the enumerable.

TASK SCHEDULERS

The TaskSchedulers folder includes 13 implementations of TaskScheduler that provide diverse types of task schedulers and additional classes that support these schedulers. Figure C-11 shows the diagram for the following classes within the TaskSchedulers folder:

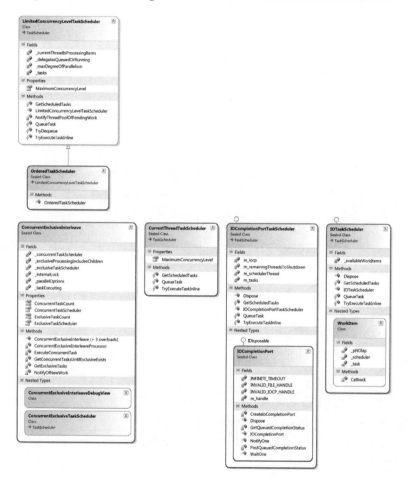

FIGURE C-11A

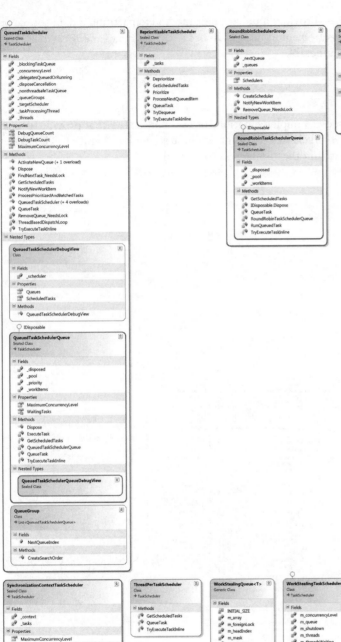

FIGURE C-11B

➤ `LimitedConcurrencyLevelTaskScheduler` — Ensures a maximum concurrency level while running on top of the `ThreadPool`. It is necessary to set the maximum degree of parallelism desired for this scheduler.

➤ `OrderedTaskScheduler` — Ensures that only one task is executing at a time. Tasks execute in the order that they were queued (FIFO). It is a subclass of `LimitedConcurrencyLevel TaskScheduler` that sends 1 as a parameter for its base class constructor.

➤ `ConcurrentExclusiveInterleave` — Provides and coordinates concurrent and exclusive task schedulers.

➤ `CurrentThreadTaskScheduler` — Runs tasks on the current thread.

➤ `IOCompletionPortTaskScheduler` — Uses an I/O completion port in order to control concurrency. This requires setting the maximum number of threads in the scheduler to be executing concurrently and the number of threads that must be available in the scheduler for executing tasks.

➤ `IOTaskScheduler` — Targets the I/O `ThreadPool`.

➤ `QueuedTaskScheduler` — Provides control over fairness, priorities, and the underlying threads used to accommodate tasks. It offers many constructors with a diverse number of parameters that allow you to control the threads to create and use for processing work items.

➤ `ReprioritizableTaskScheduler` — Changes in the priorities for previously queued tasks.

➤ `RoundRobinSchedulerGroup` — Enables the creation of a group of schedulers that support round-robin scheduling for fairness.

➤ `RoundRobinTaskSchedulerQueue` — Uses a round-robin algorithm to schedule tasks.

➤ `StaTaskScheduler` — Uses Single-Threaded Apartment (STA) threads in order to support the execution of tasks. This task scheduler allows you to use tasks with STA components. You need to set the maximum number of threads that this scheduler can use.

➤ `SynchronizationContextTaskScheduler` — Targets the `SynchronizationContext` specified as a parameter in its constructor.

➤ `ThreadPerTaskScheduler` — Dedicates one thread per task. This scheduler is especially useful when you need each task to run in a different thread whenever possible.

➤ `WorkStealingTaskScheduler` — Provides a work-stealing task scheduler. Its default parameters specify twice as many threads as there are logical cores to support the execution of tasks. However, it is also possible to specify the number of threads to use in the scheduler. This scheduler uses `WorkStealingQueue<Task>`.

INDEX